Food and Beverage Management
Third Edition

Bernard Davis, BA, MHCIMA
Andrew Lockwood, BSc, CertEd, FHCIMA
Sally Stone, BSc, MHCIMA

BUTTERWORTH
HEINEMANN

Butterworth-Heinemann
Linacre House, Jordan Hill, Oxford OX2 8DP
225 Wildwood Avenue, Woburn, MA 01801-2041
A division of Reed Educational and Professional Publishing Ltd

Ɑ A member of the Reed Elsevier plc group

OXFORD   AUCKLAND   BOSTON
JOHANNESBURG   MELBOURNE   NEW DELHI

First published 1985
Reprinted 1986, 1989, 1990
Second edition 1991
Reprinted 1992, 1993 (twice), 1994, 1995, 1996
Third edition 1998
Reprinted 1999 (twice), 2001, 2002

British Library Cataloguing in Publication Data
Davis Bernard
   Food and beverage management. – 3rd ed.
   1. Food service management   2. Hospitality industry – Management
   I. Title   II. Stone, Sally   III. Lockwood, Andrew
   647.9'5'068

ISBN 0 7506 3286 0

For more information on all Butterworth-Heinemann publications
please visit our website at www.bh.com

Typeset by Avocet Typeset, Brill, Aylesbury, Bucks
Printed and bound in Great Britain by Scotprint, Haddington

Food and Beverage Management

This book is dedicated to
Buddy,
Anna, Nikki
and Neil

Contents

Figures

Tables

Preface to the third edition

Since the publication of the first edition of *Food and Beverage Management* in 1985 and the second edition in 1991, the Hotel and Catering industry has seen many changes and developments, these being a result of natural progression within the industry, research and development and as a result of outside pressures and government legislation.

Some general trends that were identifiable during the past twelve years, and are continuing, include:

- a continuing increase in food, beverage and energy costs;
- a continuing increase in labour costs and a difficulty in obtaining an adequate number of highly skilled staff;
- an increasingly more knowledgeable customer, demanding more exciting menus, a wide range of 'healthy eating' dishes, a clean smoke-free environment and a high standard of hygiene practices from the industry;
- a continuing concern by the EC and UK Government about all aspects of food hygiene, this being evident with new legislation;
- a much wider acceptance of the use of computers throughout the industry;
- an increasing awareness of the importance of managing quality in all areas of food and beverage operations.

This third edition offers the reader two new chapters, together with a total update of the remaining chapters, with many being enlarged. Over forty new menus are included, together with numerous new tables and figures. This edition is particularly strengthened with the addition of Andrew Lockwood as a co-author – he is an established academic and author of many publications.

Food and Beverage Management continues to be an established source of reading and reference material, not only to students, but to practising food and beverage managers, controllers, and their assistants. The book has been widely accepted by universities and colleges for their degree courses in the UK and overseas, by the HCIMA as a standard textbook for the Professional Certificate, Diploma and Distant Learning, and for the Higher National Diploma. In addition, the book has been found to be a good reference source for advanced GNVQ courses.

Acknowledgements to the many colleagues and organizations who kindly contributed to the first and second editions, and to those who have given their time and assistance to this third edition. In particular, we would like to thank:

Army Catering Corps
Automatic Minibar Systems Ltd
Automatic Vending Association of Britain
Avon Data Systems Ltd
British Airways
British Hospitality Association
Brown's Restaurant and Bar
CACI Information Services
Caledonian Hotel, Edinburgh
Caterer and Hotelkeeper
Central Statistical Office
Cerco Health Services
Compass Catering
Conran Restaurants
Copthorne London Tara Hotel
Department of Health and Social Security
Dorchester Hotel
Electrolux Ltd
FDS Ltd
Gallup Organisation
Girovend Holdings Ltd
Greenalls Group PLC
Guy's and St Thomas' Hospitals
Hicks and Don
House of Commons
Innkeepers Fayre (Bass PLC)
Institute of Directors
Keynote Publications
Landmark Hotel
Langham Hilton
Leith's Events and Parties

Leith's Management
Letheby and Christopher
Marketpower Ltd
Mintel Research Services Ltd
National Health Services
Pizza Express
St Peter's Hospital, Chertsey
Surrey Commercial Services
Surrey County Council
TGI Friday's

Toby Restaurants (Bass PLC)
Virgin Atlantic

We would also like to thank all at Butterworth-Heinemann for their continued support and encouragement.

Bernard Davis
Andrew Lockwood
Sally Stone

Preface to the second edition

Since the publication of the first edition of *Food and Beverage Management*, the hotel and catering industry has come to the end of the 1980s and has already begun its progress through the 1990s. In such a relatively short period of time changes have occurred within the industry, both through its own natural progression, research and development and as a result of outside pressures and government legislation.

Some general trends that were identifiable during the past decade and are continuing include:

1 A continuing increase in food, beverage and energy costs.
2 A continuing increase in labour costs, a decline in the young labour force available for the industry and an increase in the number of part-time employees.
3 An increasing interest in healthy eating by the general public with more prominence of vegetarian dishes and menus. Also a requirement by the public for non-smoking areas to be a standard for all types of catering outlets.
4 An increasing demand and awareness by the general public for higher hygiene standards for all catering outlets. This demand being as a result of the general awareness through the media of new food legislation and of the outbreaks of food poisoning in the UK. The continuing monitoring of the above will have significant importance to the success of any catering operation in the 1990s.

This second edition offers the reader six new chapters and a total up-date of all previous chapters with many being enlarged, reflecting the growing importance of their subject areas. The new chapters are The meal experience; The marketing of food and beverages; Advertising, public relations, merchandising and sales promotion; Financial aspects; Food and beverage management in school catering; and Food and beverage management in hospital catering. *Food and Beverage Management* continues to be a source of reading material and reference to many practising catering managers, food and beverage managers, controllers and their assistants both within the UK and overseas. This edition sets out to also cover the new examination requirements for the various degree courses in hotel and catering management, the diploma and certificates of the Business and Technical Education Council and for the Hotel and Catering Institutional Management Association.

In addition, the book has been selected by the English Language Book Society since 1988 for inclusion in its hotel catering and tourism list. The English Language Book Society is funded by the Overseas Development Administration of the British Government to make available significant textbooks of British publishers to students in developing countries throughout the world.

Acknowledgements go to the many colleagues and organizations who kindly contributed to the first edition and who have again given their time and assistance to the second. Additionally, we would like to thank the following for their assistance:

AJ's Restaurants; Beefeater Steak Houses; BMRB; Boca Raton Resort and Club; *Caterer and Hotelkeeper*; Dome Cafe Bar; Electrolux Leisure Appliances; FAST International Ltd; Franchise Development Services Ltd; Gallup; Girovend Cashless Systems (UK) Ltd; Harvester Restaurants; HCTC; Hillingdon Borough Council; Horwath & Horwath; Hotel Britannia Inter-continental, London; King Edward's Hospital Fund; Liberty Street Restaurants; London Tara Hotel; Market-Power; Media Expenditure Analysis Ltd; Mintel; North West Surrey Health Authority; Pacino's Restaurant; Queen Elizabeth II Hospital; Remanco Systems Inc; Robobar Ltd; South West Thames Regional Health Authority; St Peter's Hospital, Chertsey; Surrey County Council; West Dorset General Hospital.

Bernard Davis and Sally Stone
1991

Preface to the first edition

This book has been written to explain the complexities of managing food and beverage outlets. The purpose is to examine the wide range of subject areas that come within the orbit of operational food and beverage management and to relate these to the applications applied within five broad sections of the catering industry, that is, fast-food and popular catering; hotels and quality restaurants; function catering; industrial catering; and welfare catering.

The book has been planned to cover the examination requirements for the various degree courses in Hotel and Catering Administration and Management; the Hotel and Catering Institutional Management Association; and diplomas and certificates of the Business and Technician Education Council.

In addition, the book has been written for practising catering managers, food and beverage managers, food and beverage controllers, and all their assistants who may wish to formalize and up-date their knowledge, in order to improve the profitability and productivity of their operations and to enhance their customers' satisfaction.

This book is based on our own practical experiences and from first-hand information obtained from practitioners, within both large and small companies and units, in the many segments of the industry, who so generously gave up their time to answer and discuss many of our questions while undertaking research for the book. We are also grateful to the many companies who kindly gave permission for samples of their menus to be reproduced within the book.

In particular the authors would like to express a special debt of gratitude to those people whose assistance to us has been invaluable. To Professor S. Medlik who gave valuable advice in the structuring of this book and for commenting on the early drafts of some of the chapters, and to Brian Cheeseman (Principal Lecturer, Westminster College) and Barry Ware-Lane (Operations Systems Director, United Biscuits Restaurants), both of whom made invaluable constructive comments to the final draft of the book. Also to David Airey (Lecturer, University of Surrey) for his help and advice with the first two chapters.

Acknowledgements also go to the following organisations for their help and assistance: The Peninsula Hotel, Hong Kong; The Inter Continental, London; Hilton International, London; Hyatt Carlton Tower, London; British Airways; Sweda International; Berni Restaurants; Pizza Express, New York; New York Restaurant; United Biscuits Restaurants Ltd.; The Mandarin Hotel, Hong Kong; The Broadmoor Hotel, Colorado; The Oriental Hotel, Bangkok; The Castle Hotel, Taunton; Grosvenor House, London; Sutcliffe Catering Company: Derbyshire County Council; The Department of Health and Social Security; The Home Office; The Automatic Vending Association of Britain; Multimet; Regethermic; The Hotel, Catering and Institutional Management Association.

Bernard Davis and Sally Stone
1985

1
Introducing food and beverage management

1.1 Introduction

The provision of food and beverages away from home forms a substantial part of the activities of the hotel and catering industry. Like the industry of which it is a part, food and beverage operations are characterized by their diversity. Outlets include private and public sector establishments and range from small privately owned concerns to large international organizations and from prison catering to catering in the most luxurious hotels. The hotel and catering industry as a whole ranks as about the third largest employer in Great Britain, employing 2.4 million of the total workforce. The turnover of the industry is in excess of £31,000 million. Looking at food and beverage, the annual expenditure on food from catering outlets reaches £19,500 million, clearly indicating the catering industry's importance in terms of economic activity.

If the hotel and catering industry is considered to cover all undertakings concerned with the provision of food, drink and accommodation away from home, this will naturally include all food and beverage outlets. In other words, food and beverage provision is simply one element of a broader hotel and catering industry. In conceptual terms, this raises few problems except possibly with take-away food establishments where in some cases the food may be taken home for consumption even though it is prepared and provided away from home. In practice, however, there are a number of difficulties in considering the hotel and catering industry as embracing all food and beverage establishments and outlets. This arises because, following a number of official attempts at definition, the hotel and catering industry is often considered to have a much nar-

rower scope. The official definitions exclude many food and beverage outlets. For example, the Standard Industrial Classification (CSO, 1980) gives hotel and catering a reasonably broad coverage as shown in Table 1.1, but even here parts of employee and welfare catering are either omitted or included in other sectors. This book adopts the broadest possible approach, aiming to consider all types of food and beverage operation wherever they may appear.

1.1.1 Standard Industrial Classification

For analytical purposes, economically similar activities may be grouped together into 'industries', for example into agriculture, motor vehicle manufacture, retail distribution, catering, and national government service. A system used to group activities in this way is described as an 'industrial classification'. Such a classification usually starts with a small number of broad groups of activities that are then subdivided into progressively narrower groups so that the classification can be used with varying amounts of detail for different purposes.

The first comprehensive Standard Industrial Classification (SIC) for the United Kingdom was issued in 1948. The classification was revised in 1958, in 1968 and in 1980. All the revisions have been prepared by an interdepartmental committee representing the main government departments collecting and using the statistics. Details about the SIC are published by the Central Statistical Office.

The Standard Industrial Classification provides a detailed and reliable classification of businesses into groups but, as described earlier,

Table 1.1   *Standard Industrial Classification of the hotel and catering industry*

Class	Group			Activity
Division 6			**Services**	
66			Hotels and catering	
	661		Restaurants, snack bars, cafes and other eating places	
		6611	Eating places supplying food for consumption on the premises.	
			1 Licensed places	Eating places licensed to provide alcoholic liquor with meals but not normally providing regular overnight accommodation. Any entertainment provided is incidental to the provision of meals. Railway buffets and dining car services are included. Hotels are classified to heading 6650 and night clubs etc. to heading 6630.
			2 Unlicensed places	Eating places which do not provide alcoholic liquor: ice-cream parlours and coffee bars
		6612	Take-away food shops	Fish and chip shops, sandwich bars and other premises supplying prepared food for consumption off the premises.
	662	6620	Public houses and bars	Establishments wholly or mainly engaged in supplying alcoholic liquor for consumption on the premises; the provision of food or entertainment is ancillary and the provision of overnight accommodation, if any, is subordinate.
	663	6630	Night clubs and licensed clubs	Establishments providing food, drink and entertainment to their members and guests, including residential clubs. Sports and gaming clubs are classified to heading 9791.
	664	6640	Canteens and messes	
			1 Catering contractors	School canteens, industrial canteens and other catering establishments operated by catering contractors. Canteens run by industrial establishments for their own employees are classified with the main establishment.
			2 Other canteens and messes	Separately identifiable service messes, university and other canteens not elsewhere specified.
	665	6650	Hotel trade	
			1 Licensed premises	Hotels, motels and guest houses providing overnight furnished accommodation with food and service which are licensed to serve alcoholic liquor (including bed and breakfast places).
			2 Unlicensed premises	Hotels, motels and guest houses providing overnight furnished accommodation with food and service but which are not licensed to serve alcoholic liquor (including bed and breakfast places).
	667	6670	Other tourist or short-stay accommodation	1 Camping and caravan sites. The provision of camping and caravan sites for rent. Rented caravan or chalet sites providing food supplies from a retail shop only are classified here but if the site includes a place providing prepared food it should be classified as a holiday camp .

Table 1.1 *(cont.)*

Class	Group	Activity
Division 6	**Services**	
		2 Holiday camps. Provision of chalet or caravan accommodation having on the site a place providing prepared food.
		3 Other tourist or short-stay accommodation not elsewhere specified. Holiday centres, conference centres, holiday houses, apartments, flats and flatlets. Youth hostels, non-charitable holiday homes, private rest homes without medical care.
Division 9	**Other services**	
	9310	Catering services ancillary to higher education institutions
	9320	Catering services ancillary to schools
	9330	Catering services ancillary to educational and vocational training not elsewhere specified
	9510	Convalescent and rest homes with medical care
	9611	Social and residential homes

Source: CSO: *Standard Industrial Classification*. Revised 1980.

does not give a totally comprehensive picture of the activities of the hotel and catering industry. The classification provides a consistent format for the interpretation of government statistics but it does not help to understand the complexity of food and beverage operations and their key characteristics.

1.1.2 Size and scope of food and beverage operations

The statistics that are available from different sources on the size and scope of food and beverage operations do not give a consistent picture because of the different bases used for their collection. The figures shown in Table 1.2 are collected by Marketpower Limited, one of the leading analysts of the UK catering market providing a range of services to private clients, confidential surveys and strategic studies.

Maketpower make a clear distinction between those operations run for profit and those operations run at cost. Their categories are simple and straightforward but the 'leisure' category needs a little explanation. This category includes catering provision in historic properties, gardens, museums, zoos, theme parks, cinemas, theatres, leisure centres and sports centres, clubs and events.

Looking at the number of outlets in each of the sectors, hotels has the largest and pubs has the second largest number of outlets operating for profit. However, while the number of hotels has grown slightly in the four years to 1996 the number of pubs has declined quite significantly. The leisure sector is the third largest and is growing in importance. Cafés and take-aways are the fourth largest but are reducing in size, perhaps to be replaced by a growing number of fast food operations – still a relatively small number overall. Restaurants remain reasonably static in fifth place, while the smallest sector (travel related catering) is also static. On the cost side, education has the largest number of outlets but has dropped slightly over the four years, as has the staff catering sector, which falls into third place behind the growing numbers in the health care sector. The services sector is relatively small but has grown slightly. Overall the profit side has almost three times the number of outlets than the cost side.

Looking at the number of meals served, on the profit side, pubs are by far the largest sector and have increased rapidly over the four years despite the reduction in the number of outlets. The cafés/take-aways and leisure sectors serve

Table 1.2   *Size and scope of food and beverage operations*

	Number of outlets			Number of meals served (millions)		
	1992	*1994*	*1996*	*1992*	*1994*	*1996*
Hotels	60,209	60,459	60,740	529	563	605
Restaurants	15,730	15,924	15,920	362	414	430
Fast food	1,140	1,455	1,770	500	545	594
Cafes/take-aways	33,103	32,047	30,990	1,122	1,100	1,091
Pubs	64,720	61,850	58,980	1,162	1,185	1,320
Travel	1,218	1,244	1,290	382	414	430
Leisure	45,877	46,683	47,475	935	1,071	1,099
Profit	**221,973**	**219,661**	**217,165**	**4,993**	**5,293**	**5,569**
Staff catering	23,173	22,477	21,780	1,358	1,349	1,330
Health care	21,649	22,685	23,720	765	760	755
Education	34,721	34,651	34,580	964	914	900
Services	3,148	3,194	3,260	150	149	145
Cost	**82,691**	**83,005**	**83,340**	**3,237**	**3,171**	**3,130**
Total	**304,664**	**302,666**	**300,505**	**8,230**	**8,464**	**8,699**

Source: Marketpower Catering Industry Population File, 1997

about the same number of meals but while the numbers of meals served in leisure is on the increase, the number served in cafés/take-aways is declining. Despite being the largest sector in terms of number of outlets, hotels are only fourth in the number of meals served although this would appear to be increasing. Despite the relatively small number of fast food outlets, they turn over a large number of meals placing them fifth in the table above restaurants and travel with similar and increasing numbers. Staff catering serves the most meals on the cost side of the industry but there is some evidence that this is declining slightly. The second largest sector is education, which is also declining, followed by health care, which is also declining slightly, perhaps as day surgery and short stays become more common. The smallest number of meals is served to the services and this too is declining. Overall the profit side serves almost twice as many meals as the cost sector and continues to grow reasonably strongly while the cost side seems to be on a slight downward trend.

1.1.3   A classification of food and beverage operations

It is possible to make a number of distinctions

between the many different types of food and beverage outlets. First, there is a distinction between those outlets that operate on a strictly commercial basis and those that are subsidized. A second distinction concerns the type of market served. In some cases, the market is confined to restricted groups, as for example in a hospital or prison, while in other cases the outlet is open to the public at large. A third distinction is between outlets where catering is the main activity of the undertaking, as for example in a privately owned commercial restaurant, and those where it is a secondary activity, as is the case with travel catering or school meal catering. A final distinction appears between outlets that are in public ownership and those in private ownership. To a certain extent there is a rough compatibility between the distinctions. On the one hand, captive markets tend to be in public ownership and to be a subsidiary activity of the undertaking. On the other hand, the commercial outlets tend to be in the private sector, to serve the general public and to be the main activity of the undertaking. In brief, the subsidized sector is not normally available to the public at large and normally provides catering only as an activity that is both secondary to the main business and available only to restricted groups. These broad divisions, however, do not hold true in all cases. Indeed, the

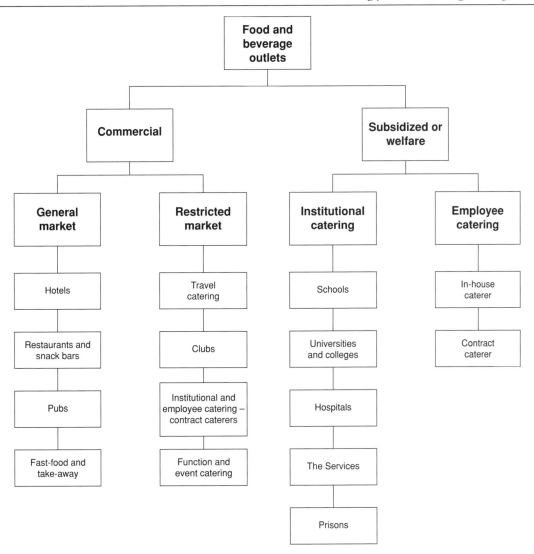

Figure 1.1   *The main sectors of food and beverage outlets*

exceptions are numerous and beyond the broad categories, they tend to devalue any generalizations.

Using some of the above distinctions, it is possible to classify food and beverage outlets into a number of broad sectors. Figure 1.1 illustrates one way of breaking down the industry into sectors. The figure shows a distinction between purely commercial operations and those which accrue subsidies in some way. The purely commercial operations may be in public or private ownership and include outlets where catering is the main activity as well as those where it is a secondary activity, as for example catering in

theatres or shops. In the case of the commercial sector, a secondary division is shown between outlets that have a restricted market and those which are open to the general public. The subsidized operations similarly may be in public or private ownership. A distinction is drawn between catering in institutions where public ownership dominates and catering for employees where private ownership is also of importance. Almost by definition subsidized catering tends to be available only to restricted markets.

As with any classification, there are of course areas of overlap. There are two of particular importance here. The first overlap concerns catering in various private schools, colleges and hospitals, and in some offices and works canteens where the catering is not in any way subsidized but run on strictly commercial lines. These outlets appear under the heading of the commercial sector as commercial catering for a restricted market, as shown in Figure 1.1. The second issue concerns the many subsidized or welfare catering outlets that are operated by catering contractors who are themselves strictly organized on commercial lines. These have not been separated in Figure 1.1 because although the operators themselves may be commercial companies, this does not affect the fact that the end product is normally subsidized for the market.

There are two reasons for using this classification here. First, it provides a very broad coverage of food and beverage outlets – broader, for example, than many of the official definitions and classifications of the hotel and catering industry. The second reason for using this classification is that it is based on distinctions that have a significant bearing upon most aspects of the operation of the catering activity. For example the difference between subsidized catering and commercial catering not only embraces differences of objectives but also covers differences in markets served, differences in organizations involved and differences in marketing and business strategy.

Using this classification, the aim here is to outline the different types of food and beverage outlets and to identify their main characteristics. This then serves as a basis for a consideration of issues of relevance to food and beverage operations in general.

1.2   The commercial sector

Commercial food and beverage outlets may be defined as those operations in which profit is a primary concern. Such outlets exist not only in private ownership but also in the publicly owned sector of the economy where, for example, a local leisure centre may seek to operate catering outlets on commercial lines. Also, it is worth noting that in the commercial sector, catering may be the main activity of the organization or it may be a secondary or additional service to customers as, for example, catering in department stores or theatres. A broad distinction can be made between catering for a restricted market and catering for a general market. In the case of the former, the market can be restricted in a number of ways: by way of membership criteria as in the case of catering in clubs or by the fact that the catering is only available to those engaged in a specific activity as in the case of travel catering or employee catering. However, there will be some overlap in some cases. For example, catering at a railway station, bus or airport terminal is normally open to the traveller as well as to the general public, while catering on the train, bus or plane itself is limited to those travelling.

1.2.1   Commercial catering for a general market

1.2 1.1   Hotels

The provision of food and beverage facilities in hotels ranges from a self-service style often used for breakfast service to full silver service used at the luxury end of the market. In resort hotels, the food and beverage facilities are often presented as one of the more important features of the hotel because the guests may be staying at the hotel for some time rather than just a night or so as may be the case in transient hotels. The types of food and beverage outlets found in hotels include silver service restaurants, licensed bars, coffee shops and snack bars, carvery and buffet restaurants, gueridon service and banqueting facilities. Some of these facilities are only available to hotel residents, or 'in-house trade', for example room service; while the others, for example coffee shops and other restaurants, are advertised externally by the hotel to attract outside custom.

1.2.1.2   Restaurants and snack bars

The primary function of commercial restaurants is the provision of food and beverages. As these restaurants do not have any in-house trade, they depend on their location and the volume of passing trade and the reputation they develop from word-of-mouth advertising. The various types of restaurants include snack bars, cafes, coffee shops, take-aways, theme restaurants, ethnic restaurants, haute cuisine restaurants, etc. These diverse types of restaurant have an equally wide range of service styles, ranging from the self-service cafeterias through to the more elaborate methods of table service (for example French, Russian, English) found in luxury restaurants, and those particular service techniques specific to speciality restaurants such as Chinese, Polynesian, Indian and Japanese. A separate bar area may be provided for before- or after-meal drinks, providing the double advantage of offering the customer a place to sit and relax away from the dining area and allowing a faster seat turnover in the restaurant.

1.2.1.3 *Public houses*

Public houses consist of a varied group of establishments, which mainly offer the general public alcoholic liquor for sale for consumption on and off the premises. The supply of food, at one time ancillary to liquor, is an increasingly dominant element in the 'product mix' for the consumer.

The characteristics of public houses are, first, that they require a magistrate's licence to operate that is only granted to suitable persons and, second, that many public houses are owned by a brewery company, providing an integration of their production with the retail distribution of alcoholic beverages.

To become more competitive and to meet customers' demands, the catering premises in most pubs have improved considerably in recent years. Some brewery companies have classified their public houses by the level of catering offered. This ranges from those offering only sandwiches through to hot and cold snacks, a cold buffet counter, a bistro-type operation, a griddle or steak bar and a full à la carte menu. The range of food items offered is mainly of the convenience food type but at times extends to the total fresh food items. Several brewery companies market specific pubs by the type of catering offered with a brand image, for example Big Steak as part of Allied Domecq Inns.

1.2.1.4 *Fast food and take-away*

This sector of the industry is concerned with the preparation and service of food and beverages quickly for immediate sale to the customer for consumption either on or off the premises. These range from the traditional fish and chip shop through a series of ethnic cuisines to the high street branded operations of McDonald's, Burger King or KFC.

At the fast food end of the market, there are a number of characteristics common to many of the outlets. First, units are usually themed around a product (for example, hamburgers) a range of products (for example, fish or pizza), or products of a country (for example, Chinese, Italian). This 'product' is very well marketed, for example from a themed product to decor and atmosphere, to the high and consistent standard of the product, to advertising on television, local radio and newspapers, to the container boxes for take-away items. Second, the method of food production is often partially or fully automated, often using commodities of the convenience type (for example, frozen chips, concentrated beverage syrups), thereby de-skilling the job and restricting the product range variable. Similarly, the method of food service is simplified and basic. Third, the pricing of the items and the ASP per customer lie within a fairly distinct known price band (for example, £3.50–£4.50). Finally, the units are often owned by large chains or are franchised.

1.2.2 Commercial catering for a restricted market

1.2.2.1 *Travel catering*

Travel catering (that is, road, rail, air and sea) has a number of characteristics not commonly associated with other food and beverage outlets. It frequently involves the feeding of a large number of customers arriving together at a catering facility, and who need to be catered for in a specific time, for example, on board a plane. The plane only carries sufficient food and beverage supplies for a specific number of meal periods. If for any reason this food cannot be served to customers, alternative supplies may not be readily available. The service of the food and beverages may be particularly difficult due to the physical conditions within the service area, for example, turbulence on board a plane. The types of restaurants described previously are usually catering for a specific and identifiable socio-economic market. Travel catering often has to cater for 'mixed markets'. Finally, there are the problems of staffing these food and beverage facilities: the extra costs involved in the transportation and service of the food and beverages; space restrictions and the problem of security while the operation is in transit. Four main types of travel catering may be identified.

- **Road catering** has progressed from the inns and taverns of earlier days used by those travelling on foot and horseback to the present-day motorway service areas and other roadside catering outlets. These service areas are often open twenty-four hours a day and have a particular problem of staffing as some employees have to be brought to and from work over a distance of twenty to thirty miles. Also, because of their isolated locations, the hours they are open and the sheer volume of numbers involved at peak periods, these service areas are also particularly prone to vandalism and littering. They do, however, provide a valuable catering service to the travelling public and their food and beverage facilities usually include self-service and waiter service restaurants, vending machines and take-away foods and beverages. High street fast food operations are also now appearing both on motorway service areas and as free-standing drive-throughs.
- **Rail catering** may be conveniently divided into two areas: terminal catering and in-transit catering. Catering at railway terminals usually comprises licensed bars, self-service and waiter service restaurants, fast food and take-away units, supplemented by vending machines dispensing hot and cold foods and beverages. In-transit catering can feature three kinds of service. The first is the traditional restaurant car service where breakfast, lunch and dinner are organized in sittings and passengers go to the restaurant car for service where appropriate seating accommodation is provided, and then return to their seats on the train after their meal. In a Pullman service, these meals are delivered direct to the seat of first class passengers only. The second type of

service is the buffet car, which is a self-service operation in which passengers go to the car and buy light refreshments over the counter. The third is a trolley service where snacks and drinks are delivered to customers at their seats. Innovative approaches to catering on trains are also in evidence such as the operation of 'Cuisine 2000' using cook-chilled foods prepared centrally, buffet cars turned into bistros on the London to Birmingham route, and on the east coast Anglo-Scottish route 'A taste of Scotland' restaurant service.

- **Airline catering** has increased and developed considerably over the past twenty-five years. Originally consisting of sandwiches and flasks of tea, coffee and alcoholic beverages, the progress to today's full and varied service has paralleled that of aircraft development itself. Like the railways, airline catering falls into two main areas: terminal catering, and 'in-transit' or 'in-flight' catering. Food and beverage outlets at air terminals usually consist of self-service and waiter service restaurants, supplemented by vending machines and licensed bars. The in-flight catering service varies considerably with the class of travel, type and duration of flight. For the economy travellers, the food and beverage portions are highly standardized with the meals portioned into plastic trays that are presented to the passengers and from which they eat their meals. Disposable cutlery, napkins, etc. may be used to increase the standard of hygiene and reduce the weight carried and storage space required. For first class travellers there is virtually no portion control. Service is from a gueridon trolley, where food is portioned in front of the customers and any garnishes, sauces, etc. are added according to their immediate requirements. The crockery used may be bone china and this combines with fine glassware and cutlery to create an atmosphere of high-class dining. A characteristic of airline catering is that this service is often contracted out to a specialist catering firm, which will supply a similar service to many airlines. The meal is usually included in the price of the fare and a particular feature is now made of cabin service facilities by different airlines. The growth in air travel has made competition fierce, and the area of food service is now a particularly competitive aspect of the total service offered by an airline.

• **Sea or marine catering** varies from the provision of food and beverages on the short sea route ferries to the large cruise or passenger liners where the catering facilities are an important part of the service offered by the shipping line and are usually included in the price of the fare. On the cruise liners the standard of catering facilities is high because they are an important sales feature in a competitive activity. On the short sea routes, however, price is usually a more important factor and because of the necessity to feed large numbers of people in a short time the catering service provided is usually of the popular and fast-food type.

1.2.2.2 Clubs

Clubs, as a sector of the hotel and catering industry, are establishments offering food and drink, occasionally with accommodation, to members and their bona fide guests. The types of clubs range from working men's clubs, to political party clubs, social clubs, sporting clubs, restaurant clubs, to the private exclusive clubs. In England and Wales, clubs are of two main types: proprietary clubs and registered clubs.

Proprietary clubs are licensed clubs, owned by an individual or company and operated by themselves for profit, and as such require a justice's licence to operate. Many such clubs resemble licensed restaurants with a substantial part of their turnover obtained from the sales of food. Another growing sector comprises sports or health clubs that offer their members sporting, fitness and leisure facilities but where food is an ancillary service.

In registered clubs the management is responsible to an elected committee. The members own all the property including the food and drink, and pay their subscriptions to a common fund. As a non-profit making club that belongs to all the members and provides a service to the members, it does not require a justice's licence to operate, simply to be registered. The turnover of members' clubs is mainly obtained from the sale of drinks that are normally sold at a competitive price as the profit element in clubs is lower than, for example, in public houses.

1.2.2.3 Institutional and employee catering – contract caterers

Institutional and employee catering will be dealt with in detail under the heading of subsidized and welfare catering, as indeed most of these types of operations are run on some form of a subsidized basis. It is worth considering, however, that in parts of the private sector such catering activities may be operated on a commercial basis. For example, in many private hospitals and private schools the catering function is operated very much with commercial objectives in mind. Increasingly, contract caterers are providing catering services to the general public on behalf of their clients, for example in leisure centres, theatres or shops.

1.2.2.4 Function and event catering

Function and event catering may be described as the service of food and beverages at a specific time and place, for a given number of people, to an agreed menu and price. Examples of function catering include social functions, such as weddings and dinner dances; business functions such as conferences, meetings and working lunches and those functions that are organized for both social and business reasons such as outdoor catering at a sports event, show or exhibition.

Function catering is found in both the commercial and non-commercial sectors of the catering industry. In the commercial sector, function catering could be a specialist organization operating in its own function facilities or an outdoor catering specialist operating in a vast range of clients' or rented facilities or within marquees, or as a separate department within a hotel. Anyone who has visited a major sporting event cannot fail to be impressed by the scale and range of catering that takes place within the 'tented village'. Indeed some visitors seem to take more interest in the food and beverage provision than in the sports event they have been invited to attend.

In the non-commercial sector, function catering is rarely the primary reason for providing the establishment with catering facilities. Such establishments include hospitals, schools, industrial cafeterias, etc. where the functions are not usually organized on a purely profit basis as they are in the commercial sector, but rather to serve a specific need of the organization. Typical examples would be Christmas functions, retirement parties, fund-raising events, etc.

1.3   The subsidized or welfare sector

Subsidized or welfare food and beverage establishments may be defined as those operations in which making a profit from the catering facility is not the outlet's primary concern. Since the operations are either completely or partially subsidized by a parent body, such establishments' primary obligation is the well-being and care of their customers or patients. Unlike customers frequenting commercial sector operations, these customers often do not have a choice of catering facilities, for example in hospitals and schools. Some non-commercial operations are subsidized by government bodies that dictate an allowance per head, or by parent companies who may have a similar arrangement.

A distinction can be made between institutional catering and employee catering facilities, for example, in hospitals and schools. Non-commercial operations embrace catering in institutions such as prisons, schools and hospitals. An important characteristic of this type of catering is that the market is not only usually restricted to the residents of the institutions but also in most cases it is captive. In addition, institutional catering may be completely subsidized. Employee catering can be in public or private ownership and covers the provision of food and beverage services to employees. The degree of subsidy in this type of operation varies considerably and in many cases the market is not entirely captive. In other words, the catering outlet may be competing with the catering facilities provided at nearby restaurants, pubs and take-aways or with food bought in by the workers from their homes.

1.3.1   Institutional catering

Institutional catering establishments include schools, universities, colleges, hospitals, the Services, and HM prisons. In some of these establishments no charge is made to certain

groups of customers to pay for the provision of the food and beverage services as they are completely or partially subsidized by various government funds. This is the part of the catering industry also referred to as the institutional sector.

1.3.1.1   *Schools*

The school meals catering service was formerly structured on a dietary basis with a daily or weekly per capita allowance to ensure that the children obtained adequate nutritional levels from their meals. Most of the schools used to operate their dining rooms on a family type service or a self-service basis with the traditional 'meat and two veg' lunch being very much the norm. There has been a shift away from this conventional arrangement to the provision of a snack-type lunch as an alternative to or replacement for the main meal. Many schools now provide 'snack meals' such as baked potatoes, pizzas, sandwiches, rolls, pies, soups, yoghurts, etc., and the children may choose from this selection in a normal cafeteria fashion.

Some areas have drastically cut their school meal service and are simply providing dining-room space for the children to bring in their own lunches from home. Whether this trend will continue in the future is debatable. It does seem likely, however, that now introduced, the snack-type meal will remain as an alternative to the traditional school meal. Many local education authorities contract out this service to specialist contract caterers.

1.3.1.2   *Universities and colleges*

All institutions of further and higher education provide some form of catering facilities for the academic, administrative, technical and secretarial staff as well as for full and part time students and visitors. The catering service in this sector of the industry suffers from an under-utilization of its facilities during the three vacation periods and in many instances at the weekends.

Universities are autonomous bodies and are responsible for their own catering services. They are, however, publicly accountable for their expenditure to the Higher Education Funding Council for England (HEFCE) which allocates them funds on behalf of the exchequer. The HEFCE's policy on catering allows for a subsidy on capital costs, that is, buildings and equipment, 'landlord's' expenses and rent and rates where applicable. Apart from a few special exemptions to named universities, they are expected to break even. University catering units have traditionally been of two basic kinds: residential facilities attached to halls that may serve breakfast and evening meals within an inclusive price per term, and central facilities that are open to all students and staff and usually serve lunches and snacks throughout the day with beverages. These catering facilities have to compete openly with the students' union services and independently staffed senior common rooms.

Residential students pay in advance for their board and lodgings. This method has been abandoned by many universities in recent years who have provided reasonable kitchen facilities in the residences to enable students to prepare and cook their own meals if they wish to. Others have introduced a pay-as-you-eat system for residential students. Unfortunately, this has led to reduced catering revenue from students.

Non-residential students are provided with an on-site catering provision that has to compete against all other forms of locally provided catering, with ease of accessibility and some level of subsidy being the main attractions. Increasingly, caterers are turning to ideas from the high street operations to attract and keep their predominantly young adult clientele.

To offset the losses incurred and to achieve a position of break-even in catering, universities have seen the advantages of making their residential and catering facilities available at commercial rates to outside bodies for meetings, conferences and for holidays during the vacation periods.

1.3.1.3 Hospitals

Hospital catering facilities have improved considerably over the past ten to twenty years with the result that new hospitals in particular are benefiting from well planned and managed catering services. Hospital catering is a specialized form of catering as the patient is normally unable to move elsewhere and choose alternative facilities and therefore special attention must be given to the food and beverages so that encouragement is given to eat the meal provided.

The hospital catering service is normally structured on a per capita allowance for patients but with staff paying for all of their meals. A decentralized approach was used in many hospitals where the patients' food and beverages were portioned at the point of delivery in the wards. This often resulted however, in patients receiving cold, unappetizing meals because of the time between the food being prepared and the patients actually receiving it. This method of food service is commonly replaced by a centralized approach that involves the preparation of the patients' trays in or close to the main production area. From here they are transported by trucks or mechanical conveyors to the various floors, and from there directly to the patients so that there should be little delay between the food being plated and served to the patient.

Another trend has seen hospital catering open for tender by contract caterers where in many instances a centralized production system for several nearby hospitals may have to be operated to be viable.

1.3.1.4 The Services

The Services include the armed forces: the Royal Navy, Army and Royal Air Force; the police and fire service, and some government departments. The armed forces often have their own specialist catering branches, for example the army catering is provided by the Royal Logistics Corp. Civil service organizations such as the Metropolitan Police force also have their own catering departments. The levels of food and beverage facilities within the Services vary from the large self-service cafeterias for the majority of personnel, to high class traditional restaurants for more senior members of staff. A considerable number of functions are also held by the Services leading to both small and large scale banqueting arrangements.

13.1.5 Prisons

The population of detainees in all penal institutions in England and Wales is more than 50,000 and continues to grow. Working on a very limited budget, the diet for the inmates is based upon fixed weekly quantities of specific named food commodities with a small weekly cash allowance per head for fresh meat and a further separate weekly cash allowance per head for the local purchase of dietary extras of which a proportion must be spent on fresh fruit. The catering within the prisons is the responsibility of the prison governor with delegated responsibility being given to a catering officer, with much of the actual cooking and service being done by the inmates themselves.

1.3.1.6   *Employee catering*

As already outlined, this is the provision of catering services to employees. The activity may be performed either directly by the employer, or subcontracted out to contract caterers. A direct or in-house catering service that is running smoothly and being well managed is unlikely to change to using a contractor. Those operations, however, that are experiencing difficulty may be wise to consider employing the services of a catering contractor but in doing so must also be sure to define exactly what is required of the contractor in terms of level of service, costs per employee head, revenue, etc.

In providing a catering service for their employees, the parent company may decide at one extreme to subsidize the facility or at the other to pass all the costs on to the customer. There are various formulas for subsidizing prices, but a general one is for the revenue from the catering facility to cover food and labour costs with the remaining costs, such as premises and equipment, fuel costs and management fees to be met by the employer. In some sectors of the industry the catering service may be provided virtually free with the employees making only a small token payment per meal.

A variety of catering styles and levels of service is found in industrial catering situations. The majority of the market is catered for by popular and fast-food facilities incorporating different methods of service, such as self-service cafeterias, buffet restaurants and vending operations. Management in large companies may also have the additional choice of waiter service facilities. At the top end of the industrial catering market, that is those facilities catering for directors and executives, the standard of food and service can equal or exceed that found in commercial high class restaurants.

Catering contractors may be employed for a variety of reasons but it is usually because the company sees itself as engaged in a certain field of industry, manufacturing for example, and therefore does not wish to involve itself in catering, or the company is dissatisfied with the existing catering service and seeks a change. In return for operating a company's catering service, the contract caterers charge a management fee, between 3 and 5 per cent of turnover being the norm. For this fee the contract caterers may install a catering facility if there is not one already there, staff the unit, and then be concerned with its day-to-day operation. Ideally, if the catering operation is being satisfactorily run within the parent company's guidelines, the catering contractors should manage the operation completely, only needing to report to the company at management meetings and other predetermined intervals.

The number of food and beverage outlets reviewed here illustrates the diversity of the hotel and catering industry. It is diverse because it caters for a varied and growing eating-out market. As with all marketing situations, it is prone to change, but although there may be shifts from one sector to another in volume terms, within the general structure of the industry the future points the way towards growth and expansion.

1.4   Cost and market orientation

It is convenient at this point to discuss the broad distinction between cost and market orientation within the hotel and catering industry, as these two terms are closely associated with the particular sectors of the industry that have been identified. Examples of cost orientation are identified in the industry particularly in the welfare sector such as catering in prisons, for patients in hospitals and often for 'in-house' employee restaurants, while market orientation examples are found in the hotels, restaurants, popular and fast-food sectors. It is arguable that all sectors of the industry would be better to employ a market oriented approach.

A market oriented business displays the following characteristics:

1 A high percentage of fixed costs, for example rent, rates, management salaries, depreciation of buildings and equipment. This high percentage of fixed costs remains fixed regardless of any changes in the volume of sales. A hotel restaurant is an example of an operation with high fixed costs.
2 A greater reliance on increases in revenue rather than decreases in costs to contribute to the profit levels of the establishment. The implication here is that in seeking to increase the business's profitability, more emphasis must be given to increasing sales (for example, by increasing the average spend of the customers or by increasing the number of customers) rather than by reducing costs. For this reason the close monitoring of all sales in a market oriented business becomes of prime importance.
3 An unstable market demand for the product, thereby requiring a greater emphasis on all forms of selling and merchandising of the product to eliminate shortfalls in sales.
4 More likely to have a more flexible pricing policy.

A cost oriented business displays the following characteristics:

1 A lower percentage of fixed costs, but a higher percentage of variable costs such as food and beverage costs. The percentage of variable costs in cost oriented establishments varies with changes in the volume of the business's sales. Employee restaurants are often found with a lower percentage of fixed costs.
2 A greater reliance on decreases in costs rather than increases in sales to contribute to the budgeted profit levels of the establishment. Thus in seeking to increase the performance level (budgeted revenue and profit) of a cost oriented business more emphasis should be given to reducing the overall costs of the operation in such areas as purchasing, portion sizes, and labour levels.
3 A relatively stable market demand for the product. In comparison to market oriented businesses, cost oriented operations enjoy a reasonably stable demand for their products.

The potential market for their products is considerably greater, so that operations such as catering outlets in industrial plants, universities and colleges are able to cater to a much wider market.
4 More likely to have a more traditional fixed pricing policy.

There are those areas of the hotel and catering industry that cannot be precisely defined as either cost or market oriented in that they display characteristics of both orientations at different times during their business. In the main, however, most hotel and catering establishments fall into one of these two categories and this has important implications for the catering and financial policies of the business, which are described later.

Service industries, such as food and beverage operations, differ from manufacturing in several ways. The customer is present at the time of both production and service. In manufacturing the customer is not present during the production process. In food and beverage operations, the customer is involved in the creation of the service that is consumed at the point of production with little or no time delay between production and service. The customer is not involved in the creation of manufactured products and there may be a considerable time lag between production and service. Services cannot be examined in advance, they are highly perishable and cannot be stored, all adding to difficulties in the quality control of service products; in manufacturing goods can be made in advance of demand and stored allowing more time for control procedures. Finally, services have a larger intangible element in many of their products than manufactured goods do and for this reason have traditionally been more difficult to quantify and evaluate.

1.5 Food and beverage management

Definitions of management are numerous with writers using different words and phrases to describe the same activity, but if allowance is made for this there is some broad agreement about managers' functions.

First, they are involved in the planning

process – setting objectives, making decisions about which direction the organization should take, that is, formulating policies. Second, managers decide how these objectives should be achieved and by whom. This involves analysing tasks and assigning them to individuals or groups. Third, managers are involved in staff motivation in such a way as to move the organization through them in the direction formulated at the planning stage, to achieve the stated objectives. Fourth, managers have a controlling function including the comparison of actual performance to that forecast at the initial planning stage and taking any necessary steps to correct any deviation from agreed objectives. The controlling may be done by observation, by analysis of accounting records and reports or by analysis of recorded statistical data.

These four management functions – planning, organizing, motivating and controlling – can be translated into the functions of the food and beverage manager. In a food and beverage department, the planning process involves the setting of several basic policies: a financial policy dealing with envisaged profitability or cost constraints of the establishment; a marketing policy defining the market to be catered for; and a catering policy defining the main objectives of operating the food and beverage facilities and the methods by which such objectives are to be achieved. Such policies would be decided at a senior level of management. The tasks needed to achieve these objectives would then be assigned to individuals who should receive job descriptions detailing the purpose of their tasks, the responsibilities of the individuals, who they are responsible to, etc. Here food and beverage managers work in conjunction with the personnel department in producing job descriptions and appointing on-the job trainers to help train new staff.

The motivation of the staff of the food and beverage department is an important function of food and beverage managers. This may be undertaken in several ways – for example, by helping individuals who are undertaking common tasks to form into groups so that a 'team spirit' may develop, by encouraging staff-management committee meetings, or at a more basic level to see that full training is given so that job anxieties are reduced for employees from the beginning.

Finally, there is the element of control in the food and beverage department. This involves the checking of actual performance against expectations or forecasts, and in the case of any wide deviations, to locate the problem area and rectify it, and to take whatever steps are possible to prevent the problem occurring again.

The functions of food and beverage managers in co-ordinating the food and beverage department are therefore numerous, and it is important that they should use all the tools of management available to them. An organization chart should be produced showing the position of the food and beverage department within the context of the total establishment. An organization chart presents graphically the basic groupings and relationships of positions, and a general picture of the formal organization structure.

In larger units, departmentalization becomes more apparent. Figure 1.2 shows the position of a food and beverage department in a large hotel. In this example, the food and beverage manager has one assistant plus three section heads. Together they are responsible for some sixty to seventy full-time staff, out of a total hotel staff of around 150.

Some units are, of course, too small to adopt anything like this type of organization structure. Indeed, in a small privately owned restaurant, it is often the owner who is 'manager' of all departments. In this instance the proprietor would also operate as the control department, monitoring all incoming and outgoing revenues and costs (see Figure 1.3).

It is also important to supplement the organization chart with a job description. A job description is an organized list of duties and responsibilities assigned to a specific position. It may be thought of as an extension of the formal organization chart in that it shows activities and job relationships for the positions identified on the formal organization chart. An example of a food and beverage manager's job description may be seen in Figure 1.4. Some organizations also produce work schedules; these are outlines of work to be performed by employees with stated procedures and time requirements for their duties. Tasks are broken down into a careful sequence of operations and timed. They are particularly useful in training new employees and for lower grade jobs, but have a limited

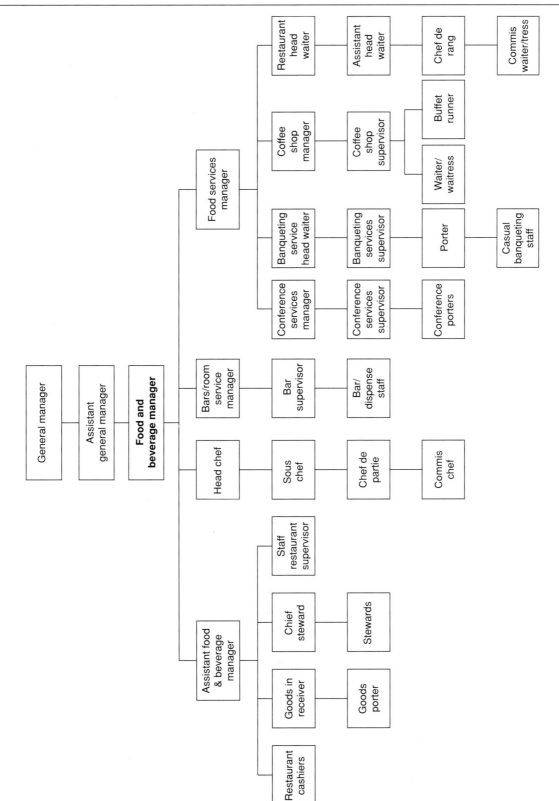

Figure 1.2 *Organization chart from a 300-bedroom four-star hotel*

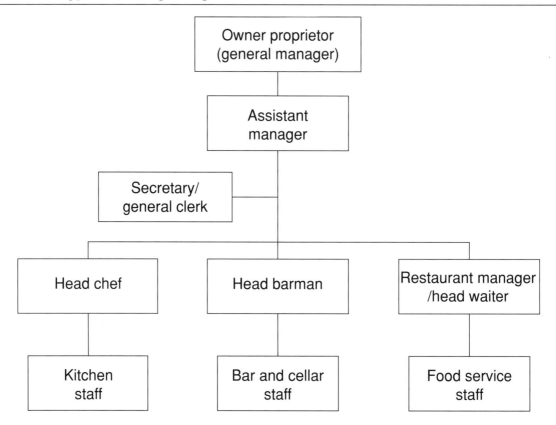

Figure 1.3 *An organization chart for a 100-seater restaurant with some function facilities and two busy bars*

application at the supervisory and management level.

Research conducted on behalf of the HCIMA by the University of Surrey (Gamble, Lockwood and Messenger, 1994), was designed to identify the types of management activities that could be seen to be typical of different sectors of the European hospitality industry. Using a critical incident methodology, the research collected situations in which managers felt that their contributions or actions had made a significant difference to the outcome of a situation; some where the manager's skills and knowledge were used well, and some where the respondents felt their skills and knowledge were lacking. These incidents were then categorized into the four key areas of managing operations, managing the business, managing people and personal skills. Each of these areas was then divided into categories. These fifteen categories represent the key areas of skills and knowledge that any manager in the hospitality industry needs in order to be effective. The categories are illustrated in Figure

1.5 and a description of the main category areas is given in Figure 1.6.

Analysing the incidents against the main category areas by level of management provides the data shown in Table 1.3. To allow for the differences in the titles and roles between industry sectors, the following management levels were used:

- Department head/junior management – managing a section within an operating unit. This would equate to the coffee shop manager in a hotel operation or the assistant manager of a fast food operation.
- Unit manager/section manager – managing a complete unit or a section within a larger unit. This would equate to a unit catering manager working for a contract catering company, an executive chef, or the food and beverage manager of a small hotel.
- General manager – overall control of one large unit composed of a number of sections or a collection of smaller units. This would equate

POINTER HOTELS (UK) LTD
Job Description

Job title:	Food and Beverage Manager
Date:	15-7-9-
Name of unit:	Great Milford Manor Hotel
Responsible to:	The General Manager
Responsible for:	All personnel within the food and beverage department.
Duties:	

1. To maintain efficient catering services within the hotel for the markets previously identified in the marketing and catering policies.
2. To maintain effective control of raw material, labour, and equipment costs used in the food and beverage departments.
3. To liaise with heads of departments in producing departmental budgets for approval by the chief accountant.
4. To be responsible for achieving required revenue and profit targets for all selling outlets whilst maintaining the agreed standards of food and beverage production and service as laid down in the catering policy.
5. To be responsible for hygiene and safety standards in the food and beverage department and ensure all legal requirements are met.
6. To liaise regularly at staff meetings with the heads of departments, together comprising the food and beverage department.
7. To be prepared to attend any other staff meetings as arranged by the general manager.
8. To liaise with the personnel department in the recruiting and training of new personnel for the food and beverage departments.

Figure 1.4   *Job description: food and beverage manager*

to the food and beverage manager of a large hotel with extensive restaurant, conference and banqueting facilities, or the manager of a small number of catering contracts.

- Regional manager – overall responsibility for a number of separate large units or geographic areas.
- Director – responsibility for the operation and management of a complete organization
- Owner/proprietor/partner.

Managing operations recorded the second highest number of incidents across the three sub-categories of managing day-to-day operations, specialist/technical areas and managing crises.

The analysis by managerial level, shown above shows a heavy emphasis in this area for the junior managers. This was strongest in day-to-day operations and specialist knowledge but when it came to a crisis the junior managers were more likely to call in their unit or general manager. Owners also get heavily involved in sorting out the crises that may occur within their businesses. Sector comparisons show that hotels and restaurants reported the heaviest emphasis on managing operations while employee catering had the lowest.

The area of managing the business included aspects of managing business performance, managing projects, managing strategic decisions

Table 1.3   *A cross tabulation of level of management against the main category areas*

Column %	Junior	Unit	General	Regional	Director	Owner	Total %
Managing operations	40.3	30.2	20.9	13.4	17.8	29.3	29.0
Managing the business	11.8	23	32.6	41.2	41.1	32	25.2
Managing people	10.7	16.4	15.9	19.6	12..3	9.5	14.4
Personal skills	37.2	30.4	30.6	25.8	28.8	29.3	31.5
Total (%)	23.2	36.5	19.6	6.3	4.8	9.6	100

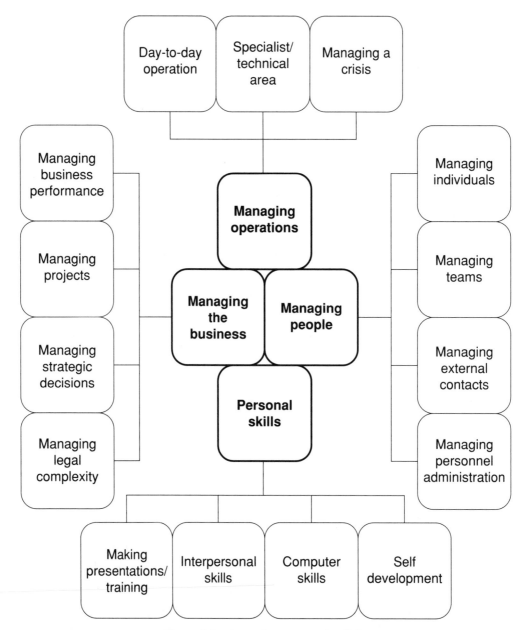

Figure 1.5   *Areas of management activity*

MANAGING OPERATIONS
This category represents those activities that form the key operational activities of the business. They are concerned with ensuring that hospitality products and services are delivered to the customer in the intended way and to the required standard. They represent the daily activity of the manager who must ensure that operations run as smoothly as possible given the constraints of a customer driven business.

MANAGING THE BUSINESS
This category represents those activities that are focused on controlling the current financial success of the business and determining its future strategic direction. The ability to monitor current performance must be developed and proposals for any required corrective action must be developed. On many occasions this will involve the implementation and supervision of a project based approach to ensure that plans are carried out. Not only must managers review current performance but they must also look forward and provide a strategic direction. At all times the business must operate within legal guidelines.

MANAGING PEOPLE
The nature of the hospitality business ensures that a large part of the manager's activity will be concerned with achieving results through others, be they subordinates, colleagues or superiors. Aside from the purely interpersonal aspects of managing people dealt with in another category, managers must be able to provide a framework within which each individual or team can contribute to the best of their ability.

PERSONAL MANAGEMENT SKILLS
The skills and knowledge that a manager in the hospitality industry requires are not restricted to the technical operation of the business or the organization of effective work activities. They must also include skills of a more personal nature which reflect not so much on what is done but more on the way that things are done. Once these skills have been acquired, the manager must continue to develop to be able to deal with new situations, new technology and new challenges.

Figure 1.6 *Description of the main management categories*

and managing legal complexity. Across the whole sample, this area was in third place behind personal skills and managing operations. More detailed analysis by managerial level reveals some significant differences. Although general managers, regional managers and directors show significantly more incidents in this area, junior managers and unit managers show a low emphasis. This suggests that managers as a whole may be becoming more business oriented but only when they have reached a position of some seniority with an organization. Comparisons across the sectors of the industry reflect this emphasis, with hotels, restaurants and popular catering, sectors with large numbers of junior managers, showing a low empha-

sis on this area but other sectors, especially contract catering and local authority services, featuring positively.

The managing people area covered managing individuals, managing teams, managing external contacts and managing personnel administration. It was therefore surprising that, given the labour intensity of many sectors of the industry and the natural importance given to this area, there were relatively few reported incidents in this area. One explanation for this anomaly is that the interpersonal skills involved in managing people are not included in this section but are categorized as more generic personal skills. Analysis across managerial level shows unit managers having the highest score in this area with junior managers and owners having low scores.

The area of personal skills includes a range of generic or transferable skills that cover making verbal or written presentations, training, interpersonal skills, using computers in management and self development. There were more incidents reported in this area than any other and most of these were in the interpersonal skills area, followed by making presentations and training. Using computers in business showed comparatively few incidents and incidents to do with self development were sadly, for an industry that seemingly values training highly, very sparse. All levels of manager reported large numbers of incidents in the area of interpersonal skills, especially the junior managers who would be new to having to handle these situations. Again there was an even spread across all sectors of the industry but a heavier than expected emphasis in popular catering or fast food. This is perhaps a reflection of the time managers spend dealing with interpersonal issues when the technological issues have been removed from consideration through systematized service delivery systems.

1.6   Responsibilities of food and beverage management

The research described above highlights the areas of activity that all managers are involved in but does not look at the specific responsibilities of the food and beverage manager. The significant contribution food and beverage sales can make towards total sales is evident but food and beverage costs can make equally significant inroads into sales. This necessitates the development of an effective system of control for all areas concerned with the food and beverage function. The development of such a total control system begins with the basic policy decisions described previously – the determination of the financial, marketing and catering policies. Working within these three broad policies of the establishment, the food and beverage department is then able to detail its objectives.

The main responsibilities and objectives of the food and beverage department may be summarized as follows:

1 The provision of food and beverage products and services catering for clearly defined markets to satisfy or exceed these customers' expectations.
2 The purchasing, receiving, storing, issuing and preparation of food and beverages within the establishment for final provision and service to the customer.
3 The formulation of an efficient control system within the food and beverage department with the purpose of:
   • monitoring food and beverage prices and achieving competitive rates while still ensuring quality standards;
   • pricing restaurant and special function menus to achieve desired profit margins;
   • compiling on a daily, weekly and monthly basis, all relevant food and beverage information on costs and sales that may be used by management for forecasting, planning, budgeting, etc.
4 Reconciling actual and forecast costs and sales, and initiating corrective action if discrepancies occur, and finding out and eliminating the causes, for example bad portion control, incorrect pricing, etc.
5 Training, directing, motivating and monitoring of all food and beverage department staff.
6 Co-operating with other departments to become a significant contributor to the organization's short- and long-term profitability.
7 Obtaining in a regular, structured and systematic way, feedback from customers, so that their comments, complaints and compliments may be taken into account to improve the overall standard of service.

These are the major responsibilities and objectives of a food and beverage department. Other minor objectives do become important during the day-to-day running of the department, but these often tend to deal with sudden crises or short-term problems and would be too numerous to mention. However, achieving all these objectives is a far from easy task when managers are faced with the inherent complexity and variability of a food and beverage operation.

1.7 Constraints on food and beverage management

The management of food and beverage departments has been described as the most technical and complex in the hotel and catering trade. The specific factors that make food and beverage management relatively more complex are due to particular external and internal pressures.

1.7.1 External factors

The external factors are often seen as the 'major' problems of the food and beverage function. They originate outside the organization and for this reason internal action can rarely solve the problem adequately, although proactive management may help to reduce their impact. Some of the major external pressures affecting the food and beverage function are listed below.

1.7.1.1 *Government/political*

- Government legislation, for example, fire regulations, health and safety acts, EU regulations.
- Changes in the fiscal structure of the country, for example, regulations affecting business expense allowances.
- Specific government taxes, for example, VAT.
- Government policy on training and employment, economic development, regional development, etc.

1.7.1.2 *Economic*

- Rising costs – foods and beverages, labour, fuel, rates and insurance.
- Sales instability – peaks and troughs of activity occur on a daily, weekly and seasonal basis.
- Changes in expenditure patterns and people's disposable incomes.
- Expansion and retraction of credit facilities.
- Interest rates on borrowed capital.

1.7.1.3 *Social*

- Changes in population distribution, for example, population drifting away from certain areas or demographic such as age structure.
- Changes in the socio-economic groupings of an area.
- Growth of ethnic minorities leading to a demand for more varied foods.
- Changes in food fashion, for example, current popularity of take-away foods, home delivery of fast foods, trends in healthy eating.

1.7.1.4 *Technical*

- Mechanization, for example, of food production and food service equipment.
- Information technology, for example, data processing in hotel and catering establishments.
- Product development, for example, organic vegetables, increased shelf life of foods through irradiation, meat and dairy produce alternatives.

1.7.2 Internal factors

Along with external factors, the food and beverage function also has many other day-to-day internal pressures. Internal problems are those originating within the organization and for this reason such problems can usually be solved adequately within the establishment if they can be identified and the root cause removed. The internal problems may be classified as follows.

1.7.2.1 *Food and beverage*

- Perishability of food and the need for adequate stock turnover.
- Wastage and bad portion control.
- Pilferage from kitchens, restaurants, bars and stores.

1.7.2.2 *Staff*

- General staff shortages and skill shortages within the industry.
- Staff shortages often coinciding with peaks of sales activity.
- Conversely, staff surpluses coinciding with troughs in sales activity.
- Absenteeism, illness, etc.
- Use of part-time or casual staff in some food and beverage departments.

- Poor supervision and training of new staff.
- High staff turnover, particularly in some areas.

1.7.2.3   Control

- Cash and credit control and collection.
- Maintenance of all costs in line with budget guidelines and current volumes of business, for example, food, beverages, payroll, etc.
- Maintenance of a tight and efficient control of all food and beverage stocks.
- Maintenance of up-to-date costing and pricing of all menu items.
- Maintenance of an efficient food and beverage control system giving analysed statistical data of all business done.

There is a dividing line between those food and beverage departments that take a proactive approach to these external and internal problems and hence function more efficiently, and those that just react to the problems only ever treating the symptoms and not the causes. It is important therefore that potential problem areas be identified in advance by management so that they can be planned for and successfully managed when and if they occur. This is only possible if there is some form of feedback from the control function back to management so that they are kept constantly aware of, first, changes occurring within the food and beverage area itself, and second, changes occurring outside the establishment that may have an effect. The types of information that management must receive to monitor the food and beverage areas are discussed in the following chapters.

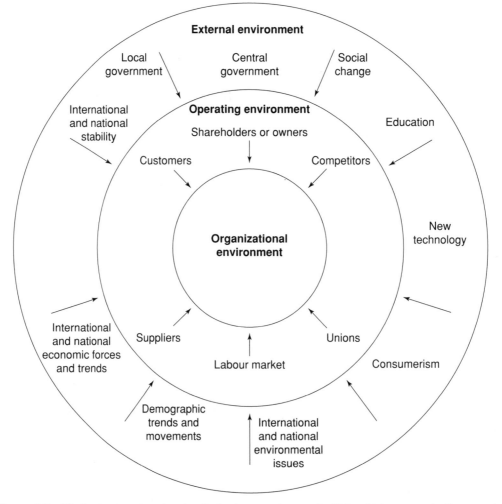

Figure 1.7   *The business system showing the business environment within which an organization operates*

Figure 1.7 shows diagramatically the potential sources of issues and problems that food and beverage managers need to be aware of if they are to maintain and improve the effectiveness of their operations. Being a food and beverage manager is a challenging and demanding job but with the clear understanding and systematic approach that the following chapters provide, it can also be a rewarding and satisfying one.

1.8 References

CSO (1980). *Standard Classification*. London: Central Statistical Office.

Gamble, P., Lockwood, A. and Messenger, S. (1994). *Management Skills in the European Hospitality Industry, 48th Annual CHRIE Conference*. Palm Springs July 27–30.

2
The meal experience

2.1 Introduction

The 'meal experience' may be defined as a series of events – both tangible and intangible – that a customer experiences when eating out. It is difficult to define exactly where a meal experience actually starts, and indeed ends, although it is usually assumed that the main part of the experience begins when customers enter a restaurant and ends when they leave. However, any feelings customers may have when they arrive at the restaurant, and when they leave, should also be taken into account and included as part of the total meal experience.

The series of events and experiences customers undergo when eating out may be divided into those tangible aspects of the product, that is, the food and drink, and those intangible aspects such as service, atmosphere, mood, etc.

These two components of the meal experience have also been labelled primary and secondary (derivative) products (Axler, 1979) but although differing in descriptive terms, the underlying concept is the same. It is the appreciation of the different components by the caterer that is important; the tangible and the intangible aspects must be integrated together to present a total product to the customer. If one or two components of the meal experience are out of harmony with the others, the whole product/service mix will be seen by the customer as a number of disjointed parts rather than as a totality.

Before customers set out to a catering facility for a meal, they may already have decided on the type of meal they want or feel would be most suitable for that particular occasion. This pre-meal experience decision may have been taken after the consideration of a number of variables and customers will choose the facility they consider satisfies all or most of their requirements. The general factors affecting a customer's choice of meal experience include the following:

1 *Social*. A social occasion is one of the most common reasons for eating out. Such family events as birthdays and anniversaries, special dates (Christmas, the New Year, Valentine's Day and Halloween), a special event (a christening and passing examinations) are all reasons for celebration and dining out. Equally, people decide to go to a restaurant for no other reason than to dine with friends. Sometimes restaurants offer a different style of meal experience, for example foreign specialities, entertainment during the meal such as films, or cabaret.

The type of meal experience and the reasons people give as to why they eat out, can be seen in Tables 2.1 and 2.2. For those people who eat out infrequently, maybe two or three times a year, the celebration of a special occasion is the most important reason. As the number of meal occasions per year rises, to over four times a year, there is a corresponding increase in the variety of reasons given, for example, to socialize with friends and relatives, as a treat for self or spouse, as a change from eating at home, etc.

2 *Business*. Meals may also be taken away from

Table 2.1 *The eating out market 1995–1999*

| | Value (£b) | | | | | Change |
	1995	1996	1997	1998	1999	1995–99
Fast food*	5.79	5.87	6.01	6.18	6.42	+10.9%
Pub catering	4.30	4.33	4.37	4.39	4.44	+3.3%
Restaurants	2.15	2.13	2.11	2.12	2.15	–
Hotel catering	1.39	1.36	1.36	1.37	1.36	−2.2%
In-store	0.81	0.80	0.80	0.79	0.79	−2.5%
Roadside	0.57	0.58	0.59	0.61	0.63	+10.5%
Other#	1.49	1.48	1.58	1.63	1.69	+13.4%
Total	16.50	16.55	16.82	17.09	17.48	+5.9%

*includes take-away.
#includes clubs, camps, casinos, mobile catering.
Source: Mintel quoted in *Caterer and Hotelkeeper*, 28 September 1995, p. 14.

Table 2.2   *Analysis of those who eat out frequently: by reason for eating out*

	Once a week		Twice a week		Three or more times a week		Frequently i.e at least once a week	
	No.	%	No.	%	No.	%	No.	%
Necessity:	56		57		67		61	
• No special reason		33		35		31		33
• I was hungry		15		16		22		18
• I always eat at that time		4		4		10		6
• I was out shopping		3		1		3		3
• I wasn't at home		1		1		1		1
Treat:	31		29		24		28	
• It was a special occasion		13		13		10		12
• It was a treat		12		10		8		10
• I was on holiday/an outing		3		5		5		4
• It was a social occasion		3		1		1		2
At home/Replacement:	7		8		2		6	
• I didn't want to cook		5		5		2		4
• I had nothing to eat at home		2		3		–		2
Business meal:	2		3		5		4	
Other reason:	4		3		3		1	
	100	100	100	100	100	100	100	100
Base	286		147		221		654	

Source: Copyright © Marketpower Limited/FDS Limited

home for business reasons. Generally speaking the level of restaurant chosen will depend on the level of business being conducted, so that the more important and valued the business, the more expensive and up-market will be the restaurant. Business lunches and dinners are still the most common, although working breakfasts and teas are also offered by some catering outlets, particularly hotels.

3 *Convenience and time.* A food service facility may be convenient because of its location or because of its speed of service. A working couple arriving home may decide to eat out rather than prepare something at home; they do not wish to travel far, nor do they want an elaborate meal, so they choose a local pizzeria, Indian or Chinese restaurant. A family out shopping at the weekend decide to have lunch in a fast-food operation in the high street. A long-distance commuter has a full meal on board a train, knowing that he will arrive home late that evening. Office workers or hospital staff with little time available decide to have lunch in the staff canteen. Housewives out shopping decide to stop for a snack in a shopping centre.

All of these are typical examples of convenience eating away from home. They are convenient sometimes in terms of location, sometimes speed, because of the limited amount of time a customer has for a meal, and very often a combination of the two. Most of the facilities used are associated with the mass-market end of the catering industry: fast-food operations; coffee shops; catering facilities in shopping centres; pizzerias; steak houses; cafeterias in leisure complexes; vending machines in schools; hospitals; offices; and other work situations.

4 *Atmosphere and service.* The atmosphere, cleanliness and hygiene of certain types of catering facilities and the social skills of the service staff can be particularly attractive to certain groups of customers. For example, wine and cocktail bars, and champagne and oyster bars in city centres appeal, in particular, to employ-

ees who have spent the day working together in offices and wish to meet together after work. The widespread use of 'Happy Hours' in such operations has further encouraged this trend for workers to go straight from their place of work to a catering outlet to socialize. These facilities are also often attractive because of their convenient locations.

5 *Price.* The price level of an operation will significantly affect the restaurant choice of customers, particularly 'impulse' buying decisions. For the majority of customers, except perhaps for those who can afford to regularly patronize high-quality restaurants, there exists a 'trade-off' point between the task and cost of preparing a meal at home, or paying for a meal out. Generally speaking, the higher the disposable income, the higher the trade-off level. For example a couple may consider it quite acceptable spending up to £30 for an impulse meal experience once a week; another couple may consider this price too high and would only be willing to pay up to £30 once a month. If they thought the meal was likely to cost more than £30 they would trade-off the meal experience at a restaurant for a meal at home, or perhaps a cheaper takeaway meal.

6 *The menu.* Finally, a restaurant's menu may appear particularly interesting or adventurous, or have been recommended, enabling customers to enjoy a different type of meal from that cooked at home.

All of these factors will at some stage affect the buying decision of customers and hence their choice of meal experience, although it is unlikely that any of these variables will operate in isolation – usually two or three factors together will influence customers' choice of operation. Once customers have decided on the type of meal they want, they will start to accumulate different expectations and anticipations. Just as customers' buying decision is influenced by a number of variables, so too is the meal experience itself.

2.2   Eating out

An analysis of who eats out and the frequency that they do, is valuable data for all caterers.

The analysis of who the customers actually are is necessary information, not only for caterers in general, operational management in particular, but also for marketing management. The size of the eating out market was illustrated in Table 2.1.

The actual reasons given by customers for eating out is also important data. An example of this type of analysis of those who eat out frequently, by frequency level, and against the overall profile, was given in Table 2.2.

The analysis of those who eat out can be done in many ways. For example, it can be done by age (Table 2.3), by socio-economic class (Table 2.4), and by the frequency of eating out – whether once, twice, or three or more times a week (Tables 2.2–2.5). Other examples of the types of analysis that may be done are by marital status, by the number of people in a household, by the number and age of children in the household, and by region within a country or of a specific area, etc.

What types of catering establishments that the public choose to eat out at, and the frequency that they do, is also valuable information. Examples of this type of market research are illustrated in Tables 2.6 and 2.7.

Major research of this nature is conducted by established market research organizations such as Marketpower Ltd, FDS Market Research Group Ltd, and Key Note, who undertake major published studies for the industry in general. Specific and confidential studies are also undertaken for individual companies. Research is also undertaken by the marketing departments of medium/large hotel and catering companies. This does not preclude the smaller-size establishment from undertaking some systematic research studies, although the sample size is likely to be smaller and the time available to do it restricted.

Ideally, basic information should provide:

1 sufficient data to aid decision-making;
2 accurate and up-to-date consumer profiles, so that an organization is more successfully able to meet the requirements of the consumer;
3 competitive analysis, so that an organization can in part measure its own performance.

Research of this nature should always be ongoing, and not just of an occasional nature.

Table 2.3 *Analysis of those who eat out frequently: by age group*

| | Contribution to those who eat out %: | | | |
	Once a week	Twice a week	Three or more times a week	Frequently i.e. at least once a week
16–24	7	15	23	14
25–34	27	22	28	27
35–44	18	16	20	18
45–54	14	21	10	14
55–64	16	13	9	13
65–74	12	11	8	10
75+	6	2	2	4
Total	100	100	100	100
Base	286	147	221	654

Source: Copyright © *Marketpower Limited/FDS Limited*

Table 2.4 *Analysis of those who eat out frequently: by socio-economic class*

| | Contribution to those who eat out %: | | | |
	Once a week	Twice a week	Three or more times a week	Frequently i.e at least once a week
AB	20	22	26	22
C1	38	30	36	36
C2	20	26	20	21
D	10	12	12	11
E	10	10	6	9
Total	100	100	100	100
Base	286	147	221	654

Source: Copyright © *Marketpower Limited/FDS Limited*

The following variables are all components of the meal experience and should individually and collectively be considered by the catering facility.

2.3 Food and drink

The type of food and drink that people choose to consume away from home depends on a number of factors which are of particular concern to customers. They include:

1 The choice of food and drink available: whether the menu is limited or extensive; whether the operation revolves around one particular product, for example, steak houses and pizzerias; or whether there is a varied choice, for example, coffee shops and wine bars.

Tables 2.6 and 2.7 show examples of the types of catering outlets visited, at least once a month, by age groupings and by gender, from a sample of 1056 adults. This shows that the majority of men and women visit catering establishments at least once a month. Public houses are the most popular eating out establishments, and are frequented by more males than females, and more by the under-45 year age groups. Despite the growth of the branded national and international fast-food companies, the fish and chip shops are second in popularity, followed by Chinese restaurants, and then fast-food establishments.

The young consumers, 16- to 24-year olds, have a preference for fish and chip shops and fast-food burger outlets, whilst the 65-plus year old group, are rather traditional, having strong preferences for public houses and fish and chip shops.

2 The quality of the product offered, for example, fresh or convenience foods: château bottled or a blended non-château bottled wine.

3 The quantity of product offered, that is, the portion sizes. For example, does the restaurant offer children's meals or smaller portions for children?

4 The consistent standard of the product: customers returning to the restaurant and repeating their order of an item would expect the product to be the same as they had eaten or drunk before.

5 The range of tastes, textures, aromas and colours offered by a food dish, or the taste, colour and aroma offered by a drink.

6 That the food and drink are served at the correct temperatures, for example, that the iced coffee is sufficiently chilled, or that hot food is hot when it reaches the customer.

7 That the presentation of the food and drink enhances the product offered. This is particularly important at all levels of catering, from cafeteria to haute cuisine service, where the visual presentation of the meal is very much part of the total experience.

Table 2.5 *Analysis of those who eat out frequently by type of outlet in which last meal or snack was eaten*

| | Contribution to those who eat out %: | | | |
	Once a week	Twice a week	Three or more times a week	Frequently i.e. at least once a week
Hotel/guest house/other accommodation	3	4	5	4
Restaurant	29	34	36	32
Fast food	11	11	9	10
Cafe/take away	24	16	11	18
Pub/club	24	29	17	23
Travel outlet	1	1	1	1
Leisure	1	–	–	1
Sports club	2	1	–	–
Work	2	3	15	7
Hospital/clinic/ care home	–	–	1	–
School/university	1	1	4	2
Total	100	100	100	100
Base	286	147	221	654

Source: Copyright © *Marketpower Limited/FDS Limited*

Table 2.6 *Establishments visited at least once a month by gender (% of respondents), 1996*

	Males	Females	Total
Public houses	38	30	34
Fish and chip shops	30	27	28
Chinese restaurants	21	22	22
Indian restaurants	15	16	15
Mexican restaurants	1	3	2
Carveries/steakhouses	9	6	7
American diners/bistros	4	2	3
Fast-food burger outlets	20	19	20
Fast-food chicken outlets	7	6	7
Pizza/pasta restaurants	18	13	16
Thai restaurants	2	1	2
Vegetarian restaurants	2	3	3
None of these	29	32	30

Base: 1,056 adults

Source: The Gallup Organization/Key Note

Table 2.7 *Establishments visited at least once a month by age (% of respondents), 1996*

	16–24	25–34	35–44	45–64	65+
Public houses	35	37	36	34	27
Fish and chip shops	48	38	30	19	14
Chinese restaurants	33	37	26	15	4
Indian restaurants	21	32	21	6	3
Mexican restaurants	5	3	3	1	0
Carveries/steakhouses	4	7	9	9	7
American diners	8	4	4	1	0
Fast-food burger outlets	46	33	21	7	3
Fast-food chicken outlets	13	15	6	3	0
Pizza/pasta restaurants	32	25	18	9	1
Thai restaurants	2	4	1	1	0
Vegetarian restaurants	5	5	3	1	1
None of these	7	12	24	41	58

Base: 1,056 adults

Source: The Gallup Organization/Key Note

8 That the price and perceived value for money are both in line with customers' pre-meal experience anticipations.

9 That the quality of the total meal experience matches or even enhances the expectations of the guests.

2.4   Variety in menu choice

The type of menu offered by an establishment and the variety of menu choice should also enhance the total meal experience. At the lower level of the market the choice of menu items in a restaurant is usually fairly limited for a number of reasons. First, price. If a customer is paying £6–£7 for a three-course meal the range of menu items that can be made available within the cost limits of such an operation is obviously more limited than in operations where the customer's average spending power is higher. Second, the amount of time taken to consume meals at this level of the market may vary between half an hour and one hour, but will rarely exceed this. Proportionately, little of this time is spent studying the menu choice. Third, it may be suggested that customers frequenting this lower level of the market may be uncomfortable if presented with a very large menu selection and may therefore prefer a more limited, but still varied menu choice.

In high-class restaurants where the average spending power is above £40 per head, the menu selection is much greater. In these establishments which encourage a luxury meal experience, the minimum amount of time customers usually spend on a meal is one and a half hours, and may often be three hours, depending on the size of the group and the occasion. The proportion of the time that may be devoted to reading the menu and selecting from the menu items is correspondingly greater. Customers frequenting these types of establishment would also expect to be offered not only a large menu selection, but also a number of chef's and house specialities and wines.

The menu choice offered by a restaurant is therefore dependent on a number of interrelated factors: the price the customer is willing to pay; the amount of time available for the meal experience; the level of the market in which the restaurant is situated and, consequently, the types of customer likely to frequent that type of operation. Further considerations affecting the choice of menu from the caterer's point of view would be the production and service facilities available, the skills of the staff, the availability of commodities and the potential profitability of the menu.

2.5   Level of service

Broadly speaking the higher the cost of the meal to the customer, the more service the customer expects to receive. In a food court where customers are spending approximately £3–£5 for a two-course meal, the degree of service received is comparatively little: customers collect and purchase their own food from particular food units, carry it to a table, and may clear their dishes from the table at the end of their meal. As the cost of the meal to customers increases so will the amount of service they receive. At the higher end of the catering market, where customers may be paying over £40 per head for a meal, full waiter silver service is most likely to be provided.

The actual service of the food and beverages to the customer may be described as the 'direct' service. Part of the restaurant's total service, however, is also composed of 'indirect' services. These include the provision of cloakroom facilities (somewhere for the customer to leave coats and bags safely); and the availability of a telephone for customer use (this is particularly important in restaurants with a large business lunch trade). It is necessary for a restaurant to identify the level of service it is going to offer in its catering establishment and to extend this standard of service throughout all aspects of the operation. Thus, if a restaurant has a very formal type of food and beverage service, usually associated with high-class operations, the other aspects of the restaurant service should be equally formal – the speed, efficiency and dress of staff; the degree of personalization and courtesy the customers receives, and so on. It is important, therefore, for a restaurant operation to consider not only the service of the food and beverages for which the staff are usually adequately trained, but also to remember the indirect service aspect of the operation, which are all part of the customer's meal experience.

2.6   Price and value for money

The concept of value for money will vary from one sector of the market to another and, indeed, from one customer to another. In the majority of cases, however, customers will frequent a restaurant not only because of its food and service, but also because they feel the price they are paying represents value for money. At the popular end of the market, inclusive (or packaged) price meals are often offered. For example, in the summer, many of the steak house operations offer rump steak and strawberries at an inclusive and competitive price, so that a prospective client is aware in advance what the main cost of the meal will be, and this will help alleviate any concern the customer may have about the total cost of the meal. At the top end of the market, menu items are often charged for separately because at this level the total cost of the meal is not such an important factor to the customer as perhaps are the other aspects of the operation, such as the standard and range of food and beverages, the level of service offered and the degree of comfort, décor and atmosphere. However, there has been some emphasis over recent years on the set price menu in quality and luxury restaurants, particularly for lunch, to attract business account meals where an idea of the cost can be ascertained beforehand.

Today, some establishments include a service charge in the price of their meals, others show it separately, while some operations do not include a service charge but leave it to the customer's discretion. Prices charged within the UK are inclusive of government taxes, while in some other countries the total amount of tax is shown separately. Some schools of thought consider that by not showing these 'added extras', such as a service or cover charge in the price of the individual menu items, customers may be encouraged to spend more because the prices will appear very reasonable; others consider that customers prefer to know exactly what they are paying for and do not like to see these 'extras' added at the end of the bill.

2.7   Interior design

The overall interior design of a restaurant is one of the first physical aspects of a catering operation that a customer will come into contact with. This first impression of the restaurant is very important. Potential customers passing by may like the look of the establishment and decide to come and eat there; customers who have actually planned to eat in the restaurant and like what they see when they enter, will feel pleased with their choice of restaurant.

The interior design of a restaurant is composed of many different aspects: the size and shape of the room; the furniture and fittings; the colour scheme; lighting; air conditioning; etc. As with the previously described aspects of a restaurant, there is a need for a sense of totality in a restaurant's interior design. The colour scheme of the restaurant should blend and balance and be enhanced by lighting arrangements; tables and chairs ergonomically and aesthetically designed so that they not only satisfy their functional purpose, but also look attractive.

The interior design of a restaurant contributes greatly to the creation of its image. A self service cafeteria in an industrial situation, for example, may consist of a very large dining area, tables and chairs of a standard design and shape, the colour scheme of the restaurant having few variations and lighting arrangements being purely functional. For this type of catering operation a consistently steady seat turnover is required, and this is encouraged by designing the interior of the restaurant so that it does not invite diners to linger over their meal; in addition a separate coffee lounge or area may be provided where customers may go afterwards and in this way vacate their seat for the next diner.

In a luxury restaurant, however, seat turnover is not so critical and, in fact, customers may be encouraged to stay in the restaurant to increase their average spend. In these types of establishment the interior design of the restaurant is made to be very comfortable: the lighting in the restaurant is quite subdued; the colour scheme has warmth and depth; there may be several particular points of interest in the restaurant, such as pictures, murals and large floral displays to hold the customer's interest; tables are farther apart, and may be separated from one another in booths or by partitions; and the chairs are so designed that the customer may sit in them for several hours without feeling uncomfortable.

The interior design of a catering facility needs to be carefully considered at the initial planning stage and if necessary professional advice sought in order to avoid costly corrective measures later. The life cycle of the operation also needs to be taken into account as this will significantly affect the financial investment in this aspect of the catering operation.

2.8 Atmosphere and mood

The atmosphere or mood of a restaurant is a difficult aspect of an operation to define, but is often described as an intangible 'feel' inside a restaurant. Not all restaurants have an obvious type of atmosphere, others try to deliberately create one. For example, luxury high-class restaurants often have a very formal atmosphere which is created by the dress and attitude of the staff, the decor of the restaurant, the service accompaniments, the type of clientele that frequent these restaurants, etc. Other restaurants such as steak houses, wine bars and pizza and pasta restaurants, try to create a relaxed informal atmosphere, and one that is very sociable to be a part of and seen in.

The atmosphere of a restaurant is affected by many different aspects of the operation. They include the décor and interior design of the restaurant, the table and seating arrangements, the service accompaniments, the dress and attitude of the staff, the tempo of service, the age, dress and sex of the other customers, the sound levels in the restaurant, whether music is played, the temperature of the restaurant, bars and cloakrooms, and the overall cleanliness of the environment and the professionalism of the staff. Again, the harmony between the product itself, the service and the overall environment is important. If one of these aspects is out of unison with the others, disharmony may result in the customer's image of the restaurant, and the customer will invariably leave feeling unsettled and remembering that one small aspect. In a high-class restaurant, for example, it is expected that linen napkins would be provided; should paper ones have to be provided customers may feel cheated when they consider the price they are paying for the meal.

2.9 Expectation and identification

A single customer or group of customers arriving at a restaurant for a meal bring with them a series of expectations regarding that restaurant – the type of service they will receive, the price they will pay, the expected atmosphere and mood of the restaurant, etc. The customer's expectations may be varied and numerous, ranging from the restaurant which the customer frequents because they want to be seen there and participate in its social atmosphere, to the small quiet restaurant where the customer may go because of its intimate and personal nature. Upon arrival at the restaurant, if the product presented to customers is in harmony with their expectations, it is very likely that they will be pleased with their choice and have a relaxed and enjoyable meal. Should customers sense disharmony, however, between their expectation of the restaurant and the actual product they find, for example, it is too intimate for the occasion, they may not enter the restaurant but choose another. If disharmony is not realized until customers are seated at the table, it is unlikely that they will leave but will have a hurried and uncomfortable meal.

There is a need for customers to be able to identify and associate themselves with a particular restaurant for a particular meal occasion. They may not always identify with the same restaurant, as their needs and expectations may vary from one meal experience to the next. For example, at a business lunch a customer may require an expensive haute cuisine restaurant with an atmosphere conducive to discussing business; such a restaurant, however, may not be suitable for the same customer to take the family to for a special occasion. A customer therefore has different needs and expectations on different meal occasions, and similarly at different times of the day, for example lunch and dinner. These alternating needs of customers should be identified by a restaurant and catered for differently; for example, the restaurant offering formal business lunches may offer special function catering in the evening when the demand for business meals is minimal. There is a danger in these situations, however, that restaurants may be led into catering for mixed markets, and it is important for a restaurant offering different levels of service at different times of the day, to keep them completely separate, and not attempt to be 'all things to all people'. Those operations that have not taken this approach invariably adjust downwards to a lower socio-economic market segment than the one to which they were originally catering.

Where different levels of markets are being catered for within the same establishment, it is sometimes possible for separate entrances to be used to service the different facilities, or functions timed so that the guests do not enter the operation all at the same time, and all require the use of the ancillary facilities simultaneously, such as cloakrooms, toilets, telephones, car parking spaces, etc. In a hotel, for example, the speciality restaurant may be situated on the top floor featuring panoramic views, while the night club may be found on the lower ground floor; both facilities operating successfully within the same establishment, but both with separate entrances, ancillary amenities and catering to different types of clientele.

2.10   Location and accessibility

The location of a food service facility may be said to be its most important feature: 'Services which are not appropriately located may not be performed at all' (Rathmell, 1974).

The situation of a catering facility must be made after careful identification of the location of the market segments to which it is catering. For example, a take-away fish and chip shop catering to a market segment identified as being couples with children of CD1 socio-economic classification (see Table 4 .1), could not be situated farther than two or three miles from this market; any distance greater than this and potential customers would consider choosing a fish and chip shop closer to their home.

The restaurant's location in relation to its present markets should not only be considered but also its location to possible future markets. For example, a city restaurant may rely heavily on a number of large local companies for the majority of its lunchtime trade; should several of these companies leave the area the restaurant's demand would be significantly affected. A roadside restaurant's trade would also be affected by the expansion or relocation of a major nearby road and consequently an increase or decrease in the volume of traffic and hence customers. The future expansion on a site with the possibility of

catering to larger or mixed markets should also be considered and incorporated into the initial planning stage whenever possible.

The accessibility to a catering operation is another important factor. Customers arriving by car will expect adequate car parking facilities. If customers have to travel by public transport, the operation should be well served by buses, trains, or taxis. If a high street take-away facility expects a large percentage of its business from passing trade there should be a heavy pedestrian flow past its doors.

2.11   Food and beverage service employees

Staff employed by a restaurant operation should complement the meal experience of the customers, and they are able to do this in a variety of ways: their social skills; their age and sex; their uniform; the tempo of their service, and so on. The number of staff serving in a restaurant is closely related to the prices charged by the establishment and the level of service that it offers. In self-service operations very few service staff are required; in some establishments the ratio of staff to customers being as low as one member of staff to twenty to forty customers. However, in the luxury haute cuisine restaurants offering full French service, the ratio may be as high as one member of staff to eight customers. These latter types of operations are, however, charging the customers for this extra attentive service and must therefore be seen to have an adequate number of staff.

Not only does the number of staff in a restaurant contribute to the meal experience, but also their attitude to customers and the tempo of their service. In a large employee cafeteria where the ratio of service staff to customers may be low and speed of throughput important, the staff are required to work at a fast and efficient speed, and where possible leave the customers to serve themselves. In a luxury restaurant the tempo of the staff is considerably slower and more relaxed because of the higher ratio of service staff to customers. It should be noted that the attitude of the staff is almost totally influenced by the management attitude and the environmental climate in which the staff are working.

The uniforms of the service staff should be appropriate for the level of the catering operation, and again this physical aspect of the restaurant must be seen to be a part of the establishment's totality. In some lower market level operations the staff may only be provided with overalls; this is in complete contrast to high-class restaurants, particularly in hotels, where there is a very strict demarcation of uniform styles according to the status of the service personnel. Additionally, such things as the level of skills of the staff, their visual cleanliness, as well as their sex, age and nationality are of importance.

At the end of the meal, staff can do a lot to reassure customers about their choice of meal experience. Because the intangible elements of a service are not visible, they are more difficult to evaluate. Customers, therefore, particularly need reassurance about the product they have purchased. Food service staff may help in several ways: at a basic level by asking if the customers have enjoyed their meal, this verbal confirmation by customers reinforces that their decision was correct in having chosen a particular restaurant; by remembering to offer customers take-home tangible items provided by the restaurant, for example, matches, sample menus, the restaurant's card; by pointing out a special promotion for a future date and enquiring whether the customer would like to make a reservation.

The type of meal experience offered by a food service facility must, therefore, be tailored around the requirements and expectations of the customer. The production of the right product – the meal experience – begins with the basic marketing questions of who are our customers and what do they want? By seeking to answer these questions, caterers are able to determine their position in the market and to offer the right product at the right price for the identified market segments. It is also important to remember that a customer's meal experience varies according to a number of factors and that the same customer's requirements may vary from one meal experience to another.

2.12 Trends in eating out

The catering industry is not by nature innovative, preferring to respond to changing tastes, rather than by being creative, which would be far too risky for operations other than those owned by large companies. The industry tends to follow the retail food industry and allows them to educate the public with cook-chill and cook-freeze meals, new flavours, textures and exotic and unusual foods.

General trends in eating out include the following:

1 An increase in interest in healthy eating by the general public. Government publicity campaigns include the publishing of such reports as the 1983 NACNE (National Advisory Committee on Nutritional Education) report, and the 1984 COMA (Committee on Medical Aspects of Food) report.
2 An increase in awareness of hygiene and cleanliness, particularly as a result of the major food poisoning outbreaks in the UK.
3 An increase in the demand for vegetarian foods, particularly by young people.
4 A decline in the general demand for red meats, with an increase in the demand for white meats, fish and pasta.
5 A growing demand for organically produced fresh foods, with a resistance to foods containing artificial additives, flavourings and colourings.
6 An increase in the demand for spicy type foods.
7 An increase in the demand for no smoking zones in restaurants.

2.13 References

Axler, B. H. (1979). *Food Service: A Managerial Approach.* Lexington, MA: DC Heath.

Campbell-Smith, G. (1989). *Marketing of the Meal Experience: A Fundamental Approach.* University of Surrey Press.

Euromonitor (1989). *The Consumer Catering Report* 1989.

Key Note (1996). *Market review – UK catering market.*

Marketpower (1995). *Who eats out?*

Mintel (1989). *Eating Out – Catering for Today's Consumer* 1989.

Rathmell, J. M. (1974). *Marketing in the Service Sector.* Cambridge, MA: Winthrop.

3
Managing quality in food and beverage operations

3.1 What is quality?

The food and beverage industry is a fast moving and exciting business. Looking at the Sunday papers, there are regular news articles about the expansion plans of new theme restaurants or multi-million pound take over deals; there are regular restaurant or hotel reviews and articles about cooking food at home. Television provides growing numbers of programs on aspects of cookery – from woks to barbecues, from cooking up a feast in twenty minutes to the real feasts of bygone eras. Cookery books, often tied to TV series, regularly top the best seller lists. The food and beverage manager faces an increasingly knowledgeable and sophisticated customer with broader tastes and experiences than ever before. These customers demand satisfaction but are increasingly difficult to satisfy.

The British Standards definition of quality (BS 4778, 1987) is 'the totality of features and characteristics of a product or service that bear on its ability to satisfy a stated or implied need'. It is these 'stated or implied needs' that the operation must satisfy. The customer translates these needs into a series of expectations of the service or product they will experience. If the restaurant meets or exceeds these expectations then the customer will feel satisfied and will feel that they have received 'quality'. If the restaurant does not meet their expectations, then there is a gap between customer expectations and the perceived characteristics of the service or product delivered to them (Parasuraman, Zeithaml and Berry, 1985) and quality will not have been provided. It is implicit in this definition that quality can exist at any level of service, from fast food to fine dining, as long as expectations of that level of service are met.

The totality of features and characteristics that go to make up the meal experience are many and varied. They consist partly of the food itself, partly the service received and partly the environment created by the decor, furniture, lighting and music. One way of looking at these characteristics is to categorize them as relating to either the product or the service and as either tangible or intangible.

The tangible elements of the product are made up of the food on the plate and the items used to serve the food on or with. The designs of the crockery, cutlery and glassware as well as the table lay-up are all part of the meal experience. The menu provides evidence of the meal experience for the customer to see before purchase by displaying a verbal description or pictures of the dishes available. It is also important to consider how well the mechanical processes that a customer comes across in a food and beverage outlet operate. These include the speed and efficiency of the EFTPOS terminal as well as the way the vending machine dispenses a cup of hot chocolate.

The intangible elements of the product include the atmosphere of the operation and the aesthetic appeal of the decor, furniture and fittings. Every restaurant and bar has its own feel. Some are designed to be warm and friendly while others can be cold or clinical. Getting the decor right to give the customer the right feelings is obviously important. The warm, dark, cluttered feel of a T.G.I. Friday's or an Exchange Restaurant is intended to give a very different impression from the clean bright business-like atmosphere of fast food operations such as Burger King or McDonald's. These intangible elements provide the feeling of comfort, of being at ease or at home that is such an important part of hospitality (Cassee and Reuland, 1983).

The intangible elements of service are very hard to tie down but are easily experienced. A genuine smile brings with it warmth and friendliness. Some restaurants manage to find ways to let their customers know that staff care about their meal, but others only succeed in letting customers know that the staff care very little. These elements simply add up to a feeling of service and of being looked after.

Although service is thought of as intangible, there are elements that are tangible. Actions that service staff carry out during service are tangible. The way the service process is arranged – Is it self service or waitress? Where do I go to pay? – is also tangible. Speed of service can be measured: although customers' perceptions of time, especially if they are waiting for something, are often wrong. The ways of talking to customers that staff use – their scripts – also provide hard evidence.

It is easiest for the food and beverage manager to control the tangible elements of the product and there is evidence (Parasuraman, Zeithaml and Berry, 1985; Nightingale, 1985) that they are more important to the customer than the intangible elements of the product. On the other hand the intangible elements of service are probably more important to the customer than the tangible elements of service but they are much more difficult for any manager to influence.

It is all well and good for an operation to meet customer requirements once, but it is no use to the customers if they receive exactly what they want on one day but, when the chef or their favourite crew member has a day off, the next visit is a disaster. The meaning of quality must also include reliability – what Crosby (1984) calls zero defects. He stresses that this is the only acceptable quality standard. Across the organization, everyone should be striving to deliver to the customer right first time every time.

Some organizations are moving away from seeing quality as simply satisfying the customer and looking to 'delight' the customer by exceeding their expectations. Deming (1982) suggests that if a customer is unhappy they will go to another supplier, but that a customer who is simply satisfied may also go somewhere else because they really have not got a lot to lose. He stresses the importance of repeat customers in generating profit. Customers who tell everyone about how great their meal was and bring their friends with them next time are worth their weight in gold. There are however some dangers in trying to exceed customer expectations. It has been suggested (Tenner and DeToro, 1992) that delight is the result of the added value of characteristics and features that customers did not expect – arousing their latent expectations. Until a few years ago nobody expected their children to be given crayons and something to draw on when they went to a restaurant. Now it is almost commonplace. This highlights the problem of escalating expectations. Little extras soon become the expected norm and new 'delights' have to be found.

Quality in food and beverage operations means reliably providing the food, service and environment that meets with our customers' expectations and where possible finding ways of adding value to exceed expectations and result in delight.

3.2   Why is quality important?

There are three main sources of pressure on businesses to pay attention to quality (Lewis 1989). First, customers are more demanding of everything they buy, as well as the way in which those products and services are delivered. Customers are no longer intimidated about complaining in restaurants and the trend to instruct service staff to check that all is well part way through the meal is asking for trouble. Second, the development of more sophisticated hard and soft technologies allows managers to offer many possible additional and convenience services, although interpersonal contact is still seen as highly valued. The effectiveness of methods such as sous-vide means that a good standard of dishes can be available from a vending machine and a microwave oven. Lastly, in an increasingly competitive and international marketplace, quality is seen as providing an edge of competitive advantage.

Many managers, however, feel that providing quality is too expensive or too much trouble to be of any real value. Zeithaml, Parasuraman and Berry (1990) propose that an emphasis on quality brings three areas of benefits.

The positive impact of quality on profit has

been shown by the Profit Impact of Market Strategy (PIMS) study (Buzzell and Gale, 1987). In this study, the single most important factor affecting a business unit's performance is the quality of its products and services, in comparison to its competitors. Walker and Salameh (1990) have shown similar results for the hospitality industry. A food and beverage operation that customers think has the quality edge over its competitors is able to boost profitability through charging premium prices. Quality provides leverage on the price/value relationship. For example, the prices charged by some restaurants, such as T.G.I. Friday's or Planet Hollywood, are above the market average but the high perceived quality of these operations keeps their value to the customer high. Over the long term, a quality advantage will result in business growth. This growth in volume will result in economies of scale and superior profit margins.

Providing high perceived value will lead to loyal customers, who will use the operation consistently over a long period and will recommend the unit to their friends. The value of long term relationships in services marketing has only recently been realized (Buttle, 1994) but good restaurateurs have always recognized the importance of repeat customers.

Quality improvement, without increasing the costs of an operation, results in operational efficiencies which more than recoup the investment. Quality costs are divided into two – the costs of conformance and the costs of non-conformance. The costs of conformance are the costs of assuring that everything comes out right and includes all efforts for prevention and quality education. The costs of non-conformance can be divided into appraisal/inspection costs and failure costs Appraisal costs are the costs of inspection to make sure that mistakes are kept down and to ensure that any mistakes that are made are identified before reaching the customer. Failure costs. are the costs of having made mistakes. They are split into internal and external failure costs. Internal costs are those incurred where mistakes are found before they reach the customer or cross the line of visibility. They include scrap, rework, downgrading and excess inventory. External failure costs are those incurred when mistakes are not found before they reach the cus-

tomer. They include such things as repair and warranty claims, providing replacement goods or services and the potential loss of future business. External failure costs are much more serious than their internal counterparts because by the time the problem reaches the customer it is already too late. While the internal failure costs of excess inventory and waste might be high, the real danger of poor quality for a food and beverage operation lies in those errors that are not discovered until they reach the customer.

Quality provides the opportunity for food and beverage operations to find a winning edge over their competitors, to ensure the long term loyalty of their customers and to improve both short term and long term profitability through cost savings and higher margins. When the benefits are so great, why is it that, with some notable exceptions, few food and beverage companies seem to have made much progress in this area?

3.3   Managing quality in food and beverage operations

The majority of the best known approaches to managing quality, from the quality gurus such as Deming, Crosby, Juran, Ishikawa, Shingo, Taguchi and others (see for example Flood, 1993), come from the manufacturing sector. The tools and techniques used in manufacturing are well proven. Increasingly, attention has been drawn to the service sector and the particular challenges faced by companies wishing to pursue service quality (see Lewis 1989; Zeithaml, Parasuraman and Berry, 1990; Gummesson, 1992). Some tools and techniques have been adapted from manufacturing to cope with the challenges and, where necessary new approaches have been developed.

Not only must food and beverage operations deal with the problems of manufacturing meals or drinks, they function also as a service operation. The resulting complexity makes managing quality in food and beverage operations more difficult but not impossible. Looking at the distinguishing characteristics of service operations Fitzgerald *et al.*, 1991 provides some interesting insights for food and beverage operations.

A large part of the hospitality provided by food and beverage operations consists of the tangible product elements of food and drink and not simply the service performance and the intangible factors that affect this interaction as is often stressed by the intangibility of a 'pure' service operation. Customers consider the tangibles such as what temperature is the food? how does it look on the plate, is the beer cold, how big is the pizza, etc.? Then there are the intangible elements of the atmosphere and service – does the customer feel secure? is the server friendly? and so on – plus the tangible service elements such as the time it takes to deliver the soup or did the waiter spill the wine?

Where food and beverage operations have a high labour content, it is hard to ensure consistent quality from the same staff from day to day, and even harder to ensure comparability between employees. Yet this will crucially affect what the customer receives. While customers expect some differences in the service they receive, they are not as tolerant of the standard of the product. A pizza served by a unit of a branded restaurant chain at one end of the country must be the same as the pizzas served in every other unit of the same chain. The customers' tolerance on the product side is lower than on the service side.

Many services cannot be inspected or tested before sale because the production and consumption happen at the same time. It is not possible to test out an airline flight or a hair cut. On the production side of food and beverage operations, the range is from simultaneous production – such as in a hibachi restaurant where cooking is done in the restaurant – to decoupled production – such as cook-chill where food is batch produced at a central location, cooled, and then distributed for later consumption. There are, however, many other possible systems in between (Huelin and Jones, 1990) and each will have their own special requirements for quality management.

A restaurant seat is a perishable product. Empty places cannot be stockpiled for a busy day sometime in the future. Once a restaurant seat has been left empty, the revenue potential of that space is lost. On the product side, raw ingredients or complete meals can be stored for short periods depending on the method of storage.

Food and beverage operations display many of the characteristics of service operations but they also have their own particular features. Providing a physical environment involves a substantial investment in premises and plant and associated fixed costs. Variable costs, however, are usually low. This cost structure means that generally the break even volume will be quite high. Passing this volume will result in high profits, but low volumes will result in substantial losses. Making the most of capacity must be a high priority to the food and beverage manager. In itself this would not be a difficult challenge if forecasting demand levels was straightforward. However, demand tends to be complex and fluctuates over time, by type of customer and by menu item. The result is a mixture of patterns that makes the forecasting and scheduling of resources very difficult.

Food and beverage production has a very short cycle of operation providing little time to monitor what is going on to correct any errors. A food and beverage operation can buy in fresh produce from the dawn markets that is prepared through the morning, on the menu for lunch and eaten by early afternoon.

When a customer enters an operation they place themselves in the care of the operation, which must employ all due diligence to ensure their safety. Food production processes deal with potentially contaminated raw ingredients with a limited shelf life. Poor handling can result in serious illness and death. The customer has very limited evidence of the hygiene standards of an operation upon which to make their choice of whom to trust.

Recent developments in catering technology have allowed some decoupling of production and service with cook-chill, cook-freeze or sous-vide methods. The industrialized service delivery system of a fast food operation ensures high speed, high volume with high consistency over a limited product range and limited human intervention. These examples of technological substitution are unusual and still the emphasis is placed on the competence of the employees who produce and serve the food.

Faced with a complex operation, the food and beverage manager is further pressured by the physical presence of the customer, monitoring progress with the expert eye of someone who has eaten many meals before. Even in home delivery operations the pressure of meeting the delivery time standard, usually between 20 and 30 minutes, represents the customer's presence.

3.4   Approaches to quality management

Given the particular characteristics described in Section 3.3 and the importance of providing quality in any food and beverage operation, there is a need for some form of systematic approach to quality. Quality and the consistency that should go with it will not happen by chance. It is the responsibility of the management team to provide a framework to encourage the delivery of this consistent quality. Although it is the operative level staff who come face to face with customers and who produce the service or prod-

uct the customer wants, it is managers who ensure that any barriers to quality are removed and that quality and quality improvement are encouraged.

The development of approaches to managing quality is shown in Figure 3.1. The diagram shows a movement from early approaches to quality relying on inspection of the finished product through quality control and quality assurance to total quality management.

3.4.1   Quality inspection

The earliest and probably the easiest approach to quality is the inspection approach. This simple approach is based on finding defects in a product or service before it reaches the customer by

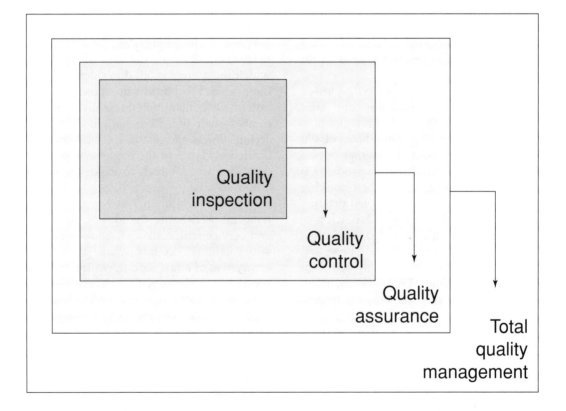

Figure 3.1   *The development of approaches to quality management*

introducing an inspection stage or stages. There needs to be some specification of what the product should be like against which the product can be checked once it has been produced. The checking would probably be carried out by staff employed mainly for that purpose. If any problems are found, that product will be rejected as non-conforming and will be sent back for rework – to put the defects right – or for scrap. Manufacturing industry has tended to rely on a separate inspection department to carry out this task, but this is not a model that has been adopted in food and beverage operations. A simple example of inspection is the head chef standing at the hot plate during a banquet passing dishes across to the staff when satisfied with the standard reached.

The focus here is firmly on identifying defects. The emphasis is on a lack of quality followed by the rejection of substandard work. The inspection becomes something the staff dread and very negative feelings can be aroused. Quality is a question of checking physical attributes off against a checklist and hoping that nothing has been missed. The emphasis is on putting things right rather than on identifying the cause of the problem and dealing with it at source.

3.4.2   Quality control

The quality control approach still centres on inspection but recognizes the need for a detailed specification and that quality checks should be made throughout the production process. Using sophisticated inspection methods at appropriate points in the production process, the approach is more likely to find errors and will correct them earlier. The emphasis is still on a find and fix mentality. Quality control will not improve product or service quality, it will only highlight when it has gone wrong. A non-conforming product or service must be produced before action can be taken to put it right and this leads to inefficiency and waste. The focus has switched for the staff onto finding others to blame for the defects to avoid the 'disciplinary' action taken against those who make mistakes. The whole focus of quality control is on mistakes. The key features of the approach are shown in Table 3.1.

3.4.3   Quality assurance

Quality assurance recognizes the inefficiencies of waiting for mistakes to happen and strives to design quality into the process so that things cannot go wrong or if they do they are identified

Table 3.1   *Quality control – key features*

Underlying principles and philosophy	Based on a philosophy of inspecting quality that concentrates on defect detection through post-production inspection.
Responsibility	Responsibility for quality is in the hands of a separate quality control department and individual inspectors.
Costs	It is assumed that there is a trade off between quality and cost – better quality will cost more. The main costs are concerned with re-work and waste.
Improvement	With a starting point of detailed product specifications and itemized costings, the focus is on the quality of the product and improvement in quality is achieved by increasing inspection to catch more deviations from the specification.
The quality chain	The customers' role in quality is uncertain but at the end of the day they are the final inspection point. Suppliers have no role in quality.
Techniques and approaches	Mainly based around the provision of detailed specifications, such as standard recipes and makes good use of checklists of inspection points as in housekeeping.
Rationale	There are few real benefits of a quality control approach but it is quick to introduce and is better than not doing anything. It also represents a first step on the quality route. There is likely to be no external recognition of this approach.

Table 3.2   *Quality assurance – key features*

Underlying principles and philosophy	Based on a philosophy of building quality into the hard systems of the operation and organizing quality into the soft systems, the focus is on producing to the design specification through the prevention of errors using in production monitoring. By stopping errors before they happen, there should be substantial cost savings.
Responsibility	The responsibility for quality may be given to a quality assurance department but it is also vested in line management who may even involve some employees.
Costs	The emphasis here is on producing the specified quality at the specified cost. By concentrating on prevention, these costs will increase but the costs involved in making errors – the failure costs – will be reduced.
Improvement	Starting with identifying the costs of quality and blueprinting or flow charting the operation, it is then possible to produce a procedure manual that will allow the introduction of variance analysis – finding out where things went wrong and why. This should lead to an improvement in quality through a clearer product specification, allied with control over the production process and the aim of getting it right first time every time.
The quality chain	The role and importance of customers are appreciated and both external and internal customer needs considered. Suppliers are also recognized as playing an important part in the quality chain and there will be detailed supplier quality agreements and some inspection of suppliers and their quality systems.
Techniques and approaches	The techniques used will include statistical process control, the use of fail-safe devices or poka-yokes, the introduction of quality teams or quality circles and a range of quality measurement tools.
Rationale	By focusing on the process of production, there should be greater control over product quality and reduced cost due to less waste and lower inventory. There will also be clear evidence of the production processes and procedures and, with staff involvement, the possibility of job enrichment. The approach will take up to two years to introduce but particularly suits those businesses wanting to compete on both cost and quality and who are probably some way down the quality road. External recognition would come for adopting systems that comply with standards such as ISO 9000.

and corrected as they happen. Lasting and continuous improvement in quality can best be achieved through planning and preventing problems from arising at source. Moving the emphasis from inspection to prevention is helped by the introduction of a number of quality assurance tools and techniques such as statistical process control (SPC), blueprinting and quality costing. The approach is also likely to include a comprehensive quality system, perhaps based on the ISO 9000 series.

In quality assurance, however, the focus is not just on systems. Effective quality assurance must involve the development of a new operating philosophy and approach; one that is proactive rather than reactive, that includes involving employees in the process from across normal departmental barriers. The key features of the approach are shown in Table 3.2.

3.4.4   Total quality management

The focus on the customer and the scale and nature of internal and external involvement are the main differences between the quality assurance and total quality management approaches. In any TQM approach, the driving force is the focus on the satisfaction of customer needs. The whole system must be directed at customer satisfaction and anything that could get in the way of delivering this satisfaction must be removed. This involves the whole organization, including suppliers, looking for ways to improve continually the products or services delivered. TQM places the emphasis on the people in the organization and their roles, through a broadening of their outlook and skills, through encouragement of creativity, through training and empowerment, in measuring their performance and find-

Table 3.3 *Total quality management – key features*

Underlying principles and philosophy	Based on a philosophy of structuring and managing quality into the whole organization of the business, the goals should be consistent satisfaction of the customer, constant improvements in products and processed leading to a highly competitive position in the market. Quality is involved in everything the business does, throughout the organization at all times.
Responsibility	The responsibility for quality is organization wide. Everyone is involved in delivering quality through a devolved strategic vision.
Costs	There is an inverse relationship between costs and quality – as quality increases the cost of quality comes down. However, cost is not really at issue. If there is a choice between cost and quality then quality will always win.
Improvement	By understanding the customers and the commitment of top management, the quality management structure is established that leads to a change in culture where continuous customer-driven quality improvement is automatic.
The quality chain	Not only are customers seen as an important part of the business, they are actively encouraged to become part of delivering quality. Suppliers are also involved in the quality effort and this may lead to strategic alliances or partnerships.
Techniques and approaches	The techniques used will include the active development of a quality culture and the development of change management, problem solving, quality analysis and quality improvement skills.
Rationale	Through guaranteed quality leading to total customer satisfaction and by competing on value and not on price, the business will achieve competitive advantage and external recognition. This approach will involve a considerable time commitment over a number of years but particularly suits long term strategies of growing market share, sustained growth and aspirations for market leadership. External recognition would come in the form of awards such as Malcolm Baldridge or the EFQM.

ing ways to improve it. The emphasis is on a management-led move towards teamwork and participation. Taking this holistic perspective can involve organizations in significant changes in their culture. It may be relatively easy to introduce new systems and procedures, but changing the culture is a much more difficult, but necessary, task. The key features of the approach are shown in Table 3.3.

3.5 Examples of quality management in food and beverage operations

The three examples that follow are drawn from three different sectors of food and beverage operations to illustrate the different problems they have to face and the various solutions they have found. Full descriptions of these cases and others can be found elsewhere (Lockwood, Baker and Ghillyer, 1996).

3.5.1 Alpha Flight Services

Alpha Flight Services (Alpha), which was established in 1958 as Forte Airport Services, is one of the leading flight caterers in the UK, serving a wide cross-section of airlines including British Airways, AirUK, Canadian Airlines, Gulf Air, and Britannia Airways, at 26 locations in the UK and Channel Islands. The division has operations in France, The Netherlands, Portugal, the USA and joint ventures in Australia and Trinidad.

Alpha services over 7500 flights per week, and is responsible for delivering around 40 million meals per year. As well as producing the meals Alpha must make sure that food and equipment are ordered, packed and loaded onto aircraft within precise time frames. As an example a Boeing 747 needs some 40,000 items to be loaded, checked and packed into predetermined stowage on the aircraft. On a long haul flight to allow for choice, dietary and religious requirements, there may be over 30 different meal types.

Close attention to detail in all parts of the operation is paramount. There is no second chance if something goes wrong. It is not possible to pop back if something is missing. If too few meals are loaded, some passengers may not get anything to eat. While some additional meals can be carried to provide some customer choice, there is simply no room to carry a large inventory of spares 'just in case'. 'Getting it right, first time, every time' is an operational credo that is particularly important to flight catering. There is only one chance to get it right. In these circumstances the focus in quality is as much on logistics and statistical process control as it is on a vision of product excellence and customer service. Although the airline passenger is the end consumer of product, it is the meal specifications as set by the client airlines that are sacrosanct. When the meal finally reaches the customer it is no longer an Alpha meal, it is now British Airways' meal or Gulf Air's meal.

In conjunction with British Airways, Alpha trialled ISO 9000 at their Woolborough Lane unit at Gatwick Airport. Alpha was the first UK flight caterer, and the third in the world, to achieve ISO 9000, but there are currently no plans to extend it to other operations. If a client airline feels they need ISO 9000, Alpha is able to discuss both the benefits and costs of achieving the standard, and to help the client airline reach a decision about whether it would bring any added value to the contract. ISO 9000 was seen by the company as a quality management system that was not far removed from the principles the company was already applying. The external audits and costs of ISO 9000 were off-putting but the company felt they could not criticize something of which they had little first hand knowledge. The company found ISO 9000 useful for a number of reasons, but primarily because it focused staff and management on very specific control processes and led them to document those processes. Essentially it involved documenting what was already being done and modifying existing documents.

The planning and control required to handle the logistics involved in delivering over 40,000 items to an aircraft within a precise period, lends itself to statistical process control techniques more than the customer service quality techniques found in other areas of hospitality. This is shown in the adoption of two manufacturing-based quality initiatives: 'zero defects' and 'just-in-time' production processes.

In 1990, a 'Code of Good Catering Practice' was introduced by the Airline Caterers Technical Co-ordinating Committee (ACTCC) providing a standardized system of operation to guarantee consistently high performance levels throughout the industry. Alpha has used the Code of Practice to measure its quality performance. The elements in the code have been turned into a detailed unit audit that forms an integral part of the management appraisal system. With increasingly strict food safety and food hygiene regulations being imposed, this unit audit is Alpha's way of ensuring that their operating procedures and management control systems remain far above the minimum standards required by the legislation. The units are assessed not on attainment, but on a penalty-based points system for evidence of not complying with the code. By awarding penalty points for non compliance rather than scoring on a percentage grade, it was felt that the units would get the message that there will be no marks given for a good effort. The achievement of the predetermined standard is the level at which their people are expected to operate, and therefore any non-compliance to that standard is then identified as an area for further improvement. The maximum score of five thousand points would shut down an operation, but this has not yet happened. In a recent audit, the best unit scored only 350 penalty points. This gives some indication of the serious commitment to zero defects that pervades the organization.

In view of the volume of meals being prepared on a daily basis, Alpha might be expected to purchase bulk supplies to maximize cost savings and protect margins. For over ten years, Alpha has been committed to a version of 'just-in-time' (JIT), an alternative method of supply that might not give the lowest unit price, but guarantees the freshest quality product at the best possible price, in direct relation to the level of service that their clients want them to provide. The JIT process is based on the idea that the cost savings generated by buying in bulk to achieve low unit costs, are outweighed by the cost of carrying the stock and, for Alpha, the loss of product quality in extended storage. Alpha uses frequent deliveries of small amounts of product as close to an 'as needed' basis as possible, to minimize inventory levels. Their manufacturing plants are built around the process rather than developing the production process around the constraints of the building. In the day-to-day operation of the plant, storage is avoided wherever possible – the raw and cooked products are delivered directly to the point of process. For example, for salad produce, there are up to three deliveries per day, each to the point of process.

The commitment to product freshness is obvious, but the gains to be made with reduced inventory levels, reduced stock rotation requirements, and increased product control are also considerable. The Gatwick operation was the first purpose-built JIT plant in the company, and stockholdings here were reduced from over twenty days to less than five days. When this is multiplied against the stock value for the whole network, substantial savings become possible and quality levels are maintained if not improved at the same time.

Alpha's approach to total quality management has been to select only those techniques and initiatives which fit their existing operating approach rather than redesigning the company around the latest programme. There are no 'buzzwords', no motivational hype, and very, very few acronym-based employee programmes. Individual TQM initiatives such as 'zero defects', 'just-in-time' and statistical process control, have been taken on board to fulfil a specific purpose in managing what is a logistically complex planning control system. Other TQM features such as 'empowerment' and 'benchmarking' are treated with a little more scepticism.

The business environment in which flight caterers operate has a strong influence on the development of management policies. For flight caterers, their prime customer is the client airline. That their products are eaten by the passenger is almost incidental. Alpha has no contact with passengers. Customer feedback comes through the airline, as do any complaints about the quality of the food. Surveys of customer preferences are carried out by the airline and passed on to the flight caterer. Although the

quality of the in-flight meal forms an integral part of the passenger's total flight experience, from the perspective of the basic mechanics of the flight itself, catering issues are very low on the list. Alpha's quality initiatives ultimately come up against the harsh reality of 'this is the amount of space available; we want this type of meal; this is the equipment we want it served on; and we want it packed in this way.' Occasionally there is some input on equipment design, but usually the meal specifications are based on the equipment that is already in place. For example, with 'SuperJumbos' carrying 600 or more passengers now appearing, communication between the airlines and their caterers has centred on 'this is the type of equipment you will have, and these are the meals we would like served'. Against these strict operating parameters, Alpha has chosen to accept the situation and focus on doing their absolute best with the specifications they are given, rather than attempting to introduce new galley styles or new types of equipment. Ultimately, Alpha delivers the product according to the level of importance that the client airline puts on that process – the more the airline is interested in service and in their passengers, the more they talk to Alpha about quality.

3.5.2 My Kinda Town Restaurants

The My Kinda Town Group, which was recently purchased by Capital Radio, is one of Europe's leading independent American theme restaurant groups, operating six separate concepts – The Chicago Pizza Pie Factory, Henry J. Bean's, The Chicago Rib Shack, Chicago Meatpackers, Tacos and Salsa! – in nineteen cities throughout the world. With a current total of thirty-three units, the groups' themes are represented through subsidiaries and franchises in the UK, France, Germany, Ireland, Spain, Belgium, Thailand, Argentina, Israel, Cyprus and Lebanon.

In 1977 the late American restaurateur and hotelier Bob Payton opened The Chicago Pizza Pie Factory in London, one of the first restaurants in Europe to sell Chicago-style deep-dish pizza. The restaurant, which was a huge success, moved in 1979 to its current larger premises in Hanover Square, London. Over the next nine years, further Chicago Pizza Pie Factory restaurants were opened in Barcelona and Paris and new concepts were created: The Chicago Rib Shack, selling prime American ribs, opened in Knightsbridge, London, in 1982, and Henry J. Bean's, an American neighbourhood bar, opened in Kensington, London in 1983. The first franchise operation was Henry J. Bean's in Aberdeen, Scotland, which opened in 1985. Other concepts have been added and expansion has continued with company-owned and franchised outlets. Chicago Meatpackers, an American family restaurant, was launched in 1987 and now has outlets in the UK, France and Germany. The UK recession in the late 1980s led the group to begin operating in Germany in 1989, where they now operate in Cologne, Dusseldorf, Hanover and Bonn through three concepts: Chicago Meatpackers, Henry J. Bean's and Tacos (a Mexican theme restaurant). In 1993, Salsa!, a Latin American bar with live music, was opened in Soho, London. On Thanksgiving Day 1994, three new restaurants were launched – a Chicago Meatpackers in Frankfurt (corporate), a Henry J. Bean's in Cologne (corporate) and a Henry J. Beans in York (franchise).

The quality philosophy at My Kinda Town is that the key to success is in looking after the basics. Customers come to MKT operations for good food, good service and a fun atmosphere, and it is up to their general managers to see that customers leave having had a good time. The group sees running restaurants as essentially a very simple business where you serve the hot food hot, the cold food cold, and everybody smiles.

Anyone going to My Kinda Town looking for vanguard quality approaches will be disappointed. The quality approach is based on a very tightly controlled operating system developed over seventeen years to monitor concepts that are now mature products. Avoiding the hype of the latest management techniques, the group focuses on the continuous improvement of what they do best. Although many of their management policies can be related to specific TQM techniques, they are rooted more in a proven track record of success than in the decision to take on external quality initiatives.

My Kinda Town recognizes the important role played by their staff in providing a quality service product to their customers and treats them accordingly. Time and energy go into the recruitment of new employees. Once recruited, effort is spent in providing them with the necessary guidance, via rules and regulations, to make sure that they know fully what is expected of them. The employment relationship remains simple – do what is asked to ensure that the customers are kept happy at all times. The focus is on providing clear guidance and on expecting consistently high performance.

Since the first franchise for a Henry J. Bean's was opened in Aberdeen in 1985, the group has expanded to thirteen franchise units based on just two of the six concepts – Henry J. Bean's and The Chicago Pizza Pie Factory. Franchise contracts are granted for between ten and twenty years and require a monthly royalty payment of between 5 and 7 per cent of sales. Franchisees to date include Scandinavian Airline Services and The Amari Group (a Thai hotel chain). To support this initiative My Kinda Town needed a fully systematized set of operating policies to maintain the consistency of the product worldwide. Attention has been given to the development of specific performance criteria rather than any explicit TQM initiatives. A customer in the Henry J. Bean's in Madrid must receive the same service as a customer in Brussels or Barcelona or Manchester, and the company's operating manuals have been developed over the years specifically to ensure that this happens.

My Kinda Town goes to great lengths to write everything down. The guiding phrase is 'If it can't be written down, it can't be measured, and if it can't be measured, it can't be controlled.' After nine years in the franchise business, there are now manuals for everything. Each department has its own manual, and staff learn the manual as part of their job. Based on this highly documented approach, My Kinda Town was one of the first restaurant companies in the UK to gain the ISO 9000 quality standard. It was the growing interest from potential franchisees that prompted this move. Showing franchisees restaurants filled to capacity was easy, but there was a need to prove that the product could be recreated anywhere in the world and operated with the same level of consistency. It was the external accreditation of ISO 9000 that would provide that proof.

The achievement of ISO 9000 proved to be relatively straightforward. With such detailed operating manuals in place, there were no major adjustments to be made, other than writing down some policies that everyone had taken for granted. Every six months there is a follow up inspection that is relatively painless and acts as spot-checking on performance.

Many features common to a TQM programme – such as quality circles, lean management structures, responsive communication systems – have been in place for several years without an explicit 'quality' label. For example, meetings are held on an informal basis rather than through a specific team structure. The chief executive attends 'MKT meeting' events at least once a year in all the units. The objective of these meetings is to keep him in touch with every member of staff in the organization, but as the company has grown, it has become difficult to avoid the suggestion of an annual 'royal tour'.

Meetings between the directors and their unit management teams follow a structured calendar to respond to training schedules and unit performance figures. At unit level, session meetings take place before the lunch and dinner service periods to ensure that everyone is kept up-to-date with menu alterations or immediate policy changes. Management team meetings take place in each unit at 4.00 p.m. every Monday and are then faxed direct to their respective director for any further action. Departmental meetings in individual units are held regularly to encourage ideas for improving the quality of services provided to the customer.

Service quality is monitored by mystery diners visiting every unit in the organization. The mystery diners fill out a six-page questionnaire to assess how well each unit has performed against predetermined performance criteria. Reports are produced monthly for head office analysis, which brings an immediate response for any unit that fails to meet the required standard. Comment cards are periodically placed on every table, with an equally rapid response for any comments about poor service or food quality.

3.5.3 Sutcliffe Catering

The Sutcliffe Catering Group forms part of the 'Services to Business' division of the Granada Group plc., alongside Granada Contract Services and Granada Vending Services. Sutcliffe has seen recent rapid expansion and is now one of Britain's largest food service management companies. The company is divided into five separate divisions operating from ten offices around the UK.

Sutcliffe draws its customers from a wide range of activities including directors' dining and staff catering, independent and grant-maintained schools, hospitals (both in the private and NHS sectors), nursing homes, public authorities, the Ministry of Defence, other government departments, and training and conference centres. To serve those markets, 20,000 staff are employed across a nation-wide client base of approximately 2300 catering contracts serving over one million meals per day.

Quality is a key element in Sutcliffe's competitive strategy to develop their customer base. They define quality as: 'achieving the highest possible standards of food and service within the policy and financial targets agreed with our clients.' It is here that the special feature of contract catering comes into play because Sutcliffe must try to satisfy the expectations of two sets of customers. First they must satisfy the client who provides some, if not all, of the funding for the catering provision and specifies the contractual parameters within which Sutcliffe must operate. Second, they must also satisfy the employees, patrons or customers of their client who actually consume the food produced. There is inherent in this relationship the possibility of conflict. The client may be looking to keep tight control of costs while the end customer will see catering as part of their benefit or service package. The two parties can often develop very different ideas about what standard of food and facilities should be provided.

To reduce the problem, Sutcliffe looks to develop a strong working relationship with their clients as a 'customer partnership'. Formal contracts establish the clients' aims, objectives and standards from the outset, but it is the working relationship, through regular meetings, open finances, and a highly visible local management team, that allows Sutcliffe to achieve and maintain high service standards and generate good referral business from their existing client base.

There has been a change in recent years from the client typically being the personnel manager of the firm to now being the finance or purchasing manager. Judgement of performance has consequently moved away from the softer area of employee benefit to a more hard nosed financial target – the ability to deliver to contract at cost. There is also a growing feeling that companies will increasingly put less subsidy into the cost of catering and expect their employees to pay more. For the end customer value perceptions will change as prices increase.

It is the catering manager who is the primary contact between Sutcliffe and the client and the primary element in Sutcliffe's quality programme – the Quality Self-Assessment (QSA). The decision was made toward the end of the 1980s to develop a formal quality system that would aim to make Sutcliffe the best at what they do by putting in place the key elements that would meet the 'food-on-the-plate' requirements of the customer and the financial and operating needs of the client. Moving away from a simple area manager administered checklist, and following a comprehensive review of their operation, the QSA audit was introduced. The QSA is based at the unit catering manager level and provides them with the documentation necessary to assess their own performance and the performance of their staff.

The QSA is in two parts. The first is a minimum standards manual which breaks down the job description of a site catering manager into six principal areas of operation:

- menu planning, purchasing, food production;
- merchandising, customer relations, service standards;
- staff and training;
- hygiene, health and safety;
- finance and administration; and
- vending.

The aim here is to meet all necessary legal requirements relating primarily to hygiene, health and safety regulations and to meet the clients' expectations. However, the manual does not specify particular cooking or presentation methods. With such a wide range of clients, Sutcliffe need to maintain flexibility and rely on the experience of craft and management staff on site. Each client is different and their individual

needs must be met.

The second part of the QSA is the self-assessment document. This is designed to enable catering managers to assess their own performance every quarter against the minimum standards set out in the standards manual. There is still an element of checking performance against predetermined criteria, but the difference is in the trust and confidence being placed in the catering manager. The QSA is not an inspection, but a reminder to help the catering manager to make sure that their unit is running at peak performance.

The natural scepticism about how accurate and honest a 'self' assessment can be has been dispelled by performance. The quarter-on-quarter results have shown gradual increases over the time the programme has been running. It would be difficult for this consistent improvement to be fixed.

Initially area managers had no involvement with the QSA but this has evolved to a position where the area manager may take part in an assessment to monitor the development of the catering manager and the unit. The clients themselves are encouraged to take part in the quarterly audit as another way of developing the 'customer partnership' relationship.

Sutcliffe's interest in formal quality procedures coincided with growing interest among their clients in the ISO 9000 quality standard. As many of their client companies already have accreditation against the standard, it was inevitable that registration for ISO 9000 would become a key element in some contract requirements. For Sutcliffe, the minimum performance criteria established in the QSA provides the groundwork for the accreditation process. Moving away from trying to put all their units through the accreditation process, Sutcliffe now has at least one unit in each division registered for ISO 9000 and the learning from those accreditations has prepared Sutcliffe for future registrations, should the individual client contract require it. When they upgraded the operations manuals of the chosen sites to meet the requirements of ISO 9000, they checked that they were right through the registration process and then subsequently updated the operations manual across the whole company. Now if a client rings up and says they want Sutcliffe to be registered then the procedures are already in place and it is almost a formality of inviting in the assessors.

The key mechanism that has allowed this to take place is the QSA. The continued fine-tuning of successive versions of the QSA document reflects the extent to which the quality message has been 'taken on board' by the Sutcliffe organization, and the extent to which the achievement of those quality goals now rests with the site catering managers.

A trend in the contract catering industry, has been to 'fixed-price' (everything provided for one price) rather than 'cost-plus' (food/labour/equipment costs + a management fee) contracts for catering services. Sutcliffe's move into this operating environment should be a smooth one. Their quality programme is geared to providing what the client wants at the price the client wants to pay, and if the clients' requirements change, the systems are designed to keep them as close to that change as possible and ahead of their competitors. The company is still in the same business of meeting the 'food-on-the-plate' requirements of the customer, and the financial and operating parameters of the client. The commitment to service excellence, continuous quality improvement, and the strength of the 'customer partnership' remains paramount as the long-term strategy of the organization.

3.6 Conclusions

The short case examples of the three companies given above demonstrate that the approaches identified earlier in the chapter are not mutually exclusive. As Figure 3.1 shows, one approach builds towards the next. Just because you have introduced a total quality management approach does not mean that you can ignore quality inspection or quality control completely, although there should now be very few defects left to find. Each company needs to build its own approach to quality that reflects its own operating environment, its own organizational culture and its own customers' special needs. Although managing quality is a complex problem to tackle, increasing numbers of companies are finding ways of building quality into their operations and improving the standards of service and products they deliver to their customers.

Those companies that do not have such a quality approach will find it increasingly difficult to compete.

3.7 References

British Standard 4778 (1987). *Glossary of quality terms*. London: British Standards Institute.

Buttle, F. (1994). Marketing and merchandising, in Davis, B. and Lockwood, A. (eds.) *Food and Beverage Management: a selection of readings*. Butterworth-Heinemann: Oxford.

Buzzell, R. D. and Gale, B. T. (1987). *The PIMS principles – linking strategy to performance*. New York: The Free Press.

Cassee, E. and Reuland, R. J. (1983). Hospitality in hospitals, in Reuland, R. J. and Cassee, E. (eds), *The Management of Hospitality*. Oxford: Pergamon Press, pp 143–163.

Crosby, P. B. (1984). *Quality without tears*. New York: McGraw Hill.

Deming, W. E. (1982). *Quality, Productivity and Competitive Position*. Massachusetts Institute of Technology, Centre for Advanced Engineering Study: Massachusetts.

Fitzgerald, L., Johnston, R., Brignall, S., Silvestro, R. and Voss, C. (1991). *Performance measurement in service businesses*. London: The Chartered Institute of Management Accountants.

Flood, R. L. (1993). *Beyond TQM*, Chichester: John Wiley and Sons.

Gummesson, E. (1992). *Quality management in service organisations*, New York: SQA.

Huelin, A. and Jones, P. (1990). Thinking about catering systems, *International Journal of Operations and Production Management*, **10**, No. 8, 42–52.

Lewis, B. R. (1989). Quality in the service sector: a review, *International Journal of Bank Marketing*, **7**, No. 5, 4–12.

Lockwood, A. J., Baker, M. and Ghillyer, A. (1996). *Quality management in hospitality: best practice in action*. London: Cassell.

Nightingale, M. (1985). The Hospitality Industry: Defining Quality for a Quality Assurance Programme – A Study of Perceptions, *Service Industries Journal*, **5**, No. 1, 9–22.

Parasuraman, A., Zeithaml, V. A., Berry, L. L. (1985). A Conceptual Model of Service Quality and Its Implications for Future Research, *Journal of Marketing*, **49**, Fall, 41–50.

Tenner, A. R., and DeToro, I. J. (1992). *Total quality management: three steps to continuous improvement*. Massachusetts: Addison-Wesley Publishing Co.

Walker, J. R. and Salameh T. T. (1990). The QA payoff, *Cornell Hotel and Restaurant Quarterly*, **30**, No. 4, 57–59.

Zeithaml, V. A., Parasuraman, A. and Berry, L. L. (1990). *Delivering service quality*. New York: The Free Press.

4
The marketing of food and beverages

4.1 Introduction

Marketing is an exchange process between an organization and its products on the one hand, and the organization's customers – its market on the other. It involves the identification and satisfaction of an organization's present and potential customers' desires and needs, and the matching of its products to them. This matching process of demand and supply is fundamental to marketing, as shown in Figure 4.1.

The British Institute of Marketing states that:

Marketing is the management process responsible for identifying, anticipating and satisfying customer requirements profitably.

Kotler (1984), whose writing on marketing is widely accepted, defines marketing as:

A social process by which individuals and groups obtain what they need and want through creating and exchanging products and value with others.

Finding out about an organization's customers requires the answers to many questions: who are our customers? what do they need? what are their preferences? what do they like or not like about our product or similar products? what do they pay and what would they pay for our product? The answers to these questions contribute to an organization's development of the right product for the right market at the right price.

4.2 The marketing concept

The marketing concept consists of a number of interrelated elements which together determine the business orientation of an organization:

1 The position of the customer as the focal point of a business is central to the marketing concept.
2 It is a positive management attitude that permeates through an organization towards the satisfaction of its customers' needs and wants.
3 It recognizes the need for an organization to increase its short- and long-term profits.
4 An organization is aware of its external environment by monitoring, analysing and responding to it.

When an organization collectively adopts the elements of the marketing concept, it is said to be marketing orientated.

In addition several other business orientations can be identified:

1 *Production orientation*. This is mostly adopted by organizations whose products are currently in demand, producing profit, and the organization is concerned with lowering unit costs by working towards a high-volume production and economies of scale. The emphasis, therefore, is towards the product, aspects such as its design, production, quality standards, costs and pricing. In the food service industry, hospitals and employee feeding were often

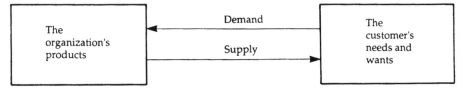

Figure 4.1 *The matching process of marketing*

production orientated, but more recently with government privatization plans and competitive tendering becoming more common, these sectors of the catering industry are having to review their business orientations and marketing strategies.

2 *Sales orientation.* This is mostly adopted by organizations whose products are not currently in great demand and the organization is concerned with increasing its volume sales. The emphasis, therefore, is towards selling and the generation of increased demand for its products. Many sales orientated businesses are of a high, fixed capital nature, for example, hotels and restaurants.

It has been suggested that no one particular orientation is right for all businesses and that under certain conditions, the adoption of any one of these orientations may be appropriate for an organization. Changes in demand, for example, may cause the operation to become either more production or sales orientated for a time, if demand is either in excess of supply, or to the contrary, there is a surplus of supply. Ultimately, however, whether in the commercial or subsidized sectors, the business is there to serve its customers, and therefore the needs and wants of the customer should never be far from the organization's central thinking.

4.3   The marketing of services

Services are generally accepted as being 'performed' whereas goods are 'objects' that have been produced. Service industries include, for example, banking, insurance, retailing and hairdressing. Manufacturing industries include those producing goods, for example, cars, tinned foods, televisions and catering equipment. Some services are highly customized. Taking the food service industry as an example, haute cuisine restaurant service is highly customized. Others are standardized, for example, McDonalds. Between these two extremes exists a range of different levels of services.

Services have a number of characteristics common to many, but not necessarily applicable to all of them. Indeed, some may not be exclusive to services. Sometimes it is necessary to look at each service separately, as although by definition all have a service element, this can be a more important feature in some industries than in others. Recognizing which characteristics of a service product are more important than others will influence the marketing of that product; its advertising and sales campaign, for example, would highlight those features which customers perceive as being important to them.

However, for the purposes of this book, the following characteristics may be said to be relevant to services in general and food service operations where applicable:

1 The customer is present at the time of both production and service. In service industries, for example, in a restaurant offering conventional food service, customers wait for the food to be prepared, are served their meal at a table and the product is consumed. There is no time delay between production of the meal and service to the customer. In the manufacturing industry, for example the manufacture of electrical goods, furniture or tinned foods, the customer is not present during the production process. There may also be a considerable time delay between the product being manufactured in a factory, delivered to a shop, its time on the shelf, being purchased by a customer, stored at home and finally being consumed.

   Exceptions in the food service industry would include cook-freeze, cook-chill and sous vide operations where production and service are separated, and only at the last stage of production is the customer present, for example the regeneration process of cook-chill meals in a school kitchen or in a hotel kitchen, prior to banquet service.

2 The customer is involved in the creation of the service. In service industries, the customer involvement is a requirement for the creation of the service, for example in hairdressers, a bank or a self-service restaurant. The degree of customer involvement can vary, simply from their presence in a coffee shop so that the meal may be served and the service element of the product completed, to a self-service vending cafeteria where customers actually contribute to the production of the service by selecting a cook-chill meal,

re-heating it in a microwave, taking it to a table, and possibly clearing away themselves afterwards.

3 The service product is consumed at the point of production. Customers go to a bank, or restaurant, for consumption of the service and, in this way, become part of the total product.

An exception in the food service industry would be take-aways where, as their name implies, the food is taken away for consumption.

4 Services cannot be examined in advance. In service industries the customer is rarely able to examine the service in advance.

Customers entering a supermarket may have a number of different brands of products that they are able to physically compare in terms of appearance, content and price. Customers using a service such as banking or a fast-food restaurant do not. In the food service industry examples of where the tangible product can at least be seen in advance include self-service food and beverage displays such as cafeterias, buffets, coffee shop trolleys and vending machines.

5 Increased contact time between service staff and customers. Because customers personally go to the operations establishment they have more personal contact time with the service staff and possibly those involved in production.

Service industries distribution channels consist of people so that the training of production and particularly service staff in customer relation skills becomes very important. Generally speaking, services which have a high personnel input tend to be more difficult to manage than those with a high equipment input, and the more customized the service, the more contact time between service staff and customers.

6 Services are perishable. An unsold hotel room for the night, or a lunchtime restaurant seat left vacant, is lost forever. Once produced, services must be consumed and, because of their perishability, services are more vulnerable to fluctuation in demand. Sales instability is typical of most catering establishments. There is often a change in the volume of business from day to day and, in many establishments, from hour to hour. This causes basic problems with regard to the quantities of commodities to be purchased and prepared, the staffing required and the availability of the components at times of production in line with the price that can be afforded in relation to the selling price.

7 Services cannot be stored. By their very nature, services cannot be stored. A restaurant open for six and a half hours during the day can only sell its services during those hours. Once closed, it cannot produce any more services to be stored and sold the next day. Peaks of activity are common in service industries. In a hotel, for example, the peaks would typically be breakfast, lunch and dinner service. Resort hotels have peak activity months during the summer and quieter months during the winter. The balance between demand and supply in a service industry is therefore critical; where demand exceeds supply, the result is lost sales and disappointed customers. In terms of marketing implications, an organization may try to spread the level of demand by pricing differentials. For example, encouraging more lunch time trade by offering cheaper table d'hôte meals, leaving the more expensive à la carte menu for evening service only; or offering a reduction in price for customers entering the restaurant before a certain hour to try and spread the peak activity time. In a manufacturing industry, stocks may be held in a factory or warehouse and moved quickly to a sales outlet which is short of stock; non-perishable goods may remain on a supermarket shelf for a considerable time. The less standardized the product marketed by the organization, the greater it is affected by differences between demand and supply. In the food service industry, for example, operations such as fast-food outlets using a high percentage of standardized convenience foods would be less affected by fluctuations in demand than a high-quality restaurant using a high percentage of fresh foods.

8 Difficulties in quality control. Because there is virtually no time delay between production and consumption of a service, the control of quality becomes very difficult. The speed at which catering operations take place

for example, relative to other manufacturing industries, allows little time for many control tasks. It is not uncommon that items ordered one day are received, processed and sold the same or the following day. It is for this reason that in large catering establishments cost reporting is done daily or at least weekly.

9 Services have high fixed costs. Service industries have a high degree of fixed costs relative to any other industries. Customers go to a service operation to purchase a product, services are not taken to customers. A hotel, a bank, a pizza restaurant will still have all the fixed costs every twenty four hours of trading whether fifty or 250 customers pass through the doors. In the manufacturing industry, supply can be increased or decreased to meet fluctuations in demand much more easily, particularly where production is highly automated.

10 Services have an intangible element. It has been suggested that services represent a performance, whereas goods are produced. Certainly different services contain different intangible elements, but they also have a tangible element in the same way as foods, for example cigarettes have an intangible element. In a fast-food outlet, a customer buying a meal is buying a highly standardized, mass-produced product that has had a high equipment input in its production and the customer will have very little contact time with the service staff. In this example the intangible aspects of the service may be said to be relatively minor. Compare this to a customer buying a high-quality meal in a high-quality restaurant. The meal may be virtually customized, it has had a high labour input in its production, and the customer may have considerable contact time with the service staff discussing the menu, and wine list, and possibly the chef; in this example the intangible aspects of the service may be perceived as being far more important to the customer. Therefore, although the intangible element is characteristic of services, it does not assume the same importance as some of the characteristics previously discussed, and is not exclusive to services only.

4.4   The marketing environment

No business operates in isolation. In a large hotel, for example, there may be a number of different style catering operations – several bars, a coffee shop, a carvery, a speciality restaurant. Although initially they may appear to operate as self-sufficient units, they do, in fact, all have a cause and effect relationship with each other. They are subsystems operating within a much larger system – the hotel. A 'system' may be defined as an interaction of all parts or subsystems, with the whole not equal to but actually greater than the sum of its parts. The food and beverage department in a hotel consists of a series of closely linked subsystems – the kitchen, bars, restaurants etc. – which, together, form the whole – the food and beverage system. The food and beverage department operates within a still larger system – the hotel – interacting with other departments such as housekeeping, front of house, etc. (see Figure 4.2). Individual operations and departments are, therefore, affected by changes in their own internal environments.

Any problems arising internally can usually be solved adequately within the establishment itself. Examples of internal problems that may arise in a catering operation include:

1 *Food and beverage:*
   (a) Perishability of food. Food purchasing, storing and issuing procedures to be checked.
   (b) Wastage and bad portioning control. Production planning, standard yields, recipes and portion sizes to be reviewed.
   (c) Pilferage from kitchen, restaurants, bars and stores. Control procedures inadequate.

2 *Employees:*
   (a) Employee shortages often coinciding with peaks of sales activity.
   (b) Employee surpluses coinciding with troughs of sales activity.
   (c) Absenteeism, illness, etc.
   (d) Use of part-time/casual employees in food service operations.
   (e) Poor supervision. Job descriptions and on-the-job training needed.

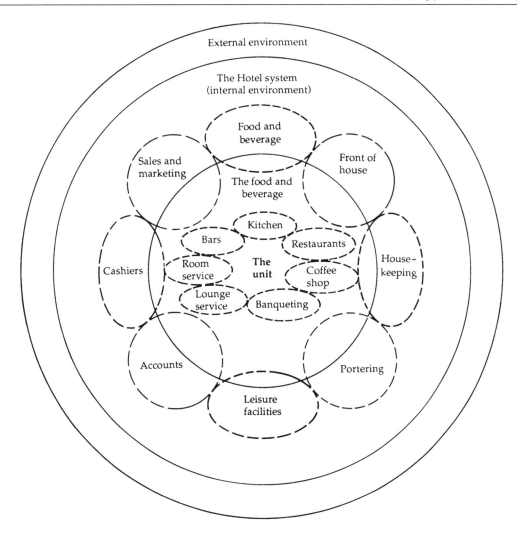

Figure 4.2 *The food and beverage system in context*

3 *Control:*
  (a) Cash collection and control. Most transactions are conducted on a cash basis in food and beverage sales outlets.
  (b) High frequency of low average spend transactions in catering operations.
  (c) Correct pricing of menus and beverage lists when food prices in particular fluctuate.
  (d) Stores control (food and liquor). Tighter financial and management controls required.

This 'system approach' can be extended beyond the realms of an individual operation. Taking the example of the hotel further, it is also

affected by external factors – its external environment – because any problems that arise are outside the organization's control and cannot be solved internally. Some of the external factors affecting a catering operation include:

(i) Political

1 Government legislation, for example fire regulations, health and safety acts, EC regulations, labelling and advertising regulations, changes in licensing laws.
2 Change in the taxation structure of the country, for example regulations affecting business expenses allowances.

3 Specific government taxes, for example value added tax.

(ii)   Economic

1 Rising costs such as food and beverages, labour, fuel, rates and insurance.
2 Sales instability, for example peaks and troughs of activity occur on a daily, weekly and seasonal basis.
3 Changes in expenditure patterns and people's disposable incomes.
4 Expansion and retraction of credit facilities.
5 High interest rates on borrowed capital.

(iii)   Demographic/social

1 Changes in population distribution, for example population drifting away from certain areas.
2 Changes in the socio-economic groupings of the area.
3 Growth in ethnic minorities leading to a demand for more varied foods.
4 Changes in food fashion, for example current popularity of take-away foods, healthy eating and diets.
5 Changes in family composition, for example smaller families with fewer children, growth of one-parent families, larger percentage of married women working, growth in the number of retired people.
6 Mobility of the market, for example increased ownership of cars, better public and private transport facilities: air; road; rail; and sea.

(iv)   Technical

1 Mechanization, for example of food production and food service equipment.
2 Computer technology, for example increasing use of microprocessors in the hotel and catering industry.
3 Product development and food processes, for example sous vide, vacuum packaging.
4 Advances in media technology, for example satellite TV, high percentage of TV and video ownership increasing advertising influence.

4.5   Market segmentation

Market segmentation is the identification of a group or groups of customers within an organization's total market. The total market may be divided into different segments, each requiring different market mixes. At one extreme there exists the mass market where an organization uses the same strategy to market its products to all segments of the market. At the other, an organization is able to identify a very specific market segment and market its products specifically to that segment.

Market segmentation is an important aspect of market planning. An organization cannot be all things to all people. To market its products cost effectively, it must clearly identify its customers and the market segments they belong to. Without this clear identification of the organization's markets, its whole marketing activity is wasted in terms of time, resources and finance.

Segmentation of the market may be viewed from two different standpoints. One is to study customers' characteristics using demographic and geographic criteria: customers' age, sex, religion, occupation, income, etc.

The other is to study customers' behaviour using psychographic criteria. Why do they buy the organization's products? What attributes of the product are important to the customer? Why do they buy our products instead of our competitors', or vice versa?

In the food service industry some of the following demographic and geographic criteria may be used to identify market segments:

1 *Geographic.* The identification of market segments by geographic area may be at international, national or local level. At the international level different cultures may not be appropriate for the introduction of certain products; regional differences of food exist within the same country; at a local level a fish and chip shop may draw most of its custom from a two or three mile radius, whereas customers may be willing to travel ten times that distance to a specialized quality restaurant.
2 *Age group.* Specific market segments may be identified in the food service industry according to their age. The younger 18-30 age group

Figure 4.3   *The marketing environment*

are more willing to experience new ideas, they like to dine and be seen in fashionable restaurants and bars. The older age group may experiment less, but could form a large part of a restaurant's repeat business.

3 *Socio-economic classification.* This is a form of general classification used by JICNARS (Joint Industry Committee for National Readership Surveys), dividing the population into six groups (A, B, C1, C2, D and E) and classifying the head of the household's occupation into the groups shown in Table 4.1. The requirements and expectations of people within each of these groups differ significantly as does the amount of money they have available and are prepared to spend.

4 *Income.* The higher the disposable income, the higher the propensity to spend more on dining out. Areas that have high percentage of ABs are, therefore, able to sustain a higher percent-

age of expensive restaurants than areas largely made up of CDs.

5 *Family life cycle.* This form of classification is based on identifying stages within the cycle of family life and how each stage affects the family's purchasing behaviour (see Table 4.2).

Generally speaking, the larger the family and the younger the children, the more restricted the purchasing power and the lower the average spend of that family.

SAGACITY is a form of analysis based on the family cycle and is used to identify different levels of socio-economic class. It divides the family life cycle into four stages: dependent, pre-family, family, and late; and further divides each stage into income and occupation (see Table 4.3).

ACORN is another commercial tool used to identify market segments, standing for 'a classification of residential neighbourhoods '.

Table 4.1 *Socio-economic grades*

Social grade	Social status	Chief income earner of household	Percentage of adult population over 15	
			Men	*Women*
A	Upper middle class	Higher managerial, administrative or professional	3.3	2.6
B	Middle class	Intermediate managerial administrative or professional	20.1	17.0
C1	Lower middle class	Supervisory or clerical and junior management, administrative or professional	26.3	28.6
C2	Skilled working class	Skilled manual workers	24.5	20.6
D	Working class	Semi-skilled and unskilled manual workers	15.7	17.1
E	Lowest income levels	State pensioners, widows, casual and lowest grade workers	9.1	14.0

Source: Research Services Ltd 1996.

The ACORN classification consists of six categories, seventeen groups and fifty-four types. It gives consumer analysis from the broadest to the finest detail, to match the varying needs of businesses. It provides the user with a matrix of consumer characteristics to be able to define the potential for marketing and planning operations (see Table 4.4).

Segmentation of an organization's market according to customer behaviour is another method that may be used. This recognizes that customers do not only buy a 'tangible' product, but they also buy a number of 'intangibles'. The organization needs to know why a customer buys its products and what value is the product to the customer. A number of 'psychographic' criteria may be considered.

First, the customer may buy a fast-food meal to satisfy a basic physiological need such as hunger. This type of purchase is closely related to the price of the meal and the customer's level of disposable income. If customers have more to spend, they buy a more expensive meal. Second, lifestyle segmentation looks at customers' backgrounds, their attitudes and opinions, their family and the community in which they live, their work and social activities etc. All of these factors affect the customer's attitude to buying decisions. Third, benefit segmentation recognizes that customers buy a product for the benefits

Table 4.2 *The life cycle of eating out (sample: 1941 adults)*

Age	Status/stage	Behaviour
15–19	Single	Eat out with friend, group of friends or family.
20–24	Courting/married	Eat out with partner alone, but also with group of friends without partner.
25–34	Married with young family	Eat out with partner alone, but also with partner and other friends.
35–44	Family children growing up	Eat out with partner alone, but increasingly also with other family members, including partners.
45–54	Children grown up	Eat out with combination of partner, family and friends; less important, friends with partner.
55–64	Pre-retirement	Greater independence from partner; eating out with friends and family more important.
65 +	Retirement	Family is dominant in eating out, with or without partner.

Source: Mintel, 1988.

Table 4.3 *SAGACITY classification*

Consumer group	Percentage of adult population over 15
Dependent white	6.9
Dependent blue	5.7
Pre-family white	6.2
Pre-family blue	4.7
Family white, better off	11.9
Family blue, better off	8.0
Family white, worse off	2.5
Family blue, worse off	6.8
Late white, better off	10.9
Late blue, better off	7.2
Late white, worse off	10.5
Late blue, worse off	17.5

Source: Research Services Ltd 1996.

that they consider are important to them, and which will satisfy their needs and wants. A customer, therefore, purchases a product from a food service facility for any number of reasons, or maybe a combination of several. Besides the factors already discussed, others including price, average spend, mode of travel, purpose of visit, may all be useful in identifying market segments. The more variables that can be identified and the more detailed the customer profile produced, the more accurate the marketing mix can be in aiming at any particular market segment.

A brief profile of a fast-food customer, for example, may be C1 socio-economic grouping, pre-family, aged between 16 and 18, living in low-status non-family area, within walking distance of unit, average spend £1.50. The customer profile for a haute cuisine restaurant sited out of a main city may read AB socio economic grouping, aged between 55 and 65, living in a better off retirement area, travels up to twenty miles by car, average spend £40.

4.6 The marketing mix

In order for the exchange process to take place in marketing, the organization must decide how to market itself to those segments it has identified, and how to influence customers' behaviour to buy. It does this by means of the marketing mix (Kotler, 1984, p. 68), which is:

> The mixture of controllable marketing variables that the firm uses to pursue the sought level of sales in the target market.

The four marketing variables that are generally accepted as being the tools of the marketing mix are the *four Ps* (McCarthy, 1981). They may be applied to food and beverage operations in the following way:

1 *Product.* The product basically consists of its tangible and intangible features. Its tangible or physical characteristics include the quality of foods and beverages produced and served, the restaurant decor, table arrangements, menu design, portion sizes, life cycle, etc. The intangible features of the product are those that satisfy the 'feelings' of the customer – the atmosphere of the restaurant, the image it wishes to portray, the attitude of the service staff.

2 *Price.* The prices charged by the catering operation are the balance between the organization on the one side with its need to achieve profitable sales, and the customers on the other with their views as to what they are willing to pay for its products. Varying price levels may be used for different products in different market segments. Pricing variables include à la carte or table d'hôte menus, whether government and service taxes are to be inclusive or exclusive, if discounts are to be given to group bookings, or reductions for meals ordered before a certain hour.

3 *Promotion.* The promotion, or communication mix, is concerned with informing the market about an organization's products and persuading them to buy. It may be on a personal level, for example service staff in a restaurant, or it may be impersonal, for example advertising or merchandising.

4 *Place.* This aspect of the marketing mix is concerned with a number of factors: the location of the catering outlet, for example, the haute cuisine restaurant, or coffee shop within a hotel; the siting of a centralized cook-chill operation and its peripheral units; the availability and accessibility of the location and product to the customers; the distribution

Table 4.4   *ACORN targeting classification – an extract*

ACORN CATEGORIES		ACORN GROUPS	% OF HOUSEHOLDS IN GB
A THRIVING		1 Wealthy achievers, suburban areas	14.0
		2 Affluent greys, rural communities	2.2
		3 Prosperous pensioners, retirement areas	2.8
B EXPANDING		4 Affluent executives, family areas	3.4
		5 Well-off workers, family areas	7.0
C RISING		6 Affluent urbanites, town and city areas	2.5
		7 Prosperous professionals, metropolitan areas	2.5
		8 Better-off executives, inner city areas	4.0
D SETTLING		9 Comfortable middle agers, mature home owning areas	13.7
		10 Skilled workers, home owning areas	10.8
E ASPIRING		11 New home owners, mature communities	9.9
		12 White collar workers, better-off multi-ethnic areas	4.0
F STRIVING		13 Older people, less prosperous areas	4.4
		14 Council estate residents, better-off homes	10.9
		15 Council estate residents, high unemployment	3.6
		16 Council estate residents, greatest hardship	2.4
		17 People in multi-ethnic, low-income areas	1.8

Source: Copyright CACI Ltd 1997.

channels and methods of transportation to be used, the inventory levels to be set.

These basic *four Ps* have been increased to *seven Ps* in recent years by Bitner (1991).

5 *Process*. The actual procedures, mechanisms and flow of activities by which the service is delivered (e.g. seating the guest, taking of food orders, dealing with questions and complaints, etc.).
6 *Physical evidence*. The environment in which the organization and the customer meet and interact, plus the tangible elements that facilitate the performance of communication of the service delivery (e.g. exterior/interior appearance of building, restaurant floor plan, decor, lighting, table layout, staff uniforms, menus, tent cards, etc.).
7 *Participants*. The individual – staff and other customers with whom the customer interacts with (e.g. hostess, restaurant manager, waiter and other customers, etc.).

Different marketing mixes are required for different market segments. In a shopping mall, for example, the marketing mix for a pasta bar would be different to that required for the coffee shop. The more segmented the market, the more detailed the marketing mix can become.

4.7 The product life cycle

The concept of the product life cycle (PLC) is that from a product's launch on to the market, until it is withdrawn, it passes through a series of stages. These four stages form an S-shaped curve and are usually described as introduction, growth, maturity and decline. Each stage has a number of particular features in terms of costs, sales, profit and competition:

1 *Introduction*. Costs at this stage are high: research and product development; stock levels to be set; advertising and sales promotion costs for the launching of the new product; managerial time and resources, etc. Sales are from first-time buyers and will be significantly affected by the success or failure of the promotional campaign. Profit is minimal, if any, owing to the high financial commitment at this stage. Losses are common. Competition is also minimal, the new product is at its infancy and many competitors choose to sit back to see the outcome.
2 *Growth*. Costs are lower as marketing research and the high initial publicity costs are more a feature of the introductory phase of a new product. Sales growth is rapid as the market expands – first-time buyers may become repeat purchasers. Profitability can be at its highest owing to increased sales and the overall reduction in costs. Depending on the success of the product launch, competition may now enter the market which has the effect of enlarging the total market for the product due to their additional advertising and promotion.
3 *Maturity*. Costs in the maturity stage may increase again, particularly in terms of promotion as the organization seeks to retain its market share. Sales gradually level out as competition from products of other companies take a share of the total market, and the growth of the organization slows. As the sales levels stabilize, so do the profits – prices are reduced in order to compete, promotional costs erode profitability levels and total demand for the product stabilizes.
4 *Decline*. As the market becomes further saturated with products, some organizations may

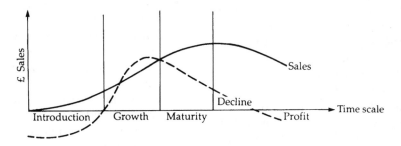

Figure 4.4 *The product life cycle*

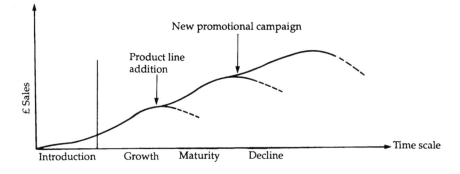

Figure 4.5 *Extending the product life cycle*

leave the market altogether. Costs become disproportionately high in an attempt to hold the company's position in the market. Sales and profit levels fall as too many products compete for an ever decreasing percentage of the market, demand falls while supply remains in abundance.

Ideally, product life cycles would be produced for all of an organization's product lines. Management need to recognize that a product will pass through various stages during its life and decisions must be made, in advance, to deal with the changes and consequences each stage brings. For example, the promotional aspects of the marketing mix will alter substantially from the introductory phase where a heavy pre-launch investment is needed, to the growth phase where expenditure may decrease significantly. If during the growth or maturity phase an addition to the product line is made, or the product altered in some way, this would again affect the promotional mix. Taking the fast-food sector of the industry as an example. The sales growth of an operation's major line (hamburgers) is seen to be declining. The operation may introduce an addition to the product line, for example a new sauce or salad item, or it may alter the product in some way, for example a new flavour or a larger-sized hamburger. Together, with a supportive advertising and sales promotion campaign, the company seeks to revitalize the market.

The effect is to sustain the growth stage of the product line. Equally, if an organization is considering entering an existing 'new' market, its product launch should coincide with the growth stage of its competitors' product life cycle; in this way it can enter the market during the product's period of rising sales. By constantly monitoring its product lines, management can attempt to continually revitalize interest in its products and sustain stable sales and profit levels.

4.8 Marketing research

Marketing research involves systematically collecting, storing and analysing information, both internally and externally, for an organization. Once the information has been collected, it may be used for the purpose of examining any aspects of the organization's marketing activities.

The use of marketing research is a problem solving approach following a number of logical stages:

(i) What information does the organization need?

For example:
- The size of the market and a breakdown of the segmentation.
- Competition and the organization's position in the market.
- Consumer behaviour. Why customers do and do not buy the company's products.
- Market feasibility study for the launching of a new product.
- Advertising research. Which advertising techniques should be used.
- The market's possible response to an increase in the products' prices.

The type of information the organization needs must be specifically identified so that valuable time and money is not wasted collecting information that will never be utilized.

(ii) Where will the information be collected from?

1 *Primary information.* Primary information is new information that the organization will usually have to go outside of its own confines to gather. Professional marketing research companies may be used or the organization can tailor-make its own. Primary information is more expensive and time-consuming because the data first has to be collected in the field before it can be analysed.
2 *Secondary information.* Secondary information is information that has previously been collected either within the organization itself or it already exists externally. Within the organization 'desk research' often highlights a number of areas that have stored information useful to marketing research, for example:

- Reservations made in a restaurant, recording client and contact name, address and telephone number, method of reservation, frequency of usage, special rates given.
- Sales records, identifying products, quantities sold, sales cycles, average spends, methods of payment, cash or credit.
- Purchasing documents, percentage of convenience and fresh foods being used, food and beverage costs and budgets compared, shortfalls, pilferage, wastage.
- Staff meetings held between management and staff.

Outside the organization, there is a wealth of information available:

- Government publications and statistics.
- Professional trade associations, publications, conferences and meetings.
- Educational establishments.
- Other publications, guides, journals, news papers and television.

(iii) How will the information be collected?

There are many sampling and interviewing techniques available for use in marketing research. The organization needs to carefully choose those that will specifically give it the type of information it requires. Examples include:

- Consumer sampling, the use of consumer panels for food tastings.
- Interviewing methods, personal or group.
- Postal and telephone questionnaires.
- Observational techniques, for example, watching where consumers choose to sit in a restaurant, their reaction when a dessert trolley is presented to them, watching the customer flow at a cafeteria counter or at a cash desk. Camera video and electronic equipment may be used here to assist the study.

(iv) How will the information be analysed?

Analysing the information largely depends on how the information has been collected and the quantity of it. Where the information is highly statistical, there are a number of specialized techniques available to process the raw data. If the research has been undertaken by a professional marketing agency, the results must be presented to the organization's management in a way that is meaningful to them; this should already have been decided upon at the initial stages of discussion. Smaller individual establishments will be involved on a much smaller scale of research and the information may be collected by the owner or a member of the management team.

(v) How will the information be utilized?

Collated and stored information is fruitless. For research information to become beneficial to an organization it must be utilized and acted upon. If a sales analysis reveals menu items unsold week after week, they should be removed from the menu and replaced. If sales from a dessert trolley are consistently low, the visual presentation, quality of foods offered, the pricing, etc. may need to be reviewed. The results of a marketing research survey or questionnaire may reinforce what the restaurant and food and beverage managers have thought for some time – now is the time to do something about it.

4.9   Market research

It is convenient at this point to distinguish between market research and marketing research. Marketing research is concerned with investigating all aspects of the marketing process. Market research is concerned with investigating markets – their size, segmentation, changes in them, etc. An example of market research is the market feasibility study.

4.9.1.   The market feasibility study

The purpose of such a study is to identify a marketing opportunity and the means of exploiting that market. The extent of a market feasibility study varies according to the needs of the situation. However, it will most likely be concerned with one of the following:

1 The identification of a gap in the eating out market and the formulation of a suitable product for it.
2 The determination of the most suitable product given a fixed location.
3 The identification of a location for a pre-determined product.

Feasibility studies also involve the analysis of a number of criteria related to the organization and its external environment.

1 Market area characteristics, for example analysis of population, levels of income, levels and type of employment, commercial and industrial activity, retail sales statistics, local tourism and transport.
2 Project site and area evaluation, for example description of site and surrounding areas, location of site to demand generators and attractions, accessibility and modes of transport, legal aspects (zoning, building restrictions, etc.) and site strengths and weaknesses.
3 Competition analysis, for example for a restaurant. Listing all competitors within x metres/miles of proposed unit and classifying by type of restaurant, ownership, type of unit, days and hours of operation, type of service offered, menu prices, number of seats, special features (live music, listed in food guides,) etc.
4 Demand analysis, for example identification

and characteristics of existing markets and market segments, future needs.
5 Recommendations for facilities and services, for example recommendations regarding the number, type and capacity of restaurants, bars and servicing departments, special architectural and design features, outline concept and broad policies.
6 Projected estimates of operating results, for example explanation as to the bases of the estimates, projections at various levels of business, relationship between revenue and operating costs, conclusions.

Caterers will eventually identify a number of groups of customers who are important to their business:

1 The regular customer who brings repeat business to the operation on a daily, weekly or monthly basis.
2 The casual customer who should be considered with the view to becoming a regular customer.
3 The function or group customer who should also be considered as an individual who may at some time come with friends or family as well as recommending additional function or group business to the establishment.
4 The potential customer who has been identified by the market research study but who has yet to use the operations facilities.

4.10   SWOT analysis

SWOT (strengths, weaknesses, opportunities and threats) is a form of analysis that may be used by organizations as part of their market planning process. It involves a systematic analysis of all aspects of the operation, both internally and externally. Strengths and weaknesses are often referred to as internal, opportunities and threats as external.

Taking a fast-food operation as an example, one of its inherent strengths may be a product's quality: customers know that from one purchase to another, they will always receive the same standard quality product. A weakness, however, may be in the limited menu choice available, or the design of the take-away packaging which does not keep the food at the correct temperature

Strengths	Weaknesses
• Good reputation • Popular products • Quality products • Unique selling points • Value for money • Skilled staff	• Poor reputation • Poor products • Low value, high price • Slow service • Unskilled staff
Opportunities • Growth potential • Niche markets • Competitive pricing • Increase product range • Efficiency update	**Threats** • Very competitive market • Limited growth possibilities • Limited finance • Increasing costs • Road work problems

Figure 4.6 *SWOT analysis – to summarize basic market research*

for a long enough time. Opportunities may exist for the extension of the menu range by offering additional products, sauces and accompaniments without having the need to purchase additional capital intensive production equipment, or to seek new and more efficient packaging within specific cost standards. Threats may be in the form of competition from other fast-food operators, or from a dramatic increase in the cost of a major raw material item to the operation, which would affect the cost of the product to the customer and the sales mix to the operation.

SWOT's use as a management tool is in its comprehensive analysis of all aspects of an organization. It would, therefore, include a detailed review of all the marketing functions discussed in this chapter, and in particular in the formulation of the marketing mix.

4.11 References

Bitner, M. J. (1991). The evolution of the services marketing mix and its relationship to service quality. In S. W. Brown, E. Gummesson, B. Edvardsson and B. Gustavsson (eds), *Service Quality: Multidisciplinary and Multinational Perspectives.* Lexington, MA: Lexington Books, pp. 23–37.

Cowell, D. (1984). *The Marketing of Services.* Oxford: Heinemann.

Davis, B. and Lockwood, A. (1994). *Food and Beverage Management – a selection of readings.* Oxford: Butterworth-Heinemann.

Kotler, P. (1984). *Marketing Management: analysis planning and control,* 5th edn. London: Prentice Hall International.

McCarthy, E. J. (1981). *Basic Marketing: a managerial approach,* 7th edn. Homewood, Illinois: Irwin.

Middleton, V. (1988). *Marketing in Travel and Tourism.* Oxford: Butterworth-Heinemann.

5
Advertising, public relations, merchandising and sales promotion

5.1 Advertising

Advertising is concerned with contacting and informing a market of an operation's product, away from the point of sale and is involved with influencing the customers' behaviour and attitude to the product before they enter the service operation.

Advertising has been defined by the American Marketing Association as:

> Any paid form of non-personal presentation and promotion of ideas, goods or services by an identified sponsor.

Its purpose, as defined by the Institute of Practitioners in Advertising (IPA) is:

> To influence a person's knowledge, attitude and behaviour in such a way as to meet the objectives of the advertiser.

The aims and objectives of an operation's advertising policy should be contained within the marketing plan. No advertising campaign ought to be undertaken unless it has been properly organized and is going to be efficiently managed. Disorganized advertising will not benefit an establishment; it may, in fact, do a great deal of harm. It is, therefore, wrong to assume that any advertising is better than no advertising.

The size of a food services advertising budget is dependent on a number of factors:

1 The nature of the catering operation, whether it is in the commercial or non-commercial sector.
2 The size of the operation. Generally speaking, the larger the commercial operation, the larger the advertising budget available.
3 The ownership of the catering facility. In a small, privately owned hotel or restaurant, the responsibility for advertising may be in the hands of the owner or manager. In a large multi-unit organization, the responsibility for advertising is either assigned to a specialist department within the organization, or given to a professional outside advertising agency.
4 The number and nature of the market segments being aimed at.
5 The amount of advertising each market segment requires to be adequately covered.
6 The type of advertising to be used. Peak time national television coverage will obviously cost considerably more than a local radio broadcast.

In some sectors of the industry advertising budgets are very large. The fast-food sector, for example, surpasses any others in the catering industry (see Table 5.1).

Of McDonald's total of £38.1m expenditure, a large percentage of this was spent on TV advertising, promoting its brand image on a national scale. Generally speaking, advertising expenditure in this sector of the industry varies from 0.5 to 4.5 per cent turnover. Companies within the hotel industry are also increasing their advertising budgets considerably.

Where small owner-managed or small groups of hotels cannot afford to individually advertise their properties and facilities to any great effect, they may group together to form a marketing consortium to achieve greater advertising impact. In the UK, for example, Prestige Hotels operates a marketing consortium with Scott Calder, its American counterpart. Such organiza-

Table 5.1 *Main media advertising expenditure by leading fast-food restaurant chains (£000), years to June 1994–96*

	1994	1995	1996
McDonald's	31,112	30,796	38,074
Burger King	7,739	8,585	5,587
KFC	5,100	6,732	8,510
Pizzaland	2,491	3,084	2,329
Pizza Hut	4,263	1,982	5,033
Wimpy	453	898	787
Bella Pasta	423	795	
Perfect Pizza	–	–	261

Source: Register-MEAL, UK Catering Market, Keynote 1996.

tions professionally produce brochures, leaflets and other sales literature which is distributed via all the consortium's establishments throughout the UK, and some times internationally. By joining together with other small or similar operations, an individual establishment benefits from being part of a large organization.

Whatever the size of the food service facility, however, advertising does have relevance and importance. In order to be effective, there must be a clear understanding of the purposes and objectives of advertising. In a catering operation these would include the following:

1 To create awareness of the product. Making the maximum number of customers aware of an operation's products, utilizing the tools of advertising available to that particular operation.
2 To create desire for the product. Customers purchase a product because of the benefits they feel they will gain from that product. Advertising, therefore, needs to create a desire for an operation's product by stressing customer benefits. The benefits of take away meals, for example, are that raw ingredients do not have to be purchased, stored, prepared and cooked. The end product is ready to eat, time is saved and cleaning up afterwards is minimal. These are some of the benefits that customers perceive as important when they buy a take-away meal, they are not just buying food for physiological needs.
3 To influence customers attitudes to the product. This may be in the short or long term.

Over a number of years, for example, an organization may wish to portray a 'caring' image towards its customers. It may choose to do this by using repetitive advertising reinforcing its caring attitude.

4 To create brand loyalty. In order to do this, a successful brand image must be created by the company, so that when customers consider buying a certain type of meal, they immediately think of a certain restaurant or fast-food operation.
5 To persuade customers to buy. This will only be achieved if the advertising campaign has been directed at the appropriate level of the market. For example, if an advertising campaign incorrectly portrays an average priced restaurant as being an expensive place to eat, customers with a lower average spending power will not choose to visit the facility because of the high-priced image portrayed; equally, customers with a high average spending power may be disappointed with their choice of restaurant. The operation's target markets must, therefore, be divided into clearly identifiable market segments. The promotional features of the marketing side can then be aimed specifically at these market segments.
6 To persuade customers to visit an operation in preference to a competitor's. Competition may be direct or indirect. Direct competition includes those operations competing for the same target market. For example, an outlet's customers may have been identified as coming from an AB middle class socio-economic group (see Table 4.1), aged between 50 to 60 years, with an average spend of £20 per head for an evening meal; direct competitors would include those establishments also aiming at this same target market. Indirect competition includes other catering operations who, although not competing for exactly the same market segment, are offering alternative catering facilities. These operations may charge prices of between £10 to £12 per head, which the identified AB middle class customers may visit occasionally for a variety of reasons such as price, convenience, etc.
7 To remind customers to buy. The objectives of an advertising campaign alter during the life

cycle of the product. For example, in the introductory phase of a product launch, creating awareness for first-time buyers is an important objective of advertising. When the product enters its growth and maturity stages and the company is heavily reliant on repeat purchases, the main objective of the advertising campaign may then shift to reminding existing and past customers to buy. This is equally applicable to operations within both the commercial and non-commercial sectors. It has particular reference in situations such as the work place where catering facilities are usually in the same block of offices or factory, and where staff may become accustomed to passing by the catering facilities and perhaps choosing to eat elsewhere. An advertising campaign to attract and remind this market segment is a particularly effective way of building up repeat business.

8 To inform the market about a product. For example, some fast-food chains now produce nutritional guides about their products which are available to customers of their restaurant and take-away outlets.

9 To provide reassurance about the product. This is particularly relevant in the catering industry where a customer often leaves a restaurant without any tangible evidence of a purchase. Customers' worries and anxieties about a product need to be allayed so that they feel they made a good purchase and will, therefore, feel disposed to make another. In the example of the nutritional guides, as well as being informative, they also reassure customers that the meals they are buying are nutritionally sound. This is particularly important with the current interest in healthy eating and diets.

10 To be ethical. From an ethical point of view, the operation's advertising must portray a truthful picture of the establishment. Customers may quite rightfully be disillusioned and annoyed if they read that a particular restaurant is offering a free glass of wine to every customer, or features some speciality drinks, only to arrive and find that the establishment has 'run out' or 'sold out' of these items.

The following advertising techniques are all applicable in some way to both commercial and non-commercial operations. However, depending largely on the sector of the industry and the size of the advertising budget available, the larger commercial organizations are able to utilize many or all of these advertising tools, whereas smaller non-commercial operations will be restricted to only a few. The major forms of advertising that may be employed by food service facilities include the following:

5.1.1   Direct mail

Direct mail involves communicating by post to specified customers; it may be directed at new and potential customers or to past or well established customers. It involves the direct mailing of personalized letters, brochures, pamphlets and leaflets, and as a form of advertising offers a number of advantages:

1 Specific customers can be targeted. For example, members of a specific profession within a defined area, members of a particular club or society, residents on a housing estate, etc. Repeat business in particular can develop by mailing personalized birthday, anniversary and Christmas cards, details of special promotions, events and offers to regular and occasional customers.

2 Direct mail is easy to introduce. It can either be initiated by the organization itself by producing its own mailing lists, or an external mail service agency or list broker may be used. It can be used by both small and large operations.

3 The feedback from targeted customers is relatively prompt and easy to appraise. Free post return cards, freephone telephone calls are usually returned soon after the direct mail shot has been received, or not at all. The use of coupons, vouchers etc. is easy to appraise in that they are normally only for use in a restricted period and the uptake can be measured easily.

4 It is a cost-effective method of advertising to specifically targeted groups of customers with very little 'wastage'.

However, direct mail also has a number of disadvantages:

1 The market must be specifically targeted or the mail shots are a complete waste of money.
2 The mail must be received, read and acted upon by the specific individual or group or all prior advertising research has also been a waste.
3 The production of good-quality mailing literature can be costly. Personalized letters should ideally be used as duplicated material has little impact and is often discarded straight away. The envelope too must encourage the recipient to open it rather than discarding it as a circular. Once the initial mail has been sent out, careful monitoring of subsequent replies is necessary; often further advertising material may need to be distributed to reinforce the initial sales literature.

The identification of the market segments to be aimed at is most important. As with marketing research, the operation may find that through its own desk research – internal and external – it can amass a considerable amount of information about its markets through restaurant reservations, sales records, trade journals, local newspapers, etc. If a restaurant is considering featuring special business lunches, for example, it may consider writing to civic and business associations and asking for their membership lists, as well as contacting any other professional groups in the area. Alternatively, a catering operation may consider using a professional mail service agency. Here again, it is important to specify exactly the section of the market to be aimed at.

Large catering organizations who have sufficient finance available are able to deal directly with advertising agencies who will totally manage an organization's advertising campaign. They will study the product to be marketed, design appropriate advertisements, and suggest possible outlets for distributing these adverts, whether through the press, on posters, direct mailing or whatever.

For the smaller organization, however, the use of a professional advertising agency for all the operation's requirements is not always feasible because of the costs involved. For the smaller organization with a limited advertising budget it may be more advantageous to identify where in the advertising campaign the operation would most benefit from professional advice and to seek this advice when necessary. The operator may decide, for example, that the two most effective ways of reaching potential markets are direct mailing and advertising in the local newspapers. Having decided on the methods of advertising and the times at which they should appear, the design of the advertisements themselves must be undertaken. At this stage even the smallest operator should consider seeking the help and advice of a professional designer.

The presentation of an advertisement in the organization's sales literature or in a local newspaper, or the layout, photography and artwork in a restaurant brochure are critical to the production of a professional piece of sales literature. When literature is being sent to potential and existing customers it is important that it projects the image of a catering operation that the owner or manager wishes to portray. Therefore even if a catering operation's financial allocation to advertising is comparatively small, a percentage of this can be well spent on employing the services of a professional designer in order to produce good-quality sales literature for the catering facility.

5.1.2   Press advertising

1 *Newspapers.* Advertising in national and local newspapers and magazines is probably one of the most popular forms of media used by catering operations. Because restaurant advertisements are generally featured together in a newspaper, it is essential that the design of an advertisement featuring a particular restaurant is such that it will stand apart from the others. As with the previously described direct mailing, advertising in the press must be properly planned and organized. If an advertisement is placed in several newspapers, records must be kept of those individuals or companies that respond to the advertisement and whether they are from the type of market segments originally aimed at. Such information is invaluable in forming a basis for planning future advertising campaigns .
2 *Magazines.* The different types of magazines in which a catering operation may choose to

advertise include professional journals and publications, business management magazines and the 'social' type magazines which are read by particular target market groups. The advantages of advertising in specific magazines are that response may be measured, they have a longer 'shelf life' than newspapers and may be re-read many times.

3 *Guides*. There are a number of 'Good Food Guides' produced in which food service facilities may wish to be included. Such well-known guides are the *AA* and *RAC* guides, *The Michelin Guide*, *The Egon Ronay Guide*, *The Good Food Guide* and the *Tourist Board Guides*. To be featured in these guides will often be as a result of passing a professional inspection by the particular organization and at times having to pay a fee for inclusion. As a method of advertising these guides have a special value in that they all have large circulation figures and are purchased by interested and potential customers and are used regularly as sources of reference for eating out occasions.

4 *Trade advertising*. Trade or 'wholesale' advertising is the selling of an operation's catering facilities through 'middle men' such as travel agents, package tour operators, etc. At present it is mainly the large hotel groups and restaurant chains who have utilized this form of external selling although it is also available to small restaurants that are privately owned. By approaching local tour operators, for example, a country restaurant may be able to secure a regular weekend lunch time trade of between twenty and thirty covers throughout the summer months. Such an arrangement not only has the advantage of increased sales for the operation, but also aids in the planning of menus, food costing, staffing levels, etc., for several months in advance. A commission fee is charged by these middle men for the provision of their services; this may vary between 5 and 12.5 per cent depending on what functions and services they have provided for the catering operation.

5.1 .3 Broadcasting

1 *Radio*. Advertising on commercial radio is mainly limited to local radio stations that broadcast within a specific radius. It may be used to advertise local take-aways, restaurants, hotels, wine bars etc. Its main advantages are that it is a very up-to-date form of advertising, not too costly and has the potential to reach a large percentage of local custom – people at work, driving cars, using personal stereos, people at home, etc.

2 *Television*. Television's major advantage over radio is its visual impact. Its major disadvantage is its high cost, particularly during peak receiving times. Its national use is limited almost exclusively to the larger restaurant and fast-food and popular restaurant chains and hotel groups, for example, KFC, McDonald's, Pizzaland. Some regional television advertising may be undertaken but at present is very limited. The use of both video cassette recorders and cable television are two further extensions of TV and their use in private homes, clubs, hotels, shopping malls etc. is increasing annually.

3 *Cinema*. Cinema advertising is also highly visual but also very localized. Catering facilities such as fast-food and popular restaurants etc. open until late in the evening are often featured, but are usually quite specific to a certain area.

5.1.4 Signs and posters

Signs and posters advertising a catering facility may be positioned either very close to it or some distance away. They are used along streets in towns and cities on hoardings, in airport lounges, railway carriages and the underground subways. External signs on main roads are particularly important for hotels, restaurants and fast-food drive-in operations who rely heavily on transient trade, and it is, therefore, important for these advertisements to be easily read and their messages understood quickly. Traffic travelling at high speeds must also be given adequate time to pull in. Posters displayed in the street, in railway carriages etc. can afford to be more detailed because passengers and passers-by will have more time available to read them.

As with all other forms of advertising, signs and posters must portray the type of image the restaurant is trying to achieve. Fast-food and take-away outlets in high street locations, for example, who are attempting to attract as much transient traffic as possible, feature large colourful signs with distinguishing logos and colours, for example, KFC, McDonalds, Wimpy etc. An up-market restaurant situated outside a town, however, would not need to use such obvious external signs, because a higher percentage of the trade would already have made a reservation and such a restaurant would, therefore, display something smaller and more discreet.

5.1.5 Miscellaneous advertising media

This includes other forms of advertising media that may be used in addition to the major channels discussed above. For example, door-to-door leaflet distribution, leisure centre entrance tickets, theatre programmes, shop windows etc.

5.2 Public relations

Public relations is a communication and information process, either personal or non personal, operating within an organization's internal and external environment. It involves the creation of a favourable environment in which an organization can operate to the best of its advantage. An organization would typically be involved internally in communicating to its customers and employees, and eventually to its customers, suppliers, sales force, local community, council and government departments, etc. Public relations has two main functions:

1 It has a problem-solving or trouble-shooting function to deal with any negative publicity. As with advertising, it is wrong to assume that any publicity is better than no publicity. Detrimental newspaper reports and letters to column writers, bad word-of-mouth and radio news publicity can all have a damaging effect on an operation's image and sales. Through a public relations exercise a company's desired corporate image can be restored.
2 It has a forward looking function to creating positive publicity for the organization and may be used at various stages during the life cycle of the facility. For example, if a fast food

unit is to be opened in a busy town centre, a public relations exercise would typically be to create a favourable environment and attitude within the local community before its opening. If this facility is specifically aiming at a younger family market, the public relations function would include informing the identified market segments of the benefits the facility has to offer to them. For example children's menus and portions will be available at reduced prices, high chairs for babies are to be provided, an informal atmosphere will exist, on certain days entertainment for the children will be organized, a young members' club will be available for those wishing to join etc.

In institutional catering, the role of public relations may be to explain to a staff committee the need for certain price increases to be passed on to the staff cafeteria, or why different products have been bought to replace existing ones etc.

The initiation of a public relations exercise should begin with the identification of that sector of the organization's environment that it wishes to communicate with; it may, for example, be a particular segment of its market, the press, local schools etc. An evaluation of the organization's existing corporate image with that sector will highlight those areas it feels are unfavourable, and would benefit from a public relations exercise. The organization may then choose the most suitable channels for communicating its messages to help create the type of environmental climate it feels would be favourable to its own company's objectives.

The choice of public relations tools to be used depends largely on the target audience, the suitability of one media over another and the budget available. They would include:

1 *Press media.* Newspapers, magazines, trade journals, brochures, leaflets, guides, press conferences, press releases.
2 *Broadcasting media.* Television, radio, cinema, promotional video and cassettes.
3 *Community media.* Sponsorship of local events, individuals, companies, exhibitions, talks, free gifts, samples.

Depending on the size of the organization, the public relations function may be the responsibility of the owner, or manager, it may be an individual's task in a medium-sized operation, a separate department within the organization consisting of a number of employees, or an external public relations company may be used.

Public relations in the hotel and catering industry has a real application whether the catering facility is a small or large operation, is independent or part of a large group, exists in the free market or captive. The importance of public relations is the ability to communicate and inform. The public image, good or bad, of a catering facility is something that develops as a result of the business activity; however, whether it is advantageous or disadvantageous to the organization can be greatly influenced by public relations.

5.3   Merchandising

The merchandising of catering operations involves the point of sale promotion of their facilities using non-personal media. Unlike advertising it is not a paid for form of communication, but like sales promotion is more concerned with influencing customer behaviour in the short term.

Once customers are inside a restaurant they have already made their decision as to the type of establishment they wish to eat in; their subsequent decisions are concerned with what particular aspects of the product they will now choose. Customers may decide to eat at a restaurant because they have seen it advertised, and will therefore bring to the restaurant preconceived ideas as to the standard of food, level of service etc., that they will receive. It is important at this stage that the point of sale merchandising of the restaurant should support its advertising campaign in order to achieve a sense of consistency and totality. For example, if the restaurant has been advertising speciality dishes for a particular week, these must be available when the customer arrives at the restaurant.

The major types of merchandising that may be employed by a catering operation include the following:

5.3.1   Floor stands

Floor stands or bulletin boards are particularly effective if used in waiting and reception areas to advertise special events, forthcoming attractions, etc. In these areas in hotels, restaurants and clubs, people may be waiting in a queue or for the arrival of other guests, and therefore have the time to read the notices on these stands. In the work place they can be placed in areas with a high throughput of pedestrian traffic, for example in corridors, and in general locations where people congregate such as beside vending machines. The announcements on these stands must be kept attractive and up to date or the messages grow old and ineffective. Some self-service operations use floor stands at the head of the waiting line to show the menu in advance and selected specialities of the day.

5.3.2   Posters

Posters have a wider circulation than the previously described floor stands. They may be displayed in reception areas, elevators, cloakrooms, in the restaurant dining area itself, in fact they may be placed in any strategic positions where people have the time available to read their messages. Consideration must not only be given to the area in which these advertisements should be placed, but also their positions within these areas. In elevators, for example, they are often placed at the back when the majority of people face forwards or look upwards as soon as they enter a lift and therefore only give a poster at the back a momentary glance. Similar thought should be given to the position of posters in reception areas; for example, their height should be at eye level and they need to be placed away from the entrance and exit doors which people tend to pass through quickly.

5.3.3   Wall displays

Illuminated wall displays are used extensively by fast-food operations showing enlarged colour photographs of the food and beverages available. They are also used by wine bars, cocktail bars and lounges and look particularly attractive at night. Blackboards are often found in pubs, bars, school cafeterias and theme restaurants where the dish of the day and other specials can be changed regularly along with their prices.

5.3.4 Tent cards

Tent cards are often placed on restaurant dining tables to promote special events, attractions, etc. They are a valuable merchandising tool because guests will almost inevitably pick the card up and read it at some point during the meal, and they may even take it away with them. They may be used to advertise special dishes or wines, or announce forthcoming events such as a Christmas Day menu or New Year party. Again, these cards should be changed regularly to hold interest and must always be up to date and clean. In hotels or other operations which have a variety of catering outlets, these tent cards are very useful in advertising the other facilities within the same establishment. In a cocktail bar, for example, tent cards may be used to advertise the à la carte restaurant, and in the restaurant the customers' attention may be drawn to special function arrangements the operation offers. This type of merchandising can help to make customers aware of the operation's alternative facilities and hence boost sales in these areas.

5.3 .5 Clip-ons

Menu clip-ons are most commonly used in restaurants to advertise speciality items, plats du jour, special table d'hôte lunches offered in an à la carte restaurant and so on; they may also be used on wine lists to promote a particular wine or region. Both tent cards and clip-ons are useful tools for the hotel or restaurant to feature the higher profit earning food and beverage items. 'Loss leaders' may be placed towards the end of the menu selection.

5.3.6 Children's menus

Children's menus and portion sizes are particularly applicable to those catering operations who attract family custom, for example resort hotels, fast-food units, medium-priced restaurants etc. In the UK the catering operations who offer this facility are generally those who cater for the lower and middle markets of the population, with higher level operations somewhat reluctant to offer this facility. In other countries in Europe,

and particularly in the USA, this is a more commonly found restaurant service, and is a useful merchandising tool as few parents wish to pay the full restaurant charge for a child when he or she eats less than half the meal.

Some restaurants offer a reduced price for children's portion sizes while others produce a separate children's menu which also contains games and puzzles to keep the children occupied while the parents are having their meal (see Figures 5.1 and 5.2). This is particularly applicable to those operations who rely heavily on family trade, and even if children's menus are not offered throughout the year, they may be worthwhile considering during the busier summer months.

5.3.7 Visual food and beverage display

It was once said that 'We eat with our eyes' and in few other situations could this be more true than in the actual cooking and presentation of the food to the customer. Visual selling in a catering operation can be enhanced by the use of several techniques:

1 *Displays.* A good display of well-presented food can do much to increase sales. Impulse buying is the purchasing of a product at a point of sale on the strength of its visual presentation, with little or no preconceived thoughts of buying that product. Good displays are necessary in any situation; customers may be encouraged to purchase more when they actually see the food and beverages, for example at self-service restaurants, buffets, carvery operations and vending machines.
2 *Trolleys or carts.* The use of trolleys or carts is another method of selling food and beverages by using display techniques. In a restaurant there may be a variety of trolleys used for hors d'oeuvres, desserts, hot and cold meat joints, liqueurs and cigars.
3 *Guéridon cookery.* A guéridon trolley in a restaurant may be used for 'finishing off' a particular dish before being presented to the customer, or it may be used to cook a complete dish, for example flambé desserts. This particular type of action presentation often encour-

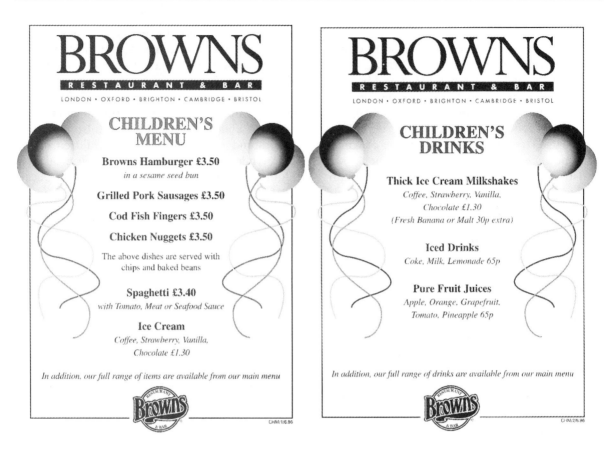

Figure 5.1   *A children's menu from Browns Restaurant and Bar*

ages other guests in the restaurant to also try these types of dishes.

4 *Other display cookery.* Some operations deliberately open up their kitchens so that customers can see their food being cooked, for example steak houses where steaks are openly grilled on a charcoal grill, and other operations which roast poultry and other meat on rotating spits. In these types of operation special attention must be given to the balance between this type of display cookery and the other items on the menu to ensure that any additional expenses, such as staffing and food costs, are justified by the increase in custom.

5 *Beverage display.* The display of beverages, alcoholic and non-alcoholic, can also contribute to impulse purchases, rather than being just a single coffee sale at the end of a meal. In a self-service cafeteria bottles and glasses of cooled fruit juices, and wine can all look inviting; in a restaurant, full wine racks,

or full bottles at the side of the buffet or carvery table have a similar visual effect.

5.3.8   Audial

Audial merchandising has fairly limited application, but can be used in situations with a 'captive' audience, for example to promote a coffee shop, pizza bar, ice-cream parlour in a shopping mall, to focus attention on a hospital's cafeteria via the hospital radio, to inform exhibition visitors in a conference centre of the catering facilities available.

5.3.9   Other sales tools

There is a variety of other internal sales tools that may be used by a catering operation. These include place mats, which in coffee shops may

Figure 5.2 *The children's menu at an Innkeepers Fayre Restaurant*

contain the breakfast menu with a reminder that the operation is open throughout the day for snacks; napkins; doilies; and pre-portioned condiments which all add to the operation's sales message. In the bars giving away cocktail sticks, matches and drink mats also enables a small part of the operation to be carried out of the establishment and may act as a reminder to customers of their meal experience several days or months later.

Through all aspects of an organization's merchandising approach, there is a very real need for it to complement its advertising campaign. Advertising the facilities will hopefully have stimulated customer interest. The role of merchandising is to convert that interest into purchases and increased sales.

5.4 Sales promotion

Sales promotion is a form of temporary incentive highlighting aspects of a product that are not inherent to it. Sales promotion may be aimed at customers, distribution channels and sales employees. It does not necessarily occur at the point of sale, although in many instances it does.

Sales promotion is used by operations for a number of reasons including the following:

1 To increase the average spend by customers and thereby increase the sales revenue.
2 To promote a new product or range of products being featured by the operation, for example offering a new flavoured milk shake in a take-away facility at a reduced price.
3 To influence impulse purchasers towards a certain product or range of products, for example featuring Australian wine at a special discount price.

4 To aid as a reminder during a long-term advertising campaign, for example on long established main menu items.
5 To help 'level' peak activities of business, for example offering a free glass of wine to customers ordering their meal before 18.30 hours.
6 To celebrate a special event, for example the New Year, Thanksgiving Day Dinner etc.
7 To 'package' together menu items at an attractive price, for example steak and strawberries. Such 'packages' are seasonal in nature but aid in directing a high proportion of customers' choices towards items of a low preparation labour content.
8 To clear slow moving stock, for example pricing specific cocktails at two for the price of one.

The types of sales promotions used are influenced by the targets being aimed at:

1 *Customers.* Sales promotions aimed directly at customers include money-off coupons, discounts or special prices during off-peak periods, free chicken meals for families, a free bottle of wine for every two adult meals ordered etc. Special events and promotions may be communicated to the customer by advertising, by direct mail, by telephone or by posters and tent cards.
2 *Distribution channels.* Promotional techniques aimed at incentivating third party agents include free restaurant meals, free gifts, competitions and the use of the hotel's leisure facilities.
3 *Sales employees.* Sales promotion incentives are similar to those listed above and include commission related sales, competitions, token and points systems occurring over an extended period to encourage an on-going sales commitment by the sales force.

Sales promotion is a marketing tool in its own right and should be planned, monitored and evaluated as such. It can be initiated either by the operation itself or by an external organization, and as with all other aspects of the marketing mix must be in line with the marketing objectives of the organization.

SPECIAL 3 COURSE MENU ONLY £6.55 UP TO 6.55PM
Only available Monday to Saturday

Including a fresh bread roll
HOMEMADE SOUP OF THE DAY
Please ask your server for today's choice.

✔ ♥ **MELON GONDOLA**
A juicy wedge of melon served with an orange twist.

GARLIC BREAD
French bread with garlic butter.

BARBECUE CHICKEN
A seasoned half roasted chicken, coated in barbecue sauce.

HADDOCK IN LEMON AND PEPPER
Grilled and served with tartare sauce.

✔ **SAVOURY PANCAKES**
Filled with mushrooms and cream cheese, topped with cheese sauce and served with a salad and garlic bread.

STEAK AND KIDNEY PIE
Cooked in a rich gravy.

◆

Ⓝ **CARAMEL APPLE GRANNY**
REGULAR ICE CREAM
FRESH FRUIT SALAD
or COFFEE

Figure 5.3 *An extract from the Henrys Table Premier House Pub Restaurant (Greenalls Group plc) illustrating the promotion of the £6.55 menu*

5.5   Personal selling

Personal selling is a paid form of promoting a facility on a personal basis. One of the main characteristics of service industries is the increased contact time between service staff and customers, and the attitudes and behaviour of an operation's service employees are important parts of the total product the customer is buying. As with the other aspects of the promotion mix, advertising, public relations, merchandising and sales promotion, the objectives, requirements and techniques of personal selling need to be fully integrated into the overall marketing policy of the organization.

Service employees are one of the most important assets of a catering operation. Too frequently waiters, bar staff, counter assistants, are seen only as 'order takers' and not as sales people. Particularly in large organizations, such as hotels which have their own sales department, it is too easy for service staff to see themselves merely as servers of the facilities' foods and beverages. The fact that an establishment may have a sales department does not relieve the catering department of its sales functions and responsibilities.

When customers enter a restaurant their first personal contact with the restaurant staff is usually the waiter who shows them to their table. How often is that same customer presented with the menu and then left to ponder for a considerable time without being asked if they would like a drink while considering the menu. A potential drink sale is lost immediately. When the waiter comes to take customers' orders there is another chance for the employee to promote the menu, perhaps the restaurant's speciality, a side salad, additional vegetables, wine to accompany the meal, rather than simply being an order taker. At the end of the meal the presentation of the dessert and liqueur trolleys can do much to revitalize a customer's palate, rather than the waiter merely asking if sweet or coffee are required.

Some establishments operate training programmes for service staff to help increase their awareness of the different ways in which they personally can contribute to an operation's sale. These training programmes can include basic sales functions of the waiter, such as asking customers if they would like a drink when they

Figure 5.4   *A T.G.I. Friday's 'happy hour' menu*

Figure 5.5   *Examples of promotional literature from Millers Kitchen Restaurants (Greenalls Group plc)*

arrive at the restaurant to more in depth sensitivity training.

Fast-food chains such as Burger King and McDonald's have highly standardized training programmes where service staff are taught selling phrases and responses that may be used when taking a customer's order. Although these highly formalized responses and situational examples are now being modified with the introduction of warmer and friendlier phrases such as McDonald's 'we've got time for you' suggesting that even in an efficiently standardized operation such as their own, they will have time for individual, personalized service.

At the other end of the catering spectrum, where there is a much longer contact time between service staff and customers, such as in haute cuisine or speciality restaurants, the 'personal touch' plays a more important role in the total service product. Also at this level, the technical knowledge of the service staff assumes greater importance.

Some operations encourage their staff to sell by providing incentives. For example, a waiter may receive a sales related bonus for every additional £5.00 spent by a customer over and above a pre-fixed average spend; the additional sale indicating that the waiter sold more food and beverages than the average for that restaurant. Incentivating service staff in this way, however, needs to be introduced with sensitivity so that the wrong type of competitiveness between staff does not develop to the detriment of the restaurant.

Whatever the level of catering operation and the amount of sales training given, there is a need for service staff to become more alert to customers' needs by listening to and observing and identifying what their needs are for that particular meal; this information may then be quantified by management for possible future action.

This aspect of personal selling is discussed as part of the meal experience (see Chapter 2).

The marketing of a catering operation must be effectively planned, organized and monitored throughout all its stages. The successes and failures of its promotional campaigns and those of its competitors, should be studied and reviewed when possible.

Good advertising, merchandising, public relations and sales promotion are difficult. They are areas of food and beverage management that often require considerable financial outlay, but which have no guarantee of success. Caterers are faced with a variety of promotional tools and techniques and whichever they choose, so will have others; they must compete therefore not only with the other facilities' catering products but also with their marketing campaigns.

Alone, advertising does not sell. It is there to stimulate interest, and to influence a customer towards buying an operation's product above those of its competitors. The customer's action is translated into a purchase at the point of sale, further stimulated by effective merchandising and possibly sales promotion techniques, all working together in a favourable environment created by good public relations.

5.6   References

Davis, B. and Lockwood, A. (1994). *Food and Beverage Management – a selection of readings.* Oxford: Butterworth-Heinemann.

Kotler, P. (1984). *Marketing Management: analysis, planning and control*, 5th edn. London: Prentice-Hall International.

Middleton, V. (1988). *Marketing in Travel and Tourism*. Oxford: Butterworth-Heinemann.

6
Food menus and beverage lists

6.1 Introduction

A primary objective of food and beverage establishments is the *selling* in its widest sense of the product: food and/or beverages. This is irrespective of whatever sector of the market one examines, whether it is an industrial restaurant, a steak bar, a hospital dining room or a carvery restaurant. The common and major aid is the menu, in all of its many forms. Once customers are on the premises of a catering establishment one of the main sales tools is some form of a menu. The other aspects which are also sales tools are the facilities provided, the degree of comfort and decor, the quality of the staff and the standard of the food and beverages available. The menu should be an extension of the three policies – marketing, financial and catering.

The marketing policy is reflected in the menu by such things as the requirements of the sector of the market that is being aimed at and the interpretation by the establishment of the needs of that market. The financial policy is reflected in the menu by the pricing and cost structure and the catering policy, by the size and type of the menu, and by the quality of the food and beverages offered (all being related to the specific needs of the identified customer).

The main aim of a food menu or beverage list is to inform customers in a clear way of what is available to them. As a sales tool it often will, by the use of well-planned and presented advertising techniques, direct the customer as to what to buy. In other words, by the means of a well-planned and presented menu it is possible to plan for a profit, or as in the case of the non commercial sector, to aid in controlling the costs while at the same time fully satisfying customer requirements. With the careful yet effective application of design, layout, typography and graphics, a menu can complement the atmosphere and type of service, and with the correct use of language and location of items, will result in a reliable and useful sales medium. The most powerful deterrents to sales are ignorance and fear by the customer. A good menu sets out consciously to assist customers by gaining their confidence and setting them at ease.

6.2 Basic menu criteria

There are a number of basic factors to be considered to ensure that a menu is to be an effective sales tool.

6.2.1 General presentation

General presentation is very important as it identifies the image and personality of that particular unit or department whether it is a steak house or a cocktail bar. The following points should be taken into consideration:

1 The menu should be *attractive*. The first impression of the menu should be that it looks interesting and inviting and that the customers will really want to read it.
2 It should be *clean*. Although this appears to be obvious it is something that is frequently ignored by caterers. If it is intended that a particular menu is to be offered frequently it is well worth considering having them either plastic coated so that they can be regularly wiped clean; or printed on inexpensive paper or card and regularly replaced or contained within a presentable and durable cover.
3 It should be *easy to read*. It is usual to use different sizes of typeface for such things as headings and the items appearing under

them. How typeface styles are used can help customers to make their choice of food and beverage items more easily. The use of attractive graphics, colour and blank space can also help with aiding customers to make their selection by directing and attracting their eye. What is not required is that a menu should resemble a page from a railway or bus timetable with its mass of information produced in an unattractive style which besides failing in so many other ways would also be annoying to the customer.

4 It should *complement the occasion.* It is necessary that the general presentation of the menu is not only in keeping with the decor of the room but also suitable and complementary to the occasion. Obvious examples are a restaurant within a holiday camp, a kosher wedding, a state banquet and bistro, where a different style and presentation are necessary for each.

5 It should reflect *current awareness.* The menu should take into consideration the current trends in eating habits, so as to be fully aware of customer requirements.

6 *Design.* By the careful use of graphics, typography and colour the menu can not only be interesting but can direct the customer's eye to specific items that the caterer wishes to sell. The design of a menu can assist in achieving the uniqueness of a particular food and beverage operation.

6.2.2 Menu content

The importance of this cannot be stressed too strongly if budgeted sales or costs are to be achieved. The content can be examined under the following headings:

1 *Language.* The language used must be in keeping with the type of operation. If a foreign language is being used it must be used accurately. As mentioned before, it is essential to keep customers at ease when making their selection and therefore frequently it will be necessary to provide a simple but accurate translation of the menu items to aid sales. A descriptive flamboyant type language is also often used on menus for themed establishments. It is necessary that customers should clearly understand what the items are, and not be left guessing.

2 *Accuracy.* A very basic requirement for all menus is that when seen by customers they are accurate as far as pricing and availability are concerned, with the correct spelling and description of dishes and drinks. It is all too common to be presented with a menu or wine list to which untidy alterations have been made in handwriting. This is not only annoying to customers but also at times leaves them with the fear that they may be being cheated by the caterer. Most, if not all, of these problems can be alleviated if more careful proofreading of the menus is done before they are printed and more care is taken when pricing items. In addition, it is not uncommon to find that the actual dishes when presented to customers do not match up to the name of the dish as on the menu, either because the caterer is not all that concerned with accuracy, or is of the opinion that poetic licence is fully permissible. However, the knowledgeable customer is not likely to return to this type of restaurant again.

3 *Pricing.* The correct pricing of all food menus and restaurant lists is very important to the success of an operation. It is essential that in total all necessary costs are covered; that the prices are attractive to the particular segment of the market that the operation is in; and that the prices are competitive in relation to the level of quality of food and drink and service offered.

There are various factors which can affect the pricing strategy operated – such things as the size and type of operation, the location, the profit required, the level of competition and the sector of the industry. In addition, the caterer would have to take into account such things as the type of menu or beverage list that is being priced, whether or not loss leaders or special offers to attract customers are used, the sales mix of items selected by customers, and the volume of business being done or forecast for each selling outlet.

4 *Sales mix.* The term 'sales mix' refers to the composition of the total sales as between the main components such as food and beverages, and also within a component such as food, to items such as appetizers and soups, fish and

meat, sweet dishes, etc. It is very important that the caterer when designing a menu or beverage list considers the importance of the actual or potential sales mix of items that the customers will choose. It is essential that the sales mix is satisfactory or it will be difficult for caterers to either cover their total food or beverage costs or to make the necessary total profit. When the sales mix of items chosen is unsatisfactory it may mean that the customers are only choosing the loss leaders or special offers; or that they are only choosing from those items which have a high food or beverage cost and a low gross profit; or that the overall average spend by customers is lower than expected or forecasted. It is necessary, therefore, that the average spend by customers is carefully monitored each day and that a sales history of all items sold is also prepared and analysed. Action to correct an unsatisfactory sales mix could be a new and carefully constructed and priced menu or beverage list; a more carefully designed menu directing the customers in their choice of items by the use of colour, graphics, space, etc. and/or by a short retraining programme on 'selling' for the service personnel.

6.2.3   Size and form

The size and shape of a menu can add to and complement the uniqueness of the facility. A food or beverage menu must be easy for the customer to handle and in no way confusing to read. The various forms that the menu can take are unlimited, from a menu chalked up on a blackboard, to a large illuminated display board with photographs, conventional menu cards, tent cards, placemats, menus printed in the shape of a fan or even handprinted onto silk handkerchiefs as mementoes for the guests at a banquet.

6.2.4   Layout of the menu

The larger the menu the more time-consuming it is for customers to make their selection of food or wine. However, if it is too short customers may not be entirely satisfied by what is offered.

Caterers need to adjust the length of their menu to the particular needs of their customers, bearing in mind that the longer a menu becomes the more management control will be necessary. What often is particularly confusing and embarrassing – unless the customer is very knowledgeable – is the length of wine lists offered in many restaurants. Unless wine lists of this type are extremely well laid out and contain additional help to customers to aid their selection, they will do very little to help the potential sales of a restaurant. The layout of a menu should take into consideration how a customer normally reads a menu. This is illustrated in Figure 6.4. This skilled use of the important areas on a menu must be utilized to enable an establishment to achieve its budgetary targets.

6.2.5   Nutritional content

The nutritional content of a menu is considered more important in the welfare sector of the industry than in the commercial sector. In the welfare sector, establishments such as hospitals, residential schools, homes for the elderly, etc., provide meals for long-stay residents; thus well-balanced nutritional meals are essential as it is unlikely that the residents will have any other source of intake of necessary vitamins, proteins, etc. In the commercial sector the vast majority of the customers will take meals at home as well as eat out in various types of restaurant. However, many more customers are becoming cautious of their dietary requirements and there is likely to be a small segment of the market who are particularly interested in, for example, the calorie content of specific menu items or in vegetarian items. To build into a menu some items which are specifically available for this type of customer can only increase the volume of business of a restaurant, providing their availability is sufficiently well-marketed to the correct market segment.

6.3   Types of food menu

Although there are many types of eating establishments offering many types of meal experiences, there are basically only two types of food menus: the *table d'hôte;* and the *à la carte.* From these two types of menus there are in practice many adaptations of each.

6.3.1 Table d'hôte menus

The table d'hôte menu is identified by:

1 Being a restricted menu.
2 Offering a small number of courses, usually three or four.
3 A limited choice within each course.
4 A fixed selling price.
5 All the dishes being ready at a set time.

This type of menu usually contains the popular type dishes and is easier to control, the set price being fixed for whatever the customer chooses, or being set depending on the main dish chosen. It is common practice in many restaurants for a table d'hôte menu to be offered to a customer together with an à la carte menu.

Table d'hôte menus can be offered for breakfast, lunch and dinners. Their many adaptations are used for:

1 *Banquets.* A banquet menu is a fixed menu at a set price offering usually no choice whatsoever to the customers, unless the client informs the caterer in advance that certain guests require, say, a vegetarian or kosher type meal, and is available to all guests at a predetermined time.
2 *Buffets.* Buffet type meals vary considerably depending on the occasion, and the price paid, from the simple finger buffet, where all items prepared are proportioned to a small size so that the customer may consume it without the use of any cutlery, to the exotic fork buffets where hot and cold food is available and where many large dishes will be carved and portioned for the individual guest. Buffets are frequently prepared for such occasions as wedding receptions, press receptions, presentations and conferences. Buffets can be classified as a form of table d'hôte menu as they offer a restricted menu, a limited choice of only what is on the buffet, a predetermined set price and all the dishes are available at a set time.
3 *Coffee houses.* A coffee house menu is a more

recent form of table d'hôte menu which is commonly used today in hotels and restaurants. This type of menu is characterized by:
(a) Being a set menu offered often for twelve to eighteen hours of the day.
(b) Being reasonably priced, with often each dish or section of the menu individually priced.
(c) Offering a range and choice of items that are suitable for snacks, light meals, lunch or dinner.
(d) Offering a limited range of foods that are either already cooked, are of the convenience type food category and require little preparation time, or are simple and quick to cook, for example omelettes, hamburgers, etc.
(e) A simplified form of service being offered, for example plate service, counter service, etc.

In some establishments the coffee shop menu may be replaced for two to three hours with a special breakfast menu offering a restricted choice when there is a need to serve a very large number of people in the shortest possible time.
4 *Cyclical menus.* These are a series of table d'hôte menus, for example for three weeks, which are repeated again and again for a set period of, for example, four months. These are often used in hospitals and industrial catering as an aid to establishing a pattern of customer demand for a menu item and as a result assist purchasing, preparation of items, and staffing requirements.

6.3.2 À la carte menus

The à la carte menu is identified by:

1 Being usually a larger menu than a table d'hôte menu and offering a greater choice.
2 Listing under the course headings all of the dishes that may be prepared by the establishment.
3 All dishes being prepared to order.
4 Each dish being separately priced.
5 Usually being more expensive than a table d'hôte menu.

6 Often containing the exotic and high cost seasonal foods.

Part of an à la carte menu may contain a *plat du jour* or 'speciality of the house' section. This consists usually of one or two main dishes, separately priced, which are already prepared and change daily. À la carte menus are, because of their size and the unknown demand of each item, more difficult to control than the typical table d'hôte menus.

A special promotion menu is a form of à la carte menu which is at times offered to the guest in addition to the à la carte menu. This type of menu is concerned with the selling of a particular part of a menu to increase the interest for the customer, to increase the average spending by the customer and in turn to increase the turnover and profit for the caterer. Promotions may be made by specially printing attractive menus for such items as:

1 Shellfish, when an increased variety of shellfish and special dishes would be made available.
2 Soft fruits, when various types of berry fruits such as strawberries, raspberries, loganberries, etc., would be featured in special dishes.
3 The game season, when pheasant, grouse, etc., would be featured in pâtés, soups, and special main course dishes.
4 Dishes cooked or prepared at the table, for example crêpes Suzette, steak Diane, etc.

6.4   The content of food menus

The content of food menus varies with the type of menu, the segment of the market it is aimed at, the occasion, the food cost available, the country or region, etc.

Table d'hôte menus are often of three to four courses only. A hotel room-service breakfast menu is illustrated in Figure 6.1.

À la carte menus often differ for lunch and/or dinner periods, although it is not uncommon for the same à la carte menu to be offered throughout the day. In the UK, for example, the heavier type items, for example thick vegetable based soups, farinaceous dishes, meat puddings, meat stews, steamed fruit and sponge puddings, would normally be found on a lunch menu; whereas the lighter and often more delicately

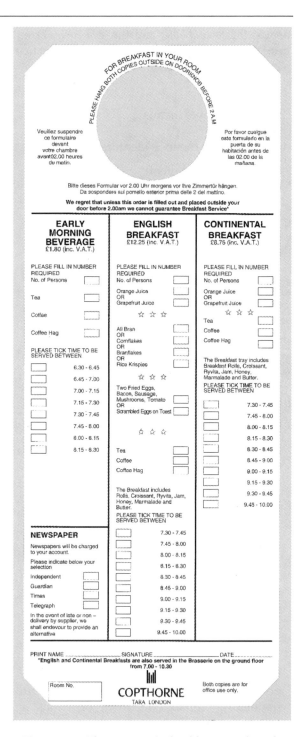

Figure 6.1   *The room-service breakfast menu from the Copthorne Tara Hotel, London*

flavoured dishes would be found on a dinner menu, for example speciality consommés, poached fish with delicate flavours and often complicated garnishes, hot and cold sweet and savoury soufflés, etc. For a full à la carte menu, the courses or sections of the menu would be divided up into a possible fourteen sections. It is from this full outline of the sequence of sections that a table d'hôte menu or a special luncheon or dinner menu could be constructed. Table 6.1 shows a full outline of an à la carte luncheon menu and Table 6.2 an à la carte dinner menu.

6.4.1　The combination of sections of the menu

The combination of the various sections of the menu depends very much on the occasion, the prices to be charged and the wishes of the customer. As illustrated in Tables 6.1 and 6.2, there is an established order of sequence of sections of the menu, which by tradition are followed. This accepted sequence enables the caterer to compile the separate courses on table d'hôte and à la carte menus and to suggest to clients suitable special and/or function menus of varying lengths.

It is very seldom the practice for all of the possible courses of a menu to be served, but as a general rule it is possible to state that when a large number of courses are served that the portion sizes are relatively small. Examples of typical menus of varying sizes, and their combinations of courses could be as shown at the bottom of the page.

6.5　Beverage menus/lists

The criteria used to prepare a wine menu, or drinks list, are the same as those used when preparing a food menu and as outlined earlier in this chapter. The use of the wine menu, or drinks list, as a selling tool cannot be emphasized enough. Customers eating in a restaurant do not have to, and will not feel embarrassed if they do not purchase a drink. It is the caterer's ability to interest and gain the confidence of customers that is likely to lead them to purchase a drink. As mentioned earlier in this book, beverages require fewer staff to process them and the profits from them are higher than those from food and so it goes without saying that this is an area that requires time and attention from the caterer to obtain the full benefit.

Beverage lists should be specifically prepared for the particular unit in which they are being sold, because the requirements vary greatly. A restaurant themed to be in the German style, offering authentic German-type food, would need to feature prominently German wines and beers. To use a general-purpose wine menu would not be suitable or likely to aid sales. What is also important with beverages is that there should be a follow-through with the correct serving temperature being adhered to and the correct traditional glassware used.

		Lunch
Two courses	–	One from sections 3, 4, 5, 6, 7, 8 or 9; and one from 11 or 13.
Three courses	–	One from sections 1, 2, 3 or 4; one from 5, 6, 7, 8 or 9; and one from 11 or 13; or One from sections 1, 2, 3, 4 or 5; one from 6, 7, 8 or 9; and one from 11 or 13.
Four courses	–	One from sections 1 or 2; one from 3, 4 or 5; one from 6, 7, 8 or 9; and one from 11, 12, 13 or 14; or One from sections 1, 2, 3, 4 or 5; one from 6, 7, 8 or 9; section 10, and one from 11, 12, 13 or 14.
		Dinner
Three courses	–	One from sections 1, 2 or 3; one from 4, 5 or 7; and one from 10 or 11.
Four courses	–	One from sections 1 or 2; section 3; one from 4, 5 or 7; and one from 10,11 or 12.
Five courses	–	One from section 1; section 2; section 3; one from sections 4, 5 or 7; and one from 10, 11 or 12; or One from sections 1 or 2; section 3; one from 4 or 5; section 7; and one from 10, 11, 12 or 13.
Six courses	–	One from section 1; section 2; section 3; one from 4 or 5; section 7; and one from 10, 11, 12 or 13; or One from sections 1 or 2; section 3; one from 4 or 5; section 6; section 7; and one from 10,11, 12 or 13; or One from sections 1 or 2; section 3; one from 4 or 5; section 7; one from 8 or 9; and one from 10, 11, 12 or 13.

Table 6.1 *A full outline of an à la carte luncheon menu*

Course of section	Examples

1 Hors d'oeuvre	(a) Fruit cocktails – Florida grapefruit, melon, etc.
	 (b) Fruits – melon, grapefruit, ugli, etc.
	     Fruit juices – orange, grapefruit, pineapple, tomato.
	 (c) Shellfish – prawns, shrimps, oysters, crabmeat, lobster, etc.
	     Shellfish cocktails – prawns, shrimps, lobster, etc.
	 (d) Smoked – salmon, trout, eel, mackerel, cod's roe, ham, salami, etc.
	 (e) Hors d'oeuvre – various.

2 Soups	(a) Consommé-double, en gelée, etc. (b) Purée – St Germain, lentils, Parmentier, etc. (c) Crême – de tomates, de volaille, etc. (d) Potage – minestrone, Scotch broth, etc.
3 Farinaceous	(a) Spaghetti, nouilles, etc. (b) Gnocchi – Italienne, Romaine, Parisienne (c) Ravioli, canneloni, etc. (d) Risotto, etc.
4 Eggs	All kinds, but excluding boiled eggs – poached, en cocotte, mollet, sur le plat, omelette.
5 Fish	Most kinds of fish are offered, but without any complicated garnishes. They are usually steamed, poached, grilled, shallow or deep fried – Dover sole, turbot, brill, whiting, mussels, scallops, salmon, whitebait, herrings, etc.
6 Entrées	Brown stews, blanquette, fricassée, meat pies and puddings, boiled meats, braised meats, braised game, fried steaks, pilaff, kebabs, vol-au-vents, etc.
7 Roasts	Beef, lamb, pork, chicken, turkey.
8 Grills	(a) Beef – fillet, châteaubriand, tournedos, filet mignon, entrecôte, rump, etc. (b) Lamb – cutlets, chops, crown chops, Barnsley chops, chump chops, kidneys, liver, etc. (c) Pork – chops, kidney. (d) Poultry – legs of chicken, spatchcock, etc.
9 Cold buffet	(a) Fish – salmon, salmon trout, lobster, crawfish, crab, etc. (b) Meat – beef, lamb, tongue. (c) Pâtés – pâté or terrines of poultry or game. (d) Pies – veal and ham, chicken, etc. (e) Mousses – ham, chicken, tomato, etc.
10 Vegetables A B	*Note:* Items found in sections 6, 7 and 8 will normally be combined in one course with the vegetables printed at this point followed by the potatoes. (a) Roasts – carrots, parsnips, swede, salsify, etc. (b) Leaves – cabbage, brussel sprouts, spinach, etc. (c) Flowers – cauliflower, broccoli, globe artichokes (d) Fruits – marrow, courgettes, aubergine, tomato, etc. (e) Seeds – beans of all types, peas, asparagus peas,etc. (f) Blanched stems – asparagus, celery, sea-kale, endives, etc. (g) Potatoes – boiled, steamed, sauté, fried, roast, creamed, etc. Hot or cold asparagus, globe artichokes, seakale, and corn-on-the-cob may be served alone as a separate course together with the appropriate sauces.
11 Savouries	Simple savouries – Welsh rarebit, roes on toast. Savoury soufflés – spinach, cheese, mushrooms, etc.

Table 6.1 (*cont.*)

Course of section	Examples
12 Sweets	(a) Puddings – fruit, sponge, milk, etc. (b) Flans – fruit. (c) Egg custard – baked, bread and butter, cream caramel, etc. (d) Pastries – gâteaux, éclairs, profiterolles, mille-feuilles, etc. (e) Yeast goods – savarin, rum baba, etc. (f) Ices – various. (g) Fresh fruit – various.
13 Cheese	A good selection of cheeses are served together with biscuits, celery, and radishes.
14 Dessert	Fresh fruits of all kinds, but with an emphasis on new season fruits whenever possible.
15 Coffee	This is not recognized as a course. Usually several types of coffee will be offered – the house coffee, Viennese coffee, instant coffee, caffeine-free coffee.

Table 6.2 *A full outline of an à la carte dinner menu*

Course of section	Examples

1 Hors d'oeuvre	(a) Fruit cocktails – Florida grapefruit, melon, etc.
	(b) Fruits – melon, grapefruit, ugli, etc.
	     Fruit juices – orange, grapefruit, pineapple, tomato.
	(c) Shellfish – oyster, lobster, prawns, crabmeat, shrimps,
	     Shellfish cocktails prawns, lobster, shrimps, etc.
	(d) Smoked – salmon, trout, eel, mackerel, cod's roe, ham, salami, etc.
	(e) Hors d'oeuvre – various, both hot and cold.
	(f) Delicacies – caviar, seagull's eggs, snails, frog's legs, etc.

2 Soups	(a) Consommé – double, petite marmite, etc. (b) Veloutés – Agnès Sorrel, Argenteuil, de céleri, etc. (c) Crème – d'asperges, de champignons. (d) Bisques – de homard, d'écrevisses, etc. (e) Cold soups – consommé, vichyssoise, crème de pois, etc.
3 Fish	(a) Shallow fried – sole meunière, filet de sole grenebloise, etc. (b) Deep fried – sole Colbert, scampi, goujons de sole, etc. (c) Grilled – sole, darne de saumon, truite, homard, etc. (d) Poached – sole Véronique, délice de flétan bonne femme, suprême de turbot cubat, etc. (e) Hot shell fish – homard thermidor, homard newburg, etc. (f) Cold fish – homard, saumon, truite, etc.
4 Entrée	(*Note*: Small, light entrée dishes with a simple garnish if at all. Vegetables are not served with an entrée if they are being served with a later course.) Vol au vent de volaille, émincée de volaille à la King, côtelette d'agneau réform, noisette d'agneau mascotte, suprême de volaille sous cloche, kebab orientale, suprême de volaille chimay, etc.
5 Rèléve	(*Note*: This is usually a joint of butcher's meat or a whole bird, poultry or game. It is usual to be served with vegetables and potatoes.) Jambon braisé au madère, selle de veau Prince Orloff, filet de boeuf Richelieu, contrefilet de boeuf Perigourdine, poulet en cocotte grandmère, poulet en casserole bonne femme, etc. Vegetables – of all types. Potatoes – all types of potato dishes.

Table 6.2   *(cont.)*

Course of section	Examples
6 Sorbet	All kinds based on the juices of most fruits such as pineapple, strawberries, raspberries, loganberries, red currants, lemons, etc., and on special wines and liqueurs such as champagne, kirsch, etc.
7 Roast	(*Note*: Like the reléve course, this is usually a joint of butcher's meat or a whole bird, poultry or game. It is usually served with a salad.) Selle d'agneau rôti, filet de boeuf rôti, poularde rôti à la Russe, faisoan rôti à la périgourdine, pluviers dorés rôti, etc. Salads – française, niçoise, opera, mascotte, etc.
8 Cold meat dish	Mousse de foie gras, galantine de faison, poulard Rose Marie, médaillons de volaille Rachel, etc.
9 A Vegetables and potatoes	(a) Roasts – carrots, parsnips, swede, salsify, etc. (b) Leaves – cabbage, brussel sprouts, spinach, etc. (c) Flowers – cauliflower, broccoli, globe artichokes (d) Fruits – marrow, courgettes, aubergine, tomato, etc. (e) Seeds – beans of all types, peas, asparagus peas, etc. (f) Blanched stems – asparagus, celery, sea-kale, endives, etc. (g) Potatoes – boiled, steamed, sauté, fried, roast, creamed, etc.
B Vegetable dish	(*Note*: Usually served hot.) Asperges, fonds d'artichauts, fénouil, soufflé aux épinards, etc.
10 Sweets	(a) Hot – soufflé palmyre, soufflé praline, soufflé Rothschild, crêpe Normande, crêpe Paysanne, etc. (b) Cold – coupe Clo-Clo, coupe Edna May, coupe Jacques, bombe Américaine, bombe Andalouse, bombe Jaffa, soufflé au citron, soufflé praline, etc.
11 Savouries	Beignets soufflé au parmesan, soufflé au parmesan, canape diane, anges à cheval, champignons sous cloche, etc.
12 Cheese	All varieties may be offered.
13 Dessert	All dessert fruits may be offered with an emphasis on new season and exotic fruits.
14 Coffee	Various types offered. (*Note*: Coffee is not considered as a separate course)

The sales of wines and cocktails in hotels and restaurants are generally lower than they should be for such reasons as poor selling, overpricing and the snobbery that goes with wines and cocktails which tend to put customers ill at ease.

6.5.1   Types of beverage menus/lists

The various types of beverage menus are numerous, but for simplicity they may be grouped as being of four kinds: wine menus; bar menus; room service beverage menus; and special promotion beverage menus.

6.5.1.1   Wine menus or wine lists

Within this general heading wine menus may be subdivided as follows:

1 *Full wine menus or lists.* This kind of menu would be used in an up-market hotel or restaurant where the customers' average spend would be high and where the time available to consume their meal would be likely to be in excess of one and a half hours. Like all menus, a full wine menu is difficult to design. Certain wines must be on the menu if a restaurant is of a particular standing; it is the

question of the selection of wines within the various types based on the manager's experience and the analysis of customer sales that make it difficult to keep a correct balance and restrict the choice to reasonable limits.

A full wine list may resemble a small book, often being of fifteen to forty pages in length. Because of the size and cost it is often the practice to have the menu contained within a quality cover and to be of a loose-leaf form so that the individual pages may be updated when required and replaced. It is also the practice for many restaurants to give a brief description of the major types of wine as well as provide a map to show the origin of the wine. The price range for this type of menu is high because of the quality of the products. The layout would usually be in the following order:

House wines
Champagnes and other sparkling wines
Red wines
White wines
Port, sherry, liqueurs
Cognac, Armagnac, gin, vodka, vermouth, whisky
Beers, lagers
Mineral waters, fruit juices.

An example of a page from a full wine list is given in Figure 6.2.

2 *Restricted wine menus or lists.* This kind of menu would be used in a middle type market operation where the demand for a full wine menu is very limited. It is also likely to be used when a highly skilled wine waiter is not required and where the waiting staff serve all food and beverages. The planning of a restricted wine menu is difficult and can best be done by an analysis of previous wine sales. It is usual that this type of menu would feature a few well-known branded wines with which the majority of customers can identify. The price range for this type of menu would be lower than that of a full wine menu and would need to bear some relationship to the food menu prices. Another feature on a restricted menu is likely to be the sale of wine by the carafe and by the glass.

3 *Banquet/function menus.* This type of menu is of

the restricted type in that it will offer fewer wines than a full menu. The contents of the menu will depend very much on the type of banqueting being done, but in general it is usual to offer a selection of wines with a varying price range so that it will suit a wide range of customers and their tastes. Again, banqueting wine menus will usually list some well-known branded wines. A point which must not be forgotten with branded wines is that customers frequently will know the prices charged for them in the local supermarket or wine store and therefore the caterer must be very careful as to the mark-up on these wines so as not to create customer annoyance.

6.5.1.2 *Bar menus and lists*

These are basically of two types: the large display of beverages and their prices which is often located at the back of or to the side of a bar and is often a legal requirement in many countries; or small printed menu/lists which are available on the bar and on the tables in the bar area. The large display of menus and prices would be in a general type of bar where the everyday type of drinks are served; the small printed menus/lists being found in lounge and cocktail bars. The cocktail bar menu/list usually contains cocktails (Martinis, Manhattans, etc.); mixed drinks (spirits with minerals); sherries and ports; liqueurs and brandies; wine (often by the glass); and minerals and cordials. The layout for a cocktail bar menu/list need not follow any set order, the emphasis for the layout being on merchandising specific items.

6.5.1.3 *Room service beverage menus/lists*

The size and type of room service menus will depend on the standard of the hotel and the level of room service offered. For a luxury type unit the menu will be quite extensive, being a combination of items from the full wine list and from the bar list. In a middle type market unit the menu is likely to be quite small, being a combination of items mainly from the bar list plus a few wines only from the restricted unit wine menu/list.

Because of the high labour costs for room ser-

CHAMPAGNE · WHITE

CHAMPAGNE

	Glass	Bottle
N.V. Quaglino's Champagne	6.75	31.75
N.V. Perrier Jouet**		37.95
N.V. Taittinger		39.95
N.V. Pol Roger		42.95
N.V. Louis Roederer Brut 'Premier'		43.50
N.V. Billecart Salmon Rose**		47.50

VINTAGE CHAMPAGNE

	Glass	Bottle
1989 Alain Thienot Rose	6.75	48.50
1989 Bollinger		66.95
1990 La Baie 'Jeques'		98.50
1990 Dom Perignon		118.00
Krug Grande Cuvee **		128.00
1991 Louis Roederer Cristal		150.00

* Half bottles available ** Magnums available

WHITE

	Glass	Bottle
	175ml	750ml
1996 Quaglino's Vin de Pays d'Oc, Domaines Virginie, France	3.25	11.75
1996 Chenin Blanc, Collards, New Zealand		18.25
1995 Corbiere del Pirineite, Alesia, Piemonte, Italy		15.25
1995 Pinot Blanc 'Cuvee Caroline', Schoffit, Alsace, France		19.95
1996 Colombard, Aston Vale, Stellenbosch, South Africa		15.25
1996 Pinot Grigio, Puiatti, Veneto, Italy		24.50
1996 Soave Classico, Pieropan, Veneto, Italy	4.35	16.95
1994 Cassis, Clos Sainte Magdeleine, Francois Sack, Rhone, France		24.75
1994 Tokay Pinot Gris 'Loerchenberg', Marc Kreydenweiss, Alsace, France		25.75
1992 Gewurztraminer, Grand Cru 'Goldert', Zind Humbrecht, Alsace, France		37.95
1995 Saint Peray, Domaine Rochepertuie, Jean Lionnet, Rhone, France		32.75

SAUVIGNON BLANC & SEMILLON

	Glass	Bottle
1996 Casablanca Sauvignon Blanc, Carico, Chile	4.25	16.95
1996 Sauvignon de Touraine, Alain Marcadet, Loire, France		15.25
1996 Echeverria Sauvignon Blanc, Molina, Chile		13.95
1996 Jordan Sauvignon/Semillon, Vallkbury Estate, South Australia	5.95	18.45
1993 Collards Sauvignon Blanc, Marlborough, New Zealand		18.75
1996 Laulaude Sauvignon/Chardonnay, Stellenbosch, South Africa		17.50
1995 Pouilly Fume, Andre Dezat, Loire, France		25.50
1996 Shaw & Smith Sauvignon Blanc, Adelaide Hills, South Australia		21.75
1995 Sancerre, Clos des Roches, Andre Vatan, Loire, France		23.75

BURGUNDY & OTHER CHARDONNAYS

	Glass	Bottle
1996 Chardonnay, Domaine La Donnaye, Southern France		14.50
1996 Montgras Chardonnay, Colchagua Valley, Chile	3.75	14.75
1996 Echeverria Chardonnay, Molina, Chile		15.95
1996 Madfish Chardonnay, Margaret River, Western Australia		24.50
1995 Chablis, Domaine de l'Eglantiere, Jean Durup, Burgundy, France	5.95	22.75
1994 Beringer Chardonnay, Napa Valley, California, USA		26.00
1995 Meursault, 'Les Tilles', Alain Coyard, Burgundy, France		27.75
1996 Hamilton Russell Chardonnay, South Africa		31.75
1995 Saint Veran, Michel Urseve, Burgundy, France		24.50
1994 Auxey-Duresses, 'Vieilles Vignes', Claude Marechal, Burgundy, France		33.50
1994 Saint Aubin, 1er Cru 'En Remilly', Marc Colin, Burgundy, France		37.50

ROSE · RED

ROSÉ

	Glass	Bottle
	175ml	750ml
1996 Chateau le Croix, Saint Emilion, France	3.75	14.50
1996 Chateau de Sours, Hugh Ryman, Bordeaux, France		17.95

RED

	Glass	Bottle
1995 Quaglino's Vin de Pays d'Oc, Domaines Virginie, France	3.25	11.75
1995 Rosso di Montalcino, Fortino Gorell, Italy		22.75
1994 Montepulciano d'Abruzzo 'Joro' Umani Ronchi, Italy		16.75
1989 Rioja Navajas, Reserva, Abellanet Spain		21.25
1995 Tempranillo, Bodegas Piedmonte, Navarra, Spain		15.30
1996 Beyerskloof Pinotage, Stellenbosch, South Africa	3.95	14.95
1994 Ravenswood Zinfandel, Napa Valley, California, USA		26.50
1994 Saintsbury Pinot Noir, Carneros, Napa Valley, California, USA		34.75
1991 Barolo, 'Monprivato', Giuseppe Mascarello, Piemonte, Italy		41.75

BORDEAUX

	Bottle
1993 Chateau Graveline-Sur-enus, Cotes de Bourg, France	18.25
1994 Chateau Petit Renouil, Canon Fronsac, France	23.50
1992 Moncet de Tropiong Mondot, Pomerol, France	32.50
1989 Chateau Malescot St Exupery, Margaux, France	38.50
1993 Chateau du Vallle, Graves, France	22.50
1993 Les Fiefs de Lagrange, Saint Julien, France	38.75

CABERNET & MERLOT

	Glass	Bottle
1993 Robertson's Well Cabernet Sauvignon, Coonawarra, Australia		21.95
1994 Robert Mondavi Coastal Cabernet, North Coast, California, USA	6.25	25.50
1996 Montgras Merlot Reserva, Colchagua Valley, Chile		17.50
1991 Saxenburg Cabernet Sauvignon, Stellenbosch, South Africa	4.75	18.95
1992 Beringer Meritage, Napa Valley, California, USA		31.75
1992 Leeuwin Estate 'Art Series' Cabernet Sauvignon, Western Australia		41.30

SYRAH & GRENACHE

	Glass	Bottle
1993 Cotes du Roussillon, Jean-Luc Colombo, Southern France	4.30	16.75
1990 Gigondas, Grand Montmirail, Denis Cheron, Rhone, France		24.75
1994 Chateauneuf du 'pge, 'Vieux Donjon' Lucien Michel, Rhone, France		33.75
1995 Crozes Hermitage, Alain Graillot, Rhone, France		29.95

BURGUNDY & BEAUJOLAIS

	Glass	Bottle
1995 Brouilly, 'La Pisse Vieille', Jean Lathuiliere, France		19.95
1996 Nicolin a Vorit, Pascol Granger, France		21.75
1996 Fleurie, Vieilles Vignes, Andre Colonges, France	5.75	22.95
1990 Pinth 'Les Charvelaves', Alain Graynd, France		29.50
1993 Beaune, 'Les Epenottes', Lauren Bollvu, France		38.75
1992 Auxey Duresses, Marechal Jacquet, France		31.75
1994 Mercurey, Emile Juillot, France		38.95
1993 Chorey 'les Beaune, Domaine Maillard, France		29.50
1994 Nuits Saint Georges, Chauvenet-Chopin, France		38.95

FINE WINES

BURGUNDY WHITE

	Bottle
	750ml
1995 Pouilly Fuisse, 'La Roche', Forest, France	42.75
1995 Santenay 'Le Gravieres', Domaine Olivier, France	39.95
1994 Chassagne Montrachet, 'Er Remilly', Colin Deleger, France	77.50
1982 Meursault 'Piere Sous La Baie', Robert Ampeau, France	92.00
1994 Puligny Montrachet, 'Le Trezie' Marc Colin, France	56.00
1995 Corton Charemagne, Michel Voarick, France	112.00
1994 Chablis Grand Cru, 'Grenouilles', William Fevre, France	54.75
1992 Chevalier Montrachet, Etienne Sauzet, France	200.00
1992 Batard Montrachet, Domaine Leflaive, France	220.00

BURGUNDY RED

	Bottle
1992 Savigny les Beaune, 'Les Lavieres', Chandon de Briailles, France	41.00
1994 Santenay, 'Les Gravieres', Vincent Girardin, France	37.50
1993 Nuits Saint Georges, Chevillon, France	85.00
1990 Clos Vougeot, Jean Grivot, France	89.50
1990 Pommard, Jean Marc Boziey, France	46.50
1989 Grands Echezeaux, Rene Engel, France	95.00
1992 Chapelle Chambertin, Domaine Ponsot, France	125.00
1978 Gevrey Chambertin, Louis Trapet, France	99.00
1993 Volnay Bonnaires, Domaine Rougat, France	145.00

BORDEAUX RED

	Bottle
1994 Chateau Smith Haut Lafitte, Martillac, Graves, France	40.00
1990 Chateau Cantel, Haut Medoc, France	52.00
1981 Chateau Pavie, Saint Emilion, France	85.00
1989 Chateau Cantemerle, Macau, France	70.00
1978 Chateau Leoville Las Cases, Saint Julien, France	135.00
1978 Chateau Grand Puy Lacoste, Saint Julien, France	97.50
1982 Chateau Palmer, Margaux, France	175.00
1928 Chateau Cos d'Estournel, Saint Estephe, France	339.00
1905 Chateau Lemur, Pauillac, France	625.00

RHONE RED

	Bottle
1987 Hermitage, Guigal, France	82.00
1992 Chateauneuf du Pape, La Vertile, France	45.00
1992 Hermitage, Gerard Chave, France	72.50
1991 Cote Rotie, Emile Champet, France	48.50
1990 Chateauneuf du Pape, Chateau de Beaucastel, France	96.00
1983 Hermitage, 'La Chapelle', Jaboinet, France	145.00
1988 Cote Rotie, Lancome, Guigal, France	295.00

CALIFORNIA & ITALY

	Bottle
1994 Ridge 'Santa Cruz' Cabernet Sauvignon, Napa Valley, California, USA	41.00
1993 Opus One, Napa Valley, California, USA	138.00
1991 Tignanello, Antinori, Italy	95.00
1993 Marcus Cabernet/Merlot, Bernardus, Carmel Valley, California, USA	44.50
1978 Robert Mondavi Cabernet Sauvignon Reserve, Napa Valley, California, USA	148.00

17.5% VAT INCLUDED   *A 5% DISCRETIONARY SERVICE CHARGE WILL BE ADDED*   *X : DENOTES WINE OUT OF STOCK*

Figure 6.2 *The wine list from Quaglino's (Conran Restaurants Ltd)*

vice staff, a practice today in many hotels is to provide a small refrigerator in each bedroom stocked with a limited quantity of basic drinks. There are many types of beverage units available specifically for use in bedrooms, some of which include a computer-based control system which automatically records the removal of any item from the unit and records it as a charge to the customer.

6.5.1.4 *Special promotion beverage menus*

This may take many forms from a free pre-function reception to promote a particular beverage, to the promotion of after-lunch and after-dinner liqueurs by the use of attractive tent cards, or to the promotion of the cocktails of the month. Fortunately assistance with beverage promotional menus is willingly given by the suppliers by providing free advertising and promotional material and by offering the particular beverage free or at a special purchase price.

6.5.2 The general rules for the serving of wines

The practice of serving a different kind of wine with each food course is seldom observed today other than for the very formal occasion or for a special gastronomic event.

The choice of wine by a customer is highly individual and the once traditional rules of what wines should only be served with a particular food are not always observed today. Some aspects of the practice that have stood the test of time and are accepted and commonly practised today are:

1 The progression of wines in a menu would be that light and delicate wines are served before

fuller bodied wines, that simple wines are served before the higher quality wines and that young wines are served before the older wines.

2 When several wines are to be served with a menu the order of serving is normally accepted as being first a dry white wine followed by a red wine and finishing with a sweet white wine .

3 Wines from several countries may be served with a meal providing that there is an affinity between the different wines and that they are accepted partners with the food.

4 Champagne may be served throughout a meal with a dry champagne being served with all courses other than with the sweet course when a semi-sweet champagne would be better suited.

5 Rosé wines may also be served throughout a menu although it would be unusual for a formal or special gastronomic occasion.

6 Dry white wines are normally served with fish, shellfish and white meats such as poultry, pork and veal.

7 Red wines are normally served with red meats, for example beef, and with game, for example all game birds, venison and hare.

8 Sweet white wines are normally served with the sweet course.

9 Port is accepted as being ideal for serving with cheese and dessert.

Table 6.3 gives a general guide to matching food to wine.

6.6 Menu merchandising

The efficiency by which menus are merchandised to customers can affect the demand for the use of the food and beverage facilities as well as influence the selection of items and thereby the

Table 6.3 *Matching food to wine*

Food	Suggested wines
Before the meal	Dry or medium sherry; Vermouth, cocktails; White wine, e.g. Chablis, Muscadet, Reisling Kabinett.
Hors d'oeuvre	No wine if food is vinegary. Anjou Rosé; Côtes de Provence; Bordeaux blanc.
Crudites	Beaujolais; Côtes-du-Rhône rouge; Chianti.
Melon	Port; Muscat; Oloroso sherry.
Grapefruit	Port; Madeira.
Pâté	Beaujolais; Chablis; Graves blanc.
Avocado	Riesling Kabinett; Graves blanc.
Foie gras	Alsace Gewurztraminer.
Caviare	Champagne.
Smoked salmon	Fino sherry; Alsace Gewurztraminer.
Smoked trout	Pouilly Fumé; Sancerre.
Consommé	Medium dry sherry; dry Madeira.
Minestrone	Chianti; Grignolino.
Pasta dishes	Chianti; Beaujolais; Côtes-du-Rhône rouge.
Shell fish	Chablis; Mâcon blanc.
Fish	Hock; Mâcon blanc; Muscadet.
Meat:	
stews/casseroles	St Émilion; Côtes-du-Rhône rouge; Châteauneuf-du-Pape.
roast meats	Beaujolais; Mâcon Rouge; Bordeaux rouge.
grilled meat	Cabernet; Hermitage; Médoc; Pommerol.
roast poultry	Bordeaux blanc; white Burgundy.
roast game	St Émilion; Napa Cabernet; Châteauneuf-du-Pape.
Desserts	Sweet Champagne; Sauternes; Côteaux du Layon.
Cheese	Châteauneuf-du-Pape; Hermitage; Côtes-du-Rhône; Sancerre; Port.

sales mix of an outlet. The menu is without doubt one of the most important sales tools that caterers have but which unfortunately they often fail to use to the best or fullest advantage. As mentioned earlier in this chapter, it is necessary for all menus to be correct against the checklist of general presentation, cleanliness, legibility, size and form, layout and content. We are concerned here with the way in which caterers can most efficiently utilize the menu to optimize their sales.

6.6.1   Methods of printing menus

6.6.1.1   *Handwritten*

This is suitable for small establishments or for exclusive establishments where the personal emphasis is important to the meal experience. Any handwritten menu should be as clear to read as a printed menu and ideally be of a good style.

6.6.1.2   *Duplicated*

There are two standard methods:

1 Duplicating from stencils is a cheap method. A stencil is typed and placed on to the duplicating machine and ink is squeezed through the stencil on to the paper.
2 Duplicating from a spirit duplicator: a 'master' is typed with a piece of hectographic carbon face up on the 'master'. The 'master' is then wound on to the duplicating machine drum and is wetted with a spirit so that a coating of the carbon is transferred on to the paper.

Both of the above methods may be used to print menus, but the standard of the printing is not that good and so the use of this method is rather limited to small, popular and industrial type outlets or for clip-on menus of popular and middle market outlets.

6.6.1.3   *Printed*

The two most common methods used by printers for the production of menus are:

1 *Letterpress.* This uses raised type or blocks clamped together, inked, and after a piece of paper is laid upon it under pressure, the image of the printing form is transferred to the paper. The advantages of this form of printing are that alterations to the type are both easy and quick and that the machines can also number and cut.
2 *Offset litho.* This is a method of printing from a flat plate which is wound around a cylinder. Using the natural antipathy between water and oil, the cylinder is dampened with water and coated with ink and the image transferred to a rubber blanket which prints on to the paper. The advantage of this form of printing is the high speed at which it is possible to operate the machine. Unfortunately a major disadvantage is that alterations are much more difficult and would require new plates and alterations to negatives.

6.6.1.4   *Desktop publishing*

This is the use of an in-house microcomputer using a desktop software package which enables the user to produce professional quality printing for daily, special offer and banquet menus and wine lists etc. and promotional pamphlets. The particular advantages of this software package include an increased internal control over printing and production; development of professional in-house quality publications; significant reduction or elimination of traditional typesetting by professional printers; a reduction in time for printing production and a significant reduction in printing costs. Common usage of desktop software packages include not only printing new menus, but the re-designing of menus, making, if necessary, daily alterations to menus, and re-pricing all or some items on a menu. This technique can be further enhanced by using a laser printer, which produces high quality professional print finish and by using a laminator to further the length of life of the menu or wine list.

6.6.2   Shape and fold of menu

The physical shape of a menu will be determined by such criteria as the number of items to be printed on the menu, the theme or style of the menu, the use of graphics, typeface and the occasion. The actual number of shapes possible is endless, from a single sheet, a central vertical fold, two parallel vertical folds, three parallel vertical folds, two/three/four vertical accordian folds, etc. to special cut-out shapes for the special occasion or sales promotion menus.

6.6.3   Size of menu

The size of the menu when printed and finished is important. Basically it should be related to the theme and style of the selling outlet. All printed menus begin as standard sheets of paper or card of standard sizes. The paper size used for printing menus in the UK is known as the 'A' series, the standard sizes being as follows:

A0 841 mm × 1189 mm
A1 841 mm × 594 mm
A2 420 mm × 594 mm
A3 420 mm × 297 mm
A4 210 mm × 297 mm
A5 210 mm × 148 mm
A6 105 mm × 148 mm
A7 105 mm × 74 mm

Long sizes
1/8 A4 210 mm × 99 mm
1/4 A4 210 mm × 74 mm

As can be clearly seen from the above, the range of the 'A' series is obtained from the largest size, A0, and halving it in size for each subsequent size.

6.6.4   Type and colour of paper or card

The type and colour of the paper or card to be used are also very important. First, paper or card of varying thicknesses may be used, the thickness of the paper chosen depending on whether it is for the cover of a menu, an insert inside a cover, etc., as well as the purpose of the menu card, for example it may be for a souvenir, or to be used daily. The thickness is by weight in grams per square metre of paper. The weights vary from 120 g/m^2 (this is about the thickness of good-quality letter paper) to 500 g/m^2 (which is of a substantial card thickness). Further to this the range of paper available is greatly increased as for each weight of paper there is a very wide range of embossed type finishes available.

When coloured stock is used, it is important that it should harmonize with the colour scheme of the outlet and also that the colour chosen should not affect the reading of the menu particularly if subdued lighting is used to help create the atmosphere. The type of paper or card chosen can also affect the readability of the menu, as absorbent, non-absorbent and glossy finished papers will all be affected differently when printed upon.

It is possible for varying finishes to be supplied to a printed menu, to either enhance its appearance, prolong its useful life, or to do both. Three common finishes are used:

1 *Varnishing*. A clear varnish is added on to the paper after completion of all printing.
2 *Lamination*. A very thin, transparent film is stuck on to the menu by a heat process on completion of all printing.

MENUS SHOULD BE EASILY READ	10pt	(TIMES Roman)
Menus should be easily read	10pt	(TIMES Italic)
Menus should be easily read	**10pt**	**(UNIVERS Bold)**
Menus should be easily read	7pt	(SABON Italic)
MENUS SHOULD BE EASILY READ	**12pt**	**(PALATINO Bold)**
MENUS SHOULD BE EASILY READ	8pt	(MELIOR Roman)

Figure 6.3   *Examples of different typefaces used in printing (illustrated in upper case and lower case) and of type sizes (measured in points)*

3 *Plasticizing.* Encapsulating the menu in two sheets of thin, clear plastic.

6.6.5   Typefaces

The style and size of the typeface and the way that the type is set will affect the readability of the menu. Usually only two or three styles of type are used on any one menu, one for the main headings or subheadings, and one for the list and description of the items. A too elegant or antique style may be confusing for customers. The type size should be such that customers will be able to read the menu without difficulty. See Figure 6.3.

6.6.6.   Layout

This is one of the most important aspects to take into consideration. It is something on which the printer can give help and guidance to the caterer but only to a limited extent. The caterer must give the printer clear instructions as to the layout of the menu as well as details of the artwork required. Ideally the caterer should provide a 'copy' of the menu, that is, a fairly accurate sketch or drawing of how the caterer envisages the printed menu. Should the caterer wish to use a designer to help prepare the menus and other promotional literature, it would be important to engage the services of a graphics designer, as a background knowledge of the printing processes is essential.

The important role that caterers play in merchandising their menu involves:

1 Studying their market and the general market trends to identify what to offer for sale.
2 Knowing what items on the menu they particularly wish to sell because of such things as low food cost, low labour cost or adding new items to increase variety in the menu and making the customers aware of this.

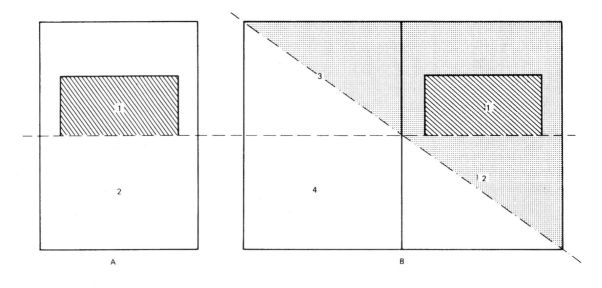

Figure 6.4   *Menu layouts and how guests read a menu*

Notes:
1 A illustrates a single sheet menu – the shaded area 1 being where the customer's eye will generally focus on picking up the menu.
   B illustrates a folded menu, or an insert to a menu. The customer's eye will generally focus on the right-hand page, first to the shaded area 1, then moving to areas 2 and 3, and finally, 4. The important selling areas are 1, 2 and 3, which in general are above the diagonal line shown in B.
2 These illustrations follow the general practice as used in the advertising industry (for example, advertisements on facing pages and above the horizontal line are normally more costly for the reasons given in 1).

Print Specification

Purchase order no.:   5432   Date 5/2/9–
Originator: Tim Walton
To: Menus Ltd, High Street, Haslemere
Deadline: 12/5/9–
First proof required: 14/2/9–
Revised proof required: 1/3/9–
Delivery date required: 12/5/9–

Job title: Tambard Restaurant Menus
Quantity required: 800 basic design 12/5/9–
                                    200 menu submitted 12/5/9–
Quantity required: 5000 miniatures

Flat size: A3 – 420 mm × 297 mm
   Miniatures: A6 – 105 mm × 148 mm
Folded size: 1 vertical central fold – 210 mm × 297 mm
   Miniatures: 1 vertical central fold – 52.5 × 148 mm

Print:
   Cover side: Hotel Motif – Tambard Restaurant
   Inside: Menu as per attached details

Bled: No – see design details attached

Materials:
   1 Make of paper: Wiggins Teape Paper Ltd
   2 Brand name: Keaykolour
   3 Colour: Sandstone
   4 Embossing: Fabric
   5 Weight: 300 g/m^2 (miniatures 120 g/m^2);

Samples: To Purchasing Manager, Pointer Hotels (UK) Ltd

Ink colours: As per artwork details attached

Artwork/layout: Details attached

Finishing: Central vertical fold
                       Gold tassel

Proofs: Galley proofs only required

Delivery instructions: To Purchasing Manager's office

Initial order: 4 × 50   (Miniatures 5 × 1000)

Stock: To be delivered by Menus Ltd

Figure 6.5   *A print specification for the printing of menus*

Note: 'Bled' is a printer's term referring to printed matter where the printing area goes right to the edge of the paper, for example a solid design or border. This requires a larger size of paper as it has to be trimmed to remove printing marks on the edge of the paper. 'Non-bled' is a printer's term referring to printed matter where the printing area does not go to the very edge of the paper, and there is the equivalent of a border to all edges.

3 Analysing previous sales for 1 above and using this information to observe how their customers read the menus and react to the use of graphics, etc. Customers generally read menus as illustrated in Figure 6.4 and it is the skilled use of these important areas on a menu that can affect sales, etc.

6.6.7   Printing and reprinting

Before engaging the services of a printer it would be necessary for the caterer to collect together all the relevant information. The use of a standard print specification, as shown in Figure 6.5, is a useful means to check that all the basic information is available. Other information which is necessary before actually going to print includes:

1 A house printing style, use of company logo.
2 Colour of menu to suit the house style, restaurant style or the occasion.
3 Quantity requirements for the next six months or twelve months.
4 Miniatures of menus to be produced as souvenirs for customers or for use as sales promotion material, etc.

The quantity to be printed is a very important decision to be made. There are several approaches to the problem when a large quantity is required over a twelve-month period, such as:

1 Printing all menus with the basic design features only.
2 Overprinting on to the prepared printed stock when required. This allows for changes in the menu to take place and for prices to be updated.

Or, alternatively:

1 Printing all menus with the basic design and menu but with no prices printed other than those required in the near future; and
2 Overprinting with updated prices as and when required;
3 Obtaining from the printer a range of press-on price transfers of a similar typeface. For the smaller caterer this allows much greater flexibility at a low cost.

The advantages of printing a large quantity of stock and later overprinting on to it are that the cost per unit (per menu) is considerably reduced plus the fact that the stock is already available and that the time taken for overprinting is minimal. It would be normal practice for the printer to hold the caterer's stock of printed paper or card.

6.7   References

Axler, B. H. (1979). *Food Service: A Managerial Approach.* Lexington MA: DC Heath.
Green, E. F., et al. (1987). *Profitable Food and Beverage Management: Operations.* Jenks, Oklahoma: Williams Books.

7
An overall view of food and beverage control

7.1 Introduction

Food and beverage control may be defined as the guidance and regulation of the costs and revenue of operating the catering activity in hotels, restaurants, hospitals, schools, employee restaurants and other establishments. The importance of food and beverage control needs considerable emphasis. In hotels, food and beverage sales often account for up to half of the total revenue, while in restaurants, food and beverage sales are the main or the only source of revenue. The cost of food and beverages in the commercial sector is usually in the region of 25–45 per cent of the total operating costs. In hospitals, schools, employee restaurants and similar operations, food and beverages are the main day-to-day expenditure, which is controlled by budgets and/or a level of subsidy, either on a total company or on a per unit basis. The amount of control is related to the size of the operation. A large group operation obviously requires much precise, detailed, up-to-date information, and its provision is often aided by the use of computers. A small operation, such as an owner-operated restaurant, often cannot afford, nor does it need, the same level of sophistication of control. In both instances the type and volume of data required needs to be selectively determined if control is to be meaningful and effective.

It is important at this stage to clarify the limitations of a control system.

1 A control system in itself will not cure or prevent problems occurring. An effective system is dependent upon correct up-to-date policies and operational procedures. But the system should identify problems and trends in the business.

2 A control system will require constant management supervision to ensure that it functions efficiently.
3 A control system will need management action to evaluate the information produced and to act upon it.

7.2 The objectives of food and beverage control

The objectives of a food and beverage control system may be summarized as follows:

1 *Analysis of income and expenditure.* The analysis is solely concerned with the income and expenditure related to food and beverage operations. The revenue analysis is usually by each selling outlet, of such aspects as the volume of food and beverage sales, the sales mix, the average spending power of customers at various times of the day, and the number of customers served. The analysis of costs includes departmental food and beverage costs, portion costs and labour costs. The performance of each outlet can then be expressed in terms of the gross profit and the net margin (i.e., gross profit minus wages) and the net profit (i.e., gross profit minus wages and all overhead expenses such as rent, rates, insurance, etc.).
2 *Establishment and maintenance of standards.* The basis for the operation of any food and beverage outlet is the establishment of a set of standards which would be particular to an operation, for example a chain of steak house restaurants. Unless standards are set no employee would know in detail the standards to be achieved nor could the employee's per-

formance be effectively measured by management. An efficient unit would have the set standards laid down in manuals often known as SOPs (standard operational procedures) which should be readily available to all staff for reference. Having set the standards, a difficult problem always for the management of an operation is to maintain these standards. This can be aided by regularly checking on the standards achieved by observation and analysis and by comments made by customers, and when necessary, conducting training courses to re-establish the standards.

3 *Pricing.* An important objective of food and beverage control is to provide a sound basis for menu pricing including quotations for special functions. It is, therefore, important to determine food menu and beverage list prices in the light of accurate food and beverage costs and other main establishment costs; as well as general market considerations, such as the average customer spending power, the prices charged by competitors and the prices that the market will accept.

4 *Prevention of waste.* In order to achieve performance standards for an establishment, targets are set for revenue, cost levels and profit margins. To achieve these levels of performance it is necessary to prevent wastage of materials caused by such things as poor preparation, over-production, failure to use standard recipes, etc. This can only be done with an efficient method of control, which covers the complete cycle of food and beverage control, from the basic policies of the organization to the management control after the event (see Figure 7.1).

5 *Prevention of fraud.* It is necessary for a control system to prevent or at least restrict the possible areas of fraud by customers and staff. Typical areas of fraud by customers are such things as deliberately walking out without paying; unjustifiably claiming that the food or drink that they had partly or totally consumed was unpalatable and indicating that they will not pay for it; disputing the number of drinks served; making payments by stolen cheques or credit cards. Typical areas of fraud by staff are overcharging or undercharging for items served and stealing food, drink or cash.

6 *Management information.* A system of control has an important task to fulfil in providing accurate up-to-date information for the preparation of periodical reports for management. This information should be sufficient so as to provide a complete analysis of performance for each outlet of an establishment for comparison with set standards previously laid down (for example, budget standards).

The amount of control necessary is related to the size and complexity of an establishment. A small owner-managed restaurant would not require the same level of control and written management information as would a large multi-outlet hotel.

Whatever the size and type of operation, the management control information required has to be limited to what is really necessary and meaningful. Therefore some selectivity is necessary to determine what exactly is required, as against producing a mass of statistical information which may be of little use or value and which may well cloud the essential basic data. The speed by which management information can be produced today with the assistance of microcomputers enables corrective action to take place very much quicker than when all the information has to be collected, collated, analysed, and presented manually.

A large unit with many selling outlets, employing a large number of staff and producing a large turnover would require quite a sophisticated control system giving often daily reports as well as weekly and periodic reports.

A small unit such as operated by a chef proprietor would require a very simple control system as the proprietor would be involved with controlling all the activities of the unit every day. The proprietor would not only have a 'feel' for all aspects of the business but would also be taking corrective action quickly whenever necessary.

7.3 Special problems of food and beverage control

Food and beverage control tends to be more difficult than the control of materials in many other industries. The main reasons for this are:

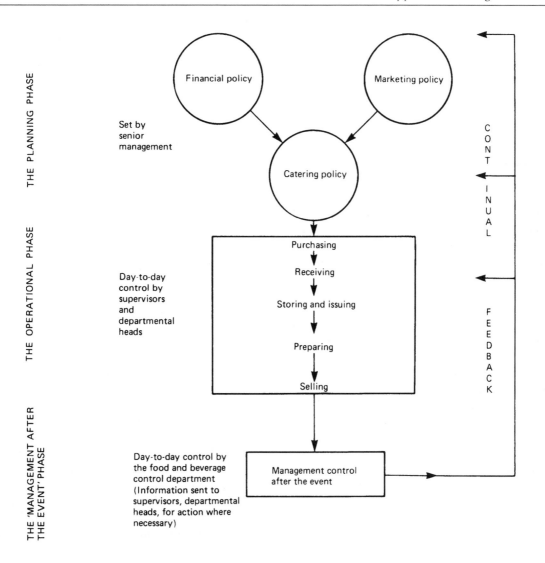

Figure 7.1   *The complete food and beverage control system*

1 *The perishability of the produce.* Food, whether raw or cooked, is a perishable commodity and has a limited life. The caterer, therefore, has to ensure that he buys produce in the correct quality and quantity in relation to estimated demand, and that it is correctly stored and processed. (Beverages are normally not as perishable as food and this contributes to their easier control.)

2 *The unpredictability of the volume of business.* Sales instability is typical of most catering establishments. There is often a change in the volume of business from day to day, and in many establishments from hour to hour. This causes basic problems with regard to the quantities of commodities to be purchased and prepared as well as to the staffing required.

3 *The unpredictability of the menu mix.* To add to the caterer's problems is the fact that in order to be competitive and satisfy a particular market, it is often necessary to offer a wide choice of menu items to the customer. It is therefore necessary to be able to predict not only the

number of customers who will be using the facility at a particular period in time, but as to what the customer's selection will be from the alternatives offered on a menu. It is seldom possible to be 100 per cent accurate, but in order to control costs effectively, it is necessary to have some method of volume forecasting as part of the total food and beverage control system.

4 *The short cycle of catering operations.* The speed at which catering operations take place, relative to many other industries, allows little time for many control tasks. It is not uncommon that items ordered one day are received, processed and sold the same or next day. It is for this reason that in larger catering establishments cost reporting is done daily or at least weekly. Further problems, particularly with perishable foods, are that with a short life for produce, items cannot be bought very much in advance of their need; and the problem of availability at times of produce relative to the price that can be afforded in relation to the selling price.

5 *Departmentalization.* Many catering establishments have several production and service departments, offering different products and operating under different policies. It is, therefore, necessary to be able to produce separate trading results for each of the production and selling activities.

7.4   The fundamentals of control

Effective control systems and procedures consist of three broad phases: planning, operational, and management control after the event.

7.4.1   The planning phase

It is difficult to run an effective catering operation without having firstly defined the basic policies. Policies are predetermined guidelines, laid down by the senior management of an organization, which outline such matters as the market or segment of the market that is being aimed at, how it is to be catered for and the level of profitability/subsidy to be achieved. Policies in general are particular to individual companies

and establishments, although in the public sector operations, there may well be broad national policies, for example for hospital catering.

A catering operation should have its policies clearly defined before it commences business, and redefined whenever a major change takes place, for example when a new theme is chosen for a restaurant to aim for a different market segment. Ideally, in a large organization the policies should be written down and periodically reviewed in relation to the current business and future trends; however, in smaller organizations there is not the communication problem of a large organization and to formally draw up and commit policies to paper is not so vital.

There are three basic policies which need to be considered:

1 The *financial policy* will determine the level of profitability, subsidy or cost limits to be expected from the business as a whole and the contribution to the total profit, subsidy or cost limit that is to be expected from each unit, and then from the departments within them. This involves the setting of targets for the business as a whole as well as each unit and the departments within them. Thus, the financial policy for a large hotel will set profit targets for the hotel, and departmental profit targets for the accommodation and catering as well as other departments. The financial policy for the catering department will set the overall target for the department itself, which will be further divided into targets for the various restaurants, bars and function facilities. The financial policy for an industrial contract catering operation will set the overall target for the operation, the level of subsidy and the level of management fee, as well as the cost limits per unit (meal or employee).

2 The *marketing policy* will identify the broad market the operation is intended to serve and the particular segment(s) of the market upon which it intends to concentrate. It should also identify the immediate and future consumer requirements on a continuous basis in order to maintain and improve its business performance. It is obvious from the above that the broad market intended to be served by a large city hotel could be broken down into the specific segments of the various types of users of,

for example, the coffee shop, the carvery, the cocktail bar, the banqueting rooms, etc. each having specific and different consumer requirements.

The interpretation of the marketing policy for a national commercial catering organization into a marketing plan for the next year may include some or all of the following objectives:

(a) *National identity* – to achieve a better national identity for all units by corporate design, and by meeting consumer expectations of what a 'popular restaurant' concept should be.
(b) *Customer* – the customer profile being the business person, shopper, tourist of either sex, aged twenty-five years or more, commonly using the high street of any major town, requiring food and beverage of good general standard, waitress served, for a typical price of £n per meal.
(c) *Market share* – to achieve, maintain or increase the percentage of 'our' market.
(d) *Turnover* – sales volume to be increased by x per cent on previous year.
(e) *Profitability* – profit to be increased by each unit by y per cent on previous year.
(f) *Average spending power* per customer to be increased by z per cent – to achieve a new average spending power of not less than £n.
(g) *Product* – the product to be maintained at a consistently high standard.
(h) *Customer satisfaction* – the net result must be the satisfaction of every customer.

3 The **catering policy**, which is normally evolved from the financial and marketing policies, will define the main objectives of operating the food and beverage facilities and describe the methods by which such objectives are to be achieved. It will usually include the following:
(a) The *type of customer,* for example high-spending business executive, low spending female shopper, short-stay hospital patient, etc.
(b) The *type of menu(s),* for example table d'hôte, à la carte, fast food.
(c) The *beverage provision* necessary for the operation.

(d) The *food quality standards,* for example fresh, frozen, canned, etc., and the grade of produce to be used.
(e) The *method of buying,* for example by contract, quotation, cash-and-carry, etc.
(f) *Type and quality of service,* for example cafeteria, counter, waiter, etc.
(g) *Degree of comfort and décor,* for example square footage per customer, type and style of décor, of chairs, tables, etc.
(h) *Hours of operation,* for example twenty four hours, seven days a week; 1200–1500 and 1800–2200 hours, Monday–Saturday, etc.

7.4.2   The operational phase

Having defined the policies (that is, predetermined guidelines), it is then necessary to outline how they are to be interpreted into the day-to-day control activities of the catering operation. The operational control is in five main stages of the control cycle. These are:

1 **Purchasing.** There are five main points to be considered.
(a) *Product testing* – to identify as a result of a series of taste panel evaluations the particular products to be used.
(b) *Yield testing* – to identify as a result of tests the yield obtainable from all the major commodities used.
(c) *Purchase specifications* – a specification is a concise description in writing of the quality, size, weight, etc., for a particular food or beverage item.
(d) *Method of buying* – by contract, quotation, cash and carry, etc.
(e) *Clerical procedures* – it is necessary to determine who originates, sanctions and places orders and what documentation is required for control.
2 **Receiving.** There are three main points to be considered:
(a) *Quantity inspection* – a person must be nominated to be responsible for physically counting and weighing goods and checking that the quantity and size of items in the delivery matches the purchase order. If there is a shortage in the delivery the pur-

chasing manager or a member of the management must be informed.

(b) *Quality inspection* – this is particularly important with perishable foods where inspection may be made by a senior chef. A head cellarman may inspect beverages. Whenever possible the items should be checked against the appropriate purchase specification.

(c) *Clerical procedures* – this is a very important aspect as all necessary documentation must follow a set procedure. It includes the acknowledgement of the receipt of acceptable goods and the delivery person's signature on a 'request for credit' note for returned goods and short deliveries.

3 *Storing and issuing.* There are four main points to be considered:

(a) *Stock records* – it is necessary to decide what records are to be kept.

(b) *Pricing of issues* – the method of pricing of the various types of issues must be decided upon so that there is consistency within the operation. Although there are many ways to price issues, it is common to use one or more of these methods: actual purchase price; selling price; simple average price; weighted average price; standard price.

(c) *Stocktaking* – the points to be considered here are the level of stock to be held; rate of stock turnover; dealing with discrepancies; identification of slow-moving items; etc.

(d) *Clerical procedures* – there is a need to determine what documentation is necessary, for example requisitions, record cards, bin cards, stocktaking reports, etc.

4 *Preparing.* This is a critical stage in the control cycle, in particular for food. There are three main points to be considered:

(a) *Volume forecasting* – a method of predicting the number of customers using the catering facilities on a specific day, and also of predicting as accurately as possible what items they will eat and drink.

(b) *Pre-costing* – a method of controlling food and beverage costs in advance of the preparation and service stages. It is done by preparing and using standard recipes

for all food and beverage items and also by using portion control equipment, for example ladles, scales, optics, standard glassware, etc.

(c) *Clerical procedures* – what documentation is required and the distribution and destination of this information.

5 *Selling.* This important stage of operational control needs to take into consideration the following points:

(a) *A checking system* – this is necessary to keep control of the number of covers sold and of the items sold. This may be done through a standard type of waiter's check system or through a till roll or in the case of hospital patients, by the summary and analysis of completed individual patient menu cards.

(b) *The control of cash* – this is vitally important. It is necessary to ensure that all items sold have been paid for and that the money is received or credit has been authorized.

(c) *Clerical procedures* – these would be necessary to control items sold and the money received or credit entitled, and would often include a restaurant checking system, meal and sales analysis, cashier's paying-in book, etc.

7.4.3   The 'management control after the event' phase

This final phase of food and beverage control is in three main stages:

1 *Food and beverage cost reporting.* As mentioned earlier in this chapter, the cycle of production is very short and the product is perishable. These factors together with the variations in demand for the product necessitate up-to-date reporting at least weekly if not daily.

2 *Assessment.* There is a need for someone from the food and beverage management team in the case of a large unit, or the proprietor or manager of a small unit, to analyse the food and beverage reports and to compare them with the budget for the period and against previous actual performance.

3 *Correction*. A control system does not cure or prevent problems occurring. When the analysis of the performance of a unit or department identifies that there is a problem, it is up to management to take the necessary steps to correct the problem as quickly as possible.

7.5 The reality of control

As has been stated earlier in this chapter, the amount of control necessary is related to the size and complexity of an operation. The larger the number of outlets within an operation, the more sophisticated should be the level of control.

However, it is important for the reader to realize the extent to which any control system can be totally efficient.

In reality no control system will be 100 per cent efficient for such basic reasons as:

1 The material product (apart from purchased beverages) is very unlikely to be 100 per cent consistent as to quality or the final yield obtainable from it.
2 The staff employed are unlikely to work to a level of 100 per cent efficiency at all times, in spite of the fact that operational manuals may exist.
3 The equipment used is also unlikely to work to the level of 100 per cent efficiency and this could well affect the yield obtainable.
4 The customers' choice of dishes can well be different at times to some of the budgeted sales mix, therefore affecting all production forecasts as well as the average spend per customer and the budgeted gross and net profit figures.

It is terribly important that the staff should see that control in some form is taking place and that on occasions there is a follow-up and action is taken on irregularities to set standards.

Further, the importance and relevance of using percentages as a yardstick necessitates that any percentages used should be directly related to the amount of money involved. A 1 per cent difference to the required budgeted gross profit may not appear very significant at first but when related in financial terms it becomes more significant. For example, in the case of a unit with a turnover of £400,000 and with a budgeted gross profit percentage of 65 per cent (that is, £260,000) a 1 per cent difference in the gross profit achievable would represent £2,600. Being aware that they are £2,600 off budget may be more meaningful to unit managers than just being aware that they are 1 per cent off target.

The management of any catering operation has to be fully aware of everything that is taking place within and outside the operation and, to be successful, needs to continually collect, analyse, and evaluate data and take any necessary steps to correct anything which is irregular to the standards set for the operation.

7.6 References

Axler, B. H. (1979). *Food Service: A Managerial Approach*. Lexington MA: DC Heath.

Green, E. F. et al. (1987). *Profitable Food and Beverage Management: Planning*. Jenks, Oklahoma: Williams Books.

Kotas, R. and Davis, B. (1980). *Food and Beverage Control*. London: Blackie.

8
Financial aspects

8.1 Introduction

Today, with the continual increases in the costs of food, beverages, labour, energy, maintenance and other overheads, most establishments operate some form of budgetary control.

A budget is a plan – expressed usually in financial and/or quantitative terms (for example, total value of payroll; number of customers, etc.) – which reflects the policies of an establishment and determines the business operations for a particular trading period. The trading period is usually of one year, but is often broken down into review (or control) periods of either thirteen four-week periods; or alternatively, of thirteen week quarters, each quarter consisting of two four-week and one five-week periods. Whichever method is adopted it is necessary that the periods remain the same so as to make it possible to compare results not only with corresponding periods in the same year, but also with the corresponding periods in earlier years. Bank holidays and special events falling into different periods each year should be noted.

The term *budgetary control* refers to a method of control where particular responsibility for various budgeted results is assigned to the managers concerned and a continuous comparison of the actual results and budgeted figures is made. When there are discrepancies between the two, it is necessary to identify the reasons for the variances and to take appropriate action. It is essential that when budgets are set they are clearly seen to be achievable, otherwise they are of little value.

The objectives of budgetary control are three-fold:

1 To provide a plan of action for a set trading period, to guide and regulate a business in keeping with its stated policies, and to maximize the full use of its resources.
2 To set standards of performance for management against which their performance can be measured.

3 To set out levels of cost responsibility and encourage cost awareness.

Budgets are prepared by the senior management of an organization in consultation with the various managers and departmental heads so as to ensure a greater level of commitment and an awareness of the aims, objectives, problems and possible weaknesses of the establishment.

8.2 Types of budgets

As can be seen from the diagram in Figure 8.1 there are various kinds of budgets that are used in food and beverage operations. Basically there are two main types: capital budgets; and operating budgets.

Capital budgets, as the name implies, are those which are concerned with the assets and liabilities of an establishment, for example equipment, plant and cash.

Operating budgets are those concerned with the day-to-day income and expenditure of an establishment and include sales, cost of sales, labour, maintenance, head office expenses, etc.

Table 8.1 shows an example of the operating statement of a restaurant for a period in the trading year, together with the allocated budget targets for that period. The breakdown of the restaurant budget identifies further the specific standards of performance required of the restaurant management. When this is set against the recorded actual performance for that period the performance achieved can be measured. It is the usual practice to show not only the actual and budget information for a period but also the cumulative information for the year to date. The cumulative figures give a smoothing effect to any irregularities in performance of past periods as well as the overall picture of performance for the year so far.

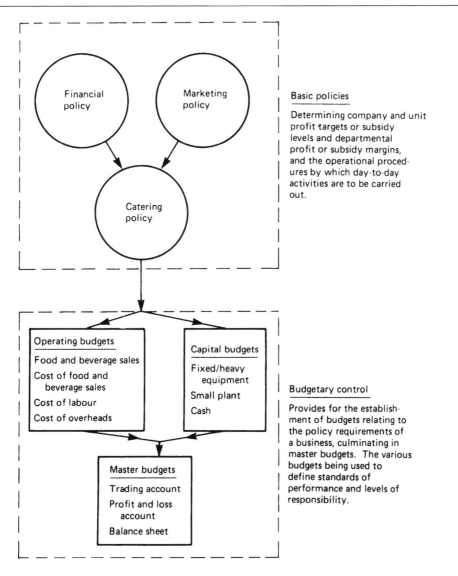

Figure 8.1   *Budgetary control as an extension of basic policies to plan and define standards against which the performance of actual results may be measured*

The above budgets are prepared not only for each unit of a business, but also are broken down into budgets for departments such as individual restaurants, bars and banqueting. It is also common practice to consolidate the above budgets into a set of master budgets such as:

1 *A master budgeted trading account* for a particular trading period showing the predetermined volume of sales, the cost of sales and the gross profit expected.

2 *A master budgeted profit and loss account* for a particular trading period showing the predetermined income and expenditure and net profit expected. This highlights unit and departmental gross profits, labour costs, overhead costs and net profit.

3 *A master budgeted balance sheet* for a particular trading period showing the assets and liabilities at the beginning and at the end of the period.

8.3   Basic stages in the preparation of budgets

For simplicity, budgeting may be seen as being in six stages. The amount of detail and sub division into departmental budgets depends very much on the type and size of the business. The basic stages are:

1 Determination of the net profit required for the business in relation to the capital invested and the risk involved. Alternatively, in the case of non-profit making establishments, the level of subsidy available or required is postulated.
2 Preparation of the sales budget. This determines the volume of sales necessary to achieve the desired net profit or subsidy and also influences the budgeted costs for food, beverages, labour and some overheads. See Table 8.1 for an example of an operating sales statement with the sales budget.
3 Preparation of administration and general budgets. These are for such items as head office expenses, advertising, rates, insurance, etc. Some of these may be regarded as fixed budgets, that is, they are not affected by any change in the volume of business, for example, head office expenses, advertising, rates, etc.; while others may be regarded as flexible budgets, that is, they are affected by changes in the volume of business, for example, telephones, laundry, etc.
4 Preparation of the capital expenditure budget which makes provision for such items of expenditure as new kitchen equipment, restaurant and bar furniture (including any installation charges), etc.
5 Preparation of the cash budget. This is regarded as the most important of the capital budgets and it predetermines the cash inflows, the cash outflows and resulting cash balance at particular points during the period.
6 Preparation of master budgets. As stated previously master budgets are prepared for the trading account, profit and loss account and the balance sheet.

Table 8.1   *An example of a restaurant operating a sales statement with the sales budget*

This period					Year to date			
Actual		Budget			Actual		Budget	
£	%	£	%		£	%	£	%
11,000	100	10,000	10	Net sales	20,000	100	21,000	100
5,500	50	4,000	40	*less* cost of sales	11,200	56	8,400	40
5,500	50	6,000	60	Gross profit	8,800	44	12,600	60
2,750	25	2,000	20	*less* wages and staff costs	4,200	21	4,200	20
2,750	25	4,000	40	Net margin	4,600	23	8,400	40
				less allocated expenses				
550	5	500	5	maintenance	1,200	6	1,050	5
220	2	200	2	head office services	600	3	420	2
220	2	200	2	other	200	1	420	2
110	1	100	1	equipment	200	1	210	
1,100	10	1,000	10		2,200	11	2,100	10
1,650	15	3,000	30	Operating profit	2,400	12	6,300	30
				(net profit)				

Note: Budgeted figures are used to compare with the actual operating results. It can be observed that the low operating profit achieved is due almost entirely to the failure to achieve the budgeted gross profit on sales in spite of an increase in sales this period.

8.4 Welfare operations

The fact that food and beverage operations in the welfare sector (for example, a hospital dining room or an employee restaurant) may not be required to make a profit in the same way that commercial restaurants are, and that they may receive some form of subsidy, does not make budgeting any less necessary. When food and beverages are being sold at or near cost prices, or are being prepared within very strict subsidy cost limits, it is even more necessary that costs be estimated very accurately than where there is a large gross profit margin which can absorb some errors in costing. When the subsidy is for such items as heat, light, repairs, maintenance, furnishings, etc., control needs to be exercised on these expenses to keep them within the limits of the subsidy.

8.5 Costs, profits and sales

8.5.1 The elements of cost

The cost of operating a catering unit or department is usually analysed under the three headings of:

1 *Material costs* – cost of food and beverage consumed and the cost of additional items such as tobacco. (Note: The cost of any food and beverage provided to staff in the form of meals is deducted from material costs and added to labour costs.) The food cost is then calculated by the formula:

opening stock + cost of purchases – closing stock – cost of staff meals = material cost

2 *Labour costs* – wages and salaries paid to all employees, plus any employer contribution to government taxes, bonuses, staff meals, pension fund, etc.

3 *Overhead costs* – all costs other than material and labour costs, for example rent, rates, insurance, depreciation, repairs, printing and stationery, china and glassware, capital equipment.

As most catering operations are subject to changes in the volume of business done, it is nor-

mal practice to express the elements of cost and net profit as a percentage of sales. A change in the volume of sales has an effect on the cost structure and on the net profit. This will be explained more fully in section 8.6.

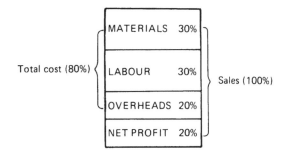

Figure 8.2 *A typical example of the elements of cost*

8.5.2 Cost groups

It is necessary to examine costs not only by their nature (material, labour, overheads) but also by their behaviour in relation to changes in the volume of sales. Using this criteria, costs may be identified as being of four kinds:

1 *Fixed costs*. These are costs which remain fixed irrespective of the volume of sales, for example rent, rates, insurance, the management element of labour costs. (See Figure 8.3.)

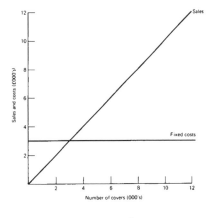

Figure 8.3 *Fixed costs*

Note: Fixed costs remain fixed, irrespective of the level of sales (for example £3,000). Typical examples of fixed costs are rent, rates, insurance, etc.

2 *Semi-fixed costs*. These are costs which move in sympathy with, but not in direct proportion to

the volume of sales, for example fuel costs, telephone, laundry. Semi-fixed costs contain a fixed and variable cost element, for example the charge for the telephone service in the UK contains a fixed cost for the quarterly charge for the rental of each phone and a variable cost depending on the number of phone calls made.

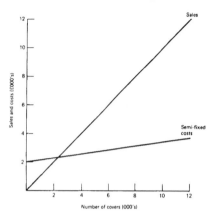

Figure 8.4   *Semi-fixed costs*

Note: Semi-fixed costs do not increase proportionately to any increase in sales. Typical examples of semi-fixed costs are fuel costs, telephone, laundry.

3 *Variable costs*. These are costs which vary in proportion to the volume of sales, for example food and beverage. (See Figure 8.5.)

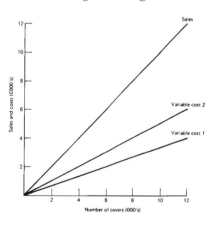

Figure 8.5   *Variable costs*

Note: Variable costs vary in proportion to the sales of a unit. Typical examples of variable costs are the cost of food and beverages. In this example sales are £1 per cover. Variable cost 1 is 33⅓ per cent of sales (£4,000 cost when sales are £12,000). Variable cost 2 is 50 per cent of sales (£6,000 cost when sales are £12,000).

4 *Total costs*. This is the sum of the fixed costs, semi-fixed costs and variable costs involved.

8.5.3   Profit

Three main kinds of profit are normally referred to in food and beverage operations:

1 *Gross profit* = total sales – cost of materials. Note: The term gross profit is often referred to as 'kitchen profit' (food) or 'bar profit' (beverages). Room hire is normally treated as 100 per cent gross profit.
2 *After-wage profit* (or net margin) = total sales – (material + labour costs).
3 *Net profit* = total sales – total costs (material + labour + overhead costs).

All of the above are normally used as measures of performance against past results and budgeted targets. For an example of the use of the three main kinds of profit used in controlling food and beverage operations see Table 8.1.

8.5.4   The behaviour of costs and profits to the volume of sales.

The behaviour of the different types of cost and profit relative to a change in the volume of sales can be identified by examining the example of a simple operating statement for a restaurant in Table 8.2. The statement shows the sales, costs and profit over two consecutive months with the May sales figure showing a 50 per cent increase in business.

8.6   Break-even analysis

It is very common for food and beverage management to be faced with problems concerning the level of food and beverage cost that can be afforded, the prices that need to be set for food and beverages, the level of profit required at departmental and unit level and the number of customers required to cover specific costs or to make a certain level of profit.

Typical questions raised are:

1 What level of sales is needed to cover the fixed costs of a unit?

2 What level of sales is required from a particular unit to achieve £x's net profit?

3 What level of sales is required to increase the net profit of a unit by £10,000?

4 What will the effect of increasing prices by 5 per cent have on net profit?

5 What will be the effect on net profit of increasing the average spend of customers by 50p per meal?

6 What increased level of sales must be obtained to cover the spending of £1,000 on advertising to promote the restaurant?

7 What will be the financial implications of discounting beverages during a proposed promotion?

8 What is the relationship between the capital invested in a restaurant and its sales and profit?

Answers to the above types of question are normally attempted by using the accepted technique of break-even analysis.

Break-even analysis enables the relationship between fixed, semi-fixed and variable costs at specific volumes of business to be conveniently represented on a graph. This enables the break-even point to be identified and the level of sales necessary to produce a predetermined level of net profit. The term break-even point may be defined as that volume of business at which the total costs are equal to the sales and where neither profit or loss is made. The technique is based on the assumption that: the selling price remains constant irrespective of the volume of business; that certain unit costs remain the same over the sales range of the charted period; that only one product (for example, a meal) is being made or sold; that the product mix remains constant in cost price and volume and that labour and machine productivity is constant.

Nearly every action or planned decision in a business will affect the costs, prices to be charged, the volume of business and the profit. Profits depend on the balance of the selling prices, the mix of products, the costs and the volume of business. The break-even technique discloses the interplay of all these factors in a way which aids food and beverage management in selecting the best course of action now and in the future.

Pricing is a multi-dimensional problem, which

Table 8.2 *The operating statement for the Endsleigh Restaurant showing the behaviour of costs and profit with a given change in the volume of sales*

The Endsleigh Restaurant		
	April	May
Number of covers	2,000	3,000
Average spend per customer	£10	£10
Total sales	£20,000 (100%)	£30,000 (100%)
Fixed costs	£3,000 (15%)	£3,000 (10%)
Variable costs	£8,000 (40%)	£12,000 (40%)
Semi-fixed costs	£6,000 (30%)	£8,000 (26.7%)
Total cost	£17,000 (85%)	£23,000 (76.7%)
Net profit	£3,000 (15%)	£7,000 (23.3%)

Fixed costs have remained the same amount of £3,000, but it should be noted that the fixed cost percentage in relation to sales has decreased by 5 per cent (from 15 to 10 per cent). The fixed costs in relation to the unit cost of production have also decreased by 5 per cent.

Variable costs have remained the same percentages of sales for both months (40 per cent) with the increase from £8,000 to £12,000 being caused by the directly proportional cost of materials to the increase in the volume of sales. The variable costs in relation to the unit cost of production remained the same at 40 per cent).

Semi-fixed costs have increased in amount from £6,000 to £8,000 but not in a direct relation to the increase in sales. In fact, as a percentage of sales, the semi-fixed costs decreased by 3.3 per cent (from 30 to 26.7 per cent).

Total costs have increased in amount from £17,000 to £23,000 but not in a direct relation to the increase in sales. As a percentage of sales, the total costs decreased by 8.3 per cent (from 85 to 76.7 per cent).

Net profit has increased in amount from £3,000 to £7,000 that is by 133 per cent while sales increased by only 50 per cent. As a percentage of total sales the net profit increased by 8.3 per cent (from 15 to 23.3 per cent).

In summary, it can be said that for each change in the volume of sales, there is an effect on the cost structure of a business as well as on the net profit. Any given increase or decrease in sales will usually be matched by a corresponding increase or decrease in the variable cost (for example, food and beverage). The other elements of cost will not in the short term be normally affected. As a result each change in the volume of sales of a business will result in a more than corresponding change in the net profit. When each of the elements of cost are related to the volume of sales as against the total costs, the changes in the cost structure of a unit become more obvious and the effect of the fluctuation in sales on net profit seen more clearly.

depends not only on the cost structure of a business and its specific profit objectives but also on the level of activity of the competition and the current business economic climate.

Example I

A restaurant has seating capacity to serve a maximum of 10,000 customers per 28-day trading period. The average spending power of the customers is £2. The fixed costs of the restaurant are £6,000 per period and the variable costs are 40 per cent of sales. The break-even chart of the restaurant would be prepared as shown in Figure 8.6. It will be seen that any number of covers served between 5000 and 10,000 will bring the restaurant some net profit. The output between the break-even point and the maximum output is known as the margin of safety. The size of the margin of safety is a measure of the stability of the profits. The higher the proportion of variable costs (to fixed costs), the greater the margin of safety, while the higher the proportion of fixed costs the narrower the margin of safety. Should the variable costs be increased (with the level of fixed costs remaining static) the break-even point will be raised resulting in a lower level of net profit and a smaller margin of safety.

8.6.1   Break-even formula

Although a break-even chart shows diagrammatically the varying levels of profit or loss from different volumes of sales, the level of accuracy of the information may at times be in doubt owing to the scale of the graph and the skill of the person drawing it. A precise break-even point may be calculated using the formula:

$$B/E = \frac{C}{S - V} = \text{units of output at the break-even point}$$

where C = the total capacity costs, that is, the costs of establishing the particular production capacity for an establishment (for example, this would include rent, rates, insurance, salaries, building and machinery depreciation)

S = sales price per unit

V = variable cost per unit

The use of the above formula is illustrated in the following example.

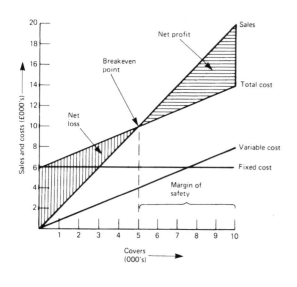

Figure 8.6   *A break-even chart*

Notes:

1 The fixed costs are £6,000 per period.
2 The variable costs are 40 per cent of sales (maximum sales are 10,000 × £2 = £20,000), that is £8,000.
3 The total cost line is derived by adding together the fixed and variable costs (£6,000 + £8,000), that is, £14,000.
4 The restaurant will make a net loss while it serves less than 5000 covers per period.
5 When the break-even point has been reached the net profit of the restaurant increases more than in proportion to the number of covers.
6 The margin of safety is 5,000 covers.

Example 2

Saudi Enterprises is considering the acquisition of the Rumble-Tum Restaurant. The purchase price is £100,000 and the directors of Saudi Enterprises expect any new purchase to show a return on capital of 18 per cent. The proprietor of the restaurant is able to provide the following information:

Rates, insurance, fuel costs, etc.	£45,000 per annum
Franchise fee	£5,000 per annum
Franchise commission	1% of turnover
Wages	£1,000 per week

The restaurant operates for six days a week and for fifty weeks in the year. *Note:* Wages are only paid for fifty weeks.

A typical day's business shows:

200 lunches served with an average
spending power of   £1.50
100 dinners served with an average
spending power of   £3.00

The maximum number of covers which it is possible to serve without physical alterations to the structure is 250 lunches and 125 dinners.

The restaurant is expected to operate at a gross profit of between 55 and 65 per cent.

Problem   Produce some standard information which would be of value to Saudi Enterprises as to whether or not to acquire the restaurant.

Solution   The solution to the problem is best dealt with in the two stages of:

1 Preparing a *profitability statement* for the restaurant when operating at gross profit percentage of 55, 60 and 65 per cent.
2 Making the calculations, using the break-even formula, to state clearly the *break-even points and their margins of safety*.

A *profitability statement* is usually prepared in the form of a table in which the different types of costs (for example, food costs, fixed costs, franchise fee costs) are deducted from a known level of sales, thus showing clearly specific types (and the calculated amount) of profit (for example, gross profit and net profit) at particular levels of sales. The value of preparing a profitability statement is that it sets out basic information in an orderly way and frequently prevents mathematical errors occurring, as mistakes are usually easily identified in a statement.

1   Purchase price £100,000
  Return on investment required £18,000
  Fixed costs:
   rates, insurance, fuel costs etc.   45,000
   franchise fee   5,000
   wages   50,000
     £100,000

Maximum number of covers

$$= 375 \times 6 \times 50 = 112,500$$

Table 8.3   *Profitability statement at maximum sales*

	Food costs		
	35%	40%	45%
	£	£	£
Sales	225,000	225,000	225,000
less variable costs	78,750	90,000	101,250
= Gross profit	146,250	135,000	123,750
less fixed costs	100,000	100,000	100,000
= Net profit	46,250	35,000	23,750
less 1% franchise commission	2,250	2,250	2,250
= Net profit (after commission)	44,000	32,750	21,500
Return on investment	44%	32.75%	21.5%

Average spend per cover

$$= \text{£}1.50 \times 200 + \text{£}3.00 \times 100 = \frac{\text{£}600}{300} = \text{£}2$$

Maximum sales possible

$$= \text{£}750 \times 6 \times 50 = \text{£}225,000$$

Typical number of covers
$$= 300 \times 6 \times 50 = 90,000$$
Typical sales
$$= \text{£}600 \times 6 \times 50 = \text{£}189,000$$

Table 8.4   *Profability statement at typical sales*

	Food costs		
	35%	40%	45%
	£	£	£
Sales	180,000	180,000	180,000
less variable costs	63,000	72,000	81,000
= Gross profit	117,000	108,000	99,000
less fixed costs	100,000	100,000	100,000
= Net profit	17,000	8,000	–1,000
(*less* 1% franchise commission)	1,800	1,800	1,800
= Net profit (after commission)	15,200	6,200	–2,800
Return on investment	15.2%	6.2%	–2.8%

Variable costs

To achieve a return on investment of 18 per cent minimum when operating at full capacity:

Maximum sales	= £225,000
less fixed costs	100,000
	125,000
less franchise commission	2,250
	122,750
less return on investment	18,000
= Money available for variable costs	£104,750

$$\frac{£104,750}{225,000} \times \frac{100}{1} = 46.55 \text{ per cent maximum}$$
variable cost permissible.

To achieve a return on investment of 18 per cent minimum when operating at typical sales:

Typical sales	= £180,000
less fixed costs	100,000
	80,000
less franchise fee	1,800
	78,200
less return on investment	18,000
= Money available for variable costs	60,200

$$\frac{£60,200}{180,000} \times \frac{100}{1} = 33.44 \text{ per cent maximum}$$
cost permissible.

2 Calculations of break-even points and margins of safety

$$\text{Break-even point} = \frac{\text{capacity costs}}{\text{sales price per unit} - \text{variable costs per unit}}$$

See Tables 8.5 and 8.6 for calculations.

8.7   Pricing considerations

The whole subject area of pricing is a complex one which unfortunately is not given the degree of priority that it requires.

The pricing of a product has to meet the objectives of an organization and aspects related to pricing will normally be found in the financial, marketing and catering policies. For example, within the financial policy of a commercial organization, the basic aim of profit to be made in relation to the capital invested will be stated. The financial policy for an establishment in the welfare sector would state the level of subsidy to be allocated to the catering department and how it was to be calculated.

Quite naturally, the approach to pricing will differ, not only between the major sectors of the industry – where normally in the non-commercial sector pricing is cost-orientated and in the commercial sector pricing is usually market-orientated – but also between organizations within these sectors. For example, a fairly new growth-orientated organization could well be concerned with increasing its sales volume (and to do so may decide to keep its prices very competitive indeed) while an established organization may well be concerned with maintaining its net profit from an established sales volume.

8.7.1   Pricing based on cost

The traditional method used to establish the price of a menu item is to calculate, ideally from a standard recipe, the food cost per unit of the particular item and to add a given percentage of gross profit to arrive at the selling price. The percentage of gross profit applied should be sufficient to cover the fixed cost element (for example, rent, rates, etc., and payroll costs); the semi-fixed element (for example, heating, telephones, etc.); and a satisfactory element of net profit.

The advantages of this method are that it is quite easy to understand it and to apply it.

The disadvantages of this cost-plus method, however, outweigh its advantages. First, the relationship between the capital investment and net profit is ignored. The net profit achieved using the cost-plus method is mainly related to the sales turnover in that the higher the volume of sales, the higher will be the net profit achieved and vice versa. Second, this method puts too much emphasis on the one ele-

Table 8.5   *Break-even point and margin of safety at maximum sales*

Food costs	35%	40%	45%
Capacity costs	100,000	100,000	100,000
Sales price – variable cost	£2.00*–0.72	£2.00–0.82	£2.00–0.92
Break-even point	78,125 covers	84,746 covers	92,593 covers
Margin of safety	34,375 covers	27,754 covers	19.907 covers
Maximum number of covers	112,500	112,500	112,500

*The average sales price per unit is £2; 35 per cent of £2 is 70p; the variable cost at 35 per cent is 72p which includes 2p commission fee.

Table 8.6   *Break-even point and margin of safety at typical sales*

Food costs	35%	40%	45%
Capacity costs	100,000	100,000	100,000
Sales price – variable cost	£2.00–0.72	£2.00–0.82	£2.00 – 0.92
Break-even point	78,125 covers	84,746 covers	92,593 covers
Margin of safety	11,875 covers	5,254 covers	– 2,593 covers
Typical number of covers	90,000	90,000	90,000

ment of cost, that is, the cost of the ingredients of a food and beverage item on a menu and only generalizes on the fixed and semi-fixed costs. Lastly, this method is unrelated to the demands of the market place and is far too rigid to use as a method in the commercial sector of the industry.

8.7.2   Pricing based on the market

The relationship between price and value for money is an important aspect of pricing. Value for money extends way beyond just the cost of the ingredients of the items chosen from a menu by a customer. The whole meal experience has to be taken into account, including such things as the atmosphere, décor, choice of menu items, level of service offered, etc.

In order to be successful and to achieve a satisfactory volume of sales, pricing has to consider three basic factors:

1 *The nature of the demand for the product.* The economic concept of the elasticity of demand is relevant here. Elasticity of demand is the sensitivity of the sales volume to changes in price. A product would be said to have an elastic demand when a small decrease in the price charged would bring a significant increase in sales or, alternatively, if a small increase would bring about a significant decrease in sales. A typical example is a change in price of 10p for products such as beer, named soft drinks, hamburgers, etc.

In the case of a product with an inelastic demand a small increase or decrease in price would not bring any significant increase or decrease in sales. A typical example might well be a change in price of 50p for products such as lobster, fillet steak, etc.; the customers who could afford these dishes would not be influenced by such a price change.

2 *The level of the demand for the product.* It is typical of most catering operations that they experience a fluctuating demand for their product

not only hourly (e.g. as seen clearly in fast-food operations), but daily (e.g. in many hotel restaurants which on some days in the week have a low customer throughput). This fluctuation of demand normally affects their volume of sales and results in the underutilization of the premises, staff, etc., highlighting the necessity for a flexible approach to be given to pricing. This practice is commonly used in the industry and serves to increase the volume of sales even if the level of profitability may not be as great as under normal conditions. Typical examples of flexible pricing are 'bargain break' weekends; 'happy hours' in bars; a sliding scale for room hire for functions depending on the day of the week; etc.

3 *The level of the competition for the product.* Competition is a factor, as much as product cost and market demand, in determining selling prices. Competition exists from not only similar type operations but also from dissimilar operations – as in most instances customers are free to choose where they go and what amount they spend. Competition can include price, normally resulting in lower gross profit margins; or quality of food, service, décor, etc. normally resulting in higher gross profit margins.

8.8 Menu pricing

8.8.1 Departmental profit margins

The approach to menu pricing must follow from the outline of the basic policies and from the determined departmental profit targets. Each department will have a significant role in the total organization and its individual profit targets will normally be unrelated. For example, in a hotel the profit required from the à la carte restaurant may well be far lower than that of its coffee shop. The existence of the à la carte restaurant may be mainly of an image status for the hotel as against being a major profit contributor. What is necessary is for the total sum of the individual departments' contributions to equal (at least) the desired contribution to the revenue for the whole establishment.

8.8.2 Differential profit margins

It is unusual to apply a uniform rate of gross profit to all of the items found on a food menu or beverage list, although this simplistic method of costing can at times still be found in the non commercial sector of the industry. In the non commercial sector of the industry one of the advantages is that where a uniform rate of gross profit is applied (for example, 60 per cent), reference to the takings can quickly show the costs at 40 per cent gross profit irrespective of the sales mix and an immediate comparison can be made to the actual usage of materials. The reasons for not applying a uniform rate of gross profit in the commercial sector are those already stated earlier in this chapter, that is, it ignores such things as capital investment; it emphasizes the cost too much; it ignores competition; etc. Further, it could distort the range of prices and values of items on a menu in that a low food/beverage cost item would end up being priced at a very low price, while a high food/beverage cost item would be exorbitantly priced. In addition, it does not allow any flexible approach to the selling of items. Differential profit margins take into account the sales mix of items from a food menu or beverage list and hopefully provide the competitive balance of prices so that in total it is attractive to the customer and achieves the desired gross profit and revenue for the department.

Table 8.7 *Differential profit margins within a food menu giving in this illustration a gross profit percentage of 65 per cent*

Description	Sales mix	Sales mix	Gross profit	Food cost	Cost of sales
	%	£	%	%	£
Appetizer	10	100	75	25	25
Main course	55	550	55	45	247
Vegetables	15	150	75	25	37
Sweets	15	150	80	20	30
Tea/coffee	5	50	80	20	10
Total	100	1000	65*	35*	350

*Weighted averages.

8.8.3 Special pricing considerations

8.8.3.1 Sales tax

Depending on the government in power, it is likely that some form of sales tax may be enforced during its period of office. It is important to the customer to know whether prices displayed or quoted are inclusive of this sales tax or not. Additionally, the caterer needs to realize that any money collected on behalf of the government has at some time to be paid to that government and that it should not be included when calculating revenue or average spend figures, etc.

8.8.3.2 Service charge

This is an additional charge, made to customers, at a fixed percentage of the total cost of the food and beverage served. The fixed percentage is determined by management, printed on the menu/beverage list, with the objective of removing from the customer the problem of determining what size of tip to give when in a particular establishment. As this charge is to be distributed to the staff at a later date, usually on a points system, it should be treated similarly to a sales tax and not included in the calculation of revenue for food and beverages or in the calculations of average spend figures.

8.8.3.3 Cover charge

This is an additional charge to a meal in restaurants to cover such costs as the bread roll and butter and items included but not priced on a menu. Care should be exercised as to whether to implement this or not as it is most likely to cause aggravation to some clients when it is applied.

8.8.3.4 Minimum charge

This is often enforced by restaurants to discourage some potential clients from using the premises and to discourage clients from taking up a seat and only purchasing a very low priced item.

8.8.4 Menu pricing applications

The exact method of pricing used by an establishment will depend on such matters as which sector of the industry the establishment is in; the level of profit/subsidy required; its basic policies; etc. It is important though to remember that the price in itself can be a valuable selling tool and a great aid in achieving the desired volume of sales.

8.8.4.1 Table d'hôte menus

This type of menu is characterized by being a restricted menu, offering a small range of courses with a limited choice within each course and at a fixed selling price. The price may be just one price for any three courses chosen, or may vary in price depending on the main course chosen.

The method of pricing chosen should take into account the departmental profit required and the differential profit margins of the menu. Based on the forecasted sales take-up by guests, the *average* should be taken to fix the price. The average may well be the true figure, rounded off, when the objective is to attract as many customers as possible to choose from the menu; or alternatively, it may be an *average plus* figure when it is being offered with an à la carte menu and it is not desired to encourage too many guests away from the à la carte menu by making the price differentiation too attractive.

8.8.4.2 À la carte menus

This type of menu is characterized by being a larger menu than a table d'hôte menu offering a greater choice of courses and dishes within each course, and each item being individually priced.

The method of pricing here is again to take into account the departmental profit required and the differential profit margins for each course and then to price each item separately using standard recipes. In addition, note should be taken of the potential sales mix within each course so as to achieve the desired profit margin.

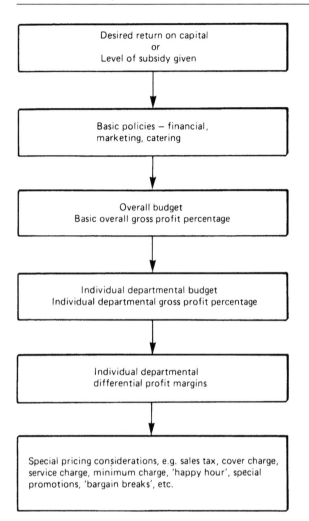

Figure 8.7   *The development of pricing*

8.8.4.3   *Banqueting menus*

This is a specific type of table d'hôte menu offering normally no choice to the customers. The specific difference in pricing this menu is that apart from the food and often the liquor, all the additional items are normally priced and charged separately. Examples of such items are flowers for each table, a band, meals and refreshments for the band, services of a toast master, hire of a microphone, printing of a special menu for the function.

The pricing of a banquet menu for a client is commonly found to have a flexible element to it, in that it is not uncommon for a banqueting manager to offer additions to a menu at no addi-tional cost to the client in order to obtain the business during a slack trading period or for a particular gap in a week. For example, the banqueting manager may offer as a free addition to the standard printed menu such things as a soup course, a sorbet, *petits fours*, etc. Further, the charge for the hire of the function room may be reduced or removed altogether (see also Chapter 19).

8.8.5   Pricing of beverages

The method used to price beverages is similar to that for pricing foods. As in the case of foods, first, the departmental profit target and gross profit percentage should be set, followed by differential profit margins based on the sales mix achievable. The sales mix breakdown depends on the type of operation and how detailed the breakdown of sales is required. The gross profit percentage of house brand beverages (that is, the particular brand of beverage that is offered to the customer, when a specific brand is not requested) is usually higher than on other brand beverages as it is normally made available by the supplier at a special discounted rate. (See Table 8.8 for an example of differential profit margins applied to a bar.)

Pricing may be more accurately calculated for beverages as little, if any, processing of the drinks takes place; drinks being purchased by the bottle (for example, beer, wine) or by a specific stated measure (for example, 6-out) from a

Table 8.8   *Differential profit margins within a beverage list giving in this illustration a gross profit percentage of 60.3 per cent*

Description	Sales mix	Sales mix	Gross profit	Beverage cost	Cost of sales
	%	£	%	%	£
Spirits	40	400	70	30	120.00
Table wines	25	250	60	40	100.00
Fortified wines	15	150	55	45	67.50
Beers	15	150	40	60	90.00
Minerals	5	50	60	40	20.00
Total	100	1000	60.3*	39.7	397.50

*Weighted averages.

bottle of known standard size (for example, wine, 75 cl). The mixing of drinks is, like food, usually prepared using a standard recipe particular to an establishment.

8.8.6 Subsidized operations

There are many operations within the non commercial sector of the industry that are subsidized in some form or other. Subsidies may take the form of completely free premises, capital equipment, services and labour or the catering department may be required to pay a percentage of these costs with the balance being the subsidy. Pricing in this situation may, for example, require the sales revenue to cover the food costs only; or food costs plus specific named expenses (for example, all labour); or food costs plus a named percentage (for example, 20 per cent) as a contribution to all overheads. Pricing in this situation is frequently done on a cost-plus basis, depending on the level of subsidy. When more than the food/beverage cost has to be recovered, it is important that prices are competitive enough to encourage a high enough volume of sales.

8.9 Profit improvement

Maintaining and improving an adequate level of profit are essential for all businesses today to survive – particularly with the increasing level of competition tempting customers not only to change from their usual type of restaurant, but also from the many other types of leisure businesses all chasing the same customers' restricted amount of disposable income.

Among the problems often facing the food and beverage manager is how can the profitability be maintained or increased. Should the prices for some or all items be increased and by how much, and/or food and beverage items costs be reduced, and/or labour costs reduced, and/or the number of customers increased, etc.

Two accepted methods of profit improvement are profit sensitivity analysis and menu engineering.

8.9.1 Profit sensitivity analysis

PSA is concerned with identifying the 'critical' or 'key factors' (i.e. the determinants of profitability) of a business and establishing how they rank in influencing its net profit. The emphasis of PSA is on net profit and the examination of those areas that responded positively to change. In order to undertake PSA the 'profit multipliers' of the business must firstly be calculated. The method is:

1 Identify the 'key factors', financial and operational of the business.
2 Assume a change in one 'key factor' at a time of say 10%, whilst holding all others constant.
3 Calculate the resulting change in net profit.
4 Calculate the profit multipliers (PM):

$$PM = \frac{\% \text{ change in net profit}}{\% \text{ change in 'key factors'}}$$

5 List the PMs in order of size.
6 Analyse the results.

See Table 8.9 for an example.

8.9.1.1 Analysis of PSA

The analysis of the results of the example 'for a commercial restaurant' given in Table 8.9, shows that by ranking the 'key factors' the revenue based factors above the dotted line, have the highest values and therefore the largest effect to the net profit, whilst the cost based 'key factors' have much less impact. This analysis stresses that the control aspects for the illustrated example factors should involve the ongoing analysis, by meal period, by day, by week, etc. of the number of customers, average spend, the sales mix, the food and beverage costs and the contribution to margins.

'Key factors' ranked by size of profit multiplier.

Price per cover	10.0
Number of covers served	5.6
Food and beverage costs	−4.0
Operational costs (fixed)	−2.6
Labour costs (fixed)	−2.0
Labour costs (variable)	−0.4

Table 8.9 *Profit sensitivity analysis: an illustration of the effect, on net profit, of a 10% increase to each 'key factor' in turn*

Key factors	Basic figures	Number of covers	Price per cover	Food & beverage costs	Labour costs – fixed	Labour costs – variable	All other operational costs – fixed
No of covers	5,000	5,500	5,000	5,000	5,000	5,000	5,000
Price per cover (£)	10.00	10.00	11.00	10.00	10.00	10.00	10.00
Total revenue (£)	50,000	55,000	55,000	50,000	50,000	50,000	50,000
Food & beverage costs	20,000	22,000	20,000	22,000	20,000	20,000	20,000
Labour costs – fixed	10,000	10,000	10,000	10,000	11,000	10,000	10,000
Labour costs – variable	2,000	2,200	2,000	2,000	2,000	2,000	2,000
All other operational costs – fixed	13,000	13,000	13,000	13,000	13,000	13,000	14,300
Total costs	45,000	47,200	45,000	47,000	46,000	45,200	46,300
Net profit	5,000	7,800	10,000	3,000	4,000	4,800	3,700
Results:							
Effect to net profit (£)		+2,800	+5,000	–2,000	–1,000	–200	–1,300
Effect to net profit (%)		56	100	–40	–20	–4	–26
Profit multiplier		5.6	10.0	–4.0	–2.0	–0.4	–2.6

8.9.2 Menu engineering

Menu engineering is a marketing orientated approach to the evaluation of a menu with regard to its present and future content, design and pricing. Its origins are based on the famous Boston Consulting Group (BCG) portfolio technique, a matrix specifically designed to analyse individual business performance in a company with a range of different business interests (see Figure 8.8). The concept of menu engineering requires food and beverage managers to orient themselves to the contribution that menu items make to the total profitability of a menu. It highlights the good and the poor performers in a menu, and provides vital information for making the next menu more interesting and appealing to the customers, and hopefully more profitable.

Menu engineering is a step-by-step procedure that focuses on the three main elements:

- customer demand – the number of customers served;
- menu mix – an analysis of customer preferences for each menu item (popularity);
- contribution margin – an analysis of the contribution margin (GP%) for each menu item.

The prerequisites to using this technique are:

- the standardization of all recipes (including the presentation), so that the food costs can be accurate;
- the accurate sales analysis of each menu item, daily and by meal period;
- the use of a personal computer, so that simple spreadsheets, with standard calculations, may be done accurately and with speed.

Using the simple matrix, menu items can be plotted, representing their performance with regard to volume (popularity) and cash contribution (profit). The four squares of the matrix commonly have names indicating the performance of items in a particular square.

1 *Stars*. Menu items *high* in menu mix (popularity) and also *high* in contribution margin.
2 *Plowhorses*. Menu items *high* in menu mix (popularity) but *low* in contribution margin.
3 *Puzzles*. Menu items *low* in menu mix (popularity) and *high* in contribution margin.

High

Popularity (sales)

Plowhorses	**Stars**
Customer perception:	Customer perception:
Over-priced, standard-type items	*Restaurant's prestige items* *Price unimportant to purchase decision*
Management action:	Management action:
• Ensure rigid specifications for purchasing, recipe and presentation are strictly maintained.	• Ensure rigid specifications for purchasing, recipe and presentation are strictly maintained.
• Locate items to a low profile position on menu.	• Feature prominently on menu.
• To increase contribution margin by 'packaging' with a high contribution item.	• Regularly promote.
	• Test price increases in 'high season'.
• Test small price increases.	
Dogs	**Puzzles**
Customer perception:	Customer perception:
Low-priced, but items dull and uninteresting	*Tempting but overpriced*
Management action	Management action
• Try revamping item.	• Reposition and feature more prominently on menu.
• If a new menu item, spend time to check if it can be improved.	• Increase merchandising.
• Review alternative menu items.	• Re-name item and change the presentation.
• Increase the price and raise status to 'puzzle'.	• Give the item 'special' status.
• Remove from menu.	

Low

Low ← **Contribution margin** → High

Figure 8.8 *Tactics for repositioning menu items – using menu engineering*

Table 8.10 *Menu engineering spreadsheet*

Menu Item	(a) Menu Mix	MM %	MM cat	(b) Sell price £	(c) Cost price £	(d)=(a)x(b) Total sales £	(e)=(a)x(c) Total costs £	(f)=(d)-(e) Total cont. M £	CM £	CM cat	Classification
Chicken	420	28	H	4.95	2.21	2,079.00	928.20	1,150.80	22	L	Plowhorse
Entrecote	360	24	H	8.50	4.50	3,060.00	1,620.00	1,440.00	27	H	Star
Fillet steak	150	10	H	9.50	4.95	1,425.00	742.50	682.50	13	H	Star
Pork chop	70	4.67	L	6.45	4.00	451.50	280.00	171.50	3	L	Dog
Seafood platter	180	12	H	8.50	4.50	1,530.00	810.00	720.00	14	H	Star
Vegetarian	210	14	H	4.95	2.20	1,039.50	462.00	557.50	11	L	Plowhorse
Chef's special	75	5	L	9.95	4.95	746.25	371.25	375.00	7	H	Puzzle
Fried cod	35	2.33	L	6.45	2.00	225.75	70.00	155.75	3	H	Puzzle
Totals	1,500	100				10,557.00	5,283.95	5,253.05	100		

Notes: 1 Potential food cost % = 50.05%

 2 Average contribution margin = £3.50

 3 Menu mix % popularity rate = (100%/No menu items) (70%) = 8.75%

4 *Dogs*. Menu items *low* in menu mix (popularity) and *low* in contribution margin.

The analysis of the data to undertake menu engineering (Table 8.10) is done using a standard computer spreadsheet package. This takes the form of a large grid compromising of rows and columns where labels, formulae and values can be entered. When in operation, the formulae and values can be changed if required, giving instantaneous recalculations of the figures, and hard copies printed and retained for easy reference. Whilst spreadsheets can be compiled by hand, the time taken would be lengthy and the opportunity to frequently undertake 'what if' exercises less likely (e.g. what would be the effect on the profitability of the restaurant with a menu of 30 main items, if the price of all the main items were to be increased by 3% or by 4%?). It should be noted here that the success in being able to move menu items 'up' the matrix to the status of a 'star' could have an undesireable effect on the profitability of the menu, simply because customers do not always behave in a rational manner in spite of the wishes of the food and beverage manager!

8.10   References

Coltman, M. (1987). *Hospitality Management Accounting*, 3rd edn. New York: Van Nostrand Reinhold.

Green, E. F. et al. (1987). *Profitable Food and Beverage Management: Operations*. Jenks, Oklahoma: Williams Books.

Kasavana, M. and Smith, D. (1982). *Menu Engineering*. Michigan: Hospitality Publications.

Kotas, R. and Davis, B. (1980). *Food and Beverage Control*. Glasgow: Blackie.

9
Purchasing

9.1   Introduction

Purchasing can be defined as 'a function concerned with the search, selection, purchase,
receipt, storage and final use of a commodity in
accordance with the catering policy of the establishment'. This suggests that the person
employed to purchase foods and beverages for
an establishment will be responsible for not only
purchasing, but also for the receiving, storage
and issuing of all commodities as well as being
involved with the purpose for which items are
purchased and the final use of them.

The purchasing function as illustrated in
Figure 9.1 is vitally important in the control
cycle. Should it be managed inefficiently it creates problems which often result in an unsatisfactory level of both costs and profit for the
establishment and dissatisfied customers. With
no specifications for commodities there would
be neither quality standards nor quantity standards resulting in over-ordering or under ordering as yields for items would be indeterminable.
The receiving department would only be able to
check on quantity and not on quality. The work
in the stores and preparation departments
would be difficult with the quality of produce
varying greatly. Finally, it would be difficult to
measure satisfactorily the performance of
departments if they were continually being provided with non-standardized commodity items.

9.2   The main duties of the purchasing manager

Quite naturally the duties will vary between
establishments, but they will usually include the
following:

1 Responsibility for the management of the purchasing office, the receiving, storage and cellar
   areas.

2 The purchasing of all commodities.
3 Ensuring continuity of supply of all items to
   user departments.
4 Finding cheaper (for same quality) and more
   efficient sources of supply.
5 Keeping up to date with all the markets being
   dealt with and evaluating new products.
6 Research into products, markets, price trends,
   etc.
7 Co-ordinating with production departments
   to standardize commodities and therefore
   reduce stock levels.
8 Liaising with production, control, accounts
   and marketing departments.
9 Reporting to senior management.

What needs to be emphasized to senior management is the importance to an organization of
an efficient purchasing department in that it
should be looked at more as a profit-orientated
department than as a general service department. £100 saved in a day by the specialized
skills of the purchasing officer is equivalent to
£100 of net profit to the organization, which frequently would only otherwise be made from the
involvement in a commercial catering activity
giving a turnover of at least £1,000.

9.3   The purchasing procedure

The procedure can be broken down into five
steps:

1 A requisition form from an authorized member of staff, for example, head chef, restaurant
   manager or from the storekeeper, informing
   the purchasing manager of low stock levels of
   items. (See Figure 10.5 for an example of a
   food requisition form and Figure 10.12 for an
   example of a beverage requisition form.)
2 The selection of the source of supply.
3 Entering into a contract with the supplier by
   phone or in writing and negotiating the price

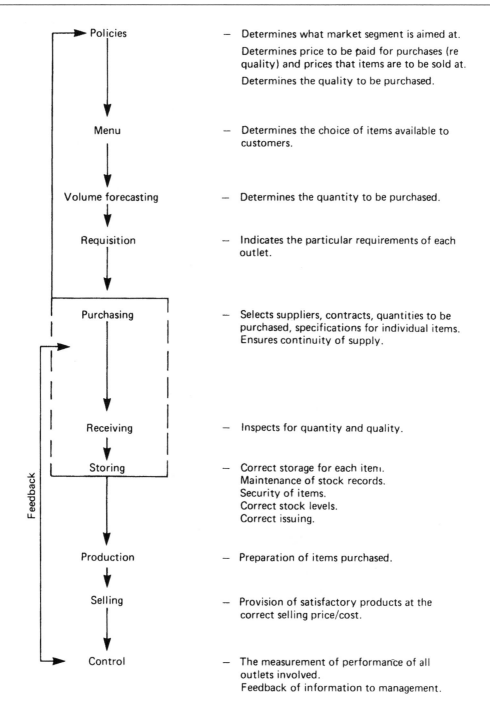

Policies	— Determines what market segment is aimed at.
	Determines price to be paid for purchases (re quality) and prices that items are to be sold at.
	Determines the quality to be purchased.
Menu	— Determines the choice of items available to customers.
Volume forecasting	— Determines the quantity to be purchased.
Requisition	— Indicates the particular requirements of each outlet.
Purchasing	— Selects suppliers, contracts, quantities to be purchased, specifications for individual items. Ensures continuity of supply.
Receiving	— Inspects for quantity and quality.
Storing	— Correct storage for each item. Maintenance of stock records. Security of items. Correct stock levels. Correct issuing.
Production	— Preparation of items purchased.
Selling	— Provision of satisfactory products at the correct selling price/cost.
Control	— The measurement of performance of all outlets involved. Feedback of information to management.

Figure 9.1 *The importance of the purchasing function*

to be paid and a satisfactory delivery performance with particular reference to the time, date, and the place of delivery.

4 The acceptance of goods ordered and the adjustment of any discrepancies in quality or quantity of goods delivered.

5 The transfer of commodities to the ordering department or to the stores or cellar.

The procedure for an establishment should reflect the type of establishment and the market it is in, for example a hospital or first-class restaurant; the location of the establishment in relation to that of its suppliers; the size of storage facilities available; the forecast of future requirements; the shelf life of the food or beverage item; and, most importantly, the establishment's or company's purchasing power. But whatever the establishment a sound purchasing policy should be implemented if satisfactory standards are to be achieved.

9.4 The selection of a supplier

A supplier can be easily selected from among those that the buyer has previously purchased from in that the quality of goods received, price and service offered would be known (see Figure 9.3). When seeking a new supplier caution must be exercised and detailed enquiries made to cover at least the following points:

1 Full details of the firm and the range of items they are selling.
2 Copies of recent prices lists.
3 Details of trading terms.
4 Details of other customers.
5 Samples of products.

Ideally, a visit should be made to any potential supplier to see the size of the company, the full range of products, the size of processing and storage facilities, the size of their transport fleet and to meet members of the management team.

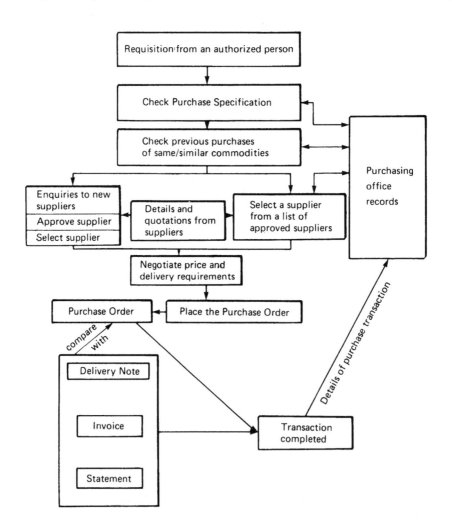

Figure 9.2 *The purchasing transaction – under the supervision of the purchasing manager*

All of this takes up valuable time for the buyer, but is essential in order to obtain a supplier with whom it is possible to have a satisfactory business relationship, who will stock the quality and quantity of commodities needed and who is able to offer a satisfactory delivery performance within an acceptable price range. This procedure would convince the supplier of the professionalism of the purchasing manager.

Having selected suppliers and placed them on an 'approved suppliers list', and after having purchased from them, it is necessary to periodically evaluate their performance using a rating system. There are three main performance criteria which are normally used in a rating system:

1 Price.
2 Quality.
3 Delivery performance.

9.4.1 Price performance

The cheapest item is not necessarily the best buy; often a cheap item is of a low quality. One supplier may specialize in lower quality goods at a lower price while another may specialize in high quality goods at higher prices. Both suppliers are specialists and both may supply the same buyer with similar goods but of different qualities. Which supplier the buyer chooses depends on the quality required – the corresponding price will then have to be paid. Price, however, is not always related to quality. The purchasing manager needs to guard against this.

The lower the price coupled with an above average quality of goods the higher is the price performance rating.

9.4.2 Quality performance

This is the ability of a supplier to supply the buyer consistently with goods of the desired quality as laid down in the purchasing specification.

Consistency in meeting the purchasing specification would give a high quality performance rating.

9.4 .3 Delivery performance

This is the ability of the supplier to meet agreed delivery times and dates with the buyer. Prompt deliveries mean that the goods will be delivered when required and when staff are available to check them efficiently for quantity and quality. Late deliveries will often add to the pressure of work at the receiving department, when other goods are also being checked in, and to possible complications in the production department.

The nearer the scheduled delivery date and time the higher the delivery performance rating.

The rating of suppliers using these three criteria provides a guide to the buyer, in an objective way, for negotiating further purchasing agreements between suppliers of similar commodities.

9.4.4 An example of a numerical supplier rating system

The numerical supplier rating system reduces price, quality and delivery performance to a mark each out of ten. The best rating that a supplier could achieve would be 10-10-10.

Price is measured by comparing the prices of each supplier for an order, over a known trading period (for example, one week, twenty eight days) against those of other suppliers of the same group of commodities. The lower the price, the higher the rating figure.

Quality is measured by the ability of the supplier to provide commodities consistently to the required specification. The performance is calculated as a percentage of the total orders made. Thus goods returned to the supplier because of poor quality would lower the rating figure.

Delivery performance would be calculated against the percentage of deliveries made on time. The majority of deliveries made on time would give a high rating figure.

A supplier rated 6–9–10 by the buying department would be understood to offer goods at a fairly high price (four suppliers being cheaper), to supply goods initially which were 90 per cent satisfactory, and to have a first class delivery record.

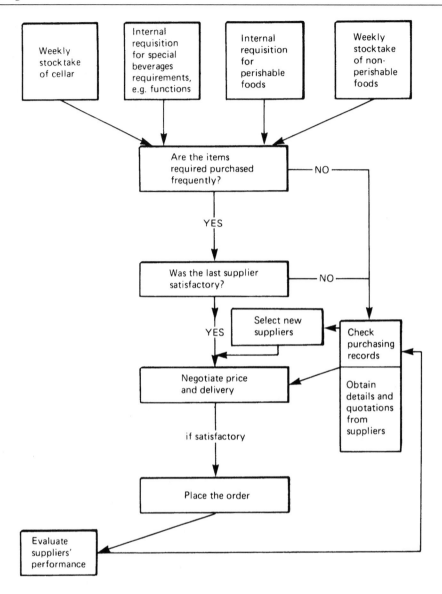

Figure 9.3   *The selection of a supplier*

9.5   Aids to purchasing

The preceding pages have attempted to reduce the complexity of the total purchasing activity to a simplified outline. There are, however, two main problems that continually confront buyers. They are:

1 Keeping up to date with what is available in all the markets in which they are dealing.
2 Keeping up to date with the current prices for all commodities. This is very important, as it enables buyers to negotiate with suppliers

more efficiently and to compare the prices that they are being charged.

In order to reduce these difficulties, buyers need to be aware of what general information services are available that will help them. These aids may be grouped under some six headings:

1 *The supply trade press.* Trade journals are published weekly and cover most of the commodities to be purchased. They give valuable current general information and indications of future trends.

2 *The commodity trade organizations.* These organizations will readily provide information to caterers about a particular commodity, such as the types available, how they should be stored and names of local and national suppliers.

3 *The catering trade press.* These papers and journals contain items of commodity news and information of present and future prices.

4 *The national press.* Leading newspapers publish commodity market news with details of the range of prices being paid in certain markets.

5 *Government publications.* These are available from agricultural departments giving a variety of information such as a national food survey response, availability of specific commodities and current food legislation.

6 *Published price indexes.* These are produced by government departments, by consumer associations and by trade journals. These indexes start from a particular date in time listing large groups of commodities and monitor the change in prices from that initial period, also recording changes on a yearly and monthly basis. This is of great significance to the caterer as it provides information of general and specific price trends and a comparison against the prices that he has paid for commodities recently.

9.6   The purchasing of foods

When purchasing food it is necessary to consider what the true cost of the item will be in relation to what the printed price list from the supplier states it to be. The true cost calculation has to take into account the invoice price less any discounts claimable; storage cost of the item (this is particularly relevant when purchasing large quantities at a special price and includes the problem of a further security risk); and the production costs. The calculation of a true cost may well indicate that it is cheaper to buy in five-case lots as against a fifty-case lot at a lower price, or that the production costs involved with an item make it too expensive to buy it in that state, and that it may be cheaper in the long run to buy the item already processed by a manufacturer.

There are seven main buying methods that may be used for purchasing foods. The particu-

lar method chosen often depends on the location of the establishment, the type and size of the business, its purchasing power and the type of food being purchased.

It is important for buyers to have accurate figures available of the consumption/usage of major items so that they may decide which method of purchasing to use and also as essential data for the negotiation of the purchasing price.

9.6.1   Purchasing by contract

There are two common types of contract used:

1 *The specific period contract* which aims at determining the source of supply and the price of goods for a stated period often of three or six months. This reduces the time and labour of negotiating and ordering to a minimum, plus it has the added advantage of assisting with budgeting and pricing, when the prices of items are fixed for a period of time. Items with a fairly stable price, such as milk, cream, bread, etc., can be contracted in this way.

2 *The quantity contract* which aims at ensuring continuity of supply of a given quantity of an essential item at an agreed price over a particular trading period. The purchase of frozen fruit and vegetables for use in a banqueting or a summer season are typical examples when the supply could be affected by the weather conditions with subsequent price fluctuations and where a quantity contract is advisable used.

A point to be noted here is that a contract is a legal document and that the conditions of the contract should be prepared by the firm's solicitors to safeguard against possible areas of dispute or, alternatively, prepared using the guidelines as laid out by one of the professional bodies.

The contract is in two parts: the general conditions; and the particular requirements or specifications.

The general conditions would include clauses such as the period of the contract, where deliveries are to be made, where invoices are to be sent, the method of payment, samples of commodities, etc. The specific conditions would normally

POINTER HOTELS (UK) LTD
Daily Market List

( ) = supplier selected

Date: **25/5/199–**

Items	On hand	Wanted	SUPPLIER			Items	On hand	Wanted	SUPPLIER		
			A	B	C				A	B	C
Fruit						Vegetables					
Apples dessert						Artichokes					
Extra class	—	40 lb				Globe					
Class 1	—	40 lb	(20p lb)	18p lb	21p lb	Jerusalem					
Class 2	—					Asparagus					
Apples cooking						Beans					
Class 2	—					Broad					
Class 3	—					French	20 lb	40 lb	70p lb	(70p lb)	72p lb
Apricots	10 lb	20 lb	(28p lb)	n/a	30p lb	Runner	—	—			
Avocado Pears						Brussel Sprouts	—	—			
						Cabbage	—	56 lb	16p lb	(14p lb)	14p lb
						Carrots	—	28 lb	(15p lb)	18p lb	16p lb

Figure 9.4   *Extract from a daily market list for fresh fruit and vegetables, with prices in brackets showing which items are to be ordered from specific suppliers*

be given as detailed specifications for particular items as explained in section 9.7 and as illustrated in Figure 9.6.

9.6.2   Purchasing by daily market list

This method is used when purchasing perishable foods on a daily basis and when it is possible to have two or more approved suppliers.

A senior member of the kitchen staff would take a quick stocktake of the foods left after each lunch service, pass this information to the head chef who would complete the 'daily market list' by entering the quantities of all items he/she requires to be purchased for the next day's business in the 'wanted' column. The list would then be processed by a member of staff in the purchasing office.

Each approved supplier would be telephoned and asked to quote a price for each of the items required. The price quoted would be based on the quality of the item required, the quantity required and the esteem placed by the supplier to supply a particular establishment. The prices quoted would be entered on to the 'daily market list' and then a decision made by the purchasing manager as to where to place the order for each item. This may result in two or three suppliers

each receiving part of the total order. An example is given in Figure 9.4.

9.6.3   Purchasing by weekly/fortnightly quotation lists

This method is used to purchase grocery items where a delivery of once a week or fortnight is adequate. The method is similar to that described when purchasing perishable foods by daily market list.

The head storekeeper would complete the stock in hand column on the master list and also fill in the wanted column for each item, based on the normal order quantity and the volume of the business expected. Meanwhile the purchasing office would send out to each grocery supplier a copy of the list on which suppliers should quote their prices. On receipt of quotations these would be entered on to a master quotation list and a decision then made about where the orders for each item are to be placed. This would be based on the requirements in the next week/fortnight, the prices quoted and the storage space available which may allow for special offers for large quantities purchased to be considered. It should be noted here that the specifications for items will usually be just by brand name of the product together with the size, weight and count. This is because the buying power of most catering companies is not large enough to interest food manufacturing companies to process foods to their specific requirements. An example of a typical form is given in Figure 9.5.

9.6.4   Purchasing by 'cash and carry'

This method is of particular interest to the medium and small establishments whose orders are often not large enough to be able to get regular deliveries from wholesalers and food manufacturers. 'Cash and carry' food warehouses are situated in all towns and resemble in layout and operation that of very large food supermarkets. The main difference is that the 'cash and carry' food warehouse is only available to traders.

The particular advantages of buying by 'cash and carry' are:

1 The warehouses are situated near to most catering establishments and their hours of business are usually longer than those of most food wholesalers.
2 Small or large quantities may be purchased at competitive prices.

3 Customers are able to see what they are buying, as against buying just from a price list or catalogue. They may also see special displays of a particular food company's products and be able to taste them.
4 Customers may use the warehouse as often as they like and in doing so keep the level of stocks held low. Also, when there is a sudden increase in their business it is easy for caterers to replace their stock.

There are two disadvantages of buying by 'cash and carry':

1 Caterers have to provide their own staff and transport to collect the items from the warehouse.
2 Caterers have to pay cash for the items they purchase.

9.6.5   Purchasing by paid reserve

This method is used when it is necessary to ensure the continuity of supply of an item for the menu which is of particular importance to a restaurant. Caterers are buying in advance a large quantity of a commodity to cover the needs

POINTER HOTELS (UK) LTD
Master Grocery Quotation List   Date: 25/5/199 –

( ) = supplier selected

				SUPPLIER					
				A		B		C	
Items		On hand	Wanted	per case	per 10 cases	per case	per 10 cases	per case	per 10 cases
BRAND	**CANNED FRUITS**								
"B & D"	Solid pack apples 6/A10's	2 c	10 CASES	13.85	(13.70)	14.00	13.75	14.10	13.95
"Lincan"	Apricot pulp 6/kilo	–	10 CASES	28.80	(28.50)	29.20	29.05	28.95	28.70
"B & D"	Apricots 6/A10's	–	5 CASES	25.30	(25.20)	n/a	n/a	25.45	25.30
"B & D"	Fruit cocktail 6/A10's	5 c	10 CASES	16.42	16.30	16.50	(16.25)	n/a	n/a
"Grosvenor"	Fruit salad 6/A10's	–	5 CASES	16.00	15.70	16.20	16.00	16.00	(15.55)
"Grosvenor"	Gooseberries 6/A10's	–	2 CASES	(15.05)	15.85	15.40	15.10	15.25	15.00
"Atlas"	Peach caps 6/A10's	5 c	15 CASES	15.16	(14.90)	15.35	15.20	15.40	15.10
"Atlas"	Peach slices 6/A10's	–	2 CASES	(15.44)	15.24	15.80	15.50	15.60	15.25

Figure 9.5   *Extract from a master grocery quotation list for canned fruit, with prices in brackets showing which items are to be ordered from specific suppliers*

for several months ahead, and requisitioning their weekly requirements from suppliers, who would hold the stock. Examples of products which are purchased by this method are frozen jumbo size pacific prawns and frozen fillets of beef.

9.6.6   Total supply

This method is relatively new. It is a method offered only by a few major suppliers who are able to offer a full supply service of all commodities to caterers. This has the advantages of only having to negotiate with one supplier; a reduced volume of paperwork; and far fewer deliveries. The main disadvantage is that of being tied to one major supplier, whose prices may not be as competitive as when using several suppliers and whose range of certain commodities may be limited.

9.6. 7   Cost plus

This is a method used frequently in the welfare sector of the industry. The establishment agrees to pay an approved supplier exactly the same price that the supplier paid for the commodities plus an agreed percentage, often l0–12½ per cent. This percentage would include the cost of handling, delivery charges, and a profit element for the supplier.

9.7   Purchase specifications for food

Purchase specifications should be used when ever possible in purchasing, in particular when purchasing by the first three methods discussed in section 9.6.

A purchase specification is a concise description of the quality, size and weight (or count) required for a particular item. Each specification would be particular to an establishment and would have been determined by members of the management team (for example, the purchasing manager, head chef and the food and beverage manager) by reference to the catering policy, the menu requirements and its price range. Copies of the specifications should be kept by the rele-

vant members of the management, the goods received clerk and the food control clerks and sent to all suppliers on the 'approved suppliers list'.

The reasons for preparing specifications are:

1 It establishes a buying standard of a commodity for an establishment so that a standard product is available for the kitchen and restaurant to prepare for the customer.
2 It informs the supplier in writing (and often aided by a line drawing or photograph) precisely what is required, and it assists the supplier in being competitive with pricing.
3 It provides detailed information to the goods received clerk and the storeman as to the standard of the foods to accept.
4 It makes staff aware of the differences that can occur in produce, for example, size, weight, quality, quantity, etc.

Unfortunately, preparing specifications in the UK and many other countries is rather difficult owing to a lack of government grading of many foods. The position has improved with the grading of fruits and vegetables produced in the EC, and with the recommended classification of carcase meat by the Meat Livestock Commission.

Specifications are easy to write when there is an official recognized grading scheme for the particular commodity. It is necessary, however, to know and understand any grading system fully to be able to obtain the maximum benefit.

When writing specifications it is convenient to write them in a standard form giving the following information:

1 *Definition of the item.* Care must be exercised here that the common catering term used by the buyer means exactly the same thing to the supplier.
2 *Grade or brandname,* for example apples grade extra class; Lea and Perrins 'Worcester sauce'.
3 *Weight, size or count,* for example pounds, hundredweights, kilos, etc.; A2⅛s, A10s, etc.; lemons 120s, pineapples 12s etc.
4 *Unit against which prices should be quoted,* for example per pound, per case, etc.
5 *Special notes for the commodity,* for example for meat it could contain details of the preparation of a particular cut of meat or details of special packaging requirements.

A point which must be noted is that while standard purchase specifications have many advantages to an establishment, there is always the problem that unless buyers are careful they can easily overspecify and buy goods of too high a standard than is really necessary and unintentionally increase the food cost.

An example of a purchasing specification for a catering cut of beef is given in Figure 9.6.

9.8 The purchasing of beverages

The purchasing of alcoholic and non-alcoholic beverages, like that of foodstuffs, has the aim to purchase the very best quality of items, at the lowest price, for a specific purpose. The purchasing of beverages should be undertaken by the purchasing manager together with such experts as the food and beverage manager, the head cellarman and the head wine waiter. As beverages will frequently contribute more to profits than foods, and as they require consider-

ably fewer staff to process them into a finished product for the customer, it is essential that adequate attention is given to this area. What is important to bear in mind always when purchasing beverages is that expensive products or products with pretty labels do not necessarily indicate or guarantee superior quality.

With beverage purchasing the following points are generally noticeable:

1 There are fewer and often restricted sources of supply.
2 The high value of beverage purchases.
3 That free advice and assistance with purchasing are given by the wine and spirit trade.
4 That quality factors are difficult to evaluate and require special training to identify them. This means setting up or attending tasting sessions several times a year.
5 There are far fewer standard purchasing units than for food.
6 There is an established standard of product. Many items like minerals, spirits, etc., will

Purchase Specification
(Striploin – special trim i.e. contre-filet)

Definition	1 Taken from a H¼ of Scotch beef
	2 Taken from a sirloin XX
Weight range	1 Between 24–28 lb (10.89–12.70 k)
	2 Average weight per delivery of 10 striploins = 26 lbs (11.79 k)
Surface fat	1 An even covering of fat not exceeding a thickness of ¾ in (19 mm)
Suet deposits	1 To be completely removed
Length of 'tops' (flank)	1 Not to exceed 1 in (25 mm)
Depth of 'eye' muscle	1 The main 'eye' muscle to be not less than 3 in (73 mm)
Gristle content	1 All small 'caps' of gristle on the underside of the 'eye' muscle to be removed
	2 'Backstrap' gristle, which is situated on top of the striploin together with its covering of surface fat to be completely removed.
Side chain	1 To be completely removed
Boning	All boning to be done cleanly so that:
	1 no bone fragments remain
	2 All bones are removed (i.e. all rib and vertebrae bones)
	3 no rib fingers remain
	4 no knife cuts deeper than ½ in (12 mm)

Figure 9.6 *An example of a purchase specification for a catering cut of beef*
Source: Bernard Davis, *Food Commodities*, 2nd edn, Butterworth-Heinemann, 1989

have a standard that will not vary over the years and items such as a well-known wine from an established shipper will be of a standard for a specific year, whereas with food items there may be several grades and a wide range of ungraded items available. In addition, food items may be purchased in different forms such as fresh, chilled, frozen, canned, etc.

7 The prices of alcoholic beverages do not fluctuate to the extent that food prices do.

A beverage selected for a wine list would not only have to be of an acceptable quality to members of the selection team, but also to the type of customer served. It should complement the food menu and be available for purchasing over a long enough period and at a price that is competitive. The continuity of supply of any wine should be established before it is added to a wine list.

There are some five main sources of supply that can be used for purchasing beverages and it is most likely that a purchasing manager would use at least two of them. The methods used for purchasing would vary between establishments because of such criteria as the type of customer; the type, size and location of the establishment; the storage facilities available; and the purchasing power of the buyer.

9.8.1   Wine shippers

These are firms that purchase wine in the country of origin and ship it to whatever country it is to be sold in. Usually shippers are concerned with the wine from a particular region only. This means that the range of products that they are to sell is limited. Further to this problem, shippers are unlikely to want to deal with customers other than prestigious establishments or the very large companies. The products of wine shippers are usually bought from a wine and spirit wholesaler.

9.8.2   Wholesalers

These are usually the subsidiary wine companies of the large breweries or independent wine companies. The brewery companies sell their own label products as a first preference to other proprietary products. Wholesalers offer a very wide range of all beverages as well as a regular delivery service to the caterer. In addition they can assist the caterer with promotional literature for both bar and restaurant sales. As the beverage supply industry is highly competitive wholesalers will also offer the following services to selected clients.

1 *Suspended debt.* Suppliers would invoice caterers for their initial cellar stock purchases, but would request payment only on subsequent purchases, the first purchase invoice being 'suspended' until the account is closed with the supplier. This has the advantage for caterers of a free loan to their business, but the drawback that they would be required to make specific beverage purchases from this one supplier only.

2 *Cellar inventory and suspended debt account.* This is similar to 1 above. The supplier will stock the caterers' cellar to an agreed level, for a specific period of time, free of charge, the opening stock levels being recorded by the supplier and the caterer. A stocktake is made by both parties at the end of the agreed period and all items used are then charged for. The supplier then makes a delivery to replenish the stock to the levels first agreed upon. The drawback to this method for the caterer is the tying of purchases to this one supplier, while the advantage is that the caterer only has to pay for what has been sold to customers and then only some several weeks after, during which time the caterer will have been able to use the money taken in the business.

3 *Publicity material.* Wholesalers will usually assist in the printing of wine lists and publicity material for promotional events.

9.8.3   Beverage manufacturers

This method of purchasing is used when the purchasing manager is able to buy in sufficiently large quantities to deal direct with the manufacturer. This is most commonly practised for the purchasing of the main spirits, minerals and beers. The advantage to the caterer is the lower

Germany

After a fairly bleak period for German wine growers who really care about the quality of their wine, there is a revival in interest for top estates. The reason is, quite simply, that Riesling is an instrument which, in skilled hands, can create wines as great as any in the world. From the delicate, slaty elegance of the Saar and Mosel, to the richer, spicy styles of the Rheinpfalz, these are wines to savour by themselves, as some of the most scintillating apéritifs you will ever find. The Pinot Blanc from Baden has another role, as the sort of balanced food wine that the Germans have been trying for so long to perfect, and are just beginning to achieve.

NIERSTEINER GUTES DOMTHAL, RHEINHESSEN, 1994
PRODUCED & BOTTLED RHEINHESSEN WINZER

£54.60 per case £4.70 per bottle Wine code: 1135

A well-made hock with the delicious, orangey flavour of really ripe grapes. Mildly medium-dry, this is the sort of wine which will appeal to almost any guest, and is ideal for serving at parties and receptions.

MONZINGER PARADIESGARTEN RIESLING, NAHE, 1995
PRODUCED & BOTTLED WEINGUT HEHNER-KILZ

£57.60 per case £4.95 per bottle Wine code: 0964

This is the sort of deliciously refreshing apéritif that will restore Germany's reputation for fine, medium-dry wines at sensible prices. With crisp acidity and the finesse that only a pure Riesling can offer, here is the solution for those who find Sauvignon Blanc too dry.
Recommended For Value

AUERBACHER FÜRSTENLAGER RIESLING KABINETT HALBTROCKEN, HESSISCHE BURGSTRASSE, 1993
PRODUCED & BOTTLED WEINGUT SIMON BURKLE

£76.20 per case £6.50 per bottle Wine code: 0963

How many wines have you drunk from the Hessische Bergstrasse region, just North of Heidelberg? Very few actually leave the area, but we are delighted that this one got away, because it displays the Riesling's marvellous complexity of flavour. Peaches, citrus fruit, slate and mineral notes all find their place, enhanced by a creamy texture and fresh acidity.

LIESER SÜSSENBERG RIESLING KABINETT, MOSEL, 1992
PRODUCED & BOTTLED WEINGUT SCHLOSS LIESER

£91.80 £7.80 per bottle Wine code: 0956

Green tinged, with a classic, slaty Riesling nose. Delicately balanced with finely honed flavours and a lingering finish. Schloss Lieser is fast becoming one of the Mosel's top estates and, with prices in this village more modest than those of its neighbours, Berncastel and Wehlen, the wines are good value. A scintillating apéritif.

GEWÜRZTRAMINER SPÄTLESE, RHEINHESSEN, 1992
PRODUCED & BOTTLED WEINGUT SCHALES

£93.60 per case £7.95 per bottle Wine code: 1064

Considering that Alsace Gewurztraminer often suffers from low acidity, it is surprising that the cooler German climate does not produce more delicious examples such as this one. Tasting of the grape itself, rather than of lychees or Turkish Delight, in this wine the fresh acidity produces a creamy, apricot character. Why not try it in a mixed case?

Figure 9.7 *An extract from the spring 1997 wine list of Hicks and Don, specialist wine merchants*

price that would have to be paid as compared to purchasing through a wholesaler.

9.8.4   Cash-and-carry

This method was discussed earlier in the chapter in relation to food. Cash-and-carry businesses offer a very limited range of spirits, wines, beers, etc. at very keen prices, but no other service. They are useful in emergencies or when special offers are being made.

9.8.5   Auctions

This is a method of purchasing that has limitations in that it usually is only for the sale of wines. It can be a useful way of buying 'end of bin' wines in small quantities from a private home or from another hotel or catering establishment. As long as purchasing managers know their wines thoroughly this can be useful source for wines for a special occasion. It would be unlikely that the quantity offered would justify this method of purchasing of wines for inclusion in a standard wine list.

9.9   Purchase specifications for beverages

The purpose of a purchasing specification is to set down in writing the standard of a product for a specific use by an establishment. This is then used by the purchasing manager to inform suppliers exactly what is required and is vital information when negotiating prices. It is also invaluable to the receiving and cellar department staff to know what to accept when deliveries are being made.

Unlike purchasing specifications for food, specifications for beverages are much simpler and to understand. The reason is that beverages are sold and purchased by the brand name label of the product, each having a consistent quality and quantity standard of content for each selling unit, e.g. barrels, kegs, bottles, splits, etc. See Figure 9.8 for an example from a beverage specification manual. As the specification is brief it can always be written in full on a purchase order. Specification for wines also includes the details of vintage and shipper.

It should be particularly noted that as the quality, consistency and quantity are virtually guaranteed the price to be paid for the product is very important as it is the one factor that is not constant. It is for this reason that close attention is given by the purchaser to offers by suppliers of special discounts for, say, five-, ten-, or twenty-case lots.

9.10   References

Davis, B. and Lockwood, A. (1994). *Food and Beverage Management – a selection of readings*. Oxford: Butterworth-Heinemann.

Hyman, H. H. (1982). *Supplies Management for Health Services*. London: Croom Helm.

Stevens, J. (1987). *Measuring Purchasing Performance*. London: Business Books.

Westing, K. et al. (1983). *Purchasing Management*. New York: John Wiley.

POINTER HOTELS (UK) LTD
Beverage Purchase Specifications

Year: 199—

| Vintage | Specification | Size | | |
		Magnum	Bottle	Half-bottle
	Champagnes			
–	Bollinger, Extra Quality, Brut	✓	✓	✓
1970	Bollinger, Extra Quality, Brut	✓	✓	✓
–	Moët & Chandon, Première Cuvée	✓	✓	–
1970	Moet & Chandon, Dry Imperial	✓	✓	✓
1969	Moet & Chandon, Cuvée Dom Pérignon	✓	✓	–
1969	Tattinger, Blanc de Blancs, Brut	–	✓	–

Figure 9.8   *An extract from a beverage specification manual*

10
Receiving, storing and issuing

10.1 Receiving of food

In many catering establishments the receiving department, mistakenly, is not considered to be a very important one, and it is often staffed by people with little or no specialized knowledge. Unless this department operates efficiently, it becomes almost a waste of time for the purchasing manager to prepare purchase specifications and to negotiate price and trading terms with suppliers. It also then becomes the weak link in the food control cycle and nullifies all effort in the rest of the control cycle.

It is important to realize that all goods being received into an establishment have a monetary value and that it is essential to ensure that exactly this value in goods is properly accounted for and received. It is also important to remember that often these goods will have a selling value several times their original purchase in price in a matter of hours.

The main objectives are to ensure that:

1 The quantity of goods delivered matches the quantity which has been ordered. This means that all goods will have to be weighed (for example, fresh fruit, vegetables, meat, etc.) or counted (for example, cases of A10s sliced peaches).
2 The quality of goods delivered is in accordance with the specification stated on the purchase form, for example checking that the grade of New Zealand lamb is correct or that a delivery of apples is of the extra class quality.
3 The prices stated on the delivery note are in accordance with the prices on the purchase order form.
4 When the quantity or quality (or both) of the food delivered is not in accordance with the purchase order or an item is omitted from the

order a 'request for credit note' is raised by the receiving clerk. When this happens with the daily delivery of perishable foods it is essential that the purchasing manager is informed, as an alternative source of supply or possible product may have to be found quickly to minimize any inconvenience to the production department. See Figure 10.1 for an example of a 'request for credit note'.
5 An accurate record is made in the 'goods received book' recording details of the delivery. An example of a goods received book is given in Figure 10.2

For these objectives to be achieved it is essential that staff employed in this department are trustworthy and fully trained in the clerical procedures and in quality inspection and also that the staff are provided with the adequate facilities to do the job properly, such as a large and well lit area, large scales with fare weights, copies of all purchase specifications and an office with a telephone. Further, whenever possible the purchasing officer should seek co-operation from the suppliers requesting them to arrive at set periods during the day, to spread the pressure of work at the receiving bay. When these objectives are not being met it can be because of short deliveries or a lower quality of produce being delivered often to that originally ordered or on the accompanying delivery note, with the receiving department staff being involved in the fraud. Unless spot checks on this area are made by a member of the food and beverage management team periodically, irregularities can go unnoticed for many weeks and be discovered only by accident or as a result of an enquiry into the reasons for the high cost of food purchased in relation to the sales.

POINTER HOTELS (UK) LTD
Request for Credit Memorandum

No: 2314

To: W. Scott
Butcher
121 High Street
DUNSFOLD

Date: 9.2.9–

PLEASE ISSUE YOUR CREDIT MEMO FOR ITEMS LISTED BELOW			£ COST £			
			Unit		Total	
14	lb	Frozen Calf Liver	3	80	53	20
50	lb	Topside of Beef	2	20	110	00

Reason: 1   Liver not delivered but invoiced

2   Beef not as per specification

Food and Beverage Controller	Accounting Dept.	Van Driver	Requested by
		Fred Reed	*Bill Smith*
			Storeman

Figure 10.1   *An example of a typical request for credit form*

POINTER HOTELS (UK) LTD
GOODS RECEIVED BOOK

Date: 5.2.9–

Delivery note no.	Supplier	Total £		Dry stores £		Meat £		Poultry £		Fish £		Staff kitchen £		Carvery kitchen £		Main kitchen £		VAT £
132	Smith	45	00	45	00													
922	Browne	120	00					120	00									
710	Walker	280	00			280	00											
312	Jones	125	00							125	00							
1213	Greene	70	00									70	00					
514	Biller	275	00													275	00	
121	Ball	125	00	75	00							50	00					
398	Cover	340	00													340	00	
179	Lawe	35	00	35	00													
	TOTALS	£1,415	00	£155.00		£280.00		£120.00		£125.00		£120.00		—		£615.00		—

Figure 10.2   *An example of an extract from a goods received book*

10.1.1   The meat tag

In the majority of catering establishments such items of food as meat, special processed meats such as hams, and fish such as smoked salmon, constitute the most expensive of the purchased foods. Because of this high cost it is not uncommon for units operating a detailed control system to set up a form of special control of these items:

Tagging expensive food serves many purposes:

1 It aids the control of expensive foods.
2 It requires the receiving clerk to weigh and record each item, and to check against the specific purchase specification weight range.
3 It assists in obtaining a more accurate daily food cost percentage figure.
4 It assists in controlling the stock levels of these items.

The operation of tagging of expensive items is as follows:

1 On receiving the items they are checked against the purchase specification as to being acceptable or not.
2 If suitable, a tag is made out for each item received, with the main information being taken from the invoice or delivery note. The weight recorded on the tag is obtained by actually weighing each item individually. An example of a meat tag is given in Figure 10.3.
3 The tag is then separated along the perforation with the control office copies being sent direct to control with the invoice or delivery note and the kitchen copy being attached by string or wire to the food item.
4 When the item is issued, at a later date, to the kitchen for use the tag attached to the item is removed and sent to control with the date of issue filled in.
5 The control office will usually operate a reconciliation of meat tags form, recording the tags received from the receiving department and from the kitchen. Thus the total value of tags of each specific expensive item would be known for:

MEAT TAG	No. 22927
Item	*Beef*
Cut	*Rib*
Total Weight	*22 lb*
Total Value	*£39·60*
Cost / lb	*£1·80*
Supplier	*Tambard Meat Co.*
Date Received	*5/2/9–*
Date Issued	*12/2/9–*

Food control Copy

= = = = = = = = = = = = = = = =

MEAT TAG	No. 22927
Item	*Beef*
Cut	*Rib*
Total Weight	*22 lb*
Total Value	*£39·60*
Cost / lb	*£1·80*
Supplier	*Tambard Meat Co.*
Date Received	*5/2/9–*
Date Issued	*12/2/9–*

Food Store Copy

Send to Food Control on day of issue to kitchens

Figure 10.3   *An example of a meat tag*

(a) Daily purchases.
(b) Daily issues to the kitchen for immediate use.
(c) Balance shown would give the stock value of those items.

RECONCILIATION OF MEAT TAGS

Item: **Beef Ribs**   *Month/period* **1/2/9–**

Date received	Tag number	Supplier	Value £	Date issued
1/2/9–	22982	Tambard Meat Co.	39.60	3/2/9–
2/2/9–	22929	Smith and Co.	36.20	6/2/9–
2/2/9–	22930	Tambard Meat Co.	38.00	6/2/9–
2/2/9–	22931	Smith and Co.	35.40	6/2/9–
5/2/9–	22932	Smith and Co.	37.80	6/2/9–
5/2/9–	22933	Smith and Co.	38.20	9/2/9–
22/2/9–	22951	Tambard Meat Co.	38.20	
22/2/9–	22952	Tambard Meat Co.	37.60	
25/2/9–	22953	Smith and Co.	36.80	
25/2/9–	22954	Smith and Co.	37.20	
25/2/9–	22955	Smith and Co.	37.90	
25/2/9–	22956	Smith and Co.	38.10	

Balance to be carried forward   **6** No.: Tag Items
Total value   **£225.80**

Figure 10.4   *An example of a reconciliation of meat tags form*

An example of a reconciliation of meat tags form is shown in Figure 10.4.

10.2   Storing and issuing food

The main objective of a food store is to ensure that an adequate supply of foods for the immediate needs of the establishment are available at all times.

Foods when accepted at the receiving department are categorized as perishable and non-perishable items. The perishable items go straight to the kitchens, where they would be stored in either refrigerators or cold rooms depending on the item. Perishable foods going direct to the kitchen are often referred to as being on direct charge in that they will usually be used within one to three days of delivery by the kitchen. Ideally, meat, fish, dairy produce, fruit and vegetables, and deep frozen foods should be stored separately from each other. However, in practice this is found only in large establishments. The non-perishable items (for example, canned foods) go to a food store where they are unpacked, checked for any damage and placed on racking. The layout for the stores normally takes the form of either:

1 Having items that are issued daily being located near to the door where issues are made, with the remainder being arranged in a logical sequence.
2 Grouping of commodities together, for example, all canned foods, dried foods, etc., each arranged into sections.

What is important, is that the layout chosen should be one that minimizes the distance walked by the storekeeper. When this is determined the stock-taking list should be printed in the same order in which items appear in the stores so as to enable stock-taking to be done quickly and efficiently.

10.2.1 Issuing of food

This should take place at set times during the day and only against a requisition note signed by an authorized person, for example head chef or restaurant manager. When the requisition is a large one it should be handed in several hours before the items are required to allow the store keeper plenty of time to collect all the food items together. See Figure 10.5 for an example of a requisition note. The pricing of issues is usually at the 'as purchased price', ignoring any small discounts. This is made easy in the case of non-per-

ishable foods by marking the current price on all items when they first come into the store. The pricing of perishable items is often done by the control office after they have been issued as they have access to the suppliers' invoices.

10.3 Stocktaking of food

The main objectives of taking stock are:

1 To determine the value of goods held in stock. This will indicate if too much or too little food is held in stock and if the total value of stock held is in accordance with the financial policy of the establishment. The total value of food held in stock is also required for the profit and loss accounts and the balance sheet, by the organization's accounts department.
2 To compare the value of goods actually in the stores at a particular time with the book value of the stock which will have been calculated with the simple formulae of:

POINTER HOTELS (UK) LTD
Food Storeroom Requisition

Department: Pastry   Date: 5/2/9–

Quantity required	Items	Quantity issued	Unit cost price £	Total cost £
1 bottle	Vanilla essence	1 bottle	2.00	2.00
2 kilo	Granulated sugar	2 kilo	0.85	1.70
3 kilo	Cake flour (1.5 K)	3 kilo	0.50	1.00
			TOTAL	£4.70

Requisitioned by: _BM Puffing_

Figure 10.5 *An example of a food storeroom requisition note*

value of opening stock + purchases during the period – requisitions made in the same period = value of closing stock

This will highlight any differences and indicate the efficiency of the storekeeper and of the system used to obtain goods when the storekeeper is off duty.

3 To list slow moving items. This will bring to the attention of the purchasing officer, the head chef, etc., those items which are in stock and for which there has been no demand, since the last stocktake. Usually these items will then be put on to a menu to sell them before they deteriorate, or returned to the wholesaler and credit obtained.

4 To compare the usage of food with food sales to calculate the food percentage and gross profit.

5 As a deterrent against loss and pilferage.

6 To determine the rate of stock turnover for different groups of foods. This is calculated by the formula:

$$\frac{\text{cost of food consumed}}{\text{average value of stock at cost price}} = \text{rate of stock turnover in a given period}$$

For example, in a 28-day trading period the cost of food consumed was £3,000. The opening stock on day 1 was £800 and the closing stock on day 28 was £700.

$$\text{rate of stock turnover} = \frac{3000}{\dfrac{800 + 700}{2}} = \frac{3000}{750} = 4.0$$

This means that in the 28-day trading period the total value of stock turned over four times and that an average of one week's stock was held during the period.

The rate of stock turnover will vary depending on the frequency of delivery, the commodity, the size of storage space available and the amount of money the establishment is prepared to tie up in food stocks.

Typical stock turnover figures for a month are at least twenty for perishable items (i.e., deliveries most days) and four for non perishable items (i.e., deliveries once a week).

Stocktaking lists should be printed in a standard format and in some way related to the lay-out of the storeroom. This is so that stocktaking can be done methodically moving around the storeroom so that nothing is missed out; also, so that it aids the checking of figure-work by facilitating the comparing of like pages with like pages from previous stock-takes to ensure that there is normally a near standard stock of items between periods.

See Figure 10.6 for an example of a food stocktaker's report and Figure 10.7 for an example of a storeroom variation report.

Stocktaking will typically be done every trading period (for example, each month, every four weeks), by staff such as the storekeeper and head cellarman, under the supervision of a member from the food and beverage management or control staff. Ideally, the stocktaking should take place at the end of a trading period and before the operational start of the next trading period. This usually means that the stocktaking will take place late in the evening or early in the morning. The end-of-year stocktake is usually done in greater detail and with some more thoroughness than for a trading period and will involve more staff, usually including the head of the control department to oversee and manage it. Professional stocktakers will often be used particularly for the end-of-year stocktake.

10.4   Receiving of beverages

The objectives for beverage receiving are similar in many ways to those of food receiving. However, as the value of beverage purchases and the ensuing profits from the sale of beverages are high, it is important that due attention is given to the receiving of beverages.

The main objectives are to ensure that:

1 The quantity of beverages delivered matches that which has been ordered. This requires a methodical approach to checking the goods against the purchase order and the delivery note. Items would be in standard units of crates, cases, etc., with standard contents of a specific size. Crates and cases should be opened to check for such things as empty, missing or broken bottles.

2 The quality inspection is simple, but again requires a thorough and methodical approach.

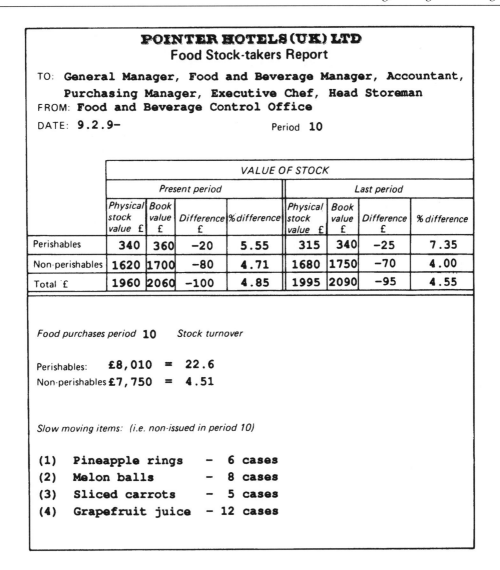

Figure 10.6 *An example of a food stocktaker's report, highlighting variances between physical and book values of stock, and also slow-moving items (possible dead stock)*

It involves such things as checking the brand name and label on each item, the alcohol proof, the vintage and shipper, against the delivery note and the purchase order.

3 The prices stated on the delivery note are in accordance with the negotiated prices shown on the purchase order form.

4 When the quantity or quality (or both) of the beverage delivered is not in accordance with the purchase order, or an item is omitted from the order, that a request for credit note is raised by the receiving clerk or cellarman.

5 An accurate record is made in the goods received book recording details of the delivery.

6 An accurate record is kept of all chargeable empties delivered and returned.

7 Deliveries of beverages are timetabled with the suppliers, often to an afternoon, when receiving and cellar staff are normally not so busy and the receiving area is free from other deliveries.

POINTER HOTELS (UK) LTD
Storeroom Variation Report

Trading period: 4

BIN no.:	ITEM	STOCK		ACTUAL STOCK		UNIT	AMOUNT
		Actual	Book	Over	Short	Cost	Over/(Short) £
93	A 2½'s Pineapple Pieces	16	18	–	2	1.20	(2.40)
87	A 2½'s Fruit Salad	22 Css	24 Css	–	2 Css	16.00	(32.00)
82	A 10's Grapefruit Juice	18 Css	15 Css	–	3 Css	4.80	(14.40)
74	Apples Solid Pack A 10's	42 Css	36 Css	–	6 Css	16.50	(99.00)
123	A 10's Carrots Sliced	17 Css	20 Css	–	3 Css	6.60	(19.80)
	Total						(£167.60)

Figure 10.7   *An example of a storeroom variation report identifying items of difference between the actual physical stock-take made and the book record of what should be held in stock*

10.5   Storing and issuing of beverages

10.5.1   Storing

Once beverages are received they must be removed immediately to the cellar and a tight level of control maintained at all times. The storage of beverages is ideally separated into five areas as follows:

1 The main storage area for spirits and red wine held at a dry and draught-free temperature of 55°–60°F (13°–16°C). This area is also used for the general collection and preparation of orders for the various bars and the storage of keg beers when there is a reasonable turnover.
2 A refrigerated area of 50°F (10°C) for the storage of white and sparkling wines.
3 A further refrigerated area of 43°–47°F (6°–8°C). This is really necessary only when the turnover of kegs is slow as otherwise they may be stored at 55°–60°F (13°–16°C).
4 An area held at a temperature of 55°F (13°C) for the storage of bottle beers and soft drinks.
5 A totally separate area, from those above, for the storage of empty bottles, kegs and crates. This area needs to be as tightly controlled as

the beverage storage area, not only because of the returnable value of the crates and bottles, etc., but to prevent free access by bar staff when an 'empty for full' bottle method of issuing is in operation.

The merchandise is unpacked in the cellar and stored correctly (table wines with an alcohol content of less than 16 per cent by volume are stored on their sides, bottles of fortified wine, spirits and vintage ports are stored upright) on shelves or racks in the same order as on the standard bottle code/bin list. The objective for preparing a standard bottle code/bin list is to eliminate the confusion of bottle sizes, spelling of names and different brands, and to establish an appropriate starting point for the control of beverages. All requisitions, inventories, wine lists, etc., are related to the code/bin list. An extract from a list could be as follows:

Bin numbers 100–149 English table wines
Bin numbers 150–199 Imported white wines
Bin numbers 200–299 Imported red wines
Bin numbers 300–399 Sparkling wines
Bin numbers 400–419 Scotch and Irish whisky
Bin numbers 420–449 Gin

To avoid confusion, the letter M is usually

assigned for magnums, H for half bottles, S for split bottles.

10.5.2 Cellar records

As the value of cellar stocks is high, it is usual for the following cellar records to be kept.

10.5.2.1 A cellar inwards book

This provides accurate reference to all beverages coming into the cellar, and posting data for the cellarman's bin cards. Whenever necessary it is a useful check against the perpetual beverage inventory ledger held in the food and beverage control or accounts office. An example is given in Figure 10.8.

10.5.2.2 Bin cards

These are provided for each individual type of beverage held in stock and record all deliveries and issues made, the cards being fixed on the shelves or racks against each beverage, the bin card numbers referring to the same bin numbers as the wine list and originating from the stan-dard bottle code list. See Figure 10.9 for an example.

10.5.2.3 Cellar control book

This provides a record of all daily deliveries to the cellar and the daily issues of each beverage from the cellar to the various bars and should cross-check with the entries on the bin cards and the perpetual inventory ledger held in the food control or the accounts office. See Figure 10.10 for an example.

10.5.2.4 Beverages perpetual inventory ledger

This master ledger, which is prepared in the control or accounts office, consists of cards (see Figure 10.11) prepared for each individual type of beverage held in stock. The purpose is to keep a daily record of any purchases of the separate types of beverages and of the quantities issued from the cellar to each individual bar or other area, and to record a perpetual inventory balance for each item. The information is obtained from the suppliers' delivery notes or invoices (adjusted at times with credit notes) and the daily beverage requisition notes from the differ-

POINTER HOTELS (UK) LTD
Cellar Inwards Book

Date. **6/2/9–**

Date	Beverage	Delivery or invoice no.	Bin code no.	Bottle	Halves	Other sizes
8/2/9–	Port	12534	505	24	–	–
8/2/9–	Sherry	9321	550	36	–	–
9/2/9–	Chianti (Red)	53911	287	12	24	–
12/2/9–	Mateus	7741	391	36	36	–
12/2/9–	Travel	7743	393	24	48	–
12/2/9–	Blue Nun	5354	192	120	24	–
12/2/9–	Crown of Crowns	5354	194	120	48	–

Figure 10.8 *An extract from a cellar inwards book*

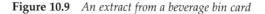

POINTER HOTELS (UK) LTD
BIN CARD

Bin No. **423**   Size: **Bottle**

Type: **White Horse Whisky**

Date	Received	Issued to bar				Balance
		A	B	C	TOTAL	
5/2/9–	12	2	–	1	3	9
7/2/9–	–	1	1	2	4	5
8/2/9–	24	2	2	2	6	23
9/2/9–	–	2	1	2	5	18
11/2/9–	–	3	2	1	6	12
12/2/9–	12	3	2	2	7	17
13/2/9–	–	2	2	1	5	12

Figure 10.9 *An extract from a beverage bin card*

ent bars. When the physical stocktaking of the cellar is undertaken, the physical stocktake figures should match to those in the perpetual inventory ledger.

10.5.2.5 *Ullages and breakages*

It is necessary for any ullages and breakages to be recorded on a standard form, together with an explanation, and countersigned by a member of the food and beverage management department. The frequency of the recording of any ullages and breakages would determine the necessity for management to take corrective action.

The term 'ullage' is used to cover all substandard beverages such as bottles of weeping wines, bottles of wine with faulty corks, unfit barrels of beer, etc., which, whenever possible, would be returned to the supplier for replacement. Breakages of bottled beverages usually occur by mishandling by cellar and bar staff.

10.5.2.6 *Empties return book*

Many of the containers of beverages such as crates, kegs, beer bottles, soda syphons, etc. are charged for by the supplier against a delivery. It

is therefore necessary that control is maintained on these charged items to ensure that they are returned to the supplier and the correct credit obtained. A container record book is required which records all containers received from the various suppliers, containers returned and the balance matching the stocktake of containers.

10.5.2.7 *Hospitality book*

This is necessary to record the issue of drinks to the kitchen and other grades of staff as laid down by the company policy.

10.5.3 Issuing of beverages

Issuing of beverages should take place at set times during the day and only against a requisition note signed by an authorized person, for example head barman, banqueting head waiter, etc. Ideally when the requisition is a large one it should be handed in several hours before the items are required to allow the cellar staff plenty of time to assemble the order together. Requisition notes are usually made in duplicate, one copy being retained by the cellarman so that

POINTER HOTELS(UK) LTD
Cellar Control Book

Date: **6/2/9–**

Bin code no. (1)	Item (2)	Unit (3)	Cost (4)	Opening stock (5)	Purchases (6)	Sub total (7)	Issues M	T	W	T	F	S	S (8)	Total issues (9)	Returns (10)	Book stock level (11)	Balance by stocktake (12)	Variances +	– (13)	Value issues at cost (14)	Value of balance c/f at cost (15)	Remarks (16)
901	Calvados	Bottle	10.50	4	6	10	–	–	–	1	–	–	–	1	–	9	9	–	–	10.50	94.50	–
914	Pernod	Bottle	9.50	10	–	10	–	1	–	1	–	–	–	2	–	8	8	–	–	19.00	76.00	–
918	Strega	Bottle	10.00	4	6	10	–	1	1	1	–	–	–	3	–	7	7			30.00	70.00	–
919	Tia Maria	Halves	4.00	14	–	14	1	1	1	1	–	–	–	4	–	10	10			16.00	40.00	–
924	Kirsch	Halves	5.00	8	–	8	–	1	1	–	1	–	–	2	–	6	6			10.00	30.00	–

Figure 10.10 *An extract from a cellar control book*

Explanation of columns

1 From a standard bottle code/bin list.
2, 3, 4, 6 From delivery note/invoice.
5 From last stocktake report.
7 Column 5 plus column 6.
8 Summation of bar requisition notes.
9 Total of all column 8 issues.
10 From credit notes.
11 From a perpetual inventory.
12 From physical stocktake.
13 Any deviations between columns 11 and 12.
14 Column 4 multiplied by column 9.
15 Column 4 multiplied by column 12.
16 Any deviations to be explained

POINTER HOTELS (UK) LTD
Beverage Perpetual Inventory Ledger

Bin No.: **129**

Type: **Chateau "Elstead"**

Size: **Bottle**

Purchase Record					Perpetual Inventory and Issue Record				Issues						
Date (1)	Supplier (2)	No. (3)	Unit cost (4)	Total amount (5)	Date (6)	Opening inventory (7)	Total purchases (8)	Total available (9)	Bar A (10)	Bar B (10)	Bar C (10)	Bar D (10)	Misc (10)	Total (11)	Closing inventory (12)
5/2/9–	Smith	36	3.20	115.20	5/2/9–	12	34	48	2	4	12	–	–	18	30
9/2/9–	Smith	36	3.20	115.20	9/2/9–	30	36	66	2	2	48	–	–	52	14
–	–	–	–	–	10/2/9–	14	–	14	2	2	–	–	–	4	10
12/2/9–	Smith	72	3.20	230.00	12/2/9–	10	72	82	2	4	48	–	–	54	28

Ullages and breakages ← (column 10, Misc)

Figure 10.11 An extract from a beverage perpetual inventory ledger

Explanation of columns:

1–4 From delivery note/invoice.
5 Columns 3 multiplied by column 4.
6 From delivery note/invoice or requisition note.
7 Same figure as last closing inventory from column 12 for previous period.
8 Same as column 3.
9 Column 7 plus column 8.
10 Distribution of issues from daily requisition notes.
11 Total of all column 10 issues.
12 Column 9 minus column 11.

entries can be made to the cellar records and then it is passed to the control or accounts office, while the second copy is retained by the person who originated the requisition and handed in with the daily takings and other control documents. See Figure 10.12 for an example of a requisition note.

The pricing of issues for beverages is different from that for food in that two prices are recorded, the cost price and the selling price. The cost price is recorded to credit the cellar account and for trading account and balance sheet purposes. The selling price is recorded for control purposes to measure the sales potential of a selling outlet using the basic formula:

opening stock + purchases – closing stock = total beverage consumed
total beverage consumed = beverage revenue

It should be noted that the above formula may be calculated for the value of stock and purchases either:

1 At cost price in order to compare the usage with the actual sales and to ascertain the profit margin and beverage gross profit.
2 At sales price in order to compare potential sales with the actual recorded sales.

It is usual for the beverage revenue to be different from the sales potential figure because of such factors as a high percentage of mixed drinks being sold or full bottle sales being made over the counter of a bar.

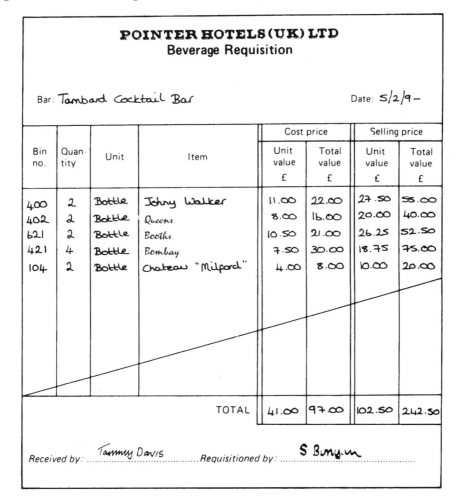

Figure 10.12 *An example of a beverage requisition form*

10.6   Stocktaking of beverages

The main objectives of stocktaking are:

1 To determine the total value of all beverages held in stock. This will indicate if too much is held in stock and if it is in line with the financial and catering policies.
2 To compare the actual value of beverages held in the cellar at a specific time with the book value of the stock which will have been calculated with the simple formula:
value of opening stock + purchases during period – requisitions during the same period = value of closing stock
3 To identify slow-moving items.
4 To compare beverage usage at cost with beverage sales in order to calculate beverage gross profit.
5 To deter pilferage and check security and control systems.
6 To determine the rate of stock turnover.

The value and volume of the closing stock are also checked against the information from the perpetual inventory ledger cards for each beverage. The stocktake should highlight any differences and indicate the efficiency of the cellar staff and the beverage control system.

The rate of stock turnover is calculated by the formula:

$$\frac{\text{cost of beverage consumed}}{\text{average value of stock at cost price}} = \frac{\text{rate of stock}}{\text{turnover}}$$

The rate of stock turnover for beverages will vary from unit to unit depending on such things as the size and type of the unit and its storage facilities, its location and whether it 'puts down' wine as an investment. An acceptable rate of turnover for a year is six, that is, the average stock held is equal to two months' supply. When the desired rate of turnover is not achieved, it is a useful exercise to calculate separately the rate of turnover for the varying broad groups of beverages held (for example, red wine, white wine, sparkling wine, spirits, liqueurs, beers and minerals), to check if turnover is particularly poor in one or more of the groups. The rate of stock turnover may be controlled by instituting 'par stocks' or stock levels based on usage, estimated demand, case sizes, and delivery times.

The stocktaking should be undertaken by staff from the control or accounts department together with members of the food and beverage management team. As is the case with food stocktaking, it is necessary that this be done at the end of every trading period and before, if possible, the beginning of the next period. This requires staff to work late at night or early in the mornings and at times at the weekends.

10.7   References

Coltman, M. (1987). *Hospitality Management Accounting*, 3rd edn. New York: Van Nostrand Reinhold.

Cracknell, H. L., Kaufmann, R. J., Nobis, F. (1988). *Practical Professional Catering*. London: Macmillan.

11
Food and beverage production methods

11.1 Introduction

Food production may be defined as that phase of the food flow (that is, from the purchasing of the foods to service to the customer) mainly concerned with the processing of raw, semi-prepared, or prepared foodstuffs. The resulting product may be in a ready-to-serve state, for example in the conventional method (cook-serve); or it may undergo some form of preservation, for example cook-chill or cook-freeze, before being served to the customer.

Beverage production may be defined as the processing of the raw, semi-prepared, or prepared beverage product, so that it is in a ready-to-serve state before being served to the customer. For example, a raw beverage product such as tea would need to be fully processed before being served, a semi-prepared product such as a cordial would require only partial preparation, and a bottled fruit juice or bottle of wine may be termed a fully prepared beverage product. The fine dividing line between food and beverage production and food and beverage service is not always distinguishable. The point at which production ends, and service begins, is often difficult to define. It is often necessary, therefore, to include certain aspects of, for example, food service when describing food production methods, in order that the production method may be seen in the context of the whole catering operation, and not in isolation.

The decision as to which food and beverage production method to use in a particular catering operation is taken at the initial planning stage – at this point the market to be catered for, and hence the type of catering facility to be offered, has been decided upon. The initial planning of a food service facility is critical to the long-term success of the operation, and one which must be afforded time, finance and commitment in order to avoid costly mistakes later.

11.2 The planning of food service facilities

The planning of food service facilities is more complex than many other types of planning projects. This is due to some of its unique characteristics, including the following:

1 The wide variety, choice and grades of raw materials available.
2 The high perishability of some raw materials.
3 The wide variety of semi-prepared and prepared products available.
4 The perishability of the end product.
5 The fast turnover of some foods, for example items delivered fresh in the morning may be prepared and served to the customer at lunchtime, and the revenue banked by the afternoon.
6 The product is rarely taken to the customer, the customer has to go to the product to purchase it, and consume it, usually on the premises.
7 The product cannot be stored for any length of time.
8 A wide variety of customers may be catered for within the same establishment.
9 There may be a variety of production and service methods in operation in any one outlet.

An inherent problem in food production planning is that customer demand for the food service facilities is not constant; the restaurant, cafeteria or fast food outlet is only in demand at certain times during the day, mainly breakfast, lunch and dinner, and this results in peak periods of activity at certain times during the day, and troughs of comparative inactivity in between. This problem is further compounded by the catering facility having to offer different menu items or 'products' for each meal period, and sometimes even a different type of food service for the different meal periods. For example, a hotel restaurant may offer a continental style buffet service for breakfast, a table d'hôte menu at lunchtime with a plated service, and an à la carte menu in the evening with silver service.

It is necessary to emphasize the importance of efficient food service planning. It involves a number of interrelated processes, each dependent on the other, which together form a totally integrated system. Cost limits are always present for each stage of the planning process, and funds are allocated specifically for the actual building, the interior furnishings, equipment, etc.; such funds must be used wisely, as short term savings often result in long-term costs. Badly planned facilities suffer daily because of initial poor planning, their poor labour utilization, loss in food quality standards, high running costs, and general lack of acceptance by customers.

11.2.1   Objectives

The first step in the planning of a catering facility is a written statement of the operation's objectives. The primary objective of a food service operation must be the provision of a catering outlet aimed at satisfying a particular market segment of the population. Allied to this main objective are the catering facility's other objectives, some taking precedence over others in different catering situations; for example, a commercial restaurant's main objective may be to maximize returns on capital in the shortest possible period, whereas an industrial cafeteria's main objective may be the provision of a subsidized catering facility in which case the net profit is no longer the most important objective.

General planning objectives can, however, be identified for all types of catering facilities and these may be listed as follows:

1 *Customer appeal.* The main objective of a catering facility is to provide a catering service for a clearly defined sector of the market. Once the sector of the market to be catered for has been identified the planning of the facility can begin.

When customers enter a restaurant, cafeteria, or any other type of food service operation, they bring with them certain expectations about the type of operation it is, the standard of food and the level of service they will receive; the image created by the catering facility must be in congruence with their image of the restaurant if the facility is to have appeal to customers. It is important that this harmonization between the customer and catering operation is extended throughout the facility. For example, in a high-class restaurant the customer would expect an extensive à la carte menu, silver service, only linen on the tables, the service staff to be correctly attired in uniforms, etc. All these individual aspects of the operation combine to portray a total picture to the customer. It is important, therefore, that at the planning stage the catering operation is planned as a whole so that all the different aspects of the production and service combine to produce a facility that is aimed at a particular market segment.

2 *Cost control.* Whatever the type of catering facility, costs must be controlled; in a catering operation these include the initial planning and building costs, and the daily running costs, such as food, labour, and fuel. Some operations are built specifically with a profit target to achieve such as commercial restaurants and cafeterias, and even those operations such as subsidized catering facilities should be aiming to keep costs to a minimum so that any 'profits' made, may be put back into the operation, and hence reduce the overall running costs of the operation.

3 *Facilitate production and service.* This involves ergonomically designing the layout of production and service areas and equipment, both in the kitchen and the restaurant and bars. Workplace design is particularly important: which equipment should be mounted; and which should be free-standing; storage facilities; the height and width of the working benches; the height, size, and shape of tables; the lighting, heating, and noise limitation requirements; etc. All of these attributes of a food service facility, if carefully planned, result in a safely designed working area and a smooth flow of employees and materials.

4 *Materials handling*. The movement of materials in a catering operation should be planned so that minimal handling is involved. Where possible the materials flow should be as direct as possible, for example from the storage area to the work bench for preparation. Cross-flows of traffic and back-tracking should be avoided as they are not only time consuming, but they are also potential accident hazards. Many aids are available to the planner when designing materials handling for a catering operation: flow process charts, string diagrams, travel charts, etc., are all aids to designing a materials-handling system that minimizes actual handling. The time spent by employees handling materials may be translated into labour costs – while the employee is transporting or moving the materials, he is not preparing them ready for sale.

Mechanical aids should be used where they will alleviate the human handling of materials, for example conveyor belts, trolleys, carts, etc. These can all be incorporated into the original plans. Any mechanical aids or labour-saving equipment should be purchased only if it is seen to be cost effective.

5 *Labour utilization*. The planning of efficient labour utilization is very dependent on the use of management tools such as work study, motion economy, etc. The tasks that are to be performed in the production and service areas of the catering operation must be identified and the most efficient method of performing those tasks analysed, so that detailed job descriptions and work schedules may be produced. The ever increasing labour costs in catering operations today necessitate the planning of efficient food production and service areas that result in greater employee productivity.

6 *Supervision and management*. At the planning stage consideration must also be given to the task of supervising and managing the catering operation, particularly the production and service employees. This involves allocating adequate time and facilities for meetings between the management and staff, training and demonstrations, etc., so that this becomes an ongoing process by management rather than something that is available to all employees at their commencement of employment, but is never refreshed.

Management of the catering facility in other areas should also be given consideration; for example, supervising the day-to-day food, labour, and fuel costs. Efficient feedback information systems need to be incorporated that are able to supply management with the type of information necessary for them to make decisions concerning the efficient running of the catering operation.

7 *Hygiene and safety standards*. Hygiene and safety standards are both factors that must be built into a catering operation at the planning stage; this is essential for the well being of both the customer and the employees. In the UK at present environmental health officers have powers to inspect and, if necessary, close premises whose hygiene standards are not high enough. The acts governing the hygiene control of premises and the current fire regulations also have to be taken into account and strictly observed by all catering establishments.

8 *Cleaning and maintenance*. Closely related to the safety and sanitary conditions of the food service facility is the consideration at the planning stage for easy cleaning and maintenance of the premises. Here a number of factors need to be taken into account: the construction and finishes of floors, walls and ceilings; the design of the equipment, such as mobile units that can be pulled clear of the wall and cleaned behind, sufficient space under the equipment so that the floor can be washed, etc. The regular maintenance of equipment is also particularly important if costly break downs and possible accidents are to be avoided.

9 *Flexibility*. Flexibility at the initial planning stage can save on an operation's long-term costs. Most catering facilities undergo some form of change during their life cycle, and advance planning for this can help the transition or change-over period considerably. Most changes in a food service operation occur in the materials being used and/or in the production techniques; for example, the introduction of a high percentage of convenience foods to an operation would reduce its labour and equipment requirements and more kitchen space would become available. Possible changes such as these should be considered at the initial planning stage, so that they may be

efficiently managed by the operation when and if they become necessary. It is not uncommon that all of the finance to plan and operate a production facility is not available initially and that the planning has to be implemented in stages when the finance is available, often over a two- to three-year period. For example, a catering operation may not be able to purchase some specific items of equipment until the second year of operation; it is important at the planning stage that this has been taken into account and that the basic services of gas, electricity, water, drainage, lighting, ventilation, etc. are fully accessible and have allowed for an increase in capacity.

If the optimum use is to be made of available money, materials, and manpower, the major requirements listed above should be used as the basis for planning a food service facility. Without adequate planning at the initial stage, the operation will lack direction and may result in trying to be 'everything to everyone'. The operation may then be faced with the situation of attempting to cater for mixed markets, for which it has not been designed, and therefore does not have the necessary facilities.

11.3 Food production methods

In examining food production methods currently in operation, reference must be made to the traditions of catering which have had a profound effect on the production methods in operation today.

Food production methods in the catering industry evolved over a period of time when there was an abundance of labour. The design of the traditional kitchen, first introduced into the UK in the latter half of the nineteenth century, grew up around the division of tasks into *parties* (similar tasks with numerous foods were carried out by a particular group of people). This was the development of the *partie* system. The rigid demarcation between the sections meant that the staffing ratio was high in comparison with the number of meals served.

During the first half of the twentieth century

there was little or no technical change in the kitchens of hotels and restaurants. Most managers and chefs had been trained in the old traditional methods which gave reasonably satisfactory results, and to them there seemed little reason to change. It is only during the last thirty years that changes in the old traditional methods have evolved. These changes were slow to appear and started in the manufacturing industry rather than in the kitchens of hotels and restaurants. Technical research was done by the major firms of food suppliers and their products slowly became accepted by the catering industry, as skilled catering staff began to be in short supply. This was further encouraged by the rising costs of space that was necessary for a traditional kitchen. Traditional kitchen tasks were beginning to disappear at increasing speed. In 1966 the first cook-freeze operation in the UK began, and from this derivatives have evolved from both cook-freeze and cook-chill methods. The following represents a study of the main food and beverage production methods currently in operation.

11.3.1 Conventional methods

11.3.1.1 *Traditional partie method*

In the conventional partie method, the majority of food is purchased raw, very little falling into what we now call the 'convenience foods' category. Facilities are provided for the receipt and storage of goods, the preparation, cooking, holding and service of food, and for dishwashing facilities (see Figure 11.1).

During each day the use of labour is intermittent, rising to a peak just before the service of each meal. The same situation exists with the cooking equipment, good utilization for short periods, but overall poor utilization of capital plant. This in turn leads to poor use of electricity and gas appliances which are often turned on in the morning and left on during the day, although only efficiently utilized for a few hours. Altogether it is an expensive way of running a kitchen; expensive because of the manpower needed to operate it, and its space, equipment and energy requirements.

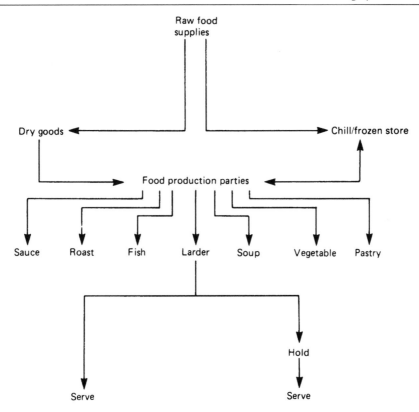

Figure 11.1   *The main division of activities in the conventional food production method*

11.3.1.2   *Conventional production with convenience foods*

Convenience foods may be introduced into a traditional production kitchen. Conventional production using convenience foods may range from a partial to a virtually complete reliance on the use of the wide variety of convenience foods now available. However, the best use of such convenience foods can only be by means of a planned catering system. It is basic to the systems approach that the operation be considered as a whole, taking into account the effects that a change in one part of the system might have on another part. Therefore, if convenience foods are to be introduced into a traditional kitchen previously using all fresh produce, the effects upon labour, equipment, space, and more important, the customer, should all be considered.

11.3.2   Centralized production methods

Centralized production methods involve the separation of the production and service components of the food flow system either by place or time or both. Food that is centrally produced is either then distributed to the point of service in batches or is pre-portioned; it may be transported in a ready-to-serve state, for example hot, or it may need some form of regeneration in a satellite or end-kitchen, for example chilled or frozen food. This form of food production became popular in the 1970s and 1980s mainly due to the demand in the welfare sector for this type of centralized production and its associated savings. However, because of the changing nature of the hospital catering service in particular, CPUs are no longer in such demand and a number have recently been closed due to their high operating costs.

BAR SERVICE

APERITIFS AND SPIRITS

A RANGE OF DRINKS FROM AROUND THE WORLD TO WHET THE APPETITE

SWEET AND DRY VERMOUTH. CAMPARI
PRIMERO AMONTILADO SHERRY
JOHNNIE WALKER BLUE LABEL WHISKY, BOURBON, RYE,
TANQUERAY GIN, BACARDI RUM, SMIRNOFF BLACK LABEL VODKA
GLENMORANGIE 18 YEAR OLD SINGLE MALT WHISKY

COCKTAILS

prepared to your choice from the range of beverages carried on board

SOFT DRINKS

a selection of traditional and modern soft drinks for all tastes

FRESH ORANGE JUICE, TOMATO JUICE, APPLE JUICE
HIGHLAND SPRING: STILL OR SPARKLING MINERAL WATER
COCA-COLA
SCHWEPPES TONIC WATER, BITTER LEMON
LEMONADE, SODA WATER, MALVERN MINERAL WATER
CANADA DRY GINGER ALE

BEERS

ALE, LAGER, LOW ALOCHOL LAGER

DIGESTIFS

AN EXCELENT SELECTION OF CLASSIC AGED DIGESTIFS AND TRADITIONAL LIQUEURS
FOR YOU TO ENJOY

GRAHAM'S 20 YEAR OLD TAWNY PORT
FRAPIN VIP XO GRANDE CHAMPAGNE COGNAC
DRAMBUIE, COINTREAU, BAILEYS, TIA MARIA
AMARETTO DI SARONNO, BENEDICTINE, GRAND MARNIER

BRUNCH

MELON AND MANGO COCKTAIL WITH
PAPAYA AND BLACK GRAPES

SELECTION OF WARM ROLLS, MADEIRA CAKE
AND AMARETTI BISCUITS

SCRAMBLED EGG WITH LINCOLNSHIRE HERBED SAUSAGE
GRILLED HAM, TOMATO, MUSHROOMS AND FRIED POTATOES

SEARED LAMB MEDALLIONS WITH ROSEMARY GRAVY
VICHY CARROTS, CELERIAC PUREE, FRENCH BEANS
AND ROAST POTATOES

VEGETARIAN AUBERGINE LASAGNE WITH ROAST
STUFFED PEPPERS AND OYSTER MUSHROOMS

CORN FED LEMON CHICKEN WITH AVOCADO GRAPEFRUIT
SALAD SERVED WITH HERBED VINAIGRETTE DRESSING

MRS BUTLERS VINTAGE FARMHOUSE LANCASHIRE, BLUE STILTON
AND FOUNTAINS GOLD CHEESES WITH CELERY, GRAPES, MELON
AND STRAWBERRY

COFFEE, DECAFFEINATED COFFEE, TEA AND HERBAL OR
FRUIT TEA WITH CHOCOLATES

AS AN ALTERNATIVE TO THE FULL MENU WE ARE PLEASED TO
OFFER A LIMITED SELECTION OF FRESHLY MADE SANDWICHES
INCLUDING SMOKED SALMON, BRIE AND ROAST BEEF WITH HORSERADISH

Figure 11.2 *Menu for a brunch served on British Airways Concorde flight from London to New York*

DINNER

APPETIZERS

Seared salmon tranche, marinated prawns and cracked wheat salad

OR

Orange and endive salad with crumbled Roquefort and Lancashire cheese

Mixed seasonal salad served with classic vinaigrette or creamy basil dressing

MAIN COURSES

Grilled fillet steak with Worcester sauce butter, red pepper, French beans and spiced potato wedges

OR

North Sea cod with Parmesan crust, fresh vegetables, new potatoes and Hollandaise sauce

OR

Confit of duck with Madeira sauce, braised red cabbage, caramelized apple
and butternut squash mustard mash

OR

Glazed Haloumi cheese and spiced leeks
accompanied by cream cheese rösti potatoes, black olives and tomato sauce

DESSERT

Diplomat pudding with caramel and double cream

Fresh fruit

Selection of English and Continental cheese served with Scottish oatcakes

Coffee, decaffeinated coffee, tea, herbal tea or fruit tea served with chocolates

Well-Being in the Air offers a healthy alternative.

BREAKFAST

Brazilian inspired "The Girl from Ipanema" energizer drink
with guava, yoghurt and banana

Citrus fruit appetizer
with cinnamon and ginger

Fruit'n Fibre cereal

Fruit yoghurt

Scrambled eggs with Lincolnshire sausages, grilled bacon rashers,
tomato, mushrooms and fried bread croûton

OR

Cheese and tomato omelet
served with asparagus, mushrooms and hash-brown potatoes

OR

Blueberry pancakes with maple syrup,
grilled Canadian bacon and tomato

Selection of warm breads and pastries including croissants,
Swiss cheese Danish pastries and carrot muffins
served with butter and preserve

Coffee, decaffeinated coffee, tea, herbal tea or fruit tea

REFRESHMENTS

Fresh seasonal fruit

Mixed grilled brochette

OR

Vegetable lasagne

Fruit yoghurt

Bakery selection of warm rolls served with butter

Coffee, decaffeinated coffee or tea

Figure 11.3 *A dinner menu – new Club World class on a British Airways flight from London to Rio de Janeiro Note*: The meals are prepared in central kitchens at a major airport, at times chilled or frozen, transported to the planes, stored and later reheated, assembled onto serving trays and served during the flight. These menus illustrate the quality of food served to passengers under severe space and time restrictions.

The advantages of centralized production include:

1 The separation of the production and service activities allows the unit to work at a consistent level of efficiency rather than 'peaks' and 'troughs' often found in a traditional kitchen.
2 By concentrating the skilled production staff at the CPU, a higher standard of preparation and presentation should be possible as satellite kitchens do not require such skilled staff.
3 Bulk purchasing reduces the raw material costs and helps reduce the overall cost per meal.
4 The introduction of a 'storage stage' between production and service allows the production unit to work to maximum efficiency and with a better utilization of staff and equipment.
5 Better working conditions and more social hours are generally available for the production teams.
6 Energy consumption can be reduced by careful scheduling and by a continuous run of single products.

The disadvantages of centralized production include:

1 The high capital investment of planning and constructing a centralized production unit.
2 Unless fully utilized the cost per meal can rise dramatically.
3 Production failures or stoppages due to power failure, hygiene problems or food contamination outbreaks can quickly escalate and have much greater repercussions than a problem in an individual kitchen.

11.3.2.1 Basic principles of cook-freeze and cook-chill systems

1 That all raw foods used should be of a good microbiological quality.

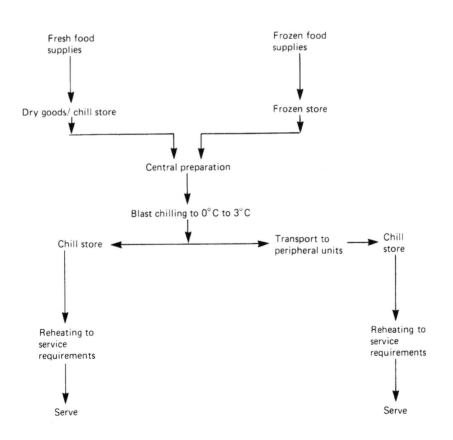

Figure 11.4 *The main division of activities in the cook-chill food production method*

2 That the initial cooking of the foods will ensure the destruction of the vegetative stages of any pathogenic micro-organism present.

3 As some micro-organisms produce spores which are not killed by normal cooking procedures, it is vital that the temperature range from + 7°C to 60°C at which these organisms can quickly multiply, must be covered as quickly as possible to restrict growth during cooking. The same attention needs to be applied when regenerating the foods.

4 Cross contamination must be avoided throughout the process, particularly between that of raw and cooked foods. Physical separation of pre-preparation and cooking areas is essential to aid this.

5 The storage and distribution conditions for cooked and chilled foods must be strictly controlled to ensure their quality and safety.

6 The reheating and service procedures for the food must be strictly adhered to, to ensure the food's safety with the temperature of all food being strictly monitored.

11.3.2.2   *The nutrition and flavour of the food*

The nutrient content and quality of any food being processed is related to:

1 *The quality of the raw food.*
2 *The general storage conditions.* Loss will occur, particularly with fresh vegetables, the longer they are stored prior to preparation or in water after preparation prior to cooking. Quality produce kept at the correct storage temperatures with as short a storage life as is conveniently possible is the ideal.
3 *The type of processing.* Any over-cooking, over-regeneration, poor refrigeration storage and any delay between re-heating and consumption all add to vitamin loss and poor palatability.

11.3.3   *Cook-freeze production*

The term cook-freeze refers to a catering system based on the full cooking of food followed by fast freezing, with storage at a controlled low temperature of –18°C or below, followed by subsequent complete reheating close to the consumer, prior to prompt consumption.

Cook-freeze is a complete food production process from the initial raw food through to the final service of the product.

- *Raw food should be purchased against a tight specification to ensure quality and consistency.* For large operations laboratory testing of all incoming foods should be a standard procedure. Inspection of suppliers' premises with regular checks on their quality and control procedures are also standard practice.
- *Food storage.* All foods should be kept under strict temperature control, in hygienic conditions until required for preparation. Care should be taken to avoid cross contamination and to ensure strict rotation of all stock.
- *Pre-preparation.* This includes all preparation of foods prior to any cooking. It is standard practice to keep this stage in the process physically separate from any further stage for hygiene and safety reasons with all staff handling raw foods to be restricted to this area.

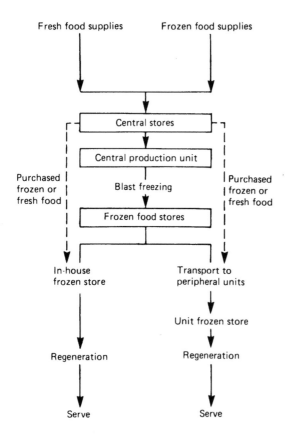

Figure 11.5   *The main division of activities in the cook-freeze food production method*

- *Cooking*. Ideally, cooking should be done in batches. The cooking must be sufficient to ensure that heat penetrates to the centre of any food and results in the destruction of non-sporing pathogens. This is achieved when the centre of the food reaches a temperature of at least 70°C and is held there for at least two minutes. This should always be carefully checked using a probe thermometer. At times it may be necessary to adjust the recipes to account for large scale batch production and to account for chemical changes in the food as a result of storage for up to eight weeks at very low temperatures.

- *Portioning*. Within a time limit of thirty minutes all hot food should be portioned into single or multi-portions prior to freezing. Whatever type of container is used the depth of the food should be restricted to a maximum of 50mm.

- *Blast freezing*. In order to preserve food quality and prevent any growth of bacteria all cooked food should be placed in a blast freezer within thirty minutes of final cooking and being portioned. Food should be frozen to at least –5°C within ninety minutes of entering the freezer and subsequently brought down to a storage temperatures of at least –1 8°C.

- *Cold storage*. The shelf life of pre-cooked frozen food varies according to type but in general may be stored up to eight weeks without any significant loss of nutrients or palatability. A simple but clearly understood system of marking every container is essential, showing the product name, batch number production and expiry date to aid stock rotation and for quality control.

- *Distribution*. All distribution should take place using chilled insulated containers for any short journeys or refrigerated vehicles for longer journeys.

- *Regeneration*. Frozen food can be thawed to +3°C prior to being regenerated, or re-generated directly from its frozen state. Food should be heated to a minimum of 70°C for at least two minutes. The service of the food should follow the regeneration as soon as possible with the temperature strictly controlled and not allowed to fall below 63°C. Food such as cold desserts will only require to be thawed prior to serv-

ing, but must be held in chiller cabinets until served.

Any foods regenerated and not consumed must be destroyed and not reheated or returned to a refrigerator.

11.3.4 Cook-chill production

The term cook-chill refers to a catering system based on the full cooking of food followed by fast chilling, with storage in controlled low storage temperature conditions just above freezing point and between 0°C to +3°C, followed by subsequent complete reheating close to the consumer prior to prompt consumption. It has a short shelf life compared to cook-freeze of up to five days including the day of production, distribution time and regeneration.

The cook-chill process involves:

- *Raw foods – storage and pre-preparation*. The purchasing, control, storage and pre-preparation of raw materials to be used in the cook-chill process have the same stringent requirements as the previously described cook-freeze process.

- *Cooking*. The cooking must be sufficient to ensure that heat penetrates to the centre of any food and results in the destruction of non-sporing pathogens. Recipe formulation is seldom necessary.

- *Portioning*. The hot food should be portioned into single or multi-portioned containers to a maximum depth of 50 mm prior to blast chilling, within thirty minutes of the cooking being completed. This is in order to preserve the appearance, flavour, nutritional quality and safety of the food.

- *Blast chilling*. All food should be chilled to between 0°C and +3°C within ninety minutes of being placed in the blast chiller. The reasons are to preserve the food quality and to prevent the growth of bacteria.

- *Chill storage*. The shelf life of pre-cooked cook-chilled foods has a maximum of five days including the day of preparation, distribution time and regeneration. The food should be stored between 0°C and +3°C in a chilled store containing only cook-chill products. This is because of the importance of maintaining this tight temperature range and to prevent any cross-contamination. A very clearly under-stood system of marking each container is essential, showing the product name, batch number and production date and expiry date, to aid stock rotation and for quality control reference.

- *Distribution.* Distribution should take place only in chilled insulated containers for short journeys or refrigerated vehicles for longer journeys. The distribution stage of this system is difficult to control effectively as an increase of temperature to +5°C is the maximum per-mitted for short journeys after which the tem-perature must quickly be brought down to between 0°C and +3°C. Should the tempera-ture reach between +5°C and +10°C before regeneration the food must be consumed within twelve hours or destroyed. If the tem-perature exceeds +10°C before re-heating the

food must be destroyed. These regulations apply equally to the storage stage as well as to the distribution stage.

- *Regeneration.* Chilled food must be regener-ated within thirty minutes after removal from its chill store. Food must be heated to a mini-mum control temperature of at least 70°C and held there for at least two minutes for reasons of palatability and safety.

11.3.5   Sous vide

Sous vide is a more recent food processing tech-nique developed in the late 1970s which lends itself readily to adaptation as a cook-chill vari-ant. The system involves the preparation of qual-ity raw foods, pre-cooking (for example, browning) when necessary, putting the raw

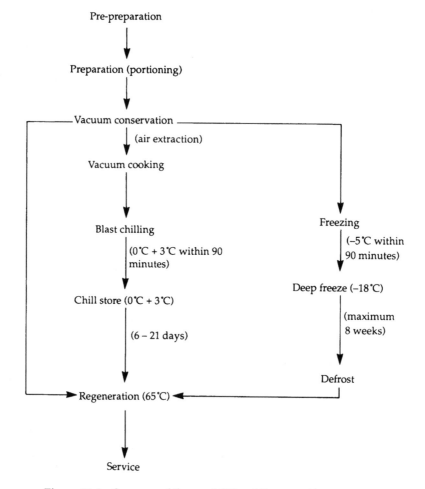

Figure 11.6 *Summary of the possibilities of the sous-vide process*

foods into special plastic bags or pouches, vacuumizing and sealing the pouches and then steam cooking to pasteurization temperatures. The food product can be served direct to the customer at this stage or rapidly chilled to +1°C to +3°C and stored at between 0°C to +3°C for a maximum of twenty-one days.

The sous vide method increases the potential shelf-life of normal cook-chill in three ways:

1 By vacuumizing the plastic bags or pouches the growth of most bacteria is restricted.
2 The food is cooked at pasteurization temperatures aiding the destruction of most microorganisms.
3 The food being sealed within the bags or pouches is protected during storage and regeneration from any cross-contamination.

The potential advantages of 'sous vide' to the caterer in addition to those offered by a cook-chill system are:

1 The flavour, palatability and nutrients are all improved, relative to normal processing, because all the contents are held within the sealed pouch.
2 The pouches provide a convenient package for safe handling and distribution, and prevent cross-contamination.
3 Shrinkage of the cooked product is reduced, increasing the yield by up to 20 per cent compared to normal cooking losses.
4 It can offer a flexible production method to catering units of all sizes with particular applications to à la carte and function menus.
5 It has a longer shelf life than cook-chill, of up to 21 days.

The disadvantages of the sous vide production method are:

1 Sous vide involves higher set-up capital and operating costs than cook-chill.
2 Its higher production costs limit its application and are prohibitive to certain sectors of the industry, particularly schools and hospitals.
3 Exceptionally high standards of hygiene are fundamental.
4 Complete meals cannot be produced as certain foods need to be processed differently, for example meat and vegetables.

11.3.6   Summary

The major food production methods currently in operation in the UK may be listed as follows: conventional or traditional (cook-serve); conventional production with the use of convenience foods: cook-freeze and cook-chill and their derivatives. There are, of course, those additional methods employed specifically by the food manufacturer, such as canning, dehydration, the use of synthetic foods etc., but these are beyond the realms of this book and are discussed adequately elsewhere.

The present trend whereby automation is increasing and fewer workers are employed, increases the demand for 'convenience' foods; quality standards are important to the caterer and the continued increase in the use of preserved and processed foods is, in part a reflection of the quality guarantees that the food manufacturer offers.

Whatever the food production system chosen, increasing costs in land values, capital and equipment, labour and raw materials demands attention to detail at the initial planning stage in order to satisfy the exact requirements of the food production system.

11.4   Beverage production methods

The term 'beverages' in this context is used to describe both alcoholic and non-alcoholic drinks. The degree of preparation necessary before these different beverages can be served to the customer varies, but in the majority of cases it is the non-alcoholic beverages that fall into the categories of raw and semi-prepared products, and the alcoholic beverages that are in the main already fully prepared.

1 *Raw beverages*. These are beverage products that require a higher degree of preparation, in comparison to the other categories, before being served to the customer. Examples of such beverages are tea, coffee, cocoa, which may require up to fifteen minutes before reaching a ready-to-serve state.

   The preparation of these raw beverage products may be away from the service area and customer, for example a stillroom in the kitchen of a large hotel, although in some speciality restaurants or coffee shops the tea or coffee making facilities may be an integral part of the total food service being offered by the catering operation.

2 *Semi-prepared beverages.* These are beverage products that do not need to be prepared from the raw product state, but neither are they ready-to-serve. Examples of semi-prepared beverages are fruit cordials which only require the addition of water; iced coffee and cocktails may also be included in this category.

The preparation of these semi-prepared beverages may also form part of the service, for example the showmanship of mixing cocktails in a cocktail bar.

3 *Fully prepared beverages.* These are beverage products requiring virtually no preparation before being served to the customer, for example bottled fruit juices, spirits, wines etc. In the majority of cases fully prepared beverages are dispensed in front of the customer, whether, for example, spirits at a bar or wines at a table.

The style of beverage production in a catering operation should be complementary to the food production method; therefore in a high-class restaurant a full range of alcoholic and non-alcoholic beverages would be available. In a cafeteria operation, however, a limited range of beverages would be offered, and such non alcoholic beverages as tea, coffee or orange squash, may actually be 'prepared' by customers themselves, for example, by the use of a vending machine or a tea, coffee or soft drinks machine.

The beverage production method in a catering operation should be afforded the same importance and consideration as the choice of the food production method. Tea or coffee, for example, are often the last part of a customer's meal and reputations can be made or marred on the taste of these beverages. Beverage production should also not be left to unskilled staff – this applies to the employees in the stillroom making the tea and coffee or the barmen mixing drinks and cocktails. The necessary requirements for good beverage production include the following: good quality raw materials – for example, a good blend of tea or coffee; the right equipment necessary for performing the job correctly – properly cleaned stills or machines, the provision of cocktail shakers, strainers etc., if cocktails are being offered; and finally, the employees must be trained for the tasks they are to perform. The standard of beverage production in a catering establishment and the standards of hygiene and cleanliness in beverage equipment should be regularly checked. The method of beverage production must be such that it will operate within the financial limits, and meet the profit targets of the establishment, as laid down in the financial policy. Mismanagement in beverage production can have a substantial effect on the establishment's gross profit, in the same way as shortcomings in food production can, and for this reason must be afforded sufficient time, consideration and finance so that a suitable method of beverage production is chosen for the particular catering operation.

11.5   References

Axler, B. H. (1979). *Food Service: A Managerial Approach.* Lexington MA: DC Heath.

Green, E. F. et al. (1987). *Profitable Food and Beverage Management: Planning.* Jenks, Oklahoma: Williams Books.

Ward, J. (1984). *Profitable Product Management.* Oxford: Butterworth-Heinemann.

12
Food and beverage service methods

12.1 Introduction

Food service may be defined as that phase of the food flow (that is, from the purchasing of the foods to service to the customer) mainly concerned with the delivery and presentation of the food to the customer, after the completion of food production. In some situations food service may include an element of transportation due to the separation of the food service facilities from the food production, for example of a centralized cook-freeze operation serving peripheral units.

Beverage service may be defined as that phase of the beverage flow wholly concerned with presentation of the beverage to the customer after the completion of beverage production. In beverage service there may be little or no element of transportation as the beverage production and service facilities are rarely separated by any real distance.

As with food and beverage production, there are a number of food and beverage service methods. It should be remembered, however, that unlike food and beverage production, food and beverage service is that part of the catering operation seen by the customer, and it is often, therefore, this aspect of a restaurant that can make or mar an establishment's reputation. The critical point at which customers' tempers fray in food service operations, is at the service counter or table. If the food and beverage service method is to be successful there must therefore be a clear understanding of the problems that occur at the food service point and hence the basic requirements that should be met by any food service method are:

1 The system chosen must be in keeping with the total concept of the catering facility and be perceived as value for money by the customer.
2 An ability to display food and beverages attractively and provide facilities to preserve the temperature, appearance and the nutritional quality of the food and beverage products, for example, buffets and carveries.
3 Offer good quality control. This is particularly important in self-service display cabinets where numerous portions of similar food and beverage products may be offered for sale.
4 Provide an efficient service. If dining in a high-class restaurant, the customer usually has more time available to consume his meal than if he is dining for example in a self service cafeteria, but even in this market of more leisurely dining the service should not be too slow.
5 Provide an atmosphere of hospitality and attractiveness; organization and cleanliness should be emphasized throughout.
6 Ensure good standards of hygiene and safety are maintained. Chances of contamination of food and equipment are increased in proportion to the number of food handlers, and the length of time the food is held. Every possible precaution should be taken to ensure correct temperatures are maintained to inhibit the growth of bacteria, ensure hand contact with food and food handling equipment is kept to a minimum, and good personal hygiene is practised by all food service staff. Also, when staff have to use equipment it must be safe for them to do so and they should have received full instructions on the operating and use of the equipment.
7 Operate within the cost and profit targets of the establishment, as detailed in the catering and financial policies.

These basic requirements should be met by any food service operation, regardless of the simplicity or elaborateness of the service method. Other more specific requirements related to particular food and beverage service methods are discussed under the various service method headings further in this chapter.

12.2   Food service methods

In order to deliver the food produced in a kitchen to the customer some form of food service is required. This may vary from full silver service in a luxury restaurant or hotel, where the food is brought to the customer's table, to a self service cafeteria where customers collect their own food from a service counter.

Traditionally, full waiter service was the predominant method of food service. However, a greater degree of informality when eating away from home, and the need for increased productivity due to rising costs, has led to other food service methods and styles being developed. These include the traditional cafeteria and its many derivatives, counter service, take-away foods, vending, and the numerous tray service systems, used particularly in the welfare sector.

The mode of food service employed by an establishment will depend on a number of inter-related factors: the type of establishment, for example whether it is an industrial cafeteria providing low-priced meals, or a high-class restaurant offering more complex and expensive dishes; the type of associated food production method, for example whether using traditional or conventional production, or a comparatively more recent method such as sous-vide; the type of customer to be catered for and the type of menu to be offered; the availability of staff and their skills; the space available; and finally, the cost and profit targets of the establishment, as determined by financial considerations.

In some operations more than one type of food service may be offered in the same establishment; for example in a large office block there may be a cafeteria for use by the majority of staff, a waiter service restaurant offering a plated meal service for use by middle management, and a silver service for top-level management. Where there is more than one level of food service offered, these different operations may be supplied from only one kitchen, although in large office blocks catering for a cross-section of customers on different levels of the building, several kitchens may have to be used.

Whatever the food service method, however, the business of eating out should be a pleasurable one. The main objective of an operation should be to present the customer with food of good quality at the correct temperature and served attractively, to ensure acceptability. The service method used must also be economically compatible with the policies and objectives of the organization. This demands efficiently designed food service facilities from the outset, taking into account all aspects of the food service operation, and particularly the market to be catered for and therefore the customer requirements.

12.3   Classification of food service methods

For the purpose of this book, the following classification of food service methods is used: self-service, waiter service and special service arrangements, as the majority of identifiable food service methods may be easily classified into these categories with very few overlaps.

12.3.1   Self-service

The simplest food service method currently in operation is the self-service method. Self-service methods may be described as those operations in which the service staff do not come to the table and serve customers their meals; customers in fact select their own food, cutlery, etc. and carry them to a dining area themselves. Such a method may be completely self-service such as in a vending operation, or it may be aided self service, for example those cafeteria operations where counter staff are available to help the customer in portioning and serving the food on to a plate.

Speed and economy are the two major reasons for choosing a cafeteria-type service – such facilities are able to serve large groups of people quickly with limited personnel. Essentially, cafeterias consist of a service counter arrangement, so that customers are able to see the food in advance of making a choice and a dining area. The counter or counters are made up of various heated and refrigerated units displaying food and beverages.

12.3.1.1 The traditional cafeteria

The traditional cafeteria arrangement consists of a straight line of counters where customers enter at one end of the line, pick up a tray and pass along the full length of the counter selecting menu items on the way. A tray rail runs the full length of the service counter on which customers rest their tray while passing along the line. The service counter and dining area are separated either by a rail or partition, and payment for the menu items selected is usually made at the end of the line where the cashier is seated.

The rate of flow through the cafeteria line varies according to a number of factors including the variety of choices offered, and hence the length of the line, the customers' familiarity with the cafeteria layout, the speed of the cashier, etc. In practical situations between four to six customers per minute can pass along a commercial single-line cafeteria, while in a cafeteria with limited choice, for example a school cafeteria, eight to ten may be the norm.

The rate of flow through a traditional cafeteria arrangement may be increased by installing more than one straight line, for example counter lines in parallel with the service facilities in between; although customer throughput may be increased still further by dispensing with the traditional straight lines and replacing them with food 'stations' or 'banks' which may be arranged in different layouts within the cafeteria. Such layouts are all encompassed within the term 'free-flow' cafeteria.

12.3.1.2 The free-flow cafeteria

This type of cafeteria design is also known as the 'hollow-square' (see Figures 12.1 and 12.2). Separated counters for hot or cold foods are usually placed along three sides of a room, with the fourth side open for traffic entering or leaving, so that a U-shape arrangement of food stations is formed. In a free-flow cafeteria, food stations may be positioned at right angles to the counter, or be staggered at an angle, forming an 'echelon' or 'saw-tooth' arrangement. Customers entering the square can go directly to the hot or cold sections without having to wait in line for their food, although during peak periods short lines may form at the most popular stations.

The beverage sections may either be placed in the centre of the square, or in the dining area itself so as to be readily accessible for the diners. Thought should, however, be given to the ease of supplying stations when the traffic area is crowded, particularly supplying centrally located stations.

The free-flow cafeteria is also able to accommodate a call-order bar where grilled and fried items are cooked to order; this is unlike the traditional cafeteria where it is essential that the line keeps moving steadily, and no allowances can be made for call-order facilities, unless they are separated out completely from the traditional line or adequate by-pass facilities are allowed.

The free-flow service method is a scatter approach to food service that is particularly useful for serving large numbers of people that arrive together. As many as fifteen to twenty customers per minute may be served in this type of cafeteria arrangement; this number may be increased once the customers have become familiar with the layout.

Payment for the meal is made as the customer leaves the free-flow area. There are usually a number of cash points available, enabling several customers to pay at the same time.

In both the traditional and free-flow cafeteria systems, the positioning of the cutlery, condiments and drinking water is beyond the cash point, so as to reduce holds-ups as much as possible. It is also important to consider the method of clearing as it is desirable that customers always see clearly what tables are free for them to sit at. Clearing can either be done by employing staff to do this or by requiring customers to clear their own tables.

12.3.1.3 The carousel

The carousel or 'roundabout server' consists of a number of rotating shelves (usually three) at different heights, all of which are approximately six feet in diameter, and rotate at one revolution per minute. Food is passed from the kitchen to a plating table still on the servery side of the carousel, from which the carousel is fed with hot and cold plated foods.

A typical carousel layout may be as follows: the bottom shelf accommodates cold foods – salads, sweets, etc. This shelf is usually pre-cooled by a refrigerator element and a crushed ice bed may be used to ensure a low temperature during the food service period. If the hot food shelf is placed above the cold shelf on the carousel, it is extended out over the lower cold shelf to ensure that the warmth from the overhead heat does not affect the cold shelf below. On the top revolving shelf bread rolls, butter, etc. may be displayed. Trays, cutlery, napkins, and beverages are usually separated out from the carousel on dispensers, although some of these items may be on one of the revolving shelves.

The carousel unit consists of a number of servery areas where the customer remains stationary, taking his choice of meal from the revolving carousel, and placing it on his tray. Payment is made to a cashier or cashiers on the restaurant side of the carousel.

The carousel may serve between 500 and 720 people an hour, between eight and twelve a minute. The customers' rate of flow depends on a number of factors – familiarity with the carousel arrangement, the range of dishes offered, the rate at which shelves are refilled by operators on the servery side, etc.

The carousel is not used to any great extent as a method of food service in the catering industry, although where it is used it would appear to be working effectively. It is a form of food service that is really only suitable for catering operations which have repeat custom, for example a staff cafeteria, rather than those operations where there are always new customers arriving who are not so familiar with the method, for example department stores. The carousel has a limited application as a method of food service, although it may be particularly suitable for some catering operations which have specific requirements or restrictions.

12.3.1.4   *Vending*

Vending today has become synonymous with selling from a machine. It is also known as 'automatic retailing' or selling from an 'electronic cafeteria' and involves a machine providing the customer with a product in exchange for some form of payment, coins, credit cards, etc.

Although vending was in evidence in the UK prior to the Second World War, mainly in the form of chocolate and cigarette machines, it was not until the 1950s that the vending of drinks and snack items really became established in this country. The markets for vended products have grown steadily over the last forty years, Tables 12.1(a) and (b) showing a detailed breakdown of vending sales 1994–1996 inclusive. In beverage vending, canned drinks, cartons and bottles have shown the greatest increase in growth over the three years to 1996 of 15%. Table 12.1 (b) shows a detailed analysis of food machines, showing snack foods have increased the greatest.

The markets available for vended products are varied and numerous and may be grouped into three main areas:

1 The *general market* vending machines and their products may be situated in areas to which the general public largely has access; for example, shopping courts, motorway service areas, garage forecourts, airports, seaports, ferries, rail and bus terminals, libraries, swimming and leisure centres, stadiums, exhibition centres, cinemas and theatres.

2 The *industrial market* includes those establishments where vending machines are provided for employers and employees in office blocks and shops, factories and sites etc. Eighty per cent of companies in the UK having installed vending machines at some or all of their premises.

3 The *institutional market* includes establishments such as hospitals and schools, prisons, sports complexes, universities and colleges and more recently hotels, replacing to some extent floor service.

The range of vending machine equipment or hardware is divisible into two major groups:

1 *Beverage venders.* Beverage vending machines have accounted for the largest share of vending sales over the last thirty years and consequently their design has been developed further than the food vending machines. This group is discussed in greater depth later in this chapter.

2 *Food vending machines or merchandisers.* Food vending machines may vend a variety of food

Table 12.1(a)   *Vending sales: beverage machines*

Machine type	1994	1995	1996	Growth in 1996 (%)	Growth over three years (%)
Traditional beverage vending machines	136,279	138,456	142,866	3.2	5
In-cup beverage vending machines	79,820	77,585	79,479	2.4	Flat
Can/carton/bottle	51,210	55,795	58,880	5.5	15
Snack/food	42,794	47,743	51,972	8.9	21
Total	**310,103**	**319,579**	**333,197**	**4.3**	**7**

Source: AVAB Census 1996

Table 12.1(b)   *Vending sales: food machines*

	1994	1995	1996
GFMs	23,802	27,074	30,612
Speciality	7,146	7,853	8,011
Total snack	30,948	34,927	38,623
Refrigerated food	11,142	11,989	12,499
Deep frozen and others	704	827	850
Grand total	**42,794**	**47,743**	**51,972**

Source: AVAB Census 1996

products – confectionery, snacks, plated meals etc., and are usually vended in one of three types of machine:

(a) *Snack machines.* Confectionery, crisps, biscuits, etc. are usually vended from an ambient temperature machine as these items have a relatively long shelf-life and do not have any special temperature requirements. Because of these factors, servicing of the machines except for restocking purposes, can be kept to a minimum thereby also reducing operating costs.

(b) *Refrigerated machines.* Snack items such as sandwiches and rolls have a limited shelf life and need to be date-stamped ('sell-by' or 'use by') and vended through a refrigerated machine. Plated foods such as salads, cold meats, etc., must be vended from refrigerated machines where the holding temperature is between 2°C and 5°C. At this temperature the food may be kept for two to four days, although some operations work on a twenty-four hour cycle only.

(c) *Hot meal machines.* Food for a hot vending

service may be vended in a number of ways. The first is the heated food vendor which will hold the temperature of the plated food at about 69°C for up to six hours. The second is the hot can vendor which usually offers a choice of items. The selection of hot canned meals, for example soups, baked beans, pasta dishes, casseroles etc., are held at a temperature of 68°C in the machine without deterioration in the quality of the food. Money is placed into the appropriate slot and the hot can is vended together with a disposable bowl and suitable cutlery to eat the food with; the can is easily opened by the use of a ring pull top. The third involves the use of a microwave oven adjacent to a refrigerated merchandiser. Cooked food is plated by kitchen staff, rapidly cooled and placed into a refrigerated merchandiser; if limited kitchen facilities are available, ready plated or semi-prepared foods may be bought in from a supplier, plated and put in the vending machine. The food is heated when placed in the microwave, which has an automatic timing device for the different foods which begins when a token or code is put into the microwave. The time taken for a meal to be heated thoroughly depends on whether it is a snack item or a full meal. Snack items being heated from a refrigerated state take between ten and thirty seconds, and a main meal between forty and sixty seconds, depending on the quantity and depth of the food, and the power supply feeding the microwave. The range of products available for hot meal vending is

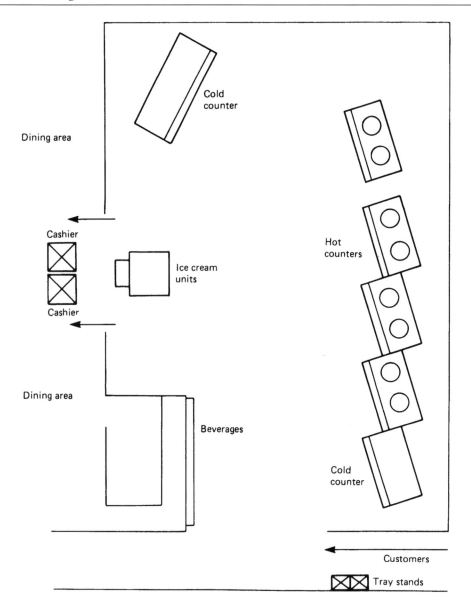

Figure 12.1   *Self-service: free-flow cafeteria*

now quite considerable although snacks and sandwiches still account for the largest percentage.

Within each of these groups the type of vending machine used will depend largely on the type of product being vended. For confectionery and pre-packed goods a simple mechanical unit with a drawer at the base of the column is all that is required; it can be free-standing, wall-mounted or be positioned on a fixed surface and does not require any electricity or water supply. Snack and sandwich vending machines require a power supply only and because their products are easily consumed, the machines can be situated outside wards, in the corridors of hotels etc., close to the customer market. Machines vending plated meals need to be situated close to the kitchen facilities and adjacent to the dining area; some banks of vending machines are sited such that the kitchen is behind the machines for ease of stocking and the dining area is in front of

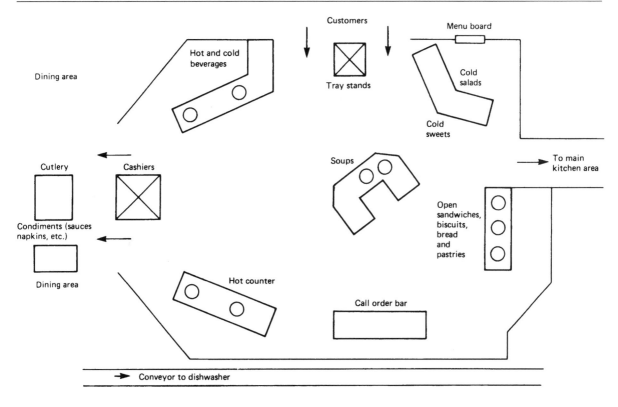

Figure 12.2 *Self-service: free-flow cafeteria*

them. These types of machines may be a rotating drum or revolving shelf design whereby a button is pushed rotating or revolving shelves until the required item is reached and then removed through a flap door.

The number of vending machines to be installed in a particular establishment will depend on the numbers to be catered for, frequency of use of the machines, the travel distance by staff to use the machines, etc. As a general rule of thumb one drinks machine is capable of serving between 150 and 250 customers. Should a full vending service be offered, that is, beverages and food items, the provision of two machines would be capable of serving between fifty and 100 customers. It is also worth noting that in many establishments vending is not used to cater for all the operation's needs, but often to simply supplement them; thus in a number of catering operations there may be a combination of a cafeteria arrangement and a bank of vending machines, the latter providing snack and beverage products, for example, which could be separated out from the main cafeteria line.

The basic question of whether to use vending machines or not should be taken after careful consideration of the organization's catering and financial policies and an assessment of what vending has to offer. The main advantages associated with vending include the following:

1 *Flexibility.* Vending can provide a twenty-four hour food and beverage service, either alone or in conjunction with other catering services. Customers can use a vending machine when they want to, rather than only when a cafeteria is open.
2 *Situation.* Vending machines can be sited close to the customer market, for example in office corridors, thus reducing workers' time away from the work place queuing for a snack or drink; customers are also more likely to take a vended drink back to their workplace and consume it there, rather than spend time away from their work, for example in a cafeteria.

Satellite vending machines can also be used to serve areas that would not normally benefit from a catering facility; for example, in a large industrial complex, machines can be sited some distance from the main kitchen and dining area.

3 *Quality control.* In terms of quality, vending machines can sell a consistent product, particularly beverages, pre-packed snacks and bought in meals from a supplier. Meals prepared in the kitchen can also be plated under tighter quality and portion control.

4 *Hygiene control.* Reduced handling of vended foods also reduces the possibilities of food contamination. Many beverage machines now also have built-in, self-clean mechanisms.

5 *Operating control.* Labour savings can be made as once cleaned and stocked vending machines should require the minimum of maintenance, thus reducing labour costs. Wastage, pilferage and cash losses should also be negligible.

6 *Speed.* Vending machines can 'sell' products quickly and efficiently, for example a hot chips machine which can vend portions of freshly prepared chips, always giving a standard product, at a standard price.

7 *Sales promotion.* Products for sale in a vending machine can look attractive and stimulate 'impulse purchases', particularly glass-fronted merchandisers (GFMs) displaying fresh fruits, sweets etc. (See Figure 12.3.)

The disadvantages associated with using vending include the following:

1 *Impersonality.* Vending machines lack the 'personal touch' and some customers will always prefer to be served food and beverages in the traditional manner rather than from a machine.

2 *Inflexibility of the product.* Initially the range of products available for vending was quite limited; today, however, vending machines offer a much wider selection, and beverages in particular can be highly customized.

3 *Reliability.* One of the major causes of dissatisfaction with vending machines in the past has been that the coin mechanism could become jammed and the machine would give no service. This is turn left the machines open to abuse and vandalism. Since their introduction

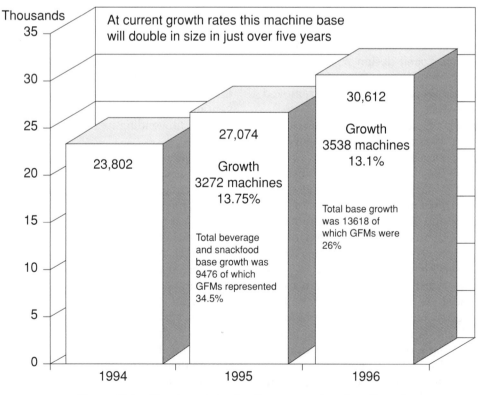

Figure 12.3 *Glass fronted merchandisers: proportion of vending sales*
Source: AVAB Census 1996

the vending machines' coin mechanism has been a mechanical device which could be regularly jammed with foreign coins, washers, etc. Today, however, the electronic coin mechanism can detect even the most accurately produced fake coins, which even when fed into the machine, do not jam it. Electronic mechanisms are constantly being improved and are incorporated into the majority of new machines. These electronic mechanisms are also capable of accepting different valued coins, displaying a running total as they are added and of giving change.

4 *Limiting.* For large-scale food and beverage service, vending machines have limitations. In some situations they are best suited as a backup to the main catering services although a bank of vending alleviates queuing and waiting time. They are also of less use in up-market situations, except in the form of mini-bars, for example in hotels.

If an organization decides to use vending as a catering facility, the next question to be answered is whether to remain 'in house', or to employ a contractor. The main cost structures for each of these groups may be itemized as follows:

Client or in-house operated service

1 Capital outlay for machine; outright purchase; lease; rented or instalment; plus depreciation of machines and loss of interest on capital. Choice of machine made by client.
2 Installation costs such as for electricity and water supplies.
3 Operating costs such as ingredients, commodities, cups, daily sales and cost records, maintenance, cleaning and servicing.
4 Selling prices set by client, all cash takings to the client.

Contract operated service

1 No capital outlay for machine – it is supplied by contractor.
2 Some installation costs paid by client, for example water and electricity.
3 Operating costs such as ingredients, commodities, cups, maintenance, cleaning, and servicing done by contractor.

4 Selling prices set between client and contractor. Reimbursement costs, direct and indirect to contractor.

In the US 95 per cent of vending installations are operated by contractors. In the UK this figure is approximately 50 per cent, although it appears to be increasing (AVAB). Any operation considering using vending as a total or part catering service needs to give careful thought to choosing a supplier; the above factors need to be taken into account, other operations using the contractor should be visited and discussions entered into with both management and staff committees as to the best way of introducing a vending system into the organization.

Vending operates in a very competitive market and a number of developments and market trends may be identified in the vending sector:

1 *Cashless systems.* The development of card operated vending has probably been the most important technological development in vending. The leading supplier of this type of system is Girovend, the main component being a credit card type of pass or card which can record the user's own data; it can be used for personnel control such as security, identity passes, attendance recording, leisure facilities, etc. For catering purposes, customers can buy any food and beverage items from a vending machine by placing their card into the machine instead of cash; their card is then debited with the amount for the items purchased.

The card first has to be loaded with credit and this can be done in a number of ways. First, supervised loading whereby a supervisor collects customers' cash amounts and loads the cards via a vending machine; the disadvantage to this method is that the handling of cash is still involved and at least one person has to be employed to do this job. Second, customers self-load their own cards with a cash value before making their purchases. By inserting the card into the loader a customer can check its balance and increase the amount by feeding the appropriate money into the machine; this method's disadvantage is that special loaders are required and cash is still handled. Third, is the direct-debit loader linked to the wages department so that a card holder may direct debit different values from his/her salary; in this way cash handling is eliminated completely.

The advantages to the customer of card vending are that it is a convenient method of payment; loose change does not have to be carried, it is not 'lost' in the machine; and, overall, a faster service can be given.

The card holders can be divided into user type groups and these categories may then be separated into different price bands. Figure 12.4 shows a breakdown of the total vending market payment systems, into cashless, free-vend and coin-operated systems. This enables different charges to be made for the same product, for example for regular employees, temporary staff, free vend for visitors etc. Cash refunds can be given to users giving up their cards, or money can be paid back into an employee account; machines can also be programmed to stop accepting stolen cards. Finally, the sales information stored in these machines can be printed out by item, price list or type of user, and a comparison between actual and cash loaded on to the cards can be given; such up-to-date information

greatly aids financial control and cost accounting.

2 *Mixed product vending.* Where the design of the machine allows, different products may be vended together and complement each other, for example, pre-packed snacks with carton juices together form a substitute for a main meal at certain times of the day. Smaller units, for example vending confectionery, can also be attached to the side of the larger machines and utilize their coin or card mechanism.

3 *Fresh brew vending.* Machines using fresh brew systems for tea and coffee ensure that a better quality end product is dispensed to the customer. In-cup drink machines where the ingredients are already in the cup also offer better hygiene, operation and servicing, control and range of products. Some beverage machines are now capable of offering 100 different selections for both hot and cold drinks and have capacities of up to 1000 cups.

4 *Space economization.* The efficient utilization of business space in offices, factories, hospitals, industrial units etc., is of great importance today. This has led many operations to criti-

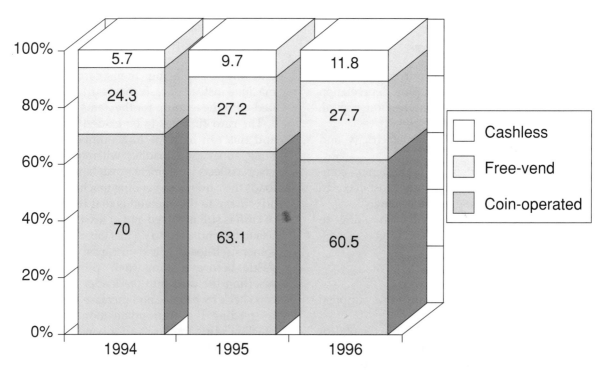

Figure 12.4   *Vending machines: payment systems*
Source: AVAB Census 1996

cally review their catering facilities and the space allocated to them, particularly where a twenty-four hour service is needed. In many situations vending is being used as a space and cost saving alternative to installing traditional catering services. Furthermore, the vending manufacturers themselves are aware of the amount of space vending machines need, and are researching ways of reducing their overall size yet at the same time trying to increase the range and quality of products they can offer.

5 *Compatibility with cook-chill.* The cook chill method of food preparation serves the vending industry well by allowing plated meals to be prepared in advance and vended for later consumption either in a chilled state, for example salads, cold meats, pâtés etc., or for use in conjunction with some type of heating system, for example microwaves.

Vending has now established itself as a method of food service that may be considered for many types of operations and situations. In some sectors of the catering industry it is employed as a total feeding system, for example staff cafeterias and rest rooms, hospital canteens etc., in others it is an economic alternative to other types of catering service at different times of the day, for example, night shifts in hospitals, twenty-four hour factories, offices, etc.

12.3.1.5 The carvery

Carvery type operations are not a new phenomenon. They were in evidence in some hotels during the earlier part of the century, but over the past five to ten years have experienced a certain revival and several large chains are now featuring them in their hotels throughout the world.

Carvery restaurants essentially offer a three course meal (exclusive of drink) at a set inclusive price. The first course is served by the waiter and usually offers a selection of five or six items. The main course is selected from the carvery counter and served by customers themselves, although usually aided by a control conscious chef. The sweet course, like the first course, is also served by a waiter.

The carvery counter may be a straight line, circular or more usually U-shaped. On this counter is placed a selection of hot meats, vegetables and potatoes, sauces and gravies. The counter itself consists of a series of hot plates and containers with the addition of overhead heat lamps to also help keep the food hot. A separate cold table may also be featured in some operations offering a selection of cold meats and salads.

Carvery style service is a speciality food service method and for this reason it has limited application. It is found mainly in hotels, private restaurants, steak houses and pubs, and may be used for special function catering. It is something of a 'fashionable' food service method in that it experiences periods of popularity and then fades into the background; at present the carvery method of food service may be said to be 'in fashion' in some sectors of the catering industry.

12.3.1.6   The buffet

The buffet is a method of food service which is a modification of true self-service. It is a food service arrangement in which foods are displayed attractively on one, or a series of tables, and presentation is an all important factor.

Customers collect a plate from one end of the table and move along it helping themselves to the foods of their choice. Buffets may be a combination of hot and cold foods, all hot or all cold. In a fork buffet cutlery is provided for the customer with which to eat the food; in a finger buffet most of the food is kept to fairly small mouth-size pieces, and little or no cutlery is provided.

Buffets may be used in conjunction with a restaurant operation or for private functions. In a restaurant style operation customers pay a fixed price for the buffet and for this price are able to return as many times to the buffet table as they would like. At private functions it is more usual to have service personnel continually circulating among the guests serving the food and the beverages and clearing tables.

Buffets are used very successfully by some hotels and restaurants for featuring special weeks, for example a Spanish week, a Scandinavian evening, etc. and for special sales promotion of, for example, foreign foods or wines. It is also an adaptable method of food service in that some operations may use buffet service for particular meal periods, for example breakfast, lunch or dinner, and revert to another type of food service for the other meals.

Buffet service also enables a facility to feed large numbers of people in a given time with less staff requirements. Compared with other types of food service, however, the buffet method can have a higher food cost; this is because good displays of food must be given which often involve presenting fairly large quantities of the items, and because it is time consuming to prepare and garnish all the buffet food in order to achieve a good display. The higher food and labour cost in the kitchen may, however, be offset by a lower restaurant labour cost as fewer service personnel are required.

12.3.1.7   *Take-away or take-out service*

The take-away, or take-out service as it is more commonly known in the US, is a method of food service that exploits to the full the concept of 'fast foods'. The products offered by these establishments are highly standardized, as are most of the features of the operations – service, sales control, product packaging, etc. The take away operation offers a limited basic menu to the customer, but within this menu there may be a number of variations on the basic items. These operations aim to achieve volume sales by offering low- to medium-priced foods, and they have become a popular segment of the catering market because they fill a need for a quick snack or meal.

The time between customers placing orders and receiving their meals, aims to be faster than any other method yet discussed; some operations aim for a thirty second service time. The customer may either take the food out of the take away to eat, or it may be consumed on the premises; a large number of so-called 'take away' outlets now provide very extensive seating areas, often for more than several hundred.

Because take-away outlets aim for a high rate of customer turnover, their situation in relation to their markets is crucial; they are usually found in high streets and main shopping centres where they have a high percentage of passing trade. Although the average spending power of customers in take-aways may be considerably lower than for some of the other food service methods

discussed, this is compensated by their high rate of customer throughput.

Today there is a wide selection of products that take-aways can offer for sale; the growth of the traditional fish-and-chip shops has now taken second place to the other types of foods now offered – hamburgers, pizzas, Chinese, Indian and Mexican food, etc.

Self-service is therefore a method of food service in which customers collect their own food from some form of service counter, in return for which they pay a lower price for the meal than they would, for example, in operations offering a waiter service. In self service operations payment for the meal is made either before the meal, for example in vending operations, or after the meal as in some cafeterias.

In the industrial sector of the catering market this method of food service has become firmly established; in the majority of cases people's main meal is in the evening, so that they only require a snack-type short lunch which a self service operation can adequately provide. In the welfare sector this utilitarian method of food service is also used extensively, leaving the more leisurely dining to that part of the day which is not associated with work.

12.3.2   Waiter service

Waiter service involves the transportation and service of food to the customer – whether at a table, counter or bar – rather than customers collecting their own food. This method of food service has also been termed 'aided' or 'personalized' service.

In terms of customer throughput the traditional waiter service to a customer seated at a table is a much slower method of food service than the self-service methods. However, with waiter service speed and price are no longer necessarily the most important factors governing the selection of the food service method. Other factors now become more important both to the caterer and the customer – the provision of a more elaborate service, more leisurely dining facilities, a wider variety in menu choice, etc.

12.3.2.1 *Counter or bar service*

This method of food service is an appropriate example to illustrate the transition between self-service and waiter service, as it offers the informality of the self-service methods, and yet also combines that degree of extra service given to the customer commensurate with waiter service.

In bar service customers sit on stools or chairs at a counter, the shape of which may be a straight line, or as is more usual, U-shaped. The latter shape allows the waiter to serve a considerable volume of trade single-handed. The average sized U-shape counter accommodates between ten to fourteen customers, served by one member of staff; larger counters catering for between twenty to twenty-eight customers may be manned by two staff. This type of food service is not designed for large groups of people arriving at once, but for a steady stream of people arriving alone, in couples, or even in parties of between four and six. With these numbers being the average size of the party, the seat turnover using a counter arrangement may be considerable.

The covers are laid up and cleared in front of the customer by the waiter behind the counter. Orders are taken by the waiter and dispatched to the kitchen; here the food is plated, which is then brought to the counter and placed before the customer. The distance between the food production area and the counter is usually minimal which facilitates easy handling of the food and hence speed of service to the customer. In some U-shaped counter arrangements, usually those serving between twenty to twenty-five people, there may be a central island on which are placed a variety of cold dishes for the first and sweet courses. This enables the waiters to serve the customers very rapidly, offers a good display of foods which may encourage impulse buys, and leaves the kitchen staff only the main courses to prepare to order; this last factor has a particular advantage if the kitchen is servicing not only the counter arrangements, but also other restaurant facilities.

12.3.2.2 *Table service*

Table service is a method of food service in which the waiter brings customers' food to the table and places it in front of them, either pre-plated, or if it is silver service, served with a salver on to a plate and then placed in front of customers. Table service is the most leisurely of the service methods so far discussed; customers may still take as little as half to three-quarters of an hour to eat their meal, but are more likely to take between one-and-a-half to two hours, and may even take three to four hours, often depending on the size of the party.

There are basically two types of menus available in table service from which customers may select their meal. The first is the à la carte menu in which all the items on the menu are individually priced and customers select and combine dishes according to their choice. The other is the table d'hôte menu which consists of a number of items combined together to produce a set meal, at a set price. A set table d'hôte menu may, for example, include a choice of two appetizers, three or four entrées including vegetables, and a choice of two or three sweets; a beverage, for example coffee, may also be included in the price. The use of the term table d'hôte is today frequently replaced by the term 'fixed price menu'.

There are a number of different styles of table service, these include the following:

1 *American service* in which the guest's meal is portioned and plated in the kitchen, brought into the restaurant by the waiter and placed in front of the customer.

2 *French service*, which is the most elaborate of the table service methods, involves preparing the guest's food in the kitchen, arranging it on silver salvers which are then brought into the dining room and placed on a small cart called a *guéridon*. On this guéridon is a small heater called a *réchaud*, used for heating or flaming the guest's food, which is then served from the silver salvers on to the guest's plate and placed in front of the guest.

3 *The Russian style of service* illustrates the food service method commonly referred to as silver service; the food is prepared and portioned in the kitchen and placed on to silver salvers which are then taken into the restaurant. A dinner plate is placed in front of the guest and the food is served on to the guest's plate.

4 *English service*, which is the least common of

all the table service methods described and is usually only used for private functions. The food is prepared in the kitchen, but not portioned, instead the complete joint of meat, for example a whole turkey, is presented to the guests before carving. The host or one of the service personnel then carves and portions the meat and places it on to a plate with the vegetables, and the plate is then placed in front of the guest.

These are the four main traditional methods of table service, although variations do of course occur within the different styles. Service carts, for example, are not used exclusively in the French style of service, they may be used in a number of the other service styles, although not perhaps to the same extent. Some of the following food service methods are also, in the strict sense of the word, table service, but they have been included here by the titles under which they are more commonly known, as within these following methods different types of table service may be used.

12.3.2.3   Banquet service

Banquet service is usually associated with large hotels, although today many food service operations are employing this type of food service as a profitable sideline, for example hospitals, colleges and universities and small restaurants.

The variety of table arrangements used in banqueting service are numerous, using either round, square, rectangular and other interlocking-shaped tables; if there is a 'top' table on which sit the host and the most important guests this table is usually served first. The number of people that may be catered for in banqueting service can be as small as six to eight for a private dinner party, to a large convention of several thousand people. The food served to the customer may either be pre-plated in the kitchen (American service) or portioned on to the plates in front of the customers (Russian service). A further method is to use one of these types of service for the meat/fish main course and to allow customers to help themselves to the vegetables and accompaniments placed on the table in service dishes with the necessary serving equipment.

The advantages of this food service method are that the number to be catered for is known well in advance; the specific time of dining is also known; and a set menu for a set price is established. This enables the service of large numbers of people to be undertaken by a comparatively small number of service personnel, usually one waiter serving between ten and twelve customers.

12.3.2.4   Room and lounge service

Room service is a method of food service which, like banqueting, is most commonly associated with the larger hotels, although some motels and smaller hotels do also offer a degree of room service. Today, however, even in the larger hotels, it is not a method of service that is as common as it was in former years.

From the customers' point of view, hotel guests do not usually choose to eat their meals in their rooms, they prefer either to use the hotel's restaurant facilities, or to dine outside the hotel. From the management's point of view it is a method of food service that is very expensive to provide – a great deal of time and cost is involved in serving customers in their rooms, particularly if a full meal service is offered; for this reason most hotels offering room service today only offer a very limited menu selection or snack items only. The high cost of providing a floor service includes the basic problem of a fluctuating demand with the need to have staff always available to provide the service, the lifts to transport the food from the kitchen, as well as the need for trollies, tables, trays, heating plates, etc. Furthermore, the special requirement of service pantries on most floors necessitates valuable revenue space being used for food production, which could be more efficiently contained and organized elsewhere, thus releasing service area pantries for other uses.

Today, the provision of lounge service is almost exclusively confined to up-market hotels and to resort-type establishments. With many of the larger middle market hotels offering day long coffee shop service, the need for hotels to offer food and beverage refreshments in the lounge areas has been reduced. Like room service, the provision of lounge service is highly labour intensive, distance from the production area may be considerable, and demand uptake by the customer can fluctuate greatly.

12.3.2.5   *Car or drive-in service*

Car service commonly consists of two types of service: the first where customers remain in their vehicles in the drive-in area to consume their meal; and the second where customers buy their food and beverages and then leave the drive-in to consume them elsewhere. The former type of car service operations have not increased in popularity in the last ten to fifteen years, although there are still many operations in the US where they are almost exclusively still found.

Waiters (usually called carhops) take the customers' orders and return with the food placed on trays – these fit on to the car door or steering wheel. The customers eat their food in their cars, the carhops removing finished trays. Payment for the meal is made directly to the carhops.

This method of food service has declined in popularity for almost the same reasons as room service; mainly because it is a very labour intensive service method with often a long distance between the production area and the customer, also because people generally prefer to eat their meal, if only a snack, at a counter or table in a dining area, rather than in a car. Today, many drive-in operations are now providing a restaurant or dining space for their customers, so that they do have an alternative to eating in their car.

The second type of car service is an extension of the fast-food system of take-away and involves customers ordering their requirements from a menu board which are transmitted usually via a microphone at the entrance to the drive-in. Customers then drive to the exit where they collect their purchases and pay at the same time. These fully computerized systems allow a rapid throughput of customers and parking areas do not have to be provided, unless the drive-in is also offering dining facilities. This method of drive-in take-aways is growing in popularity faster than the original concept as it does at least allow customers a choice of where to consume their meals.

Waiter service is therefore a method of food service in which customers receive some form of personalized service from the catering facility, in return for which they pay a higher price for the meal than would be paid, for example, in a self-service operation. On a simplified scale, the higher the cost of the meal to the customer, the more service the customer expects.

There are a limited number of establishments today which offer the elaborate, traditional service styles described, particularly the true French service; rising costs, especially labour costs, have to a great extent limited this type of service out of the market, although there will always be a small section of the total market that is able to pay the high prices charged. The majority of restaurants offering a waiter service today use either the American or Russian styles of service, depending upon the price the customer is willing to pay.

12.3.3   Special service arrangements

In some catering situations it is a necessity for the prepared food to be transported and served directly to the customer – it may, for example, be a patient in a hospital ward, a passenger on board a plane, or an elderly person living at home. In such cases as these, 'special' service arrangements may be used. There are a number of special service arrangements available and in the majority of cases are based on similar concepts and have very similar characteristics; it is convenient, therefore, to take a particular sector of the catering industry, the welfare sector, and to discuss the special service arrangements found in hospitals, as it is in these types of catering situations that most special service arrangements are found.

12.3.3.1   *Centralized tray service*

Today, there are a number of centralized tray meal systems available for use in hospital catering. Although differing from each other in certain aspects, the basic menu selection procedure for patients is very similar. Menu cards are distributed to patients on the previous day; patients can then make their own selection of food for the following day from the choice on the menu card. Also included on the card are the desired portion sizes of the meal and any particular dietary requirements customers may have.

The menu cards are collected from the wards and returned to the catering officer who then prepares a production schedule for the following day based on the number to be catered for, the quantity of food to be produced, etc. Individual diet cards are then prepared for every patient in the hospital; these are later placed on the tray before it moves along the conveyor belt, so that the operatives can read exactly what is to be given to each patient.

When the food has been prepared for a particular meal period, the food is loaded into heated or refrigerated *bain-maries* which are wheeled up to the conveyor belt and plugged into a mains socket to keep the food at the correct temperature throughout the service period. Cutlery for the meal is wrapped in a napkin (or pre-wrapped cutlery may be used) and placed on to a tray with the patient's menu card. The trays automatically move along the conveyor belt and the next item to be placed on the tray is some form of heated plate receiver, on top of which is then placed the conventionally styled plate. As the tray moves along the conveyor belt the operatives place the requested menu item and portion size on to the plate. By the time the tray reaches the end of the conveyor belt a complete meal has been assembled; one or two supervisors then check the tray's items against the menu cards before putting lids over the plates and placing the completed tray into the mobile holding cabinets, or tray trolleys, which are then sent to the wards. Using this special service arrangement several hundred complete meals can be prepared in a very short time and with constant supervision (see Figure 12.5). Depending on menu selection, dietary requirements, garnishes etc., 500 tray meals can be completed in one to one and a half hours. If a cook-chill conveyor belt is being used, the ambient temperature of the kitchen should be 5°C or below.

The tray systems utilizing this basic concept include the Ganymede, Finessa and Heatrex concepts. In all these systems the food is kept hot by the use of some form of heated plate receiver on top of which is placed the conventionally styled plate, from which patients eat their meal.

Some other service arrangements do not heat the food container to maintain food temperatures, but rely instead on heat insulation, for example the Temprite concept. Because the

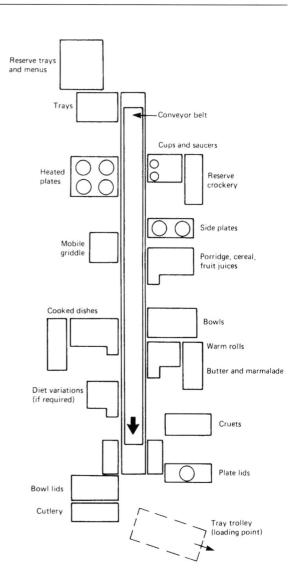

Figure 12.5   *Breakfast tray service layout: the Ganymede*

Temprite containers neither heat nor cool the food placed into them, it is particularly important for the food to be placed into the moulded trays at the proper temperatures, and covered quickly. If this procedure is followed carefully the change in food temperature is not significant for some time. The Temprite system is currently used in a variety of catering situations ranging from transporting thirty lunches from an organization's main kitchen to a district office fifteen minutes away, to providing hospitals in the UK, France and Germany, catering for between 700 and 900 meals per serving.

There are, of course, other special service arrangements, found particularly in hospitals in the US. Differential heating containers (DHC), for example, use metallized shielding over prepared trays to control the input of microwave on the various components of a meal. Other arrangements also include those that are almost totally computerized – from the analysis of the patients' meal choice to the assembly of the patients' trays. At present, however, the sophistication and cost of such special service arrangements are limiting factors to their more widespread use.

Special service arrangements are generally recognized as being a most effective way of serving 'captive audience' customers. One of their main aims is to provide meals that are both standardized and nutritionally balanced; using such systems as have been described these objectives can be achieved. Centralizing tray service preparation saves duplication of space and equipment, rationalizes labour requirements, and individual meals can be ordered to suit customer requirements. As well as the above savings there may also be savings on food costs due to centralized portion control, and elimination of waste from excessive ordering.

It should be remembered, however, that where special service arrangements are used, such as in hospitals, customer satisfaction is of particular importance. The presentation of the tray, food arrangement, colour combination, garnishes etc. are also therefore important factors to be taken into account so that encouragement is given to the patient to eat the meal provided.

12.3.4   Trays

The use of a tray in a food service facility has several purposes: first, the transportation of the customer's food and beverages from the service counter to the table whether in cafeteria or waiter service; second, it can be used as an aid to portioning control, for example in airline catering and more recently school catering where 'indented' trays are used; third, it can be used in the removal of dishes from the place where the customer has dined, to the dish washing area; and finally, it can be an aid to advertising by printing an establishment's logo actually on the tray and cross advertising this with outer outlets of the operation, for example a department store's different catering facilities.

The catering situations in which trays may be used as an aid to food service vary therefore from self service cafeteria arrangements using plastic trays, to high-class restaurants using silver trays, to travel catering situations where complete meals are served on a tray, for example on board a train or plane.

12.3.4.1   *Tray size and design*

The standard size of trays used extensively in catering establishments is $18 \times 13\frac{1}{2}$ in (45.7×34.3 cm), almost accounting for 80 per cent of sales, this being the width calculated to be the most practical for a person to pass through a standard 2 ft 6 in (76 cm) doorway. Tray sizes do, however, vary from $4\frac{1}{2} \times 6\frac{1}{2}$ in tip trays which may be used for presenting restaurant bills to customers, or as small liqueur trays, to $23\frac{1}{2} \times 18$ in (59.8×45.7 cm) used for banqueting service. The size of the tray may be limited by the material of which it is made, for example in steel anything larger than the 16 in (40 cm) tray is almost too heavy for handling, and at this size, too, polystyrene becomes too flexible.

The use of trays in catering situations is an integral part of the food service system and a number of factors must therefore be taken into consideration before choosing a particular type of tray for any catering operation:

1 The size of the tray in relation to the customers using them (for example, whether it is small children in school catering, or large adults working in a factory).
2 The shape of the tray in relation to the tables, that is, whether square, rectangular or round. (For example the Vickeray circular tray is designed so that a number of these trays can fit closely together to form a circle on a round table.)
3 The cost of the trays with a view to their expected life cycle.
4 The purpose of the trays. (For example, large rectangular trays would not be suitable for the service of beverages in a hotel bar; if the trays are to be used for transporting beverages the use of anti-skid tray mats may be considered.)

5 The method of disposal, whether the trays will simply be stacked on a trolley, or if a lowerator is to be used the tray dimensions must be precisely defined.
6 The manufacture of the trays (for example fibreglass, wood, polypropylene etc.) and whether the trays need to be dishwasher safe.
7 The size of the tray has to be chosen bearing in mind the size and type of crockery and glassware that the customer choosing a typical meal would use.
8 The colour combinations of the trays in relation to the type of establishment and the decor used should be taken into account. Simulated timber designs still comprise over 85 per cent of sales mainly through a re-ordering habit; today, however, there is a variety of colours and patterns used in tray design, which are not only attractive but may also be used to differentiate between different types of restaurant service offered by a large catering facility, or may be used in hospital catering to differentiate between different dietetic needs.

Finally, a combination of self-service and waiter service is now becoming more popular in some catering operations. Customers select their first course from a buffet arrangement, order their main course from the counter or from the waiter, which is then served to them pre-plated at their table, desserts and coffee subsequently being ordered and served in the same way. Harvester Restaurants for example operate this type of service. Customers make their own salad selection from a salad cart, their main courses and dessert being selected from the menu. Alternatively, customers may order their meals from a counter, giving the operative their table number, and the food is then served to them at their table, for example Millers Kitchen; desserts are ordered in the same way. This 'assisted' or 'aided service' enables more customers to be served by fewer service staff as the waiters' time is not divided between taking orders and service as the customers themselves place their own orders. Refrigerated dessert displays are often situated adjacent to the ordering counter which can result in an increase in impulse purchases by the customer waiting to give his dessert or coffee order.

12.4   Beverage service methods

Beverage service is an area which is sometimes neglected by catering operations, although it can be a most lucrative part of the total catering service, if approached and managed in the correct way.

The method of beverage service employed by a catering establishment should be complementary to the food service method. In a high class haute cuisine restaurant, for example, it is common to find an adjacent cocktail bar for pre-dinner drinks, where the customer is served at the bar or table by a waiter; after the meal beverages are served at the customer's table, or served in a separate coffee lounge. In a catering facility operating a self-service method of food service, customers would either help themselves to beverages as they moved along the cafeteria line, serve themselves from a vending machine, or be served by an operative behind the counter. There is not often a separate coffee lounge in self-service restaurants, although where space requirements permit, one may be provided to help increase customer throughput.

12.5   Classification of beverage service methods

As with the previously described food service, there are basically two main types of beverage service: self-service, and waiter/bar person service. Unlike food service, however, there are no special service arrangements designed specifically for the service of beverages other than a bar or dispense bar, although beverage service is of course included as part of those special arrangements described earlier, such as in hospital catering.

12.5.1   Self-service

Self-service beverage methods are those in which customers collect their own beverages from a counter or machine, rather than a waiter serving beverages to the customers at tables. Such a method may be completely self-service, such as the vending of beverages, or it may be aided such as in the traditional cafeteria arrangement where an operative would portion drinks into cups and glasses and hand these to the customers.

12.5.1.1 The cafeteria

In traditional cafeteria arrangements beverages are included in the main counter line, usually at the end, just before the cashier. The serving of beverages is, however, recognized to be one of the slowest points in the cafeteria line and the tendency now is to separate the beverages out from the main line completely and to serve them from a separate counter. This 'breaking down' of the traditional cafeteria line is carried further in the free-flow cafeteria arrangements which consist of a series of individual counters of which beverages are one.

In some cafeteria arrangements the beverage counters may actually be sited in the dining area. This is an attempt to speed up the throughput of customers in the main cafeteria area to the dining area. Such beverage stations may either be manned by counter staff or vending machines may be used.

12.5.1.2 Bar or counter service

This method of beverage service is most commonly found in public houses or hotels and restaurants which have licensed bars, customers purchasing their drinks at the bar and then usually carrying them back themselves to a table for consumption. Payment for the beverage is made directly to the barperson. A growing trend in this type of service is the use of computerized automatic measuring devices for beers, spirits, and soft drinks, together with an emphasis on displaying and merchandising beverages.

12.5.1.3 The carousel

Pre-portioned cold drinks may be offered for sale on a carousel. These are usually situated on the refrigerated shelves and such beverages as glasses of wine, fruit juices, milk, iced coffees, etc. may be featured. Hot beverages such as tea and coffee would be dispensed from a separate counter either adjacent or close to the carousel, or again may be sited in the main dining area.

12.5.1.4 Vending

Beverage vending machines may vend hot or cold drinks separately or together in the same machine and may also dispense alcoholic and non-alcoholic drinks. (Alcoholic vended beverages are studied in the next section under room service.)

1 Hot non-alcoholic beverage machines vend coffee, tea, chocolate and sometimes soups. They offer a range of variations, for example with and without sugar, creamers or whiteners, beverages of different strengths, fresh brew leaf teas, ground and continental coffees etc.
2 Cold and non-alcoholic beverage machines vend a variety of drinks, mainly syrup and concentrate based, although some powders are used. Examples of cold drinks being vended include still and carbonated bottle waters and juices, cartoned milks and milk shakes, fruit and health drinks, and canned products such as Coca-Cola and Pepsi which it is estimated account for 90 per cent of the canned drink vending market.
3 Hot and cold non-alcoholic beverage machines were developed to meet the growing need for cold drinks in some establishments already using vending machines, yet who did not require a machine vending cold drinks only. Packages of cold vending drinks were therefore designed that could be fitted into most existing hot drinks machines with little difficulty.

Beverage vending has a considerably wide application within the catering industry. First, it may be used in those operations offering a total vended service such as hospitals, where both food and beverages are sold through vending machines. Second, beverage vending may be used as a supplement to an existing method of food and beverage service, such as in cafeteria arrangements where all the food is served in a traditional line, but the beverages are separated out and dispensed from vending machines. Finally, beverage vending may not be used within the actual restaurant operation itself, but it may still be used as part of the establishment's total catering facilities – for example by siting individual or banks of beverage vending machines throughout the office block, factory layout, or as a supplement to, or in place of, a floor service in hotels.

12.5.1.5 Room service

Beverage service in hotel and motel rooms is most commonly waiter service, although many establishments have now installed mini-bars or small automatic dispensing machines (also called Bell Captains), from which guests may obtain a drink. A limited choice of alcoholic and non-alcoholic drinks and snacks are placed in the mini-bar, guests simply removing any drinks they may require. The mini-bars may be free-standing or, alternatively, they can be built into existing furniture. A recent development is the introduction of glass fronted mini-bars to promote impulse consumption; these units may be connected with a light that comes on with the room light, or they can react to any light in the room, for example the bathroom light being switched on during the night.

There are a number of mini-bar systems available today and payment for items consumed may be made in several ways.

1 The purchase may be automatically registered at the cashier's office and debited directly to the customer's account. The beverages consumed are itemized on the guest's bill, which can also show the time of purchase and the cost. The advantages of this totally computerized system are that every selection from the mini-bar is immediately registered so that the hotel has few lost sales, the guest does not have to be disturbed for a daily stock check of the mini-bar and detailed information such as sales analysis, value of stock held, refill and maintenance requirements etc. is all available to management (see Figures 12.6 and 12.7). Its major disadvantage is the high cost of installing such a system although this has to be weighed against the savings made in reducing labour costs and the number of lost sales, the increase in efficiency and security to both guests and the hotel, and the additional control information generated for management.

2 On the morning of the guest's departure, the mini-bar is checked and the customer's account debited for drinks consumed. This form of control may either be totally manual or it can be aided by the use of a portable system to process the data normally manually recorded. The manual system is a lengthy process involving the checking of all mini bars within the hotel on a daily basis and recording by hand those that have been used, those in use, mini-bars requiring re-stocking etc. With this 'honesty bar' system, however, the guests are either required to remember their purchases from the machine or the mini-bars must be checked early enough so that the customer's account can be correctly debited before leaving the hotel. With such a system, lost sales can sometimes therefore run at a high level.

This manual approach has been greatly improved by the use of hand held terminals, such as those made by Electrolux. The mini bar management system (MMS) is a portable system used by the mini-bar attendant to record consumption from the mini-bars. By using a bar code reader and a bar chart listing the products in the mini-bar, the data can be recorded and relayed to the invoice printer by telephone or read directly (see Figure 12.8). This information can then be prepared as an individual receipt for the room account or entered directly on to the guest's account. As with the totally computerized system, there are labour savings to be made and it can also provide detailed up-to-date management information. Its major advantage over the totally computerized system is its reduced installation cost as it can use existing telephone and electrical cables. Such a system does, however, still require an attendant to physically check the mini-bars daily although a system can be installed whereby an attendant can see those rooms where the mini-bar has been opened, which need to be serviced etc., via a central display console; this is not only labour saving but also reduces guest disturbance.

3 The guest may purchase a drink by placing the correct amount of money into the machine and removing the beverage item as with a normal vending machine.

Mini-bars therefore exist as a supplementary service to room service and are used by guests at different times of the day when they

```
RoboBar Version
Sales Analysis


RoboBar sales from 30-Apr-9  23:53 01 to 31-May-9  23:57:33

Sequence numbers 200836 to 206557

Active filter summary
      Selection Criteria              Sequence number
      Start Sequence Number           200836
      End Sequence Number             206557
      Tax included                    Yes (Gross)
      Refunds Included                No
      Sorted by                       Sales Value

Sales Analysis

   Name                Sales        %     Total Revenue        %
   STILL WATER          1660    29.44          4150.00     23.74
   1/2 CHAMPAGNE         110     1.95          2365.00     13.53
   DELUXE WHISKY         264     4.68          1584.00      9.06
   BEER                  520     9.22          1560.00      8.93
   DIET COLA             642    11.39          1284.00      7.35
   COLA                  633    11.23          1266.00      7.24
   SPARKLING WATER       453     8,03          1132.50      6.48
   MIXED NUTS            294     5,21          1029.00      5.89
   ORANGE JUICE          457     8.11          1005.40      5.75
   VODKA                 157     2.78           706.50      4.04
   GIN                   148     2.63           666.00      3.81
   TONIC WATER           194     3.44           310.40      1.78
   1/2 WHITE WINE         14     0.25           217.00      1.24
   TOMATO JUICE           92     1.63           202.40      1.16
                        5638                  17478.20
```

Figure 12.6 *An example of a RoboBar mini-bar sales analysis*
Source: Automatic Minibar Systems Ltd

may not want to call or wait for room service. Operated and managed efficiently mini-bars can be an independent profit centre generating additional revenue for the hotel.

Welcome trays or hospitality bars are now increasingly found in hotel rooms. These basically consist of a base which can be free-standing or fixed to a unit, or wall-mounted for extra safety and security, a kettle, an ingredient dispenser which would contain sachets of coffee, tea, sugar, pots of milk and cream and sometimes packets of biscuits, and a detachable tray with cups, saucers, spoons and a teapot. Welcome trays are essentially a free service provided by hotels so that guests may make themselves a hot drink at any time without calling for room service.

```
RoboBar Version
Daily Analysis Report


Daily Analysis from 01-May-9 to 31-May-9

    Total Sales                                    : 17478.20 (14875.06)
    Start Vend Sequence Number                     : 200836
    End Vend Sequence Number                       : 206557
    Number of installed bars                       : 240
    Number of active bars                          : 229
    Available room nights                          : 7440
    Occupied room nights                           : 6148
    Security locked room nights                    : 1
    Unlocked room nights                           : 6147
    Average percentage occupancy                   : 82.63
    Percentage occupancy at end of period          : 80.42
    Used bar nights                                : 1521
    Average percentage use                         : 24.74
    Average sale per room                          : 2.35 (2.00)
    Average sale per occupied room                 : 2.84 (2.42)
    Average sale per unlocked occupied room        : 2.84 (2.42)
    Average sale per used bar                      : 11.49 (9.78)
```

Figure 12.7   *An example of a RoboBar mini-bar daily analysis report*
Source: Automatic Minibar Systems Ltd

12.5.1.6   The buffet

Beverage service in buffet-type arrangement is usually waiter service, although in some cases pre-portioned drinks may be on display on the buffet table to encourage sales. Such beverages that may be offered include glasses of wine, fruit juices, iced coffee, etc.

12.5.1.7   The take-away

In take-away operations, beverages are usually served to the customer with the food ordered. When the customer's order has been prepared, the food and beverage items are packaged and handed to the customer. Like the food products offered for sale by the take-away operations, the beverage products are also highly standardized, often offering a limited number of beverages, with a number of variations, for example the take-away may offer six or eight different flavoured milk shakes. The disposable contain-

ers used for the beverages all carry the operation's theme or logo, e.g. McDonald's, so promoting the company's brand image.

Self-service is therefore a method of beverage service in which customers collect their own beverages from a service point rather than waiters bringing beverages to them. In the majority of industrial catering situations today, self-service is the most commonly adopted method of beverage service, because it can aid in speeding up customer throughput, and for this reason beverages are usually separated out from the main food service counter.

12.5.2   Waiter/waitress service

Waiter/waitress beverage service methods are those in which beverages are transported and served to the customer, whether at a table, counter or bar, by a member of the service staff. It is a method of beverage service more commonly associated with higher priced catering facilities rather than some of the self-service operations previously described, and hence is more widely found in haute cuisine and other full service restaurants.

12.5.2.1   Counter or bar service

In bar service customers may either sit on stools or chairs at the counter or bar and be served directly by the bar staff, or they may sit at individual tables within the bar area and be served by waiting staff who collect the drinks from the bar for the customer. The former method of beverage service in which the customer may remain seated at the bar or table, is most commonly used in public houses and coffee-shop styled catering facilities. The latter method is widely used in hotel bars and other restaurants which often feature a separate bar for pre- and after-dinner drinks. In both catering situations the bar is acting as a sales tool for the establishment and must therefore look attractive and feature an appropriate selection of beverages for that particular type of operation and the market at which it is aiming.

12.5.2.2   Dispensing machines

For the convenience of classification those automatic machines dispensing alcoholic and 'mixer' beverages, may be termed dispensing machines, while those offering non-alcoholic beverages may be termed vending machines. Automatic dispensing machines may be used to accurately dispense exact amounts of alcoholic beverages, the types of dispensing machines varying from the very simple to the very sophisticated. In many, the machine's controls are set at the amount required to be dispensed, the bottle is placed inverted into the machine, and the machine will measure and dispense the portions set on the machine. In the more sophisticated machines cocktails may even be mixed and then dispensed.

The use of automatic dispensing machines has several advantages; each portion is accurately measured so there is no overpouring or under pouring; standard drinks are always served to the customer; some dispensing machines can pour and mix drinks quicker than a barperson; if the machines meter the number of drinks dispensed, a precise check may be made on the number of drinks served and the amount of money taken by the bar; their use cuts down breakages, wastage and theft; bar layouts can become more compact and save on space requirements; and finally, those machines that not only meter and dispense drinks, but also maintain a perpetual stock inventory are a very useful tool for re-ordering and management control.

12.5.2.3   Table service

In the context of this classification table service is being used to describe the service of beverages at the customer's dining table. The customer's order for beverages is taken at the table and the beverages usually collected from the side of the bar or from a dispense bar, which is out of sight from the customer. A dispense bar is a bar for dispensing beverages to service staff, and not directly to customers; because it is not a visual sales tool of the establishment, it is not usually designed to be aesthetically appealing but very functional, as it often has to serve a number of restaurant and other beverage sales outlets in the establishment, for example in a hotel. In some restaurants a trolley or cart may be used for the service of beverages to tables, particularly after the meal when liqueurs are served. The use of such a beverage cart is not only an aid to the service of the beverages but is also an important visual sales tool.

12.5.2.4   Banquet service

Beverage service at banqueting functions is often very similar to food service in that specific beverages have already been chosen and are served at set times during the course of a meal, to accompany certain foods. Pre-meal drinks in banqueting may either be served by the service staff, for example taking trays of drinks round to the guests, or a bar offering a selection of drinks may be arranged in the room used for guest assembly, and the guests can buy directly from this. During the meal the wines pre-chosen by the host are served, and after dinner beverages such as coffee and liqueurs are also served at the guests' tables. This above system is referred to as an 'inclusive bar'. Any other beverages ordered by the guests are not usually included in the cost of the banquet meal and are therefore paid for separately by the guests. The alternative to an inclusive bar is a 'cash bar' when no drinks have been pre-ordered and all drinks are paid for by the guests themselves. It is a common practice, however, that in the reception area for a banquet the wine waiters will have set up a table so that customers can choose, and at times pay for, their wines in advance.

12.5.2.5   Room and lounge service

In waiter service operations the customer orders the required beverages from room or floor service and the drinks are taken to the room; payment may be made directly to the waiter, or as is more usual, is debited to the customer's account. Although self-service machines are being used in some establishments waiter service is still the most common method used for room service.

As with the service of foods in hotel lounges, beverage service is gradually being confined to the more expensive hotels; some other grades of hotels, resort establishments and pubs, however, do use the service of morning coffees and afternoon teas as a means of extending their service times.

12.5.2.6   Car or drive-in service

In drive-in operations beverages are served to the customers at the same time as they receive their food. The beverages and food are placed on trays from which customers eat in their cars; the trays are removed by the waiters or carhops when the customers have finished. Alternatively, the customer may take the beverages away for consumption.

12.5.2.7   Coffee carts

The use of coffee carts or tea trolleys for the service of beverages has been included here because within this type of service beverages are often served directly to customers at their desk or table. This method of beverage service is still being used today in office blocks and factory

buildings although to a large extent it is being replaced by vending.

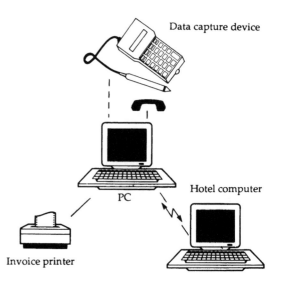

Figure 12.8   *The Electrolux mini-bar management system*
Data can be entered using either the keyboard or an attached bar code scanner. Cues are displayed on the portable data terminal (PDT) indicating the data to enter. When the data has been gathered, the PDT is connected to a telephone or directly to the computer to transmit data to the host computer for processing.
Source: Electrolux Leisure Appliances, Electrolux Ltd.

12.5.2.8   Liqueur trolleys

Liqueur trolleys may be used in a variety of restaurants and hotels and are usually brought to the customer's table at the end of a meal. An attractively stocked and interesting display of liqueurs can often stimulate customers' interest and increase alcoholic beverage sales.

The waiter method of beverage service is therefore most commonly used in higher priced catering establishments, although it does have an application in a number of other catering situations. By definition this type of beverage service is more labour intensive than the type required in self-service operations. In haute cuisine restaurants for example, employing the French method of food service, in which the food is presented to the guest before service, a similar method of beverage service also exists; the service of wine, for example, would be very similar in style and formality – the wine being presented to the customer and tasted before it is served to the other guests. This type of service contrasts with self-service operations where guests not only help themselves to the food they would like, but also to the beverages. In the majority of catering situations, therefore, the style of beverage service reflects the style of food service, so that the two are complementary to one another.

12.6 References

Axler, B. H. (1979). *Food Services: A Managerial Approach.* Lexington MA: DC Heath.

Automatic Vending Association of Britain (1996). *Census vend inform.* Automatic Vending Association of Britain.

Green, E. F. et al. (1987). *Profitable Food and Beverage Management: Operations.* Jenks, Oklahoma: Williams Books.

13
Food and beverage production control

13.1 Introduction

Food and beverage production control may be regarded as consisting of four basic stages of pre-control which together should reduce wastage and therefore reduce higher costs than necessary from over-production, loss of business opportunity from a shortage of items being available, and loss of revenue from giving excess portion sizes.

The four basic stages are:

1 Production planning.
2 Standard yields.
3 Standard recipes.
4 Standard portion sizes.

When the four basic stages are practised in a food and beverage operation they should aid management in controlling costs, setting standards and achieving customer satisfaction. The production of beverages needs to be tightly controlled as the contribution to profits from beverages is usually higher than that from food.

13.2 Food production control

13.2.1 Production planning

Production planning, or volume forecasting as it is also known, is the forecasting of the volume of sales for an establishment, for a specified time period, for example a day, a week or a month.

The aims and objectives of production planning are as follows:

1 To facilitate food cost control for the establishment.
2 To facilitate the purchasing of foodstuffs, particularly perishable items, and ensure appropriate stock levels are maintained.

3 To reduce the problem of food that is left over and how it is to be re-used, or customer dissatisfaction when insufficient foods are available.
4 To gear production to demand by forecasting the number of meals to be served for a given meal period, for example the number of dinners to be sold in a particular catering outlet for a period of seven days; and on a more detailed level, to predict the number of menu items that will be taken by a specific number of customers.
5 To enable a comparison to be made between actual and potential volume of sales, and for corrective action to be taken if necessary.

An initial forecast is made either at a set period in advance, for example a month, or when the major food orders are placed. This initial forecast estimates the total number of meals to be sold by the establishment and the estimated total of each menu item. In the case of a large hotel with a variety of catering outlets, a more detailed forecast would be made for each individual outlet. Factors that need to be taken into account at this stage are the season, and hence the weather forecast for that time of year; past popularity of menu items; major events occurring in the area – fêtes, shows etc., that are likely to attract a larger than average number to the establishment's normal catchment area, any sales campaigns currently being promoted by the operation, etc.

The initial estimate is later adjusted, usually one or two days prior to the day of production, so that a more accurate forecast may be made. On the basis of this updated information, any changes that may need to be made with regard to staff scheduling, food purchases and requisitions etc., should be made as soon as possible.

There are a number of aids or management tools that may be employed by an establishment to assist the forecasting and planning of production.

13.2.1.1 *Cyclic menus*

These are a series or set of menus that are repeated at set periods of time by a catering outlet; for example, menus may be planned for a three-week cycle, and at the end of the three weeks the same menus would be repeated. Generally the longer the period of time between the menus being repeated, the shorter the choice of menu items: for example, a menu offering only two or three main courses would need a cycle of between twenty to twenty-four days to avoid early repetition, whereas a menu offering a choice of six or seven main course items may only need a cycle of between ten to twelve days. The type of catering establishment must therefore have an influence on the length of the cyclic menus being offered. For example, in a hospital with an average stay of just over a week, a two or three week cycle may be appropriate; whereas for guests staying at a resort hotel or people living in residential establishments such as homes and universities, a larger cycle menu would be necessary to avoid repetition and monotony.

The main advantages of the cyclic menus may be as follows:

1 Repetition of menu items aids in the preparation of standard recipes, procedures for preparation, etc., in the production kitchen. This repetition is also instrumental in the establishment of standard training procedures, efficient work flows, good utilization of equipment, etc.
2 Staff scheduling and rostering may be accurately calculated when fairly precise production requirements are known. This enables labour requirements to be increased or decreased according to the forecast production needs, and this in turn helps to reduce kitchen and restaurant labour costs.
3 With a set range of menus available, customer preferences for certain items will soon become apparent, and this in turn will aid further production forecasting and planning by the establishment and aid in reducing purchasing and production costs.
4 By analysing sales, certain dishes may be iden-

tifiable as being very popular. Should this happen, full advantage should be taken of this with the aim of establishing a reputation for the dish.

The main disadvantages of cyclic menus may be as follows:

1 The range of menu items offered may be too repetitious and hence become monotonous for the customer if the cycle is too short for the type of establishment so that, for example, the same foods are offered on the same day each week. It can also become monotonous for the staff if the menu is limited, resulting in staff boredom and lack of motivation and flair.
2 The cycle menus must be reviewed and if necessary rewritten where appropriate, to take advantage of seasonal foods, special offers, etc., otherwise food costs could increase substantially.

13.2.1.2 *Sales histories*

These are detailed records showing actual sales of menu items for a catering outlet. Ideally, the actual sales should be recorded alongside the forecast sales for comparative and future forecasting purposes.

Sales histories should be recorded on a daily basis which is then totalled at the end of the week; this is so that a backlog of data to be processed does not develop and so that information may be relayed to management as soon as possible on how accurate the forecasting has been. Where there is more than one catering outlet in an establishment, separate sales histories should be kept for each one; this is particularly useful for comparative purposes of, for example, sales of specific menu items which may be selling particularly well in one outlet and could therefore be extended to another.

The recording of sales histories can be a very labour intensive task so that in a number of large establishments it has now become considerably more economical to buy several electronic cash registers which automatically produce sales histories for the catering outlet as well as performing the normal cash register functions.

See Figure 13.1 for an example of a volume forecast/sales history form.

POINTER HOTELS (UK) LTD **Volume Forecast**								
Monday **6/2/9–** to Sunday **13/2/9–**								

	MONDAY		TUESDAY		WEDNESDAY		THURSDAY	
	Estimated	*Actual*	*Estimated*	*Actual*	*Estimated*	*Actual*	*Estimated*	*Actual*
Restaurant								
Lunch	40	48	55	58	60	64	70	
Dinner	85	81	90	94	90	98	85	
Coffee shop	125	135	120	128	125	132	120	
Breakfast	180	195	180	197	160	148	155	
Lunch								
Dinner	110	115	125	136	120	104	115	
Functions	240	235	–	–	–	–	140	
Lunch	–	–	320	310	120	115	–	
Dinner								
Specials	–	–	–	–	–	–	–	
Staff meals	15	15	15	15	15	15	15	
Breakfast	52	50	55	52	55	55	52	
Lunch								
Dinner	42	40	48	46	40	42	44	
Total meals	889	914	1008	1036	785	773	796	

GENERAL COMMENTS:

Figure 13.1 *A volume forecast form, showing the estimated number of meals to be served in each selling outlet daily, and the actual meals served*

Note: This form would also be of use as a combined volume forecast/sales history form. The volume forecast for each outlet should be taken to the next stage when the forecast sales for each menu item should be prepared.

The other aids available to management for production planning are more specific to the actual production process, and these are discussed below.

13.2.2 Standard yields

The standard yield of a particular food product is the usable part of that product after initial preparation, or the edible part of the product after preparation and cooking; for exam-

ple, the standard yield for a whole fillet of beef is the number of fillet steaks that will be available for cooking and final sale to the customer after the fillet is trimmed and any unwanted meat removed. Any usable trimmed meat should be taken into account with the standard yield.

In large establishments buying in large quantities of food per week, standard yields may be available for almost all the commodities – meat, fish, vegetables, etc. In smaller establishments standard yields may only be determined for the more expensive cuts of meat or fish such as whole fillets, lobsters, salmon, etc. The development of standard yields by an establishment has a number of advantages:

1 Standard yields determine the most appropriate and advantageous size/weight to buy a particular commodity in.
2 They assist in determining the raw material requirements for the production levels anticipated from the production forecasts, and therefore act as an aid in the purchasing of the establishment's foodstuffs.
3 They act as a 'double check' for the purchasing department. Should an unsatisfactory delivery of meat, for example, be made to an establishment and is unnoticed at the receiving bay, this delivery is subject to a second 'checking' procedure in the kitchen where the meat should yield a standard number of portions.
4 They act as a safeguard against pilferage or wastage occurring in the kitchen as the actual and potential yields can be compared and this acts as a measurement of the efficiency of the production department.
5 Finally, they are an aid to accurate food costings for particular dishes offered on an establishment's menu, as the cost factor can be established (see Figures 13.2 and 13.3).

13.2.3 Standard recipes

A standard recipe is a written schedule for producing a particular menu item, specifying the name and quantity of the item to be produced, the constituent ingredients necessary for its production, and the method of preparation. This is the basic information contained in a standard recipe although it may also include such information as the costings of the dish, its nutritional value, etc. Detailed recipe cards are usually kept in the food and beverage control department for cost and price updating, only the basic information needing to be included on those cards that are displayed in the production area – often together with a photograph of the end product. (See Figure 13.5 for an example of a standard recipe form.)

The use of standard recipes by an establishment has a number of advantages.

1 Accurate food costings can be determined for particular dishes and from this the cost per portion may be calculated. It is necessary to have the food cost of a dish for the purpose of pricing it for sale to the customer, in order to make the required gross profit. For some items it is not possible to make a gross profit, of, for example, 65 per cent, whereas for other items the gross profit made may be higher; by having this type of information, the food and beverage department is able to balance the menu prices so that overall the necessary gross profit is obtained from the menu.
2 In certain institutional establishments, such as hospitals, it is important to know the precise nutritional value of the dishes being given to certain patients. By itemizing the ingredients for a particular dish the nutritional value of it is easily calculated.
3 They are an aid to purchasing and internal requisitioning. By taking into account the following day's production forecast requirements the head chef is able to use the standard recipes to calculate the quantities of foodstuffs he/she will require the following day. In some catering establishments the head storeman may have a copy of the standard recipes and when the next day's forecast requirements are sent, the head storeman is responsible for calculating the quantity of foodstuffs that need to be sent to the kitchen.
4 Standard recipes are particularly useful in the preparation of items in the kitchens, both as a reminder to present staff of the preparation procedure, and also as an aid to the training of new employees. More importantly the use of standard recipes in the production area ensures that the customer will always receive a standardized product.
5 Standard recipes are an aid to menu planning. New additions to the menu, for example, may be accurately costed and balanced with the other items on the menu, not only in terms of price, but also in appearance, flavour, colour, etc.
6 They may be used as a basis for compiling standard portion sizes which, if used in conjunction with standard recipes and standard yields, will together form the basis of a very effective production control system.

YIELD TEST SUMMARY REPORT

ITEM. **Canadian Smoked Salmon**
PURCHASE SPECIFICATION: **437**
STANDARD RECIPE No.: **520**
TOTAL RAW WEIGHT AS PURCHASED: **3 lb 4 oz**
COST PER lb.: **£7.00**

Cooking and preparation details	Weight lb	Weight oz	Percentage original weight
As purchased weight	3	4	100
Less initial trimming		9	17.3
Presentation weight	2	11	82.7
Less unservable weight and skin		11	21.2
Total servable weight	2	0	61.5

Ratio of servable weight to original weight

$$= \frac{\text{servable weight}}{\text{original weight}} = \frac{2 \text{ lb } 0 \text{ oz}}{3 \text{ lb } 4 \text{ ox}} = \frac{32}{52} = 61.5\%$$

Cost per servable lb

$$= \frac{\text{as purchased price per lb}}{\% \text{ original weight}} = \frac{£7.00}{61.5\%} = \frac{£7.00}{0.615} = £11.38$$

Cost Factor

$$= \frac{\text{cost per servable lb}}{\text{as purchased price per lb}} = \frac{£11.38}{£7.00} = 1.626$$

Portion Cost (at 2 oz portion size)

$$= \frac{\text{cost per servable lb}}{\text{no. portions per servable lb}} = \frac{£11.38}{\frac{16}{2}} = £1.42 \text{ pence}$$

Figure 13.2   *An example of a yield test summary report showing the essential basic information that should be calculated for all major food items on a menu*

```
                        YIELD AND PRODUCT TEST REPORT


    ITEM:   PINEAPPLE

    Brand:   Rosebrooke; pineapple rings in syrup

    Country of origin:   South African produce; Cayenne variety

    Price per can:   £3.50              Size:   A.10

    Nett weight:   6 lbs 12 ozs

    Liquor content.   45 fl ozs

    Drained weight of contents:   4 lbs 2 ozs

    Approx. cost per lb of solids:   51.85 pence

    Approx. cost per oz of solids:   3.24 pence

    Approx. cost per ring of solids:   7.78 pence

                        Score

                        Eating quality................ (Max 25 pts) ....  20
                        Flavour ......................... (  "   20 pts)....  15
                        Tenderness ................... (  "   20 pts) ....  18
                        Colour ........................... (  "   15 pts) ....  12
                        Blemishes ...................... (  "   10 pts) ....   9
                        Wholeness ..................... (  "   10 pts) ....  10

                        Maximum 100 .............. Total        ....  84

    Remarks and opinions

    An excellent sample of rings, 3 in. in diameter with a count of 45 per
    can;  slightly tart without acidity and with a glazed appearance, free
    of blemishes making an attractive dessert fruit.

    Summary


    Price per lb           Cost per oz          Count           Score

    40.74 pence            3.24 pence           45              84
```

Figure 13.3 *A typical example of a yield and product test report*
Note: Tests of this kind require to be undertaken each year when a new season's supply is available

BUTCHERING AND COOKING TEST REPORT

NAME OF ITEM: **Fillets of Beef** GRADE: **Frozen − Irish**
PIECES: **10** WEIGHT: **51 lbs 0 oz**
PRICE PER LB: **£3.50** DEALER: **Endsleigh & Co.**
TOTAL WEIGHT PRICE: **£178.50** DATE OF TEST: **24/7/9−**

Item	Weight lbs	Weight oz	Ratio %	Cost Per lb £	Cost Total £	oz Pence
Raw yield						
Initial raw yield	51	0	100	3.50	178.50	21.875
Less bones fat, trim	10	8	20.59			
Saleable raw weight	40	8	79.41	4.41	178.50	27.56
Breakdown						
Trimmed fillet	30	0	58.82	5.26	157.80	32.875
Hamburger meat	6	0	11.76	1.50	9.00	9.37
Stroganoff	4	8	8.82	2.60	11.70	16.26
Total						
Cooked yield						
Saleable raw weight						
Shrinkage						
Saleable cooked weight						
Breakdown						
Total						

Raw or cooked portion cost and portion cost factor

Name of dish	Portion size (RTC)	No. of portions	Cost per portion £	Total cost £	Cost factor
Filet mignon	4 oz	120	1.315	157.80	0.3757
Châteaubriand	16 oz	30	5.26	157.80	1.50286
Filet de boeuf rôti	8 oz	60	2.63	157.80	0.7514
Total					

Figure 13.4(a)   *An example of a typical butchering and cooking test report showing alternative data for an uncooked cut of meat*

BUTCHERING AND COOKING TEST REPORT

NAME OF ITEM: **Fore-rib of beef** GRADE: **Scotch–1st quality**
PIECES: **1** (boneless) WEIGHT: **22 lb 0 oz**
PRICE PER LB: **£2.80** DEALER: **Rosebrook**
TOTAL WEIGHT PRICE: **£61.60** DATE OF TEST: **12.12.9–**

| Item | Weight | | Ratio % | Cost | | |
	lbs	oz		Per lb £	Total £	oz Pence
Raw yield						
Initial raw yield	22	0	100	2.80	61.60	17.5
Less fat, trim	2	0	9			
Saleable raw weight	20	0	91	3.08	61.60	19.25
Breakdown						
Total						
Cooked yield						
Saleable raw weight (or saleable wt)	20	0	91	3.08	61.60	19.25
Shrinkage	3	8	17.5			
Saleable cooked weight	16	8	75	3.73	61.60	23.33
Breakdown						
Total						

Raw or cooked portion cost and portion cost factor

Name of dish	Portion size (RTC)	No. of portions	Cost per portion £	Total cost £	Cost factor
Roast beef f					
à la carte	12 oz	22	2.80	61.60	1.0
table d'hôte	8 oz	33	1.87	61.60	0.6679
Total					

Figure 13.4(b) *A typical example of a butchering and cooking test report for a cooked item, for example roast fore-rib of beef (boneless)*

Unit	Ingredients	Date: 5/2/8–		Date:		Date:	
		Price per unit	Amount	Price per unit	Amount	Price per unit	Amount
		£	£				
1¼ kg	Topside of Beef	1.50/kg	1.88				
2½ l.	Brown Stock	0.05/1.	0.13				
125 g	Meat Dripping	0.50/kg	0.06				
½ kg	Caster Sugar	0.20/kg	0.10				
1 kg	Sliced Onions	0.40/kg	0.40				
1 l.	Beer	0.60/1.	0.60				
125 g	Flour	0.25/kg	0.03				
	Total cost		£3.20				
	Cost per portion		£0.16				

RECIPE: CARBONADE OF BEEF **POINTER HOTELS (UK) LTD** STANDARD RECIPE No.: 321

QUANTITY: 20 Portions   PORTION SIZE: 112 g (raw weight)

Preparation and Service
1.   Cut meat into thin slices.
2.   Season with salt and pepper and pass through flour.
3.   Quickly colour on both sides in hot fat and place in casserole.
4.   Fry onions to a light brown colour.
5.   Add to the meat.
6.   Add the beer and sugar and brown stock to just cover the meat.
7.   Cover with tight fitting lid and cook in oven at 175°C until meat is tender. Approx. 2 hours.
8.   Skim and correct seasoning.
9.   Serve in casserole dish.

Figure 13.5   *An example of a standard recipe*

13.2.3.1   Recipe files

A number of management tools may assist in the forecasting and planning of the establishment's food production requirements – cyclic menus, sales histories, standard yields, standard recipes and standard portion sizes. It is difficult to emphasize too much the need to have this valuable information logically and neatly assembled so that it is available at any time to the personnel who need to use it.

Recipe files should be maintained by the establishment containing the type of information that has just been described. These files may be assembled in two ways: the first is manually, and the second is by the use of a computer.

1 *Manually.* Cards of a standard size may be maintained containing details of all the individual dishes offered on the establishment's menu or menus. Such details would include, for example, the standard recipes for the particular dishes and their standard portion sizes.

The file would then need to be classified, for example, under such headings as meats, vegetables, desserts, etc., and each dish numbered so that any particular item may be easily located.

This system of maintaining a recipe file is, however, very labour intensive; every time it is necessary to alter the details of a dish in any way, the recipe card must firstly be located, then the changes handwritten or typed, and the card then placed back into the recipe file. Should the management wish to change the menu completely, a detailed list of all the menu items, their gross profits, etc., would be needed and this would take a considerable amount of time as it would have to be prepared manually. This system is also very open to human error and in a large establishment could take up a considerable amount of space.

2 *By computer.* Some establishments are now using computers to store their recipe files. The same amount of detailed information must first be collected, but here instead of writing

the details on to cards, the information is typed into a computer.

A great deal of information may be programmed into a computer, and certainly more than could ever be contained on individual cards – nutritional standards, food characteristics, budget allocations and constraints, and so on. Once the computer has been programmed and fed this huge amount of data, it can very quickly produce information that it would take one person several days or weeks to collate. In rewriting a whole new menu for example, the computer may be asked to find the optimum combination of menu items within given constraints, such as to list at least fifteen main dish items that will give a gross profit of 65 per cent, for the next three months, based on current prices. Such a task would take the food and beverage department a considerable amount of time and even then the optimum combination may still not have been achieved. A computerized recipe file can of course also be used for simple day-to-day tasks, such as stores ordering and requisitioning – a print out from the computer being sent to the head storeman, instead of a handwritten stores order.

In terms of labour costs alone, therefore, the savings achieved by the use of a computerized recipe file can be considerable. These long-term savings should be seriously considered as a viable alternative to the manual system even though the cost of setting up such a computerized system may be initially more expensive.

13.2.4 Standard portion sizes

A standard portion is the quantity of a particular food item that will be served to the customer; the quantity may be measured in terms of ounces (for example, a 4 oz portion of meat), or a numerical quantity (for example, one bread roll per person). The portion sizes of the food items are determined by management in conjunction with the heads of both the kitchen and restaurant departments.

Standard portion sizes in the operation may be established in several ways.

1 By buying in pre-portioned food items, for example 8 oz rump steaks, pre-wrapped packs of butter and condiments, etc.
2 By buying in food items in bulk and portioning them in the production kitchen before service, for example, pre-plating salads to be served in a display cabinet in a cafeteria line.
3 By portioning food items as they are being served to the customer, for example, food in hot *bain-maries* in a cafeteria line being plated and served when the customer requests the food item.

In establishments operating more than one level of service, there may be varying portion sizes for the same food items, for the different catering outlets. For example, in a hotel the coffee shop offering a table d'hôte menu may serve a 6 oz rump steak, while the silver service restaurant offering an à la carte menu would serve an 8 oz steak.

Standard portion sizes, like standard recipes, are an aid to food costing, as once the standard portion size has been established the gross profit may be calculated for that dish. Any fluctuations in the sizes of the portions, for example serving larger portions, will therefore be reflected in the restaurant's gross profit, particularly so if this is occurring with a number of menu items.

It is important also to provide kitchen and restaurant staff with the correct portioning equipment, so that if the customer is to receive 3 oz of vegetable, the operative has a 3 oz ladle to serve the vegetable with. Spot checks should also be regularly made to ensure that the correct portioning equipment is being used; often if a certain sized ladle goes missing, the operative will simply use another which could be 1 or 2 oz larger. As with standard recipes, details of the standard portion sizes should be made readily available to all necessary employees. The food and beverage costing department should regularly review the portion size of a particular food item with reference to its current price, as it may be necessary either to reduce the standard portion size if the cost of a particular food item has increased substantially; increase the selling price; or possibly, remove the dish from the menu for a period until the cost price is acceptable. In the kitchen and restaurant the standard portion sizes of a dish are often combined with the standard recipes, and together they may be displayed on a wall chart to which all employees may refer.

There are therefore a number of techniques that may be employed by an establishment to assist in the planning of food production requirements. If these techniques are to be used effectively they must be co-ordinated, so that from standard yields standard recipes are written, and from these standard portion sizes are established, and so on. These management techniques are also applicable to different size establishments – from the small thirty-bedroom hotel to the large international hotel chain; the only difference is in the degree of sophistication, as the principles remain very much the same.

13.3   Beverage production control

The planning of beverage production is a comparatively more simple task than the planning of food production for a number of reasons. First, unless the catering outlet is a wine bar or similar, the main reason customers are frequenting the establishment is for the purpose of having a meal, so the purchasing of drink is of secondary importance to the customer; and, second, beverages, with few exceptions, are non-perishable and therefore do not deteriorate over a long period, in fact in the case of wines for example, they may even improve.

Although beverage production control is not so complex as food production control it may still, however, employ several of the same management techniques. For the purpose of comparison beverage production control may be discussed under the same headings as food production control.

13.3.1   Production planning

Production planning, or volume forecasting, is the forecasting of the volume of sales for an establishment for a specified period and the detailing of the volume of sales for each outlet such as a dispense bar, cocktail bar, cash, and inclusive function bars, etc.

The method is more straightforward than that for food because the product is usually non-perishable and therefore there is very little waste,

and also the product is generally purchased in a ready-to-serve state. It is common practice to have established par stocks for all selling outlets. A standard par stock is a predetermined number of bottles of each item and brand used in a particular bar, and the size of the par stock is calculated to be sufficient to meet the demand for a busy day plus a safety factor. The main purpose of a standard par stock is to help determine the average daily consumption of a bar, to assist with requisitioning, and to promote good control over the stock.

13.3.1.1   Sales histories

These records may be kept by a catering establishment to monitor their beverage sales, and from these develop lists of the most requested drinks. It may be that 90 per cent of the outlet's mixed drinks orders, for example, comes from this beverage list, while the remaining 10 per cent will consist of a variety of other drinks. Such information may be used for future purchasing planning or as a basis of special promotions featuring varieties of these popular mixed drinks etc.

13.3.2   Standard yields

The standard yields of beverage products may, with few exceptions, be accurately calculated, because for the majority of beverages there is little wastage and all the contents of, for example, a bottle of spirits may be used. For the purpose of beverage control all beverages bought in to an establishment should have standard yields calculated, on which the pricing of each drink may be based, and to control wastage and pilferage. If, for example, a 75 cl bottle of wine is bought in, allowing 15 cl of wine to a glass, five good measures should be obtained.

13.3.3   Standard drink recipes

Standard recipes should also be compiled for the majority of beverage products offered for sale by the establishment. Like standard yields, standard recipes may be very accurately produced as all the contents of a drink may be itemized on the standard recipe (see Figure 3.6).

POINTER HOTELS (UK) LTD

Recipe No.   304

Beverage Recipe: Scaramouche Cooler

QUANTITY: 1   Portion Size: 12 oz

| Unit | Ingredients | Date 5/2/9— | | Date | | Date | |
		Price per unit £	Amount £	Price per unit	Amount	Price per unit	Amount
2.5 cl	VODKA 70 cl bottle	11.00	0.39				
2.5 cl	Fresh orange juice	0.20	0.10				
1.0cl	Fresh lemon juice	0.18	0.06				
1 split	Bitter lemon	0.20	0.20				
1 in.	Piece orange peel	–	–				
1 in.	Piece lemon peel	–	–				
1 slice	Orange	0.10	0.02				
	Total cost		0.77				
	Selling Price		1.85				
	Cost Percentage		41.6%				

Preparation and Service

1.   Half fill a 14 oz tall tumbler with ice cubes.
2.   Add vodka, orange and lemon juice.
3.   Fill with bitter lemon and stir.
4.   Twist orange and lemon peel over drink and add to glass.
5.   Cut orange slice and fasten to rim of glass.
6.   Serve with tall cocktail stirrer.

Figure 13.6 *An example of a standard beverage recipe*

Obviously only a certain number of standard recipes may be produced for an establishment, and this is where the sales histories discussed earlier may be particularly useful – they do at least ensure that the recipes for the most popular drinks have been standardized. With such a variety of components with which to make different drinks, it would not be practical to write standard recipes for every possible combination; so the bar staff should be provided with a book or books chosen by management on how to prepare those varieties of drinks that may be rather unusual or rare. Computer terminals and visual display units may be used in bars where the mixing and service details of various drinks can be displayed to order giving a speedier visual recipe than using a book.

Bar staff should also be provided with the correct equipment for measuring and mixing drinks. Standard bar equipment would include such items as a fruit knife and board, sticks for cherries and olives, ice bowls, fruit squeezers, a cocktail shaker and stirrer, etc.

13.3.4   Standard portion sizes

As with standard recipes, standard portion sizes for beverages should be easier to control than those for food products. With some beverages, for example a bottled baby orange juice, all the contents of the bottle will be emptied into the customer's glass. Other beverages such as spirits need to be measured before being poured into the customer's glass, the use of optics being an accurate method.

Another aid to control the portion size is to use standard glassware for specific drinks. This not only helps staff to become consistently accurate when free pouring drinks but it prevents customer dissatisfaction when they may receive the correct portion size but served in a larger glass when it appears the portion size is smaller than the previous drink.

13.3.4.1   *Automatic beverage dispensing machines*

A more recent method for controlling accurately beverage costs and ensuring standard portion sizes is to use automatic beverage dispensing machines. The bottles of beverage are inverted and connected with small bore pipes within a locked storeroom, to each selling outlet. The advantages of this method are numerous, but include the following:

1 The drink size is pre-set and the drink automatically measured.
2 The yield is consistently higher than when using other methods as the bottles drain completely into the dispenser.
3 Each drink can be metered by the selling outlet. This helps with inventory control and the calculation of estimated bar revenue.

4 It prevents bar staff from handling bottles. Every drink that they need for a customer is obtained by just pressing the correct drink button on the dispenser.
5 Many beverage dispense machines are connected to microcomputers so that they can measure the drinks, dispense, display the prices, print the guest's bill, as well as maintain the inventory and analyse drink sales.

Unfortunately, there are some disadvantages in using beverage dispensing machines, such as:

1 Unsuitability for certain types of beverage operations, for example a cocktail bar in a luxury type hotel where the clientele expect personal service with the mixing of their drinks.
2 The cost of installing dispensing machines is high, although the higher level of control should help to repay the initial costs relatively quickly.
3 In general they are only suitable for use in bars with a very high volume of sales and where the customer is not so concerned with traditional bar service.

The management techniques used in beverage production planning are therefore very similar in concept and method to the techniques used for food production planning; if anything even tighter standards may be laid down for beverage production for the reasons already discussed. A similar recipe file for beverages may also be produced – either manually or by use of a computer and again the use of a computer for beverage planning should be seriously considered for the long-term cost savings and tighter control it can offer the establishment.

13.4   Reference

Green, E. E. et al. *(1987). Profitable Food and Beverage Management: Operations.* Jenks, Oklahoma: Williams Books.

14
Food controlling

14.1 Introduction

The main objectives of food cost control were detailed in Chapter 7 as being:

1 The analysis of income and expenditure.
2 The establishment and maintenance of standards.
3 The pricing and quotations of menus.
4 The prevention of waste.
5 The prevention of fraud.
6 Information for management reports.

This chapter aims to deal with the 'after the event' phase of the control cycle, that is, the phase following the routine operational stages of the cycle, namely purchasing, receiving, storing, issuing, production and service (see Chapters 9 to 12.) It will deal with the analysis of expenditure and income, and the methods used to calculate daily and period food costs, to-date costs, and potential costs as well as the information for food and beverage management reports.

14.2 The essentials of a control system

It is important when examining an existing control system or preparing to install a system into a new operation that the following points should be borne in mind.

1 Any control system should be comprehensive and cover all the outlets of an establishment and all stages of the food control cycle.
2 The cost of maintaining the system should be in relation to the saving to be made, the level of sophistication of the control system usually increasing with the increase in the volume of sales and the complexity of the menu.
3 The control system should be easy to operate and to be understood by all levels of staff.
4 The control system should be seen by staff to be working. That is, that management act in a positive way to adverse trading results and follow up on future results to check if the corrective action taken is effective.
5 To be effective the information produced must be accurate and up-to-date.

14.3 Calculation of food cost

There are several basic terms which need to be emphasized with regard to the calculation of food costs, such as:

1 *Food cost.* This refers to the cost of food incurred in preparing the meals served.
2 *Food cost percentage.* Refers to the percentage of the revenue from sales incurred in preparing the meals, that is, the cost of food as a percentage of sales of food.
3 *Gross profit or kitchen gross profit.* The excess of sales over the cost of food expressed as a percentage, or in financial terms.
4 *Potential food cost (or sales).* The food cost (or sales) under perfect conditions. This may be expressed as a percentage or in financial terms.

14.4 Methods of food control

14.4.1 Weekly/monthly food cost report

The following is an example for the calculating of the monthly food costs for an operation where detailed information is not thought to be necessary, or for a small or owner-managed unit where the control is an everyday part of the manager's activity, in order for the operation to be successful. The weekly/monthly food cost report is almost a reconciliation report on an activity that is tightly controlled daily by management (see Table 14.1).

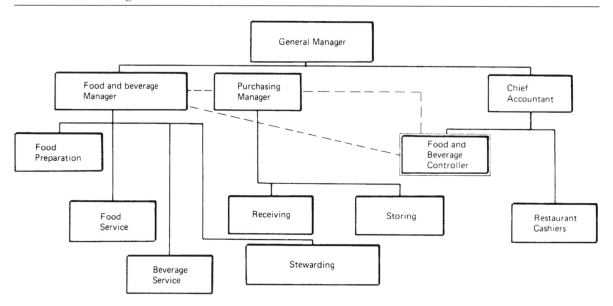

Figure 14.1   *An extract from the organization chart of a large hotel showing the relationship of the food and beverage control department to other departments*

Note: The broken line indicates close co-operation to be maintained between the various departments to obtain maximum control and operating results

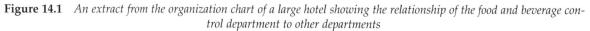

Table 14.1   *A weekly/monthly food cost report*

	£
Opening food stock level a.m. Day 1	2,220.00
plus Total purchases for period (Day 1-28)	10,934.00
Sub total	13,154.00
Less Closing food stock level, Day 28	2,116.00
= Total cost of food consumed	11,038.00
Total food sales	29,251.00
Food cost percentage = 37.74%	

The advantages of this method are:

1 It is simple and quick to produce.
2 It can give an indication of the general performance of the unit.

The disadvantages though are:

1 This information is only produced after seven or twenty-eight days of operation.
2 It provides no intermediate information so that any undesirable trends (for example, food costs too high) may be corrected earlier.

3 It does not provide the daily or to-date information on purchases, requisitions and sales that a unit with an average of £1,000 a day turnover should.

14.4.2   A daily food cost report

This food cost method is suitable for a small-to medium-sized operation, or one where a not too sophisticated method is required, or where the costs involved in relation to the savings to be made do not justify a more involved method.

Table 14.2 shows an example of this basic food cost report for twenty-eight days. The following is a step-by-step procedure on compiling the report.

Step 1   Prepare a chart on column paper as set out in Table 14.2 and complete entries on a day-to-day basis as follows.

Step 2   Column 3. Begin by entering the opening stock value (that is, the closing stock value at the end of the last period). On subsequent days enter in this column the difference between column 5 and column 6 of the previous day, for example the entry in column 3 on March 3rd is £2,635.50 – £370.00 = £2,265.50.

Step 3   Column 4. Enter the total of all goods purchased and received on that day. *Note:* On Sundays there is no purchasing done and therefore no entry made.

Step 4   Column 5. This is the total of columns 3 and 4 for that day.

Step 5   Column 6. This is the total of all goods requisitioned by the chef on that day. *(Note:* Some of the items requisitioned may be for pre-preparation on the same day but for selling on subsequent days.)

Step 6   Column 7. This is the total food sales as recorded by the cashier/manager and will consist often of cash plus credit accounts. *Note:* Any government taxes that are required to be charged against food sales have been excluded from this figure.

Step 7   Column 8. This is obtained by dividing column 6 by column 7 and multiplying by 100 to convert to a percentage (for example, March 2nd £370 ÷ £980 = 0.3775, 0.3775 x 100 = 37.75)

Step 8   Column 9. This is the to-date total of all food purchases, that is, the sum total of all purchasing for the period to date.

Step 9   Column 10. This is the to-date total of all food requisitions for the period.

Step 10   Column 11. This is the to-date total of all food sales for the period.

Step 11   Column 12. This is obtained by dividing the figures from column 10 by figures from column 11 of the same day and multiplying by 100 to convert to a percentage.

The advantages of producing this basic food report are:

1 It is simple and easy to follow.
2 It gives a reasonably detailed account of the general performance of the business on a day-to-day basis.
3 It records the daily stock level, daily purchases, daily food requisitioned and daily food sales and enables the daily food cost percentage to be calculated. This information is used for preparing to-date totals (that is, running totals to date).

4 The to-date food cost percentage smooths out the uneven daily food cost percentages and highlights the corrective action to be taken, if necessary, early in the month. The uneven daily food cost percentage is often caused when food is requisitioned on one day to be processed and sold on subsequent days.

The disadvantages of this basic food report are:

1 Although simple and easy to prepare, the report relies heavily on the accuracy of the basic information to be collected, for example the total of daily purchases, daily requisitions, etc.
2 It is not totally accurate as it ignores such things as the cost of the staff meals; food transferred to bars, for example potato crisps, nuts, salted biscuits, trays of canapes, etc. which are given away free in the bars to customers and items such as lemons, limes, etc. which are included in certain drinks; and beverages transferred to kitchens, for example wine, spirits, beer, etc. for use in the cooking of specific dishes.

14.4.3 A detailed daily food cost report

This food cost report is a development of the previous report and refines the accuracy of the report by taking into account the cost of beverages transferred into the kitchen, the cost of food transferred out of the kitchens to the bars, and the cost of employees' meals. Table 14.3 shows an example of a detailed daily food cost report.

The advantages of this type of report are:

1 It is more accurate than the two previous food reports illustrated in Tables 14.1 and 14.2 in that it includes additions to the cost of food for beverages transferred to the kitchen (for example, cooking wine, etc.) and deductions for the cost of food transferred from the kitchen to the bars (for example, lemons, oranges, olives, nuts, etc.) and for the cost of all employees' meal. It also separates purchases into those that go straight to the storerooms and those that go direct to the kitchen and are charged immediately to the kitchen. The result of these additions and subtractions is that the true cost

Table 14.2   *A daily food cost report*

1	2	3	4	5	6	7	8	9	10	11	12
		Today	*Today*	*Today*	*Today*	*Today*	*Today*	*To-date*	*To-date*	*To-date*	*To-date*
Date	*Day*	*Opening food storeroom inventory*	*Purchases*	*Total food available*	*Food requisitioned*	*Food sales*	*Food cost*	*Food purchases*	*Food requisitions*	*Food sales*	*Food cost*
March		£	£	£	£	£	%	£	£	£	%
1	M	2,220.00	320.50	2,540.50	290.00	820.00	35.37	320.50	290.00	820.00	35.37
2	T	2,250.50	385.00	2,635.50	370.00	980.00	37.78	705.50	660.00	1,800.00	36.66
3	W	2,265.50	404.00	2,669.50	440.00	1,100.00	40.00	1,109.50	1,100.00	2,900.00	37.93
4	T	2,229.50	480.00	2,709.50	480.00	1,050.00	45.71	1,589.50	1,580.00	3,950.00	40.00
5	F	2,229.50	890.00	3,119.50	404.50	1,005.00	40.25	2,479.50	1,984.50	4,955.00	40.05
6	S	2,715.00	202.50	2,917.50	535.00	1,490.00	35.91	2,682.00	2,519.50	6,455.00	39.09
7	S	2,382.50	–	2,382.50	240.00	720.00	33.33	2,682.00	2,759.50	7,165.00	38.51
8	M	2,141.50	380.00	2,522.50	310.00	920.00	33.70	3,062.00	3,069.50	8,085.00	37.96
9	T	2,212.50	402.00	2,614.50	395.00	1,015.00	38.92	3,464.50	3,464.50	9,100.00	38.07
10	W	2,219.50	425.00	2,544.50	345.00	925.00	37.30	3,889.00	3,809.50	10,025.00	37.99
11	T	2,229.50	464.00	2,763.50	427.00	1,160.00	36.81	4,353.00	4,236.50	11,185.00	37.87
12	F	2,336.50	844.00	3,180.50	463.00	1,220.00	37.95	5,197.00	4,699.50	12,405.00	37.88
13	S	2,717.50	185.00	2,902.50	512.00	1,405.00	36.44	5,382.00	5,211.50	13,810.00	37.73
14	S	2,390.50	–	2,390.50	265.00	690.00	38.41	5,382.00	5,476.50	14,500.00	37.77
15	M	2,125.50	365.00	2,490.50	315.00	840.00	37.50	5,747.00	5,791.50	15,340.00	37.75
16	T	2,175.50	495.00	2,670.50	405.00	1,085.00	37.33	6,242.00	6,196.50	16,425.00	37.77
17	W	2,265.50	445.00	2,710.50	465.00	1,290.00	36.05	6,687.00	6,661.50	17,715.00	37.60
18	T	2,245.50	492.00	2,737.50	380.00	990.00	38.38	7,179.00	7,041.50	18,705.00	37.64
19	F	2,357.50	904.00	3,261.50	440.00	1,015.00	43.35	8,083.00	7,481.50	19,720.00	37.94
20	S	2,821.50	143.00	2,964.50	547.00	1,407.00	38.88	8,226.00	8,028.50	21,127.00	37.99
21	S	2,417.50	–	2,417.50	237.00	604.00	39.24	8,226.00	8,265.50	21,731.00	38.03
22	M	2,180.50	345.00	2,525.50	327.00	850.00	38.47	8,571.00	8,592.50	22,581.00	30.05
23	T	2,198.50	305.00	2,503.50	435.00	1,105.00	39.37	8,876.00	9,027.50	23,686.00	38.11
24	W	2,068.50	485.00	2,553.50	403.00	1,090.00	36.97	9,361.00	9,430.50	24,776.00	30.06
25	T	2,150.50	463.00	2,613.50	393.00	1,050.00	37.43	9,824.00	9,823.50	25,826.00	38.04
26	F	2,220.50	865.00	3,085.50	485.00	1,350.00	35.93	10,689.00	10,308.50	27,176.00	37.93
27	S	2,600.50	245.00	2,845.50	525.00	1,490.00	35.23	10,934.00	10,833.50	28,666.00	37.79
28	S	2,320.50	–	2,320.50	204.50	585.00	35.04	10,934.00	11,038.00	29,251.00	37.77
Totals			10,934.00		11,038.00	29,251.00		10,934.00	11,038.00	29,251.00	37.77

Closing stock 2,116.00

Proof of inventory

Opening stock	2,220.00
plus Purchases	10,934.00
Sub total	13,154.00
minus Requisitions	11,038.00
Closing stock	2,116.00

Explanation of columns
 1 Date.
 2 Day of week.
 3 Stock level at beginning of each day. The opening stock for the first day of a new period is the closing stock figure from the previous period. Subsequent days are calculated from column 5 minus column 6 of previous day.
 4 Total of all food produced and delivered on that day.
 5 Total of column 3 plus column 4.
 6 Total of all food requisitions for that day.
 7 Total daily food sales obtained from till readings.
 8 Column 6 divided by column 7, expressed as a percentage.
 9 Running totals of column 4.
10 Running totals of column 6.
11 Running totals of column 7.
12 Column 10 divided by column 11, expressed as a percentage.

of the food sold to customers is more accurate than previously.

2 The accuracy of the to-date food cost percentage is refined to take into account all daily transactions and these figures should be fully relied upon to be the basis against which corrective action may be taken.

The disadvantages of this type of report are that it is more detailed than the previous reports and it relies very much on the accuracy of the collected information, for example the collection of all the requisition notes and the accurate extensions of the pricing of items; the collection of the goods received sheet and the checking of it against delivery notes, credit notes, invoices, etc.

14.4.4 Calculation of the potential food cost

The potential food cost is the cost of the food under perfect and ideal conditions. The potential food cost of an operation is the principal and most effective method of evaluating the actual food cost. Any variance higher than 1 per cent between the potential and actual costs should be investigated. The potential food cost may be calculated in a variety of ways, but because of time it is usually costed per menu for each selling outlet twice a year or more frequently if the menu changes. This means that the potential figures will differ between breakfast, lunch and dinner menus and between selling outlets, where the prices of items may vary (see Figure 14.2).

The calculations are in three main steps.

1 For each individual menu item multiply the number of portions actually sold during a 'sample' week as determined by the restaurant sales analysis, by the potential food cost per portion (Figure 14.3), to obtain the total potential cost of food sold for that week.
2 Multiply the same portions actually sold, as above, by the menu selling prices, and arrive at the potential total sales.
3 Divide the potential total food cost by the potential total food sales and arrive at a figure which, when expressed as a percentage, is the potential food cost percentage.

To be able to do the above calculations it would be necessary to have the following information to hand:

1 A detailed sales analysis of all items sold in the various outlets, together with their selling prices.
2 Standard recipe cards of all the menu items costed out (Figure 13.5).
3 Summary of potential food cost (Figure 14.2), obtained from the standard recipe cards.
4 Average market price for the main ingredients taken from invoices, food marketing reports or food cost indices reports.

It is not unusual for there to be a difference between the actual and the potential food cost figures. Usually the actual cost of the food sold is higher than the potential for such reasons as food being a perishable commodity, the difficulty of being exact when forecasting food production requirements and that a small amount of waste is almost unavoidable. Any large differences in the figures will reflect a lack of adherence to established standards, or pilfering or sheer carelessness resulting in an excessive amount of waste. As stated earlier, any variance in excess of 1 per cent should be investigated.

14.5 Food control checklist

It would not be possible to state in a book what corrective action should be taken when standards are not being met as the operating and trading conditions would vary from one establishment to another. It is possible, however, to produce a control checklist, similar to the one below, to act as an *aide-mémoire* when trying to identify the reasons for any variance in standards, the checklist being a summary of the control procedures which should be used. Any control procedures not being used would be a weak link in the chain of control.

14.5.1 Menu

1 Suitable for present market segment.
2 Takes into account current trends in customer eating habits.

POINTER HOTELS (UK) LTD

Tambard Coffee Shop

SUMMARY OF POTENTIAL FOOD COSTS   PERIOD: 3/4 – 4/12   MEAL: Dinner

Menu item	1 Cost of main ingredient	2 Cost of pre-preparation	3 Cost of surrounding items	4 Potential cost of one portion	5 Unit sales value	6 Food cost	7 Abstracted no. sold	8 Potential total cost	9 Actual total cost	10 Potential total sales	11 Actual total sales
	£	£	£	£	£	%		£	£	£	£
Taramasalata	0.35	0.11	0.04	0.50	1.85	27.03	250	125.00	–	462.50	–
Chilled orange juice	0.18	–	0.05	0.23	0.65	35.38	80	18.40	–	52.00	–
Chilled tomato juice	0.16	–	–	0.16	0.60	26.67	60	9.60	–	36.00	–
Pate du chef	0.40	0.08	0.05	0.53	1.30	40.77	150	79.50	–	195.00	–
Soup of the day	0.18	0.05	0.02	0.25	0.75	33.33	210	52.50	–	157.50	–
Chilled melon	0.45	–	0.02	0.47	1.60	29.37	60	28.20	–	96.00	–

Figure 14.2 *An extract from a summary of potential food costs for a coffee shop for a specific period of time*

Explanation of columns

1–4 Information obtained from standard recipe forms.

5 From current menu.

6 Column 4 divided by column 5, expressed as a percentage.

7 From coffee shop sales analysis.

8 Column 4 multiplied by column 7.

9 This would seldom be calculated. The final actual total food cost figure would be taken from the food cost report for the period.

10 Column 5 multiplied by column 7.

11 This would seldom be calculated for each individual item. The final total sales figure would be taken from the food cost report for the period.

3 Menu is interesting, imaginative, changes during the year, takes into account the major food seasons, assists greatly in selling.

4 Accurately priced, competitive, takes into account the labour content in the production and service of dishes.

14.5.2   Purchasing, receiving, storing and issuing procedures

1 Purchase specifications used for all main items.

2 Purchase orders made for every purchase; the exception possibly being to the daily order of fresh fruit and vegetables.

3 All purchases made from nominated or approved suppliers.

4 Deliveries timetabled whenever possible so that quantity and quality checks may be efficiently carried out.

5 All deliveries to be recorded in the foods received book and credit notes obtained for

any variance between what is stated on the delivery note and what is actually delivered.

6 All deliveries of food to be entered into bin cards/ledgers on the day of delivery.

7 Issues of all food from the stores to be against authorized, signed requisitions only.

8 Entry to food stores to be restricted to authorized personnel.

14.5.3   Food production

1 Yield and product testing practised to establish and measure standard of products.

2 Production to be related to volume forecasts.

3 Maximum use to be made of standard recipes.

4 Efficient scheduling of production to be made so as to ensure maintenance of quality of dishes produced.

5 All equipment to be regularly maintained so as to ensure the standard yields and quality of dishes are maintained.

POINTER HOTELS (UK) LTD

Tambard Restaurant.

POTENTIAL FOOD COSTS   APPETIZERS: Shrimp Cocktail

Date	Standard portion size	Factor base	Factor per portion	Cost/lb AP	Cost of main ingredient	Cost of pre-preparation	Cost of surrounding items	Standard cost of one portion	Selling price	Food cost %	Remarks
1	2	3	4	5	6	7	8	9	10	11	12
				£	£	£	£	£	£	%	
5/2/8-	10 each	PS803	0.125	1.60	0.20	0.10	0.15	0.45	1.25	36	
6/5/8-	10 each	PS803	0.124	1.85	0.23	0.12	0.15	0.50	1.25	40	Review Selling price
5/8/8-	10 each	PS803	0.124	1.80	0.23	0.12	0.16	0.51	1.50	34	
7/11/8-	10 each	PS803	0.125	2.20	0.28	0.14	0.20	0.62	1.70	36	

Figure 14.3 *Potential food costs for shrimp cocktail*

Explanation of columns

1 Date.
2 Standard portion size.
3 Factor base: description of raw material from which dish is prepared or purchasing specification reference.
4 Factor per portion: column 6 divided by column 5.
5 Cost of 1 lb of raw material as purchased.
6 Cost of main ingredient.
7 Cost of pre-preparation.
8 Cost of surrounding items – shredded lettuce, brown bread and butter, lemon wedge.
9 Standard cost of one portion – total cost of main ingredient, preparation and surrounding items.
10 Selling price.
11 Food cost percentage.
12 Remarks.

14.5.4 Food service

1 Food service standards established and practised.
2 Standard portion sizes adhered to.
3 Standard portion size equipment always available.
4 Careful control made to all food sent to restaurant, for example sweet and carving trolleys, etc. All unsold food to be accounted for and returned to the kitchen.

14.5.5 Food control procedures

1 Check and marry up all delivery notes, credit notes, invoices and goods received report.
2 Check arithmetic to all paper work.
3 Check correct discounts are being allowed.
4 Check delivery notes to bin cards/ledgers.
5 Maintain certain charges and credits for period inventory.
6 At set periods complete a full inventory of all chargeable containers.
7 At set periods complete a full stocktake of all food stores and food held in the kitchens and compare to ledgers.
8 Prepare a stocktaking report and stocktake variance report.
9 Maintain up-to-date food control reports.

The major reasons for food cost (and gross profit) variances from the established standard for a unit include the following:

1 Inaccurate arithmetic to paperwork. This also includes the paperwork of suppliers.
2 Inefficient stocktaking.
3 Poor revenue control. Lack of systematic procedures and practices.
4 Poor menu. Unrelated to market conditions and requirements, lack of sales analysis and up-dating of menu.
5 Poor purchasing, resulting in higher food costs, overstocking and wastage.
6 Poor receiving, inferior goods being accepted, short weight of goods being signed for.
7 Poor storing, poor rotation of stock resulting in wastage, poor security.

Table 14.3   *A detailed daily food cost report*

1	2	3	4	5	6	7	8	9
		Today	*Today*	*Today*	*Today*	*Today*	*Today*	*Today*
Date	*Day*	*Stock levels at beginning of each day*	*Storeroom purchases*	*Total food available in storeroom*	*Food requisitioned*	*Direct purchases*	*Beverage transfer to kitchen*	*Cost of food used*
March		£	£	£	£	£	£	£
1	M	2,220.00	120.50	2,340.50	90.00	200.00	–	290.00
2	T	2,250.50	200.00	2,450.50	185.00	185.00	5.00	375.00
3	W	2,265.50	204.00	2,469.50	240.00	200.00	5.00	445.00
4	T	2,229.50	380.00	2,609.50	380.00	100.00	10.00	490.00
5	F	2,229.50	690.00	2,919.50	204.50	200.00	–	404.50
6	S	2,715.00	202.50	2,917.50	535.00	–	10.00	545.00
7	S	2,383.50	–	2,382.50	240.00	–	10.00	250.00
8	M	2,142.50	200.00	2,342.50	130.00	180.00	5.00	315.00
9	T	2,212.50	302.00	2,514.50	295.00	100.00	15.00	410.00
10	W	2,219.50	325.00	2,544.50	245.00	100.00	10.00	355.00
11	T	2,299.50	264.00	2,563.50	227.00	200.00	23.00	450.00
12	F	2,336.50	444.00	2,780.50	63.00	400.00	13.00	476.00
13	S	2,717.50	185.00	2,902.50	512.00	–	8.00	520.00
14	S	2,390.50	–	2,390.50	265.00	–	15.00	280.00
15	M	2,125.50	265.00	2,390.50	215.00	100.00	25.00	340.00
16	T	2,175.00	295.00	2,470.50	205.00	200.00	15.00	420.00
17	W	2,265.50	345.00	2,610.50	365.50	100.00	15.00	480.50
18	T	2,245.00	292.00	2,537.00	180.00	200.00	20.00	400.00
19	F	2,357.00	504.00	2,861.00	40.00	400.00	10.00	450.00
20	S	2,821.00	143.00	2,964.00	547.00	–	13.00	560.00
21	S	2,417.00	–	2,417.00	237.00	–	13.00	250.00
22	M	2,180.00	145.00	2,325.00	127.00	200.00	3.00	330.00
23	T	2,198.00	105.00	2,303.00	235.00	200.00	15.00	450.00
24	W	2,068.00	285.00	2,353.00	203.00	200.00	17.00	420.00
25	T	2,150.00	263.00	2,413.00	193.00	200.00	7.00	400.00
26	F	2,220.00	565.00	2,785.00	185.00	300.00	15.00	500.00
27	S	2,600.00	245.00	2,845.00	525.00	–	15.00	540.00
28	S	2,320.00	–	2,320.00	204.50	–	5.00	209.50
Totals			6,969.00		7,703.50	3,965.00	317.00	11,355.50

Closing stock 2,115.50

Proof of inventory			*Proof of cast*	
Opening stock	2,220.00		Opening stock	2,220.00
plus Storeroom purchases	6,969.00		*plus* Storeroom purchases	6,969.00
			Direct purchases	3,965.00
Total	9,189.00		Beverage to kitchen	317.00
minus Requisitions	7,7073.00			
			Total	13,471.00
= Closing stock	2,115.50		*Minus* Employee meals	655.00
			Food to bars	70.00
			Closing inventory	2,115.50
			= Cost of food sold	10,630.50

10	11	12	13	14	15	16	17
Today	*Today*	*Today*	*Today*	*Today*	*To-date*	*To-date*	*To-date*
Cost of employee meals	*Transfers of food to bars*	*Cost of food sold*	*Food sales*	*Food cost*	*Cost of food sold*	*Food sales*	*Food cost*
£	£	£	£	£	£	£	£
35.00	–	255.00	820.00	31.09	255.00	820.00	31.09
25.00	–	350.00	980.00	35.71	605.00	1,800.00	33.61
30.00	5.00	410.00	1,100.00	37.27	1,015.00	2,900.00	35.00
25.00	5.00	460.00	1,050.00	43.81	1,475.00	3,950.00	37.34
30.00	5.00	369.50	1,005.00	36.76	1,844.50	4,955.00	37.22
30.00	5.00	510.00	1,490.00	34.23	2,354.50	6,445.00	36.52
25.00	–	225.00	720.00	31.25	2,579.50	7,165.00	36.00
20.00	–	295.00	920.00	32.06	2,874.50	8,050.00	35.55
20.00	–	390.00	1,015.00	38.42	2,264.50	9,100.00	35.87
20.00	–	335.00	925.00	36.22	3,599.50	10,025.00	35.90
25.00	5.00	420.00	1,160.00	36.21	4,019.50	11,185.00	35.93
20.00	5.00	451.00	1,220.00	36.96	4,470.50	12,405.00	36.03
20.00	–	500.00	1,405.00	35.59	4,970.50	13,810.00	35.99
20.00	–	260.00	690.00	37.68	5,230.50	14,500.00	36.07
30.00	5.00	305.00	840.00	36.31	5,535.50	15,340.00	36.08
20.00	5.00	395.00	1,085.00	36.41	5,930.50	16,425.00	36.10
20.00	–	460.50	1,290.00	35.66	6,390.50	17,715.00	36.07
20.00	–	380.00	990.00	38.38	6,770.50	18,705.00	36.19
25.00	5.00	420.00	1,015.00	41.38	7,190.50	19,720.00	36.46
25.00	5.00	530.00	1,407.00	37.67	7,720.50	21,127.00	36.54
20.00	–	230.00	604.00	38.08	7,950.50	21,731.00	36.58
20.00	–	310.00	850.00	36.47	8,260.50	22,581.00	36.58
20.00	–	430.00	1,105.00	38.91	8,690.50	23,686.00	36.69
20.00	–	400.00	1,090.00	36.69	9,090.50	24,776.00	36.69
25.00	5.00	370.00	1,050.00	35.24	9,460.50	25,826.00	36.63
20.00	10.00	470.00	1,350.00	34.82	9,930.50	27,176.00	36.54
20.00	–	520.00	1,490.00	34.90	10,450.50	28,666.00	36.45
25.00	5.00	179.50	585.00	30.68	10,630.00	29,251.00	36.34
655.00	70.00	10,630.50	29,251.00	36.34	10,630.00	419,870.00	36.34

Explanation of columns

1 Date.
2 Day of week.
3 Stock level at beginning of each day. The opening stock for the first day of a new period is the closing stock figure from the previous period. Subsequent days are calculated from column 5 minus column 6 of previous day
4 Total of all food produced and delivered on that day. (Note: Not including direct foods to the kitchen – see column 7).
5 Total of column 3 plus column 4.
6 Total of all food requisitions for that day.
7 Total of all food purchased and delivered on that day which went on direct charge to the kitchen, for example fresh meat, poultry, fish, fruit, vegetables, etc.

8 Total of all beverage requisitions made by the kitchen for use in food production.
9 Totals of columns 6, 7 and 8.
10 Total of all food requisitions made to produce employee meals.
11 Total of all bar requisitions for food, for example oranges, lemons, nuts, crisps, etc.
12 Column 9 minus (column 10 plus column 11).
13 Total daily food sales obtained from till readings.
14 Column 12 divided by column 13, expressed as a percentage.
15 Running totals of column 12.
16 Running totals of column 13.
17 Column 15 divided by column 16, expressed as a percentage.

```
┌─────────────────────────────────────────────────────────────────────┐
│                  POINTER HOTELS (UK) LTD                              │
│                    Jambard Restaurant                                 │
│                                                                       │
│                                        DATE  5/2/9-                    │
│        CARVING TROLLEY REPORT                   LUNCH/DINNER           │
│  ┌──────────────────────────────────────┬──────────────────────────┐ │
│  │        Number ribs used          6   │                          │ │
│  │        Total raw weight issued  108 lb  0 oz                     │ │
│  │        Total cooked weight issued 65 lb  8 oz                    │ │
│  │                                      │                          │ │
│  │ Minus  Weight of bones returned   8 lb  8 oz  Number portions sold│ │
│  │        Weight of meat trimmings   2 lb  0 oz                     │ │
│  │        Weight dripping/fat        4 lb  8 oz        106          │ │
│  │                                      │                          │ │
│  │        Total of returned items   15 lb  0 oz                     │ │
│  │                                      │                          │ │
│  │  Net servable weight             50 lb  9 oz                     │ │
│  │  Net servable yield  %              46.76%                       │ │
│  │  Unsold cooked rib returned       2 lb  0 oz                     │ │
│  │  Actual weight meat sold         48 lb  8 oz                     │ │
│  └──────────────────────────────────────┴──────────────────────────┘ │
└─────────────────────────────────────────────────────────────────────┘
```

Potential portion size: 8 oz
Potential portions at 8 oz: 97
Potential at 16 portions per rib: 96
Potential at 17 portions per rib: 102
Actual portions per rib: 17.67
Difference in number portions sold: +9
Difference per portion size.   -0.7 oz

Signed: Wor Bone

Food Controller

Figure 14.4 *An example of a report form used to control the sale of roast beef from a carving trolley*

Notes:
1 Average weight of the rib of beef is 18 lb.
2 The figure of 47.76 per cent yield of servable meat is a check against the purchase specification and processing method.
3 The unsold cooked rib returned would be a check on the accuracy of the volume forecast. The 2 lb of cooked rib returned represents 23.76 per cent of the whole cooked rib of average weight 10 lb 14½ oz.
4 The figures show that the carver served nine more portions than he should have as against the potential figures, and also that customers on average were served 0.7 oz less than they should have been.

8 Failure to establish and/or maintain standards for volume forecasting, standard recipes, standard yields and standard portion sizes.
9 Failure to account accurately for all staff and management meals.
10 Food control not being seen by staff to work, resulting in staff failing to maintain desired standards.

14.5.6 Checklist for the smaller operation

A quick checklist for the smaller operation for food cost (and gross profit) variances from the established standard would include the following:

1 Check the arithmetic of all major figures (that is, food report, stock report, etc.)

2 Re-check stock figures and total, and in particular look for unusual figures in relation to the norm. The percentage of the total consumption of each category of commodities (meat, poultry, fish, dairy, fresh vegetables, etc.) should be constant for any given menu over a period. Once a standard has been established, variations from it will indicate a problem, for example if the meat consumption percentage was up it could well indicate pilferage, fraud, wastage or an increase in price and management attention should be focused towards this.

3 Re-check sales figures and check against meals served.

4 Check for unusual variances in sales. This could be caused by a major change in the weather, a national holiday, etc.

5 Check for unusual changes in the sales mix.

6 Check for unusual changes in price of major and costly food items.

7 Check stores, refrigerators and wastebins for evidence of overpurchasing, over preparation and unnecessary wastage.

8 Check on meals taken by staff.

14.6 Reference

Kasavana *(1984). Computer Systems for Food Service Operations.* CBI. New York: Van Nostrand Reinhold.

15
Beverage controlling

15.1 Introduction

The objectives of beverage control are similar to those of food control. In simple terms it is to determine and report on the actual and the potential sales and costs for each beverage outlet and to take corrective action where necessary.

As mentioned earlier in the book, beverage control is simpler than food control for many reasons including:

1 There are a fewer number of beverage items to handle than food.
2 Beverages are purchased in standard unit sizes of known standard qualities.
3 Beverages are not as highly perishable as foods.

It is important however, that strict control of beverages is maintained at all times for such reasons as:

1 The danger of bar staff appointing themselves as 'unofficial partners', e.g. a barman paying no overheads and no wages yet, if bringing in bottles of spirits and selling them and pocketing the money, is devoiding the unit of that amount of sales and profit.
2 It is easier for bar staff to steal money than it is for food staff.
3 Beverages are more tempting than food to many staff.
4 Beverages are, in the main, more expensive, and contribute more to profit than food items.

15.2 Calculation of beverage cost

There are several basic terms which need to be explained with reference to the calculation of beverage costs:

1 *Beverage cost*. This refers to the cost of the beverages incurred in preparing the drinks served.
2 *Beverage cost percentage*. This refers to the cost of beverages sold as a percentage of sales of the beverages.
3 *Gross profit or beverage gross profit*. The excess of sales over the cost of the beverage expressed as a percentage or in financial terms.
4 *Potential beverage cost (or sales)*. The beverage cost (or sales) under perfect conditions; this may be expressed as a percentage or in financial terms (see Figure 15.1).

15.3 Methods of beverage control

There are many different methods in use today to control costs, the various methods depending on the size of the operation, the volume of business, owner or managed operation, etc., and the level of sophistication of control required. Each of the different methods in use could be classified under one of the following six basic types of beverage control systems. Whatever method is adopted, it would be of little value unless the previous steps of control had been efficiently implemented and enforced, that is, the control of purchasing, receiving, storing and issuing; production planning; the establishment of standard yields, standard recipes, standard portion sizes and inventory.

15.3.1 Bar cost system

This system is similar to that for the basic food cost report and the detailed food cost report in Chapter 14. It may be produced for each bar separately or for all of the beverage operations as

Potential Sales Report

BAR: Tambard Cocktail   DATE: 1/2/9– to 7/2/9–

Explanation	Total cost	Total sales potential
	£	£
Inventory at 1/2/9–	248.00	679.45
Plus Bar requisitions for period 1/2/9– to 7/2/9–	1,470.00	3,585.37
Minus Transfers out to other bars	28.00	87.50
Total available beverages	1,690.00	4,177.32
Minus Inventory at close 7/2/9–	242.00	672.00
Adjustments for:		
Mixed drink sales		102.00
Bottle sales		25.00
Total	1,448.00	3,378.32
Actual sales recorded 1/2/9– to 7/2/9–		3,349.50
Difference		28.82

Ratio of actual cost to:

Actual sales revenue	43.23%
Potential sales revenue	42.86%
Difference (minus)	0.37%

Action to be taken: 1. Check all figures and arithmetic
                        2. Check mixed drink sales allowances

Figure 15.1   *An example of a potential (standard) sales report for a bar*

illustrated in Table 15 .1 (a) and (b) . The reader will notice that in both examples issues to and from the bar and the stocktake of each bar have been at cost price. In Table 15 l(b) the report does not include the opening and closing stocktake of the individual bars, it assumes that any beverage issued is for sale that day. The report in Table 15.1 (a) is time-consuming but may be deemed necessary when the desired gross profit is not being achieved and when wanting to check in some detail on the performance of individual bars in a unit. Many of the problems which necessitate an investigation of a bar are mentioned at the end of this chapter.

Table 15.1(a)   *An example of a beverage control report for a bar*

1	2	3	4	5	6	7	8	9	10	11	12	13	14
		Today	Today	Today	Today	Today	Today	Today	Today	Today	To-date	To-date	To-date
Date	Day	Bar opening inventory	Bar requisitions	Total beverage available	Transfers of food to bar	Transfer of beverage to kitchen	Bar closing inventory	Cost of beverage sales	Beverage sales	Beverage cost %	Cost of beverage sold	Beverage sales	Beverage cost %
February		£	£	£	£	£	£	£	£	%	£	£	%
1	M	320.50	180.50	501.00	5.50	10.00	355.00	141.50	365.00	38.77	141.50	365.00	38.77
2	T	355.00	225.00	580.00	7.00	12.00	320.00	255.00	605.00	42.15	396.50	970.00	40.88
3	W	320.00	165.00	485.00	4.00	4.00	285.00	200.00	495.00	40.40	596.50	1,465.00	40.72
4	T	285.00	215.00	500.00	7.50	12.50	264.00	231.00	554.00	41.70	827.50	2,019.00	40.98
5	F	264.00	286.00	550.00	9.50	16.50	296.00	247.00	606.00	40.76	1,074.50	2,625.00	40.93
6	S	296.00	327.00	623.00	12.50	8.50	256.00	371.00	942.00	39.38	1,445.50	3,567.00	40.52
7	S	256.00	144.00	400.00	4.00	9.00	288.00	107.00	281.00	38.08	1,552.50	3,848.00	40.35
Total week 1	–		1,542.50	–	50.00	72.50	–	1,552.50	3,848.00	–	1,552.50	3,848.00	40.35

Proof of cast

Opening stock		320.50
	plus Bar requisitions	1,542.50
	plus Food to bars	50.00
Total		1,913.00
	minus Beverages to kitchen	72.50
	minus Closing stock	288.00
Cost of beverage sold		1,552.50

Notes:

This report is in respect of one bar only.

1 It is more accurate than Table 12.1(b) as it involves taking stock daily and making extensions.

2 It produces an accurate record of materials costs and revenue, and takes into account transfers in and out of the bar.

Explanation of columns

1 Date.
2 The day.
3 From physical stocktake of bar on closing of previous day.
4 Total beverage requisition by the bar on the day.
5 Column 3 plus column 4.
6 Total of food requisitions required by the bar.
7 Total of kitchen requisitions of beverages from the bar.
8 Total of physical stocktake of bar on closing.

9 (Column 5 column 6) – (column 7 column 8).
10 Total of bar sales recorded, obtained from accounts department.
11 Column 9 divided by column 10, as a percentage.
12 Running total of column 9, to date.
13 Running total of column 10, to date.
14 Column 12 divided by column 13, as a percentage.

15.3.2   Par stock or bottle control system

This is a simple yet effective method of beverage control and is particularly useful for the smaller type operation where there are few full-time control staff. The following points should be noticed.

1 The level of par stock is established for each bar, that is, to establish for each beverage the number of bottles required for a busy day plus a small safety factor. This number is determined to be the stock level to be held in the bar at the beginning of the service each day. To simplify the system only full bottles are counted, partial bottles are not counted.

2 The number and type of empty bottles are noted each day, this being the amount and type to be requisitioned for the day.

3 The potential sales are based on the quantities issued at selling price and are compared to actual revenue received.

Table 15.1(b) *An example of a beverage report for a unit operating several selling outlets*

1	2	3	4	5	6	7	8	9	10	11	12	13	14
		Today	Today	Today	Today	Today	Today	Today	Today	Today	To-date	To-date	To-date
Date	Day	Opening beverage storeroom inventory	Beverage purchases	Total beverage available	Total beverage requisitions	Transfers of food to bars	Transfers of beverages to kitchen	Cost of beverage sold	Beverage sales	Beverage cost %	Cost of beverage sold	Beverage sales	Beverage cost %
February		£	£	£	£	£	£	£	£	%	£	£	%
1	M	2,600.00	240.00	2,840.00	440.00	10.00	20.00	430.00	1,300.00	33.08	430.00	1,300.00	33.8
2	T	2,400.00	400.00	2,800.00	650.00	30.00	30.00	640.00	1,800.00	35.56	1,070.00	3,100.00	34.52
3	W	2,150.00	1,200.00	3,350.00	710.00	20.00	20.00	710.00	1,920.00	36.98	1,780.00	5,020.00	35.46
4	T	2,640.00	320.00	2,960.00	620.00	15.00	25.00	610.00	1,640.00	37.19	2,390.00	6,660.00	35.89
5	F	2,340.00	140.00	2,480.00	580.00	5.00	50..0	590.00	1,720.00	34.30	2,980.00	8,380.00	35.56
6	S	1,900.00	1,800.00	3,700.00	820.00	20.00	30.00	310.00	2,180.00	37.16	3,790.00	10,560.00	35.89
7	S	2,880.00	–	2,880.00	420.00	10.00	10.00	420.00	1,110.00	37.83	4,210.00	11,670.00	36.07
Total Week 1	–		4,100.00	–	4,240.00	110.00	140.00	–	–	–	4,210.00	11,670.00	36.07
Closing stock 2,460.00													

Proof of cast

Opening stock	2,600.00
plus Beverage purchases	4,100.00
plus Food to bars	
Total	6,810.00
minus Beverages to kitchens	140.00
minus Closing stock	2,460.00
Cost of beverages sold	4,210.00

Notes:
1 This report may be used when there are several outlets.
2 It is not that time-consuming, as separate daily bar stock-taking is not done.
3 On a daily basis, the control is not 100 per cent accurate.

Explanation of columns

1 The date.
2 The day.
3 Column 5 minus column 6 of previous day.
4 Total of all beverages purchased as per invoices.
5 Add column 3 and column 4.
6 Add all bar requisitions together.
7 Total of all requisitions of food by various bars.
8 Total of all requisitions of beverages by the kitchen.
9 Columns (6 7) column 8.
10 Total of all bar sales, obtained from accounts department.
11 Column 9 divided by column 10, as a percentage.
12 Running total of column 9, to date.
13 Running total of column 10, to date.
14 Column 12 divided by column 13, as a percentage.

4 Adjustments to be made to the initial selling price if many mixed drinks are sold. This may only be necessary if the difference between the potential and actual sales figures gives cause for investigation.

The particular advantages of this system are its simplicity and ease of operation. The system assumes that over a short period the level of par-tial bottles remains relatively constant so that it becomes unnecessary to count each bottle's contents to determine the total sales. Theoretically the sales value of today's issues should equal yesterday's revenue. This would be unlikely, however, but over a short period the sales value of issues to date should equal the revenue to date figures.

15.3.3   Potential (or standard) sales value system

This system is designed to control beverage sales and therefore beverage costs by setting a sales value on each bottle item carried in stock. The revenue value of each bottle is based on the standard size of the drink, the contents of the bottle and the selling price for each drink. The sales value of each drink is called the potential (or standard) sales value. The system requires as a basis for its operation, established standards for a bottle code number system, drink recipes, drink sizes, glassware and par stocks. Whenever the bottle size, drink size or recipe change a new calculation must be made and recorded, as this can affect the price of a drink and should require the price to be reviewed.

The various calculations which have to be made to establish the potential sales values are concerned with:

1 *Full bottles of spirits.* The potential sales value of a full bottle of spirits, etc. which at times may be sold over a bar is equal to the selling price established by management. As little handling is involved in selling a full bottle, its price will usually be lower than when sold by the individual glass.
2 *Spirits etc. sold by the glass.* The sales value for a bottle of spirits, wine, etc. which is to be sold by the glass is calculated as in the following example.

Potential sales value for a bottle of whisky:

Size of bottle	70 cl
Size of a straight drink	2.5 cl
Selling price per drink	£1.50
Number of drinks per bottle	28
(as determined by management)	

$$\underset{\substack{\text{(number of} \\ \text{drinks)}}}{28} \times \underset{\substack{\text{(selling price} \\ \text{per drink)}}}{£1.50} = \underset{\substack{\text{(potential} \\ \text{sales value} \\ \text{of one bottle)}}}{£42.00}$$

3 *Soft drink and mineral water sales.* The potential sales value of soft drinks, etc. depends on the pricing policy of the establishments; it could, for example, be:
   (a) A fixed price when sold on its own or when with another drink, for example gin and tonic water.
   (b) At a lower price when served as part of a mixed drink, for example a straight 2.5 cl drink of whisky may cost £1.50; a split bottle of dry ginger may cost £0.45; as a mixed drink whisky and dry ginger may be priced at £1.50 and not £1.95 as would be the case in (a) above.
   (c) The cost of soft drinks is included in the price when selling spirits.
   It should be noted that if a lower or inclusive pricing system is adopted, adjustments must be made when preparing the control sheets so that an accurate potential sales figure is calculated.
4 *Cocktails, etc.* If all drinks served to customers were sold as straight drinks or full bottles, it would be simple to calculate the potential sales value. When drinks are sold as cocktails containing two or more high selling price items it often requires an adjustment to be made when preparing the control sheet.

When the sales of mixed drinks on analysis are found to be low, there would be little need to go into great detail to calculate the allowances for the various mixed drinks. It is only when the actual money taken in the bars differs from the potential sales value by say more than 2 per cent that detailed analysis of sales and allowances needs to be done.

15.3.4   The inventory or 'ounce' system

This method is recognized as the most accurate (non-automatic) method of determining the amount of beverage sold. It is used at times when investigating the cause of an unacceptable difference recorded between the actual and potential results in a beverage report. It is, however, a complicated and difficult system to operate for large units with a full range of beverage services unless aided by a mini computer. The system requires:

1 An accurate and detailed analysis of all sales by type and brand of drink sold, for each selling outlet.
2 The calculation of the actual consumption of each type and brand of drink based on the daily physical stocktake, giving opening and closing stock levels of bars, plus any issues,

and minus any transfers out to other bars. All drinks sold are converted back to the number of ounces of each type and brand of drink sold using the standard beverage recipes. The total consumption of each kind of drink per sales bill has then to be compared with the actual consumption determined from the physical inventory and any adjustments.

The main disadvantages of this control system are:

1 The time required to analyse sales and to take stock levels daily.
2 The time required to calculate the daily consumption for each selling outlet.
3 Additional difficulties if a large number of mixed drinks are sold and if drinks of different sizes are sold in each selling outlet.

15.3.5   Banqueting and function bar system

Should the banquet department have its own storage and bar areas it can operate and be controlled in the same way as any other bar. If, however, a bar has to be set up for each separate banquet or function, it will be necessary for an authorized person to requisition for each event from the main cellar and then immediately at the close of the event to return all unsold beverages. Bottles issued would be the quantity issued from the cellar for that function. Bottles returned are the bottles and part bottles (calculated in tenths of a bottle) unused and returned to the cellar. The number of bottles issued minus bottles returned should be equal to the number of bottles and part bottles used. The actual cost is the purchase price paid per bottle, or half or split. The potential sales per bottle would be the selling price per drink multiplied by the standard number of drinks per bottle.

It would be normal practice for the bar staff at a function not to be paid until the actual and potential sales calculations had been made and found to be satisfactory.

15.3.6 Automated beverage dispensing system

There are many types of mechanical and automated beverage dispensing machines available, all designed to assist management in controlling beverage costs. The advantages and disadvantages of this system have been outlined earlier in section 13.3.4. As a method of controlling beverages it is very efficient, but the question of the cost of the installation and its suitability for some types of operation may preclude it from being considered.

15.4   Control checklist

As mentioned earlier in this book, there are two kinds of control with which we are concerned:

1 *Operational control.* That is the day-to-day control procedure of purchasing, receiving, storage, issuing, production and selling.
2 *Post-operational control or control after the event.* This is the examination of what took place in the various outlets and the comparison of these results with the various standards set by management and the determination of what corrective action must be taken if necessary.

As with food control, a beverage control checklist, similar to the one below, can be produced to act as an *aide-mémoire* to help identify the reason(s) for variances in standards.

15.4.1   Purchasing, receiving, storing and issuing procedures

1 Purchase specifications prepared for all main items.
2 Purchase orders completed in detail for every purchase made.
3 Purchases made from nominated or approved suppliers only.
4 Deliveries timetabled for a slack period so that quantity and quality inspection may be efficiently carried out.
5 Copy of purchase order sent to delivery point for checking against deliveries.
6 All deliveries entered on to the goods received report and credit notes obtained for any variance between goods and delivery note.
7 Credit notes obtained for all returned empties and ullages.
8 All deliveries to be entered on to bin cards, etc. on day of delivery.

9 Issues of beverages to be against authorized signed requisition only.
10 Cellar ledger and any other records kept to be up to date and accurate.
11 Access to cellar restricted.
12 Check that all bottles are stamped with the establishment stamp and are correct bottles for the particular bar. Check bottle disposal area contains no 'foreign' bottles.

15.4.2   Bar procedures

1 Bar stock to be replenished by written and authorized requisitions, or by using a 'full for empty' bottle system.
2 Bars to use standard recipes, standard drink sizes and glassware.
3 Bars to sell 'house brands' for all drinks unless specifically requested by the customer, as they will normally give a higher gross profit. 'House brands' may, for example, be determined by a brewery owning a chain of pubs, restaurants and hotels, when it would quite naturally wish to sell its own products in preference to those of its competitors; or by a company that has no liquor ties but negotiates a price advantageous contract with a supplier. In both cases the prices paid for the particular 'house brand' would normally be lower than if purchased otherwise.
4 Check that all bar sales are properly recorded.
5 Periodically check proof of liquor in open bottles if tampering is suspected.
6 Check that beverage price lists are displayed and freely available to customers.
7 Check frequency of 'breakages' recorded.
8 Check 'shortages' or 'overs' recorded by accounts department for each bar.
9 Check that bar staff have no access to till rolls, etc.

15.4.3   Beverage control procedures

1 Check and cross-reference delivery notes, credit notes, invoices and goods received report.
2 Check arithmetic to all paper work.
3 Check correct discounts are being allowed.
4 Check delivery notes, etc. to cellar inwards book.

5 Maintain beverages perpetual inventory book.
6 Maintain container charges and credits for period inventory.
7 At set periods complete a full inventory of all chargeable containers, for example crates, kegs, soda syphons, etc.
8 At set periods complete a full inventory of cellar and compare to beverages perpetual inventory book.
9 Prepare a stocktaking report of value and type of goods, rate of stock turnover, etc.
10 At set periods complete a full inventory of the stock of each bar for beverage control reports.
11 Maintain daily and to-date beverage control reports, the amount of detail depending on the size of the unit and the volume of business.
12 Prepare end of period beverage reports for management and highlight any problem areas for corrective action.

As mentioned earlier, beverage control is not so difficult or involved as food control. What at times is a problem is the dishonest employee and this is usually difficult to detect. The typical problems are bar staff who:

1 Bring in their own bottles of spirits, etc., sell the contents to customers and then pocket the money. This results in a busy bar with disappointing cash takings!
2 Drink at work. Bar staff who help themselves to the odd drink soon get into the habit of it unless it is quickly detected. This results in lower than should be cash takings or customers having short measure drinks which 'compensate' for the bar staff free drinks.
3 Fail to 'ring-up' each drink sold and pocket the money taken from the client. This results again in lower cash taken.
4 Provide free drinks for friends, again, resulting in lower bar takings.
5 Dilute drinks. When a group of customers order their third or more 'round of drinks', they are less likely to identify weak drinks, the difference being pocketed by the bar staff.
6 Under-charge the customer. The customer, being an accomplice of the bar staff, orders a drink, pays for it and is then given change

POINTER HOTELS (UK) LTD
Food and Beverage Controller's Report

Period 3
26 February, 199- to 25 March, 199-

Food sales	£
This Period	40,302
Last Year	39,818
Cumulative This Year	167,809
Cumulative Last Year	148,062

Food cost	%
This Period	35.6
Last Year	37.0
Cumulative This Year	34.9
Cumulative Last Year	35.4

Beverage sales	£
This Period	20,581
Last Year	22,795
Cumulative This Year	94,132
Cumulative Last Year	85,151

Beverage cost	%
This Period	36.8
Last Year	39.6
Cumulative This Year	36.1
Cumulative Last Year	36.7

Food inventory levels	£
This Period	3,590
Last Year	4,720

Rate of Inventory Turnover	
This Period	3.0
Last Year	3.2

Beverage inventory levels	£
This Period	18,850
Last Year	21,200

Rate of Inventory Turnover	
This Period	0.4
Last Year	0.5

Figure 15.2 *The summary page taken from a food and beverage controller's report for a four-week period*
Note: The report would include, for example, a detailed food report (Table 14.3), a detailed beverage report (Tables 15.1(a) and (b)), a stocktakers report (Figure 10.6), and a detailed beverage inventory report (Figure 10.11)

in excess of what it should be. This results in bar takings being lower than they should be.

7 Short-change customers. This is the all too common problem of bar staff giving customers less change than they should do and pocketing the difference for themselves.

If the spirits are on optics, or beers, spirits and minerals automatically dispensed to controlled measures, any discrepancy will almost certainly mean an error in cash handling made deliberately or by carelessness.

The above types of problems are usually only discovered when good beverage control procedures are in operation, the identification of the dishonest employee being made as a result of such steps as changing bar staff duties and shifts, taking daily bar inventories, changing till drawers during a busy shift and checking the cash with the till reading, and by observation of the bar by an unknown member of the management or security staff. The above only highlights the necessity for the personnel department to carefully interview and take up several references before employing any new bar staff.

15.5   References

Coltman, M. (1987). *Hospitality Management Accounting*, 3rd edn. New York: Van Nostrand Reinhold .

Kasavana, M. L. (1984). *Computer Systems for Food Service Operations*. CBI. New York: Van Nostrand Reinhold.

16
Revenue control – control systems – operating ratios

16.1 Introduction

In many of the previous chapters continual mention has been made of controlling costs, both of food and beverages. The control of revenue is equally important.

To control the revenue of a unit, particular attention must be paid to the major factors which can have an influence on the profitability. Therefore it is essential to control the main factors which can affect the revenue of a business, such as the menu-beverage list, the total volume of food and beverage sales, the sales mix, the average spend of customers in each selling outlet at different times of the day, the number of covers served and the gross profit margins.

It is important to note, particularly in commercial operations that somewhere in the total control system there is a need for the accountability of what has been served to the customer and the payment for what has been issued from the kitchen or the bar.

The payment for food and beverage may be made in many forms such as cash, foreign currency, credit cards, cheques, travellers' cheques, luncheon type vouchers and signed bills.

All staff handling cash should be adequately trained in the respective company's methods. It is a common practice for a cashier's or waiter's handbook/manual to be produced so that an established procedure may be followed with the specific aim of ensuring that cash security is efficiently carried out at all times. A typical handbook/manual would contain information on the standard procedure to be followed for such things as:

1 *Opening procedure* – instructions here would include procedures about checking the float, having a float of specific denominations, checking the till roll, recording waiters' bill pad numbers, etc.
2 *Working procedure* – instructions on how to accept payment and the procedure to follow.
3 *Closing procedure* – instructions on any documentation and recordings to be completed, cashing up, recording of credit cards, cheques, etc.
4 *Procedure for accepting foreign currency* – what currency is to be accepted, how to obtain the current exchange rates, how this is to be recorded, etc.
5 *Procedure for accepting credit cards* – which credit cards are to be accepted, how they are to be checked, method of processing credit cards for payment, recording of credit vouchers, etc.
6 *Procedures for accepting vouchers such as luncheon vouchers* – which vouchers are acceptable, how this is to be recorded.
7 *Procedure for accepting cheques* – how cheques are to be made out, customers to produce a valid cheque guarantee card, checking that signatures correspond, etc.
8 *Procedure for accepting travellers' cheques* – what travellers' cheques are acceptable, what currencies are acceptable, witnessing and checking signatures, how this is to be recorded.
9 *Procedure for a complimentary or signed bill* – check against current list of authorized persons and their signature, how this is to be recorded.

There are two basic approaches to recording and controlling food and beverage sales.

1 *A manual system,* which is commonly used in small and in exclusive type catering units.
2 *An automated system,* which is commonly used in units with several outlets, in units with a very high volume of business and in up-to-date companies with many units.

16.2   Manual systems

16.2.1   Sales checks

One of the simplest steps to take when attempting to establish sales control procedures is to require that each item ordered and its selling price are recorded on a waiter's sales check. See Figure 16.1 for an example of a sales check. Using some form of a check system serves the following functions:

1 To remind the waiting staff of the order they have taken.
2 To give a record of sales so that portion sales and sales mixes and sales histories can be compiled.
3 To assist the cashier and facilitate easy checking of prices charged.
4 To show the customer a detailed list of charges made.

An additional aid is to use numbered checks and control these tightly, recording all cancelled and missing checks (see Figures 16.1, 16.2 and 16.3).

It is more common to find *duplicate* or *triplicate checks* being used as an aid to control for the following reasons:

1 They provide the kitchen, buffet, or bar with a written record of what has been ordered and issued.
2 They authorize the kitchen, buffet, or bar to issue the food and/or beverage.
3 They provide the opportunity to compare the top copy of the check with the duplicate to ensure that all that has been issued has been charged and paid for.

16.2.2   The cashier's role

In addition to following precisely the unit's procedure for the handling of all revenue transactions within the restaurant or bars, it is normal practice for the cashier working a manual system to be required to complete the following:

1 To issue check pads to the waiting staff prior to a meal period, to record the numbers of the checks issued in each pad, and obtain the waiting staff's signature for them; and on the completion of the meal period to receive from the waiting staff their respective unused check pads, record the numbers, and sign for the receipt of those returned. This information to be recorded on the check number issue control sheet (see Figure 16.2).
2 To check the pricing, extensions and subtotals of all checks and to add any government tax charges and to enter the total amount due.
3 To receive and check money, credit or, when applicable, an approved signature in payment for the total amount due for each check.
4 To complete the missing check list for each meal period. This is an aid to the cashier in controlling what checks are used. The respective check numbers on the list are crossed out when payment is made. When a missing check is identified, investigation to be carried out to find the reason for this, and if no satisfactory explanation is forthcoming, to inform a member of management on duty. Missing checks to be marked on the missing check list (see Figure 16.3).
5 To complete the restaurant sales control sheet (see Figure 16.4) for each meal period. This form requires that all revenue received (or its equivalent) is recorded under specific headings such as cash, cheques, credit card transactions, etc. From this control sheet basic data – such as the number of covers served or the average spend per customer on food and beverages – is quickly obtained.
6 To complete the necessary paying in of all cash, etc. in accordance with the unit's established practice. This could be direct to a bank whether a small independent unit, or a unit of a large company, or to the head cashier's office if a large unit with many outlets. See Figure 16.5 for an example of a daily banking and till control sheet.

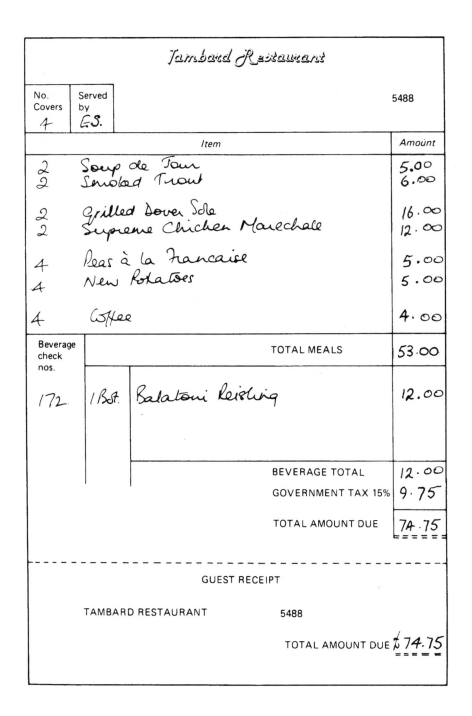

Figure 16.1   *An example of a guest check*

CHECK NUMBER ISSUE CONTROL SHEET

Date	Checks issued	Check returned	Waiter/Waitress signature	Cashier signature
Feb.1	0548 – 0599	0562 – 0599	Ned Smith	M. O'Neill
	0423 – 0499	0442 – 0499	Bill Bloggs	M. O'Neill
	0172 – 0199	0193 – 0199	Henry Tops	M. O'Neill
	1283 – 1299	nil	Neil Jones	M. O'Neill
	0800 – 0899	0804 – 0899	Neil Jones	M. O'Neill

Figure 16.2 *An example of a check number issues control sheet*
Note: The waiting staff sign for the pads of checks issued at the beginning of a meal/beverage service period and return the unused ones to the cashier who signs for the receipt of them

MISSING CHECK LIST

Date 5.2.9–   Lunch/Dinner

100	150	(200)	250
101	151	201	251
(102)	152	202	252
103	(153)	203	253
104	154	204	254
105	155	205	255
106	156	206	(256)
107	157	207	257
108	158	208	258
109	159	209	259
(110)	160	210	260
111	161	211	261
112	162	212	262
113	163	213	263
114	164	(214)	264
115	165	215	265
116	166	216	266
	167	217	267

Figure 16.3 *An example of a typical missing check list*
Note: This would be kept by the cashier, who would circle on this sheet the opening check number of each waiter's pad and then cross off each subsequent number when a check is used. The last check number used would also be circled for easy reference.

Restaurant Sales Control Sheet

Date 15.2.9–   Lunch/Dinner

Check nos.	Waiter nos.	No. covers	Food £	Beverage £	Other £	15% £	Total £	Cash	Credit card £	Cheque	Other charge
			Sales								
023	4	2	21.00	7.00	–	4.20	32.20	–	32.20	–	–
714	9	3	37.00	11.00	–	7.20	55.20	–	55.20	–	–
641	7	2	23.00	8.00	–	4.65	35.65	–	–	35.65	–
910	8	5	64.00	22.00	7.00	13.95	106.95	106.95	–	–	–
134	4	2	24.00	–	–	3.60	27.60	–	–	–	Room 427 27.60
653	7	4	52.00	16.00	–	10.20	78.20	–	78.20	–	–
Totals		85	977.50	212.50	32.00	183.30	1,405.30	360.00	480.00	202.00	180.00

Figure 16.4 *An example of a restaurant sales control sheet used to summarize the sales at the end of a meal period*

Daily Banking and Till Control Sheet   No. 34350

Date

UNIT ....   DEPARTMENT ....

Banking summary	£	p	Bank slips	£	p
Total daily trade					
Less credit trade					
Less weeks petty cash					
TOTAL BANKING £			TOTAL BANKING £		

Till controls	Till 1 £	p	Till 2 £	p	Till 3 £	p	Till 4 £	p	Till 5 £	p	Total £	p
Closing reading												
Opening reading												
Total rung on till												
PLUS cash over												
LESS cash under												
TOTAL DAILY TRADE £												

Attach bank slips and return to Chief Cashier/Accountant

Unit Manager/ess ....
(signature)

REMARKS:

Figure 16.5   *An example of a daily banking and till control sheet*

16.2.3   Problems of the manual system

In brief, the basic problems of controlling any food and beverage operation are:

1 The time span between purchasing, receiving, storing, processing, selling the product, and obtaining the cash or credit for the product, is sometimes only a few hours.
2 The number of items (food and beverage) held in stock at any time is high.
3 A large number of finished items are produced from a combination of the large number of items held in stock.
4 The number of transactions taking place on an hourly basis in some operations can be very high.
5 To be able to control the operation efficiently, management ideally requires control in formation of many types to be available quickly and to be presented in a meaningful way.

The full manual control of a food and beverage operation would be costly, time consuming and data produced would frequently be far too late for meaningful management action to take place. Certain aspects of control such as regularly up-dating the costings of standard recipes,

Table 16.1 *Food and beverage department – percentage of revenue*

	UK		London		Provinces		Scotland		Wales	
	1996	*1995*	*1996*	*1995*	*1996*	*1995*	*1996*	*1995*	*1996*	*1995*
Food sales										
(% of total revenue)										
Lower quartile	22.8	24.5	14.6	15.1	25.9	27.8	24.7	24.9	27.5	29.2
Median	27.9	29.3	17.2	17.7	29.7	30.9	31.1	32.1	28.4	32.8
Upper quartile	32.9	34.2	19.6	19.7	33.3	34.9	34.8	35.1	38.6	41.9
Beverage sales										
(% of total revenue)										
Lower quartile	9.3	9.3	4.6	4.6	10.2	10.4	11.3	11.1	10.6	13.0
Median	11.9	12.1	6.0	6.1	12.4	12.9	13.7	14.1	12.8	16.1
Upper quartile	14.6	15.1	7.8	7.6	14.7	15.4	16.4	16.6	16.5	21.1
Other food										
& beverage sales										
(% of total revenue)										
Lower quartile	2.0	2.0	1.3	1.3	2.7	2.9	1.5	1.6	1.9	0.6
Median	3.5	3.6	2.5	2.3	4.1	4.3	2.9	2.3	3.3	1.2
Upper quartile	5.1	5.1	4.2	4.4	5.9	5.7	3.8	4.0	3.4	3.0
Total food										
& beverage sales										
(% of total revenue)										
Lower quartile	36.3	36.9	20.5	21.3	41.1	42.3	41.0	40.4	41.1	44.2
Median	44.5	45.8	26.1	26.7	46.0	47.4	48.6	48.8	42.7	59.2
Upper quartile	51.2	53.0	31.8	29.9	51.8	53.8	52.8	53.7	56.3	65.1
Food cost of sales										
(% of food revenue)										
Lower quartile	30.1	30.6	28.5	29.3	30.5	31.1	29.9	29.7	31.4	31.5
Median	31.6	32.2	30.4	30.7	31.8	32.6	31.7	31.3	32.7	32.6
Upper quartile	33.2	34.1	32.6	32.3	33.2	34.2	34.0	33.4	33.2	34.9
Beverage cost of sales										
(% of beverage revenue)										
Lower quartile	27.6	28.7	25.4	25.9	28.2	29.5	27.8	28.7	28.2	30.3
Median	29.6	31.2	27.3	28.3	29.9	32.1	29.9	31.2	30.5	32.9
Upper quartile	31.5	34.0	29.3	30.6	31.6	34.5	31.7	33.4	35.7	36.2
Food & beverage										
payroll										
(% of food & beverage revenue)										
Lower quartile	25.6	25.4	27.9	28.4	25.1	24.9	26.1	27.2	26.7	26.5
Median	28.3	28.1	34.4	35.0	27.5	27.2	28.8	28.7	28.5	27.8
Upper quartile	31.6	31.7	42.4	41.9	30.4	30.1	32.8	32.0	31.0	30.9
Other expenses										
(% of food & beverage revenue)										
Lower quartile	4.8	3.7	7.5	5.5	4.5	3.4	4.7	4.4	5.9	2.9
Median	6.4	5.1	9.1	8.4	6.0	4.7	6.4	5.6	6.2	4.2
Upper quartile	8.3	7.1	11.3	10.5	7.8	6.6	7.2	7.1	6.6	5.7
Total expenses										
(% of food & beverage revenue)										
Lower quartile	59.2	59.9	63.7	64.3	57.8	59.0	60.8	60.7	61.7	62.0
Median	63.1	64.2	70.0	72.0	61.3	62.5	66.2	65.0	62.1	64.5
Upper quartile	68.6	69.1	81.3	81.9	85.7	67.2	69.9	70.2	67.6	67.1
Departmental										
operating profit										
(% of food & beverage revenue)										
Lower quartile	31.3	30.9	18.7	18.1	33.7	32.8	30.2	29.8	32.4	33.4
Median	36.0	35.8	30.0	28.0	37.1	37.5	33.5	35.0	37.9	35.4
Upper quartile	40.3	40.1	36.3	35.7	40.8	41.0	39.2	39.3	38.3	38.6

Note: amounts do not necessarily add to totals shown

Source: BDO Hospitality Consulting – United Kingdom Hotel Industry 1997

Table 16.2   *Food and beverage department – amount per available room*

	UK		London		Provinces		Scotland		Wales	
	1996	*1995*	*1996*	*1995*	*1996*	*1995*	*1996*	*1995*	*1996*	*1995*
Food sales										
Lower quartile	5,230	5,039	4,051	3,851	5,624	5,396	6,004	5,314	5,905	5,550
Median	7,376	7,104	5,678	5,264	7,785	7,387	8,203	6,848	7,576	6,339
Upper quartile	10,076	9,551	8,008	7,321	10,159	9,596	10,061	9,528	12,298	10,973
Beverage sales										
Lower quartile	1,975	1,803	1,210	1,143	2,220	1,984	2,578	2,133	2,237	2,059
Median	3,143	2,839	1,775	1,769	3,432	3,051	3,556	3,177	3,024	3,327
Upper quartile	4,850	4,514	3,602	3,136	4,818	4,400	5,216	4,773	5,090	5,888
Other food & Beverage sales										
Lower quartile	504	451	488	397	577	536	379	389	496	120
Median	971	854	889	945	1,162	956	753	569	655	236
Upper quartile	1,627	1,373	1,486	1,507	1,694	1,462	1,104	1,030	1,082	632
Total food & beverage sales										
Lower quartile	8,062	7,545	6,120	5,622	8,949	7,703	9,276	8,293	8,616	7,877
Median	11,443	10,574	8,144	8,085	12,037	11,113	11,617	11,199	11,521	9,764
Upper quartile	16,163	14,950	13,563	11,292	16,284	15,259	15,951	14,779	17,388	16,717
Food cost of sales										
Lower quartile	1,634	1,536	1,230	1,118	1,791	1,604	1,781	1,625	1,892	1,838
Median	2,331	2,240	1,634	1,475	2,508	2,315	2,472	2,232	2,428	2,073
Upper quartile	3,294	3,114	2,301	2,236	3,266	3,196	3,376	2,952	4,178	3,684
Beverage cost of sales										
Lower quartile	567	563	336	326	655	615	765	722	686	665
Median	895	902	502	465	977	954	1,052	1,000	1,024	1,100
Upper quartile	1,446	1,420	1,017	748	1,430	1,420	1,612	1,541	1,739	1,897
Food & beverage payroll										
Lower qartile	2,351	2,091	1,994	1,807	2,418	2,184	2,591	2,411	2,363	2,080
Median	3,325	2,999	2,912	2,380	3,400	3,016	3,238	3,154	3,278	3,015
Upper quartile	4,551	4,160	4,900	4,421	4,411	4,097	4,769	4,185	4,643	4,480
Other expenses										
Lower quartile	482	308	484	290	475	324	466	306	647	304
Median	721	495	702	528	716	479	788	649	745	436
Upper quartile	1,001	824	1,517	1,835	973	761	1,021	1,000	778	543
Total expenses										
Lower quartile	5,299	4,710	4,224	3,801	5,445	4,906	6,058	5,395	5,474	4,767
Median	7,166	6,690	5,647	5,204	7,627	7,042	7,239	7,250	7,114	6,658
Upper quartile	10,045	9,445	9,303	8,848	9,922	9,414	11,046	9,615	10,725	10,787
Departmental Operating profit										
Lower quartile	2,561	2,407	1,285	1,151	3,020	2,541	2,930	2,570	2,996	2,785
Median	4,039	3,857	2,467	2,178	4,331	4,202	4,096	3,798	3,879	3,606
Upper quartile	5,872	5,381	3,960	3,750	6,142	5,626	6,000	4,943	6,055	5,930

Note: amounts do not necessarily add to totals shown

Source: BDO Hospitality Consulting – United Kingdom Hotel Industry 1997

calculating gross profit potentials, and providing detailed sales analysis would seldom be done because of the time and labour involved.

A manual system providing a restricted amount of basic data is still widely used in small- and medium-sized units although they are likely to be replaced in the near future by machine or electronic systems.

The day-to-day operational problems of a manual system are many and include such common problems as:

1 Poor handwriting by waiting staff resulting in:
   (a) Incorrect order given to the kitchen or dispense bar.
   (b) Wrong food being offered to the customer.
   (c) Incorrect prices being charged to the customer.
   (d) Poorly presented bill for the customer, etc.
2 Human error can produce such mistakes as:
   (a) Incorrect prices charged to items on a bill
   (b) Incorrect additions to a customer's bill
   (c) Incorrect service charge made
   (d) Incorrect government tax (for example VAT) charge made.
3 The communication between departments such as the restaurant, dispense bar, kitchen and cashiers has to be done physically by the waiting staff going to the various departments. This is not only time consuming but inefficient.
4 Manual systems do not provide any quick management information data, any data produced at best being normally 24–48 hours old, as well as being costly to produce.
5 Manual systems have to be restricted to the bare essentials because of the high cost of labour that would be involved in providing detailed up-to-date information.

16.3 Machine systems

16.3.1 Pre-checking systems

Pre-check machines are somewhat similar in appearance to a standard cash register and are designed to operate only when a sales check is inserted into the printing table to the side of the machine.

The machine is operated in the following way.

1 A waiter has his/her own machine key.
2 A check is inserted into the printing table and the particular keys, depending on the order taken, are pressed giving an item and price record as well as recording the table number, the number of covers and the waiter's reference number.
3 A duplicate is printed and issued by the machine which is then issued as the duplicate check to obtain food and/or beverages.
4 For each transaction a reference number is given on the sales check and the duplicate.
5 All data is recorded on a continuous audit tape that can be removed only by authorized persons at the end of the day when the machine is cleared and total sales taken and compared to actual cash received.

The advantages of the system are:

1 The sales check is made out and a record of it made on the audit tape before the specific items can be obtained from the kitchen or bar.
2 Analysis of total sales per waiter is made on the audit tape at the end of each shift.
3 No cashier is required as each waiter acts as his/her own cashier, each keeping the cash collected from customers until the end of the shift and then paying it in.
4 As each waiter has his/her own security key to operate the machine, there is restricted access to the machines and no other way by which pre-checks can be provided and used in exchange for items from the kitchen or bar.

16.3.1.1 *Pre-set pre-checking system*

This is an up-date on the basic pre-check machine. The keyboard is much larger than the previous machines, and has descriptive keys corresponding to all items on the menu which are pre-set to the current price of each item. A waiter pressing the key for, say one cheeseburger would not only have the item printed out but also the price. A control panel, kept under lock and key, would enable management to change the price of any item, if required, very quickly. It is also possible to have a running count kept of each item recorded and at the end of a meal period by depressing each key in turn to get a print out giving a basic analysis of sales made.

16.3.2 Electronic cash registers (ECRs)

These are very high speed machines which were developed mainly for operations such as supermarkets and were further adapted for use in high volume catering operations. Figure 16.6 show a customer's bill produced on an ECR. The particular advantages of these machines are that they will:

1 Price customers' checks through pre-set or by price look-ups.
2 Print checks, including the printing of previously entered items.
3 Have an additional special key so that the pre-set price can be changed during promotional periods such as a 'happy hour' in a bar.
4 Provide an analysis of sales made by type of product and if required by hour (or other similar period) of trading (see Figure 16.7).
5 Provide an analysis of sales by waiter per hour or per shift period.
6 Analyse sales by method of payment, for example cash, cheque, type of credit card, etc. (see the banking report in Figure 16.8).
7 Complete automatic tax calculations and cover and service charges.
8 Provide some limited stock control.
9 Provide waiter checking-in and checking out facilities.
10 Provide facilities for operator training to take place on the machine without disrupting any information already in the ECR.
11 Restrict access to the ECR and the till drawer by the key or code for each operator.
12 Have rotating turret displays of prices charged to individual customer transactions. This is of particular value in self-service and counter operations.
13 Eliminate the need for a cashier, by requiring each waiter to be responsible for taking payment from the customers and paying in the exact amount as recorded by the ECR at the end of each shift.

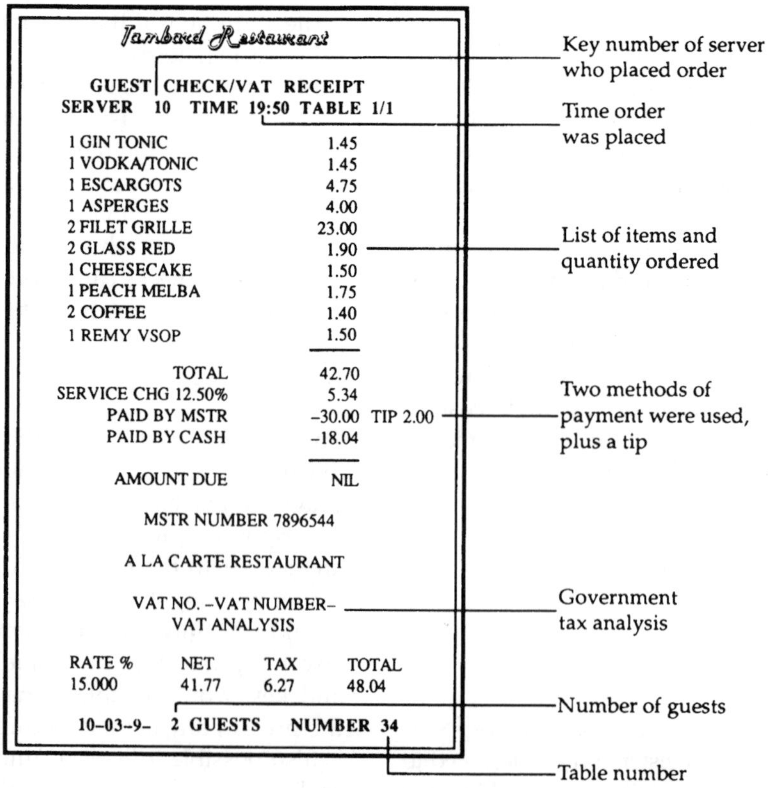
GUEST CHECK/VAT RECEIPT
SERVER 10 TIME 19:50 TABLE 1/1

1 GIN TONIC	1.45
1 VODKA/TONIC	1.45
1 ESCARGOTS	4.75
1 ASPERGES	4.00
2 FILET GRILLE	23.00
2 GLASS RED	1.90
1 CHEESECAKE	1.50
1 PEACH MELBA	1.75
2 COFFEE	1.40
1 REMY VSOP	1.50
TOTAL	42.70
SERVICE CHG 12.50%	5.34
PAID BY MSTR	-30.00 TIP 2.00
PAID BY CASH	-18.04
AMOUNT DUE	NIL

MSTR NUMBER 7896544

A LA CARTE RESTAURANT

VAT NO. -VAT NUMBER-
VAT ANALYSIS

RATE %	NET	TAX	TOTAL
15.000	41.77	6.27	48.04

10-03-9- 2 GUESTS NUMBER 34

Figure 16.6 *An example of a customer's bill produced on a Remanco ECR model*
Source: Remanco Systems Inc.

Electronic cash registers are not without their problems and it is important to consider the following prior to selecting an ECR for purchase.

1 Is it suitable for the type and size of operation it is to be used in?
2 Cost – how does this compare with other models of similar capacity?
3 Is it an up-to-date model or is it about to be superseded?
4 What on-site training will be offered if this model is purchased?
5 Can this ECR be linked to similar ECRs as part of a network or directly to a micro computer?
6 Maintenance. How foolproof is this machine? What level of maintenance is normally expected? Can simple maintenance be done by staff for example, changing of the printing ribbon, etc.?
7 What safeguards (for example, battery override) are standard or optional to the model when power failures occur? (The memory of the day's business could be lost in a power failure causing a serious loss of control.)
8 What built-in security features are included so as to restrict access to commands, re-setting, and disclosure of information to authorized personnel?
9 Will this particular model of ECR function perfectly when near to other powerful electrical equipment?
10 Does this model of ECR have a seal-in keyboard to restrict dust and moisture, which could result in the keys of the ECR operating intermittently?

SALES STATISTICS

ESTABLISHMENT: Pointer Hotels (UK) Ltd
DATE PRINTED: 14/7/9–
TIME PRINTED: 13:32
JOURNAL FILE: 9JA26A

OUTLET/TIME	GUEST	CHECK	TOTAL	ADJUST	VAT TOT	EX VAT	FOOD	BEVERAGE	TOBACCO	SERVICE	OTHER
BAR											
BREAKFAST	0	0	0.00	0.00	0.00	0.00	0.00	0.00	0.00	0.00	0.00
LUNCH	21	78	230.88	–6.64	30.22	200.66	76.20	0.00	131.10	0.00	0.00
DINNER	307	328	1713.69	0.00	223.66	1490.03	313.10	0.00	1176.93	0.00	0.00
	328	406	1944.57	–6.64	253.88	1690.69	389.30	0.00	1308.03	0.00	0.00
RESTAURANT											
BREAKFAST	155	107	1080.80	0.00	140.73	940.07	940.07	0.00	0.00	0.00	0.00
LUNCH	31	18	155.07	0.00	20.23	134.84	120.13	0.00	14.71	0.00	0.00
DINNER	71	43	518.15	0.00	67.61	450.54	375.17	0.00	75.37	0.00	0.00
	257	168	1754.02	0.00	228.57	1525.45	1435.37	0.00	90.08	0.00	0.00
COFFEE SHOP											
BREAKFAST	40	20	179.75	0.00	23.43	156.32	154.06	0.00	2.26	0.00	0.00
LUNCH	14	5	71.75	0.00	9.36	62.39	34.13	0.00	28.26	0.00	0.00
DINNER	113	82	770.50	0.00	100.37	670.13	577.17	0.00	92.96	0.00	0.00
	167	107	1022.00	0.00	133.16	888.84	765.36	0.00	123.48	0.00	0.00
TOTAL											
BREAKFAST	195	127	1260.55	0.00	164.16	1096.39	1094.13	0.00	2.26	0.00	0.00
LUNCH	66	101	457.70	–6.64	59.81	397.89	230.46	0.00	174.07	0.00	0.00
DINNER	491	453	3002.34	0.00	391.64	2610.70	1265.44	0.00	1345.26	0.00	0.00
	752	681	4720.59	–6.64	615.61	4104.98	2590.03	0.00	1521.59	0.00	0.00

Figure 16.7 *An example of sales statistics produced at the end of a day's trading for a hotel's bar, restaurant and coffee shop*
Source: Remanco Systems, Inc.

```
╔══════════════════════════════════════════════════════════════════════════╗
║                           BANKING REPORT                                   ║
╚══════════════════════════════════════════════════════════════════════════╝
```

ESTABLISHMENT: Tambard Restaurant
DATE PRINTED: 13/7/9–
TIME PRINTED: 17:09
JOURNAL FILE: 9AP25A

	PAYMENT METHOD	NUMBER	TOTAL	TIP	INCL. TIP
1	CASH	137	1223.19	0.00	1223.19
2	CHEQUES	3	36.85	0.00	36.85
3	ACCESS	7	143.52	3.09	146.61
4	VISA	11	175.84	2.30	178.14
5	AMERICAN EXPRESS	7	136.72	8.80	145.52
6	DINERS CLUB	3	63.14	0.00	63.14
7	TRUMPCARD	0	0.00	0.00	0.00
8	ROOM CHARGE	591	5749.16	32.24	5781.40
9	REST ROVER DISC VOU	0	0.00	0.00	0.00
10	VOUCHER	0	0.00	0.00	0.00
1	F & B DISC VOU	0	0.00	0.00	0.00
2	LUNCH VOUCHER	0	0.00	0.00	0.00
3	CARTE BLANCHE	0	0.00	0.00	0.00
4	LEDGER	0	0.00	0.00	0.00
5	DEPOSITS	0	0.00	0.00	0.00
6	NOT USED	0	0.00	0.00	0.00
7	TRUMPCARD DISCOUNT	0	0.00	0.00	0.00
8	VOUCHER DISCOUNT	0	0.00	0.00	0.00
9	DEPT. TRANSFER	0	0.00	0.00	0.00
10	WALKOUT	2	28.80	0.00	28.80
	TOTAL	761	7557.22	46.43	7603.65

Figure 16.8   *An example of a banking report showing the different methods of payment received*
Source: Remanco Systems, Inc.

16.3.3 Point-of-sale control systems

At a basic level a point-of-sale control system is no more than a modern ECR with the additional feature of one or several printers at such locations as the kitchen (or sections of the kitchen) or dispense bar. Some systems replace the ECR with a 'server terminal' (also called 'waiter communication' systems), which may be placed at several locations within a restaurant, and is a modification of an ECR in that the cash features are eliminated making the terminal relatively small and inconspicuous.

The objectives for having printers are:

1 To provide an instant and separate clear and printed order to the kitchen or bar, of what is required and by and for whom (see Figure 16.9)
2 To speed up the process of giving the order to the kitchen or bar.

3 To aid control, in that items can only be ordered when they have been entered into the ECR or terminal by an identifiable member of the waiting staff and printed.
4 To reduce the time taken by the waiter in walking to the kitchen or bar to place an order and, as frequently happens, to check if an order is ready for collection.
5 To afford more time, if required, for customer contact.

Printers are at times replaced by VDU screens. Server terminals are part of a computer-based point-of-sale system. These special terminals are linked to other server terminals in the restaurants and bars within one system and, if required to, also interface with other systems so that, for example, the transfer of restaurant and bar charges may be made via the front office computer system. The advantage of a computerized point-of-sale system is that it is capable of processing data as activities occur, which makes it possible to obtain up-to-the minute reports for management who can be better informed and able to take immediate and accurate corrective action if necessary.

This type of point-of-sale control system has been taken one step further with the introduction of hand-held terminals. Remanco's electronic server pad (ESP), for example, is a palm-size unit which uses radio frequencies to communicate from the guest's table direct to the kitchen and bar preparation areas (see Figure 16.10). The use of such a terminal offers a number of advantages: food and beverage orders are delivered faster and more efficiently to preparation sites; waiters in turn can attend more tables; with a two-way communication service staff can be notified if an item is out of stock; all food and

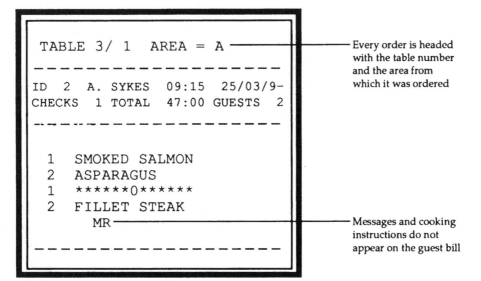

TABLE 3/ 1   AREA = A ——— Every order is headed with the table number and the area from which it was ordered

ID 2 A. SYKES   09:15   25/03/9–
CHECKS 1 TOTAL   47:00 GUESTS 2

    1   SMOKED SALMON
    2   ASPARAGUS
    1   ******0******
    2   FILLET STEAK
         MR ——— Messages and cooking instructions do not appear on the guest bill

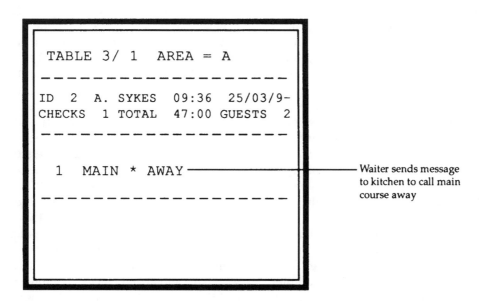

TABLE 3/ 1   AREA = A

ID 2 A. SYKES   09:36   25/03/9–
CHECKS 1 TOTAL   47:00 GUESTS 2

    1   MAIN * AWAY ——— Waiter sends message to kitchen to call main course away

Figure 16.9 *Examples of order dockets*
Source: Remanco Systems Inc.

beverage items ordered are immediately charged to the guest's bill, which is accurate and easy to read; finally, operations can reassess their labour utilization and efficiency, certain members of the service staff, for example, can take the simple orders, while others can spend more time with customers to increase food and beverage sales.

The ESP is a completely noiseless terminal with orders being entered alphabetically, numerically or by using pre-set codes. When not being used and the unit is closed, its design resembles a conventional order pad, compact and light in weight that can easily be carried around by service staff. It is currently being utilized in a variety of situations, including restaurants (for example, Smollenskys Balloon, London); coffee shops (for example, the Tower Hotel); and in lounge areas (for example The Chelsea and The Churchill hotels).

16.3.4   Microcomputers

Before the invention of the microprocessor only a few large organizations were able to justify the high cost of a computer system. In the hotel and catering industry these systems were mainly applied to areas such as the front office, and reservations in particular, as well as for many aspects of the accounting function. The very complex area of food and beverage management including purchasing, storing, stock control, standard recipes, menu planning, pricing, sales analysis, etc. received scant attention from computer firms.

The information required by food and beverage management, to be efficient, is demanding in terms of computer programming, storage and retrieval of data. The move from manual systems, to systems aided by mechanical cash registers, to systems aided by the many types of ECRs, has led to the evolution of totally computer-aided control systems.

The reason for this evolution is simply that the computer equipment necessary for a food and beverage control system is getting smaller, more powerful, cheaper, more reliable, less complex for an operator to use, and relevant software packages are available. The equipment required is of two kinds:

1 *Hardware*. The physical unit comprising the computer unit itself, plus VDU, printers and hard disk drives.
2 *Software*. The computer programs designed and written to fulfil a specific purpose.

From the user's perspective, software is seen as being in two major categories:

1 *Packages* – software that is bought in from a computer firm and is already pre-programmed to perform a specific function, for example payroll, stock control, etc.
2 *User-developed programs* – software which is designed by the food and beverage management staff or by company staff with or without the assistance of computer programming expertise.

In addition, computer firms are marketing *turnkey* systems which are pre-programmed software packages designed to serve a particular sector of the industry or to perform a particular function; they may also come with the necessary hardware. The basis of this marketing approach is that it would be far too expensive to purchase computer hardware and then employ computer programming staff to write a specific set of programs for a unit or company.

The problem with total packages and systems is that they will have been prepared for a very general market so as to be of a wide appeal, and a generalist approach to solving a problem or presenting data will have been taken. With the diversified nature of the hotel and catering industry and the highly personal manner in which many businesses are operated, many of the packages are not entirely acceptable. However, turnkey systems and some carefully selected packages are being successfully used, particularly in the small- to medium-sized operations and companies where often the menu size and ingredients used are not that large and also when a significant proportion of the food purchased is of the pre-prepared and pre-packaged kind. At this point it is significant for the reader to identify both those large and small companies who have a total and efficient computerized food and beverage control system as well as those companies who are still relying very much on a mixture of a manual system enhanced with ECRs.

The cost of a computerized system would include:

1 The system hardware.
2 The system software.
3 The cost of additional or special programming.
4 The cost of training staff and payroll costs.
5 The cost of running a dual system whilst the new system is run-in and initial problems ironed out.
6 The cost of maintenance which should be by contract whenever possible.
7 The cost of supplies, for example computer paper, etc.

Careful planning is necessary by an organization prior to selecting the hardware and software best suited to its needs from the wide range of models and packages available. The following steps should be taken to ensure that the most suitable system is purchased.

1 Analyse the present system for its strengths and weaknesses. By careful analysis determine exactly what the information requirements are for all areas of the organization's operation and management.
2 In general terms summarize the equipment specifications by reference to the information requirements.
3 Select a list of potential suppliers and request literature. Follow this with a request of a presentation of their equipment and if still interested ask for a full demonstration.
4 Obtain from a short list of potential suppliers full details of companies using their equipment and packages. Visit some of these companies and talk to the management and the operators.
5 Check if the programs are simple to understand in that the operator is continually guided through the system with unambiguous prompting on the VDU screen. Also that well-prepared training manuals are included with the equipment.
6 Check if the supplier takes overall responsibility for both the hardware and software performance and maintenance.
7 Check if the supplier can modify the software packages to the particular requirements of the organization.
8 Conduct a financial analysis of alternative

short-listed suppliers' equipment and select a supplier.
9 Have the system put into full operation with the suppliers' training and technical staff standing by to assist with initial problems as they occur. If an existing control system is in operation, this should be continued for a period until the new system is working correctly and all staff training fully completed.

The advantages of a carefully selected micro computer-based information system for a catering operation are in its ability to provide for management's easy and quick access to accurate and complete information related to the total (or part of the) business at any time that it is required, thus allowing management more time to evaluate the information produced and take action quickly when required.

16.4 Operating yardsticks used in controlling

Besides the general operating ratios that have been used earlier in this chapter, for example food cost in relation to food sales, beverage cost in relation to beverage sales, etc., there are many more that are used and found to be of value. The following is a brief explanation of those that are frequently used.

16.4.1 Total food and beverage sales

The total food and beverage sales should be recorded, checked and measured against the budgeted sales figures for the particular period (for example week or month).

The analysis of these figures is usually done daily for large establishments and for those that are not operating a manual control system. The analysis would show separately the food sales and the beverage sales per outlet and per meal period.

The importance of this yardstick cannot be emphasized enough other than to remind the reader that it is cash and cash only that can be banked and not percentages or any ratio or factor figures.

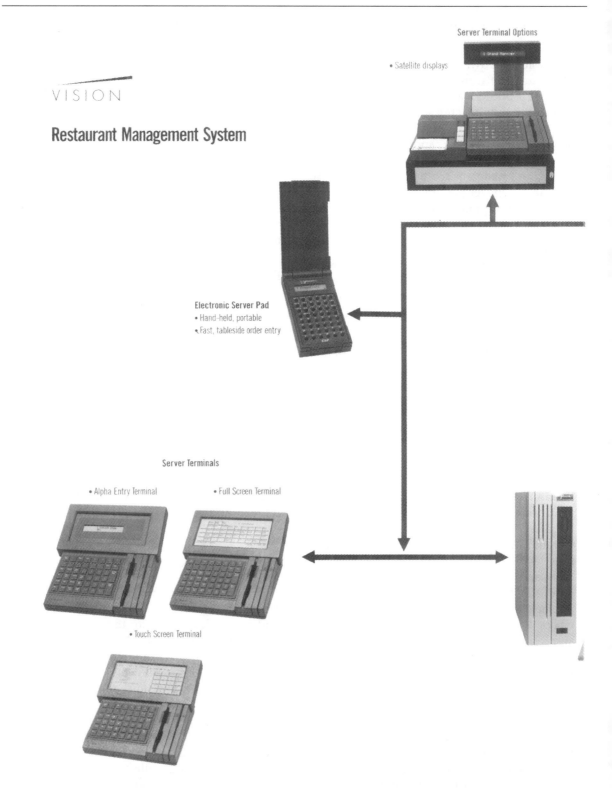

Figure 16.10   *The 'Vision' restaurant management system, integrating the electronic server pad in a fully computerised hotel system*
Source: Remanco Systems Inc.

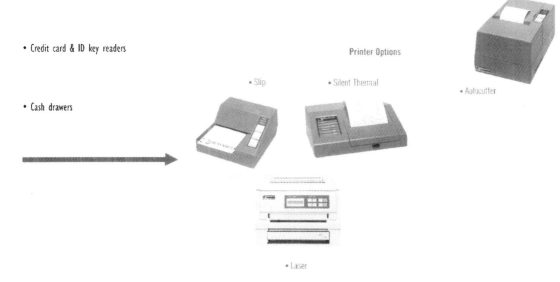

• Credit card & ID key readers

Printer Options

• Slip

• Silent Thermal

• Autocutter

• Cash drawers

• Laser

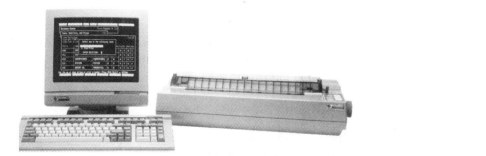

Back Office
• Industry-standard hardware
• Full relational database
• Remote Service
• Supports multiple users

Communications
• Hotel front desk
• Remote office access
• 2 way reporting and control
• On-line and batch reports

```
*********************************************
SUMMARY FOR CATEGORY:   2
ITEM      ITEM      QNTY    TOTAL    GROSS
NUMBR     NAME      SOLD    SALES    MARGN
---------------------------------------------
    1 CLUB SANDWICH 129    509.55   251.55
    2 FILET MIGNON  138   1373.10   683.10
    3 FRUIT PLATE     6     29.70    14.70
    4 HAMBURGER      14     35.00    17.50
    5 OMELETTE       10     39.50    19.50
    6 QUICHE          5     24.75    12.25
    7 ROAST BEEF     20    159.00    79.00
    8 SOLE            7     48.65    24.15
    9 SIRLOIN STEAK  37    294.15   146.15
   10 STEAK&MUSHRM   12     54.00    27.00
   30 CAESAR SALAD   19     47.50    23.75
   31 SIDE SALAD     10     10.00     5.00
   32 SPINACH SALAD   4      7.80     3.80

CATEGORY  2 SALES TOTAL:          2632.70
CATEGORY  2 PERCENT COST OF SALES: 50.34
*********************************************
*********************************************
SUMMARY FOR CATEGORY:   5
ITEM      ITEM      QNTY    TOTAL    GROSS
NUMBR     NAME      SOLD    SALES    MARGN
---------------------------------------------
  500 BLOODY MARY   12     27.00    13.56
  501 COLLINS        3      6.75     3.39
  503 MARTINI        4     11.00     3.60
  504 SCREWDRIVER    9     20.25    10.17
  600 CAMPARI       13     19.50     9.75
  601 GIN           12     21.00    11.16
  602 BEEFEATER      8     18.00     9.04
  606 SCOTCH         5      9.75     4.75
  607 CHIVAS REGAL   3      7.50     3.75
  608 VODKA          5      8.75     4.75
  700 DRAMBUIE       8     14.00     7.44
  703 PERNOD         4      7.00     3.60
  704 TIA MARIA      4      7.00     3.48
  800 COURVOISIER    4     10.00     5.00
  801 HENNESY        1      2.25     1.13
  802 REMY MARTIN    6     16.50     8.10

CATEGORY  5 SALES TOTAL:           206.25
CATEGORY  5 PERCENT COST OF SALES: 50.22
*********************************************
*********************************************
```

Figure 16.11 *An example of a print-out of the analysis of sales at the completion of a meal period*

16.4.2   Departmental profit

As mentioned in Chapter 7, departmental profit is calculated by deducting the departmental expenses from the departmental sales, the expenses being the sum of the cost of food and beverages sold, the cost of labour and the cost of overheads charged against the department, and the profit being usually expressed as a percentage of the departmental sales, for example:

$$\frac{\text{departmental profit (£1,200)}}{\text{food and beverage sales (£8,000)}} \times \frac{100}{1} = 15\%$$

The departmental profit should be measured against the budget figures for that period.

16.4.3 Ratio of food/beverage sales to total sales

It is worthwhile for food and beverage sales to be separated from each other and to express each of them as a percentage of the total sales. This would be a measure of performance against the established standard budgeted percentage as well as indicating general trends in the business.

16.4.4   Average spending power

This measures the relationship between food sales and beverage sales to the number of customers served. If food sales are £350 and the number of customers served is seventy, the average spend by each customers is £5. The average spending power (ASP) for beverages is usually related to the number of items recorded on the till roll, rather than to the number of customers, and the total beverage sales. Thus if £600 is the recorded beverage sales and an analysis of the till roll showed that 400 drinks had been sold, the average spend per drink would be £1.50. What is different here is that a customer may order several drinks during an evening and therefore the average amount spent on a drink is more important than the ASP per customer. To calculate the ASP for bottled wine sales in a restaurant or at a banquet though could be a useful exercise.

16.4.5   Sales mix

This measures the relationship between the various components of the total sales of a unit, for example:

Sales mix	%
Coffee shop sales	
food	20
beverages	5
Restaurant sales	
food	25
beverages	15
Banqueting sales	
food	20
beverages	10
Cocktail bar sales	
beverages	5
	100

MENU ITEM	COST	SOLD AT	GROSS PROFIT	% COST	TOTAL SOLD	TOTAL INCOME	TOTAL COST	TOTAL PROFIT
CALC COST	31.09%							
REAL COST	30.99%							
UP/DOWN	0.10%							

PERIOD TO DATE APRIL 19—

NEW PRICES, NEW FOOD COSTS, ACTUAL SALES.

MENU ITEM	COST	SOLD AT	GROSS PROFIT	% COST	TOTAL SOLD	TOTAL INCOME	TOTAL COST	TOTAL PROFIT
TOMATO SPAG	0.63	3.05	2.02	23.75	472	1439.6	297.36	954.47
MEAT SPAG	0.77	3.05	1.88	29.03	799	2437.0	615.23	1503.9
SEAFOOD SPAG	0.71	3.05	1.94	26.77	467	1424.4	331.57	907.00
SPECIAL SPAG	0.77	3.05	1.88	29.03	262	799.10	201.74	493.13
TOM/MEAT SPAG	0.70	3.25	2.13	24.77	261	848.25	182.70	554.91
TOM/SEA SPAG	0.74	3.25	2.09	26.18	41	133.25	30.34	85.53
TOM/SPEC SPAG	0.70	3.25	2.13	24.77	15	48.75	10.50	31.89
MEAT/SEA SPAG	0.71	3.25	2.12	25.12	46	149.50	32.66	97.34
LEG OF LAMB	1.70	5.95	3.47	32.86	421	2505	715.70	1462.5
FISH	1.03	4.95	3.27	23.93	271	1341.5	279.13	887.35
RIBS	1.24	4.35	2.54	32.78	960	4176	1190.4	2440.9
PEASANT POT	1.32	3.95	2.11	38.43	542	2141	715.44	1146.2
FISHERMANS PIE	0.96	3.95	2.47	27.95	475	1876.3	456.00	1175.5
STEAK PIE	1.09	3.95	2.34	31.73	1365	5391.8	1487.9	3200.6
CHICKEN PIE	1.03	3.95	2.40	29.99	595	2350.3	612.85	1430.8
TURKEY	1.16	4.35	2.62	30.65	407	1770.5	471.87	1067.7
SIDE SALAD	0.24	0.90	0.54	30.67	414	372.60	99.36	224.64
MUSHROOMS	0.30	1.05	0.61	32.86	123	129.15	36.90	75.40
GARLIC BREAD	0.12	0.55	0.36	25.09	1170	643.50	140.40	419.17
JACKET POTATO	0.13	0.90	0.65	16.61	579	521.10	75.27	377.86
VEG OF DAY	0.20	0.90	0.58	25.56	88	79.20	17.60	51.27
CLUB	0.76	3.05	1.89	28.66	527	1607.4	400.52	997.18
PASTRAMI	0.87	2.95	1.70	33.92	132	389.40	114.84	223.77
RUBENS	0.88	2.95	1.69	34.31	100	295.00	88.00	168.52
HAMBURGER	0.68	2.55	1.54	30.67	243	619.65	165.24	373.59
CHEESEBURGER	0.71	2.85	1.77	28.65	252	718.20	178.92	445.60
BACONBURGER	0.95	3.15	1.79	34.68	148	466.20	140.60	264.79
CHOCOLATE CAKE	0.30	1.05	0.61	32.86	772	810.60	231.60	473.27
APPLE PIE	0.33	1.05	0.58	36.14	246	258.30	81.18	143.43
STRAWB SHAKE	0.33	0.95	0.50	39.95	169	160.55	55.77	83.84
COFFEE SHAKE	0.33	0.95	0.50	39.95	108	102.60	35.64	53.58
+ BANANA	0.08	0.20	0.09	46.00	168	33.60	13.44	15.78
+ MALT	0.08	0.20	0.09	46.00	56	11.20	4.48	5.26
CROISSANT	0.26	0.75	0.40	39.25	64	48.00	16.38	25.36
PAIN CHOC	0.30	0.75	0.35	46.00	35	26.25	10.50	12.33
DAILY SPECIAL	0.95	3.25	1.88	33.62	385	1251.3	365.75	722.29
SPEC SWEET	0.30	0.95	0.53	36.32	151	143.45	45.30	79.44

SUMMARY

COST OVERALL	31.09%	. . . SIDE ORDS	24.35%
. . . SPAGS	26.59%	. . . SANDS	30.55%
. . . SALADS	30.29%	. . . SWEETS	32.15%
. . . M/COURSE	32.00%		

Figure 16.12 *An example of a monthly food analysis sheet produced on a small personal computer*

In addition, a sales mix may be calculated for the food and beverage menus for each outlet under group headings such as appetizers, main course items, sweet course, coffees, etc.; and spirits, cocktails, beers and lagers, etc. This would not only highlight the most and least popular items, but would at times help to explain a disappointing gross profit percentage that occurred in spite of a good volume of business; the reason often being that each item is usually costed at different gross profit percentages and if the customers are choosing those items with a low gross profit this would result in the overall gross profit figure being less than budgeted for.

16.4.6 Payroll costs

Payroll costs are usually expressed as a percentage of sales and are normally higher, the higher the level of service offered. It is vital that they are tightly controlled as they contribute a high percentage of the total costs of running an operation.

Payroll costs can be controlled by establishing a head count of employees per department, or establishing the total number of employee hours allowed per department in relation to a known average volume of business. In addition, all overtime must be strictly controlled and should only be permitted when absolutely necessary.

16.4.7   Index of productivity

This is calculated by the formula:

$$\frac{\text{sales}}{\text{payroll (including any staff benefits costs)}}$$

The index of productivity can be calculated separately for food sales, beverage sales or for total food and beverage sales.

The use of the term 'payroll costs' in the formula includes not only the appropriate payroll costs, but also any other employee benefits such as employers' pension contributions, medical insurance, etc.

The index of productivity would vary depending on the type of operation, for example a fast food restaurant with a take-away service would have a high index of productivity, as the payroll costs would be lower than a luxury restaurant employing highly skilled and expensive staff with a high ratio of staff to customers, which may have a relatively low index of productivity.

As payroll costs can be controlled and should be related to the forecasted volume of business, a standard index of productivity can be established to measure how accurately the two elements are related.

16.4.8   Stock turnover

This has been mentioned previously in the book. It is calculated by the formula:

$$\text{rate of stock turnover} = \frac{\text{cost of food or beverages consumed}}{\text{average stock value (food or beverage) at cost}}$$

The rate of stock turnover gives the number of times that the average level of stock has turned over in a given period.

Too high a turnover would indicate very low levels of stocks being held and a large number of small value purchases being made. This is costly and time consuming for whoever does the purchasing as well as costly for the purchases as no price advantage can be taken of the standard quantity offers made by suppliers. Too low a turnover would indicate unnecessary capital tied up in an operation and therefore additionally a larger control and security problem.

16.4.9   Sales per seat available

This shows the sales value that can be earned by each seat in a restaurant, coffee shop, etc. As in section 16.4.10, the seat is the selling point and is required to contribute a certain value to turnover and profits.

16.4.10   Rate of seat turnover

This shows the number of times that each seat in a restaurant, coffee shop, etc. is used by customers during a specific period. Thus, if in a 120-seater coffee shop 400 customers were served in a three-hour lunch period, the rate of seat turnover would be 400 divided by 120, that is, 3.33. As the coffee shop staff can only sell food to customers while they are seated at a table, the importance of the rate of seat turnover is highlighted.

16.4.11   Sales per waiter/waitress

Each waiter/waitress will have a known number of covers for which he/she is responsible. This would vary depending on the style of food and beverage service offered. As salespeople for the restaurant or coffee shop, their takings should be of a predetermined target level so as to contribute to a satisfactory level of turnover and profit.

16.4.12   Sales per square foot/metre^2

This is self-explanatory in that the space of all selling outlets needs to be used to its best advantage so as to achieve a desired turnover and profit. This can be calculated on a square foot/metre basis. As the square footage per customer varies with the type of food and beverage service offered, so must the costs to the customer so that an establishment is earning the desired turnover and profit per square foot of selling space.

16.5   Reference

Coltman, M. L. (1987). *Hospital Management Accounting*. New York: Van Nostrand Reinhold.

17

Food and beverage management in fast-food and popular catering

17.1 Introduction

Fast-food and popular catering may be defined as that sector of the catering industry primarily concerned with the preparation and service of food and beverages quickly, for immediate sale to the customer. Examples of fast-food and popular operations include take-aways such as hamburgers and fish and chip operations, coffee shops, snack bars, self-service cafeterias, public house catering, steak houses, etc.

In terms of UK sales, sandwiches accounted for just over 25% of total sales in 1994, burgers almost 21%, pizza and fish and chips between 14% and 15% (see Table 17.1). Between 1990 and 1994 the value of the fast-food market increased by 26%, accounting for 52.1% of all restaurant sales in the UK. Almost 50% of adults visited a fast-food operation at least once a month and 73% visited a take-away over the same period. Future growth is expected as the major brands expand, particularly via franchising so that the year 2000 will see a 24% increase at current prices taking the 1994 value.

Although differing from one another in certain aspects, these catering outlets have a number of characteristics which are common to all these types of operations – they offer a limited menu range; the operation may be centred around one particular product, for example, a hamburger, or offer a limited range of products as found, for example, in coffee shops and cafeterias; the food and beverages sold are of a consistent standard and quality with a high percentage of convenience and ready prepared foods being used. These operations cater mainly for the relatively lower average spend markets with lower prices

being charged than those found in other food and beverage establishments; there is a low ratio of service staff to customers with many of these operations being a form of self-service; consumption of the food may be on or off the premises; less rigid meal times are observed by these establishments, with some form of menu usually available throughout the day; and finally, all aspects of the operation are highly standardized, leading to a high volume throughput with resulting economies in food, labour and other operating costs.

Table 17.1 *The UK fast-food/take-away market by product sector (£m at RSP and %), 1994*

	£m	%
Sandwiches	1348	25.7
Fish and chips	744	14.2
Burgers	945	18.0
Pizza	774	14.8
Chicken	343	6.5
Other	1088	20.8
Total	5342	100

Source: Key Note 1995 Market Report: fast food and home delivery outlets

These characteristics of fast-food and popular catering operations are displayed to a varying extent by the different types of operations. In take-away outlets, for example, characteristics such as the limited menu range, the lower prices charged, and the low ratio of service staff to customers are more evident than in other popular operations such as public houses, where the menu range is larger, higher prices are charged

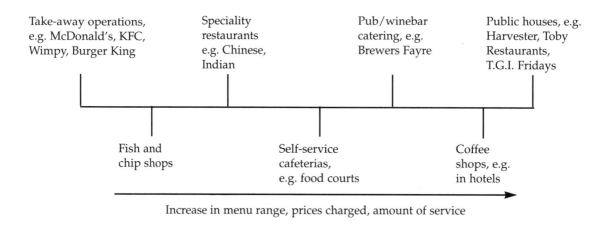

Figure 17.1 *The range of fast-food and popular catering outlets*

and waiter service to the table may be the norm. Therefore within the fast food catering market there are different levels of operation, which vary from the take-away operations such as McDonald's and Burger King at one end of the scale, to catering establishments such as public houses at the other end (see Figure 17.1). However, because these different types of operations do display similar characteristics they may be conveniently grouped under the umbrella term of fast-food or popular catering outlets, although it is important to realize the range of establishments within this sector.

Unlike some establishments the provision of food and beverages is usually a fast-food or popular catering operation's only activity, and therefore the establishment has few alternative uses; industrial cafeterias, for example, are often able to offer function facilities at the weekends or in the evenings when the cafeteria would otherwise be unused. For the majority of fast-food and popular catering operations, however, this alternative is not available and they must therefore rely heavily on their day to-day operation during which time they must maximize their sales potential. For this reason, the location of fast-food and popular catering operations is par-

ticularly important, as they must be aimed at attracting a large volume of trade to generate a high turnover. These catering establishments are usually sited either in town centres such as in high streets, near cinemas, sports centres, shops etc., and in motorway service areas, airports and railway stations, which are primarily aimed at passing traffic, or situated in residential areas which rely heavily on local and passing trade.

17.2 Basic policies – financial, marketing and catering

In any food and beverage operation there are a number of basic policy decisions that need to be made at the initial planning stage, before the establishment begins operating or whenever major changes of operation are to take place. These are the financial, marketing, and catering policies.

Fast-food and popular catering establishments may be independently operated, in which case the individual operators are responsible for compiling their own policies or, as is more usual, they may be part of a large organization.

Table 17.2 *Major UK restaurant and fast-food operators, 1994–95*

Company	Key brands	Outlets
Allied Domecq[b]	Big Steak, Wacky Warehouse, Exchange	270
Bass[b]	Toby, Harvester	278
Bright Reasons PLC	Pizzaland, Bella Pasta, Pizza Piazza	190
City Centre Restaurants PLC	Deep Pan Pizza, Garfunkels, Chiquito, Caffé Uno UK Diner, Raja Mama's, Nachos	205
Granada	Happy Eater, Little Chef, Welcome Break, Granada	400[b]
Grand Metropolitan	Burger King	380
McDonald's	McDonald's	650
Pelican	Café Rouge, Dome	100
Pepsico	KFC	367
Pizza Express	Pizza Express	94
Scottish & Newcastle[b]	Chef & Brewer	1,600
Whitbread	Beefeater, T.G.I. Friday's Pizza Hut[a], Brewers Fayre	875

[a] Pizza Hut in the UK is a joint venture between Whitbread and Pepsico

[b] Restaurant operators within public house estates, including many outlets also serving food

Source: Key Note 1996 Market Report: restaurants

17.2.1 Franchising

The size of these large organizations also allows them to offer franchise arrangements to prospective franchisees. Franchising is an arrangement in which the franchisor grants to the franchisee a licence to use particular commercial methods of operation which he has developed. The franchisee contributes the necessary capital to start up an operation, effort and motivation to run the establishment, and agrees to be controlled by the franchisor; the franchisor in return contributes to the training of the franchisee, the procedures of operation and other managerial expertise. Franchising arrangements are particularly applicable to fast-food outlets because of the way in which these operations lend themselves to standardization and duplication and in this way encourage the development of franchising within the large chain operations (see Table 17.3).

The advantages to the franchisee are:

1 It offers the opportunity for immediate entry into business.
2 It offers immediate entry into a particular market with a proven successful 'package', that is, a brand product.
3 Assistance is offered in finding and evaluating sites.

Table 17.3 *Company-owned and franchised operations for selected fast-food chains (% share), 1993/1994*

	Company owned outlets	Franchised outlets
McDonald's	85	16
Burger King	37	63
KFC	28	72
Wimpy	3	97
Domino's	–	100
Spud-u-Like	43	57

Source: Key Note 1995 Market Report: fast-food and home delivery outlets

4 Assistance is given with initial layouts, shop fitting specifications, and advice with planning applications.
5 Assistance is given with initial training of management and staff.
6 The franchisor provides menus, and sells (or nominates suppliers) all food, beverage, small equipment, etc. to the franchisee.
7 The franchisor provides all operational documents.
8 The franchisor provides regional and national promotional support.
9 The franchisor provides regular advice and assessment.

The advantages to the franchisor are:

1 It enables the franchisor to expand the business with speed using the franchisee's investment capital.
2 It enables the franchisor to achieve market penetration with relative ease and speed using the franchisee's capital, time and energy.
3 It reduces the number (if any) of development staff to find sites and to be involved in lengthy openings of new units.
4 It increases the benefits to the franchisor by providing significantly greater market exposure of the product.
5 It enables the franchisor to be the required supplier of the food, beverages, disposable commodities, equipment and at times fixtures and fittings, to the exclusion of competitors' products in all forms.
6 It enables the franchisor to have the franchisee under a period contract, to pay for entry into the franchise, to pay a commission fee based on turnover, and often to pay a specific percentage of turnover towards regional and national advertising and promotions.

17.2.2   Financial considerations

Fast-food and popular catering establishments have a number of characteristics which enable their particular business orientation to be identified. Relatively speaking, they do not require such a high initial capital outlay (relative to other sectors of the industry), nor a high percentage of fixed costs, although they do normally have a higher percentage of variable costs. Although the products offered for sale by these establishments are perishable, they are not as perishable as similar food and beverage products offered by other types of catering establishments; this is mainly due to the high level of convenience foods used by popular catering outlets, and the fact that often most of the foods are 'cooked to order' and do not have to be prepared sometime in advance; also because the products are not so highly perishable, these operations do not suffer from such sales instability as do hotels, for example, and they therefore have a lesser degree of dependence on market demand. All these factors contribute to making the fast-food

and popular catering operations both cost-orientated (to control costs tightly) and market-orientated (to ensure the volume of business in a very competitive sector of the industry).

In these lower average spend operations, the cost of the meal to the customer is an important variable in determining the sales of the operation; because fast-food and popular operations demonstrate a very elastic demand, an increase in an establishment's prices of, for example, 10 per cent, is likely to have a substantial effect on its sales. Variable costs in fast-food operations account for a large part of the product's selling price and the range of price discretion is consequently low. The prices charged by these establishments must therefore be carefully calculated, particularly in relation to competitors' pricing levels. The average spend per customer can be relatively low, ranging from £3–£4 in take away operations up to £15 per head in public houses, although these relatively low average spends are compensated for by the volume sales achieved.

The financial policies of fast-food operations would include the envisaged profitability of the establishment and the way in which it may be achieved, by controlling costs, balancing selling prices against volume sales, determining the profit margins on the food and beverage items, etc.

17.2.3   Marketing considerations

The growth and development of popular and fast-food catering in the past fifteen years have brought an increasing awareness of the importance of marketing to this sector of the industry. With the growth of gross and disposable incomes, together with an increase in eating away from the home by all sectors of the general public, the potential to develop in these areas, not previously exploited, was identified.

The marketing policy for the modern popular and fast-food organization is the key to success in this sector of the industry. A study of many of these organizations provides an outline to the marketing policy which may be discussed under the variables of product, promotion, place, price, process, physical evidence and participants.

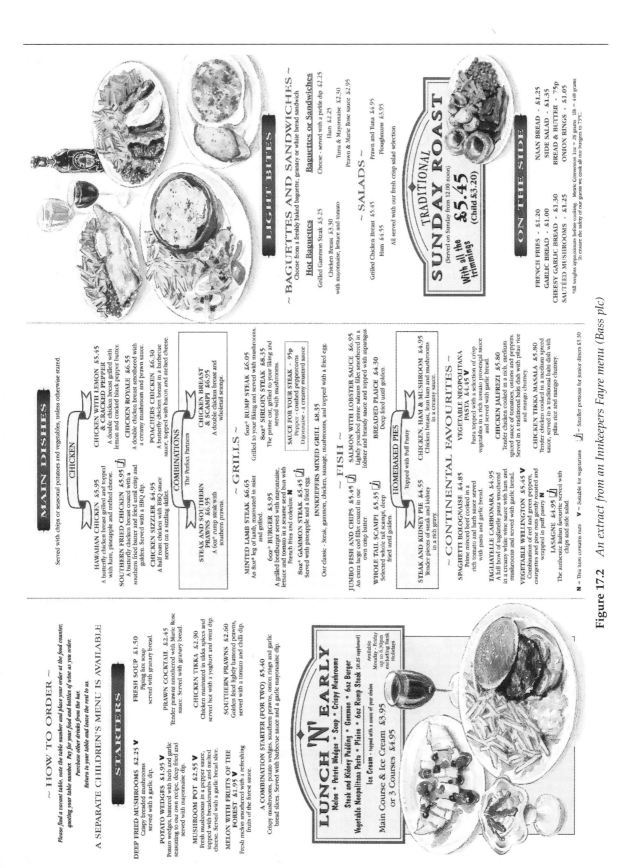

Figure 17.2 An extract from an Innkeepers Fayre menu (Bass plc)

Wines

Toby offers a comprehensive selection of wines from around the world – the perfect complement to your meal.

Whites

5. Kron Prinz Liebfraumilch Qba (9.5%)
A medium sweet German white wine.
£7.75

6. Piesporter Michelsberg Qba (9.5%)
A light soft-flavoured medium dry wine from the Mosel Valley.
Bottle - £8.25   Half bottle - £4.45

7. Lambrusco Bianco Corelli (4.0%)
Light, fresh with a slight sparkle and pleasantly sweet.
£6.95

8. Chapel Hill Chardonnay (12.5%)
A buttery, ripe flavour enhanced by fermentation with American oak.
£8.50

9. Muscadet AC Chateau De La Ragotière (12.0%)
A crisp, dry wine with a high balanced fruit flavour.
£10.50

10. Chablis AC Paul Dupressior (12.5%)
A crisp, firm dry white wine from Burgundy.
£12.50

11. Lindemans Chardonnay (13.0%)
A rich creamy white wine with a welcome spiciness.
Bottle - £9.95   Half bottle - £5.25

TOBY HOUSE WINES

Superb value at £6.95

Alexis Lichine Vin De Pays
A range of quality French wines.

WHITE
A choice of 1. dry 2. medium dry or 3. medium sweet (11.0%)

RED
4. Light (11.5%)

House wines by the 175ml glass
£1.95

CHAMPAGNE & SPARKLING WINES

12. Lanson Black Label NV (12.0%)
A Grand Marque Champagne for those special occasions.
£23.95

13. Asti Spumante DOCG (7.0%)
A sweet and very fruity sparkling wine. Great for parties.
£10.75

LOW ALCOHOL

14. Eisberg German (0.05%)
A slightly sparkling low alcohol medium sweet wine.
Bottle - £6.25   175ml Glass - £1.65

Mineral Water
Natural Mineral Water, served with ice and lemon.
Small Bottle - £1.25   Large Bottle - £1.95

Wine Taste Guide
All white and rose wines are coded from very dry, to very sweet.
All red wines are coded according to their fullness from light and easy drinking to the fullest bodied, richest wines.

The percentage figure shown is the alcohol by volume content of the wine (subject to vintage variance).
All wine is sold by the 75cl bottle or 37.5cl half bottle.

Reds

15. Valpolicella DOC (11.0%)
A classy fruity red Italian wine.
£7.50

16. Libertas Merlot (13.0%)
Soft and plummy with superbly drinkable fruit flavours - a rare South African merlot.
£8.45

17. Rioja Reserva (12.5%)
A soft, fruity and mellow Spanish wine.
£11.95

18. Mouton Cadet AC (12.5%)
A round and full fruit wine with depth of flavour and delicate bouquet of classic mature bordeaux.
Bottle - £11.95   Half bottle - £6.50

19. Côtes Du Rhone AC (12.5%)
A full-flavoured, soft fruity wine.
Bottle - £8.45   Half bottle - £4.95

20. Mateus Rosé (11.0%)
A fruity, medium sweet rosé wine with a gentle sparkle.
£9.25

A full range of bar drinks or hot and cold soft drinks is also available.   Our staff will be pleased to serve you.

All items subject to availability.   Service charge is not included.   All prices include VAT at the rate of 17.5%, subject to change and revised customs and excise duties.

We aim to provide the highest standards of food, service and value for money.
If any aspect of your Toby visit is unsatisfactory, please inform a member of staff who will ensure the problem is rectified immediately.

Toby Restaurants, Hagley House, 83 Hagley Road, Edgbaston, Birmingham B16 8QG.

TCR 2/97

Figure 17.3 *The wine list from a Toby Restaurant*

1 The **product** for the fast-food and popular catering sector has two easily identifiable tangible characteristics: a high degree of standardization and of theme. It includes not only the menu, but also the quality of the food and beverages, its methods of production, the portion sizes, and the method of service and presentation as well as the general layout/design of the individual unit, the décor, and ambience.

Typically, fast-food units are brightly lit with a high standard of hygiene and cleanliness, for which this sector is generally well known; identifiable brands of colour scheme are used (green, yellow, and red colours being evident) and the menu being themed around one main food item such as hamburgers, pizzas, etc. Popular catering units are similar, although as their pricing levels and the average spend per meal increases, the amount of investment spent on the décor theme increases as well as the space allocation per cover.

2 The **promotion** techniques used by fast-food operations are usually very direct and obvious. Many operations use specifically designed logos and colours which become representative of that level of operation in terms of standard of food, service, etc. These colours and logos are used extensively in most aspects of the establishment, the external facia, interior decor, service accompaniments and so on, and in take-away operations on the disposable wrappers used for packaging the foods and beverages. By continually reinforcing the image of the operation through these different aspects, the organization is able to develop a form of *association advertising* so that when an organization's logo is seen by a customer, it is immediately associated with that particular organization. Particular to this sector of the industry are the number and variety of give-aways, such as car stickers, key fobs, children's badges, balloons, fancy hats, etc. with an organization's logo, clearly displayed, for example McDonald's meal boxes.

3 The **place** refers to the way by which the products and premises are made readily available to the customers at the appropriate time and location. Location is of prime importance to business success in the fast food and popular catering sectors where customers are unlikely to travel too far for this type of meal experi-

ence. For example, a typical fish and chip shop is unlikely to be successful unless it has a local residential population of not less than 5000 within a two or three mile radius, nor would a public house steak operation be successful unless it has a local residential population of not less than 75,000 within a five to ten mile radius. The importance of being on a major A or B class road with easy and adequate car parking facilities is also essential.

4 The **price** is a very important element also to success in this sector of the industry. Customers will tend to be cost conscious and to be aware of the prices charged' by competitors for similar items. Any significant increase in price could well result in a significant decrease in sales. The price must be seen by these customers as giving good value for money together with a consistent and standard product of good quality.

5 The **process**, that is the service delivery of the product in fast-food catering, presents a problem, particularly in the take-away sector, in that the staff-to-customer time can be very limited. For product and staff development it is important to obtain feedback from an operation's customers. Why do customers frequent that type of operation? How many times a week do they use it? What are their likes and dislikes about the products offered? Would they like to see any additions made to the menu? The obtaining of this type of information can be costly and would require in most cases the services of a specialist market research team. An inexpensive and valuable method is to get the customers to complete a simple but well prepared questionnaire, that may be printed on the back of the customer's bill or on a separate sheet. An example of a typical questionnaire is given in Figure 17.6.

6 The **physical evidence** incorporates all the tangible elements of the fast-food establishment such as the table arrangements, decor and lighting, staff uniforms, menu design, etc.; popular catering establishments are particularly skilled in offering totally themed environments.

7 The **participants** are those people the customer interacts with, whether restaurant staff or other customers. The highly standardized nature of

fast-food operations extends to personnel training and interaction with customers so that in this sector of the catering industry the 'how' element of service is often well documented in company training manuals, for example how to greet and seat customers, take orders, deal with complaints, etc.

17.2.4   Catering considerations

17.2.4.1 *Type of customer*

Although the majority of fast-food and popular operations cater for the middle 'mass' markets, it is dangerous to define these markets too specifically, as customers from other market segments do also buy from these type of operations for a variety of reasons. Perhaps a more appropriate question to ask therefore is, 'What sort of meal experience are customers seeking when they enter a fast-food or popular catering operation?'

In a take-away establishment it may be suggested that customers seek this type of operation as no more than a 'filling station', a sales outlet that they may enter at any time during the day and purchase food and beverages immediately, either to be consumed on the premises, or elsewhere at their convenience. This type of informal eating or 'grazing' has increased during recent years prompting an increase in the demand for fast-foods and convenience style eating. In other types of popular catering establishments, customers may require something more than simply refreshment. Shoppers in a department store, for example, will often purchase a beverage and a snack not only for refreshment but also so that they may sit down and rest. At the higher spending level of the popular catering sector, customers will frequent restaurants such as public houses and theme restaurants for different reasons again. Here they would expect a larger menu choice, waiter service at the tables, a better standard of décor and some form of restaurant atmosphere; in return for this the customers would pay a higher price for their meal. Customers' needs may therefore vary considerably from one type of fast-food operation to another.

Broadly speaking, fast-food and popular catering establishments have a fairly limited market area to which they cater. A take-away fish and chip shop, for example, may have a market area of up to a two mile radius; beyond this distance potential customers would not travel to this particular operation, but would choose one closer by. Other types of popular catering restaurants have a slightly wider catchment area, for example of up to a five mile radius but again beyond this distance the extra cost involved in travelling to the operation outweighs other benefits. The market area of these types of operation is therefore critical in the siting of an establishment, particularly if the operation must rely on repeat business from the surrounding area, rather than a high percentage of passing trade.

The type of customer likely to frequent these operations will vary in terms of sex, age, socio-economic grouping and so on; from this type of information an operation may build up a customer profile – this is a description of the type of customer likely to frequent a particular operation. For example, a customer profile for a Chinese take-away situated in a residential area may read as follows; customers coming from a B and C1 socio-economic grouping, both sexes, young to middle-age group who are willing to experiment with different foods, often with young children, a high proportion of car ownership willing to travel three to four miles to the operation, and an average spend of £5.00 per customer. Once this type of customer profile has been established, the operation's advertising and merchandising campaigns can become more meaningful because the market segments have been identified and the campaigns can be aimed directly at these. Customer profiles are also very useful if an operation is considering expanding and opening a similar operation in another area. It may have been established, for example, that a population of between 4000 and 5000 is necessary to support a fish and chip take-away operation; with a knowledge of the customer profile and the number needed to support an operation, different areas can be reviewed as possible future sites.

17.2.4.2   *Type of product/menu*

A fast-food and popular type operation may be centred around one particular product, for example a hamburger, a croissant or baked potato; or it may offer a range of products as, for example, is

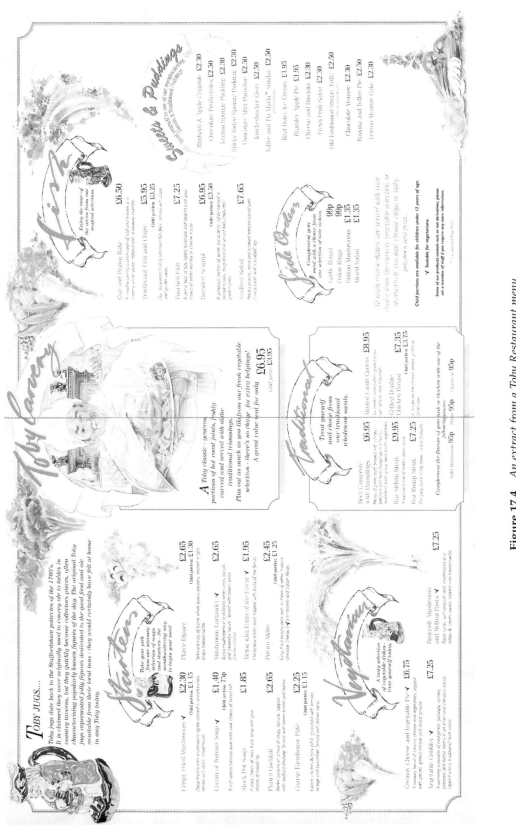

Figure 17.4 An extract from a Toby Restaurant menu

found in coffee shops and cafeterias. Those operations that feature one or two standard food items achieve menu variety by featuring the standard item in a number of different ways. For example, if a food court outlet is offering jacket potatoes as its main food item, it may offer eight or ten different fillings to achieve variety; similarly, hamburger operations offer a variety of accompaniments and garnishes with their standard hamburger. The majority of take-away operations have traditionally been of this nature, that is featuring one particular product such as chicken, pizza, fish and chips, croissants, baked potato, etc. There has been an identifiable trend however, in the past few years, of these types of operations broadening their product base and product mix in order to offer customers more choice and encourage sales growth. McDonald's, for example, now feature pizza on their menus so that customers who may traditionally have only frequented Pizza Hut or Pizza Express, can now also consider McDonald's as an alternative.

Other types of fast-food and popular operations offer a range of products; these vary from the high street coffee shop offering mainly specific hot and salad-type products, to the large self-service cafeterias in office blocks and factories, featuring a wide variety of hot and cold foods. Where popular catering establishments offer a variety of products, they can be sold as complete meals, for example plates of salad; an entrée and two vegetables; sausage, egg and chips, etc. In higher spend establishments such as public houses, the meal is offered less 'pre-assembled', for example the main meat item such as rump steak, may be offered with a choice of french fries, saute potatoes or jacket potatoes and a similar variety of accompaniments for example vegetables or a salad.

The products sold by fast-food and popular catering operations are highly standardized and portion controlled, particularly in take-away operations. The larger organizations, such as McDonald's, have vertically integrated their supply chains, controlling food production through to product sales, ensuring total product control and specification. Other companies may buy in pre-prepared and packaged products from the food manufacturers and sell them directly to the customer, for example pre-wrapped pies, biscuits, butter, etc. In this situation the fast-food operation closely resembles a retail trading outlet

in which it has bought from the wholesaler and is selling to the customer without altering the product in any way.

This is a particularly useful way for an operation to increase its menu range without increasing the work load on the kitchen staff or requiring additional space or equipment to prepare a menu item with fresh produce.

The menu as a sales tool is important in any food and beverage operation, but is particularly so in these types of operations where staffing levels are reduced to a minimum and the operation's only vehicle for selling its products is via its menu and visual displays. In situations such as takeaways where contact time with the service staff is minimal, the menus are featured very prominently, usually with pictorial representation of the dishes.

In fast-food operations every item on the menu is priced, either individually or as a complete meal, the price range being relatively limited; in take-aways for example, the lowest priced item may be 70p for a beverage and £4 for the most expensive item. In popular restaurants inclusive two- and three-course meals may range from £10 to £15. All prices shown are usually inclusive of any surcharges such as government taxes and service charges, so that there are no 'hidden' extras. In take-away operations such as McDonald's, Burger King, Wimpy etc., all transactions are on a cash payment basis; only in the higher priced popular catering outlets, for example public houses and pizza restaurants, are credit facilities accepted.

Finally, the product packaging should complement the other aspects of the operation and help to reinforce its image. The packaging of the product includes the direct packaging of the food, for example the crockery on which the food is presented, or the containers and bags in which the food is taken away, the service accompaniments such as the menu itself, tableware and cutlery napkins, straws etc., and the more indirect packaging such as the restaurant décor, the staff and their uniforms, the seating arrangements, and so on. Some forms of packaging have a dual role: the disposable ware used by take-away operations, for example, not only has a functional purpose but can also be a very useful form of external advertising for the operation.

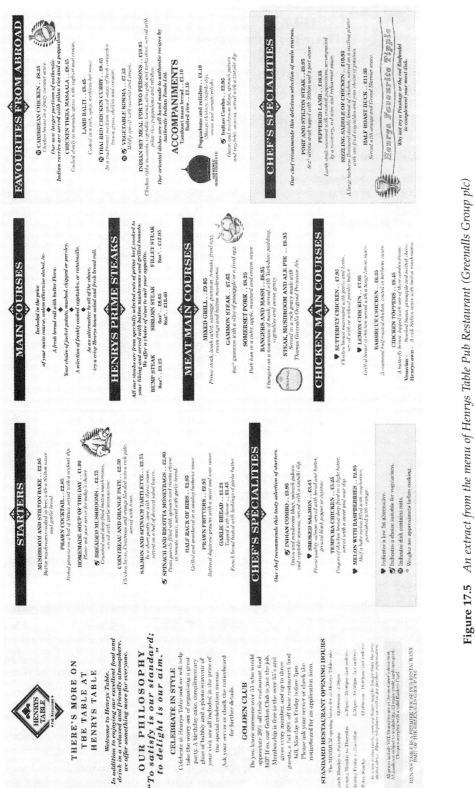

Figure 17.5 An extract from the menu of Henrys Table Pub Restaurant (Greenalls Group plc)

PRIMO PIZZA
Please pay at the cash desk
No. 991234

WE VALUE THE OPINIONS OF OUR CUSTOMERS AND WOULD
APPRECIATE YOUR CO-OPERATION IN COMPLETING
THIS SIMPLE FORM.
THE INFORMATION GIVEN WILL HELP US TO HELP YOU –
OUR CUSTOMER

Gradings A = Excellent,   B = Good,   C = Fair,   D = Poor

Please circle below your gradings

Range of items on menu	A	B	C	D
Speed of Service	A	B	C	D
Friendliness of Service	A	B	C	D
Atmosphere	A	B	C	D
Cleanliness	A	B	C	D

Please grade the products you purchased

Home Made Soup	A	B	C	D
Toasted Sandwich	A	B	C	D
Regular Pizza	A	B	C	D
Pastrami Pizza	A	B	C	D
Ham Pizza	A	B	C	D
Green Pepper Pizza	A	B	C	D
Ice Cream	A	B	C	D

Additional Comments

Name ....

Address ....

THANK YOU FOR YOUR ASSISTANCE

Figure 17.6   *An example of a questionnaire used by fast-food catering organizations*

17.2.4.3   *Food production styles*

The food production styles used by fast-food and popular catering operations are dictated to a large extent by the high percentage of convenience and ready prepared foods used by these establishments. The convenience foods used include pre-portioned items; frozen, dehydrated, and canned foods; and any other items that are purchased by the establishment with little or no further preparation necessary before they can be sold to the customer.

In these operations it is not so much a question of whether or not to use convenience foods, but of those available which ones to use and to what extent. The amount of convenience foods used by an establishment will depend on a number of factors: the cost of buying in manufactured foods compared with the cost of producing the same products on the premises; the standard of food that the establishment wishes to offer; the variety of menu items to be offered; whether the additional costs of buying manufactured foods is offset by savings in production and labour costs, etc. Generally speaking, however, the advantages gained by using convenience products in fast food operations do warrant their extensive use in these types of establishments.

Like most aspects of these operations, food production is highly standardized. Standard purchasing specifications are used to buy in the food and beverages, they are prepared according to standard recipes, and from these standard yields are obtained. Portion control and costing are very tightly controlled. Some of the kitchens in these operations are in fact no more than 'finishing kitchens'; they are designed to serve mostly bought-in pre-prepared foods quickly and efficiently. The kitchen area, a non-revenue earning aspect of the operation is reduced to a minimum, so that the revenue earning side of the operation can be maximized. This style of food production is seen at its extreme in take-away operations where the kitchen space requirement per customer is kept to an absolute minimum.

As the popular catering establishment becomes more elaborate in terms of menu variety, style of service etc. so the variety in food production methods used is increased and the space and equipment requirements become greater. Whereas in take-away operations all but a few of the food items are centrally produced either by a food manufacturer or the organization's own central kitchens, in cafeterias, snack bars, coffee shops, etc. less pre-assembled foods are usually bought in and more are produced on the premises themselves. The food production methods used by these latter establishments are more conventional, although a high percentage of convenience foods, such as frozen, dehydrated, cook-chill and sous-vide products may still be used.

The equipment used in these catering establishments is geared to fast production and service. Some equipment is common to most types of fast-food operations, such as pressure fryers, convection ovens, high pressure steamers, griddles etc.; while other production equipment may be specific to particular operations, such as an automatic buttering machine in a sandwich bar, or a conveyorized grill for cooking hamburgers in a take-away operation. Some self-service cafeterias today incorporate a call order bar which can achieve a very rapid throughput by offering a selection of cook-to-order items that can be prepared very quickly, e.g. omelettes, fried minute steaks, etc. The equipment needed here may be as little as a deep fat fryer, a griddle plate, a small salamander, one or two boiling rings and a bread toaster, and this limited equipment would be capable of producing several hundred call order meals over a meal period.

Wherever possible, the equipment used in fast food operations is rationalized, thereby reducing the amount of kitchen space necessary, and increasing the food service area of the operation to achieve high customer throughput. Also the trend in recent years is to have modular equipment, making it easier to relocate or replace and up-date equipment without having to redesign a kitchen or having to relocate several items of equipment.

17.2.4.4   Food service styles

A variety of food service styles are used by popular catering establishments depending on the type of establishment, the speed at which the customers must be served, the type of menu offered, etc. The service styles used by these types of operations include waiter service, self-service, traditional and free-flow cafeterias, buffets, call-order bars and vending. In takeaways and most industrial cafeterias, self service methods are employed, in which customers present themselves at a counter, and either help themselves to the foods displayed, or are served across the counter with the desired food and beverage items. Speed of customer throughput is important, some hamburger take-aways aiming at a thirty second service time to customers. In the more restaurant-like establishments there is a longer time interval between the customer ordering the food and receiving it. There is also a more leisurely dining atmosphere and customers may take between one and two hours to consume their meal, for example, in public houses, compared with five to fifteen minutes in take aways or fast-food operations. Some takeaway operations and restaurants now use facsimile transmission (fax) to send their menus and daily specialities out to local organizations who in turn send their orders back by fax; either to be collected later in the case of takeaways, or to be ready at pre-set times in the case of restaurants.

Few à la carte menus are offered by catering establishments within this sector of the industry, and where they do exist are in establishments with a fairly large variety of menu choice. More commonly found are operations such as public houses which offer table d'hôte menus usually featuring two-course and three-course lunches and evening meals for a set price, with additional courses being offered but individually priced. A customer's food and beverage order may be relayed to the production area in a vari-

MENU

MARGHERITA 360p
mozzarella cheese, tomato
NAPOLETANA 425p
mozzarella cheese, tomato, capers, anchovies, olives
MUSHROOM 420p
mushrooms, mozzarella, tomato
NEPTUNE 660p
tuna, anchovies, olives, capers, onion, tomato (no cheese)
FIORENTINA 490p
spinach, free range egg, parmesan, garlic, olives, mozzarella, tomato
VENEZIANA 420p
onions, capers, olives, pine kernels, sultanas, mozzarella, tomato
(A discretionary 25p is included which is paid to The Veneziana
Fund on your behalf.)
MARINARA 500p
anchovies, garlic, tomato, olives, (no cheese)
GIARDINIERA........................ 585p
sliced tomato, mushrooms, olives, pepperonata, leeks,
parmesan, petits pois, mozzarella, tomato
FOUR SEASONS 620p
mushrooms, peperoni sausage, capers, anchovy, olives,
mozzarella, tomato
CAPRICCIOSA 605p
ham, pepperonata, anchovy, free range egg, capers,
olives, mozzarella, tomato
LA REINE 485p
ham, olives, mushrooms, mozzarella, tomato
SICILIANA 605p
anchovy, ham, artichokes, olives, garlic, mozzarella cheese, tomato
AMERICAN 580p
peperoni sausage, mozzarella, tomato
AMERICAN HOT 610p
peperoni sausage, hot green peppers, mozzarella, tomato
QUATTRO FORMAGGI 415p
four cheeses, tomato

extra tuna, peperoni sausage	*per item*	95p
any other pizza ingredients as an extra	*per item*	75p

LASAGNE PASTICCIATE 575p
layers of pasta with Bechamel, cheese, bolognese sauce
and parmesan
CANNELLONI........................ 575p
rolls of pasta filled with ricotta cheese, spinach
and parmesan
HAM & EGGS "PizzaExpress".......... 410p
two free range eggs, ham, tomato, baked dough balls
SALADE NICOISE "PizzaExpress"........ 610p
tuna, free range egg, anchovies, capers, olives, lettuce
tomato, cucumber, dressing and baked dough balls
MOZZARELLA & TOMATO SALAD 595p
with baked dough balls

SIDE ORDERS

GARLIC BREAD "PizzaExpress" 125p
baked dough sticks brushed with garlic butter
BAKED DOUGH BALLS 125p
MIXED SIDE SALAD 210p
MOZZARELLA & TOMATO SALAD 260p

WINES

HOUSE WINE
  BY BOTTLE 75cl *red or white* 890p
  ½ BOTTLE 37.5cl *red or white* 485p
  BY GLASS 175ml *red or white* (11%/12% a.b.v.) 240p
CHIANTI *Straccali* Litre Flask 1275p
CHIANTI *Frescobaldi* 75cl 995p
VALPOLICELLA *Maso Laito* 75cl 995p
½ VALPOLICELLA *Maso Laito* 37.5cl ... 545p
BARBERA D'ASTI *Ceppe Storici* 75cl 1025p
FRASCATI *Fontana Candida* 75cl 965p
½ FRASCATI *Fontana Candida* 37.5cl ... 570p
CHARDONNAY *Araldica* 75cl 1035p
VERDICCHIO *Casal di Serra* 75cl 1025p
PROSECCO *Zonin* 75cl 1340p
CHAMPAGNE *Mercier* 75cl 2375p
PERONI BEER *Nastro Azzurro* 5.2% a.b.v. 33cl .. 215p
APERITIF............................. 140p
SCOTCH 40% a.b.v. GIN, VODKA 37.5% a.b.v. 25ml .. 155p
BRANDY *or* LIQUEURS 40% a.b.v. 200p
tonic, dry ginger or bitter lemon 105p
TOMATO JUICE *"PizzaExpress"* 110p
ORANGE JUICE 110p
MINERAL WATER *San Bernardo* 50cl 130p
COCA-COLA, LEMONADE 105p
MILK................................ 75p
COFFEE   *filter* 95p
       cappuccino 145p
       espresso 125p

DESSERTS

DUOMO DI BOSCO 285p
FRESH FRUIT SALAD 260p
CHOCOLATE FUDGE CAKE 255p
TORTA DI PERE 255p
CHEESECAKE 255p
all of the above are served with cream, ice cream or mascarpone
TIRAMI SU 245p
ICE CREAMS:
CASSATA 240p BOMBE 240p TARTUFO 295p

PRICES INCLUDE VAT
THERE IS NO SERVICE CHARGE
All gratuities go to your waiter or waitress.
An optional service charge of 10% will be
added for parties of 7 or more.
PizzaExpress hopes that you have enjoyed your pizza
Your comments will be welcomed by
our Manager, or by the Directors at
PizzaExpress, Kensal Road, London W10 5BN
Telephone 0181-960 8238

NOW OPEN IN HERTFORD, REIGATE AND SEVENOAKS

PEI 060197

Figure 17.7 *A Pizza Express menu*

ety of ways – at a call order bar customers themselves will order their food choice directly from the 'kitchen'; in take-away operations the orders are often relayed to the production area via a microphone system; in popular catering establishments offering waiter service, the waiter takes customers' orders to the kitchen.

In take-away operations the customer's food and beverage items are wrapped and packaged in disposable containers and customers usually have a choice of either eating their food immediately, or taking it away to be consumed later. Where disposable ware is not used, such as in coffee shops and cafeterias, the customer's meal is plated and then served. Silver service is rarely found in popular catering establishments. Service accompaniments, that is, tableware, condiments, etc. are of a functional nature, although in take-away operations these are again disposable and condiments, sauces, etc. are usually sold or given free in pre-portioned packs.

The service equipment used by the staff may be very specialized. In addition to using portion control equipment such as ladles and scoops, specially designed pieces of equipment may be used by particular operations. In take-aways, for example, french fry scoops have been designed which not only exactly measure portions of chips, but also aid the opening of the bags into which they are poured. With this one piece of equipment numerous portions of this food item can be prepared within a very short space of time.

A variety of seating arrangements may be used in popular catering establishments although these are usually dependent upon the type of operation, and hence the space allocated per customer. Snack bars and coffee shops usually allow between 9 ft^2 (0.84 m^2) and 12 ft^2 (1.12 m^2) per person in the service area, self service cafeterias between 12 ft^2 (1.12 m^2) and 16 ft^2 (1.49 m^2) per person. Tables and chairs may be free-standing or banquette arrangements may be used, where seats and tables are permanently fixed either built along walls or in island groups, an economical use of space. Where a bar or U-shaped counter arrangement is used, the seating is again usually fixed, although it is not such an advantageous use of space because separate circulation space is necessary for service staff behind the counter. Special provisions are usually made for children in fast-food operations; these include simple aspects of

service such as providing high chairs, children's cutlery, half-portions of foods, etc.

In some popular catering establishments self-clearing of dishes is found. In take-away operations which can offer quite extensive dining facilities, everything except the customer's tray is disposable and the customer simply empties the tray contents into a refuse bin and stacks the tray. In self-service operations the customer may be required to simply remove the tray from the table and place it on a shelf on a mobile trolley or place it on a conveyorized belt which runs from the dining room to the dishwashing area. In those operations with personal service, the service staff remove soiled dishes from the customer's table. In popular catering establishments such as take-aways, with a high percentage of disposable ware used, the amount of space made available for dishwashing is minimal; as the establishments become more elaborate, both in terms of production and service, the area needed for dishwashing also increases.

The majority of fast-food operations are designed around a food theme or particular product and this factor combined with heavy customer usage and throughput causes such operations to have a more limited life cycle than other types of catering outlet. Take-away operations with their colourful and bright decor and furnishings have a limited life of about two to three years. Commercial coffee shops and snack bars have a slightly longer life of four to five years, and the more restaurant-like operations such as public houses may require little change for five or six years. After these periods of time the operation may become somewhat 'dated' and need to be refurbished as well as be reviewed in terms of current trends, competition from similar types of establishments, and so on.

The number of themed restaurants has increased significantly in recent years as eating out has become a social activity for more people. Families in particular have been targeted and many traditional pubs are having to diversify by adding dining areas or becoming restaurants. Whitbread for example recently acquired the Pelican Group, owner of the Cafe Rouge, Dome and Dragon Inns, whose outlets can either operate on independent sites or can be incorporated into converted pubs. There has been a steady decline in traditional drinking in pubs; by introducing food, the customer has been attracted back and sales from public house restaurants have increased (see Table 17.4). In London, themed restaurants recently opened include Planet Hollywood, The Radio Cafe, Babe Roth's, Internet Cafes and the Rainforest Cafe and mega-restaurants include Mezzo, operated by Conran, and the 300-seat L'Odeon and Football Football.

Table 17.4   The public house restaurant market (£m, 1991–995)

	1991	1992	1993	1994	1995
£m	680	720	782	855	931
% change year-on-year	–	3.9	8.6	9.3	9.8

Source: Key Note 1996 Market Report: restaurants

17.2.4.5   Organization and staffing

Staffing levels in fast-food operations are, where possible, kept to a minimum. The ratio of service staff to customers is dependent upon a number of factors which include the type of establishment, the range of menu items, and the prices charged. The labour intensity of an operation is particularly related to its price level; broadly speaking, the higher the price of the meal to customers, the more service they expect to receive. Take-away operations, for example, have a very low service staff to customer ratio, one service staff member serving several hundred customers over a peak lunch time period. This ratio increases as the operation becomes more sophisticated so that in waiter service establishments, for example, one waiter may only serve twelve to sixteen customers.

The amount of service staff contact time with customers is also dependent upon the type of establishment. In take-away operations for example, contact time is very limited. The counter staff or crew are mainly involved in taking customers' orders and serving the food and beverages straight from the production area to the customer. In self-service cafeterias and waiter service operations, the amount of contact time between the service staff and the customer increases proportionately.

In order to achieve high volume sales fast food operations must offer a standardized product that can be prepared and served quickly and efficiently. To do this all aspects of the operation are, where possible, deskilled so that they can be performed rapidly by unskilled labour; for example, because of the high percentage of convenience foods used in the kitchens the production staff need no longer be trained chefs.

There is little reliance on skilled craftsmen on the production or service side of fast-food operations which enables labour costs to be controlled. The type of staff fast-food operations employ often includes a high percentage of part-time labour and workers who may be employed only for one season; for these reasons these types of establishments may experience a higher staff turnover than other catering establishments.

The training of staff in fast-food operations usually revolves around training them quickly and completely for a number of specific tasks; in this way individuals become part of a team and can alternate when needed between production and service tasks, at the same time giving them variety in their jobs. Illustrations and pictures of menu items are usually displayed in the production and servery areas which act as guides and reminders for the personnel working in these areas, leaving little to the discretion of the employee.

Pictorial representation of the foods and beverages sold by the operation is often used in training programmes, and is particularly useful when training foreign staff.

Where an operation is independently operated the owner or manager would be responsible for the training of the staff; where it is group owned the staff would follow a strict training programme organized by the parent company, for example Wimpys, McDonald's, etc.

The number of management personnel in a fast-food operation depends to a great extent on the size of the establishment. For example, a high street take-away with a seating capacity of several hundred may have one manager, several assistants and up to six supervisors – one or two for the production lines, one for the counter, and two in the dining area itself. In a large popular catering operation with several outlets such as a licensed bar offering snack items, a steak bar and a carvery, these different outlets would have separate management teams.

Stn	Bill	PLU Description	Qty	Total	Ser.	Tbl	Time	Cov.	Status
1	16535	Stella Artois	1	2.00	1	0	10:22	0	Paid
		Stella Artois	1	2.00					
		Heineken	1	1.70					
		Coors Extra Gold	1	2.00					
		Coors Extra Gold	1	2.00					
		Half Stella	1	0.90					
		Half Stella	1	0.90					
				=========	CA	12.00			
				11.50					
		Change		0.50					
1	165636	Fosters Ice	1	2.00	2	0	10:28	0	Paid
		Sol	1	2.10					
		Smk Salmon Mousse		12.60					
		Gruyere Tart	1	2.50					
		Canneloni	1	3.00					
		Canneloni	-1	-3.00					
		Seafood Linguine	1	6.95					
		Chicken & Tarragon	1	4.95					
		Sun Dried Tomato	1	0.00					
		Glass House Red	1	1.80					
		Glass Dry White	1	1.80					
		Choc. Amaretto Tri	1	2.10					
		Exotic Fruit Salad	1	2.10					
		Choc. Amaretto Tri	2	4.20					
		Choc. Amaretto Tri	-2	-4.20					
		Expresso	2	1.60					
				=========	CA	30.50			
				30.50					
1	165637	Glass House Red	1	1.80	3	0	10:29	0	Paid
		Glass Dry White	1	1.80					
		Cheese & Biscuits	1	1.80					
		English Cheddar	1	0.00					
		Stilton	1	0.00					
		French Brie	1	0.00					
		Cheese & Biscuits	1	3.00					
		Stilton	1	0.00					
		French Brie	1	0.00					
		La Roule	1	0.00					
				=========	CA	9.60			
				9.60					
1	165638	Half Stella	1	0.90	1	0	10:31	0	Paid
		Half Coors	1	1.00					
		12oz Sirloin	1	12.00					
		Medium	1	0.00					
		Lattice	1	0.00					
		Salad	1	0.00					
		French Dressing	1	0.00					
		Cajun Chicken	1	5.95					
		Chips	1	0.00					

Figure 17.8   *An example of an audit trail*
Source: Avon Data Systems Ltd

PLU	Description	Qty	Amount	Qty	Voids	Qty	Totals	Buy in	Gross Profit
001	Stella Artois	2	4.00	0	0.00	2	4.00	0.57	3.43
002	Heineken	1	1.70	0	0.00	1	1.70	0.11	1.59
003	Coors Extra Gold	2	4.00	0	0.00	2	4.00	0.04	3.96
008	Budweiser	14	28.00	-13	-26.00	1	2.00	1.25	0.75
010	Fosters Ice	3	6.00	-2	-4.00	1	2.00	1.25	0.75
012	Michlob	2	3.60	0	0.00	2	3.60	2.67	0.93
015	Sol	2	4.20	0	0.00	2	4.20	2.67	1.53
035	Rioja	1	9.00	0	0.00	1	9.00	2.50	6.50
040	Pinot Noir	1	9.50	0	0.00	1	9.50	3.00	6.50
042	Glass Dry White	2	3.60	0	0.00	2	3.60	0.80	2.80
045	Glass House Red	2	3.60	0	0.00	2	3.60	0.80	2.80
047	Jack Daniels	1	1.50	0	0.00	1	1.50	0.57	0.93
065	Southern Comfort	2	3.00	0	0.00	2	3.00	1.27	1.73
066	Archers	1	1.40	0	0.00	1	1.40	0.50	0.90
068	Baileys	1	1.40	0	0.00	1	1.40	0.50	0.90
086	Glass Coke	1	0.80	0	0.00	1	0.80	0.68	0.12
087	Lge dash coke/lemo	4	1.20	0	0.00	4	1.20	1.04	0.16
097	Perrier	1	1.00	0	0.00	1	1.00	0.85	0.15
101	Elderflower Presse	1	1.20	0	0.00	1	1.20	1.02	0.18
102	Smk Salmon Mousse	2	5.20	0	0.00	2	5.20	1.20	4.00
103	Gruyere Tart	2	5.00	0	0.00	2	5.00	4.26	0.74
104	Canneloni	2	6.00	-1	-3.00	1	3.00	2.55	0.45
115	12oz Sirloin	1	12.00	0	0.00	1	12.00	10.21	1.79
120	Medium	1	0.00	0	0.00	1	0.00	0.00	0.00
123	Chips	2	0.00	0	0.00	2	0.00	0.00	0.00
125	Lattice	1	0.00	0	0.00	1	0.00	0.00	0.00
126	Salad	1	0.00	0	0.00	1	0.00	0.00	0.00
127	Vegetables	2	0.00	0	0.00	2	0.00	0.00	0.00
132	French Dressing	1	0.00	0	0.00	1	0.00	0.00	0.00
134	Sun Dried Tomatto	1	0.00	0	0.00	1	0.00	0.00	0.00
138	Cajun Chicken	1	5.95	0	0.00	1	5.95	5.06	0.89
139	Seafood Linguine	2	13.90	0	0.00	2	13.90	11.82	2.08
142	Pork & Calvados sc	1	6.95	0	0.00	1	6.95	5.91	1.04
145	Chicken Curry	1	4.95	0	0.00	1	4.95	4.21	0.74
146	BBQ Spare Ribs	1	6.45	0	0.00	1	6.45	5.49	0.06
148	Chicken & Tarragon	1	4.95	0	0.00	1	4.05	4.21	0.74
154	Cream	1	0.00	0	0.00	1	0.00	0.00	0.00
157	Apple Tarte Tartin	1	2.00	0	0.00	1	2.00	1.70	0.30
159	Raspberry Pavolva	1	1.90	0	0.00	1	1.90	1.62	0.28
160	Profiteroles	1	2.10	0	0.00	1	2.10	1.79	0.31
162	Exotic Fruit Salad	1	2.10	0	0.00	1	2.10	1.79	0.31
163	Choc. Amaretto Tri	3	6.30	-2	-4.20	1	2.10	1.79	0.31
165	Cheese & Biscuits	2	6.00	0	0.00	2	6.00	5.10	0.90
166	English Cheddar	1	0.00	0	0.00	1	0.00	0.00	0.00
167	Stilton	2	0.00	0	0.00	2	0.00	0.00	0.00
168	French Brie	2	0.00	0	0.00	2	0.00	0.00	0.00
170	La Roule	1	0.00	0	0.00	1	0.00	0.00	0.00
187	Expresso	2	1.60	0	0.00	2	1.60	1.36	0.24
192	Half Stella	3	2.70	0	0.00	3	2.70	1.13	1.58
194	Half Coors	1	1.00	0	0.00	1	1.00	0.85	0.15
		89	185.75	-18	-37.20	71	148.55	94.12	54.43

```
Total Sales        148.55
Less Discounts       0.00
Plus Gratuities      0.00
                   -------
                   148.55
```

Figure 17.9   *An example of a PLU report*
Source: Avon Data Systems Ltd

(a)

```
-----------------------------------------------------------------------------
Department                  Sarah's Bar        TOTAL        EX. VAT       VAT
-------------------------    ------------    ------------    ------------  -----------
   Lager                         31.15          31.15           26.51       4.64
   Draught Beers                  0.00           0.00            0.00        0.00
   Bottled Beers                  0.00           0.00            0.00        0.00
   Alcopops                       0.00           0.00            0.00        0.00
   Baby Fruit                     3.40           3.40            2.89        0.51
   Baby Mixers                    0.00           0.00            0.00        0.00
   Spirits                        7.30           7.30            6.22        1.08
   Liquors                        0.00           0.00            0.00        0.00
   White Wine                    25.70          25.70           21.87        3.83
   Red Wine                       0.00           0.00            0.00        0.00
   Starters                      78.60          78.60           66.87       11.73
   Main Course                    0.00           0.00            0.00        0.00
   Sweet                          0.00           0.00            0.00        0.00
   Vermouth                       0.00           0.00            0.00        0.00
   Spirits                        0.00           0.00            0.00        0.00
   Coffee & Tea                   2.40           2.40            2.04        0.36
   Tobacco                        0.00           0.00            0.00        0.00
   Starters                       0.00           0.00            0.00        0.00
   Main Courses                   0.00           0.00            0.00        0.00
   Desserts                       0.00           0.00            0.00        0.00
   Tea/Coffee                     0.00           0.00            0.00        0.00
   Bar Snacks                     0.00           0.00            0.00        0.00
   Discos                         0.00           0.00            0.00        0.00
   Other Tips                     0.00           0.00            0.00        0.00
-------------------------    ------------    ------------    ------------  -----------
             Sub Total          148.55         148.55          126.40       22.15
Gratuities                        0.00           0.00            0.00        0.00
Discounts                         0.00           0.00            0.00        0.00
-------------------------    ------------    ------------    ------------  -----------
             TOTAL              148.55         148.55          126.40       22.15
```

```
=================================================
Vat Analysis                    VAT         Net
-------------------          --------    ----------
Tax Rate 1   17.50%            22.15       126.40
Tax Rate 2    0.00%             0.00         0.00
Tax Rate 3    0.00%             0.00         0.00
Tax Rate 4    0.00%             0.00         0.00
Tax Rate 5    0.00%             0.00         0.00
```

Figure 17.10(a) *Example of a departmental report*
Source: Avon Data Systems Ltd

17.3   Control and performance measurement

Controlling and measuring the performance of a food and beverage establishment presupposes the existence of standards against which the operation's performance may be measured. Such standards are contained in the financial, market-ing and catering policies. If an operation is inde-pendently operated it is the owner who will establish these standards; if it is group owned the operation will be governed by policies from the head office.

The control of any food and beverage opera-tion may be divided into two main areas: the on going or operational control; and the after-the event or post-operational control. Operational control will follow the previously described food and beverage control cycle – purchasing, receiv-ing, storing, issuing, preparation and selling. Within each of these stages standards are laid down against which certain aspects of the oper-ation may be measured; for example, to measure the purchasing function of the establishment standard purchase specifications, portion sizes, and yields may be used (see Chapter 9 for more detailed examples).

The information obtained from the sales aspect of the control cycle is the first step in post-

(b)

```
=====================================================================================
Analysis Codes                  Sarah's Bar                    Total
===========================     ===================     ===================
Wine                                 25.70                       25.70
Beer                                 31.15                       31.15
Alcopops                              0.00                        0.00
Soft Drinks                           5.80                        5.80
Tobacco                               0.00                        0.00
Tea/Coffee                            0.00                        0.00
Spirits                               7.30                        7.30
Food                                 78.60                       78.60
<NOT USED>                            0.00                        0.00
<NOT USED>                            0.00                        0.00
<NOT USED>                            0.00                        0.00
<NOT USED>                            0.00                        0.00
<NOT USED>                            0.00                        0.00
<NOT USED>                            0.00                        0.00
<NOT USED>                            0.00                        0.00
<NOT USED>                            0.00                        0.00
<NOT USED>                            0.00                        0.00
<NOT USED>                            0.00                        0.00
===========================     ===================     ===================
Sub Total                           148.55                      148.55

<NOT USED>                            0.00                        0.00
<NOT USED>                            0.00                        0.00
===========================     ===================     ===================
TOTAL                               148.55                      148.55
```

Figure 17.10(b)   *Example of an analysis report*
Source: Avon Data Systems Ltd

operational control. Although this is also described as control after the event, the time between the event and control is critical. The measurement of an operation's performance should begin as soon after the event as possible; if it is not, any impact the instigation of a control procedure should have will be lost.

Generally speaking, the speed at which information is gathered for control and performance measurement is perhaps at this time still most efficient in the popular and fast-food sector of the catering industry. This is mainly due to the commercially-orientated attitudes adopted by the large group companies which control the majority of popular catering establishments, and the fact that they are offering highly standardized products which aid tight control. Computerized data processing is used to a considerable extent particularly by com-

panies operating take-away establishments. Their fast and efficient information gathering begins at the purchasing function with computerized stock control and continues through all aspects of the control cycle. Sales information is gathered at the sales counter where electronic cash resisters are used to record and analyse sales figures. The information that may be obtained from these registers includes a breakdown of the sales of individual items, the total sales of all the items, the number of customers served, the average bill, opening and closing stock inventories, etc. Daily figures are easily totalled to give weekly or period-end totals. This type of detailed information that may be gathered at the end of the day's trading, is of great use to management in identifying specific problem areas that can be acted upon very quickly.

Figure 17.11   *Examples of (a) a server report, (b) a time report,*
(c) a voids report and (d) a short bill report
Source: Avon Data Sytems Ltd

```
=========================================================================================
(a) Server                    Total Sales        Discounts        Gratuities        Totals
    ------------------ ---------------- ------------------ ----------------- -----------
    001   Sarah                  78.30             0.00             0.00            78.30
    002   Steve                  30.50             0.00             0.00            30.50
    003   Shauna                 39.75             0.00             0.00            39.75
    ------------------ ---------------- ------------------ ----------------- -----------
                                148.55             0.00             0.00           148.55

=========================================================================================
(b) Time From - To         Gross       Trans       Average
    ------------------   =========   ==========  ============
    00:00 - 01:00             0.00          0          0.00
    01:00 - 02:00             0.00          0          0.00
    02:00 - 03:00             0.00          0          0.00
    03:00 - 04:00             0.00          0          0.00
    04:00 - 05:00             0.00          0          0.00
    05:00 - 06:00             0.00          0          0.00
    06:00 - 07:00             0.00          0          0.00
    07:00 - 08:00             0.00          0          0.00
    08:00 - 09:00             0.00          0          0.00
    09:00 - 10:00             0.00          0          0.00
    10:00 - 11:00*           73.45          4         18.36
    11:00 - 12:00            75.10          3         25.03
    12:00 - 13:00             0.00          0          0.00
    13:00 - 14:00             0.00          0          0.00
    14:00 - 15:00             0.00          0          0.00
    15:00 - 16:00             0.00          0          0.00
    16:00 - 17:00             0.00          0          0.00
    17:00 - 18:00             0.00          0          0.00
    18:00 - 19:00             0.00          0          0.00
    20:00 - 21:00             0.00          0          0.00
    21:00 - 22:00             0.00          0          0.00
    22:00 - 23:00             0.00          0          0.00
    23:00 - 24:00             0.00          0          0.00

=========================================================================================
(c) Server Name   PLU Sc.  Description           Qty  Amount  Bill No   Station       Time
    -----------   =======  ===================   ===  ======= ========  ===========   ======
    Steve         104      Canneloni               1    3.00  165636    Sarah's Bar   10:24
    Steve         163      Choc. Amaretto Tri      2    4.20  165636    Sarah's Bar   10:27
    Shauna        010      Fosters Ice             2    4.00  165641    Sarah's Bar   10:32
    Shauna        008      Budweiser              13   26.00  165641    Sarah's Bar   10:32

    Summary
    ========
    Server Name   No. of voids     Total Value
    -----------   ============     ============
    Steve         3                       7.20
    Shauna        15                      30.00

=========================================================================================
(d) Stn Bill    Total   Ser. Tbl Time  Cov. Method 1: Method 2: Method 3: Method 4: Method 5: Method 6:
    -------------------------------------------------------------------------------------
    1   165635 11.50   1   0   10:22  0   CA   12:00      Change   0.50
        165636 30.50   2   0   10:28  0   CA   30.50
        165637  9.60   3   0   10:29  0   CA    9.60
        165638 19.85   1   0   10:31  0   CA   20.00      Change   0.15
        165641 16.20   3   0   11:03  0   CA   17:00      Change   0.80
        165642 49.95   1   0   11:06  0   VI   46.95
        165643 13.95   3   0   11:07  0   CH   13.95
    GRAND      =======
      TOTAL    148.95
```

```
-----------------------------------------------------
Payment Type        Sarah's Bar        Totals
------------------  ---------------  ----------
Cash  . . . . . .          86.65         87.65
Access  . . . . .           0.00          0.00
Visa  . . . . . .          46.95         46.95
Misc. Crds  . . .           0.00          0.00
AMEX  . . . . . .           0.00          0.00
Cheque  . . . . .          13.95         13.95
Mastercard  . . .           0.00          0.00
Foreign . . . . .           0.00          0.00
                    ---------------  ----------
        TILL TOTAL:       148.55        148.55

Discounts . . . .           0.00          0.00
Gratuities  . . .           0.00          0.00
Sales Lgr . . . .           0.00          0.00
Room Post . . . .           0.00          0.00
                    ---------------  ----------
  . . . . . . .            148.55        148.55

Membership Bills outstanding.             0.00

No. Trans . . . .              7

Average Spend . .          21.22
```

Figure 17.12   *An example of a banking report*
(including ASP)
Source: Avon Data Systems Ltd

Point-of-sale (POS) computer systems are continually being updated and improved, giving more detailed information at faster speeds. These systems are modular so that additions and modifications can be made, for example the addition of a visual display unit (VDU), operating remote printers etc. Thermal printing is also used so that printer ribbons are no longer needed, high quality non-degrading receipts and print outs are produced and the machine is quieter during operation.

These POS systems can work in isolation in individual units or be linked via a restaurant analysis and information system (RAIS) to a central control unit enabling management to monitor and control the individual sales outlets. Communication is two-way: the transmission of operating data from unit POS systems to the centrally located personal computer; and from the computer to POS terminals for programme changes or information to unit managers.

RAIS systems provide complete operations reports (daily, weekly, monthly etc.), enabling any one of the units, for example take-aways,

steak restaurants, to be called at any time and information retrieved (for example, sales, cash levels, employee activity, inventory levels). Banquet (Avon Data Systems Limited) is a computer software program allowing terminals in different locations around an establishment to handle a number of sales or transactions including drinks, meals and services. The systems can track tables, allowing multiple bills per table. Bills can be transferred from one area to another, for example from the bar to the restaurant, and if linked to a hotel management system, added to a guest's room account. Figures 17.8 to 17.12 are examples of the type of control reports and information that is available to management following the food and beverage sales made during an operation's meal period. This type of control efficiency, currently used by fast-food operations in particular, is paving the way for control in the hotel and catering industry in general.

17.4   References

Golden Square Services Ltd (1985). *The Successful Franchise: A Working Strategy*. Aldershot: Gower.

Housden, J. (1983). *Franchising and other Business Relationships in Hotel and Catering Services*. Oxford: Butterworth-Heinemann.

Key Note (1995). *Market report: fast food and home delivery outlets*. London: Key Note Publications.

18
Food and beverage management in hotels and quality restaurants

18.1 Introduction

Hotel food and beverage management may be described as one of the most complex areas of the catering industry because of the variety of catering outlets that may be found in any one hotel. The different types of catering services associated with hotels include the following: luxury haute cuisine restaurants, coffee shops and speciality restaurants, room and lounge service, cocktail bars, banqueting facilities and staff restaurants. (Banqueting is described in the following chapter and staff catering separately at the end of this chapter.) Additionally, some hotels will provide a catering and bar service to areas of the hotel such as swimming pools, and health complexes, discos, and other leisure areas as well as often providing some vending facilities. Quality restaurants are also included in this chapter as they may be discussed in conjunction with the luxury restaurants found in hotels.

Quality restaurants are those establishments whose sole business is restaurants and who offer very high standards in all aspects of their operation – an extensive à la carte menu, silver service, good quality facilities and décor, service accompaniments, etc. The luxury restaurants found in hotels may therefore be defined as quality restaurants, although there are also those operations found outside hotels and which are usually independently owned and operated.

The type and variety of catering outlets in hotels will depend to a large extent on the size of the hotel. Small hotels of up to thirty to forty bedrooms may have a licensed bar, and a restaurant which may offer a limited table d'hôte or à la carte lunch and dinner menu. A medium-sized hotel of up to 100 bedrooms would usually have a licensed bar and two restaurants; these may include a grill room/coffee shop offering a table d'hôte menu and a separate à la carte restaurant. The bar in this size of hotel may also offer a limited selection of snacks. Today, room service in these small- and medium-sized operations is limited; facilities for tea and coffee making within the room are more usually provided as an alternative. In the large hotels with several hundred bedrooms, the largest variety of catering outlets is found – the traditional haute cuisine restaurant alongside the more unusual speciality restaurant; lounge and cocktail bars; several coffee shops, some offering a very limited selection of snacks, others offering more substantial menu items; and varying degrees of room service.

However, it should be noted that for many hotels, the importance of the food and beverage department in operating an à la carte restaurant and a twenty-four hour room service, neither of which may be significant net profit contributors, is essential for the hotel to obtain a four or five star grading, with their input of service and facilities enabling the hotel to significantly increase its prices for accommodation. In so doing the hotel is more likely to be able to increase its total revenue and net profit figures.

The different types of catering outlets in hotels depend not only on the size of the operation, but also on its nature and the market for which it is catering. A medium-sized resort hotel, for example, where a guest's average length of stay may be two to three weeks, may need to offer a variety of food and beverage facilities to cater for the guests' different and changing needs during their stay. A transient hotel, however, such as one situated near an airport where the guest's average length of stay may be one or two nights, may only need to provide comparatively limited catering facilities.

The percentage of restaurants today that may be described as quality restaurants is small; indeed it may be as little as 3 to 5 per cent of the total number of restaurants in all sectors of the catering industry. However, the narrow market for which quality restaurants cater will continue to be present in the future, because there will always be that percentage of the eating-out market that demands the highest standards in all aspects of a restaurant operation, and can afford to pay the high prices charged. As for the future demands for catering services in hotels, this is closely allied to the demand for hotel accommodation itself. The continually growing tourism industry both in the UK and abroad guarantees a future demand for some form of hotel accommodation to be provided for tourists, and with this a demand for food and beverage services.

18.2 Basic policies – financial, marketing and catering

18.2.1 Financial considerations

The business orientation of hotels and quality restaurants is determined by a number of factors which are characteristic of these types of operations. Hotels and quality restaurants are characterized by the need for a high capital outlay and have a correspondingly high percentage of fixed costs; the perishability of their product; and a demand for that product that is unstable. All these factors lead to a high dependence of these operations on the demands of the market, so that hotels and quality restaurants may be said to be highly market-orientated. In comparison to the welfare sector cost-orientated operations, hotels and quality restaurants are therefore more dependent on their market for the survival of their operation, and this has important implications for their basic policy making decisions.

Hotels and quality restaurants are profit orientated and this is reflected in their financial poli-

cies. The financial policy of a large hotel for example may stipulate that the gross profit (GP) to be achieved by the hotel's coffee shop and lounge service is 65 per cent, the grill room 60 per cent and the à la carte restaurant and room service 70 per cent. The higher GP levels of the à la carte and quality restaurants are mainly due to the lower variable costs of these operations and the need to cover the higher staff costs. The differential profit margins to be obtained by the different menus would also be laid down for each outlet; for example, an 8 oz rump steak in the hotel's grill room may be required to achieve a 50 per cent GP, whereas the same menu item in the à la carte restaurant may achieve a 70 per cent GP.

The high percentage of fixed costs associated with the quality restaurants and other catering outlets in hotels, affects the margin of safety of these operations; this is the difference between the operation's breakeven point and its maximum potential output. High fixed cost operations have a smaller margin of safety than those with lower fixed costs, so that a drop in the volume of sales would seriously affect the profitability of high fixed-cost establishments. In addition, the wide range of price discretion that is available to hotels and quality restaurants further complicates their pricing structure. The balance between the price level of these establishments and their volume of sales must therefore be carefully calculated, and this again would be contained in their financial policies.

Generally speaking the average spend of customers in hotel catering outlets, is higher than in similar catering operations found outside an hotel. This is particularly evident with reference to the hotel's high ASP quality restaurants, but also in the less expensive outlets such as coffee shops; here the ASP of the hotel customer may again be higher than in comparable operations found for example in a town's high street. The higher prices charged by these types of catering facilities result in higher sales per employee, and a higher revenue per trading hour. In fast-food operations with their lower ASP per customer, the long trading hours of these establishments are often necessary in order to achieve high volume sales. In the catering outlets of hotels similar long trading hours are not characteristic of all the facilities; the lower ASP coffee shops may stay open for most of the day, but the higher ASP restaurants in the hotel, like the quality restaurants found outside, will only open for the lunch and dinner periods, approximately three hours and four to five hours respectively. In the larger hotels some form of food and beverage service is generally available twenty-four hours a day and most of the catering facilities are usually open seven days a week; quality restaurants situated outside the hotel, however, may only open six days a week. The catering policy of the hotel or quality restaurant in conjunction with the financial policy of the establishment will, however, determine the opening hours of the operation based on such information as revenue per trading hour, sales per employee per hour, etc.

The average spend per customer varies according to the type of catering outlet. In a coffee shop or lounge service of a hotel which usually offer limited food and beverage items, the ASP may be in the £10 to £16 range; in the à la carte restaurant of a hotel or other quality restaurants, the ASP may range from £30 to £60 per customer. Payment for food and beverages in hotels may be made in several ways. If customers are residents the charges may be debited to their hotel account. Alternatively, payment may be made on a cash or credit basis. Generally speaking, the higher the price level of a restaurant, the more likely that credit facilities will be available. Some hotels and quality restaurants include a service charge in the price of their meal, while others leave it to the discretion of the customer. This is the sector of the industry where the practice of tipping is most commonly found and the 'trunc' system of sharing pooled by the employees.

In the higher ASP operations, the cost of the meal to the customer is not such an important variable in determining the sales of the operation; broadly speaking, the higher the price level of an operation, the less elastic its demand. The demand for those catering facilities offered by quality restaurants and hotels (specifically the à la carte outlets), therefore tends to be relatively inelastic, that is, a large change in price will not have a very substantial effect on the sales of the establishment. This characteristic of hotels and quality restaurants has important implications for the marketing policies of such establishments; if they cannot compete with other cater-

ing operations on the basis of price, they must look to the other aspects of their operation, such as food quality and standard of service as a basis for competition.

18.2.2   Marketing considerations

Because of the narrowness of the market for which quality restaurants cater, the marketing policies of these operations are able to quite clearly identify their market and target their advertising and merchandising campaigns at this market level. The marketing policy of a hotel however is considerably more complicated because of its variety of catering outlets and the corresponding variety in the types of customers these facilities will attract; the customer frequenting the hotel's coffee shop for example, may not be the same customer to use the hotel's à la carte restaurant. The danger of catering for mixed markets within the same establishment must therefore be recognized and planned for accordingly. The marketing policy of a hotel may vary with different times of the year because it can see opportunities for marketing its catering facilities to different markets. A hotel in a coastal resort, for example, may cater largely for families and groups of tourists during the summer months, during which time its catering facilities may be well patronized. In the winter months, however, this market may no longer be available and the hotel may therefore alter its marketing policy and promote its catering facilities as part of banqueting and conference 'packages'. In this way the hotel's catering facilities may be utilized throughout the year without the danger of mixing its markets, and adversely affecting the hotel's total image, whilst also ensuring a consistent revenue and maximum utilization of the hotel's capital equipment.

A hotel's marketing policy will also contain its intentions with regard to its resident and non-resident markets. For example, is the hotel going to concentrate mainly on trade generated from within, that is, residents, or to what extent is it going to attempt to attract outside custom? Some hotels aim almost exclusively at the resident guest and may offer comparatively limited catering facilities, compared with those hotels seeking to also attract the non-resident customer by

A LA CARTE MENU

CHILLED FRUIT AND VEGETABLE JUICES

Tomato, Apple, Prune, Pineapple or Passion Fruit	£3.50
Fresh Orange, Grapefruit, Carrot or Cucumber	£4.00

REFRESHING FRUITS

Fresh Fruit Salad	£6.50
Melon, Papaya, Mango or Berries in Season	£8.50
Tropical Fruit Platter	£12.00
Fresh Grapefruit	£3.80
Stewed Apples, Prunes or Apricots	£3.80
Pink Grapefruit segments with Raspberries	£6.50

CEREALS

Crunchy Nut Cornflakes, Cornflakes, Rice Crispies, All Bran, Grapenuts, Fruit 'n' Fibre, Bran Flakes, Weetabix, Sugar Puffs, Alpen, Shredded Wheat, Porridge — £3.50

FROM OUR BAKERY

Apple Scones, Blackberry Muffins, Croissants or Danish Pastries	£3.20
White and Wholemeal Toast or Assorted Rolls	£2.80

EGG DISHES

Boiled, Poached, Scrambled or Fried served with Grilled Tomato	£4.50
Omelettes: Plain, Cheese, Mushroom, Ham or Herbs	£7.40

ACCOMPANIMENTS

Streaky or Back Bacon, Pork or Beef Sausages, Grilled Mushrooms, Gammon Steak, Black Pudding, Breakfast Roesti — £4.00

BREAKFAST FAVOURITES

Dutch Apple Pancake with Blueberry Compote	£12.50
Scottish Pancake with Maple Syrup or Honey	£12.50
Waffles with Maple Syrup or Honey	£12.50
Coddled Egg with Tomato	£6.50
Scrambled Egg with Smoked Salmon and Chives	£12.00
Grilled Breakfast Steak	£16.00
Pan-fried Lambs Kidneys	£11.00
Grilled Kipper Herring	£9.50
Poached Smoked Haddock	£10.50
Fish Kedgeree	£9.50
Bagel with Smoked Salmon and Cream Cheese	£11.00

BEVERAGES

Tea – English Breakfast or China with Milk or Lemon	£3.80
Coffee – Dorchester Blend Filter, Decaffeinated, Espresso, or Cappucino with Milk or Cream	
Hot Chocolate	£3.80
Mineral Water (250 ml)	£2.50

Service and Tax included

TRADITIONAL ENGLISH BREAKFAST

Freshly squeezed Fruit Juice or choice of Cereals

Two Farm Eggs, Fried, Scrambled or Poached served with Tomato and your choice of Bacon or Sausage

or

Grilled Kipper Herring or Poached Smoked Haddock

served with

Toast and a selection from our Bakery

Tea or Coffee

£17.50

CONTINENTAL BREAKFAST

Freshly squeezed Fruit Juice
Our Bakery Selection
Tea, Coffee, Hot Chocolate or Milk

£14.50

DORCHESTER LÉGER BREAKFAST

(Low in fat and cholesterol)

Freshly squeezed Orange or Grapefruit Juice

Bircher Müesli
(made with low fat yoghurt)

Fresh Fruits and Berries

Low Fat Cottage Cheese

Egg-white Omelette with Herbs or Mushrooms

served with

Wholemeal Rolls, Brown Toast and Pumpkin Muffins with Marmalade and Soya Margarine

Tea or Coffee with Skimmed Milk

£17.50

Service and Tax included

Figure 18.1 *A breakfast menu from the Grill Room, the Dorchester Hotel, London*

offering a wider range of catering outlets – restaurants, bars, banqueting facilities, etc.

In contrast to the very often direct and obvious advertising of fast-food establishments, particularly take-away operations, the advertising and merchandising techniques used by hotels and quality restaurants have traditionally been more discreet and subtle; this is particularly evident with the advertising of quality restaurants which are aiming at an up-market clientele and the techniques used are appropriately sophisticated. For example, advertising in quality magazines – obtaining free write ups of the restaurant in quality newspapers and magazines – joint promotion with credit card companies. These can enhance the type of image the restaurant is trying to create. In the lower ASP catering outlets of hotels, such as coffee shops or wine bars, the advertising of these facilities may be more direct, often because to a large extent these types of facilities are attempting to attract passer-by traffic. In both the lower and higher ASP outlets in hotels there is a tendency today for an alternative entrance to the catering facility to be available directly from the street, in addition to an inside entrance which would be used mainly by hotel guests. By having the street entrance, more pedestrian traffic is encouraged to use the catering operation without feeling awkward in walking through the hotel foyer to the catering facility.

'Crisscross' advertising is a technique available to hotels where there is more than one type of catering facility in the hotel; for example, the cocktail bar may use tent cards to advertise a special promotion week in the à la carte restaurant. Where the hotel is part of a large organization, inter-hotel advertising may be used which usually features the catering outlets of the group's hotels in the company sales literature which is distributed to all hotel units throughout the country, and sometimes abroad. It is also possible to advertise the food and beverage facilities of the hotel in conjunction with its other services; for example, a number of large hotel chains now offer 'bargain week ends', where for an inclusive price a guest may stay at the hotel for two or three days on *demi pension* or *en pension* terms. Where quality restaurants are situated in establishments with accommodation, gourmet and wine weekends may be offered

during off-peak winter months. Discounts are given to hotel residents dining in the à la carte restaurant, a free bottle of wine is offered with the meal, or two meals for the price of one during the quieter weekdays. It is important therefore for all possible advertising techniques to be reviewed for the marketing of catering outlets, as they may often not only be marketed in isolation, but also may be advertised in conjunction with the establishment's other facilities such as accommodation.

18.2.3   Catering considerations

18.2.3.1   *Type of customer*

The profile of a customer frequenting a quality restaurant is very likely to be different from the profile of a customer frequenting a fast-food take-away operation. In the latter case it has been suggested, the customer sees the take-away as little more than a 'filling station', somewhere that food and drink can be bought to satisfy some immediate basic need. Customers frequenting a quality restaurant, however, will be desiring a considerably more in-depth meal experience; they will be visiting a quality restaurant because they have a greater interest in the quality of food and beverages they are buying, the standard of service and décor, etc. and because they can afford to pay more for their meal. This same type of customer is also likely to patronize the à la carte and haute cuisine speciality restaurants of hotels. A customer profile for a quality restaurant operation may for example be: customers coming from socio-economic groupings A and B, middle to older age group, both sexes, willing to experiment with unusual dishes, expecting a selection of 'house specialities', a high percentage of car ownership willing to travel up to twenty to thirty miles to dine, ASP £30–£60 per head.

Customers patronizing hotel catering facilities may be conveniently divided into two main groups: residents, and non-residents. The ratio between these two groupings will vary from one hotel to another, although generally speaking the resident guests will generate considerably more business than the non-residents, the ratio being as high as 85:15 in some hotels. 'In house' sales are often generated by conference and banqueting guests staying in the hotel, and block bookings by tours who may be staying at the hotel on half-board terms. Resident guests may be further sub-divided into business and non-business cust-omers; these different types of customers are likely to frequent the different levels of catering facilities in the hotel. The business traveller on an expense account, for example, is more likely to patronize the more expensive à la carte restaurant than is a family staying at the hotel who would probably use the less expensive coffee shop.

Resident guests may be staying at a hotel on a variety of different terms and these will affect to what extent they will use the hotel's catering facilities. The most commonly used hotel rate is for bed and breakfast which charges for the overnight accommodation and includes either a continental or full English breakfast. Guests staying at a hotel under this rate will usually have their breakfast in the hotel dining room but will not often return to patronize the hotel's other restaurant facilities, at least not on a regu-lar basis, as it would then be more advantageous for them to be staying at the hotel on other terms. These other terms include half-board (demi-pension) and full-board (en pension) rates. Half-board arrangements include accom-modation and two other meals, usually breakfast and then either lunch or dinner. Full board or inclusive terms include accommodation and three other meals – breakfast, lunch and dinner; sometimes at resort hotels en pension terms also include afternoon teas. These fully or partially inclusive terms are advantageous to hotels as they guarantee a certain percentage of restaurant custom which is advance booked and which may be catered for relatively easily by offering set table d'hôte menus.

Non-resident trade will depend to a large extent on the situation of the hotel. If it is sited in a town or city within close proximity to local office blocks and business firms, a considerable amount of trade may be generated from here; civic lunches, business meetings, etc. may account for a large percentage of the hotel's restaurant trade. Even if the hotel is situated sev-eral miles out of town, because of this very fea-ture it may still be able to attract local business trade out to its catering facilities. Quality and well-known restaurants in particular have a wider market area than any other level of food and beverage operation. These types of restau-rants generate custom because of their reputa-tion and customers are willing to travel a considerable distance to these establishments.

For chance trade a hotel must be situated where there is a heavy pedestrian traffic passing by; even where this is the case, chance trade does not usually account for more than 1 or 2 per cent of a hotel's main restaurant custom, although a considerably higher percentage of passing trade may use its lower ASP catering facilities, for example the hotel coffee shop. A well signposted and spacious hotel car park will at times attract chance trade. The low percentage of chance trade usually associated with the more expen-sive quality restaurants is, however, compen-sated by the high percentage of advance bookings made for seats in these operations. This is in contrast to the previously described fast-food operations where, particularly with take-aways, chance trade accounts for a higher percentage of total custom.

18.2.3.2   *Type of product/menu*

The food and beverage products offered by a hotel will depend on the type of customer fre-quenting the establishment and the market being catered for. In a hotel catering mainly for the commercial or business traveller, the follow-ing facilities may be found: a coffee shop or spe-ciality restaurant featuring a popular priced menu where the guest may have a meal that is served reasonably quickly, in a pleasant and relaxed atmosphere and which is not too expen-sive; a higher priced à la carte restaurant with a higher standard of service and quality of food, with a more sophisticated atmosphere and a more extensive menu; and one or two bars, one of which may be a cocktail bar that is situated adjacent to the à la carte restaurant. Room ser-vice in these types of hotels is usually very lim-ited and where it is provided is restricted mainly to beverages, a few snack items or light meals.

In a resort hotel, or one that is catering mainly for non-business and holiday guests, the cater-ing services of the establishment fulfil a different role. In a hotel catering mainly for the business traveller the catering services often have a purely functional nature, for example the hotel's

The Dining Room
St Valentines Day Dinner & Dance

"Menu for Him"	*"Menu for Her"*

Native Colchester Oysters with
a Chilli Salsa
or
Warm Salad of Venison with Wild Mushrooms,
Champagne Vinaigrette

~ ♥ ~

Cream of Celery Soup with Black Truffle
or
Glazed Ravioli with
Veal Sweetbreads & Apples

~ ♥ ~

Roast Breast of Guinea Fowl with Thai Basil and
Blackbean Sauce
or
Poached Fillet of Turbot with a Lobster Jus

~ ♥ ~

Iced Passion Fruit Soufflé with Sugar Straws

~ ♥ ~

Coffee, Tea & Infusions
"Delice d'Hommes"

Salad of Scottish Lobster with
a Spicy Mango Compote
or
Traditional Caesar Salad with
Poached Quail Eggs & Crispy Croutons

~ ♥ ~

Cream of Celery Soup with Black Truffle
or
Ravioli of Tofu & Chinese Vegetables,
Ginger Sauce

~ ♥ ~

Panfried Breast of Chicken with
Morels & Lemon Grass
or
Steamed Fillet of Dover Sole with a
Tomato & Olive Fondue

~ ♥ ~

Chocolate Box of Pleasures

~ ♥ ~

Coffee, Tea & Infusions
"Delice de Dames"

£90.00 per couple

We are also pleased to offer, with the best wishes of Pol Roger,
the following most romantically priced champagnes

Pol Roger, White Foil Brut NV £25.00 per bottle
Pol Roger Rosé 1988 £45.00 per bottle
Pol Roger Cuvée Sir Winston Churchill 1986 £65.00 per bottle

ALL PRICES ARE INCLUSIVE OF VALUE ADDED TAX
GRATUITIES ARE AT OUR GUESTS DISCRETION

Figure 18.2   *The St Valentines Day Dinner and Dance menu from the Landmark Hotel, London*

Luncheon and Supper Specialities	
Chef's Recommendation	
Salad Niçoise	£10.00
Tomato and mozzarella salad with fresh basil, virgin olive oil and balsamic vinegar	£11.00
Warm Stilton and leek tart	£10.50
Smoked Scottish salmon	£15.50
Fresh tortilla with chicken and tomato salsa	£11.00
Linguine with seafood	£12.50
Traditional English Fish & Chips	£13.50
Seasonal mixed salad with Stilton, Yoghurt or Dorchester Dressing	£8.00
Sweets and Cheese	
English and Continental cheese platter	£8.50
Almond tart with home-made honey ice-cream	£8.50
Exotic fruit salad with mint	£8.50
Passion fruit and strawberry brulée	£8.50
White and dark chocolate mousse	£8.50
Bread and butter pudding	£8.50

Vegetarian Menu

Hot and cold appetisers

Warm Stilton and leek tart
£10.50

Linguine with mixed vegetables
£10.50

Feuilleté of asparagus with a light butter sauce and mixed peppers
£15.50

Terrine of Ribblesdale goat's cheese and vegetables
£9.80

Selection of Mediterranean Appetisers
£14.50

Falafel - deep-fried chick pea cakes with sesame seeds served with a yoghurt sauce
£10.50

Oriental vegetable salad with salsa noodles
£9.50

Cannette with pesto and potato
£12.50

à la carte restaurant may be an ideal setting for business meetings; in a resort hotel, however, the catering outlets are usually seen as part of the entertainment facilities of the hotel. In these establishments the food and beverage services offered by the hotel have a different role because of the guest's length of stay and particular attention should therefore be paid to such aspects of the operation as menu variety. Hotels offering full board and half board terms can have a high percentage of long-staying guests, where the guests' average length of stay may be several weeks. Cyclical menus may be used by these hotels and are very useful for volume forecasting and planning; for example, in a hotel where the guests' average length of stay is two to three weeks, a cyclical menu based on a twenty-eight day cycle would be appropriate.

The menus of catering outlets in hotels may either be centred around one particular product, for example, steaks in a grill room, or as is more usual, offer a range of menu items. The greatest range of menu items is found in the à la carte restaurants of hotels; even in similar quality restaurants found outside hotels there is rarely

Caviar

'Sevruga'
The smallest of the Caspian Sea sturgeons produces the small eggs that are dark grey in colour and have a delicate flavour

28g   £28.00   50g   £39.00

Krug Grande Cuvée
The harmony of two impeccable flavours
£14.00 per glass

'Oscietra'
with 20-80 kg in weight this medium sized sturgeon produces dark grey to golden-coloured eggs that develop a fine and unique flavour

28g   £34.00   50g   £48.00

Krug Vintage 1985
A pure and unique relationship
£16.50 per glass

'Beluga'
The rarest and most exclusive caviar from the Caspian Sea. A simply delightful experience

28g   £63.00   50g   £95.00

Krug Clos du Mesnil 1985
The Royal composition
£23.50 a glass

Figure 18.3   *An extract from the menu from the Promenade Restaurant at the Dorchester Hotel, London*

Figure 18.4   *A menu from the Members' Dining Room, House of Commons, London*

this same range available. Traditionally haute cuisine hotel restaurants have offered a very extensive menu, sometimes with up to 200 menu items. The trend today, however, is away from such a large menu range to a more limited number of items, say, of up to 100, which are changed seasonally. In this way food costs are more easily controlled mainly because of the reduction in food losses and wastage and all menu items re-priced where necessary. Cyclical menus are rarely used in quality and haute cuisine hotel restaurants; instead the menus are usually written for a set period, for example, three to six months, and then changed.

The menus offered by quality restaurants both inside and outside hotels, are mainly à la carte although some operations offer table d'hôte menus for specific meal periods, such as Saturday and Sunday lunches, in order to try to attract extra custom. In some restaurants these

menus are written in French; where French terms are used on the menu the English translation should be given and if possible some form of description so that the customer understands exactly what he is ordering. This decision as to the language to be used should be part of the marketing policy and be particularly related to the market segment being catered for.

Menu layout and design are important aspects of any restaurant operation because its menu is a sales tool which should be representative of the type of image the operation is trying to project. The menus used in quality restaurants and hotel speciality restaurants are very often large and grandiose which reinforce an image of sophistication that these types of restaurants are trying to create. The typeface used on the menus is usually traditional with the names of the menu items in one style of print and the translations or descriptions often in italics underneath. For à la carte menus all items are individually priced, although some seasonal foods such as game dishes may be marked 'market price' and would vary in price according to the time of year and their availability. House specialities may either be a permanent feature on the menu and be changed when the menu is completely re-written, or they may be changed weekly and advertised on the menu.

Because of the volume of trade that passes through the lower ASP outlets of hotels, such as coffee shops, the menus in these operations are physically handled to a greater extent than are the menus in quality restaurants. Hard wearing menus must therefore be used in these levels of operations so that they do not deteriorate in appearance; laminated finishes, for example, are often used so that the menu surfaces may be wiped clean. The time spent by a customer in reading a coffee shop menu is considerably less than a customer would spend reading an à la carte menu. The menu layout in the hotel's lower ASP outlets should therefore pay particular attention to the grouping of the items on the menu and the highlighting of the high GP food items most prominently.

A number of quality restaurants both inside and outside hotels are now speciality restaurants in which the menus are centred around either a specific food, for example sushi in a Japanese restaurant or a particular country, for example Spanish restaurants. Other hotel restaurants feature speciality foods from the region in which the hotel is situated; this is a particularly useful way for the smaller country hotel to market its catering facilities in a slightly unusual way. Some regional and national tourist boards will often include establishments that are featuring traditional English food, in their tourist brochures and other sales literature; in this way the smaller hotel is able to achieve a considerably wider range of advertising than it would have been able to on its own.

The products offered by quality restaurants and other catering facilities in hotels are less standardized than the products of fast-food operations. Generally speaking, the higher the price level of a catering outlet the less standardized are its products. In hotels, therefore, the lower ASP coffee shop operations would feature more standardized products than the high ASP à

la carte restaurants. In some of the more transient-type hotels, the food and beverage operations have been streamlined, and standardized pre-portioned products are served directly to the guests; on a breakfast buffet for example prepacked breakfast cereals, preserves, cartons of milk and cream, biscuits and cheese may be offered. Where a hotel is part of a large group the organization may have its own central purchasing and supply department so that the individual hotel unit would be supplied with the majority of its items from there. In the independently operated hotel or quality restaurant, however, it is dependent upon individual owners to find reliable suppliers who are able to provide food and beverage items of a consistent quality and standard.

The life cycle of quality restaurants and other catering outlets in hotels, is generally longer than operations in other sectors of the industry – for example, fast-foods. In hotels the life cycle of the coffee shop or grill room operation would be the shortest with about four or five years before the catering facility needed to be substantially changed. The à la carte restaurant, however, like other quality restaurants, may have a considerably longer product life cycle of six to ten years. This longer life cycle does not suggest that during these years no aspect of the operation should be altered; there should be a constant awareness of changes in the market, competition, etc. at all times. The life cycle relates more specifically to the interior and exterior décor of the operation which are usually the most costly aspects to alter substantially in any way.

18.2.3.3 *Food production styles*

The most widely used method of food production in the kitchens of quality restaurants and hotels is still the conventional method of production, based on the *partie* system. The partie system is a method of kitchen organization in which production is divided into separate areas according to the type of food being produced. In a large hotel kitchen, for example, there may be as many as seven main production parties: roast; vegetables; larder/salads; poultry; fish; soup; and sauces, and each of these sections may be further subdivided depending on the quantity of food to be produced by the partie. Although the

The ORIENTAL Restaurant

HOT AND COLD APPETISERS

Shredded roast duck, chicken and fresh fruits with onions served in cold peanut sauce	£13.00
Deep-fried mixed sea food wrapped in rice paper with mango	£17.50
Sliced prawns and fresh asparagus with ginger and lemon sauce	£19.00
Deep-fried soft shell crab with chilli pepper and herbal salt (1 piece)	£9.50
Mixed Oriental platter — deep fried crab claw, soya chicken and steamed scallops	£12.50
Steamed scallops with black bean or garlic sauce (two pieces)	£8.00
Boiled prawns and chicken dumplings with ginger and spring onion sauce	£9.00
Shredded beans and with mixed vegetables served in chilli and lime juice	£7.50

ROAST — BARBECUE

Roasted Peking duck (served in two courses; for between two and six people)	£42.00
Warm roasted Lamb with pickled vegetables	£17.50
Honey cured barbecued pork	£12.00
Soya chicken with sweet yellow beans	£12.50
Cold jelly fish with sesame seed	£18.50
Roasted duck with sweet ginger and cucumber	£16.50

SOUPS

Hot and sour soup	£8.00
Double boiled cabbage and black mushroom soup	£7.50
Braised beancurd and assorted seafoods soup	£7.50
Chicken and vegetable soup with straw mushrooms	£7.50
Sweet corn soup with crab meat	£8.00

SHARK'S FIN
(Imported directly from Hong Kong)

Baised superior shark's fin with crab meat	£38.00
Braised shark's fin soup with mixed seafood	£18.00
Double boiled superior shark's fin soup with chicken and hearts of Chinese cabbage	£35.00

ABALONE
(Imported directly from Hong Kong)

Braised whole superior abalone with oyster sauce	£45.00
Braised slices of abalone with broccoli florets	£22.00
Braised slices of abalone with black mushrooms	£22.00
Steamed abalone stuffed with prawn mousse in brown sauce	£26.00

SEAFOOD

Stir-fried prawns and garden greens with chilli	£21.00
Deep fried lobster in a tangy barbecue chilli sauce	£35.00
Sautéed lobster with ginger and spring onion	£35.00
Fried prawns with cashew nuts in lemon sauce	£21.50
Stir-fried scallop with snow peas	£17.50
Deep-fried sole with chilli bean sauce and asparagus tips "Oriental Style"	£27.00
Steamed fillet of seabass with black bean sauce and spring onions	£26.50
Wok-fried squid with pineapple and pepper	£17.00

Service and Tax included

All meats are cooked to refuse from smoking during meals

The ORIENTAL Restaurant

POULTRY

Deep-fried crispy skin chicken	£16.50
Sautéed chicken and snow peas with oyster sauce	£16.00
Fried pigeon in orange sauce	£13.50
Deep-fried boneless chicken in lemon sauce	£14.50
Stir-fried boneless pigeon with young ginger and pineapple	£15.50
Sautéed breast of duck with fresh asparagus	£17.50
Wok-fried duck with black pepper	£17.50

BEEF AND PORK

Wok-fried slices of beef with shredded Chinese pastry in oyster sauce	£24.00
Stir-fried beef with lemon grass and black pepper	£21.00
Medallions of beef Cantonese style	£24.00
Shredded pork with bamboo shoots in sea special sauce	£16.50
Marinated pork ribs bathed in barbecue sauce	£15.00
Deep-fried marinated spare rib in chilli pepper and herbal salt	£15.00

VEGETABLES

Stewed vegetables with fungi and bean sprouts	£10.50
Stir-fried bean curd with ground beef in chilli sauce	£11.50
Sautéed assorted vegetables	£8.00
Braised bamboo shoot and Chinese mushrooms in chilli sauce	£12.50
Wok-fried bean curd with minced chicken in oyster sauce	£7.50
Chinese garden greens in crab meat sauce	£12.50
Hot pot of braised aubergines, salted fish and diced chicken	£7.00
Shiitake mushrooms and snow peas in oyster sauce	£7.00
Stir-fried white cabbage with garlic	£7.50
Stir-fried green asparagus	

RICE AND NOODLES

Fried rice with chicken and salted fish	£11.00
Fried rice with prawns and assorted meats wrapped in lotus leaves	£10.00
Fried rice Fookien style	£11.00
Stir-fried egg noodles with bean sprouts	£8.00
Fried white noodles with shredded duck and mixed greens	£16.50
E-fu noodles with crab meat sauce	£12.00
Pan-fried rice noodles with shredded barbecue pork and mixed vegetables	£10.00
Oriental special fried rice	£12.00

No monosodium glutamate is used in the preparation of these dishes

Chef: Simon Yung   Manager: Jimmy Mau

Service and Tax included

Figure 18.5 The menu from the Oriental Restaurant, the Dorchester Hotel, London

WEEKEND MENU

SOUP & SANDWICHES

Leek & potato soup (hot or cold)	3.75
Smoked salmon sandwich	5.75
Suffolk sweetcured bacon & tomato sandwich*	4.95

FISH & SHELLFISH

Smoked haddock, spinach & cheese pie*	4.95
6 Irish rock oysters +	7.00
Loch Fyne smoked salmon with caraway bread	8.00
Fish & chips with mushy peas	9.50
Crab mayonnaise	9.50
Half lobster mayonnaise	13.00
Dublin Bay prawn mayonnaise	12.00

+ We do not recommend the consumption of spirits with oysters

MEAT DISHES

Pie of the day (15 minutes)	8.50
Rare roast beef salad with french beans, onions & horseradish	7.00
Cumbrian air dried ham with spiced pear & rocket	6.00
Rump steak, horseradish butter & chips* 8oz	12.95

PUDDINGS

Pudding of the day	3.95
Cambridge burnt cream	3.95
Sticky toffee pudding, toffee sauce	3.95
Bread & butter pudding	3.95
Ice creams & sorbets	3.95
Selection of British & Irish cheeses	5.00

* These dishes not available between 3pm and 6pm

17.5% VAT INCLUDED

WEEKEND BRUNCH

(Available Saturday & Sunday, 12 noon to 3pm)

2 Courses 13.95
3 Courses 16.25
(One drink per person included)

-

Pint of Theakston's best or Beck's bier
Greyhound
(Brut de Chardonnay, Cointreau & grapefruit juice)
Freshly squeezed orange juice
Bloody Mary

-

English muffin, Loch Fyne smoked salmon,
poached egg & dill hollandaise
Smoked haddock fishcake, lemon mayonnaise
Cumbrian air dried ham, celeriac & mustard

-

Sausages with black pudding, bubble & squeak,
tomato relish
Fish & chips with mushy peas
Corned beef hash with fried egg, spiced beans

-

Rhubarb & custard tart with poached
rhubarb & ginger
Sticky toffee pudding, toffee & rum sauce
Cambridge burnt cream

(All brunch items are available individually by request)

COFFEE

Espresso	1.65
Double espresso	1.95
Cappuccino	1.85
Filter	1.50

12.5% DISCRETIONARY SERVICE CHARGE WILL BE ADDED

Figure 18.6 *An extract from the Butlers Wharf Chop House menu (Conran Restaurants)*

APPETISERS	MAIN COURSES	PUDDINGS
Cornish Crab Cakes on an Avocado and Pimento Relish	Grilled Red Mullet with a Tapenade Crust on a raft of Baby Leeks with New Potatoes	Terrine of Two Chocolate Mousses
Winter Vegetable Soup with Chervil Dumplings	Poached Pavé of Scottish Salmon with Hollandaise Sauce and New Potatoes	Caramel Bananas in a Puff Pastry Case
Traditionally Oak Smoked Scottish Salmon served with Gros Campagne Bread and Caper Butter	Half a Lobster with Mango and Celeriac Salad, Chive Vinaigrette	Nougatine Parfait
Tagliatelle Pasta with a Sun Dried Pimento Cream and Greens	Grilled Dover Sole with New Potatoes, Garden Vegetables and Dijon Butter Sauce	A Choice of Sweets and Fresh Fruits from the Trolley
Salad of young Spinach Leaves with Lardons of Bacon and Country Bread Croutons	Supreme of Maize Fed Chicken with Bubble and Squeak	Selection of Dairy Ice Creams and Sorbets
	Rosette of Lamb on a Compote of Mediterranean Vegetables	Cheese from the Trolley

ALWAYS AVAILABLE		
	Gressingham Duck Breast in a puff-pastry case with Savoy Cabbage and Madeira Jus	* * *
Chilled Ogen Melon	Loin of Venison with a Truffle and Peppercorn Sauce served with a basket of Winter Vegetables and Swede Purée	Coffee with Petit Fours
Grilled Scottish Salmon with market Vegetables and New Potatoes	Skirt Steak of Beef with Pont Neuf Potatoes and a Tabasco and Parsley Butter	A Selection of Assorted Leaf Teas
Plain Omelette with selected Vegetables and Chips	"The Churchill" Mixed Grill from Sea and Meadow	
Grilled Fillet or Sirloin Steak with seasonal Vegetables and Bearnaise Sauce	A Dome of Roasted Aubergine with Peppers and Garlic	
	Seasonal Salad	
	Selected Market Vegetables	

10/96

Figure 18.7 *Menu from the Churchill Room, House of Commons, London*

other production styles such as cook-chill and sous-vide are making inroads into this previous bastion of hotel tradition, these inroads are mainly in specific areas, for example function catering, where they may be used to complement the traditional methods rather than replace them.

Where a conventional or traditional method of food production is used in the kitchens of quality restaurants and hotel à la carte restaurants, it is used in conjunction with the highest standards of fresh foods available and a low percentage of convenience foods. For the lower price level outlets, however, such as a hotel's coffee shop or bar snack service, a higher percentage of convenience foods may be used in the kitchen.

Where convenience foods are used by hotel kitchens the quality of the food and beverage products is very dependent on the supplier. Where the hotel is part of a large organization, this may have its own centralized production unit and so the quality of foods can be very tightly controlled. An individual operator, however, is reliant on the quality produced by the food manufacturer from whom he is buying. Today a number of food manufacturers are selling higher quality convenience foods, for example pâtés, coq au vin, beef chasseur, etc. which

TSAR'S

First Courses

Potato and Mushroom Soup served in its own Shell
£5.20

Warm Duck Salad with Sauté Potatoes, fresh
Raspberries and Beetroot on a bed of Mixed Leaves
£7.80

Marinated Herrings with an Onion Vodka Salad
£6.90

Salmon and Crab Tartare　£8.80

Grilled Tiger Prawns with a Chilli Vodka Dip　£8.80

Gravad Lax with a Sweet Honey and Mustard
Dressing　£8.80

Main Courses

Chicken Kiev with a Tomato and Garlic
flavoured Vodka　£11.60

Fillet of Beef Stroganoff with Rice Pilaff　£13.90

Baby Rack of Lamb with a Sour Cherry Sauce,
Sweet Pepper Potato and Baby Vegetables
£15.50

Roasted Fillet of Venison with a Cumin Sauce
£18.20

Fillets of Sole with Spinach and Oyster Mushrooms
£17.90

Steamed Salmon with a Tomato and
Vodka Fondue　£13.60

Desserts

Potato and Nut Dumplings with a Lemon Sauce and Minted Soured Cream　£3.90

Black Cherry flavoured Vodka Brulée　£5.10

Strawberry and Vodka Ice Cream glazed with a Warm Sabayon　£6.20

Hazelnut Chocolate Cake with Orange and Chocolate Vodka flavoured Sauce　£4.90

Freshly Brewed Coffee　£2.90
Black Russian Tea　£2.90

Prices are inclusive of VAT and Service Charge

Figure 18.8　*A menu from the Tsar's Restaurant and Bar, the Langham Hilton, London*

fill a market gap for a particular level of operation. The types of catering operations which use these products are mainly those catering for the middle market such as the currently popular cafe and wine bars and bistros, etc. In these operations which may offer two-course and three-course inclusive meals for between £10 and £18, food and labour costs must be very tightly controlled and the use of these types of convenience foods aids in this. It is important that where convenience foods are used in a kitchen based on conventional production methods they should be introduced and utilized as part of a totally planned catering system. This involves taking into account not only the financial aspects of the operation, but also having different equipment to make the best use of them, and preparing staff for their introduction.

In some of the older style establishments which are using convenience foods, there are often large production areas which have not been substantially altered for twenty or thirty years; these large kitchens are particularly found in the independently operated establishments which may have had a relatively low injection of capital over a number of years. The production equipment is usually outdated, and consequently where convenience foods have been introduced, they are not being used as efficiently as they may be. In these types of establishments convenience foods may not be an aid to the establishment's production; for these types of foods to be an asset in a kitchen they must be introduced in a planned and systematic way.

Where a hotel has a number of different catering outlets, these may be served either from one central kitchen or by a number of separate kitchens, although where possible, duplication of kitchen areas is avoided because of the high capital costs involved. In hotels which offer room service, however, a separate floor kitchen may be installed with limited production equipment, which is able to supply beverages and small snacks and hence remove the load from the main kitchen. The equipment used in the kitchens of hotels and quality restaurants will depend to a large extent on the menu being offered. Those operations featuring a limited coffee shop and snack item menu will have a correspondingly limited range of kitchen equipment, designed to cook or regenerate food and beverage items rapidly for immediate service. Those kitchens serving quality restaurants with an extensive à la carte menu and which are using almost totally fresh food products, will have a far greater range of preparation equipment.

As mentioned earlier, where the more modern methods of production have been introduced to the kitchens of hotels they are mainly used in specific areas. Cook-chill, for example, is partic-

ularly applicable to banquet catering and is discussed in the next chapter. The types of frozen products used by hotels can be individual portion packs, such as a boil-in-the-bag duck à l'orange, or it can be ten-portion cheesecakes to be featured on the dessert trolley of the hotel's coffee shop. Where a hotel is not part of a group, but is still sufficiently large, it may be able to liaise directly with a food manufacturer to produce food items to its own specifications, and in this way assure itself of a consistent standard and quality product. Some bought-in convenience foods for the catering outlets of hotels are therefore highly standardized when they arrive at these establishments. Many of the products purchased for use in quality restaurants, however, will be very special to the particular restaurant and its menu and only purchased in small quantities at a time, for example local wild mushrooms, local river or sea fish etc.; this results in less highly standardized products being served in the higher priced operations than in the lower priced restaurants found in hotels.

Although at present the conventional method of food production is still the most widely used in the kitchens of quality restaurants and hotels, these traditional kitchens and their high capital outlay and running costs are becoming less common. Today, the economic production unit is steadily growing larger and it will become less and less feasible to justify kitchen methods which cost more than comparable results from the factory or other centralized production units. In the future, particularly in the lower priced catering outlets of hotels, the localized kitchen will only produce those foods that are demonstrably better in terms of quality, economy and convenience.

18.2.3.4 Food service styles

The variety of food service styles used in hotels is dependent upon the different types of catering outlets in the establishment. In a small hotel, for example, where one restaurant is used for the service of all meals, and features table d'hôte menus for lunch and dinner, plated meals may be served to the guests by service staff. In a large hotel, however, with four or five different types of outlets, there can be a corresponding variety in the service styles. Breakfast service in the hotel, for example, can be on a self-service basis in the coffee shop, or waiter service in the main restaurant. For lunch and dinner the coffee shop can serve a limited selection of plated snacks and meals directly to customers at their table, and the outlet may also incorporate a self-service buffet or carvery. The hotel grill room or themed restaurant could feature a table d'hôte menu with plated meals, and the à la carte restaurant would offer silver service, both with waiter service. In addition to the main dining areas the hotel bar can offer a limited snack service and the hotel could also offer room service facilities; because room service is, however, a highly labour intensive and time-consuming method of food service, the majority of hotels offering room service today usually provide only a very limited menu selection, except for the large luxury establishments; the room service menus often containing some items from the main restaurant menu. This same variety of service styles is not, however, found in quality restaurants. This level of operation usually only offers a similar service style to that found in the à la carte restaurants of hotels, that is, silver service to the table.

Food service styles are not only dependent on the type of catering operation, but also on its price level. Generally speaking, the higher the price level of an operation, the more elaborate and sophisticated the service style becomes. In the lower ASP catering outlets of hotels, customers select their food and beverage items, and either remain at the counter to consume their meal, or return to a table. At the other end of the market, namely, in quality restaurants both inside and outside hotels, these operations are based almost exclusively on waiter service to the customer's table. In these quality restaurants a variety of table service methods may be employed, although French and Russian service are the two styles most commonly used.

As the sophistication of food service styles increases with the price level of an operation, so too do beverage service styles. The service of wines, for example, is considerably more elaborate in an à la carte quality restaurant than in an operation featuring a table d'hôte menu. In a quality restaurant an extensive wine list would be available and a wine waiter would serve the wine throughout the duration of the meal. In a lower ASP catering outlet a more limited wine list would be offered and the service of the wine would usually be by the member of staff serving at the customer's table, rather than a separate wine waiter. Adjacent to quality restaurants may be a cocktail bar or some other form of bar where beverages are served to customers at individual tables. In the lower ASP operations, this bar arrangement is not often found; patrons for the table d'hôte restaurant would usually use the main hotel bar.

Customer throughput will vary considerably from one catering outlet in a hotel to another. In the coffee shop and lower ASP operations seat turnover may vary from half an hour to one and a half hours; a faster customer throughput during the lunch time period is often achieved where a high proportion of trade is from local offices and the customer's total lunch hour is only one hour. In the à la carte restaurant of a hotel the lunch time seat turnover is generally quicker than in the evening, again because a large percentage of trade is often business with a fairly limited lunch hour. In the evening seat turnover is usually slower in all the different catering outlets, particularly in quality restaurants where guests may spend three or four hours in the restaurant. In these levels of operations beverage service after the meal, such as coffee and liqueurs, may be in a separate coffee lounge; this enables seats to be vacated in the dining area, is conducive to a more leisurely meal experience and helps increase seat turnover, without making customers feel they are being hurried.

Although some catering outlets in hotels are self-service, this food service style is rarely accompanied by a self-clearing of dishes, as is found in some other sectors of the industry. Where self-service is used in buffet or carvery restaurants, service staff remove the customers' dishes from the table, as they do in waiter service operations.

As the price level of a restaurant rises, in addition to the quality and variety of menu items increasing, the intangible aspects of the operation also become more important. In quality restaurants, for example, the atmosphere of the restaurant now plays a more important role in the customer's total meal experience. This is affected by many factors including the speed of

LONDON • OXFORD • BRIGHTON • CAMBRIDGE • BRISTOL

BREAKFAST
(11 am 12 noon Mon – Sat)

Freshly Squeezed Orange Juice £2.15

Traditional English Breakfast £5.65
*bacon, egg, sausage, tomato, black
pudding and mushrooms, with toast*

Granary Toast £1.15
with local jam and butter

TEA TIME
(3 pm – 5.30 pm)

**Traditional Cucumber or Egg and
Cress Sandwiches** £2.25

Cheese on Toast £2.15

Toasted Crumpets £2.15

Freshly Baked Scones £2.35
local jam, butter and clotted cream

COFFEE AND TEA

Regular *Black or White* £1.05

Espresso £1.05

Cappuccino £1.15

Double Espresso £1.15

Fresh Decaffeinated £1.15

Mocha £1.15

Cafe Latte £1.25

Pot of Tea per person £1.15
*Darjeeling, Lapsang Souchong, Ceylon,
Jasmine, Earl Grey, English Breakfast, Fruit*

Iced Tea £1.45

Iced Coffee £1.45 *with cream* £1.75

Hot Chocolate
Regular £1.15 *Mint* £1.65 *Rum* £2.45

Liqueur Coffee *from* £2.75

COLD DRINKS

Pure Fruit Juices £1.20
*Orange, Apple, Grapefruit,
Pineapple, Tomato*

Freshly Squeezed Orange Juice £2.15

Elderflower Pressé £1.70

Coke or Diet Coke £1.20

Lemonade £1.20

Ginger Beer £1.20

Milk £1.20

Mineral Water *(small)* £1.20 *(large)* £2.65

Aqua Libra £1.85

NON-ALCOHOLIC COCKTAILS

Pussy Foot £2.85
*Peach nectar, lemon juice, grenadine and
the yolk of an egg shaken on ice and
topped with soda*

Virgin Mary £2.85
Tomato juice, lemon juice and seasoning

Hobson's Choice £2.85
Apple, citrus juices and cassis on ice

BROWNS T-SHIRTS £8.50	**BROWNS TEA TOWEL** £3.50
BROWNS BASEBALL CAP £8.50	**BROWNS UMBRELLA** £19.50

**A service charge of 10%
will be added to parties
of 5 or more**

**In fairness to customers
having meals, the sale of side
orders, coffee, teas etc.
may be restricted**

O/P/1/11.96

Figure 18.9 *An extract from a menu from Browns Restaurant and Bar*

BROWNS

R E S T A U R A N T & B A R

LONDON · OXFORD · BRIGHTON · CAMBRIDGE · BRISTOL

BOTTLED BEERS

Heineken £1.90	Peroni £2.05	Michelob £2.20
Boddingtons £2.20	Kronenbourg 1664 £2.15	Budweiser Budvar £2.20
Stella Dry £2.15	Low Alcohol Lager £1.85	Becks £2.20

WHITE WINE

	HOUSE WINE	Glass	Half	Bottle
1	**Côtes du Roussillon** Pierre de Marca *Southern France* (12.5% abv) *Attractive bouquet, a well made uncomplicated, dry wine*	£1.60	£4.75	£8.65
2	**Dalwood** Medium Dry *South East Australia* (12% abv) *A fragrant, well balanced and full flavoured wine*	£1.80		£9.65
3	**Monferrato Bianco** *Italy* (10.5% abv) *Crisp with appley fruit and a clean finish*	£1.85		£9.95
4	**Semillon Chardonnay** Stewart Point *South Australia* (11% abv) *Well balanced wine with good citrus and light fruit flavours*	£1.95		£10.45
5	**Chenin Blanc** Mount Pearl *South Africa* (12% abv) *Fresh, off dry and attractively full flavoured*			£11.55
6	**Three Choirs** Estate Premium *England* (10% abv) *Fresh and fruity, medium dry. Estate bottled in Gloucestershire*			£11.95
7	**Chardonnay** Domaine Virginie *Southern France* (12% abv) *A full flavoured and fruity Chardonnay*			£12.55
8	**Sauvignon de Touraine** Domaine des Chézelles *France* (12% abv) *Almost perfect Sauvignon from Noyers sur Cher in the Loire*	£2.35	£6.95	£12.95
9	**Chardonnay** Wolf Blass *South Australia* (14% abv) *Lively fruit with oak flavours combine perfectly for long finish*		£7.45	£13.85
10	**Sauvignon Blanc** Morton Estate *New Zealand* (11% abv) *Elegant Gooseberry aroma, and well balanced tropical fruit flavours*			£15.15
11	**Saint-Véran** Domaine de Luc Terrier *France* (13% abv) *A neighbour of Pouilly Fuisse, this vineyard produces dry stylish Burgundy*			£19.85
12	**Gewurztraminer** Moulin Blanc AC, Dopff 'au Moulin' *France* (12.5% abv) *Fine, dry spicy wine, with a beautiful perfumed flowery nose*			£21.95
13	**Chablis** 1ᵉʳ Cru Vaillons, Domaine Raoult *France* (13% abv) *From the Premier Cru vineyard of Vaillons, with immediate attractive fruitiness*			£27.85
	DESSERT WINE			
14	**Sauternes** Baron Philippe de Rothschild *France* (12.5% abv) *Sweet balanced richness, delicious as an aperitif or with puddings*	£3.95	£11.75	

RED WINE

	HOUSE WINE	Glass	Half	Bottle
15	**Côtes du Roussillon** Pierre de Marca *Southern France* (12.5% abv) *Chunky and full, without being heavy*	£1.60	£4.75	£8.65
16	**Montepulciano D'Abruzzo** *Italy* (12% abv) *Full of rich berry fruit characteristics*	£1.80	£5.35	£9.65
17	**Shiraz Cabernet** Stewart Point *South Australia* (12% abv) *Warm and well rounded with good fruit and soft tannins*	£2.00		£10.95
18	**Señorio de Los Llanos** *Spain* (12.5% abv) *Soft rounded fruit with a gentle oaky flavour*	£2.10		£11.45
19	**Pinotage** Mount Pearl *South Africa* (12% abv) *Full bodied, lots of colour and plenty of fruit*			£11.75
20	**Good Ordinary Claret** AC Berry Brothers *France* (12% abv) *A wine of classic Bordeaux style, mature and mellow*	£2.15	£6.50	£11.95
21	**Salice Salentino** Riserva Francesco Candido *Southern Italy* (13% abv) *Packed full of ripe, rich fruit with soft tannins and subtle oaky character*			£12.45
22	**Cabernet Sauvignon** Wolf Blass *South Australia* (13% abv) *Soft and full flavoured, with subtle oak ageing*		£7.55	£13.95

Figure 18.10 *An extract from a wine and drinks list from Browns Restaurant and Bar*

service, which is generally more relaxed and at a slower pace, service accompaniments, the décor of the restaurant, and so on. Quality restaurants are generally tastefully decorated with specific colour schemes and lighting arrangements being used to create the desired atmosphere. Indoor plants are often dispersed around the room which help to divide the room into smaller and more intimate areas; fresh flowers may also be used as part of the table decorations.

At this level of operation the customer may also be purchasing some form of entertainment as part of the meal experience. In its simplest form this may be live background music, but at a more sophisticated level it may either be a cabaret, or an inclusive dinner-dance arrangement offered by the restaurant. In these restaurants room design must be flexible to cater for these special functions. In the case of a dinner dance, some form of flooring is usually laid over the carpet for the dancing area, or a dance floor may be concealed below the carpet, which can easily be removed. In restaurants offering this entertainment facility, air conditioning is often provided in the dining area, and indeed this is now becoming a standard feature in most quality restaurants.

The service accompaniments used in the hotel's coffee shop and table d'hôte restaurants are usually of a functional nature, designed to withstand a fairly high usage due to the speed of customer throughput. As the level of restaurant operation becomes more sophisticated, however, so do the service accompaniments. In quality restaurants for example the tablecloths and napkins used are linen, and the cutlery and crockery also of a high standard. Other service accompaniments and equipment would be specifically related to this level of operation because of the type of menu it offers, for example, a guéridon trolley for flambé work.

The seating arrangements used by catering outlets in hotels will depend to a large extent on the level of operation. For the hotel coffee shop and table d'hôte restaurant, free standing and banquet seating arrangements may be used, with between 12 and 18 ft^2 (1.12 and 1.67 m^2) being allowed per person in the dining area. In quality restaurants banquet seating is rarely found, although permanently fixed wall seating is used, which enables the dining space to be uti-

lized more efficiently. In those operations with free standing seating, up to 20 to 22 ft^2 (1.86 to 2.05 m^2) per person may be allowed, the extra space being essential where guéridon and dessert trolleys are used.

18.2.3.5 *Organization and staffing*

Staffing organization in hotels and quality restaurants depends to a large extent on the size of the establishment and the level of service being offered; the larger the operation and the more staff employed, the greater the departmentalization and specialization of the catering personnel. In a small hotel with one restaurant offering a limited menu, there may be as few as five or six production staff and a similar number of service staff; this would constitute the catering department. In a large hotel, however, with a number of catering outlets, the catering department may consist of several hundred personnel. In the smaller hotel little staff hierarchy would be present; in the larger hotel a very clearly defined hierarchy would be identifiable for each catering outlet.

As the staff hierarchy in a catering operation increases, so does the specialization of the staff functions. The *head chef* of a large hotel or quality restaurant may therefore have several *sous chefs* who would deputize in his absence, and under the sous chefs would be the *chefs de parties;* these are each responsible for the main sections in the kitchen – roast, vegetables, fish, larder, pastry, soup and sauces, etc. The chefs de parties may have several *commis,* or assistant chefs, reporting to them, depending on the size of the section, and finally there can be a number of general apprentices working in the kitchen in any one of these sections. In the large kitchens organized on this traditional partie system, each section is quite autonomous; in smaller kitchens where less specialization is found, the kitchen staff may be required to perform a variety of tasks that would normally be associated with specific sections in a large production area. The head chef of a large kitchen is usually involved to a far greater extent with the administrative side of the operation, rather than in the physical preparation of meals. In a small establishment, however, the head chef is more involved in the production of restaurant meals, leaving the majority of the

Rhône

			750ML	375ML
42.	Côte du Rhône Villages			
	Château Goudray	1992	£21.00	£18.00
43.	Châteauneuf-du-Pape			
	Clos des Papes	1993	£42.00	£27.00
44.	Châteauneuf-du-Pape			
	Château de la Font du Loup	1988	£35.00	
45.	Crozes Hermitage			
	Georges Duboeuf	1989	£19.00	
46.	Cornas, Jean-Luc Colombo	1991	£49.00	

Burgundy

COTE DE BEAUNE

47.	Côte de Beaune Villages, Louis Jadot	1994	£28.00	
50.	Chorey lès Beaune			
	Les Confrelins Arnoux Pere et Fils	1991	£38.50	£18.95
51.	Corton-Pougets Grand Cru			
	Louis Jadot	1987	£64.00	
53.	Volnay les Santenots 1er Cru			
	Eric Boigelot	1990	£62.00	
54.	Savigny les Beaune les Bourgeots			
	Domaine Simon Bize et Fils	1993	£37.00	
55.	Savigny les Beaunes 1er Cru les Lavières			
	Domaine Chandon de Briailles	1991	£39.00	£20.00
56.	Pommard 1er Cru, Grand Clos des Epenots			
	Domaine de Courcel	1989	£72.00	
57.	Pommard, Moillard	1990	£59.00	
49.	Cuvée Maufoux	NV	£17.00	

COTE-DE-NUITS

58.	Gevrey Chambertin Vieilles Vignes			
	Jean-Pierre Marchand	1993	£46.00	
59.	Gevrey Chambertin, Moillard	1993	£56.00	
60.	Nuits St Georges, Jean Chauvenet	1992	£55.00	
61.	Charmes Chambertin Grand Cru			
	Bouchard Père et Fils	1985	£73.00	
62.	Clos Vougeot Grand Cru			
	Bouchard Père et Fils	1985	£87.00	
63.	Chambolle Musigny Clos du Village Monopole			
	Domaine Antonin Guyon	1990	£62.00	

9

Figure 18.11   *An extract from the wine list from the Landmark Hotel, London*

administration to the hotel owner or proprietor.

On the food service side of catering operations a similar staff hierarchy is found according to the size of the establishment. In a large operation, for example, the staffing organization for a lunch or dinner service in a quality restaurant serving eighty or more covers, from an à la carte menu, may be as follows: the restaurant manager or his assistant, one head waiter, two chef de rang, one wine waiter, one commis wine waiter, and three commis waiters. In a smaller operation, however, there may only be the restaurant manager or head waiter, and several assistants, with no separate staff hierarchy for beverage service.

Unlike the independently operated quality restaurant, a catering outlet in a hotel is one of many departments within the establishment. In a large hotel unit the catering department may consist of several restaurants and bars, the kitchens, room service, banqueting and staff catering. In this operation the food and beverage manager would be responsible for the co-ordination of each of these different outlets in line with the hotel's financial, marketing and catering policies. The manager would also be responsible for the co-ordination of the catering department with the other areas of the hotel. For example, in an establishment employing several hundred staff, there is likely to be a separate personnel department. By co-ordinating with the food and beverage department, personnel may become almost entirely responsible for the employing of the lower grades of staff, such as commis waiters and chefs, leaving the food and beverage manager to only become involved in the employing of supervisory and management staff for the food and beverage department.

Because of the high degree of departmentalization in large hotels, the food and beverage manager is able to delegate responsibility to a far greater extent to other heads of departments; these would include such personnel as the head cellarman, the headstoreman, the chief steward and so on, who would all have their own specialized functions and would report to the food and beverage manager. The food and beverage manager would in turn report directly to the general manager of the hotel, and be required to attend meetings with the other heads of departments, over which the general manager would preside. In the smaller hotels of up to fifty bed-

rooms where there is considerably less specialization because of the size of the operation, the owner or proprietor of the hotel may have a very small management team; in hotel operations of this size there may only be two assistant managers, one responsible for the food and beverage department, the other the front of house.

The ratio of service staff to customers will depend largely upon the type of catering outlet and the level of service being offered. In a hotel coffee shop, for example, with limited waiter service, the ratio may be as low as one waiter to twenty customers. As the service style becomes more elaborate, however, so the number of service staff increases; thus in a quality restaurant the ratio may be as high as one waiter to six to ten customers. Service staff contact time also increases with the ratio of staff to customers. In quality restaurants, for example, service staff are not only involved in 'taking orders' as they are, for example, in take-away operations; in quality restaurants customers may require explanations of certain dishes, such as the house specialities, and the service staff would be expected to be knowledgeable about these menu items.

Because a substantial percentage of trade in quality restaurants is repeat trade, customers appreciate being served by familiar staff, and this is recognized by these establishments. Most of the staff employed by these operations are therefore full-time, with little part-time labour being used.

The level of skill of food and beverage employees in hotels will depend largely on the type of catering outlet with which they are associated. The hotel's coffee shop, for example, using a high percentage of convenience foods, may only require comparatively unskilled labour in both production and service areas. In the hotel à la carte restaurant and other quality restaurants, highly skilled labour is necessary; both in the kitchen where a high percentage of the food used is fresh and is prepared from the raw state on the premises, and in the restaurant where silver service is commonly used.

The rates of pay are usually higher for food and beverage staff employed in quality restaurants, particularly for production staff and management personnel. Some high ASP operations still offer lower rates of pay to the food service staff, leaving the remainder to be supplemented by gratuities from customers, although this practice is becoming less common. Generally speaking the greater the responsibilities of an employee in a catering operation, the higher the rates of pay. The head chef of a large hotel or quality restaurant would therefore receive a considerably higher salary than, for example, the head chef of a small hotel.

The training of food and beverage employees will also depend on the level of operation in which they are employed. Most of the tasks associated with the preparation and service of foods in a hotel coffee shop, for example, are usually simplified so that comparatively unskilled labour may be used which assists in keeping labour costs down. Training of these employees is therefore usually limited to preparing and serving the coffee shop's menu items quickly and efficiently. Considerably greater skills are, however, required by the food production and service staff who are employed in the upmarket quality restaurants. The skills needed by these staff often take a number of years to acquire and the training of these employees is therefore a much longer and in depth process; trainee chefs for example may be apprenticed to large hotel kitchens for several years.

18.2.3.6 Staff catering

Staff catering facilities will vary from one operation to another; in some establishments little or no provision is made by the establishment to provide food and beverage facilities for staff, while in other operations it is very much a fringe benefit of the organization and facilities may be quite extensive. Decisions made regarding staff catering will be contained in the establishment's financial and catering policies. The financial policy would determine such factors as the number of meals per day to be provided for the employees, whether these are to be provided free or at what percentage cost to the employees, etc. The catering policy would in turn stipulate the standard and quality of food to be provided, whether cyclical menus are to be used and so on.

In small hotels and quality restaurants there is rarely a sufficiently large number of catering staff employed to warrant the provision of a separate dining area. In the large hotels, however, where there may be several hundred employees,

separate staff catering facilities need to be provided. Where there is a large number of staff to be catered for, separate food production and service staff may be employed by the hotel to prepare and serve food for the establishment's employees; these staff would be independent of the main kitchen and restaurant staff.

Some hotels operate two levels of staff catering. The first is for the majority of the hotel employees, up to supervisory and middle management level. The staff restaurant is usually operated on a self-service cafeteria basis and there is often a choice of two to three items for each course. Vending machines can also be situated in this dining area offering a selection of snack items and beverages. The second level of staff catering would be for senior management personnel for whom a separate dining area would be provided with a higher standard of décor, service accompaniments, etc. Waiter service is usually provided in this dining area. Where a separate dining area is not available for this level of personnel, senior management can take their meals in the hotel's coffee shop or grill room; a number of tables in the restaurant can be designated for staff which can be used when the restaurant is not busy or before the normal service starts.

Where staff catering facilities are provided by an establishment they can be accounted for in a variety of ways. The most common method adopted is to provide the meals free of charge to employees, allowing a certain amount per employee per week; the cost allowed is usually based on an average cost for the value of staff food consumed per meal period. This method ensures that a standard allowance for staff meals is made per employee, so that staff feeding costs cannot be used by the kitchen to mask inefficiencies in the overall food costs for the week. In some operations staff meals are charged 'at cost' to the employee which can be with or without a percentage mark up to cover overheads, etc. In other establishments a flat charge per meal is made either at the point of sale, or a deduction made at source from the employee's wages. Where staff meals are being provided free or at discounted rates, they represent a cost to the establishment. The cost of employee meals should therefore be deducted from the cost of food used, to calculate the true cost of food sold;

the same figure is later added back on the profit and loss account or gross profit analysis as an operating expense. This accounting procedure does not affect the final profit figure, but does give a more realistic figure for the cost of food sold by the establishment.

In quality restaurants situated outside hotels, allowances need only be made for meals consumed by the operation's food production and service staff. In hotels, however, staff catering includes meals for all the hotel staff, and is not confined to food and beverage personnel only. In these establishments the cost of the staff meals can be debited to the catering department in a number of ways. The most widely adopted method is to debit the food and beverage department for all staff meals taken by hotel employees. Some establishments, however, debit the individual departments, such as front office, housekeeping, catering, etc. for the meals consumed by their personnel. This transfer of costs from one department to another again does not affect the hotel's final profit, only departmental ones, and does allow a more accurate cost and profit analysis of the individual hotel departments.

Staff catering not only includes the main meal provided by an establishment, but also any other periods such as tea and coffee breaks during which time food and beverages are provided for employees. Tea and coffee breaks can be dealt with in a variety of ways. Employees may be allowed to leave their departments and have their break in the staff cafeteria where beverages and snacks are being served. In some establishments beverages may be brought to the employees in their offices and departments, although this service is usually only available to senior management personnel, or in departments where it may be inconvenient for staff to leave. In other operations individual vending or other beverage making machines may be positioned in certain departments from which employees may obtain drinks during the day. Other staff drinks may be purchased by employees, usually from the hotel's dispense bar; these can either be sold at cost, or at cost plus a small mark-up, depending on policy.

The type of staff catering facilities that may be provided by an operation is therefore very much dependent on the size of the establishment, and its basic policy decisions regarding this area of food and beverage service. Where staff meals are provided, however, they should be of a good quality and a consistent standard. The using of leftover items for example from the hotel's other catering outlets, may be an effective way of reducing food costs, but they should not be relied upon as the main source of staff meals, rather as a supplement to them. Many hotel staff rely on the meal provided at work for their main meal of the day, and as such it should be nutritious and varied.

Finally, where staff meals are available for several hours over a meal period, they should remain a consistently good quality throughout this service time; this ensures that staff coming into the cafeteria towards the end of service will receive meals of the same standard, and largely the same choice, as those staff at the beginning of service received.

18.3 Control and performance measurement

The control and performance measurement of catering outlets in hotels will be determined by its established basic policies. In a large hotel the catering department is one of many departmental accounts and must conform to the standard accounting system adopted for the establishment as a whole. In quality restaurants situated outside hotels the control and performance measurement of these operations is very often specific to those particular establishments.

Because hotels and quality restaurants are profit-orientated establishments, the main yard sticks against which these operations will be measured are their profit levels to be achieved. The gross profit levels to be achieved by quality restaurants situated outside a hotel, for example, may be similar to that of a hotel's à la carte restaurant, as an example between 65 and 70 per cent. Although for independent quality restaurants the profit level may only be as high as 65 per cent because these operations do not have the same high percentage of fixed costs associated with hotels.

Where a restaurant or hotel is privately owned, its performance is measured against standards laid down by the owner or governing body, which may or may not be contained in a formalized policy document. Large hotel groups today, however, produce manuals or other written documents in which the company's basic policy decisions and standards for the hotel units are contained. These 'Manuals of Procedures' may either relate to the complete food and beverage control cycle, or to specific areas such as the purchasing of food and beverage items, or the training of food production and service staff. Also contained in such a manual would be the types of reports and other documents that need to be produced by the establishment and at what time intervals these should be sent to the company's head office. For example, the manual may state that on a weekly basis the individual units are required to produce a *summary of weekly trading*, showing such basic information as the food and beverage sales and costs for the hotel's different catering outlets, the number of covers, the GP percentages for the restaurants and bars, etc. At the end of every trading period, which may be four weeks, a more detailed report may be required showing a more in-depth breakdown of sales and costs; at the end of a quarter, that is, three trading periods – a complete *profit and loss account* may be required; and finally, for the year ended a *balance sheet* for the whole catering department.

The sophistication of food and beverage control in an establishment will depend to a large extent on the size of the operation. The larger the establishment the greater the room for error because of the number of stages in the control cycle and the amount of information obtained at each stage. Generally speaking, therefore, the larger the organization and the more information that is needed regarding its operation, the more sophisticated the establishment's accounting system must become. For this reason it is more common to find standard manuals of procedures being used in large hotels, particularly those that are group owned, than in the smaller independently operated hotels (although such manuals are equally applicable to these smaller establishments).

The vast majority of hotels and restaurants today use ECRs of a wide range from the very basic 'stand alone' model where a single machine stands on the cashier's desk or on a bar counter to record all transactions, to the sophisticated point-of-sale control system based either on ECRs with the additional feature of one or several printers or VDU screens at such locations as the kitchen, bar and cellar, or on a computer point-of-sale system. This employs a micro computer which is pre-programmed to convert data into a range of management reports. The system collects data on an automatic basis through the 'server terminals' of a special design (being relatively small and having no cash tills) and is also linked by printer or VDU screen to the kitchen, bar and cellar. These special terminals are linked together via the computer to other 'server terminals' in the restaurants and bars and, if required, the terminals can be interfaced with other systems so that, for example, the transfer of restaurant charges to a guest's hotel bill can be made via the front office computer. The particular advantage of a computerized point-of-sale system is that it is capable of processing data as activities occur which makes it possible to obtain up to the minute reports so that the management are better informed and can take more immediate and accurate corrective action if necessary.

The performance of the food and beverage departments in hotels may be measured against the performance of other hotels. This information is available in the published statistics report of the major hotel and catering consultancy firms.

18.3.1   Outsourcing

Today, in line with current thinking and trends, hoteliers are also exploring alternatives to the overall management and operation of their hotel food and beverage facilities. Just as competitive tendering in schools and hospitals has prompted a huge increase in the contracting out of catering in those sectors, so an analogy can be drawn in the hotel industry where the search for alternative methods of food and beverage management is initiating an interest in the concept of outsourcing.

An increasing number of hotels are looking critically at their restaurant operations and the returns from them, particularly in comparison with the revenue from the accommodation side of the operation. As an example, a three- or four-star UK hotel of between 100 to 150 bedrooms can expect a departmental return on investment (DROI) for the food and beverage department of approximately 7 per cent, compared to the rooms department of 13 per cent.

Alternatives to the direct management of a hotel's food and beverage outlets include the following outsourcing options:

1 *Lease or rental agreements*. A third party operates a catering outlet for example a restaurant or bar, paying either a fixed fee or a percentage of income, share of profit, etc. to the hotel. A specific rental agreement may be made for a particular restaurant, or lease arrangements made for a number of the hotel's catering outlets. Examples include 'The Restaurant', Hyde Park Hotel, operated by Marco Pierre White and 'Trader Vics', Hilton Park Lane, operated by Trader Vics.

2 *Contracting out*. This is very similar to a lease arrangement although the third party may operate more than one of the hotel's food and beverage catering outlets including staff feeding. Again a fixed rental fee may be charged by the hotel or a percentage of food and beverage turnover or profit, or a combination of charges agreed. Examples of contracted out food and beverage services include T.G.I. Friday's operated by Carlson Restaurant Brands Worldwide and Beefeater Restaurants operated by Whitbread Inns in Travel Inns throughout the UK.

3 *Franchising*. Hotels operate a restaurant or bar under a franchise agreement, the franchise fee being upwards of 5 per cent of the outlet's turnover. The franchiser My Kinda Town has its brand Henry J. Bean's in a number of hotels around the world including Stakis Hotel, York and the Amari Hotel, Bangkok. Under a franchise agreement the hotel itself becomes responsible for the day-to-day operation and management of the restaurant which is significantly different to a third party employing their own staff and operating the outlet. Careful consideration must therefore be given by the hotel management in terms of integrating a franchised unit into the existing hotel structure, both in physical terms – is it compatible with, or does it enhance the hotel's desired image? – and in human resource terms – the type of catering personnel employed in a franchised outlet; for example, employees in T.G.I. Friday's would be different from the staff employed in the hotel's à la carte restaurant and salaries may also be significantly different.

Where two strongly branded concepts have come together in a joint venture, considerable success has been achieved; by taking a branded concept and introducing it to a hotel, both parties have benefited. Carlson Hospitality Worldwide for example are introducing a scaled down version of the T.G.I. concept into their hotels. Called 'right sizing' the core concept remains the same and becomes a brand extension, in this instance called a 'Friday's American Bar' which can be installed into smaller venues and establishments. Choice Hotels International in the USA are now introducing a food court concept called 'Choice Picks' consisting of a number of modular branded outlets which can be put together in different ways depending on the location and the market.

This concept of a partnership between a branded restaurant concept and a hotel group is not dissimilar in principle to the partnership concept between school or hospital caterers and contractors and may well prove to be the better commercial alternative for both parties rather than a win or lose situation for either one.

18.4 References

Cracknell, H. L., Kaufmann, R. J. and Nobis, F. (1988). *Practical Professional Catering*. London: Macmillan.

Medlik, S. (1989). *The Business of Hotels*, 2nd edn. Oxford: Butterworth-Heinemann.

Pannell Kerr Forster Associates (1996). *Hotel food and beverage – for prestige or for profit?* PKF Worldwide.

19
Food and beverage management in function catering

19.1 Introduction

Function catering may be described as the service of food and beverages at a specific time and place, to a given number of people, to an agreed menu and price. This form of catering may also be described as banqueting, although the term function catering is generally regarded as the wider terminology as not all functions may be called banquets. Examples of function catering include social functions, such as wedding buffets and dinner dances, business functions such as conference meetings and working lunches, and those functions that are organized for both social and business reasons such as outdoor catering at a show or exhibition.

The variety of function events ranges from providing a bar in a reception area where delegates for a conference are able to assemble before their meeting, to large formal banquets of over 1000 where six to eight-course meals are served. Function events also range from those that are very informal (for example, a children's birthday party, a retirement party) to those that are very formal (for example, masonic dinner, livery dinner, lunch or dinner of a professional body, etc.). Function catering may be the *raison d'être* of an establishment, that is a specialist function organization; it may be quite divorced from the establishment's main function, such as a hospital or factory; or the function facilities may be one of a number of catering services offered by an establishment, for example a hotel. In the latter case the type and variety of the function facilities will depend largely on the size of the hotel. Small hotels of up to thirty bedrooms, for example, may be able to provide small rooms capable of catering for a limited number of guests, or it

may not be able to offer any facilities at all. Medium-sized hotels of up to 100 bedrooms may have several function rooms and suites which in total can accommodate several hundred guests. In the large hotels of over 300 bedrooms the greatest variety of function facilities is usually available which are often able to cater for several hundreds of guests in many of its function rooms. The type of function facilities found in an establishment will also depend on the level of market for which it is catering. A luxury hotel situated in a major city, for example, will offer a wider range of function facilities than a small hotel situated in a local town; in the latter example there is unlikely to be the same level of demand from the surrounding population as there would be for function facilities in a large city.

Function catering is found in the commercial and non-commercial sectors of the catering industry, and in both of these sectors the nature of function facilities available will vary considerably from one establishment to another. In the commercial sector only a small percentage of function catering is of a truly high class *haute cuisine* nature, and where it is found is usually associated with those operations offering a similar standard in all aspects of the establishment, such as luxury hotels; the high standards offered by these types of function establishments and their associated price structure, inevitably limits the market to which they can cater. The largest market for function catering is usually associated with the middle range establishments, both in terms of price and standards of facilities offered; such establishments would include medium-sized hotels, the function rooms of public houses and department stores, independent restaurants, etc. At the lower price range of the function market, limited catering facilities would be available offering a similarly limited variety of functions.

In the non-commercial sector function catering is rarely the primary reason for providing the establishment with catering facilities. Such establishments include hospitals, schools, industrial cafeterias, etc. where the functions are not usually organized on a purely profit basis as they are in the commercial sector, but rather to serve a specific need of the organization. In the non-commercial sector functions are sometimes organized as a service or goodwill gesture to promote the social and welfare activities of a company or institution, such as retirement presentations, anniversary parties, school balls, etc. With these types of functions only a small percentage of the total cost of the event may be passed on to the guests. This should not imply that cost limits are not applied to these types of functions, merely that they are usually only truly costed if, for example, the facilities are being hired to customers outside the organization, or if profit-making is the specific purpose of the function, such as in a fund raising event.

There are those types of functions that are not easily assigned to either of the above sectors and may therefore be described as belonging to the semi-commercial sector. In this sector of the function market the majority of events are organized on a non-profit basis; however, there are exceptions to this general rule and functions may be required to meet a predetermined profit level, for example, university catering. For most of the year functions held at universities are mainly organized on a non-profit basis; such events include student and staff socials, inauguration lectures, degree ceremonies, etc. During the vacation period, however, other types of functions may be organized by the university catering department and these would be costed on a profit basis. These types of functions are usually arranged in conjunction with the other services provided by the establishment; for example, an increasing number of university establishments are now offering conference 'packages' in which business organizations may hire lecture theatres, accommodation, and catering facilities as a total product, all within the university confines. For these types of events the university caterer would be expected to cost

fully the catering component of these packages.

The typical hotel function or banqueting 'season' runs between the months of October and May with the busiest months being December and January. For the rest of the year some of the facilities may be used for providing separate restaurant facilities for tour groups who normally have limited time available for meals and whom the hotel may wish to keep apart from the normal day-to-day restaurant business. The function facilities may also frequently be let on a day or half day basis for such occasions as antique shows, trade exhibitions, fashion shows, etc. where the requirement of food and beverages may be very limited.

This function season is more noticeable in certain types of establishments, particularly those organizations whose sole purpose is function catering, and those that offer purpose built facilities such as hotels. In other establishments such as public houses, department store restaurants, industrial cafeterias, etc., the function season is not so evident, as existing dining facilities are usually adapted for function events rather than specific facilities being available; however, even these types of operations are still likely to experience peak periods during the year when the function facilities are in greater demand than at other times. This characteristic fluctuating of demand associated with function catering has implications for such establishments' basic policy decisions, and these are discussed below.

19.2 Basic policies – financial, marketing and catering

Policy decisions relating to function catering are largely determined by a number of characteristics inherent in this type of catering. The first is the season. Usually, the hotel banqueting season extends from October to May, a peak business trading period of eight months. The second is the concentration of events during these months, which are mainly at weekends, particularly Friday and Saturday events, during which time an operation must seek to maximize its sales potential. Third, a considerable amount of information is available to the caterer in advance of the organized functions; this includes the number of guests to be catered for and for which

From the Director General

1997 INSTITUTE OF DIRECTORS ANNUAL CONVENTION

LUNCH BOX MENU

Field Mushroom and Pesto Tart with Tomato and Asparagus Salsa
✱✱✱
Grilled Salmon Bois Boudran
Grilled Mediterranean Vegetable Salad
Minted Cous Cous

Roll and Butter
✱✱✱
Mandarin Gateau with Apricot Coulis

VEGETARIAN LUNCH BOX MENU

Roast Asparagus, Leek and Plum Tomato Salad with Balsamic Dressing
✱✱✱

Field Mushroom and Pesto Tart with Mesculum Salad
Grilled Mediterranean Vegetable Salad
Minted Cous Cous

Roll and Butter
✱✱✱
Mandarin Gateau with Apricot Coulis

Figure 19.1 *The Lunch Box menu, served to 2400 delegates at the Royal Albert Hall by Letheby and Christopher*

BUFFET LUNCHEON MENU 1

A plated first course of:

Layered terrine of vegetables & cheese
with arugula salad

SALAD BUFFET

Oriental style seafood salad
Chicken tandoori & penne
Potato, dill & cucumber salad
Mediterranean vegetable salad

PRESENTED ON SILVER CHAFFING DISHES

Peppered beef with soya beans & Thai basil
Salmon ravioli with lemongrass & kafir
Fried rice with baby prawns & garden peas

DESSERTS

Baked apple & sultana cheesecake
Assorted miniature French pastries
Fresh seasonal fruit salad
Filter coffee

The above menu is priced at £44.00 per person

BUFFET LUNCHEON MENU 2

A plated first course of:

Terrine of grilled salmon,
three tomatoes & shrimp salad

SALAD BUFFET

Grilled & marinated vegetables
Landmark Caesar salad
Curried rice salad with pineapple
Farfalle with tomatoes, basil & ham
Spicy beef salad with sesame seeds

PRESENTED ON SILVER CHAFFING DISHES

Fillet of brill with herb crust, spinach & new potatoes
Ragout of chicken with button mushrooms,
pearl onions and red wine sauce
Lentil & potato samosa's scented with
turmeric & cummin

DESSERTS

Seasonal fruit tranche
Individual sherry trifle
Frangipane tart
Filter coffee

Figure 19.2 *Two buffet luncheon menus from the Landmark Hotel, London*

meal periods, for example lunch or dinner; their time of arrival and departure; the menu they are to be given; and the price being paid per guest. This large amount of pre-event information enables the organization of functions to be pre-planned to considerable detail, including the profit levels to be achieved. This in turn aids in the control of functions as the standards set before the event may be used as yardsticks against which the performance of a function may be measured.

The basic policies relating to function catering are usually quite specific to this form of catering. If function trade is an establishment's only source of business then the policies laid down will only relate to this type of trade. In other establishments, however, such as hotels, the function facilities may be one of a number of catering outlets, although even in these organizations the banqueting department will often have policy decisions relating specifically to this department.

19.2 .1 Financial considerations

Function catering is most commonly associated with the commercially orientated sector of the catering industry and this is reflected in the financial policies of function catering establishments, which are mainly profit-orientated. Such aspects as the gross profit levels to be achieved would be contained in the financial policies. Generally speaking the gross profit percentage achieved in function catering is higher than that achieved by other catering outlets, such as coffee shops or haute cuisine restaurants. In function catering a gross profit percentage of between 65 and 75 per cent may be required depending on the type of establishment, the average spending

BUFFET DINNER MENU A

(Minimum numbers 50 guests)

Appetizers

Terrine of Provençale vegetables with pesto

Cutlets of salmon, dill & vegetable vinaigrette

Plum tomatoes with bocconcini cheese & balsamico

Rillettes of duck with pickled vegetables

Soup

Soup of the day or clients choice

Salads

Chefs selection of three salads with mesculin
leaves & dressings

Main Courses

Oriental beef with water chestnuts & cashews

Seafood fricassee with potato scales

Aubergine Charlotte, pimento vinaigrette

Shrimp fried rice & vegetable ragout

Desserts

Fruit puddings with berry coulis

Whisky trifle

Baked apple & sultana cheesecake

Cheese

Selection of English country cheeses
with walnut bread & biscuits

Filter coffee

The above menu is priced at £47.00 per person

SERVICE AND TAX INCLUDED

1/97

BUFFET DINNER MENU B

(Minimum numbers 50 guests)

COLD BUFFET

Combination of three marinated Scottish salmons
Rollmop herrings & prawns
Smoked trout fillets
Rare Angus beef with horseradish
Supreme of chicken jardiniere
Honey glazed loin of ham with asparagus
Continental charcuterie & sausages

SALADS

Flaked salmon with fine beans & cos lettuce
Bang Bang chicken
Bow type pasta with pesto dressing
Beef tomato with bocconcini
Artichoke & marinated peppers
Salad of mesculin leaves and dressings

HOT BUFFET

Fricassee of monkfish, woodland mushroom risotto
Blackened beef with Oriental stir fry
Dartois of corn fed chicken truffle sauce

DDESSERTS

Summer pudding with Drambuie cream
Mirror of individual desserts
Seasonal berries & fruits with zabaglione
Baked apple & & sultana cheesecake

Cheese

A fine selection of British & Continental cheeses
with deli style breads, celery & grapes

Filter coffee & petits fours

The above menu is priced at £49.95 per person

1/97

SERVICE AND TAX INCLUDED

Figure 19.3 *Two examples from the banqueting buffet dinner menu suggestions from the Landmark Hotel, London*

power of customers, the standard of food and beverages and the level of service offered, etc.

The average spending power of guests for different types of functions can, in the majority of cases, be calculated in advance. The ASP will comprise the cost of the meal and may often include beverages served during the function as well as a proportion of the cost for the provision of printed menus, place names, flowers, a toastmaster, band, etc. Items that may not be included in the cost of the event may be the pre-dinner drinks which can be purchased at the bar before the meal, and after-dinner drinks such as liqueurs and cigars.

The financial policy will also determine the pricing structures for the different types of functions offered by the establishment. For example, the operation may not make a separate charge for the hire of the function room or banqueting suite, but include this in a set price per head for the meal. Other establishments may have a set

price per guest and, in addition, make a separate charge for the hire of the room. Where a guest wishes to hire a function room and does not require any other services of the establishment, the client would be charged for the room hire; if, however, a customer requests a bar to be available in the room, or purchases some other service from the organization, the policy decision may be not to charge for the hire of the room. A flexible pricing policy is advocated in order to maintain a competitive edge and to obtain a high level of business throughout the year.

The pricing structure for an establishment's function catering facilities will be largely determined by its cost structure, with particular reference to its fixed and variable costs. This is most in evidence in the non-commercial sector where functions may not be fully costed, that is not taking into account the fixed costs of the operation. Where the costing of function menus is based mainly on covering food and labour costs, it is important to remember that both of these increase with the size and quality of function offered. However, due to the volume of sales the food and labour costs as a percentage of actual sales will slightly decrease; it is necessary therefore to not only consider the food costs per function but also the potential benefits to be gained from a reduction in labour costs. There are a variety of pricing structures that may be used for costing functions, the adoption of any one being determined by such factors as the type of organization, the standards of food and beverage service to be offered, and the cost structure of the establishment.

19.2.2 Marketing considerations

The marketing policy of a function establishment will determine the different markets at which the facilities may be aimed, and how best to market any special characteristics of the establishment. For example, if the operation is situated in a city centre it may be marketed as being in close proximity to surrounding business firms and commerce. Alternatively, the function facilities may be situated outside a busy city or in a resort town and the operation may then be marketed making a particular feature of this. Different selling techniques will also be used for the various markets being catered for. For example, to sell the facilities to the business market direct mail shots may be used which are sent to specific firms and companies. To reach the non-business market, however, catering for weddings, birthdays, etc. local newspaper advertising may be used.

By marketing an establishment's function facilities the other services offered by the same establishment may also benefit from an increase in trade. In hotels, for example, function catering can be a very profitable aspect of the establishment as it may not only generate business for the banqueting department, but also for the hotel's other departments such as rooms and catering; reduced room rates and meal discounts are often offered to those guests attending a function at a hotel. Conversely, the other services of the establishment may help to market its function facilities. For example, if a hotel is aiming specifically at the business sector, this market may be encouraged to use a particular hotel if it is offered other facilities that would interest its employees or guests such as a swimming pool, squash courts, etc.

An organization offering function facilities may either be catering to a resident or a non resident market. The resident market would consist of those guests who are staying at the establishment, such as at a hotel for a conference and are usually on demi-pension or en pension terms. The non-resident market would consist of those guests coming to the establishment for a specific function, for example a wedding reception but not requiring overnight accommodation.

A marketing policy should also contain details relating to an establishment's competitors and recommend a periodic review of other function facilities to keep abreast of current developments and trends. In the same way as a potential restaurant customer may study the menus and price lists of a number of restaurants before deciding on a particular one in which to have a meal, the organizer of a function is likely to visit a number of establishments and obtain quotations before making a firm function booking. Such quotations are usually very similar in terms of price, the main differences being in the additional services each operation can offer. Thus if function managers are to obtain function trade it is important for them to be aware of the types of services other function establishments can offer so that they can attempt to give 'added value' and be more competitive. This involves careful consideration of the customer's needs and matching the facilities of the establishment to best serve the client.

In the marketing of an operation's function facilities the function manager or secretary should be aware of who the 'buying agent' is for the particular organization being contacted. For example, it may be the general manager's secretary who is responsible for booking a firm's functions, or if the organization is sufficiently large it may have its own specialized department to deal with this so that the caterer may contact this department directly. The organizer of the function will at some stage wish to see the facilities to be hired and it is important that the first impressions are favourable ones. The function manager should therefore try and ensure that the organizer of the function sees the room

POINTER HOTELS (UK) LTD
General terms and conditions: functions

1 If the hotel is prevented from performing its obligations in respect of any booking for any cause outside of its control, it shall be entitled to cancel any such booking without liability but, if so requested, the hotel will use reasonable endeavours to transfer the booking to another of the hotel's establishments satisfactory to the client.

2 In the event of cancellation of any booking by a client, the client shall pay to the hotel a cancellation fee for each day (or part of a day) and for each suite or room in respect of which the booking was made, calculated at the room hire rate appertaining at the time of cancellation, provided always that the amount of cancellation fees payable may be waived or reduced by the hotel in respect of the same period or part of a period, such waiver or the amount of any reduction to be at the sole discretion of the hotel.

3 The hotel reserves the right to require payment of a deposit at any time prior to the holding of a function, the amount of which will be determined by the hotel. Should the customer fail to pay such deposit within seven days of being requested to do so, the hotel may treat the booking as having been cancelled by the client.

4 Final numbers attending functions should be notified to the function office twenty-four hours prior to the commencement of a function. This number will be the minimum figure charged.

5 Accounts for all functions must be paid within seven days of the receipt of the account.

6 The hotel accepts no responsibility for loss or damage to any item of equipment, furniture, stock or any other property brought on to the premises by the client or persons authorized by the client.

7 The hotel shall make no alteration of any sort to the accommodation and shall, at his own expense, make good any and all damage arising in any way from this hiring whether damage is to the suite or room or to the hotel, however such damage be caused and by whosoever it is caused.

8 The client shall be responsible for the orderly conduct of the function and shall ensure that nothing shall be done which will constitute a breach of the law or in any way cause a nuisance or be an infringement of or occasion or render possible a forfeiture or endorsement of the licences for the sale of wine, beer, spirits or for music and dancing. In particular, the client shall ensure that there is no illegal betting or gaming.

9 The hotel reserves the right to approve any person engaged by the client to perform any duty of any sort or to entertain at the function, such approval not to be unreasonably withheld.

10 No food, wine, beer or spirits may be brought into the hotel by the customer or the customer's guests for consumption on the premises, unless the prior consent of the hotel has been obtained and, if the hotel so requires, an additional charge paid.

11 All meetings must terminate within thirty minutes of the finishing time stipulated in any booking.

12 The correspondence between the hotel and client shall be taken as confirmation of the customer's agreement with and acceptance of the foregoing terms and conditions. An exchange of letters constitutes a contract.

Figure 19.4 *An example of the general terms and conditions required by hotels for clients using the hotel's function facilities*

being considered for hire, arranged and laid out for a function. In this way the client is able to gain an appreciation of the function room in terms of décor, layout, standard of service accompaniments, etc., which are all sales tools in helping to create a favourable impression to the organization's advantage, and hence aid in selling the function facilities.

A marketing plan (that is, the interpretation of the marketing policy into a plan of action for a specific period, for example one year, five years) for a large city hotel could include such headings as:

1 *Finance* – this would give the targets of turnover and profits set for the period.
2 *Productivity* – this would set the targets of productivity and performance by the sales staff.
3 *Promotions*
   (a) *General* – this may state to increase business in all established areas by, for example, 10 per cent. The plan also details how this is to be achieved.

DECORATED BUFFET

MENU ARRAN

Chilled and Dressed Lobster Mayonnaise
Caledonian Smoked Salmon and Cream Cheese
Baskets of Seasonal Melon filled with fresh Berries
Barbary Duck and Foie Gras Terrine stuffed with preserved Walnuts

*

Whole decorated Scottish Salmon
served with Lemon Mayonnaise and poached Asparagus
Honey Roasted and decorated Gammon
served with Cranberries and Pineapple Chutney
Roast Barron of Angus Beef carved on and off the bone
served with Horseradish Mousse
Galantine of Orange glazed Turkey stuffed with Vegetables and Sage

*

Celeriac Swiss Cheese and Apple Salad
Cherry Tomato and Pinenut Salad dressed with Basil
Cucumber and Dill Salad marinated in Yoghurt and Garlic
Potato, Ham and Shallot Salad with Chives
Asparagus and young Sweetcorn Salad dressed with Olive Oil
Radichio Salad
Cos Lettuce Salad
Crisp Iceberg
Oak Leaf and Lollorosso Salad

*

Steamed New Potatoes with Mint
Buttered Baby Barrelled Vegetables
Scottish Salmon Koulibiac served with Lobster Butter Sauce
Roast Sirloin of Angus Beef served with Traditional Roast Gravy

*

Caledonian Hotel Grand Chocolate Torte
Traditional Croquem Bouche with Caramel and Dipped Fruits
Fresh and Preserved Fruits flavoured with Alcohol and Syrup
Selection of Pompadour Charlottes and Pastries
Specially Selected French and Local Scottish Cheese
displayed with Fresh Fruit and Home Baked Bread

*

Coffee

£48.00

This menu is available for 50 or more guests
a supplement may be required for less.

One ice carving is also displayed on this buffet.
The purchase of additional ice carvings are available on request.

This menu is a full traditional decorated display buffet
with all reasonable refinements.

Figure 19.5   *A decorated buffet menu from the Caledonian Hotel, Edinburgh*

(b) *Special* – this may state the specific forms of promotion to be undertaken this period, for example aimed at the local ethnic community, aimed at local/national sporting clubs, etc.

(c) *Facilities* – this may be aimed at marketing certain facilities which are new, or have been recently refurbished or which in the past period have had a low occupancy record.

(d) *Development* – this may be the development and promotion of a new package plan, for example a new package for business meeting rooms together with special rate meals; or bargain break weekends for guests attending a function in the hotel over a weekend period.

4 *Research* – this could be the collection, analysis and evaluation of data relevant to competitors' business.

The advertising of an establishment's function facilities may either be specifically concerned with this form of catering or it may be in conjunction with the advertising of the establishment's other amenities, such as in a hotel. The organization should ideally utilize a variety of sales tools to promote its facilities, for example brochures, photos and slides of different function arrangements, and layouts for different occasions. Good visual presentation is particularly important in the advertising of function facilities; functions are usually organized for a specific occasion, whether it be a product launch, a business convention or a twenty-first birthday celebration, and the organizer is therefore keen to make it a memorable event and will be impressed by effective visual presentation of the function facilities and by receiving personalized attention and service.

Sample function menus produced by an establishment need to be of a good quality and appearance as the customer will often wish to take them away to study before deciding on the function menu. These sales tools should also be of a standard consistent with the level of operation and the type of image it is trying to project. Function 'folders' containing details of all the different facilities offered by an establishment are often produced by organizations which may be distributed to prospective clients advertising

the establishment's function facilities.

A function 'folder' often colour-coded for easy reference by the client, would most likely be composed of the following:

1 An envelope type folder with the company's logo, title and address clearly displayed.
2 A personal letter from the function/banqueting manager to the client.
3 A list of function rooms together with details of the numbers that could be accommodated for different types of functions, for example a formal lunch or dinner, a dinner dance, a buffet type reception, a theatre-style conference/meeting, etc.
4 Plans of the room with basic dimensions, position of power points, telephone points, ceiling heights, etc.
5 Sample menus for lunch, dinner, buffets, meetings etc.
6 Details of audio-visual equipment available for meetings, for example lecterns, microphones, overhead projectors, screens, etc.
7 Details of accommodation facilities available, often at special rates for guests attending a function/meeting.
8 Coloured postcards of the hotel/function rooms.
9 Relevant simple maps and parking arrangements where necessary.

19.2.3 Catering considerations

Based on the guidelines laid down in the financial and marketing policies, the different types of menus to be offered by a function organization would be contained in the establishment's catering policy. Suggested function menus and 'packages' are often compiled by establishments which can be sent to prospective clients. These set menus will usually achieve a pre-determined gross profit percentage and therefore any alterations to such menus, such as to accommodate specific customer requirements, must be carefully considered so as to ensure the required gross profit percentage is maintained. The price structure of such menus is based on a number of factors relating specifically to food and beverages, such as the type and quality of food to be offered, the percentage of convenience foods to

Whether it's a Dinner Dance, a Banquet, a Cocktail Party, or a Wedding Reception, you couldn't be better placed.

Our banqueting suites, the Shannon and the Liffey, are tastefully decorated in pastel shades of pink and grey. Each suite can be made into smaller replicas of itself, by means of a system of sliding soundproofed panels, so providing an ideal setting for your function no matter how large or small. "Flexibility" is our formula for success.

A highly sophisticated lighting system has been installed to allow for every alternative in both mood and atmosphere at the touch of a button.

The Shannon and the Liffey have their own portable dance floors, tailor-made to suit your needs.

We offer an extensive range of menus from which to choose – finger buffet through to gala dinner. However, we relish a challenge to create any menu you may wish.

There are many services that we can supply – toastmasters, bands, entertainers, guest speakers, floral arrangements, individual gifts and many, many more – let us arrange this for you.

Professional planning and management, excellent cuisine and service, attention to every detail until the last guest leaves – this is your guarantee of success.

To ensure this, we will assign a member of our Banqueting Team to you from your first enquiry, through the planning stage, and during the function itself.

BANQUETING SUITES MAXIMUM CAPACITY

	LIFFEY SUITE (3 sections)			
		1	2	3
DINNER	240	80	80	80
DINNER/DANCE	180			
BUFFET (SIT DOWN)	180	60	60	60
BUFFET (FORK)	360	100	100	100
BUFFET (FINGER)	400	120	120	120
COCKTAIL PARTY	450	120	120	120

	SHANNON SUITE (3 sections)			
		1	2	3
DINNER	300	100	100	100
DINNER/DANCE	270			
BUFFET (SIT DOWN)	250	80	80	80
BUFFET (FORK)	500	150	150	150
BUFFET (FINGER)	600	170	170	170
COCKTAIL PARTY	650	200	200	200

Figure 19.6   *An extract from the publicity material available for client functions*
Source: The London Tara Hotel

be used, whether a free drink is to be included in the price, etc., in addition to such factors as the method of service, standard of décor and so on.

The catering policy would also stipulate such aspects of the operation as the trading hours of the function establishment, or if it is an industrial cafeteria, for example, the periods during the week that the restaurant would be available for function use. With reference to trading hours, many operations limit themselves by only offering their facilities for lunch and dinner periods, with the result that for the rest of the day the function facilities are not used. The operation's trading hours may be substantially increased, however, by utilizing the other periods of the day and thus achieve a higher sales revenue per trading day. Other types of functions that may be considered include morning coffee meetings, afternoon teas, after theatre meals and so on.

The establishment should not only consider increasing its daily trading hours, but also its business at specific times during the week. For example, it may offer a reduction in the cost of functions held on week days as compared with the same type of events being organized at weekends. In the lower price level operations the demand for functions is more elastic; that is, a change in the cost of a function is likely to affect the demand for this catering service. At this level of operation therefore the marketing of the establishment's function facilities at a cheaper rate during the week may prove to be successful. However, at the higher price level of the market the demand is relatively inelastic, that is a substantial change in the cost of the function will not necessarily result in a correspondingly large change in demand. At this level of operation therefore the offering of a cheaper weekday rate may not be particularly attractive and the establishment must look to other aspects of the operation such as the standard of food and beverages and service or special facilities to try and increase its sales.

Purpose-built function establishments or those operations offering function facilities are thus able to utilize their facilities for considerably longer trading periods than are other types of catering outlets, for example restaurants. They are often able to cater for more diverse markets as the problem of mixed markets is not so common in this type of catering. This is mainly due to functions being specific events for specific groups of people, as compared with other types of catering outlets, such as restaurants, which may be catering for a variety of customers during any one trading period. Exceptions to this general rule are those functions at which different groups of people hire individual tables at a dinner dance evening, for example Christmas and New Year's Eve dinner dances. At these types of events there may be ten or fifteen independent parties of guests at the same functions, all celebrating different occasions, such as twenty-first birthdays, anniversaries, etc. However, these types of functions are not as common as those events organized for a specific group of people for a specific event, where a banqueting suite or function room is hired solely for their use.

As the price level of functions increases, so the food and beverage products being offered become more sophisticated. In the high ASP functions of £40–50 per head the meal may consist of six or eight courses with a selection of wines to accompany the different foods; after-dinner liqueurs may also be included in this price. In the lower ASP operations of between £15–25 per head, the function meal may consist of three or four courses and at this price level one set wine may only be served throughout the meal.

At the majority of functions the beverages to accompany the guests' meal are chosen in advance, often by the host. The beverage list, like the menus being offered, generally increases in variety with the price level of the function, particularly with reference to the choice of wines. Generally speaking, however, the function wine list should be relatively limited, concentrating mainly on good quality wines for the prices charged by the establishment, and for which supply is consistent. It is not unusual to include in the list the house wines of the establishment and to have them specially labelled. If a bar is set up for a function the beverage list should again concentrate on the most popular pre- and after-dinner drinks and liqueurs, rather than hold an extensive stock for which there may be little demand. Here again it is common practice for the house brands to be included in the list.

Additionally, it is not uncommon for the client to request a wine or liqueur that is not held in stock; special requests of this nature being part of the service to the client. If, however, customers wish to supply some or all of their alcoholic beverages, such as wines and liquor, then a decision has to be made as to whether to allow this or not, and if so what 'corkage' charge is to be made. Decisions of this nature depend very much on the total value of the individual function.

For those purpose-built establishments such as conference buildings and halls, function events are the only products to be offered by these operations. In other establishments, such as industrial catering situations, the ability to offer function catering is an additional service the catering department may be able to make available. In this way the organization is able to utilize more efficiently facilities which may otherwise be left unused during certain periods of the day or week. Function events also enable an establishment to make special presentations of food and beverages that are different from the standard menus usually offered; for example, special menus being provided for Christmas Day meals, anniversaries, etc. In hotels which offer table d'hôte and à la carte menus, functions may again enable production staff to display their skills and experiment with new dishes.

The life cycle of function facilities may range from five to ten years, usually depending on the standard of décor and furnishings at the end of this period. Generally speaking, few function facilities are designed on the basis of a gimmick or special feature because of the comparatively limited life cycle of such decor. Function rooms and suites are more usually designed and furnished to basic standards which can then be adapted as appropriate for different functions to achieve a desired atmosphere or effect.

19.2.3.1   Type of customer

Guests attending a function are usually there for a specific occasion – a business luncheon, a dinner dance, a wedding reception or whatever. In this respect function guests differ from customers frequenting other catering facilities, such as restaurants, who may not be eating out for a specific occasion but perhaps to only fulfil some more basic need. Where the function is of a social nature, for example a dinner dance, the meal

experience of the guest is an important and integral part of the function. At those functions organized for non-social or business occasions, it may be suggested that the actual meal experience of the guests does not feature so prominently because it is not the primary reason for the function event. The meals provided for delegates at a conference for example, should be of such a nature that they can be consumed in the limited time usually available so that the delegates may return to the day's business fairly quickly. Where the function is of a mainly celebratory nature, however, more creative food and beverages may be offered as there is usually more time available both to the caterer to serve the meal and to the customer to appreciate it.

At any one function there may be a variety of customers in terms of sex, age, socio-economic grouping and so on. At a conference lunch of several hundred guests for example, there may be a spectrum of customer profiles ranging from the more senior to the junior delegates. At a company Christmas social there may again be a similar mixture of management and staff personnel. Indeed, the only common factor to all the guests at a function may be the purpose of the function; this in turn usually helps to alleviate the problem of mixed markets to which the establishment may be catering at any one event.

In function catering, as indeed with other forms of catering, it is important for the establishment to not only be able to identify its customers, but also its non-customers. In the marketing of function facilities an operation can afford to be more flexible than other types of catering outlets can. It is able to do this by identifying a range of market levels to which it may cater and then offering a corresponding variety of products in terms of price, standard of food and service, to these different market levels.

The average spending power of customers at a function will depend mainly on the nature of the event. The cost of the function per head will have been decided upon in advance by the function organizer in conjunction with the caterer. At some functions this cost may not only include the meal itself, but also pre-dinner drinks, after-dinner liqueurs, coffees, etc.; examples of functions organized on this basis include conference lunches and dinners and wedding receptions. At functions such as dinner dances, however, a con-

SCOTTISH MENU

Reekit saumon wi' a hairst o' ither wat'ry beesties
(Smoked Tay Salmon with Prawns)

* * *

Cock-a-Leekie

* * *

"Chieftain o'the Pudding Race" haggis, neeps and tatties
an a nippie tae helpit a' slide ower
(Haggis, Bashed Neeps and Tatties
served with a small Whisky)

* * *

Ane or twa bitties of roastit Aiberdeen Angus
(Roast Sirloin of Aberdeen Angus
with a Brew Wine Sauce)

A pucklie o'bil't vegies, an ane or twa chappit mealiie tatties
(Seasonal Fresh Vegetables
Braised Ayrshire Potatoes)

* * *

Cranachan wi'freet an' Atholl sals
(Caledonian Cranachan
with Blackcurrant Sauce)

* * *

A tassie o' black bean bree wi' ane or twa sweeties
(Coffee and Whisky Truffles)

£45.00

VEGETARIAN OPTION

STARTERS

Galia Melon with Champagne Sorbet and Mint Syrup

Plum Tomato and Rosemary Soup
scented with Garlic and finished with Double Cream

Avocado Pear, baked with Basil Butter
filled with a hot Vegetable Salsa

Salad of crisp Iceberg Lettuce
with a sweet Mustard Dressing,
crisp Croutons and shaved Parmesan

MAIN COURSES

Broccoli and Wild Mushroom Strudel
served with a Bell Pepper and Vodka Sauce

Vegetable Bake
(seasonal baby Vegetables
bound in a Herb and Garlic Custard
served with Tomato Fondue)

Brochette of marinated Provencale Vegetables
served with Butter Tagliatelle
and hot Garlic Vinaigrette

Puff Pastry Feuillete of Asparagus and Woodland Mushrooms
bound in Tarragon Cream Sauce.

One starter and one main course
to be chosen for a group of vegetarians

Figure 19.7   *An example of a Scottish dinner menu, with the vegetarian option, from the Caledonian Hotel, Edinburgh*

siderable amount may be spent by the guests at the function in addition to paying the set price per head. Where it is likely that the customers will purchase additional beverages, cigars, etc. the prices charged by the establishment should be carefully calculated so as not to be prohibitive to the type of customers attending the function and the price range they are able to afford. This is particularly important to take into account at those events catering for a variety of market levels and their respective customer profiles and range of spending power, at the same function.

It has already been suggested that a function may be catering for either a resident or a non resident market. In some operations the resident market may be said to be captive. A day's business meeting organized at a conference centre, for example, would usually include morning coffee, luncheon, afternoon tea and perhaps an

evening meal in its programme. These meal periods would be arranged for specific times during the day so that the main purpose of the conference may be apportioned as much time as possible; for example, the delegates may be allocated one hour for lunch during which time they would be expected to consume their meal and return to the day's meeting.

Unlike the customers frequenting other types of catering facilities such as restaurants where there may be a high percentage of chance trade, function trade is almost entirely booked well in advance. Indeed, for many functions the guests may know in advance what their meal is going to consist of. The few exceptions to this general rule of booking functions in advance are usually found where there is a resident market, for example in hotels. Guests staying at a hotel may either be attending a conference at the hotel or

FORK BUFFET MENU FIVE

Honeydew Melon with Mango Puree and Seasonal Fruits
Tomato and Basil Soup with Gruyere Cheese

***

Honey Roast Ham with glazed Pineapple
Smoked Trout Fillets with Creamed Horseradish
Caledonian Sausages with Onion Gravy and Creamed Potatoes

Tomato and Chive Salad
Pasta Salad
Green Salad
Coleslaw
Salad Leaves

***

Chef's choice of Gateau
Selection of Cheese decorated with fresh fruit

***

Coffee

£21.00

FORK BUFFET MENU SIX

Chicken Liver Pate with Oatcakes
Leek and Potato Potage with Chicken and Chives

***

Danish Salami with Pickled Vegetables
Marinated Seafood with Belgian Endive
Casserole of Beef and Smoked Bacon
flavoured with Thyme and Claret

Potato and Chive Salad
Tomato Salad
Cucumber Salad
Coleslaw
Tuna and Sweetcorn Salad

***

Chef's choice of Gateau
Selection of Cheese decorated with fresh fruit

***

Coffee

£21.00

Figure 19.8 *Examples of the fork buffet menus from the Caledonian Hotel, Edinburgh*

elsewhere, and decide to have a smaller meeting one evening at the hotel. Should a small private room be available the guests could use this room with little or no advance booking being made and this may then be termed 'chance' function trade.

It is also important to remember that many functions are of an annual type, for example a company's annual dinner dance, annual general meeting, annual sales conference, etc. The relevance here is to recognize that a lot of business may be potentially repeat business and therefore attention to detail at functions is of vital importance.

Furthermore, at many events there may be potential customers who may be considering the establishment for their own future function events, if particularly impressed by the organization and its catering facilities.

19.2.3.2 Type of product/menu

The type of menu offered by an establishment specializing in function catering will depend on a number of factors including the market level being aimed at and the pricing structure adopted. In some establishments a relatively narrow market may be catered for, while in others a wide range of menus may be offered for different levels of markets. In the industrial sector for example where large firms employ several thousand employees, a wide variety of function menus may be offered at the senior management level; for the majority of employees less varied three and four course set menus may be available at cheaper prices.

The different menus available will also depend on the nature of the function. At a wedding reception buffet for example, emphasis should be on providing an attractive display of food and beverages that are able to retain their appearance and quality throughout the reception. The menu offered at a sit-down conference luncheon, however, would be quite different as the food and beverages are fulfilling a different role. The type of menu offered may therefore vary according to whether it is of a purely functional nature, or whether it is to have a mainly entertainment value.

The menu being offered at a function is usually only one aspect of the total event. For example, at a product launch or business meeting the emphasis of the function may not be the provision of the meal itself, whereas at functions such as gourmet evenings where the event is arranged around the meal the purpose of the function may be said to be the food and beverages themselves.

Such aspects as service to the guests should not be neglected once the meal has been com-

SWINGING 50s HOGMANAY PARTY

Menu

Potted Hock
with toasted plain bread

*****

Oeuf Sur la Plat
Baked Eggs cooked with Smoked Haddock
and Arbroath Smokie Cream topped with
Hollandaise Sauce

*****

Haggis with Neeps and Tattie Bridie
finished with Whisky and Chive Sauce

*****

Braised stuffed Rump of Orkney Beef
finished with Claret Sauce, steamed Leek Dumpling
and braised Cabbage balls

*****

Strawberry Milk Shake Bavoise
with candied Fruit Tartlet and Marshmallow Sauce
finished with Candy Floss

*****

Coffee and Gob Stoppers

Dress – Lounge Suits or 50s
Cocktails at 7.30 pm
£65.00 - non residential
£130.00 - residential

The price indicated above is for one guest and includes Swinging 50s Dinner Dance, overnight accommodation (sharing a twin or double room) and full Scottish breakfast on New Year's Day 1997 and VAT.

NEW YEAR'S DAY BRUNCH

Wake up! - the party is not over, join us for a dazzling Jazz Brunch. We will keep you entertained with our Grand Finale to the celebrations.

Menu

Selected Juices Served on Ice
Honeydew Melon with Fresh Figs
Half Ogen Melon with Strawberries
Selection of Fresh Fruit and Berries
Preserved and Poached Fruit Compotes

*****

Oak Smoked Salmon and Chicken
Honey Cured Duck Breast
Smoked and Preserved Scottish Fish and Meats

*****

From the Baker
Fruit, Plain and Coconut Scones, Pancakes,
Danish Pastries, Croissants and Batch Rolls
A Selection of Continental Breads

*****

Scrambled Eggs and Smoked Salmon
Lyonnaise Potatoes
Sautéed Black Pudding with Apple
Grilled Tomatoes, Hash Browns
Bubble and Squeak
Grilled Lamb Chops, Grilled Bacon
Caledonian Bangers and Mash
Pan Fried Minute Steak
Cabbie-claw of Sole
Haggis with Neeps and Tatties
Steak and Mushroom Pie
Selection of Vegetables and Potatoes

*****

Sticky Toffee Pudding with Caramel Sauce
Fresh Fruit Salad, Caledonian Cloutie Dumpling
Whisky Trifle, Selection of Sorbets and Ice Creams

*****

Scottish and Continental Cheeses

£30.00 per guest
under 14 - £18.00
11.00 am - 3.00 pm
Live Jazz

Figure 19.9 *Examples of Hogmanay celebration menus from the Caledonian Hotel, Edinburgh*

pleted and attention must also be paid to the smaller aspects of the function such as the provision of place names, menus, seating plan, etc. for the guests. It must therefore be remembered that the customer is buying a total 'product' and not just one aspect of it.

Function menus may be compiled in a variety of ways. Perhaps the most common method is to offer set three and four course menus for a set price; the minimum number of courses is usually three plus coffee. Second, the caterer may list certain groups of items together and allow organizers of functions to decide their own menu, for example six or eight choices for each course –

appetizers, main dishes, vegetables, salads and sweets – may be offered from which organizers would compile the menu. All the menu course items offered would have the same approximate food cost, although for the higher cost items such as salmon, a small additional charge may be made if this was chosen as the main dish. Third, a similar list as before of available food items may be offered by the establishment although each item would be priced individually rather than grouped together according to price; the function organizer would again be responsible for compiling the menu from the à la carte selection. Finally, some operations do not require a set menu to be decided upon in advance but allow the guests on their arrival to choose their meal from a selection of menu items. As many as eight or ten choices of both appetizers and main dishes may be available for the guests to choose from; these are usually fairly standardized items that have been prepared in advance and only need to be reheated or garnished prior to service. In these operations the dessert course is usually a choice from the sweet trolley which is brought to the guest's table.

Whereas the menus offered by restaurants or other types of catering outlets may be altered quite regularly, for example every three or six months, the menus available for functions generally have a longer life cycle. This is mainly due to only a fairly limited amount of function trade being on a truly repeat basis and this does not therefore necessitate a short-term change of the establishment's menus. The major exception to this are those functions such as business lunches which may be organized by a local firm; with the majority of social functions, however, these are mainly 'one off' events organized once or twice a year.

19.2.3.3 *Food production styles*

The conventional method of food production is still the most widely used method in function catering; it is employed in the small establishments catering for fifty guests and the larger operations catering for over 500. Where the conventional method of food production is used the kitchen is divided into parties each producing specific items for the menu. If plated food service is being used the guests' meals are pre-plated in the kitchen and served directly to the table in the dining area. The silver service method is however more widely used in function catering; for this style of service the kitchen is required to arrange portions of food, usually of ten or twelve, on to platters and dishes which may then be taken to the guest's tables and served onto their plates. Each partie is therefore responsible for preparing certain food items which are assembled at the servery area before being taken by the food service staff.

Because function catering is based on a predicted number of meals to be served and the menu is known in advance, a considerable amount of pre-planning can be done by the kitchen prior to the function. This characteristic of function catering allows a number of other food production styles to be employed in function kitchens that are not always suitable for use in other catering situations. These other styles of food production include cook-chill, sous vide and cook-freeze and are methods that are being increasingly used by function kitchens. Where the cook-chill or sous-vide methods of food production are used all meals may be prepared in advance of demand and therefore production can be scheduled to gain the best use of equipment, space and running costs. There is virtually no menu limitation with this method, and where the kitchen is not purpose-built for cook-chill production it may be integrated into the existing system; it does not require heavy capital outlay and the food may be chilled on existing china used by the catering operation.

From a management point of view, however, the cook-chill and sous vide methods of food production must be more tightly controlled and supervised as a threat of possible bacteria contamination is more real than with other food production styles; also, due to the large numbers of guests usually being catered for at functions, it could be the source of a potentially large food poisoning outbreak. Special attention must therefore be given to the temperature of chilled food (between 0°C to 3°C) and to the general standards of hygiene in the production area.

Because of the large capital outlay required to operate a cook-freeze operation, it is a production method that is confined mainly to large groups and organizations that serve a number of

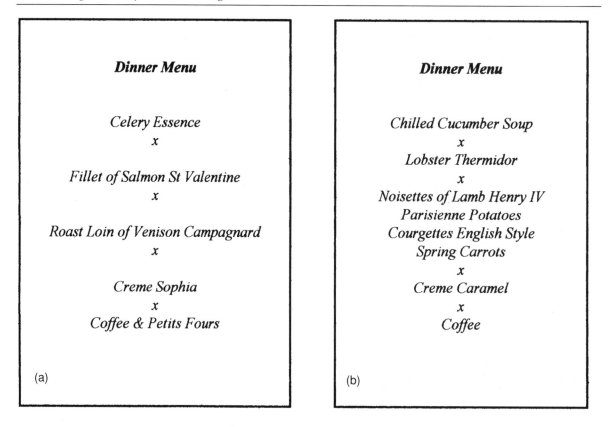

Figure 19.10   *Example of function dinner menus served by the Army Catering Corps. (a) To celebrate the 47th Annual Dinner for the ACC Officers' Dining Club at St Omer Barracks, Aldershot. (b) The final dinner menu served at an Officers' Mess of the British Army of the Rhine, West Germany, in the presence of Her Majesty the Queen, the Guest of Honour*

function establishments. The same advantages accrued to the cook-chill methods of food production may be applied to the use of cook-freeze for function catering; bacteriological hazards in particular are considerably reduced, the normal storage temperature for frozen foods being −18°C and below and at this temperature no microbiological growth can occur. The major disadvantages to the more widespread adoption of this method, however, are the very large capital outlay required to install the system and the high running costs involved in terms of energy requirements; both of these factors translated into costs are prohibitive to its use in the majority of function establishments. Furthermore economies can be gained in function catering by preparing meals several days in advance; by preparing them several weeks in advance relatively few further economies are gained. There are also limitations to the foods that can be pre-

pared and frozen, particularly some delicate sauces and garnishes. For these reasons where cook-freeze is employed by individual function kitchens it is limited in its use, mainly to standard menu items that by experience have been proven to freeze well. The alternative is for the larger organizations to operate their own cook-freeze operations completely independent of the function establishments but which can supply them with staple food items usually available on the function menus.

Catering for function events may be a kitchen's sole task, or it may be one of a number of catering outlets served by the kitchen, as, for example, in hotels. Where a kitchen is producing food and beverages for a number of different catering outlets, the same method of food production is usually employed for all the catering facilities; in a hotel, for example, the conventional method of food production may be used

LEITH'S

MENUS

FINGER BUFFET

Crostini with:
Roasted Cherry Tomatoes and Mozzarella
Gravadlax with Lemon
Chicken with Tarragon Mayonnaise

Leek and Mustard Pies
Barquettes of Herbed Cream Cheese with Tomato and Red Onion
Baby Yorkshire Pudding with Rare Roast Beef and Horseradish
Smoked Salmon and Quails' Egg Tartlets with Dill Mayonnaise
Bresaola with Mustard Fruit on Rye
Filo Tartlets of Bang Bang Prawns

Hot

Sausages with Rowanberry Chutney
Mini Baked Potatoes with Gruyère and Smoked Ham
Thai Crab Cakes with Coconut and Chilli Dip
Lamb Koftas with Yoghurt and Mint Dip
Courgettes filled with Gorgonzola and Tomato
Filo Parcels with Mushrooms and Chives
Duck and Spinach Tartlets
Chicken, Mozzarella and Black Olive Spring Rolls

Sweet

Glazed Strawberry Tartlets
Mini Coffee and Chocolate Eclairs

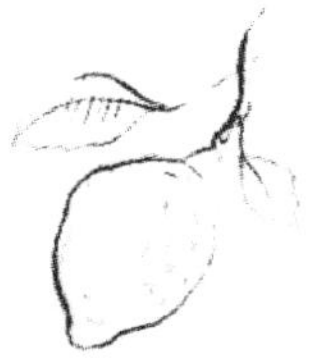

Figure 19.11   *An example of a finger buffet menu served at the Science Museum, London by Leith's Events and Parties*

LEITH'S

MENUS

Salad of Asparagus and Quails' Eggs
Chervil dressing

Poached Scottish Salmon with Fennel and Cardamom
Buttered New Potatoes with Soft Herbs
Fine Green Beans with Toasted Almonds

Filo Baskets filled with Macerated Berries in Balsamic Vinegar
Strawberry Syllabub

Coffee
Homemade Petits Fours

***

Timbale of Crab and Avocado
Herb Mayonnaise

Fillet of Beef sautéed in Basil with Mozzarella and Pesto Crust
Light Tomato Sauce

New Potatoes with Mustard Grain Butter
Courgettes, Sugar Snaps and Baby Squash

Cinnamon Biscuits with Poached Apples and Rhubarb
Orange Custard

Coffee
Homemade Petits Fours

Figure 19.12   *Examples of silver service menus offered by Leith's Events and Parties*

to service the hotel's coffee shop, the à la carte restaurant and the banqueting facilities. In some of the larger kitchens where it is easier to divide the production area according to the various types of catering outlets, different food production styles may be used to serve the different catering facilities; for example, the conventional method of food production may be used for the hotel coffee shop and à la carte restaurant, and cook-chill used for function catering. The more recent methods of food production are, however, usually associated with purpose-built function establishments or those that have been able to build a new style production kitchen specifically to serve its function facilities.

Because of the volume production of standardized dishes at functions, this form of catering also lends itself particularly well to the use of convenience foods. The different types of convenience foods that may be used include dehydrated stocks and soups; tinned fruits; frozen meats and vegetables; pre-prepared desserts, for example gateaux, etc. As with other catering facilities the convenience foods used may either be purchased directly from a food manufacturer, or from a company's central supplies if the establishment is part of a large group.

The supporting departments to the main production area are particularly important in helping to ensure the smooth running of functions. The clearing of soiled dishes after a function, for example, results in peak loads being placed upon the dishwashing or ware-handling area. The equipment and staff of this department must therefore be fully equipped and geared to coping with these peaks of activity, particularly if crockery from one function is needed for another one later in the day. In such cases as these the turnaround time of the equipment must of necessity be very rapid.

The equipment used in the kitchens of function catering establishments will depend to a large extent on whether the kitchen has been purpose-built to cater specifically for functions or whether it must serve a variety of catering outlets. In the latter case the equipment used may not have been designed to cope with the heavy peak period usage associated with function catering, and particular attention must therefore be paid to scheduling the use of equipment between the function and other catering

facilities of the establishment. Where the production area has been specifically designed for function catering the problem of equipment scheduling usually only arises if there are a number of different function facilities to be served. Generally speaking, where the conventional method of food production is employed, specialized equipment is not used, most of the equipment being larger editions of equipment found in the majority of kitchens. Where specialized methods of food production are used, however, specific types of equipment may be required. For example, if the Regethermic cook-chill method of food production is used, specially designed porcelain or aluminium meal dishes are required into which the prepared foods are placed and stainless steel or black coated aluminium lids are used as covers. Immediately prior to service the food is then heated to service temperature by placing these dishes into a purpose designed trolley/oven unit; the oven heating system is based on quartz radiant heaters placed to ensure even and simultaneous heat distribution on both the porcelain dish or stainless steel cover. This, however, is a purpose-designed method of food production, utilizing specialized equipment which may be too expensive to purchase except for the larger function establishments. In such cases as these similar methods of food production, based on the same principles, may be employed by smaller establishments without the more expensive specialized equipment; this is providing adequate attention is paid to the temperature of the food, the standards of hygiene in the production kitchen and overall control by management.

19.2.3.4 Food service styles

There are essentially two styles of food service used at functions. The first is the buffet arrangement where the guests will usually serve themselves from a display of food and beverage items. The second is the more formal 'sit-down' function where guests are served at their tables by food service staff; this latter style may be further subdivided into those functions where plated meals are served and those at which silver service is used.

Where a self-service buffet arrangement is employed, eye appeal to the guests plays an important role. The buffet table or tables, for example, should be placed so that an attractive food and beverage arrangement is seen by the guests as they enter the room; if several buffet tables are being used the different courses may be pre-arranged on the various tables. Where foods are to be left on display it is particularly important that the foods selected are those that will keep their quality and appearance throughout the function and that the proper equipment is available to keep the foods hot or cold as required. In addition to the buffet tables, there are usually a number of occasional tables, and chairs placed around the function room for use by the guests. The number of tables and chairs that may be needed varies according to the type of buffet and the number of guests. Fork buffet functions, for example, require a greater number to be available so that the guests may sit down at the tables and eat their meals; at finger buffets fewer tables are necessary because the guests are usually able to stand and eat their food quite comfortably. Whatever the type of buffet, however, some table and seating arrangements should be provided on which guests may place their glasses, plates, etc.

The other main food service style used in function catering is waiter service to the table. For lower ASP functions, or wherever the situation demands, the food may be pre-plated in the production area and then served directly to the guests. However, the more widely adopted service method at functions is the Russian or silver service style. In this method the food is brought to the guests' tables on platters and salvers and then served from these on to the guests' plates.

This is a slower method of food service than the previously described American style but it is generally regarded as the more sophisticated. The food may be brought into the function room in a variety of ways. The most commonly adopted method is for the service staff to first go to the hotplate or servery area in the kitchen and collect the plates to be placed in front of the guests; the menu items are then also collected from the servery area, taken into the dining room and served onto the guests' plates at their tables. This method may be further subdivided into two stages: commis waiters or 'bussers' bring the plates and food items into the dining area and place them on sideboards, trained service staff would then serve the food to the guests at the tables. Alternatively, heated or refrigerated trolleys may be taken into the function room before the guests arrive and when they are seated the hot and cold food would then be removed from the trolleys and served. Some food items may be on the table when the guests arrive, for example, roll and butter; where a cold hors d'oeuvre is being served this can also be on the table.

Beverage service in function catering may be divided into service to the guests' table in the function room, and service to the guests in a separate area such as a reception room. Some large function establishments have a permanent bar in a reception area, others may erect a bar for a specific function at the request of the organizer. Where a separate bar is set up payment for drinks may be made in one of two ways. If it is a cash bar the guests pay for their drinks directly to the bar staff; if it is an open or inclusive bar where the cost of the drinks is included in the price of the function, no cash payment is made by the guests.

In some establishments, for example small hotels, there may be insufficient room available for a separate reception area to be provided; in these establishments therefore the hotel bar may be used for guest assembly. Beverage service to the guests' table will depend largely on the numbers being catered for and the level of sophistication of the function. For the large formal functions usually associated with the higher ASP operations, separate beverage staff would be responsible for serving wines and other beverages at the table; where separate beverage staff are not employed, the food service staff would serve the beverages during the meal. It is normal practice for food service staff to be employed just for the service of the meal, and beverage service staff to be employed up to the end of a function.

Whatever the food service style adopted, the top table at a sit-down function, or the most important guests at a formal reception, should always be served first and accorded the most attention by the service staff. The table and seating arrangements at sit-down functions are governed by a number of factors – the nature of the function, for example business or social; the numbers to be catered for; the size of the room; special requests by the organizers; etc. The different table arrangements available include the T-shape and U-shape, the latter being particularly suitable for business lunches; where large numbers are involved a top table and sprigs may be used or a series of round tables each accommodating between eight to ten guests, again with a top table. The space allocation per guest will vary from one type of function to another although, generally speaking, for sit-down functions an allocation of between 12–16 ft^2 (1.12–1.49 m^2) per person is usually allowed and between 10–12 ft^2 (0.93–1.12 m^2) for buffet functions.

A feature of table arrangements peculiar to function catering is that after each function the room layout is changed ready for the next function; this is unlike other catering facilities which usually remain unaltered from one meal period to the next. Because the table and seating arrangements are changed on such a frequent basis careful consideration must be given to the use of easy folding tables, stacking chairs, etc. which are all aids to the more efficient function organization. This, as can be envisaged, causes problems regarding storage of this equipment, and also for the cleaning of function rooms as it frequently has to be done late at night or in the early morning.

In function catering flexibility of room design is particularly important. The room design should be flexible so that it can not only offer different table arrangements for different functions, but also so it is able to accommodate specialized equipment, fittings and furnishings etc. that the organizer may wish to include. The size of the function room will obviously limit to a large extent the different arrangements and services it is able to offer, so that smaller establishments would not be expected to provide as wide a range of facilities as the larger operations. In the larger function establishments extensive facilities are often available which are achieved by combining a number of the establishments' function rooms or suites.

The service accompaniments used in function catering should be of a hardwearing and functional nature, yet at the same time remain aesthetically attractive; this latter aspect is particularly important in function catering where large expanses of cutlery, crockery, etc. are usually on display which creates an impression, favourable or otherwise, as the guests enter the function room. Where an establishment's function facilities are one of a number of the organization's catering outlets, as for example in a hotel, the service equipment used for functions is usually specific to that department, that is, linen, crockery, cutlery, etc.; the banqueting department is then responsible for its own equipment and the stocktaking of these items.

Unlike other types of catering outlets (for example, coffee shops or à la carte restaurants) function catering is the provision of food and beverages for a specific number of people who have booked a function room or banqueting suite for the duration of the service period (for example, lunch or dinner). Thus in function catering the question of seat turnover does not really arise. Once the guests are seated at a function they remain there for the whole meal period and are not replaced by other customers (an exception may be a two-sitting luncheon at a business conference). Generally speaking, however, once a function has been sold, the establishment is guaranteed a set number of customers at a set price. The length of a meal period in function catering is similar to the service periods of other types of catering outlets, that is one-and-a-half to two-and-a-half hours for lunch and between three and four hours for dinner; where entertainment is provided at the function, for example a dinner dance the function may extend for a longer period, of up to five to seven hours.

Other services may be offered by the function caterer in addition to the service of food and beverages. The function organizer, for example, may require a toastmaster or a band for a evening function, and where possible the establishment should be able to provide, or at least recommend, someone reputable and reliable. It should be remembered that where an establishment can satisfy all or most of a client's requirements, this will be appreciated by organizers who would otherwise have to assemble these different components of the function for themselves.

19.2.3.5 *Organization and staffing*

Staffing organization in function catering is governed by a number of factors which include the size of the establishment and hence the number of staff permanently employed, and the numbers to be catered for at any one function which may involve additional staff being employed. In an establishment dealing specifically with function catering, or a large hotel with a banqueting department, a function manager would be employed who is responsible for the organization of functions. In smaller establishments such as a hotel of thirty bedrooms offering a small private room for functions, the owner or proprietor of the hotel may work in conjunction with the food and beverage manager/assistant manager or the restaurant manager to organize function events.

In the larger establishments the function department usually consists of a small core of permanent staff who are able to cope with the majority of the establishment's functions, and who may be supplemented by a number of casual or 'on call' staff for larger functions. The permanent staff may comprise the following personnel. The *function manager* who is responsible for all function catering administration; they would be involved in meeting the clients and discussing such aspects of the function as the cost per head, the food and beverages to be served, the seating plan, any special requirements, etc. In some establishments there may be a separate function sales manager who is specifically concerned with the marketing of the establishment's facilities.

Once a firm booking has been made, details of the function event should be sent to the other personnel in the function department involved in organizing the event. This would include the *head chef,* the *head food* and *wine waiters,* and if the function is to take place in an establishment where departments other than the food and beverage department is involved, such as in a hotel, several other departments should also be notified, for example *reception, hall porters,* etc. To aid them with the administration arrangements function managers may have one or two assistants, depending on the size of the establishment, but almost definitely a *function secretary.* They would be responsible for distributing function memos informing specific personnel of function events and may in the function manager's absence, be responsible for showing clients the establishment's facilities, discussing function arrangements, taking provisional bookings, etc.

The function *head waiter* is mainly responsible for dealing with the more practical aspects of functions such as ensuring the table and seating arrangements in the function room or suite are correct, liaising with the *head wine waiter* to discuss the complementary service of the food and the wines, engaging casual or part time staff for the function and briefing them before the event about their stations, the menu, special requirements and so on. This pre-function briefing is an important aspect of any function as it is often the only time that information relating to the event can be relayed to all the function staff together. Such aspects as station allocation, menu translation, the collection points for the food and in what order they are to be served would all be discussed at this briefing.

In addition to the function management team, there would be a small core of permanent food service staff who would be able to deal with the establishment's smaller functions, such as morning coffee and afternoon teas, small luncheon and dinner parties, etc. Where additional part-time or casual staff are needed to supplement the permanent staff, the engaging of such personnel is often undertaken by head waiters; they will usually have a list of the names and addresses of those willing to work at functions, and in the majority of cases these are female. The hours of work and rates of pay for the part-time staff are stated in advance and where the function continues after midnight the establishment will usually pay their taxi fare home.

The function head wine waiter would have similar responsibilities to those of the head waiter although not on such a large and detailed scale. Their duties would include the employing of casual beverage service staff such as dispense bar staff or staffing a bar set up for pre-dinner drinks. The head wine waiter would also be responsible for allocating floats to the beverage staff if cash sales were to be made during the course of the function, such as liqueurs and cigars.

The permanent function staff employed by an establishment must have the appropriate skills for serving at functions and where necessary additional training may be given to these employees by the function management. Comparatively little formal training is, however, received by part-time staff and therefore an establishment engaging casuals for a function is quite dependent on the skills they have acquired mainly through experience. This is important so that the organization not only knows their practical skills, but also their general attitude towards working at functions; for example, such aspects as the clearing away after a function may be left to the permanent function staff who would soon become disgruntled with these arrangements. Careful consideration should therefore be given to the employing of part-time staff by a function organization.

The ratio of food and beverage staff to guests will vary according to the nature of the function. If a self-service buffet is being offered, fewer food service personnel are required as large numbers of customers can be served by a comparatively limited number of service staff; once the food has been placed onto the buffet table only a few service staff are needed to remain behind the buffet arrangement to help serve the food, carve joints, etc. leaving the majority of staff to clear tables, serve drinks, etc. The ratio of service staff to guests at this type of function will be approximately one to twenty or thirty guests. At a more formal sit down function the ratio is higher, usually one member of staff to eight to twelve guests. Considerably fewer beverage staff are needed at functions, one member of staff to twenty to thirty guests being an average ratio; at some functions if the beverage staff are not particularly busy they may help the food service staff, such as with clearing tables.

The staffing organization for the kitchen will depend on the method of food production used by the establishment. Where the conventional method is used the kitchen personnel are divided into parties. If function catering is one of a number of catering services offered by an establishment, for example in a hotel, there may be an independent head chef for functions in addition to the head chef for the whole establishment. Where other methods of food production are being used, however, this rigid demarcation of staff into parties is not usually found. If cook-chill is being used for example, the production staff may be preparing food for a function three days in advance; in this type of operation the kitchen personnel would mainly be concerned with the preparation and chilling of large numbers of food items rather than work-ing towards the preparation of complete meals ready for immediate service.

In those establishments offering extensive function facilities a separate staff team may be necessary in addition to the food production and service staff. This team would mainly consist of porters, carpenters, lighting technicians, etc. whose work is of a supporting nature to the function. Other staff may also be employed for those functions large enough to warrant their services, for example cloakroom attendants, toastmasters, etc.

The style and sophistication of management found in function catering will depend largely on the type of establishment and the size of the function facilities. In large purpose built conference centres or those establishments with large function facilities, the management need to have more specialized knowledge than would normally be required of catering managers on other types of catering facilities; such detailed knowledge would include exact room specifications, electricity and other power points, the different seating arrangements available, acoustic and sound insulation, lighting levels, the hiring of specialized equipment and so on. In catering establishments such as industrial situations where the management is concerned not only with function catering but also with a variety of other catering services, the same level of expertise as found in purpose-built establishments is not usually present.

19.3 Control and performance measurement

As with other types of catering outlet, the size and ownership of the establishment in which catering events are held will determine to what extent basic policy decisions exist. Generally speaking, the larger the operation, or if it is a purpose-built function establishment, the more likely it is that policy decisions relating to this form of catering will be contained in a formalized document. Where such policies do exist, the performance of the function facilities can be measured against the standards contained in them.

The booking of a function event may begin in very much the same way as a client may book a

Daily Banquet Diary

Date 4.2.9–

Day Monday

Room	Time	Estimated numbers	Client address telephone	Type of function	Price	Details
Main Ballroom	A.M. P.M. 18.30 for 19.00	200	W.Smith 99 Main Street, Godalming, Surrey 0468 – 23112	Dinner/dance Menu B7	£24	Dinner 19.00 Cash bar 21.00
Churchill Suite	A.M. P.M. 18.00	320	High Flair, North Street, Westminster 0243 – 8787	Fashion show with finger buffet Menu F4	£12	Room hire £400 Cash bar 18.00
Continental Suite	A.M. 12.00	80	A. Browning, 21 Park Lane Greychester 4921 – 6792	Wedding reception Buffet Menu D9	£18	18 inch silver cake stand required 12 bottles house champagne
	P.M. 17.30 for 18.00	55	B.Ball & Co, 45 High Drive, Haslemere 0428 – 719432	Retirement dinner Menu B8	£24	Cash bar 17.30

Figure 19.13 *An example of a daily banquet diary. This is the initial record used for all function business, recording tentative and confirmed bookings. It is from this diary that a weekly functions list would be prepared and sent to all appropriate departmental heads*

POINTER HOTELS (UK) LTD

Function Instruction Sheet

NAME Surrey Gundog Association   *FUNCTION TYPE* Dinner Dance
ORGANIZER Tammy Davis   *No EXPECTED* 350
ADDRESS Tambard Kennels, Milford   *STARTING TIME* 19.30   *SERVING TIME* 20.00 hrs
   DEPOSIT REQUIRED £1,000
TEL No Milford 121234   *DATE DEPOSIT PAID* 5/9/9-
TAKEN BY B. Smith   *TOTAL PRICE PER COVER* £28.00   *VAT* Ex. VAT
DATE OF FUNCTION 5/10/9-   *VAT* 15%
ROOM Ballroom   *DATE OF ENQUIRY* 5/2/9-

MENU @ £24.00

Consommé Double en Tasse
Paillettes Dorées

Suprême de Turbotin Walewska

Filet de Boeuf en Croûte
Sauce Périgourdine

Pommes Parisienne
Haricots Verts au Beurre

Ananas Frais au Kirsch

Coffee

		Charge			Charge
☐	Hire of room	n/c		Menu	£40.00
☐	Flowers	35 x £6	☐	Printing	
☐	Candelabra	n/c	☐	Table Plan and Cards	n/c
☐	Toastmaster	–	☐	Board & easel	–
☐	Spotlights	n/c	☐	Lectern	–
☐	Bands	£500	☐	Projector	–
☐	Band supper	8 x £10	☐	Photographer	n/c
☐	Tape	–	☐	Changing rooms	n/c
☐	Microphone	n/c	☐	VAT	15%
☐	Cabaret	£570	☐	Invoice no.	5432
☐	Cake	–	☐	Piano	n/c
☐	Stand & knife	–	☐	Platform	n/c

SPECIAL REQUIREMENTS

COFFEE
TEA   All beverages and tobacco   Extension of licence to 01.00 hrs.
WINES   to be paid cash by
LIQUEURS individual guests.   No Top Table
CIGARETTES
CIGARS   35 x 10 covers

4 vegetarians, table no. and guests'
names to be notified

ACCOUNT INSTRUCTIONS   Guest (2)
General Manager
Asst. Manager
F. & B. Manager
Purchasing Manager
Control Office
Chef
Front Office
Head Porter

This is your confirmation and contract for your
forthcoming function.
A guaranteed number of guests for meals must be given
not later than 48 hours prior to the function.

PAYMENT IS DUE WITHIN 14 DAYS AFTER THE FUNCTION

Please sign and return one copy.

IVOR MONEY

(AUTHORIZED SIGNATURE)

Figure 19.14 *An example of a function instruction sheet completed after the initial enquiry by the banqueting/function manager*

restaurant table. The host or organizer contacts the catering facility and ascertains whether a certain number of guests can be accommodated at the establishment on a particular day at a specified time. After this initial enquiry, however, the similarity between these two types of catering outlets becomes less evident. By its very nature a function event involves considerably more detailed and critical organization than does a restaurant meal. It involves the development of a series of logical procedures and timings which must be precisely executed if the function is to be a success. Taking a simple example, if a menu item is not available in a restaurant for a particular meal period, the guest may choose an alternative dish; at a function, however, where all the different aspects of the event have been organized specifically for that occasion, it is not a simple matter to make last minute alternative arrangements, particularly because of the large numbers usually involved. The strict planning and organization for function catering must therefore encompass all aspects of the operation and this begins with the initial customer enquiry.

The first of a series of documents to be drawn up by the caterer for every function should be a function checklist. This comprises a list of the services offered by an establishment and those that the client wishes to make use of would be noted accordingly. The checklist serves as a reference document for caterers and enables them to identify all the client's needs; it is updated at each meeting between caterers and organizers of the function until it is finally completed sometime before the event. At this stage the relevant details from the checklist would be transferred from this document to another function form or memo which is then distributed to the appropriate personnel – the head chef, head waiter, head wine waiter, etc. Where the function is being held in a hotel the other departments that may be informed would include the front office, reception and cashiers, the hall porters, the hotel's bar if a separate one is not being arranged for the function, and so on.

At one of the initial meetings between the client and the caterer an estimate of cost for the function will be discussed. At this stage this is not a formal quotation which must be made clear to the client as additional services and hence costs are almost inevitably requested as

the date of the function approaches, and these must all be added to the total cost. When all the details of a function are agreed, a final quotation is prepared by the caterer and sent to the function organizer. If the quotation is accepted, a deposit and acceptance of the booking should be returned to the establishment, the deposit charge being set by the financial policy of the operation.

The costing of functions will depend largely on the type of establishment in which the function is to be held. For example, if it is an establishment in the welfare sector of the industry, the caterer may only be required to cover the basic food costs. If the banqueting department is one of several catering departments in a hotel, only direct costs that is, food and labour, may be debited to the function. Where function trade is an establishment's sole source of revenue, however, all costs including overheads would be charged to the function. Generally speaking, because functions are complete events in themselves, and each one is different, they are usually individually costed; this is an important source of information against which the performance of a function may be measured, and by studying these costings potentially weak areas may be discovered. For example, the costing for a function may be simply broken down as follows: food cost 35 per cent, labour cost 30 per cent, overheads 15 per cent. Should the labour cost increase to 33 per cent the organization may re-examine the staff to customer ratios it uses as a basis for setting staff levels; or if the overheads for functions increase to 17 per cent, the operation may review the ancillary services it is offering to see if a suitable charge is being made for these additional facilities. As with the other aspects of the establishment, if the operation is part of a large organization, the costings and profit levels to be achieved by the establishment will be determined by the head office; for the independently operated establishments, however, the costings must be done by themselves.

Unless a cash bar is set up for a function, or beverages are purchased from the beverage staff for cash, the majority of payments for functions are made on a credit basis. The final settlement of the cost of the function is usually made several weeks after the event, and for some large functions considerable amounts of money may be involved. This could substantially affect the cash flow of the catering establishment and for this reason accounts sent to the client should be carefully itemized so that the exact breakdown of the cost of the function may be clearly seen. The final account is also usually one of the last pieces of correspondence between the client and the caterer and should therefore continue to reflect the image of the organization.

Control is needed not only of the financial aspects of the function, but also of the guests themselves. Where a function is being held for 500 or 1000 guests this is a large number to control and the establishment must be properly organized before their arrival. For example the reception area should be adequately signposted and the directions to other facilities such as the lifts, cloakrooms, etc. should also be clear. If more than one function is being held in an establishment, strict segregation of guests is needed. This is particularly important where different levels of markets are being catered for and is aided if the establishment has more than one function entrance; segregation of markets may also be extended to other aspects of the operation, for example the cloakrooms, etc.

The performance of a function establishment may be measured in a number of different ways and against different yardsticks. In a city centre hotel for example, the final profit from a function will determine by and large the success of the event. In an industrial catering situation the final profit made, or the ability to cover specific named expenses such as food, beverage and labour costs, may not be the criterion against which the success of a function is measured. For example, an industrial firm may organize a Christmas party for its employees and the success of this type of function would be the goodwill generated by the parent company; a wine shipper may organize a wine and cheese evening for some of its more important clients and the success of this event would be the sales promotion achieved by the company.

Finally, function catering involves the production of a considerable amount of documentation for each function event and this is a very useful exercise against which the performance of the function can later be measured. In this respect function catering is quite unique. In few other catering situations are events so well-documented from the initial enquiry to settlement of the final account which then provides a useful source of information for the future planning of functions by the establishment.

19.4 Outdoor catering

Outdoor catering is a specialized from of function catering and may be organized in several ways. It may either be offered by hotels and restaurants as an additional service to the operation's main function or it may be the organization's raison d'etre. In the first instance a hotel or restaurant may organize such events as luncheons, wedding receptions, afternoon teas at a local show, etc. The type of product and service offered would be limited to the knowledge and capabilities of the in-house catering team and the equipment and staff available. The potential pitfalls of this type of outdoor catering are numerous in terms of staff limitations, transportation and correct handling of the food and beverages, additional equipment needed and correct costings for the total event and finally the overall control of the operation away from the establishment's everyday management and control procedures. For these reasons this type of outdoor catering is usually limited to the smaller or more local events which do not overstretch a hotel or restaurant's resources and capabilities.

Secondly, outdoor catering may be organized by specialist organizations who operate by far the largest number of outdoor catering events in this sector of the catering industry. Some of these professional outdoor caterers are individuals who may only have a refrigerated van and employ one or two extra staff for specific events; the range of products and services they can offer are limited. At the other end of the scale, large specialist outdoor caterers such as Ring & Brymer may cater for thousands of customers over several days at national events, for example, Wimbledon, Royal Ascot and the Royal Horticultural Show. The organization and management needed by these companies are very similar to a banqueting department in a large hotel or a conference centre and in addition would have to take into account a number of factors specific to outdoor catering:

- The location of the event, whether a semi-permanent site is being used where limited services are already in situ in terms of water, sanitation, heating and lighting, or whether a marquee is to be erected and these essential services brought in.
- The transportation of the food and beverage items, the distances involved and whether heated or chilled trucks are needed.
- The additional hygiene problems associated with food being transported and held at the correct temperatures and the added worry of possible power failures on a temporary site; the losses and pilferage that can occur at any stage during transportation and the setting up and the difficulties of ensuring back up facilities and supplies and staffing miles away from the organization's main base.

The additional cost involved in supplying outdoor food and beverage facilities are reflected in the cost of outdoor events which by their very nature must be higher than supplying the same or similar product in an organization's banqueting hall or restaurant. Further, the additional management time and control needed must also be included in the costings and is critical to the success of an outdoor catering event.

19.5   Reference

Taylor, D. (1983). *How to Sell Banquets*. London: Hutchinson.

20
Food and beverage management in industrial catering

20.1 Introduction

Industrial catering, also called 'industrial feeding' and 'employee feeding' may be described as the provision of catering facilities at a place of work for use by the organization's employees. The catering facility may range from vending machines supplying a limited variety of beverages and snacks, to a waiter silver service restaurant with an extensive menu. In the majority of establishments the provision of a catering service is more important in terms of its functional purpose rather than its entertainment value, as the catering amenities represent a place of refreshment and rest for those employees who choose to use the facilities.

Catering facilities in industrial firms first began to appear in the nineteenth century when there was shown to be a correlation between the physical and mental health of employees and the catering and other welfare facilities provided for them. Today industrial catering facilities have emerged as an important fringe benefit to employees, particularly where highly subsidized or completely free meals are still provided.

Catering amenities are an important aspect of industrial situations and as a department in an organization can evoke the emotional feelings of the employees. Companies are appraised on the type of facilities they provide for their staff, and it is a service that once provided should not be allowed to fall below its initial standards. This is particularly important where companies have developed and employed more staff over a number of years without due consideration to the catering service which has long since become over-stretched. Where possible, therefore, when the staff numbers to be catered for are initially

calculated, a provision should be made for the possible expansion of the catering facilities, should the employee numbers increase by a certain percentage. If they increase by a very large proportion the organization's basic financial, catering and marketing policies may need to be revised.

Unlike other forms of catering outlets such as hotels, restaurants, high street take-aways, etc. where catering may be the main or only function of the establishment, the catering facilities in industrial situations such as factories, office blocks, hospitals, etc. are an ancillary service to the main function of the organization. The two main methods by which catering may be organized in such industrial situations are direct management or contracted out. Direct management is where the parent company chooses to establish and operate the catering facilities itself. The second method involves the parent company employing a firm of contract caterers to operate and manage the catering department for them. In the first situation the parent company is completely responsible for the type and standard of catering service it provides; the catering department thus becoming another department in the organization that is under its direct control and management.

Where contract caterers are employed the organizationof the catering service is transferred to an outside firm. Contract caterers are individuals or firms who undertake the responsibility of operating and controlling a company's catering facilities within that company's guidelines for a specified contract arrangement. Contract caterers are usually engaged for a specific period of time, after which the contract may be renewed or dissolved as both parties wish.

Contract caterers are involved in all types of industrial catering situations, ranging from the small independent concerns to the large multinational organizations and may become involved for different reasons: for example, the organization's dissatisfaction with the existing services; complaints about the standard of catering have been made at staff meetings and repeated attempts to improve the facilities have failed, or the company does not wish to become involved in operating the catering facilities itself or recognizes that it does not have the expertise and so engages the services of contract caterers.

The contract catering industry in the UK has experienced an overall increase of almost 7 per cent in the total number of outlets operated from 1966 to 1997 (see Table 20.1), state education at 32 per cent, healthcare at 21 per cent and public catering at 6 per cent showing the largest increases. Business and industry have shown a marginal increase largely due to a reduction in the overall number of offices and factories and a streamlining of workforces. In the cost sector, the contract caterer's traditional market, there has been an increase in the total number of outlets served of just over 2 per cent (see Table 20.2), healthcare increasing by 43 per cent and state education by 17 per cent.

The possible advantages of using contract caterers include the following. Establishing and operating catering services are the main functions of contract caterers and as such they can have a more professional approach than many of those organizations who try to operate their own catering facilities; this professional attitude and approach are reflected in the standards of facilities provided and in more effective cost control; in addition to a well-organized catering department, other financial benefits can accrue because of the purchasing power of large contract caterers, such as cost savings, products prepared to the company's own specifications, etc. However, there are also a number of possible disadvantages in employing contract caterers. First, unless a particular catering contractor firm is recommended, or has a good reputation, an

Table 20.1   *UK contract caterers: number of outlets 1990–1997, followed by per cent of total for the year*

	1997 %	1996 %	1995 %	1994 %	1993 %	1992 %	1991 %	1990 %
Business and industry	7,586 45.4	7,574 48.5	7,473 50.0	7,132 59.7	7,671 72.7	7,775 74.7	7,058 75.2	7,089 82.6
Healthcare	483 2.9	397 2.5	459 3.1	405 3.4	379 3.6	337 3.2	365 3.9	250 2.9
State education	6,140 36.7	4,957 31.7	4,603 30.8	2,383 19.9	490 4.6	450 4.3	465 4.9	242 2.8
Independent schools	545 3.3	578 3.7	579 3.9	587 4.9	733 7.0	620 6.0	610 6.5	492 5.7
Local authorities	357 21.	451 2.9	295 1.9	261 2.2	362 3.4	463 4.5	362 3.9	262 3.1
Ministry of Defence	395 2.3	393 2.5	267 1.8	265 2.2	210 2.0	190 1.8	132 1.4	68 0.8
Public catering	1.034 6.2	971 6.2	1,002 6.7	619 5.2	475 4.4	324 3.1	233 2.5	116 1.4
Oil rigs[a]	182 1.1	311 2.0	263 1.8	302 2.5	242 2.3	246 2.4	163 1.7	62 0.7
Total	16,722	15,632	14,914	11,954	10,562	10,405	9,388	8,581
% increase	+7.0	+5.0	+25.0	+13.0	+1.5	+11.0	+9.0	

[a] includes training centres and construction sites

Source: British Hospitality Association Contract Catering Survey 1997

Table 20.2 *UK contract caterers: number of meals served 1990–1997, followed by per cent of total for the year*

	1997 %	1996 %	1995 %	1994 %	1993 %	1992 %	1991 %	1990 %
Business and industry	455	465	456	408	401	325	321	305
	41.0	42.7	43.5	43.4	49.8	49.7	52.6	62.8
Healthcare	121	81	77	65	68	41	42	29
	10.9	7.4	7.4	6.9	8.5	6.3	6.9	6.0
State education	206	172	163	94	31	33	26	15
	18.5	15.8	15.5	10.0	3.9	5.0	4.3	3.1
Independent schools	8.4	99	99	100	111	81	66	59
	7.6	9.1	9.4	10.6	13.8	12.4	10.9	12.1
Local authorities	17	18	15	20	28	31	30	32
	1.5	1.7	1.4	2.1	3.5	4.7	4.9	4.5
Ministry of Defence	86	92	86	92	67	56	47	22
	7.7	8.4	8.2	9.8	8.3	8.6	7.8	4.5
Catering for the public	128	134	130	120	69	62	50	24
	11.5	12.3	12.4	12.8	8.6	9.5	8.3	4.9
Oil rigs, etc.[a]	14	28	23	41	29	25	27	10
	1.3	2.3	2.2	4.4	3.6	3.8	4.3	2.1
Total	1,111	1,089	1,049	940	804	654	609	486
% increase	+2.0	+4.0	+12.0	+17.0	+23.0	+7.0	+25.0	

[a] includes training centres and construction sites

Source: British Hospitality Association Contract Catering Survey 1997

unsuitable contractor may be engaged unknowingly by a parent company; second, should the catering facilities not reach the required standards then the engaging company is not able to make any necessary changes immediately but must work through the catering contractors, that is, the organization loses direct control. Finally, a management fee and/or a percentage of the turnover is taken by catering contractors which would not normally have to be paid by the parent company if it was operating its own catering service. Therefore if the services of a catering contractor are being considered, a thorough investigation should be undertaken including visiting other facilities being operated by the contractors to see the type of facilities and standards achieved elsewhere.

Employee feeding is provided in all sectors of the industry, the nature of the catering facilities varying considerably from one establishment to another. Traditionally contract catering was mainly confined to operations such as factories, office blocks, department stores, sports centres,

etc., with the welfare and other institutional establishments (for example, hospitals and schools) mainly operating their own catering facilities; however, this situation has now changed considerably due to the introduction of competitive tendering. The majority of catering companies operate catering services in a number of organizations, and some large contractors are responsible for over 1000 firms.

Recently there have been a number of trends in industrial catering which may be identified, which will affect the type of facilities provided in industrial situations. The first is the move away from the 'factory canteen' image of former years to the more professional and commercially operated facilities. This trend has become particularly noticeable over recent years during which period an increasing number of organizations, in particular service companies such as oil, banking and insurance have led the way in providing good catering and social amenities. The second trend is the increase in the number of industrial catering facilities being built away from the centres of large towns and cities due to the increasing cost of land. This in turn is encouraging the development of new industrial estates in areas where land is considerably cheaper. Where these new sites are being developed there are often few other local amenities and it has thus become necessary for new organizations to provide a range of industrial catering facilities for their employees. Thirdly, there is a noticeable move away from the provision of totally and heavily subsidized catering to nil subsidy catering, that is the establishment pays for the provision of the building and capital equipment but the operating costs must be covered by sales from the catering outlet.

The life cycle of industrial catering facilities is generally longer than for similar types of facilities in other sectors of the industry; this is mainly due to the provision of a catering service not being the *raison d'être* of any industrial organization, unlike hotels, independent restaurants, etc. Consequently the catering department does not usually receive large influxes of capital to update its facilities as often as it would perhaps like, and in times of economic crisis the catering department is nearly always one of the first to suffer in terms of investment. The life cycles of the different catering facilities will therefore vary from between five to fifteen years depending on the type of catering outlet, the degree of usage, the capital available, and the organization's basic policy decisions.

The different variety of catering facilities that may be available in an industrial situation include some or all of the following:

1 *A cafeteria.* Single, straight line or free-flow. Used by the majority of employees. Providing light and full meals, snacks, and beverages.
2 *Coffee or snack bar.* Providing light meals only, that is, snacks and sandwiches and beverages. Mainly used for morning coffee and afternoon teas, and for those bringing their own meals to work.
3 *Plated service restaurant.* Open at main meal periods only. Offering more variety in the choice of foods and beverages, and higher standards of food and service. Used mainly by middle management.
4 *Silver service restaurant.* Open for main meal periods and often for morning coffee and

afternoon teas. Highest standards of food and service. Used mainly by senior management.
5 *Vending machines.* May be a supplement to or in place of a catering facility. Frequently vending may be the only catering service available during nights and at week-ends. May vend main meals, for example chilled pre-plated dishes ready to be reheated or snack items such as pre-wrapped sandwiches, rolls, tea, coffee, etc. May be sited within the main dining area or in strategic positions around the office block or factory. Used by any grade of employee.
6 *Remote catering facilities.* Smaller catering services situated away from the main amenities. The food may be transported to these satellite facilities in heated trolleys, or small peripheral kitchens may serve these smaller dining areas. Trolley or cart service to employees at their place of work is also still used in office blocks and factory complexes.
7 *Conference/function facilities.* Plated or silver service may be used. Available for business meetings during the day and social functions in the evening and at weekends. Patronized by all levels of employees.

20.2 Basic policies – financial, marketing and catering

The extent to which basic policy decisions are contained in a formalized document will depend largely on whether the organization's catering is operated by the parent company or whether it is contracted out to an independent catering firm. In the first situation the parent company is responsible for formulating its own basic policies. Where contract caterers are employed the parent company will determine the broad guidelines within which it and the contract caterers must work to formulate the basic policies. The basic policy decisions are determined by the objectives the company is attempting to achieve in providing a catering service for its employees. For example, if an organization only wishes to provide limited refreshment facilities such as vending machines, then the type and size of these catering amenities will be considerably less than those of a company who sees its catering service as being an additional service to its employees and which can also be used for social functions.

There are a number of reasons why a company may provide a catering service for its employees. The office block or factory may be situated where there are few alternative catering facilities and it must therefore provide some form of catering service, for example isolated industrial estates; it may be for prestigious reasons, acting as an added benefit to prospective employees, particularly in areas where there is keen competition for labour; the company may need to provide some form of catering service to staff at their place of work because it is of such a nature that it cannot be left for any long period, for example continuous process industries; or the organization may see the provision of a catering service as a social responsibility to its employees, particularly as the meal received at their place of work may be the employees' main meal of the day.

20.2.1 Financial considerations

Once a company has decided to provide a catering service the financial policy will determine the amount of money to be invested in the catering facilities. Some companies consider the provision of a catering service as a valuable and important contribution to the welfare of their employees and are proud of the standards they achieve. Other companies have different views and feel that as little money as possible should be invested. However, once a company has opted to provide a catering service then the best possible facilities should be sought with the finance available.

Catering services in industrial situations range from being provided completely free of charge to those in which the total cost of the meals is passed on to the customer. In between these two extremes a variety of pricing structures are used, some covering the direct food costs only, others covering food and labour costs. The extent to which prices are subsidized by the parent company will depend on its financial policy. Where catering facilities are provided on a non-profit making basis, but still take into account all indirect costs such as heating, lighting etc., the food costs may account for more than 50 per cent.

Where the prices charged aim to cover the food costs only, the prices may be considerably lower. The trend today, however, is away from providing heavily subsidized catering facilities and making them more self financing by requiring the customers to contribute more to the costs.

The catering service at the headquarters of Scottish Widows in Edinburgh is an example of the way in which a subsidized service can be reduced over a number of years. The aim of the company is to achieve 'nil subsidy', that is, cash sales are to cover operating costs including food, labour and sundries whilst the catering costs of occupancy (building space), capital equipment and energy will be met by the parent company. The original annual subsidy of £210,000 has been reduced by over 50 per cent during the first phase through a combination of limiting menu choices, staffing cutbacks, more self-service and a small tariff increase. The free tea trolley service has been abolished and replaced by vending using the 'smart cards' cashless payment system offering the employees one free drink a day and vending sales average 2.5 cups per person per day. Snack items and sandwich sales have increased over the more expensive meat and two vegetable meals. The trend towards nil-subsidy catering will continue as subsidies are cut by companies striving to reduce their catering costs.

Working within the limits set by the financial policy, the size and variety of catering facilities will be determined by the number of employees expected to use the catering services. Few industrial situations are the same and therefore the percentage usage of catering facilities varies from one establishment to another; it may be as low as 10 per cent in some organizations and over 70 per cent in others with the norm being between 25 and 35 per cent; generally the higher usage of the catering facilities occurring when the percentage of catering subsidy per meal is highest.

There are a number of factors which can affect the total number of employees likely to use the restaurants, cafeterias etc. and any one of these may be more important in one situation than in another. The level of subsidy is probably the most influential factor, with a higher percentage of employees using the amenities when they are free or highly subsidized, than if they are not. Alternative catering facilities are also important particularly if the establishment is situated in a busy high street where there are other restaurants, snack bars, take-aways etc. which are readily available. Other factors are the location and accessibility of employees' homes to their place of work – the closer they are the more likely women employees in particular are to go home at lunchtime; the accessibility of the facilities in relation to all the organization's departments and offices, as there are the distance and convenience factors to be considered. The siting of the catering facilities should therefore be an important consideration at the initial planning stage. Unfortunately in some buildings the catering service is afforded whatever space is available or an area that no other department can utilize. The result is cafeterias and restaurants that are badly designed ergonomically, they are not conveniently sited for patrons to use, and because of these factors they suffer from poor uptake and subsequent financial problems.

20.2.2   Marketing considerations

The trend towards industrial catering facilities becoming more customer oriented is reflected in the marketing attitudes of these establishments. Gradually a more determined approach is being taken particularly by contract caterers, and industrial catering facilities are now being 'sold' to the employees. In addition to advertising the amenities using posters, leaflets, etc. some companies now give new employees several days' free meal tokens to encourage them from the time they join the company to use the facilities; other companies give away a certain number of free meal tokens each month. In this way it keeps the employees in contact with the catering department, generates goodwill and also acts as a reminder to the employees of the existence of the catering facilities.

Customer loyalty schemes, popular with airlines and hotel groups, are also being used by contract caterers. For example Sutcliffe Catering has launched a Summertime Fun Days promotion in 1500 of its 2000 units, customers receiving a stamp every time a meal is purchased. Once collected to a certain value, these stamps can be used as discounts in other parts of the Granada Group such as Little Chef restaurants and Forte

hotels. By promoting a customer loyalty scheme Sutcliffe aims to reward customer loyalty, increase average spend per customer and to attract new customers – the increase in overall sales helping to contribute to reducing the client's catering costs and subsidies.

In the case of contract caterers, business may be obtained either through word of-mouth advertising or direct advertising. Word-of-mouth advertising can be an important source of trade for contract caterers, particularly once a good reputation has been established by a company. Direct advertising by contract caterers would include advertising in trade journals, selective mail shots and generally identifying those business magazines and circulars which may be taken by the type of companies contract caterers are interested in; for example, a large contracting firm may only be interested in catering for companies with over 1000 employees, and so would aim its advertising campaign at this size of market.

Market research in industrial catering can be particularly effective because the potential market for the catering facilities is often captive or semi-captive and is therefore relatively accessible. Research can take a number of forms; it may either be a large in-depth project and an outside agency may be engaged, or the company may do its own market research which is usually quicker, cheaper and more interesting. If the organization decides to undertake its own research, questionnaires can be distributed to all its staff to be completed. On analysis the results can prove to be valuable sources of information as they often obtain the views of the silent majority and are a source of objective information. This is particularly important where organizations may be under pressure from certain groups to provide catering facilities which in reality would be over-sized for the number of employees to be catered for. In cases such as these the objective information obtained from questionnaires may be taken along to meetings and help in discussing more realistic demands.

The type of questions used to form these questionnaires may include some of the following: How often do you use the restaurant? If you do not use the restaurant, what is your main reason? – it may be because of the atmosphere, poor choice, service etc. and a training need may be identified. How long does it take you to get to the restaurant? – in an establishment of several thousand it may take a considerable period of time. What type of food do you prefer? On what basis do you make your choice? How much do you spend? How long do you usually spend in the restaurant? – it may be a social gathering place or just somewhere to eat and leave quickly. Would you like to be able to buy wrapped or take-away foods? – a lost main meal sale may be partially compensated by a sale of a snack item. If you do not use the restaurant what do you use? – employees may be buying snacks outside the organization and again those could be provided by the establishment. Do you have a main meal in the evening? Are there any changes/introductions you would like to see made? and so on. By the careful compiling of this type of questionnaire a great deal of data can be collected about the use of the catering facilities.

Information may also be obtained on the profiles of customers using the services, that is, sex, age, marital status, their position in the company, etc., and also on those customers who may be termed 'floaters', that is, those employees who sometimes use the restaurant and sometimes do not. In many establishments it is this sector of the market that may be most influenced by an advertising campaign promoting the facilities and help to increase the number of employees using the catering services. Market research may therefore be used to discover people's attitude towards the existing catering services and also if new facilities or changes are being considered a similar type of survey may be used.

Finally, feedback can be obtained from an organization's employees not only through formalized surveys and questionnaires but also via channels within the organization such as staff councils and committees. Indeed it is probably in the industrial catering sector that people are the quickest to air their opinions regarding the catering facilities and may be generally more critical. It is important therefore that there should be some feedback through these committees in answer to any questions that may be put to the catering department, just as when surveys have been conducted the results should be communicated to the employees and some form of action be seen to be taken.

20.2.3 Catering considerations

The catering policy will determine the standards of food and beverages to be provided for the different levels of catering facilities, such as a higher percentage of fresh foods to be used in the silver service restaurant than in the cafeteria. When setting the hours of service for the catering amenities particular reference should be made to the type of catering service to be provided for the evening shift; for example, the self-service cafeteria may be closed and vending facilities provided instead.

The catering policy in conjunction with the marketing policy will also determine the other uses for the catering facilities. For example a large industrial cafeteria may be used for welfare activities such as retirement presentations and Christmas parties; it may also be used for company meetings, lectures given by visiting speakers, etc.

The trend today is away from providing separate catering facilities for each of the different grades of staff in the organization; the majority of new industrial catering facilities being built may be used by all grades of staff, regardless of their status in the organization. The major exceptions to this, however, are executive dining rooms which are used by senior management only and for entertainment purposes.

In addition to itemizing the type, size, variety, etc. of the catering facilities to be provided, the basic policy decisions should also include the procedure to be followed should any aspect of the catering service need to be changed or altered in any way. Such alterations may include the expansion or reduction of the amenities, due to an increase or decrease in the number of the organization's employees.

20.2.3.1 *Type of customer*

In industrial catering situations the customers using the facilities are mainly the organization's employees with few establishments allowing their services to be used by the general public. In this respect the markets for industrial catering facilities may be described as more selective than the markets to which other sectors of the industry usually cater. This situation is sometimes referred to in terms of free, semi-captive and captive markets, each denoting the degree of freedom customers have in choosing where to take their custom. To take two examples. A customer working in a large city centre may have a variety of catering facilities from which to choose, while an employee working on an industrial estate or a construction site many miles from the nearest town would only have the catering facilities at the workplace to use. Between these two extremes of free and captive markets, the semi-captive market exists where the customer has a degree of choice as to which catering facilities to use.

The total market available for industrial catering facilities may be quite restricted and this may be further limited as the individual catering facilities usually cater to quite specific groups of employees. The demarcation of markets between the facilities may be achieved through the pricing structure, but in the majority of situations it is achieved by use of the organization's staffing structure. In a large company situation, for example, this allows the senior management to use the executive dining room, the middle management to use the waiter service restaurant, and the cafeterias, coffee bars, etc. for the clerical and administration staff to use. Such a system does not, however, allow a similar upward flow of customers, for example allowing junior employees to use the middle management's waiter service dining room. Because of this segregation of employees according to their status level in the company, the problem of mixed markets does not really arise; a natural division of socio-economic groups evolving depending on the employee's position in the company. Indeed, it is usually only at social functions such as retirement presentations, Christmas parties, etc. that these 'barriers' disappear and the different market levels mix together freely.

Due to the large numbers usually involved in industrial catering, it is a sector where a small percentage change in the number of customers using the catering facilities can result in a large increase/decrease in actual numbers for any one meal period. For example, in an office block of 1000 people, 450 on average may use the cafeteria daily for their main meal; a sudden change in the weather may deter many employees from leaving the building at lunch time and thus increase the percentage usage by 10 or 15 per cent which is an additional 100 or 150 customers to be catered for.

With few exceptions customers in an industrial catering situation are patronizing the catering facilities to fulfil a basic need, for example hunger or thirst, and not purely for social purposes. The few exceptions to this general rule include the entertaining of visiting guests, lunchtime birthday celebrations, etc. For this reason employees in industrial situations are seeking a different meal experience to the one they would desire if they were going out for an evening meal. Customers in industrial situations require a meal of a good standard and quality, at an acceptable price, and one that can be comfortably consumed in the amount of time they have available for their meal. This last factor of time may be critical in some catering situations and must be carefully calculated to allow patrons sufficient time for their meal although still achieving the necessary seat turnover. Seat turnover will vary from one type of catering facility to another, generally decreasing as the service style and food become more elaborate. In an industrial cafeteria the seat turnover may be two to three times per hour; in a snack bar where patrons go for a cup of coffee after their lunch or a snack meal it may be five to six times per hour; in a waiter service dining room with plated food service it may be once an hour and in a dining room where silver service is used it may be as low as a third to a half time per hour.

Because the meal experience in an industrial catering situation is different from the type experienced in other catering outlets, the employees in an organization have different requirements of the facilities provided. First, they will be seeking consistent value for money, perhaps more so than they would be in other catering outlets such as a restaurant where they may be taking an evening meal. Second, if employees do not consider they are getting value for money, or if the standards of food and service are not to their satisfaction, they are more likely to voice their opinions. Customers who have poor meals in their cafeteria may not only complain to the catering management, they may also discuss it with other colleagues; if they too have had a similar meal experience ill feeling towards the catering service can soon develop with a subsequent drop in custom. In this respect patrons of industrial catering facilities may be more critical of the service provided at their place of work than of similar restaurant facilities elsewhere.

The ASP of customers in industrial catering will depend on the type of catering facility and to what extent the service is subsidized. Some companies supply meals completely free, others make a nominal charge, for example 50p, and others pass the full cost on to the customer so that a two-course luncheon may cost over £3. Where the catering service is provided completely free, this usually includes foods and non-alcoholic beverages only; if employees wish to purchase alcoholic beverages that may be available, these must be paid for by the employees themselves. The daily income received from the catering service is sometimes supplemented by special function events; at these functions the ASP of patrons may vary from between £5 to £25, depending on the nature of the event and the type of customers. Again function catering may be completely subsidized by the parent company or at least the total direct costs borne by the employers. On these occasions the market being catered for will often be mixed in terms of socio-economic grouping, age, sex, job level in the company, etc.; it will also usually include guests from outside the organization such as friends, families, etc. of the employees.

20.2.3.2 *Type of product/menu*

Due to the wide variety of catering facilities found in industrial catering situations, a corresponding variety of products are usually also offered. In industrial cafeterias the menus available are generally more limited in terms of choice than are the menus offered in comparable commercial operations. In an industrial situation for example, the cafeteria menu may consist of two or three starters, including fruit juices and soup; two or three main dishes, for example fish, meat and a vegetarian dish; in addition a wide range of salads and snacks are nearly always available, and two or three desserts usually including ice cream and cheese. The table d'hôte menu offered in a waiter service restaurant and the à la carte menu in a silver service restaurant would also be comparatively limited. By streamlining and often simplifying the menus available the catering management is able to achieve an

acceptable speed of food production and service and more easily control the food costs.

Unlike other types of catering facilities in which the same menu may be available for three to six months, in industrial situations the menu is usually changed daily. This is particularly applicable to hot starters, main courses and desserts; those items that are nearly always available would include soup, fruit juices, salads (whether plated or as part of a buffet arrangement), desserts and cheese. Because of the very short cycle of the menus offered there is a considerable amount of flexibility afforded to industrial caterers. In addition to offering different standard dishes daily, special diet foods and beverages may be introduced, such as low calorie or vegetarian foods; the industrial caterer should be able to take advantage of special discounts on foods from the food suppliers and pass the benefits on to the customers in the form of lower prices and by doing so increase the facilities uptake.

Higher expectations from a more educated consumer have placed demands on caterers to provide a greater variety of choice and higher standards in industrial catering situations. This is particularly noticeable in relation to the use of branded products by contract caterers which has recently increased significantly, see Table 20.3. Other areas which have seen an increase in popularity include vegetarian and ethnic foods, calorie-counted meals and healthy eating, see Table 20.4.

Table 20.3 *Branded outlets operated by UK contract caterers*

	1997	1996	1995
In-house/own brands	810	506	147
High street/franchises	80	65	26

In some large industrial situations where a variety of catering facilities are available, portion sizes may vary from one outlet to another. For example, in a factory complex the size of the meal given to the manual workers in one canteen would usually be larger than the same meal offered in another cafeteria to female office staff. Some employees may wish to bring their own lunches and snacks, etc. from home to eat at

Table 20.4   *Future trends in UK contract catering*

| | Forecast increase in activities | |
	Current year %	Previous year %
Vegetarian food	89	86
Healthy eating	85	86
Ethnic food	85	79
Customer care	85	83
Theme days	85	72
Marketing expenditure	81	86
Training expenditure	81	66
IT expenditure	81	76
Calorie-counted food	77	76
Staff levels	74	48
Breakfasts	63	48
Developing in-house brand	59	62
Single status feeding	48	55
Public sector activity	37	38
Trolley service	29	24
Overseas business	22	21
Developing high street brands	11	21
Night shifts	7	14

work, and it should be a policy decision by management whether or not to make available separate dining facilities for this purpose or to allow food to be brought in and consumed in the dining areas. It may be argued that by allowing food to be brought on to the premises from outside these employees are not purchasing anything from the company's cafeteria. However, beverages are usually bought from the cafeteria by these employees and sometimes desserts. It is not really valid to suggest that by prohibiting food to be brought into the company's cafeteria these employees will have to purchase something from the organization's catering service; if they have decided that they wish to bring in their food for financial, medical, or whatever reasons, prohibiting this may only cause ill will. Also the percentage of employees who wish to bring in their food should be quite insignificant and if it is not, then the management should be reviewing the existing catering service as it may not be providing the type of facilities the majority of employees want.

A recent growth area in industrial sites has been the introduction of convenience stores, sometimes in addition to a company's existing catering facilities and in others to replace them.

Eurest, for example, has opened thirty 'Stop Gap' shops, some including branded outlets such as Upper Crust and Deep Pan Pizza, and plans to continue opening further outlets; Gardner Merchant operates eighty 'Work Shop' units in diversified industrial sites and universities. The convenience stores are generally situated near the organization's main entrance or the catering facility itself so that it receives maximum potential customer exposure. It may be argued that these convenience stores take business away from the restaurant or cafeteria but generally they are offering a different type of product, for example a snack or sandwich, and a sale is made on site as opposed to an employee buying the same product outside the organization and bringing it in. Convenience stores are also seen as providing an additional service to a company's employees and a way of reducing a client's subsidies.

In some industrial cafeterias beverage service may only consist of non-alcoholic beverages such as tea, coffee, cold drinks, etc. In other operations particularly those in large office blocks, a bar offering alcoholic beverages may be available; for a director's dining room a separate bar area would usually be installed. The service of beverages for after the meal, such as coffee after lunch, can be served in a separate area to the main dining room. This method encourages customers to vacate their restaurant seats and hence increase the seat turnover.

An attempt should be made to try to achieve a reasonably relaxed atmosphere in the dining room thus encouraging customers to feel refreshed after their meal. This may be achieved, first, by allowing a sufficiently long meal break in which the employees may consume their meal comfortably and, second, by providing pleasant restaurant facilities for them to dine in. It is a characteristic of human nature that if an area looks clean and tidy when a customer arrives, more effort and care will usually be taken in ensuring that it stays in that same condition. However, if customers enter a dining area and find dirty crockery and utensils on the tables left by previous patrons then customers are not particularly encouraged to clean away their dining implements when they have finished eating. Consideration should also be given to the décor and furnishings of the restaurant. Tables and chairs, for example, need to be durable but can still be attractive; if they are to be used for company meetings where long rows of tables and chairs may be required, interlocking tables and fold-away chairs would also be needed.

20.2.3.3 *Food production style*

Whereas a variety of food service styles may be employed in any one industrial catering situation, the conventional cook-serve method of food production is still the most widely used for serving all the different types of outlets, for example cafeterias, restaurants, vending machines etc.

As in the kitchens of the other sectors of the industry, this involves the division of the kitchen tasks into parties, each being responsible for the production of a certain group of food items. Unlike other catering outlets, however, such as in hotels, restaurants or those involved in functions, industrial catering may involve a considerably longer holding time between production and service, particularly where the kitchen is supplying a cafeteria outlet. In this food service arrangement the food may often be kept hot in large quantities in the service line for most of the service period. Where the conventional kitchen is supplying a plated or silver service restaurant, however, then the food is either pre-portioned directly on to the customer's plate in the kitchen or on to serving salvers or platters. In large office blocks catering for several thousand employees the executive or senior management dining room may be situated away from the other catering facilities. In such situations as these where the distance separating the different facilities is considerable, the executive dining room will usually have some form of separate kitchen.

Although the conventional method of food production is still the most widely used, the cook-chill method and to a lesser extent cook freeze, are being used in the industrial sector. Cook-chill has a particular application in industrial sites such as factories which have a main administration/office block and in addition a number of satellite workshops, factories etc. With the cook-chill method the food is prepared in a central production area and may then be transported to finishing kitchens where it is reheated and served. A similar arrangement can also be used for the cook-freeze method which has an additional advantage in that the food can be transported greater distances because of the temperature at which it is held, thus serving a wider area.

The high volume of standardized dishes in the majority of industrial catering establishments lends itself to the use of convenience foods particularly in the cafeteria-type outlets which may be catering for several thousand employees over any one meal period. The foods used may be purchased directly from a central production unit. Some large contract caterers, and indeed companies operating their own catering facilities have a strong purchasing power and are able to order food and beverages directly from the food manufacturers to their own specifications, for example, cuts of meat, sausage rolls, pies, etc. and many other pre-portioned and pre-prepared food items.

In the main production area the cooking equipment is mainly of the heavy industrial type, for example large convection ovens, bratt pans, fryers, steamers, etc. For the industrial sector the equipment available should be able to cope not only with the production of large quantities of food items that may be held in the cafeteria line throughout the service period, but also with those items that must be cooked in batches to retain their freshness, for example fried foods. The use of smaller individual items of equipment such as microwaves is not so widespread in large industrial kitchens because they are only able to cater for a limited number of customers. They are particularly valuable however for snack bars, call order bars, etc. which may be a feature of a cafeteria arrangement and in finishing and satellite kitchens. Where methods of food production other than the traditional system are used, such as cook-chill or cook-freeze, specialized production equipment is necessary, such as the use of forced air convection ovens for the reheating of frozen foods.

As with function catering, the clearing away of soiled dishes at the end of each meal period is critical, particularly where large numbers are involved. In this sector of the industry conveyor belts and carousels may be used to remove the trays of dirty utensils from the food service area, such as a cafeteria, to the dishwashing area.

LEITH'S

STAFF RESTAURANT LUNCH MENU
Chef - Sally-Anne Knief

<u>SOUP</u>	*	Cream of Tomato and Basil Soup
HOT MAIN COURSE	*	Grilled Salmon with Cucumber and Apple Salsa
SALAD MAIN COURSE	*	Seafood Salad with Lime and Coriander Dressing
	**	Carrot and Courgette Roulade with Cream Cheese and Chives
	**	Bruschetta with Roasted Mediterranean Vegetables
	*	Smoked Trout with Lemon and Dill
PASTA DISH		Lasagnette with Lardons, Mushrooms, Cream and Crispy Fried Sage
SNACK DISH	**	Homemade Leek and Red Leicester Pastie
POTATOES	**	Roasted New Potatoes with Garlic
VEGETABLES	***	Broccoli Florets
	*	Honey Roasted Carrots
SALADS		Spinach with Feta Cheese and Olives Tomato, Red Onion and Red Pepper Salad Five Bean Salad with Celery and French Parsley Cracked Wheat, Cucumber and Tomato Salad with Mint and Coriander Mange Tout, Beansprout and Carrot Salad with Soy and Ginger Dressing
HOT SWEET		Cherry and Walnut Sponge with Vanilla Sauce
COLD SWEET		Summer Fruit topped Cheesecake

*   LOW FAT
**   HIGH FIBRE
***   LOW FAT & HIGH FIBRE

Figure 20.1   *An example of a staff restaurant menu served by Leith's Management in one of their City of London units*

20.2.3.4   *Food service styles*

The most widely used method of food service in industrial catering today is the self-service cafeteria. Traditionally the straight line arrangement was most commonly used but the free-flow system is now more common as it allows a considerable number of customers to enter the cafeteria and begin to make their choice of food and beverage items at the appropriate service points. In some establishments this system may have to cater for several hundred employees all arriving at the same time, for example from large factories. Numbered among the different food service points there may be several specialist bars serving selected food items; for example a salad or sandwich bar where a light meal or snack may be obtained quite quickly, or a call order bar offering mainly hot meals and snacks. A call order or grill bar will serve those items of food that can be cooked or reheated rapidly, particularly if a microwave is among the equipment used; the foods offered would include omelettes, jacket potatoes, mixed grills, pizzas, etc.

Second to the self-service arrangement is the plated method of food service in which the customer's food is plated in the kitchen and brought to their table by a waiter. Because this is a slower method of food service and more costly to provide, it is mainly confined to a fairly limited number of employees, usually those of a certain status within the organization such as the middle management upwards.

The use of the silver service is again restricted in this instance to mainly senior management only. The use of vending machines has increased during recent years although mainly for the service of beverage and snack items. Where vending is used plated main meals are still often served by counter staff, although chilled meals from vending machines are more popular than are hot meals. Where a full catering service is not provided at certain times of the day, for example for the night shift, machines vending main meals may be provided.

The carousel method of food service is used in industrial catering situations although not to any great extent, for a number of reasons. First, one carousel can only cater for a limited number of customers, after which more than one unit would need to be provided and this can prove expensive; second, only a limited number of customers can choose from the carousel at any one time, unlike the free-flow arrangement for example, which because of the number of service points, allows a larger number of customers to make their choice at the same time; third, the space needed for a carousel involves not only the space in the dining room area but also a similar amount of space in the production area; finally, a considerable back up staff is needed in the kitchen to keep the carousel well stocked with food items so that there are few, if any, labour savings. However, it is an effective food service method where it does not have to cater for too large a number of customers. It may also be useful for siting in odd-shaped areas for which other arrangements may not be suitable; for example, it may be fitted into the corner of a dining area which has limited space available. Other food service styles are used in industrial catering establishments although these are usually for specific occasions, for example buffet self-service arrangements for functions, etc.

Food and beverage items which are ready for service may be transported to the cafeteria or restaurant in a variety of ways. Where the production area is situated directly behind the cafeteria line the prepared food may either be passed through serving hatches or physically carried to the service points. Where the distance between production and service areas is greater, heated or refrigerated trolleys may be used which can be connected to the electrical system on arrival at their destination and so keep the food at the correct temperature until required for service. Where the distance is considerably greater, for example on large industrial estates, heated or refrigerated trucks may be used with the food being kept hot or refrigerated as before.

Beverage service in industrial catering may either be self-service, such as in vending, straight line or free-flow cafeterias, or waiter service to the table. In some large office blocks a bar serving alcoholic and non-alcoholic drinks may be provided and may also offer a limited menu of snacks and sandwiches.

Where large numbers are being catered for, the time for meal periods will usually allow for more than one sitting. Seat turnover may therefore be quite crucial as some employees will only have a limited meal break in which to consume their

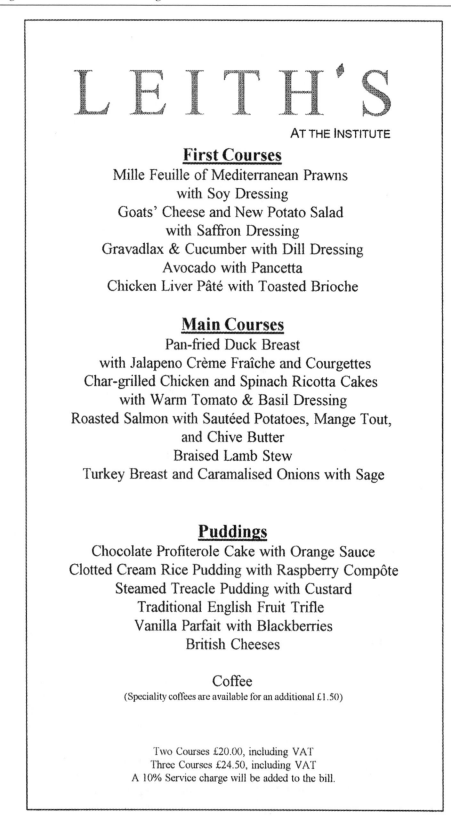

Figure 20.2   *Example of a menu for Leith's restaurant at the Institute of Chartered Accountants*

meals and return to their place of work. Because of this time constraint the slowest points of cafeteria or other food service arrangement should be critically studied and improved upon where possible. The slowest points in a cafeteria line usually include the service of beverages and the cash desks at the end of the line. The adoption of free-flow service points has done much to alleviate these slow areas, although where a traditional straight line is used these two points may still be separated out from the main line. To speed up the service of beverages there may either be a separate beverage service counter situated near to the main cafeteria arrangement or it may be sited within the dining area itself; in the latter arrangement the beverage station could be manned by food service staff or it may consist of a bank of vending machines. The cashier's stand can also be sited away from the main cafeteria line, and in any case the cashier should be given sufficient room to view more than one tray at a time. In this way the cashier may in fact be processing up to two trays at the same time: collecting money from the first person, and taking mental note of items on the second tray ready to register their prices.

The methods of payment used in industrial catering situations include the following:

1 Cash payment after the meal has been collected but before it is consumed, for example cafeteria arrangements.
2 Cash payment after the meal has been collected or served to the table and consumed, for example waiter service restaurants.
3 By purchasing tokens up to a certain value before the meal, to be exchanged in one of the establishment's catering outlets. These tokens are usually priced for two or three set courses, for example a starter and main course, or a main course and dessert, or all three courses. Where no charge is made for the meals provided a similar token system may be used, one for every day of the month, and these are given to every employee at no charge; each day employees use the restaurant, a token is removed from their card, or it is marked accordingly, so that it is no longer valid.
4 By using an 'electronic money' system, such as Girovend, in order to eliminate the handling of cash. All employees or members of an orga-

nization are issued with a card which is pre-encoded by the company's in-house control unit. The information held by the card includes the holders' user group number, the tariff number that they will be charged under and any allowances for free or subsidized purchases. The card holders are then able to load their cards with as much value as they wish at validation units. Either coins or bank notes may be used. However, an increasing number of companies link the validation units or loaders to the payroll computer to centrally deduct the amounts from salaries. Once the card has a monetary value the card holder is able to make purchases from any of the system's operated tills or vending machines. Digital displays on the units show the current card balance and the amount being spent; on completion of the purchase the new card balance will be shown.

Over recent years a number of trends have emerged which have affected the demand for industrial catering facilities and so shaped future food service styles. The introduction of flexible working hours or 'flexi-time' to the industrial sector has had an enormous impact. Flexi-time requires employees to be at work between certain hours, for example 10.00 a.m. 4.00 p.m., but they may begin work anytime after 8.30 a.m. and finish by 6.00 p.m., providing the required number of total hours per week are worked; this enables employees to choose whether to finish work early one day, or stay late another, or work longer hours for several weeks in order to earn a complete day off, etc. Due to this flexible-time scheduling many employees now take a much shorter lunch break so that they may leave work early. This has resulted in an overall decline in the number of main meals taken at work and an increased demand for more snack type facilities such as sandwich bars which sell take-away food, only 44 per cent of working people taking a proper daily lunch break. The average working lunchbreak is now 33 minutes; in 1990 39 per cent of the working population took half an hour or less for lunch, in 1994 this had risen to 51 per cent (see Figure 20.3). Where main meals are being provided there is a need for these to be served in a shorter time period and therefore the slower traditional line counter is being replaced

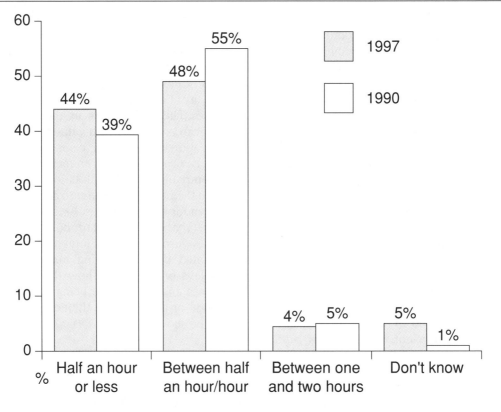

Figure 20.3   *The working lunch: time taken for lunch*
Source: Eurest Lunchtime Report 1997

by the echelon free-flow design which has a faster customer throughput.

The national average spend at work per customer on food at lunchtime is £1.45 (in London this rises to £1.79), an increase of 17 per cent over four years. Of this total, 40 per cent of employees spend less than £1.00 on their lunch, a reflection of the popularity of snacks and sandwiches (see Figures 20.4 and 20.5).

The increase in the number of women now going out to work has also led to a change in the overall demand for main meals in industrial catering facilities. Many female employees utilize their lunchtime to go shopping and therefore only require a snack at lunchtime, their main hot meal being eaten in the evening with their families. Combined with this has been the growing interest generally in our daily eating habits, and this trend has led overall to more people eating less; female employees in particular are more diet conscious today and demand lighter meals, salads, etc. at work.

Finally, mainly due to the increased cost of land, there has been a dispersal of industry away from major cities and towns, to areas where land is cheaper. Firms are also able to obtain building and training grants from the government by taking work to regions with high unemployment. This dispersal of industry has meant that for some companies the majority of their employees now live within a short commuting distance. Previously when the companies were sited in large cities a far higher percentage of their workforce would have been long distance commuters, preferring to live outside of the city and travel in daily. This is significant as long distance commuters generally need a main meal at lunchtime, more than do those employees who travel a short distance; this is because they have their breakfast earlier and are therefore in need of substantial refreshment by lunchtime. Short distance commuters, however, have breakfast comparatively late and may only need a snack lunch which they bring with them, eating their main meal in the evening.

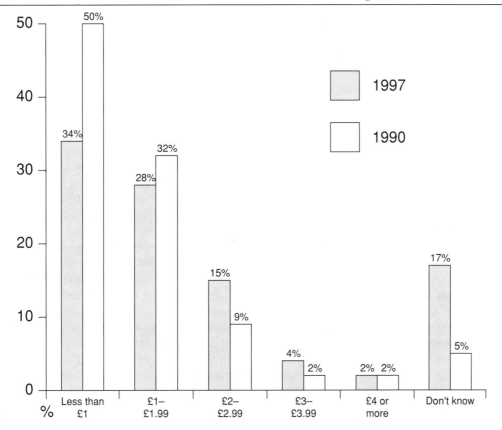

Figure 20.4   *The working lunch: average spend per customer*
Source: Eurest Lunchtime Report 1997

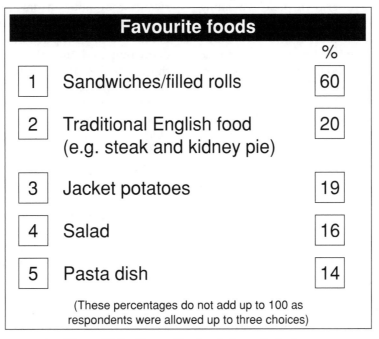

Figure 20.5   *The working lunch: favourite foods*
Source: Compass. Lunchtime Report 1994/5

The general trend today, therefore, is away from the heavier main meal at lunchtime towards a lighter snack-type meal. This has important implications for those new office blocks, factories, etc. which are currently incorporating catering facilities in their design, and for those existing catering services which in some establishments may be reduced as the original demand and sales mix have changed from when the first basic policy decisions were made.

20.2.3.5 *Organization and staffing*

The staffing of the catering department in industrial establishments is usually organized in one of two ways. First, it may be organized along the lines of other departments in the establishment using the same basic staff hierarchy structure, or, second, it may be an autonomous department within the organization with its own staffing and management hierarchy. In the first situation the catering department is seen as one of the departments in the establishment using to a large extent not only a similar personnel structure but also similar costing and budgeting techniques, marketing activities, etc. However, where the catering department is viewed as being separate from the main establishment in terms of organization, it will then also have its own policies relating specifically to that department. Whatever the catering department's internal structure, however, it is still usual for it to be responsible to the personnel department and through this to a more senior management level. The catering department is often ultimately the responsibility of personnel as it is an aspect of the organization that is concerned with the welfare of the company's employees. The management personnel in industrial catering may either be selected by the parent company through the personnel department or if it is operated by contract caterers a management team would be engaged by them.

The size of the catering department and the staffing organization necessary are determined by the size of the industrial catering facilities. A large industrial firm employing several thousand employees, for example, may have a catering department of approximately 150 staff comprising food production and service staff and the management team. A smaller company, however, employing several hundred employees

may only require about twenty-five catering staff. Economies of scale can therefore be made in terms of labour savings as the greater the number to be catered for, the smaller relatively the number of catering staff required and thus the ratio of staff to customers is reduced.

The staffing ratio of service personnel to customers also varies from one type of outlet to another. In the directors' dining room, for example, where silver service may be used, the ratio of customers to staff can be as low as eight customers to every one waiter. In the middle management or supervisory dining room where plated service is often used, the ratio may increase to fifteen to twenty guests for every one waiter. In the cafeteria with a self-service system the ratio is more difficult to quantify but may be as high as thirty to fifty guests for every one member of staff.

Generally speaking the hours worked by staff in the industrial sector are more 'social' than those worked by staff in other sectors. This is mainly due to the majority of offices and factories working a standard five-day week Monday to Friday with weekends free; catering staff are therefore able to work straight shifts through the day. Exceptions to this include continuous process industries that must be staffed twenty-four hours a day, seven days a week; examples of these organizations include office blocks with computer systems and heavy extracting and manufacturing industries. For these sectors of the industry a twenty-four hour catering service is also required and therefore a night shift is usually provided although sometimes an extended vending service only is available.

Because a large number of companies only provide one main meal a day, for example lunch, they really only require a full complement of catering staff during the morning for preparation work and for the actual service period; a skeleton staff is then able to cope with any afternoon teas and snacks. This busy period of 10.00 a.m.–3.00 p.m. is often organized by employing part-time labour engaged for a set number of hours. These hours are particularly attractive to working mothers who are able to leave and collect their children from school before and after work. During the school holiday periods the industrial companies may either provide crèches for the children so that the mothers may continue working or if this is not possible other part-time labour may have to be found, for example students on vacation. A higher percentage of women also tend to hold supervisory and managerial positions in industrial catering than in other sectors of the industry. This is again mainly due to the more convenient working hours which are such that women can combine a managerial position with running a home.

The number of part-time staff employed in contract catering rose by 9 per cent during 1966 from 35,000 to 38,428 whilst the number of full-time staff dropped by nearly 6 per cent from 97,765 to 92,663. For the purpose of comparison, the British Hospitality Association assumed two part-time employees to be the equivalent of one full-time employee, a total overall drop of 3.1 per cent in the number of staff per outlet (see Table 20.5). For the corresponding period the number of outlets and meals served increased indicating a tighter control on labour costs and improved productivity as the number of staff per outlet fell from 7.4 to 7.7.

Due to the high percentage of part-time labour often being used in industrial kitchens only the higher echelons of production staff usually need to be craft trained. The everyday preparation work can be performed by relatively untrained employees and this is further aided by the high percentage of convenience foods used in these kitchens. By employing non-craft employees where possible in both the production and service areas, labour costs are able to be kept down. Where higher standards of skills are needed to provide a wider selection of foods requiring more skilled work, for example in the directors' dining room, separate production and service staff may be employed for this type of catering outlet.

The organization of the catering department will depend on the number and variety of catering facilities provided but where there is more than one type of facility each outlet would usually have its own restaurant supervisor or manager. Often several cafeterias and restaurants can be served by one large production area which would be managed by the head chef and a number of *sous* or second chefs. If the industrial layout was such that more than one production area was needed to serve the different outlets then a number of 'head' chefs may be employed. Overseeing both the production and service areas is the catering manager who is mainly responsible for the financial aspects of the department as well as the standards of service and who would liaise with the head chef and restaurant manager on such matters as budgeting and costing, menu formulation and selection and so on.

The concept of facilities management is also becoming widespread in the industrial sector whereby the catering contractor not only organizes and manages a company's catering requirements but also a range of other needs depending on the client. This may include such areas as cleaning, housekeeping and laundry, security, buildings and maintenance, gardening and waste disposal. Table 20.6 lists the range of support services offered by catering contractors. Some large organizations have their own facilities management division, for example Gardner Merchant provides a FM service to groups such as British Gas, the Ford Motor Company and the BBC.

The training of food production and service staff will depend on whether the parent company is operating its own catering facilities or whether contract caterers are being used. Where a company is direct catering, its own personnel department would be responsible for the train-

Table 20.5   *Employees in UK contract catering: number of staff per outlet*

	1997	*1996*	*1995*	*1994*	*1993*	*1992*	*1991*	*1990*
Number of outlets	16,722	15,632	14,941	13,354	10,552	10,405	9,388	8,583
Number of staff[a]	111,875	115,430	113,606	105,436	91,802	90,880	81,500	74,813
Number of staff per outlet	6.7	7.4	7.6	7.9	8.7	8.7	8.7	8.7

[a]Full-time equivalents for years 1994–97
Source: British Hospitality Association

Table 20.6   *UK contract catering: range of support services*

	Number of outlets	
	1977	1996
Bar	355	394
Cleaning	950	635
Housekeeping	349	461
Maintenance	45	46
Building property management	18	13
Laundry	204	243
Shops	334	235
Reception	72	72
Social Clubs	48	52
Security	62	60
Gardening	82	65
Waste removal	44	74
Postal	17	19
Road sweeping	28	30
Medical	6	15
Distribution	12	19
Fire	3	11
Other	326	534
Total	2,855	2,978

Source: British Hospitality Association

ing of the catering staff; where contract caterers are employed they would engage and train their own staff. Most large industrial contractors have a standard training programme and all catering employees would also undergo a basic induction course to the company. This induction and training programme is very important in the recruitment of new employees. Research has shown that the most critical period for a newly engaged employee is the first few weeks with the company. During this initial period the possibility of employees leaving the company is increased if they are unsure of exactly what their job entails because it has not been explained to them or if they have not been trained in how to do their job. It is therefore important that all catering employees be given some form of induction to the company and a very clear job description outlining the tasks they are expected to undertake and the responsibilities they will have. It is not sufficient to expect new employees to try and find out for themselves what their job entails 'as they go along'. An appreciation of this problem has lead to governments setting up training boards which

can monitor and assist the training programmes for individuals and companies.

In the UK the Hospitality Training Foundation (HTF) provides information and support on training by collaborating with trade and professional bodies, educational establishments, employers and trade unions. The HTF has a charitable status and aims to 'help the hospitality industry raise standards and improve performance by understanding and capitalizing on the benefits of training, and to help secure an adequate flow of new entrants to the industry through a co-ordinated approach to careers promotion'. The HTF has three trading divisions, the Hotel and Catering Training Company (HCTC) involved in organizing youth and adult training programmes; the Hospitality Awarding Body awarding NVQs and SVQs; and the Stonebow Group offering training, consultancy and management development, some courses being sponsored by the government and others by the European Social Fund (ESF).

Through the HTF in the UK it is possible for a wide range of employees to obtain training and if successful, certification at craft level and at managing the training function. All of these qualifications being widely recognized throughout all sectors of the industry.

The provision of uniforms for catering staff also helps individual employees to identify with the organization for which they work, whether it is the parent company directly or a catering contractor. In the latter case most catering contractors are keen to provide uniforms for their staff because it promotes the company's image and increases the contractor's profile in the industry.

Finally, it is important that the catering department is represented on the company's staff committees and councils. This enables a two-way flow of information to take place, with any department in the company able to express their views regarding the catering facilities and allowing the catering department to answer any suggestions, problems or grievances that may be put forward to them.

20.3   Control and performance measurement

In order to measure the performance of a catering department, standards must be laid down against which actual results may be measured. It must not be assumed that the level of sophistication is necessarily a function of the size of the organization (although generally the larger companies do have more documented control and performance policies), rather it is a function of the parent company's attitude towards the catering department and the management personnel who are responsible for it. Standards should be documented in the form of policies which contain the objectives of the organization in providing the catering facilities and the parameters within which the catering department must function, documented in the form of budgets.

In formulating a catering budget the services being provided within the establishment must first be identified, for example the directors' dining room, vending facilities, overtime meals, etc. The menus for the respective outlets must be reviewed and if possible weekly or monthly cycle menus may be introduced. These are of particular value when used in conjunction with sales histories and volume forecasting techniques, both of which have particular application in establishments in the industrial sector where the number of customers using the catering facilities is often quite constant from day to day. Third, the sales and costs for the catering service must be itemized for each outlet; in a large industrial company there may be a number of different sales points including beverage vending machines, snack bars and tea trolley services, in addition to the more substantial facilities, such as cafeterias and dining rooms. The costs incurred by the catering department would include some or all of the following: food costs, wages and salaries, cleaning materials, maintenance, replacement of equipment, fuel costs, decoration and refurbishing charges and so on. Having assessed the income and expenditure for the catering department for the coming year a reasonably realistic figure can then be obtained for the operation's expected profit, or loss. This is a highly generalized sequence of steps for formulating a budget, but illustrates how a rough framework can be drawn up fairly quickly within which a more detailed analysis can take place. For example, in assessing the department's sales figures each outlet could be further broken down according to the menu structure,

for example soups, grills, fish, vegetables, etc. and the differential profit margins calculated for each group of menu items. In this way high GP items may be identified and incorporated into other menus and low GP items excluded or used to a lesser extent.

In addition to producing detailed financial accounts, attention should also be given to the everyday control of the catering department; this begins with the goods being ordered and delivered to the establishment and is complete with the sale of the food items. When the goods are first delivered to the establishment they must be checked against the order forms and entered in some form of goods inward book which can be periodically examined by the catering manager and by the company's auditors. Where possible stocks of food and beverages should be kept to a minimum for a number of reasons. First, the operation's capital is tied up which can adversely affect its cash flow; second, high stock values mean an unnecessarily high insurance to cover any risks to the goods; third, there is an increased risk of spoilage due to bad stock rotation. As a rough guide the turnover rate for perishable items should be about twenty during a 28-day period and for non-perishable items once during a 28-day period. Fourth, there may be an increased risk of pilferage; and finally, it encourages staff to use more than may be necessary because of the large quantities being held. Generally speaking, therefore, stockholding should not be encouraged and as a rule of thumb should be no more than one and a half times a week's takings. The stores being held should also relate to the operation's menu structure, and to safeguard this a Goods Issues Book should be kept to check that the goods being delivered to the establishment are actually used by it.

The control cycle is complete at the end of the service period when a sales reconciliation has been compiled comparing actual consumption with the quantity of food produced by the kitchen;this information is usually documented on a sales reconciliation sheet which can then be sent to the food and beverage control department. This is a far more satisfactory piece of control information than, for example, other physical checks such as plate counts which can be interfered with too easily. Where an establishment has more than one catering outlet sales reconciliation sheets may be produced for all the sales points, that is, cafeterias, dining rooms, vending operations, tea trolley services, etc.

The methods of payment used by different catering facilities each warrant a different type of control system:

1 In some operations only cash payment is accepted which is paid directly to the cashier at the end of the cafeteria line. In others, luncheon vouchers may be used in part or total payment for the meal.

2 Payment may also be made directly to a member of the service staff in waiter service restaurants or at a sufficiently high managerial level patrons may only need to sign their bills at the end of the meal and no cash is exchanged, except perhaps for alcoholic drinks. In-house credit cards may also be used, enabling patrons' accounts to be directly debited so that no cash payment occurs.

3 In some operations no cash is handled within the catering outlet; instead patrons purchase meal tokens prior to entering the restaurant, according to the number of menu items they wish to have. However, the token system is not as widely used today as it could be in industrial catering, for a number of reasons. First, there is the additional administration involved in producing the tokens; second, tighter control is needed to ensure that the meals are being exchanged for tokens and not being given away to some customers free of charge; third, physical control is needed so that today's meal tokens cannot be 'recycled' for tomorrow's meals; and finally, once a customer has chosen the menu items and purchased the required number of meal tokens, the 'impulse buying' factor is removed from the cafeteria line.

4 The use of cashless systems in industrial catering situations enables detailed sales information to be produced for performance evaluation by management. All GiroVend units for example, record in memory the value of the sales by product, user group and user's operating tariff. Figures 20.6 and 20.7 are examples of product turnover information from a 'GiroVend for Windows' (Microsoft) system and have itemized the weekly and monthly sales by GiroCard or cash and given

a report on the subsidies and guest card refunds operating during that particular time period. Data from each of the systems point of sale or loaders is transferred to the control unit for full management accounts and to update the audit system.

All reports contain an audit voucher number which increases in strict numerical order each time a report is taken, enabling a check to be made that all reports are consecutive (see Figure 20.8).

20.3.1 Measurement of performance of contract caterers

All of the previous detail is relative to the measurement of performance by caterers of their unit(s), whether it is an in-house catering situation or a contract caterer.

The measurement of performance by a client of the catering contractor is something which may be done periodically but should always be reviewed well in advance of the end of the current contract period, so that should the present contractor be found unsuitable, time would be available to seek out a new contractor.

The measurement of performance would include the following:

1 *Relationship.* A satisfactory business relationship during the period of the contract, between the client and management of the catering contractor.

2 *Cost to the client.* The maintenance of the operation within the agreed prescribed limits, for example for food costs; this could have been agreed on a per head of employee, or per employee served, basis. The cost of other operational expenses could be on a comparative basis with previous trading periods or related to the number of meals served.

3 *Prices paid for raw materials.* The prices paid for all food and beverage items to be seen to be of an acceptable fair level. Comparisons of prices paid would easily be made against published prices of major wholesalers and price indices published in the major trade journals. The level of discount given by the catering contractor for food and beverage items is usually only a small percentage of what the contractor

GiroVend®
© 1994-1996 GiroVend Holdings Ltd.

Licenced to:
SmartCard '97

Audit Summary REPRINT
Level 2 Weekly Audit (2)
Audit Number : 30
Audit From : 13/01/97 11:54:32
Audit To : 21/01/97 12:56:10

Machine		GiroCard					Cash				Summary	
#	Vchr	Sales	Subsidy	Refund	Loading	Payout	Sales	Subsidy	Refund	Overpay	GV Bal	Cash Box
Vending/Tills with product breakdown												
1	30	136.87	0.00	0.00	511.37	0.00	0.00	0.00	0.00	0.00	374.50	511.37
39	30	137.75	0.00	0.00	221.43	0.00	0.00	0.00	0.00	0.00	83.68	221.43
Section Total:		274.62	0.00	0.00	732.80	0.00	0.00	0.00	0.00	0.00	458.18	732.80
Coin/Notes loaders												
10	30	0.00	0.00	0.00	778.50	0.00	0.00	0.00	0.00	0.00	778.50	778.50
11	30	0.00	0.00	0.00	804.00	0.00	0.00	0.00	0.00	0.00	804.00	804.00
12	30	0.00	0.00	0.00	407.00	0.00	0.00	0.00	0.00	0.00	407.00	407.00
Section Total:		0.00	0.00	0.00	1,989.50	0.00	0.00	0.00	0.00	0.00	1,989.50	1,989.50
Guest card refund units												
0	30	0.00	0.00	0.00	176.12	3.00	0.00	0.00	0.00	0.00	173.12	173.12
Section Total:		0.00	0.00	0.00	176.12	3.00	0.00	0.00	0.00	0.00	173.12	173.12
Grand Total:		274.62	0.00	0.00	2,898.42	3.00	0.00	0.00	0.00	0.00	2,620.80	2,895.42

GiroVend®
© 1994-1996 GiroVend Holdings Ltd.

Licenced to:
SmartCard '97

Audit Summary REPRINT
Level 2 Weekly Audit (2)
Audit Number : 31
Audit From : 21/01/97 12:56:10
Audit To : 24/01/97 19:05:33

Machine		GiroCard					Cash				Summary	
#	Vchr	Sales	Subsidy	Refund	Loading	Payout	Sales	Subsidy	Refund	Overpay	GV Bal	Cash Box
Vending/Tills with product breakdown												
1	31	118.15	0.00	0.00	504.35	0.00	0.00	0.00	0.00	0.00	386.20	504.35
39	31	145.14	0.00	0.00	229.63	0.00	0.00	0.00	0.00	0.00	84.49	229.63
Section Total:		263.29	0.00	0.00	733.98	0.00	0.00	0.00	0.00	0.00	470.69	733.98
Coin/Notes loaders												
10	31	0.00	0.00	0.00	723.50	0.00	0.00	0.00	0.00	0.00	723.50	723.50
11	31	0.00	0.00	0.00	687.00	0.00	0.00	0.00	0.00	0.00	687.00	687.00
12	31	0.00	0.00	0.00	409.00	0.00	0.00	0.00	0.00	0.00	409.00	409.00
Section Total:		0.00	0.00	0.00	1,819.50	0.00	0.00	0.00	0.00	0.00	1,819.50	1,819.50
Guest card refund units												
0	31	0.00	0.00	0.00	150.86	4.86	0.00	0.00	0.00	0.00	146.00	146.00
Section Total:		0.00	0.00	0.00	150.86	4.86	0.00	0.00	0.00	0.00	146.00	146.00
Grand Total:		263.29	0.00	0.00	2,704.34	4.86	0.00	0.00	0.00	0.00	2,436.19	2,699.48

Figure 20.6 *Extracts from GiroVend weekly audits, to be transferred to the monthly audit*

GiroVend®	Audit Summary REPRINT
© 1994–1996 GiroVend Holdings Ltd.	*Level 3 Monthly Audit (3)*
Licenced to: SmartCard '97	Audit Number : 9 Audit From : 03/01/97 17:53:42 Audit To : 01/02/97 18:57:56

Machine		GiroCard					Cash				Summary	
#	Vchr	Sales	Subsidy	Refund	Loading	Payout	Sales	Subsidy	Refund	Overpay	GV Bal.	Cash Box

Vending/Tills with product breakdown

#	Vchr	Sales	Subsidy	Refund	Loading	Payout	Sales	Subsidy	Refund	Overpay	GV Bal.	Cash Box
1	9	480.64	0.00	0.00	1,936.53	0.00	0.00	0.00	0.00	0.00	1,455.89	1,936.53
4	9	41.66	0.00	0.00	0.00	0.00	0.00	0.00	0.00	0.00	-41.66	0.00
32	9	167.93	0.00	0.00	0.00	0.00	0.00	0.00	0.00	0.00	-167.93	0.00
33	9	128.27	0.00	0.00	0.00	0.00	0.00	0.00	0.00	0.00	-128.27	0.00
36	9	129.98	0.00	0.00	0.00	0.00	0.00	0.00	0.00	0.00	-129.98	0.00
37	9	869.45	0.00	0.00	0.00	0.00	0.00	0.00	0.00	0.00	-869.45	0.00
38	9	665.54	0.00	0.00	0.00	0.00	0.00	0.00	0.00	0.00	-665.54	0.00
39	9	546.82	0.00	0.00	873.95	0.00	0.00	0.00	0.00	0.00	327.13	873.95
40	9	528.34	0.00	0.00	0.00	0.00	0.00	0.00	0.00	0.00	-528.34	0.00
41	9	601.68	0.00	0.00	0.00	0.00	0.00	0.00	0.00	0.00	-601.68	0.00
42	9	425.90	0.00	0.00	0.00	0.00	0.00	0.00	0.00	0.00	-425.90	0.00
45	9	408.83	0.00	0.00	0.00	0.00	0.00	0.00	0.00	0.00	-408.83	0.00
51	9	94.65	0.00	0.00	0.00	0.00	0.00	0.00	0.00	0.00	-94.65	0.00
61	9	635.69	0.00	0.00	0.00	0.00	0.00	0.00	0.00	0.00	-635.69	0.00
62	9	1,005.75	0.00	0.00	0.00	0.00	0.00	0.00	0.00	0.00	-1,005.75	0.00
63	9	542.50	0.00	0.00	0.00	0.00	0.00	0.00	0.00	0.00	-542.50	0.00
64	9	843.25	0.00	0.00	0.00	0.00	0.00	0.00	0.00	0.00	-843.25	0.00
65	9	961.38	0.00	0.00	0.00	0.00	0.00	0.00	0.00	0.00	-961.38	0.00
66	9	363.70	0.00	0.00	0.00	0.00	0.00	0.00	0.00	0.00	-363.70	0.00
67	9	350.85	0.00	0.00	0.00	0.00	0.00	0.00	0.00	0.00	-350.85	0.00
68	9	201.65	0.00	0.00	0.00	0.00	0.00	0.00	0.00	0.00	-201.65	0.00
Section Total:		**9,994.46**	**0.00**	**0.00**	**2,810.48**	**0.00**	**0.00**	**0.00**	**0.00**	**0.00**	**-7,183.98**	**2,810.48**

Other Vending/Tills

#	Vchr	Sales	Subsidy	Refund	Loading	Payout	Sales	Subsidy	Refund	Overpay	GV Bal.	Cash Box
3	9	427.22	0.00	0.00	0.00	0.00	0.00	0.00	0.00	0.00	-427.22	0.00
9	9	154.75	0.00	0.00	0.00	0.00	0.00	0.00	0.00	0.00	-154.75	0.00
14	9	35.60	0.00	0.00	0.00	0.00	0.00	0.00	0.00	0.00	-35.60	0.00
16	9	221.55	0.00	0.00	0.00	0.00	0.00	0.00	0.00	0.00	-221.55	0.00
Section Total:		**839.12**	**0.00**	**0.00**	**0.00**	**0.00**	**0.00**	**0.00**	**0.00**	**0.00**	**-839.12**	**0.00**

Coin/Notes loaders

#	Vchr	Sales	Subsidy	Refund	Loading	Payout	Sales	Subsidy	Refund	Overpay	GV Bal.	Cash Box
10	9	0.00	0.00	0.00	3,081.50	0.00	0.00	0.00	0.00	0.00	3,081.50	3,081.50
11	9	0.00	0.00	0.00	2,858.50	0.00	0.00	0.00	0.00	0.00	2,858.50	2,858.50
12	9	0.00	0.00	0.00	1,399.00	0.00	0.00	0.00	0.00	0.00	1,399.00	1,399.00
Section Total:		**0.00**	**0.00**	**0.00**	**7,339.00**	**0.00**	**0.00**	**0.00**	**0.00**	**0.00**	**7,339.00**	**7,339.00**

Guest card refund units

#	Vchr	Sales	Subsidy	Refund	Loading	Payout	Sales	Subsidy	Refund	Overpay	GV Bal.	Cash Box
0	9	0.00	0.00	0.00	820.80	33.67	0.00	0.00	0.00	0.00	787.13	787.13
Section Total:		**0.00**	**0.00**	**0.00**	**820.80**	**33.67**	**0.00**	**0.00**	**0.00**	**0.00**	**787.13**	**787.13**

| *Grand Total:* | | *10,833.58* | *0.00* | *0.00* | *10,970.28* | *33.67* | *0.00* | *0.00* | *0.00* | *0.00* | *103.03* | *10,936.61* |

Figure 20.7   *Example of a GiroVend monthly audit*

receives, and it is for this reason that the client needs to monitor the prices paid, as suppliers will willingly inflate prices and then discount them to the contractor to an agreed level.

4 *Maintenance of standard of product.* The standard of product achieved by the contractor on a day-to-day basis, should be at least of an acceptable consistent level. This can be measured by the number and type of comments received often from a users' committee and by the percentage of uptake by the employees.

5 *Maintenance of hygiene standards.* The standard of hygiene set by the client and achieved by the contractor should be as high as is operationally practical. This should be regularly measured by the catering contractor with the results available for the client, but also by the local environmental health department for the

GiroVend	**Product Turnover REPRINT**
© 1994-1996 GiroVend Holdings Ltd.	**Level 3 Monthly Audit (3)**
Licenced to:	Audit Number : 9
SmartCard '97	Audit From : 03/01/97 17:53:42
	Audit To : 01/02/97 18:57:56

	Quantity	*Value*
Machine: **Central Purchasing Drinks (38)**		
Product:		
Hot Water (22)	997.00	19.94
UNKNOWN DRINK (23)	4,304.00	645.60
Machine Total: Central Purchasing Drinks (38)	5,301.00	665.54
Machine: **Central Purchasing Drinks No4 (4)**		
Product:		
Hot Water (22)	19.00	2.66
Kenco Coffee (1)	260.00	39.00
Machine Total: Central Purchasing Drinks No4 (4)	279.00	41.66
Machine: **Central Purchasing Food (63)**		
Product:		
Snack item .25p (27)	119.00	29.75
Snack item .35p (29)	482.00	127.20
Snack item 30p (28)	144.00	43.20
UNKNOWN PRODUCT (0)	1,079.00	342.35
Machine Total: Central Purchasing Food (63)	1,824.00	542.50
Machine: **Group Finance Drinks (33)**		
Product:		
Cappuccino (6)	58.00	8.70
ChocoMilk (9)	19.00	2.85
Esspresso (7)	7.00	1.05
Hot Chocolate (8)	14.00	2.10
Hot Water (22)	61.00	1.22
Kenco Coffee (1)	686.00	102.90
Tetley Leaf Tea (4)	63.00	9.45
Machine Total: Group Finance Drinks (33)	908.00	128.27
Machine: **Marketing Drinks (32)**		
Product:		
Cappuccino (6)	154.00	23.10
ChocoMilk (9)	59.00	8.85
Esspresso (7)	14.00	2.10
Hot Chocolate (8)	18.00	2.70
Hot Water (22)	34.00	0.68
Kenco Coffee (1)	811.00	121.65
Tetley Leaf Tea (4)	59.00	8.85
Machine Total: Marketing Drinks (32)	1,149.00	167.93
Machine: **P2 Basement Drinks (40)**		
Product:		
Hot Water (22)	380.00	7.54
UNKNOWN DRINK (23)	3,492.00	520.80
Machine Total: P2 Basement Drinks (40)	3,872.00	528.34
Machine: **P2 Basement Food 1 (2000) (64)**		
Product:		
Vend food 60p (83)	246.00	134.75
Vend food 70p (84)	149.00	94.25
Vend food 80p (85)	173.00	122.25
Vend food 90p (86)	109.00	92.65
Vending food 20p (80)	282.00	54.00
Vending food 35p (81)	207.00	68.95
Vending food 40p (88)	282.00	103.60
Vending food 45p (82)	398.00	172.80
Machine Total: P2 Basement Food 1 (2000) (64)	1,846.00	843.25
Machine: **P2 Basement Food 2 (1200) (65)**		
Product:		
UNKNOWN DRINK (23)	3,400.00	961.38
Machine Total: P2 Basement Food 2 (1200) (65)	3,400.00	961.38

Figure 20.8   *Example of a detailed GiroVend product turnover reprint*

	Quantity	*Value*
<u>Machine:</u> **The Link Drinks (37)**		
Product:		
Hot Water (22)	340.00	6.80
UNKNOWN DRINK (23)	5,755.00	862.65
Machine Total: The Link Drinks (37)	6,095.00	869.45
<u>Machine:</u> **The Link Food 1 (1200) (61)**		
Product:		
Snack item .25p (27)	894.00	223.50
Snack item .35p (29)	217.00	75.95
Snack item 18P (25)	63.00	11.34
Snack item 30p (28)	1,086.00	324.90
Machine Total: The Link Food 1 (1200) (61)	2,260.00	635.69
<u>Machine:</u> **The Link Food 2 (2000) (62)**		
Product:		
Vend food 60p (83)	371.00	204.05
Vend food 70p (84)	332.00	215.80
Vend food 80p (85)	203.00	152.25
Vend food 90p (86)	100.00	85.00
Vending food 20p (80)	278.00	55.60
Vending food 35p (81)	187.00	65.45
Vending food 40p (88)	155.00	62.00
Vending food 45p (82)	368.00	165.60
Machine Total: The Link Food 2 (2000) (62)	1,994.00	1,005.75
<u>Machine:</u> **Warehouse Drinks (36)**		
Product:		
Cappuccino (6)	157.00	23.55
Fizzy Raspberry (13)	58.00	8.70
Hot Water (22)	19.00	0.38
Kenco Coffee (1)	87.00	13.05
Kenco Decaff (2)	217.00	32.55
LEMON TEA (92)	344.00	51.60
Tetley Leaf Tea (4)	1.00	0.15
Machine Total: Warehouse Drinks (36)	883.00	129.98
Grand Total:	*49,636.00*	*9,994.46*

Figure 20.8   *(Contd)*

client, together with any complaints by the customers.

6 *The ability of the contractor to provide extra services.* This could be the provision of back up facilities by the contractor for such things as providing a kitchen and restaurant design service, providing technical advice on energy saving, providing a customer satisfaction survey and analysis, etc., as well as being up to date with current trends in modern business practice, catering trade practice, etc.

The performance of contract caterers can be measured against the standards detailed in the client contract. There are various types of contracts which may be employed, either individually or as a combination.

Traditionally the 'cost-plus' contract has been the most popular arrangement whereby all costs relating to the catering service are met by the client and in addition a management fee is paid to the contractor. However, over recent years this type of contract has declined sharply (see Table 20.7) as clients become more budget and cost conscious and look to contract caterers to help them reduce their catering subsidies. This client-driven shift is particularly noticeable in the welfare sector where fixed price tenders are required so that tender bids can be compared against each other. Fixed price contracts involve the client paying a set price for the catering service and require the caterer to undertake some financial risk, because if they underestimate the cost of the service they bear the excess financial burden.

Other types of contract include performance guarantee contracts ensuring costs do not exceed a certain amount, for example a client may only subsidize labour and overheads, the caterer being responsible for other costs. Partnership contracts involve the client and caterer agreeing on the partnership ratio and then sharing the subsequent costs and revenue of the catering service. Finally, concessionary rent contracts require

the contractor to pay a rental fee to the client in order to operate the catering service; this may be based on a percentage of profit or turnover or be a fixed amount.

Table 20.7 *Types of catering contract in the UK*

	1997	1996	1995	1994
Cost plus	6,762	7,637	7,925	7,958
Contract with performance guarantee	1,342	950	654	529
Fixed price	8,070	6,224	5,493	4,018
Partnership	131	86	101	72
Concession rent	671	735	741	777
Total	16,722	15,632	14,914	13,354

Source: BHA Contract Catering Survey 1997

20.4 Reference

British Hospitality Association (1997). *Contract Catering Survey*. London: Marketpower.

Koudra, M. Industrial and Welfare Catering 1970–1980. MPhil Thesis, University of Surrey. Unpublished.

Compass. The Eurest Lunchtime Report 1997.

21
Food and beverage management in school catering

21.1 Introduction

Welfare catering may be defined as that sector of the catering industry primarily concerned with the preparation and service of food and non-alcoholic beverages, the cost of which is not normally or totally passed on to the consumer. This sector includes schools, hospitals, homes for the young, the elderly, the underprivileged, prisons, etc. Because there may be little or no alternative catering facilities available to these customers, they may defined respectively as semi-captive or captive markets. Furthermore, they may represent mixed markets in terms of age, sex, socio-economic classification, nationality, religion etc.

Although differing from one another in certain aspects, the welfare catering sector has a number of characteristics which are common to many of these types of operations:

1 They are governed and affected by national and local government changes in policy. Establishments such as state schools, hospitals and prisons are part of the public sector of the catering industry and are directly affected by government changes in financial policies, level of subsidies, nutritional standards, etc. Recently passed government acts in particular have had a significant effect on the school meals and hospital services; their implications are dealt with in more detail later in this chapter.

2 Financial budgeting is tightly controlled by national and local government authorities. Until recently public sector catering operations have been controlled through government designation of cost limits and budgets, suppliers that may be used, wages set through national trade union agreements, etc. The historical trend is now being altered by the introduction of local financial management, for example delegating financial control to individual schools, and to local health authorities.

3 Nutritional standards are particularly important in the welfare sector. When school meals for example, were introduced in the early 1900s, they had an important role to play in providing adequate nutrition to school children. Today, although the school meals service has altered greatly, nutritional standards are still important. Hospital and prison catering, too, has a large responsibility in this field, particularly where patients or inmates do not have alternative catering facilities available to them, and are therefore reliant on the institutions for their total feeding requirements.

Welfare catering is also faced with the problem of providing sufficient variety and choice in the number of menu items that may be made available, working within limited financial budgets. Variety of choice has particular relevance in captive market situations such as welfare establishments.

4 The social importance of the welfare catering service. Initially, the social role of the school meal service was to provide school children with nutritionally balanced meals at lunch time. Today, its social role has expanded to accommodate a number of identifiable current trends; these include an increase in the number of smaller, snack-type meals being taken, a rise in the percentage of working mothers, an increase in the number of families no longer sitting down together in the evening for their main meal. In many cases this has led to school lunches becoming the children's

main meal of the day and one of the few social meal occasions that may be had; because of this many schools still see school meals as an important part of their pupils education.

5 Mixed markets are often catered for in welfare catering operations. In commercial situations, different market levels may be identified using criteria such as social, age, geographic, income, etc., and the different market segments catered for accordingly; in schools, hospitals, old people's homes and other institutions, such segmentation does not occur, all levels of markets are catered for together and in much the same way. School head teachers, doctors and senior medical staff may have separate dining facilities but in the majority of situations, all 'customers' are provided for together in welfare establishments. Thus, what may be acceptable and appeal to one school child, or hospital patient, may not appeal to another. In few other areas of the catering industry is a service faced with catering to such varied and possibly mixed markets within the same catering facilities.

6 Service periods are rigidly observed. Due to the strict daily timetable of schools, hospitals and prisons, meal periods are equally strictly observed. In a school, for example, serving between two to three hundred children, the lunchtime service may only extend from 12.30–1.15 p.m. A commercial operation serving a similar number of customers may remain open for up to three times that service time. Welfare establishments often do not have the flexibility to serve for longer periods – the school hall may be used as the dining room and needed for other activities after lunch; doctors' visits, medical check-ups have to be adhered to in hospitals, etc. In commercial operations a greater degree of flexibility is available.

7 Large-scale production methods are used. Because of the large number of customers that have to be served within a limited service period, large-scale production methods are often employed and utilized by welfare establishments, in particular cook-chill and cook-freeze. These methods have led to many operations, but not necessarily all, making savings due to economies of scale.

8 Meals may be served in non-restaurant surroundings and by non-catering staff, for example patients in hospital wards, children in school gymnasiums, halls, classrooms etc. Increasingly, however, where space and finance permit, restaurants and cafeterias of a more permanent nature are replacing antiquated school dining facilities, and able hospital patients are encouraged to eat their meals in a communal dining or lounge area, away from the ward environment. Frequently meals may have to be transported considerable distances to satellite kitchens and so mobile trolleys may also serve as temporary service counters.

Catering services in schools as we know them today are the result of considerable development since the Second World War. The standards reached are high in spite of the problems caused by the different governments whose attitude to the welfare services in the UK have not been consistent.

21.2   The school meals service

A brief resumé of the history of the school meals service in the UK and the government legislation and reports that have affected it will highlight the speed at which the service has developed:

- *Pre-1906.* Meals provided only to some children on a voluntary basis by charities.
- *1906.* The Education (Provision of Meals) Act, empowered local education authorities to provide and aid the provision of meals free and at reduced charges for necessitous children and at a charge not less than the food cost for other children.
- *1914–1918.* Provision of school meals temporarily expanded on a great scale but declined from 1915 with the government discouraging the provision of meals.
- *1919–1938.* Expenditure on school meals and milk rose fourfold, while the parental contribution decreased from 73 per cent to 42 per cent reflecting the emphasis on free and subsidized meals.
- *1939–1945.* The government encouraged the development of the provision of school meals.

In 1943 grants up to 100 per cent to build and equip school canteens were given. The 1944 Education Act and the Provision of Milk and Meals Regulation required local authorities to provide school meals in all maintained schools.

- *1955 and 1966*. Nutritional standards of school meals were updated. Methods of food service and the range of meals provided were increased.
- *1967*. The school meals service was financed by the local authority rate support grant and not solely by the government.
- *1973*. Re-organization of local government from 197 to 115 bodies.
- *1976–1979*. The government reduced its contributions to the cost of school meals.
- *1980*. The Education Act no longer required local authorities to provide meals of specific nutritional standard. More emphasis by some authorities was placed on the provision of snack meals and a variety of meals at varying prices. Parental contribution increased as local authorities increased the prices for meals; local authorities no longer required to provide school meals except for children of families receiving supplementary benefit.
- *1983*. The NACNE Report (National Advisory Committee on Nutrition Education) published its report 'Proposals for nutritional guidelines in Britain' recommending a reduction in fats, sugar, salt and alcohol and an increase in dietary fibre; it also set nutritional guidelines to the year 2000.
- *1984*. The COMA Report (Committee on Medical Aspects of Food Policy) published its report 'Diet and cardiovascular disease' outlining recommendations for a healthy diet.
- *1986*. The Social Security Act was introduced and free school meal arrangements changed, cash payments were introduced to families receiving family credit.
- *1987*. Under the Local Government Act, local authorities were obliged to open Direct Service Organization (DSOs), for example school meals, to compulsory competitive tendering, that is, allowing both private commercial firms and 'in-house' caterers to compete for school meals catering contracts.
- *1988*. The Education Reform Act introduced Local Management of Schools (LMS), devolv-

ing financial responsibility to some school heads.
- *1992*. The School Meals Campaign was launched calling for the reintroduction of nationally agreed nutritional standards for school meals; supported by more than 50 national organizations

21.3   Basic policies – financial, marketing and catering

21.3.1   Financial considerations

Since the Local Government Act 1988 and the introduction of compulsory competitive tendering (CCT), the school meals service has undergone major changes. Under the CCT local authorities are obliged to open school meal catering to competitive tendering; this is part of an overall government policy of offering many local authority domestic services out to tender. 'In-house' school meal services now have to compete against private catering contractors at both national and local level.

Initial reaction from national catering organizations was not necessarily favourable. Firstly the size of the welfare sector and the high cost of tendering did not encourage contract caterers to bid for many school meal contracts; secondly employees in particular are loyal to in-house arrangements which some contractors felt could affect the operational efficiency of many operations; thirdly, in many educational establishments, schools, universities and colleges, their financial year consists of three 12-week periods of operation, with non-operational gaps of 3–6 week periods in between. Many catering contractors were against term only contracts, with holiday breaks reducing the cost-effectiveness of the service they could offer. Further to this problem a number of contractors felt that in order to make the school meals service more cost-effective, increases in prices would need to be made which could affect the level of uptake.

For these reasons a number of the larger contractors looked at other ways of possibly offering their services. Firstly they did not bid for the total school meals service in a borough or county, but for part of it, for example carefully selected schools or groups of schools. Secondly, instead of competing against in-house services, private contractors began to offer their commercial experience in the form of consultancy to in-house operations. Most school meal contracts are still operated by direct service organizations (DSOs), that is, in-house teams.

However, after a 'settling in' period and a reappraisal of the schools meals market during the recession years, contract caterers have realized the potential growth prospects in educational establishments. This has resulted in a huge increase in the number of state schools being catered for by contract caterers from 450 in 1991 to 4653 in 1995. In some local education authorities (LEAs) the catering service may even be divided between the in-house team and the contract caterers, for example, a private contractor providing the main school meals and the DSO providing packed lunches. These contracts last for between 4–5 years so that over half of the original contracts awarded in the early 1990s are currently in their second round of tendering.

21.3.2 Marketing considerations

The complete area of marketing had, until fairly recently, been somewhat ignored in the school meals service. In the late 1970s nearly 65 per cent of school children were having school meals, by 1991 this figure was down to 42 per cent. This declining number of children taking school lunches was causing a threatening downward spiral, as fewer children bought school meals so they became less economic to provide.

To counteract this dramatic drop in demand, local authority school meal services began studying ways of reversing this decline and increasing sales. Taking a marketing approach, school meals campaigns have begun by finding out what their customers want, and marketing research has produced some interesting results. The results have shown that children want less queueing, a relaxed environment to eat in, more choice, value for money, the food to be prepared from fresh ingredients, more healthy dishes to choose from, and the opportunity to buy larger portions if they want. The traditional meat-and-two-veg lunches no longer appeal to today's school meal customers. Children are more

widely travelled, they have often experienced many new foods, tastes have changed, snack-type meals are more popular and there is a far greater variety of foods for children to choose from. They are bombarded on a daily basis by 'food marketing' – McDonald's, Wimpy, Burger King, Pizzaland, etc. – on television, radio and video, in newspapers, magazines and comics, in the high street, and on buses and trains. School meals are competing with organizations with large marketing budgets.

Different authorities have approached this problem in different ways although all have had to take a more marketing-orientated approach.

Many local authorities have produced information packs to distribute to schools which contain posters, leaflets, sample menus and recipes, question and answer sheets, etc. to be distributed to parents and children, and to be discussed in the classroom (see Figures 21.1 and 21.2). In areas with large foreign communities, translation packs are also available.

Publicity material uses the children's language of today to describe the school meals; the interior design and ambience of the cafeteria or restaurant also takes into account today's tastes and preferences; pop music is played at a level the children enjoy; posters and pictures decorate walls and T-shirts, sweat shirts, caps and badges with the school logo are sold. Publicity media such as local radio and press are also used; in-school magazines and inserts are all additional marketing tools, as are guest celebrity appearances to open new school dining facilities. Competitions have been organized with prizes ranging from the best colouring for the younger children to best essays for the older age group. These types of competition can be organized at a local level, by individual schools, and at national level, with prizes including a family trip to Disneyland (see Figure 21.3).

In the late 1980s a nationwide FEAST (fun eating at school today) campaign was launched, coordinated by a national committee representing regional committees and local authorities. Today this has been largely superseded by the National School Meals Week which aims to raise the overall interest and awareness of the school meals sector.

Figure 21.1   *An example of Surrey County Council's spring term menu 1997, based on a six-week menu cycle*

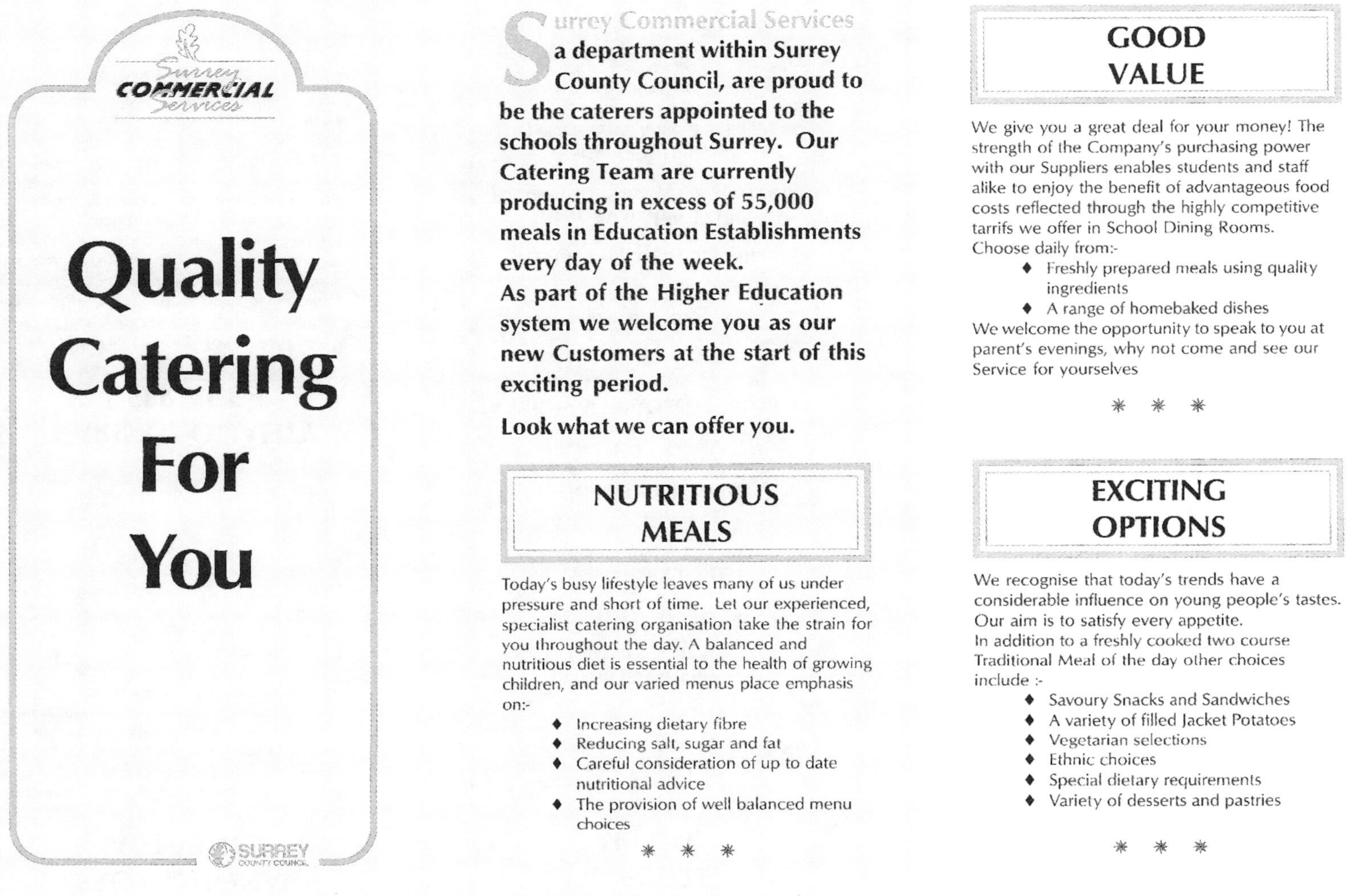

Quality Catering For You

COMMERCIAL Services

Surrey Commercial Services a department within Surrey County Council, are proud to be the caterers appointed to the schools throughout Surrey. Our Catering Team are currently producing in excess of 55,000 meals in Education Establishments every day of the week.

As part of the Higher Education system we welcome you as our new Customers at the start of this exciting period.

Look what we can offer you.

GOOD VALUE

We give you a great deal for your money! The strength of the Company's purchasing power with our Suppliers enables students and staff alike to enjoy the benefit of advantageous food costs reflected through the highly competitive tarrifs we offer in School Dining Rooms. Choose daily from:-

- ◆ Freshly prepared meals using quality ingredients
  - ◆ A range of homebaked dishes

We welcome the opportunity to speak to you at parent's evenings, why not come and see our Service for yourselves

✳ ✳ ✳

EXCITING OPTIONS

We recognise that today's trends have a considerable influence on young people's tastes. Our aim is to satisfy every appetite.

In addition to a freshly cooked two course Traditional Meal of the day other choices include :-

- ◆ Savoury Snacks and Sandwiches
- ◆ A variety of filled Jacket Potatoes
- ◆ Vegetarian selections
- ◆ Ethnic choices
- ◆ Special dietary requirements
- ◆ Variety of desserts and pastries

✳ ✳ ✳

NUTRITIOUS MEALS

Today's busy lifestyle leaves many of us under pressure and short of time. Let our experienced, specialist catering organisation take the strain for you throughout the day. A balanced and nutritious diet is essential to the health of growing children, and our varied menus place emphasis on:-

- ◆ Increasing dietary fibre
- ◆ Reducing salt, sugar and fat
- ◆ Careful consideration of up to date nutritional advice
- ◆ The provision of well balanced menu choices

✳ ✳ ✳

SURREY COUNTY COUNCIL

Figure 21.2 *An example of promotional material supplied by Surrey Commercial Services detailing their services*

APPETITE APPEAL

Tasty well balanced meals are features of the extensive range offered in our Cash Cafeterias. Our menu compilation is constantly updated to reflect todays lifestyle.

"Dish of the Day"
Pork & Pineapple Pepperpot served with Rice
(Tender Pork in a Spicy Sauce)
*

Vegetarian Choice
Vegetable & Bean Lasagne
(Layers of pasta and beans in a creamy sauce)
*

Individual "Pot" Meals
Cauliflower Cheese au Gratin
(served with a slice of crusty garlic bread)
*

A Variety of Filled Jacket Potatoes
Tuna - Baked Beans - Cheese
Mushroom - Bacon

Served with Seasonal Vegetables or Salads of the Day

Freshly Prepared Salad Bar

Also Available Daily
Freshly made Sandwiches and Filled Rolls
Hot and Cold Snacks
A Selection of Drinks and Juices
Cakes and Pastries
Biscuits and Cookies

For further information contact

SURREY COMMERCIAL SERVICES
HIGHWAY HOUSE
21 CHESSINGTON ROAD
EWELL
KT17 1TT
Telephone
0181-541-7391

PROMOTIONAL ACTIVITIES

To maintain interest and encourage awareness in the dining room, our marketing team are continually developing new ideas to enhance the service to our customers.
We organise :-

◆ Special Theme Days to compliment School activities
◆ Fun Days with Competitions
◆ Money Saving Offers
◆ Active Marketing of Healthy Diets for Young People

✳   ✳   ✳

CARING, QUALITY SERVICE

Surrey Commercial Services has evolved from a 50 year old history in Education Catering, and has achieved an expert understanding of the unique demands of this business and the importance of our customers needs.
We strive to provide the right atmosphere for relaxed sociable mealtimes - especially during an exciting but sometimes anxious period in a student's life.
Our policy of developing close partnerships between pupils, teaching staff and our on site catering teams enables us to tailor our Service to the individual needs of each School.

✳   ✳   ✳

Figure 21.2   *An example of promotional material supplied by Surrey Commercial Services detailing their services*

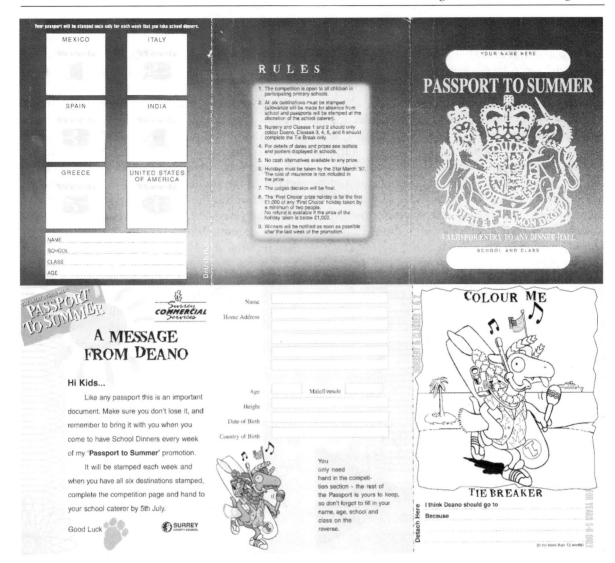

Figure 21.3   *An example of a competition organized by Surrey County Council called 'A Passport to Summer'*

21.3.3   Catering considerations

21.3.3.1   *Type of customer*

In the school sector of the welfare industry the majority of its market is still a captive one. The balance has altered somewhat over recent years with the availability of alternative catering facilities close to schools and the increase in the number of packed lunches now being taken from home, but for the majority of children, the school catering service is often the only one available to them during the day. This poses problems for the school caterer of maintaining high standards of food production and service and ensuring that the menus are varied and interesting. The school meals service caters for staff and children: in primary schools, children's ages vary from approximately 5 to 11 years and may include some nursery children; and in secondary schools from 12 to 16 or 18 years (although different local authorities may have differently structured age bands). The social classification of the parents varies with the catchment area and the level of education offered. In certain areas the majority of the children may be from immigrant families from many different countries and of different religions and requiring specific types of food and meals which are outside the normal range of school meals provided.

The major difference between catering for primary and secondary school children is that in secondary schools the customers are also the consumers; school children of secondary school age make their own food and beverage selection and consume the meal. In primary schools it is more usual for parents to be the customers and the children the consumers. Generally speaking, choice is more limited at primary school age, and the initial decisions of whether to have a full school lunch, a packed lunch supplied by the school or to take a packed lunch from home, would previously have been made by the parents. In primary schools the school meals advertising and publicity campaigns are consequently often directed at the parents, promoting such features as the benefits of providing healthy school meals to young children, the time saved in not having to prepare school lunchboxes, the value for money of the luncheons, etc. These effective publicity campaigns are often the result of social training courses initiated by the local authorities.

The school meals service in Devon is operated by Direct Services and is currently trying to increase school meal uptake from 55 per cent to 60 per cent. In September 1996, 86,000 leaflets were sent out to parents of primary school children aimed at increasing the parents' awareness of the school meals service. Devon Direct Services (DDS) organized a holiday prize draw to encourage response which resulted in a 8.2 per cent return rate, that is 7000 of the leaflets had been read and returned. The cost of £2000 was divided between DDS and the sponsors who had their logos on the leaflets and in turn benefited from receiving feedback from parents and DDS.

21.3.3.2   *Type of menu*

The menu for the school meals service until 1979 was required to provide for all pupils who wanted it, a varied, attractive and sustaining midday meal. Other primary objectives contained in the Department of Education and Science report of *Catering in Schools* intended to meet the social, educational and nutritional needs of school children. The meat-and-two veg

meal which was considered standard and capable of providing school children with a nutritious and substantial meal is fast disappearing and is being replaced by the more popular type of foods and snack meals.

In the 1980s two government-sponsored reports were produced which have both been concerned with British diet and the effects on the health of the nation. The first, the *NACNE Report 1983* recommended a reduction in the level of intake for fat, sugar and salt of 10 per cent and an increase in the intake of dietary fibre of 25 per cent, the *COMA Report 1984* made similar recommendations. More recently in 1994 two further reports, the Health of the Nation and the Nutritional Aspects of Cardiovascular Disease, were produced and these two reports plus today's current interest in diet and healthy living and fitness, have led to an overall increase in the use of whole grain bread, and rice, jacket potatoes, fresh fruit and vegetables where possible and a reduction in the amount of sugar used in desserts and puddings.

Due to the changes occurring within the school meals sector, a number of alternatives to the traditional service are being used by local authorities, including:

1 Changing the normal school hours to the continental system of 8.30 a.m.–2.30 p.m. with two 20-minutes breaks for snacks during the school day, and not providing any main meals.
2 Operating a cash cafeteria system with food and beverage items individually priced so that pupils may choose and buy whatever they want. In local authorities where this has been tried, it has resulted in a significant uptake of meals, although because the meals are put together by the children themselves, there is less control on their nutritional intake.
3 Shortening lunch breaks to 35-minute periods, and offering limited snack-type meals only, ensures that children do not have time to leave school and use other catering outlets, and the limited kitchen facilities needed reduce overhead and labour costs.
4 Buying in or preparing on-site a variety of packaged lunchboxes, containing such items as sandwiches, a piece of fruit, a yogurt, a biscuit or cake and a drink. The provision of these lunchboxes has the advantage of requiring the

very minimum of kitchen and dining staff.

They are popular with the children because they receive foods they have pre-selected, know that they like, and yet there is still an element of surprise every day. Parents also like them because the children are receiving a balanced meal that is good value for money, they do not have the daily chore of shopping, preparing and filling the lunchbox, and, finally, the school is responsible for the cleaning, sterilizing and storing of lunchboxes. For the local authority it is a cost effective way of providing lunch to those children who would otherwise bring a packed lunch from home.

21.3.3.3 Food production styles

Although the variety of food production styles used in the school meal service varies, the most widely used method is still the conventional cook-serve. As in the kitchens of other sectors of the catering industry, the kitchen is divided into 'parties', each being responsible for the production of a certain group of food items; in smaller kitchens the number of divisions may be fewer, but the responsibility for the production of the group of food items is correspondingly larger.

In recent years other methods of food production have been introduced to help solve the problems of labour, food, energy and transport cost, the introduction of newer methods having originated from research and experimentation in the welfare sector itself and not from what one might have expected, the commercial sector.

The following points have particular relevance to the welfare sector and influence the food production and service methods used by the school meals service:

1 The importance of providing a nutritional meal for growing school children.
2 The stringent cost limits within which the sector has to operate.
3 The large numbers that have to be fed within a short space of time.
4 The distance between the production kitchen and the service point to the customer, for example at some schools food may be produced in a central kitchen twenty miles away from the service point. This highlights the problems of:

(a) Transporting the food quickly, safely and at the correct temperatures.
(b) The considerably longer holding time between production and service and the problems that go with it of decreasing nutritional value, tiredness in taste and appearance, the dehydration of the food, as well as maintaining the correct temperature to hold and serve the food.

Methods such as cook-freeze have the advantages of providing food of a high nutritional value, with considerably reduced bacteriological hazards, and food that can be reconstituted by semi-skilled staff. It also divorces production from service allowing a much better utilization of equipment and labour with a higher productivity. If food production is centralized it can result in the cold store acting as a buffer between production and service and also allows considerable economies of space, equipment and staff costs at peripheral units. The biggest disadvantage to cook-freeze is the high initial capital cost, and that to benefit from economies of scale, central production units (CPUs) have to be used on a continual basis which is not always required by a school meals service.

Cook-chill is also used but not to the extent of cook-freeze, mainly because of the limited storage life of the prepared meals. Also, the trend in secondary schools towards snack-type cash cafeterias does not lend itself so easily to cook-chill. This method of food production serves primary schools better where demand is known in advance and standard quantities and meals can be batch produced.

Central production units are also used and can vary in their methods of operation from buying in from food manufacturers, frozen and chilled foods and distributing them to the peripheral kitchens, to producing their own cook-freeze and cook-chill items. Many CPUs will operate using a mixture of all of these methods together with a central buying function for the total range of convenience foods.

21.3.3.4 Food service styles

The mode of food service used in a school will depend on a number of interrelated factors: the size and type of unit, for example a primary or secondary school; the food production method utilized; the type of customer, staff or school child; and the type of snack or meal to be served.

Food service styles for school meals are changing. Until recently, the method most commonly used was the family service. The food was prepared in the kitchen and portioned into dishes in units of six, eight or ten; the unit size depending on the number of students able to sit at a table. The food was then portioned out on the plates usually by a helper for small children or by the 'head' of the table. This method was used extensively as it was seen to meet a valuable social and educational need for children. The development of self-service cash cafeterias in secondary schools has now firmly superseded the traditional service and has developed from a limited choice of meal at a fixed price to a wide range of snack and main meal items each individually priced and paid for to a cashier at the end of the counter. This later development has evolved as a result of students requiring a wider choice of foods and beverages with a wide price range, the popularity of snack-type items and also by the school meals organizers reacting to a marked drop in customer uptake.

In primary schools the traditional set meal service is still the most widely used form of food service, with 55 per cent of LEAs in England serving set meals. In secondary schools the self-service cafeteria has replaced the traditional service, 75 per cent of LEAs providing a cafeteria only service, compared with 20 per cent in primary schools. By contrast only 2 per cent of LEAs serve set meals in secondary schools.

It has been suggested that since the introduction of cash cafeterias, the nutritional standard of school meals has declined, and that left to choose for themselves, children will choose 'chips with everything'. However, in many situations if the school does not provide this type of service, the children would simply take their custom to the high street shops and buy there; re-imposing the traditional meat-and-two-veg meal would only lead to an even greater fall-off in sales. By actively educating and encouraging children in the classroom and cafeteria to create their own nutritionally balanced meals, and by the use of differential pricing in the cafeteria, sensible eating can at least be encouraged. School Nutrition Action Groups (SNAGs) and school food committees are becoming more widespread in schools and allow pupils, caterers, teachers and school managers to work together to provide a better type of catering service in schools. The 1996 Gardner Merchant School Meals Survey confirm that where such committees are found in schools, improvements are seen both in perceiving school meals as healthy and in the number of pupils supporting the service.

Where there is a food committee the frequency of eating a school meal is 2.63 times per week compared with 2.56 times per week without a committee; 82 per cent of pupils perceived their school meals as being healthy, against 66 per cent of pupils interviewed without a food committee; the numbers choosing fresh fruit for dessert rises from 6 to 16 per cent, whilst the frequency of chip eating falls from an average of 2.9 times per week to 2.7 when a school has a food committee.

Although pupils' tastes cannot be completely influenced, school nutritionists and food committees can at least ensure that the meals they provide are lower in fat, salt and sugar and that higher fibre foods and whole grain products are used, for example lower fat crisps and chips, yogurts, puddings and desserts made with reduced sugar, wholemeal bread and brown rice, ice-cream made with reduced sugar, milk etc. In this way school children are offered nutritionally balanced meals while still being of the type and variety they like and want.

21.3.3.5   *Organization and staffing*

The organization and staffing of the school meals service has undergone changes since the introduction of compulsory competitive tendering (CCT) in the late 1980s and early 1990s. Local authorities are now required to put their schools' catering service out to tender; this is undertaken by a client who acts on behalf of schools. The client specifies the service, advertises the contract in the trade press, approved journals and *OJEC* (*Official Journal of EC*), receives the tenders, evaluates them and awards the catering contract.

An example of an organization chart for a typical county authority is shown in Figure 21.4; Surrey County Council's school meals are provided by an in-house team. The organization and staffing levels for the catering services will be determined by the catering contractor

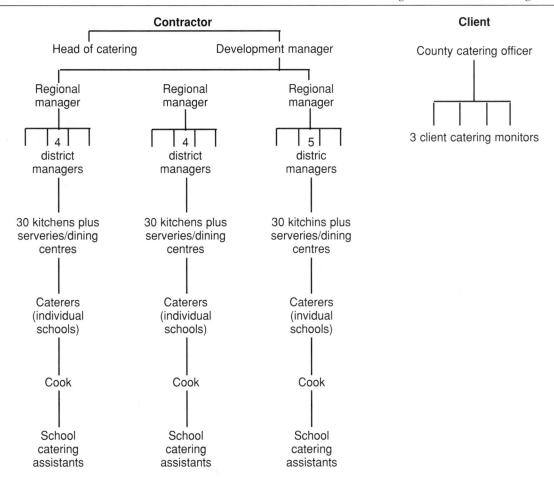

Figure 21.4 *Surrey County Council: organization and staffing chart*

although staffing numbers and staff to customer ratios will be of basic economic efficiency and be similar from one organization to another.

21.4   Control and performance measurement

The type of control systems used in the school meals service varies from one authority to another, as indeed do the prices charged for the school meals, ranging from 65p to £1.20, and the uptake of lunches, from 30 to 95 per cent, depending on the area of the country.

The budgeting for the school meals is generally the responsibility of the local education authority (LEA) although this can be devolved to the individual schools if they opt for Local Management of Schools (LMS).

With the introduction of the Education Act 1980 and the local authorities no longer being required by law to provide a two-course meal within specified nutritional and price limits, the school meal service has of necessity become more marketing orientated by offering the children a wide range of foods, particularly snack type meals. The introduction of loss leaders, the importance of sales mix analysis, the use of differential profit margins for lunch menus are all performance and analysis tools which are being utilized to enable the school meal service to operate and be controlled more efficiently. Differential pricing for example, can not only increase sales but also encourage children to eat the more nutritious foods; in some cafeterias, for example fresh fruit is sold virtually at cost price, while the price of portions of chips is weighted, that is, increased to discourage their purchase in preference to healthier foods.

In terms of control at the point-of-sale, the introduction of cashless systems, i.e. magnetic stored-value cards, has proved beneficial in some cases. Parents are able to buy the cards or pay into a weekly account which is debited directly by the school meals organizer. The problems associated with cash are reduced, for example lunch money being lost, wrong change being given, pilferage of floats, the banking of money, etc. It also discourages children from going elsewhere and spending their lunch money outside of school and parents know the school lunch money is being spent correctly.

Cashless systems offer an effective form of control as all sales information and cash received is immediately stored and analysed in an electronic cash register (ECR). School meals organizers are also enthusiastic as they see this type of system as a means of chanelling school lunch money to actually being spent at school.

Cashless systems are also a very useful aid in stocktaking, sales mix analysis and menu compilation.

The main disadvantages associated with cashless systems are the high initial capital costs if the hardware is purchased or the on-going leasing costs if it is rented. This type of system is only practical in secondary schools and it is difficult to eliminate cash totally so some banking will always need to be done. However, a number of local authorities are looking at the systems currently available on the market and feasibility studies are being done.

With the introduction of tendering and following the award of a contract for a specific period, the measurement of the service provided needs to be carefully monitored, taking into account a number of criteria, which have already been discussed in Chapter 20. These would include the cost to the client, the meeting of the specification, the maintenance of standard products, quality, hygiene etc., and could be equally well applied as yard sticks whether the service was being operated by private contractors or had remained 'in-house'.

21.5   References

British Hospitality Association (1995). *Contract Catering Survey 1995*, London: British Hospitality Association.

Education Act 1987. HMSO.

Local Government Act 1987. HMSO.

NACNE Report 1983. HMSO.

COMA Report 1984. HMSO.

The Caroline Walker Trust (1992). *Nutritional Guidelines For School Meals*. London.

22
Food and beverage management in hospital catering

22.1 Introduction

In Chapter 21 the general characteristics of the welfare sector were discussed; these are equally applicable to both the school meals and hospital catering services. In addition, however, hospitals have several other factors which need to be taken into account when considering the provision of a meals service:

1 For the majority of hospital patients there are no alternative catering facilities available to them so that, in effect, they become captive consumers. In certain situations, for example, distance from a town, the time of day, these terms may also be applied to the staff.
2 Modified therapeutic and medically prescribed diets are often needed in addition to the normal dietary meals being produced. The provision of such meals involves additional supervisory and managerial time and control, increasing the unit cost of producing special meals.
3 Flexibility is needed in terms of production and service in the event of additional admissions from casualty, early discharges, large scale emergencies etc.
4 The catering service is not seen as a priority in the overall planning and financial budgeting of hospitals, although customer satisfaction with hospital meals is recognized as being beneficial in terms of patient recovery – good presentation, quality and service of hospital food encouraging patients to consume and enjoy their meals.
5 Hospital meals are not sold in cash terms to the patients but form an integrated part of the total hospital package of customer care. For the hospital caterer, patient satisfaction cannot therefore be measured in terms of sales receipts, so other ways of measuring response to the catering service must be used, such as customer satisfaction questionnaires, wastage control, etc.

These additional factors combined place a further responsibility on the unit catering manager to provide attractive, appetizing and nutritious meals for both patients and staff under increasingly stringent financial constraints.

22.2 The hospital catering service

A brief resumé of the recent history of the hospital catering service is as follows:

- *Pre-1948.* Hospitals are administered by voluntary organizations (religious and charitable) and by local authorities.
- *1948.* The modern hospital service as we know it today was created when the state formally assumed responsibility for most hospitals with the National Health Act 1946 coming into force. All hospital services were co-ordinated, centrally financed and controlled by regional boards. This led to the creation of a new post in hospital services, that of the catering officer.
- *1963.* The Platt report, *Food in Hospitals,* highlighted the many problems of old, out dated hospitals and kitchens, lack of food control, excessive waste, loss of vitamins and other nutrients through bad cooking methods being used, poor administration and poor standards of hygiene and cleanliness. Recommendations included raising the status of hospital caterers

and making them responsible for all aspects of food and the control and supervision of all staff in these areas.

- *1968–1972*. The Salmon Committee investigated the state of health service catering. Some of the recommendations were implemented with the re-organization of the National Health Service (NHS) in 1974.
- *1974*. Re-organization of the NHS resulted in fifteen regional authorities in England each with its area and district authorities. This resulted in a better management structure and catering being accepted as a profession within the NHS.
- *1979*. Report of the Royal Commission on the National Health Service published as *Cmnd 7615* provided the first comprehensive review of the NHS since 1956. The report recommended that the service could be improved by changes in the administrative structure to make it more responsive to patients' needs, less costly, and a better service to work in.
- *1979*. Consultative paper, *Patients First,* on the structure and management of the NHS in England and Wales was published.
- *1983*. The Rayner Scrutiny Report on *The Cost of Catering Services in the National Health Service* was published.
- *1986*. The McCarthy Report on *A Review of Hospital Catering,* King Edward's Hospital Fund was published.
- 1988. Local Government Act opening DSOs to competitive tendering.

22.3   Basic policies – financial, marketing and catering

22.3.1   Financial considerations

The financial policy for National Health Service catering is controlled by the Department of Health and Social Security which sets cost levels for the provision of the catering services. The cost levels in the main are concerned with the cost for the provision of food on a unit cost allowance for a full week. Current guidelines per meal are 60 per cent for food cost and 40 per cent to contribute towards overhead costs; in the NHS hospitals today,

average food spend per patient is approximately £1.70 per day. This is for the provision of two meals per day, lunch and evening meal; breakfast and beverages are funded from another budget allowance.

Initially, each year a financial allocation is made available to operate the catering facilities. The total figure is not a consistently fixed amount, as when being calculated, the figure would be based on the average number of persons being fed. Any major changes in these numbers would have to be taken into account and adjustments made to the budget.

In some areas the regional health authorities are allocated funds which are then distributed through their district health authorities to individual hospital units. Unit general managers within each district then distribute the funds to the necessary hospitals with a responsibility to ensure that as far as possible a standard service is provided to the patients in all the hospitals under the same control. However, for the individual catering manager or financial controller, there is little that can be done to influence the overall financial policy or budget. In other areas there has been a move away from this traditional funding either because a hospital has trust status or because contract caterers are responsible for the hospitals catering budget. The majority of hospitals in the UK are funded directly by the NHS, others operate under a trust status although still funded by the NHS, and the remaining units are private hospitals managed by private health care companies, such as BUPA.

Overhead costs, in particular wages and salaries, are controlled by the recommended staffing ratios and the nationally negotiated rates of pay. The financial policy for hospitals would include the financial guidelines for the provision of food not only for patients, but also for all the various groups of staff employed who since 1969 have been required to pay for their meals, although subsidised meals for staff are also provided. In some hospitals where staff cafeterias have been opened to visitors and the public, the financial policy would also contain the different pricing details for these two groups of customers, for example visitors may pay 20 to 25 per cent on top of the standard staff prices. It would also detail charges to be made for functions such as wedding receptions, luncheons, dinners, room hire etc. to different categories of users, such as staff and non-staff, local health authority and other health authority, commercial etc.

22.3.2 Marketing considerations

Like the school meals service, marketing in hospital catering has, until fairly recently, been somewhat ignored. However, with recent cutbacks and financial pressure being placed on the public sector as a whole, hospitals are being forced to look at ways of increasing their revenue, and decreasing their costs still further. In particular, a customer-orientated approach is being adopted by hospital catering managers in order to take the hospital catering service through the 1990s.

The marketing of hospital meals may be considered for:

1 The patients.
2 The staff.
3 The general public and visitors.

22.3.2.1   *The patients*

The patients form the major part of a hospital's market. Menu items, ordering procedures, menu cycles, etc. have for some time been included in guideline booklets and standard procedure manuals. Today, however, more detail is being included about marketing the hospital catering service – from the initial patient check-in to the hospital, to their final discharge. The introduction of the NHS Patient's Charter in April 1995 now obliges hospitals to give patients a written explanation of the catering services and standards they can expect during their stay. Figure 22.1 shows extracts from the Patient's Charter 1995 from a typical NHS hospital, relating to the catering services. A standard tray layout both descriptive and pictorial, should be contained in a standard document for staff, together with additional guidelines such as 'all trays and tables to be clean and unmarked; all cutlery to be clean and matching; blue and white crockery to be used at ward level – chipped and cracked crockery to be replaced; cruets full and matching'. Appearance and presentation of hospital meals should be given particular attention. Meal acceptability may be reviewed with the aid of patient questionnaires, personal interviews by catering staff or dieticians etc.

In terms of patient care, the marketing of the hospital catering service may be studied using the headings previously discussed as the tangible and intangible elements of the food service product (Chapter 4). Where research has been conducted into patients' reaction to the standard of hospital meals, the response has generally been favourable relating to the quality of food and beverages provided. In hospital catering the tangible product – the meals themselves – may in fact need little review and change; the quality of the food produced in hospitals in particular has improved over the last twenty years.

Today, the intangible aspects of the product are now receiving further study and attention; the atmosphere of the ward or dining area, the attitude of the service staff, the consideration of the patients' apprehension to their stay in hospital, being served a meal in bed, dining alone and in strange surroundings, the patient's worry of not understanding the menu terminology and ordering a wrong dish etc. The recognition of these intangible aspects of the meal experience and an attempt to allay the worries and fears of the patients go a long way towards improving hospital patients' enjoyment of their meal and overall satisfaction with the catering service provided.

22.3.2.2   *The staff*

The staff form the second largest market in hospitals. The marketing of hospital catering facilities to staff is mainly concerned with promoting the use of in-house services. Sales promotion is probably the most widely used method of increasing sales by constantly reminding the hospital staff of the facilities available and encouraging the staff to use them: notices and posters on staff boards in changing rooms and rest rooms, special features in staff magazines, discount vouchers in wage packets, tent cards on tables are all methods that may be used. Merchandising techniques include attractive food and beverage displays in the cafeteria or restaurant such as buffets and cold counters, salad bars, cold drinks machines etc.

CATERING SERVICES

From April 1995, if you have to stay in hospital, you can expect to be given a written explanation of the hospital's patient food, nutrition and health policy and the catering services and standards you can expect during your stay.

The standards will mean that:

- you have a choice of dishes, including meals suitable for all dietary needs;
- you have to order no more than your next two meals in advance;
- you have a choice of the size of portion you want;
- you are given the name of the catering manager;
- you have help if you need it, to use the catering services, for example, menus printed in other languages and large print. This help should be readily available.

MEALS

The day begins early in hospital with morning tea at approximately 6.30 am. However, we shall try not to disturb you if you are asleep.

Mealtimes are:	Breakfast	7.30 am – 8.30 am
	Lunch	12.00 noon – 1.00 pm
	Supper	5.00 pm – 6.00 pm

You will also be offered drinks mid-morning, mid-afternoon and at bedtime. You can choose what you wish to eat at each mealtime and we can provide special meals (Kosher, Halal, vegetarian, etc). You may also be visited by one of the hospital dietitians if your treatment involves a special diet related to your medical condition.

If you have any suggestions or comments about the catering service, please ask to see the catering manager who will be happy to discuss these with you.

Figure 22.1   *Extracts from the Patient's Charter 1995*

22.3.2.3   *The general public and visitors*

The general public and visitors is not an area in the hospital catering service that has traditionally been exploited to its fullest potential, although some hospitals have found that marketing their facilities to the local community and visitors has brought in extra revenue. The two major stumbling blocks to this area of marketing are often, first, the hospital's location, and, second, the general public's image of hospital catering. In some cases hospitals are situated outside of a town or city so that the possibility of attracting the local community out to its catering facilities is negligible; visitors to patients, however, may still be catered for. Second, the marketing of hospital catering facilities to the general public is not an easy task as it is not an area of the industry immediately associated with an attractive image and quality food and beverages. However, a number of hospitals have met with considerable success in this area. Examples include Guy's Hospital London, which has hospitality suites on the twenty-ninth floor, taking advantage of its fine views over the city. The suite is available for both staff and non-staff hire and is priced accordingly, able to cater for up to 200 people for a formal meal and 250 people for a stand up reception. Figures 22.2–22.5 show the banqueting services room capacities at Guy's and St Thomas' Hospitals together with examples of a selection of menus ranging from a finger buffet to a sit down dinner and vegetarian alternatives.

22.3 .3 Catering considerations

22.3.3.1 *Type of customer*

We have already noted that for the hospital catering service three divisions of customer may be identified: patients; staff, and visitors. Hospital patients can be further divided into categories of medical, maternity, surgical, geriatric, orthopaedic and pediatric, ENT, neurological, mentally and physically handicapped plus a number of other special cases. Some hospitals have patients of each category, some hospitals with three or four of the categories, while others may specialize in one type only. In addition, the age groups will often be mixed, their socio-economic backgrounds being of all levels, and in some cases of varying and particular ethnic origins.

The hospital staff are mainly categorized by their occupations: medical, nursing, house keeping, portering and domestic staff, senior medical and administrative personnel sometimes having their own separate dining room facilities. Visitors may be divided into those requiring a full-course luncheon or dinner, possibly dining with patients they are visiting, and those wanting only a snack or beverage item. As visitor catering has been identified as an area of further potential sales, more hospitals in the future may be providing better food and beverage facilities for this sector of their market.

22.3.3.2 *Type of menus*

In general the menus will be table d'hôte type menus with up to three main course choices, one of which would be vegetarian. In particular, for some hospital patients, there will be restrictions made by the medical staff as to the type of diet they are allowed. The types of diets required for hospital patients may be classified into the five main groupings of:

1 *Full or normal diets.* A patient is permitted to eat any kind of food cooked by any of the usual methods. Figure 22.6 gives examples of the menus offered to patients on normal diets at St Peters Hospital, Chertsey, offering a choice of three main courses and three desserts.
2 *Light diets.* These are for patients who have been very ill but are beginning to take solid foods again. The meals should be small and the dishes light, that is, easily eaten, swallowed, and digested, for example fruit juices, soups, porridge, minced beef, poached fish, egg dishes, pureed vegetables, rice puddings, ice-cream, fruit jellies, etc.
3 *Soft diets.* These are for patients who can eat ordinary food but require it to be pureed or minced. This may be because of dental problems or because they may have difficulty in feeding themselves.
4 *Modified (or therapeutic) diets.* These are diets adapted from the normal hospital menu and used as part of the medical treatment. The diet must contain all of the nutrients required for a balanced diet unless the patient is not allowed specific nutrients. The designing of the normal hospital menu so as to allow items to be chosen by patients who require modified diets is important as it reduces the production problem of these diets. It is also important that before normal menu items are allowed for modified diets, the standard recipes are agreed by the caterer and the dietician and then strictly adhered to. Modified diets include diabetic, low fat, low salt, high energy, etc. Figure 22.7 is an example of a days' therapeutic menus, showing the various diets that have to be catered for.

	THEATRE STYLE	BOARDROOM	'U' SHAPE	STAND UP RECEPTION	SIT DOWN DINNER	DINNER DANCE
Governors Hall	200	40	40	250	125	90
Grand Committee Room	–	24	–	50	24	–
North Wing Committee Room	–	16	–	25	14	–
South Wing Committee Room	–	24	–	–	30	22
Shepherd Hall	200	40	40	250	200	160
Consultants Dining Room	25	26	24	80	26	–

	THEATRE STYLE	BOARDROOM	'U' SHAPE	STAND UP RECEPTION	SIT DOWN DINNER	DINNER DANCE
Robens Suite	100	40	36	180	120	80
Emily McManus Dining Room	–	16	–	20	14	–
Emily McManus Lounge	–	12	–	30	–	–
Court Room	40	24	20	50	40	–

Figure 22.2 *Banqueting services room capacities, Guy's and St Thomas' Hospitals, London*

FINGER BUFFET MENUS

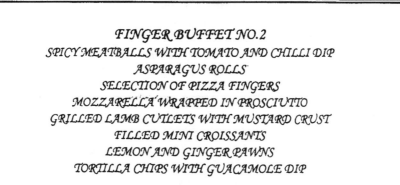

FINGER BUFFET MENU NO. 1
MINI CROQUE MONSIEUR
SCAMPI WITH TARTAR SAUCE
STUFFED VINE LEAVES
CHEESE AND RED ONION TARTLETS
VEGETABLE SPRING ROLLS
COCKTAIL CHIPOLATAS WITH A DIJON DIP

FINGER BUFFET NO. 2
SPICY MEATBALLS WITH TOMATO AND CHILLI DIP
ASPARAGUS ROLLS
SELECTION OF PIZZA FINGERS
MOZZARELLA WRAPPED IN PROSCIUTTO
GRILLED LAMB CUTLETS WITH MUSTARD CRUST
FILLED MINI CROISSANTS
LEMON AND GINGER PAWNS
TORTILLA CHIPS WITH GUACAMOLE DIP

FINGER BUFFET NO. 3
PROFITEROLES FILLED WITH STILTON, CELERY AND APPLE STUFFED VINE
LEAVES
DEEP FRIED MUSHROOMS WITH CHEESY BACON DIP
CHICKEN AND ASPARAGUS PASTRIES
GOUJONS OF COD WITH TOMATO SAUCE
GARLIC WEDGES WITH PESTO DIP
AVOCADO & WALNUT TARTLETS
GRILLED LAMB RIBLETS WITH ROSEMARY
MINI ROLLS FILLED WITH EGG AND CRESS
SMOKED SALMON AND ROAST BEEF
GHERKINS AND OLIVES

Figure 22.3 *Finger buffet menus from Guy's and St Thomas' Hospitals, London*

DINNER MENU NO.6

Artichoke Heads with a Walnut Vinaigrette

Paupiette of Plaice poached in Chardonnay served with a Seafood Sauce

Grilled Supreme of Aylesbury Duck with a Red Wine & Cassis Sauce

Lyonnaise Potatoes

Creamed Swede & Carrots

Brandy Snap Baskets filled with Champagne Sorbet and Fruits of the Forest

Coffee & Petis Fours

DINNER MENU NO.7

Traditional oak Smoked Scottish Salmon with Lemon,

Capers, Olives and salad Garnish

served with Thinly Sliced Brown Bread & Butter

Meallions of Lamb Fillet pan fried with a sauce of english Honey,

Red Wine and a hint of Rosemary

Minted New Potatoes

Glazed Leeks

Creme Brulee with warm Morrello Cherries in Syrup with Brandy

Mature Cheddar, Caerphilly and Bresse Blue

with Celery and Grapes

Coffee & Petis Fours

DINNER MENU NO.8

Smoked Salmon filled with Flaked Crab Meat served on a bed of salad leaves

Pan Fried Fillet of Beef served on a Crouton with Glazed Shallots

in a rich Port Wine Sauce

Sauteed Poatotes

Turned Carrots

Caramelized Orange Slices in Cointreau with a Lime Creme Fraiche

Stilton with Celery & grapes served with Bath Olivers

Coffee & Petis Fours

DINNER MENU NO.9

Leek and Gruyere Cheese tartlet with a Basil Vinaigrette

An array of fresh Shellfish, pan fried with Garlic, Onion, Capers,

Peppers and tomatoes

Fillet of Beef with a Pate of Mushrooms wrapped in pastry

with a Shallot Sauce

Chateau PotatoesCauliflower

Baby Cararots

Passion Fruit Syllabub with Tuillie Biscuts

Brie, Wensleydale and Danish Blue

with Celery and grapes

Coffee & Petits Fours

Figure 22.4   *Dinner menus from Guy's and St Thomas' Hospitals, London*

VEGETARIAN ALTERNATIVES

STARTERS

Grilled Haloumi with a Caper and Coriander Vinaigrette

Tagliatelle tossed in garlic with Mushrooms and Walnuts

Fresh Aparagus with a Sorrel Hollandaise Sauce

Artichoke Heads with a Walnut Viniagrette

Seasonal Melon with Exotic Fruits steeped in Port

MAIN COURSES

Red Pepper with Vegetable Couscous

Honey Soy Kebabs with Fuity Pilaf

Penne Pasta with a Ggorgonzola, Tomato, Cream and Bail Sauce

Spinach and Leek Pancakes with a White Wine and Mushroom Sauce

Potato and Herb pie

Figure 22.5 *Vegetarian menu from Guy's and St Thomas' Hospitals, London*

2SERVE ST PETERS HOSPITAL   WEEK THREE FRIDAY

FRIDAY LUNCH		FRIDAY SUPPER	
Soup		Soup	
Meatballs in Tomato Sauce	D	Roast Chicken	D
Breaded Fish	D	Vegetable Goulash	D
Harvest Vegetable Pie	D	Minced Chicken	DS
		Cottage Cheese & Apricots	
Poached Fish	DS	Sandwich	D
Cottage Cheese & Apricots		Chicken With Sage and Onion	
Sandwich	D	Sandwich	D
Chicken With Sage and Onion			
Sandwich	D	Gravy	DS
Peas	DS	Mixed Vegetables	DS
Sweetcorn	S	carrots	DS
Chips		Roast Potatoes	D
		Boiled Rice	D
Creamed Potatoes	DS	Creamed Potatoes	DS
Apple Crumble & Custard		Strawberry Sponge & Custard	S
Cheese & Biscuits	D	Pineapple	D
Diet Yoghurt	DS	Sugar Free Rice Pudding	DS

D = Suitable for Diabetics
S = Suitable For Soft Diets
Kosher and Halal Meals are available on
request

**If you have any comments or problems
regarding the food please ask to speak to a
Hotel Services Manager**

2SERVE ST PETERS HOSPITAL   WEEK THREE SATURDAY

SATURDAY LUNCH		SATURDAY SUPPER	
Soup		Soup	
Lasagne	D	Spicy Pork Sausage Casserole	D
Braised Liver & Onions	D	Cauliflower Crumble	D
Vegetable Quiche	D	Minced Pork	DS
Minced Chicken	DS	Shaved Ham & Tomato Sandwich	D
Shaved Ham & Tomato Sandwich	D	Egg Mayonnaise Sandwich	D
Egg Mayonnaise Sandwich	D		
Gravy	D		
Cauliflower	DS	Broccoli	DS
Green Beans	DS	Peas	DS
Saute Potatoes		Parsley Potatoes	DS
Creamed Potatoes	DS	Creamed Potatoes	DS
Mincemeat Pie and Custard		Mandarin Conde	S
Toffee Mousse	S	Orange Jelly	S
Low Sugar Apple Fool	D	Low Sugar Raspberry Jelly	DS

D = Suitable for Diabetics
S = Suitable for Soft Diets
Kosher and Halal Meals are available on
request

**If you have any comments or problems
regarding the food please ask to speak to a
Hotel Services Manager**

Figure 22.6 *Examples of normal diet lunch and dinner menus, St Peter's Hospital, Chertsey*

THERAPEUTIC MENUS WINTER 96

SUNDAY		MAIN	POTATO	VEGETABLE	DESSERT
PUREE/SWALLOWING	LUNCH	Puree Ocean Pie (Base Only)	Puree Creamed	Puree Peas	Chocolate Mousse
	SUPPER	Chicken Chasseur	Puree Creamed	Puree Cauliflower	Raspberry Jelly
LOW FAT	LUNCH	Roast Lamb 2oz	Boiled	Peas	Raspberry Jelly
	SUPPER	Chicken Chasseur (no fat)	Boiled	Cabbage	Chocolate Mousse
REDUCING	LUNCH	Roast Lamb 2oz	Boiled	Peas	Low Sugar Rhubarb Fool
	SUPPER	Chicken Chasseur (no fat)	Boiled	Cabbage	Chocolate Mousse
LOW SALT	LUNCH	Roast Lamb	Roast	Peas	Sultana Sponge
	SUPPER	Ocean Pie	Boiled	Cabbage	Chocolate Mousse
LOW POTASSIUM	LUNCH	Roast Lamb	Soaked Boiled	Peas	Chocolate Mousse
	SUPPER	Minced Chicken	Soaked Boiled	Cabbage	Raspberry Jelly
LOW PROTEIN	LUNCH	Roast Lamb (2oz)	Roast	Cauliflower	Sultana Sponge
	SUPPER	Vegetarian Ravioli	Boiled	Cabbage	Strawberry Sponge
GLUTEN FREE	LUNCH	Roast Lamb	Roast	Peas	Rhubarb Fool
	SUPPER	Chicken Chasseur	Boiled	Cabbage	Raspberry Jelly
LOW RESIDUE/LOW FIBRE	LUNCH	Roast Lamb	Boiled		Raspberry Jelly
	SUPPER	Minced Chicken	Boiled		Chocolate Mousse
ADDITIVE FREE	LUNCH	Roast Lamb	Roast	Peas	Rhubarb Fool
	SUPPER	Ocean pie	Boiled	Cabbage	Yoghurt
HIGH ENERGY	LUNCH	Chicken Chasseur	Roast	Peas	Strawberry Sponge
	SUPPER	Ocean Pie	Roast	Baked Beans	Sultana Sponge

23/01/97

Figure 22.7 *Therapeutic menus, St Peter's Hospital, Chertsey*

5 *Special diets*. These are for patients who for particular medical reasons must not be fed from the normal hospital menu. Their meals will be prepared separately by a diet cook usually working under the supervision of a dietician.

The menus for hospital staff would be similar to those prepared for industrial restaurants in that they would offer a limited choice of foods and beverages at varying prices, particular care being paid to the fact that at times the staff are also a captive market and some may be resident.

Today's market for the hospital catering service is a mixture of the more traditional group of customers who prefer a more traditional type of menu, for example meat and two vegetables, and a less traditional younger market wanting something different and willing to experiment. Catering for mixed markets and their conflict of needs makes the task of balancing the patients' menu requirements in a captive environment a difficult one for the hospital caterer.

22.3.3.3   *Food production styles*

As in the school meals service, conventional production is still the most widely used method of food production in the hospital catering service. Food and beverages are traditionally prepared and then distributed to the patients and staff using either a centralized or a decentralized food service system. Particular attention must be given to nutritional and dietary standards, maintaining the food at the correct temperature during its transportation and delivery, and finally the meal presentation to the customer.

Capital intensive schemes such a cook-freeze and cook-chill have also been introduced into the hospital catering service over the past thirty years to help meet public sector cost constraints. Such schemes have been initiated both by local authorities and private contractors who have won hospital contracts.

Where hospitals have cook-chill and cook freeze capacities greater than their requirements, hospital caterers are finding ways of marketing their excess production facilities as revenue raising projects, in order to generate additional revenue for the hospital catering service. At St Peters hospital in Chertsey for example, the hospital itself has an uptake of approximately 40 per cent of the hospital's cook-chill CPU output, a further 40 per cent is taken up by other hospitals and the remaining 20 per cent is sold to outside commercial organizations such as airlines and breweries. Its cook-freeze unit is also able to use its excess production facilities to meet third party work.

22.3.3.4   *Food service styles*

In the hospital catering service more than one food service style will often be offered in any one unit. For example, there may be a waiter service for senior medical and administrative staff, a cafeteria service for all other staff, a tray service for patients and a vending service for use by visitors, staff and patients. The use of vending machines for hospital staff on night duty in particular has increased in order to make revenue savings.

In hospital catering there are basically two methods of food service distribution to the patients; decentralized, and centralized. Decentralized service involves the preparation of the patients' trays or plating of food away from the main production area. Bulk quantities of food are loaded into heated or refrigerated food trucks and distributed to the hospital's floor kitchens and wards. At the floor kitchens and wards either trays are set up and served to the patients or the meals are plated in the ward by patient service assistants and served directly to the patients. Menu cards are delivered to patients in the morning with their breakfast with a selection of lunch and and dinner menus for the coming day. This type of hostess service at ward level is popular as patients have a choice of foods at the time they are going to eat. Under a centralized system the patients would already have had to have chosen what they would like the day before, or worse, would already have had their selection made for them by an outgoing patient. This method of food service, however, has a number of disadvantages:

1 Duplication of service equipment in the main production kitchen and at the individual floor kitchens.
2 Closely associated with the above is the double handling of food that occurs in the two kitchens.

3 Quality deterioration of the food occurs if it is left too long in the food trucks and the temperature of the food may alter considerably by the time the food reaches the patient.
4 The space required for the floor kitchens may be better utilized for other hospital facilities.
5 Staffing requirements are high to operate the floor kitchens, and the number of supervisory staff needed may also be duplicated.

Centralized service involves the preparation of the patients' trays in or close to the main production area. From here they are transported by trucks or mechanical conveyors to the various floors and from there directly to the patient. This method of food service has a number of advantages:

1 Duplication of service equipment and double handling of food at the floor kitchen is eliminated .
2 Supervision of the trays is considerably easier both from the point of view of dietary control and actual presentation; the presentation of the food is done by staff directly under the control of the catering officer.
3 The quality of the food the patients receive is considerably improved as there is little service delay from the time the trays leave the kitchen to when they reach the patients.
4 The space previously occupied by floor kitchens is made available for alternative hospital uses.
5 Dishwashing facilities may also be centralized with further savings in terms of space and cost, improved hygiene standards and a reduction in noise levels near the wards.

There are a number of centralized tray meal systems available for use in hospital catering and, although differing from each other, the basic menu selection procedure for patients is very similar. Menu cards are distributed to patients on the previous day so that patients can then make their own selection of food for the following day from the choice on the menu card. Also usually included on the card are the desired portion size of the meal and any particular dietary requirements the customer may have.

The menu cards are collected from the wards and returned to the catering officer who then produces a production schedule for the following day based on the number to be catered for, the quantity of food to be produced, etc. Individual diet cards are then produced for every patient in the hospital which are later placed on the tray before it moves along the conveyor belt and the meal is assembled. In this way several hundred complete meals can be prepared in a very short time and with constant supervision.

The trays are then loaded into some form of mobile trolley unit and taken directly to the wards and served to the patients. This minimum of delay ensures that the meal is presented to the patients at its best in terms of appearance, temperature, quality and nutritional standard. A more recent alternative to centralizing or decentralizing food service in hospitals has been the buying in of ready prepared meals, either chilled or frozen, and regenerating them at ward level. This reduces the production requirements of the hospital unit considerably, especially compared with the very high capital set up costs of a CPU. Central production units and their associated savings are only truly viable if they are fully utilized. Any dormant time increases the cost per unit meal which in turn leaves them less viable as a production unit. In fact some CPUs today have become so under utilized that the only economic alternative has been to close them down. As more and more hospitals are now adopting trust status and are becoming more autonomous, the system of one CPU serving a number of NHS hospitals is becoming less common as the individual hospitals are now able to negotiate their own terms.

For staff, the most widely used method of food service in hospitals is the self-service cafeteria, supported often by a waiter service of plated meals for those who are prepared to pay a little extra to contribute to the additional labour cost and also by a 24-hour vending service usually just for hot and cold beverages and simple snack items. The self service cafeteria is often of a multi-purpose type so that it can adequately cope with the full range of meals from breakfast, lunch and dinner. This type of cafeteria is often a straight line with separate built-in call order and beverage facilities, or a free-flow arrangement. Both of these styles have been explained in detail earlier in Chapter 12.

22.3.3.5 *Organization and staffing*

The organization and structure of the hospital catering service are under change at the time of writing this book. As long as government and local authority financial support remains for this service, it will always be subject to change by whichever political party forms the government at national and at local authority level.

The traditional organizational structure of regional and district authorities with individual hospital catering managers reporting to a district management team is becoming significantly less common. Over 90 per cent of NHS hospitals now have trust status and the remaining 10 per cent will gradually move across over the next few years. Today a new type of internal organizational structure has evolved in hospitals in response to cash shortages and cutbacks within the NHS and the opening of hospital contracts to competitive tendering.

The Rayner Report in 1983 recognized that 'If the NHS wants its catering managed as efficiently as is found in a good hotel, it must integrate it with other hotel services'. The concept of grouping all ancillary services under one hotel manager was further supported in the McCarthy Report 1986 which recommended that 'A single individual should assume responsibility at unit level for patient and staff services, as a hotel services manager.' The hotel services concept unifies all ancillary services in a hospital into one department. Its definition differs slightly around the country but basically includes some or all of the following services: catering, domestics, portering, linen and laundry, reception, residences, telecommunications, security, hairdressing, goods distribution, etc. The hotel services manager is responsible for co-ordinating the services under one umbrella.

Where this approach has been adopted, it has resulted in a number of benefits accruing to the different departments, and the overall organizational efficiency of the hospital:

1 Management is able to oversee all the ancillary services and utilize manpower most efficiently. Shortfalls or a high demand in one area can be levelled out by bringing in or taking out staff as necessary. Better utilization of staff resources results in an overall decrease in costs, due to less overtime being needed, for example, in one department, while another area is over-staffed.

2 Increased flexibility within the ancillary services gives better job satisfaction to the workforce with better motivation, communication, status and future job prospects for the employees. Management has also benefited from having more varied responsibilities, with a more general managerial approach being adopted by hotel services managers.

3 Having all services under one management results in faster decision making, numerous individual department heads no longer having to be brought together.

4 Traditional 'rivalry' between departments is reduced or removed, individual departments working together as one team under one management to provide all non-medical services; blame cannot be passed from one department to another when shortfalls occur.

5 Hygiene standards are improved; domestic staff serving patients, for example, receive the same hygiene training as food production staff, seeing themselves as part of the total food service process rather than having an isolated service-only role.

22.4 Control and performance measurement

The control systems used in the NHS catering service can range from those hospitals where control is undertaken by the hospital finance department, to those where control is managed by the hospital catering or contract manager. The level of sophistication of the control system is partly a function of the size of the individual hospital.

Catering managers need to have an update on their budget and actual costs and to be able to follow the food market prices so that seasonal, special offers, or alternative foods may be taken advantage of. It is only with current food control information and a developed knowledge of food market prices and trends that the caterers are able to operate within the financial limitations set by the NHS and yet still provide an acceptable level of service.

The control of hospital staff catering is similar

to that used in industrial catering. The costing may be structured in a number of ways:

1 The provision of a meal for staff within a fixed price level, as determined by union negotiation, with the costing being 75 per cent of the price charged to the food cost of the item, and 25 per cent being a contribution to the overheads.
2 The provision of other staff meals on a 60: 40 basis.
3 The provision of food and beverages for a wide range of hospital functions, for example staff Christmas parties, buffets for various types of occasions, etc. These are usually costed out on a 60: 40 basis at least depending on the policy of the hospital district, but often on a food cost plus all catering wage costs for the preparation, cooking, serving, clearing, washing-up etc.
4 The provision of vending and other retail type foods, for example confectionery, biscuits, etc. These items would usually be costed with a low percentage mark-up on the food cost owing to the items being very competitively priced outside the hospital service.

Daily, weekly and monthly control information must be collated for performance measurement. All areas of the catering service should be monitored and include: hygiene and food handling, the control of food service at kitchen level, financial control and efficiency for food and catering staff, menu content for patients and staff, meal service control at ward level and customer awareness. Where standards are not being met, the original objectives that were established for that particular area of the catering department should be reviewed and a programme of action initiated to bring the results in line with the standards as quickly as possible. Only by the setting of clearly defined targets and guidelines can hospital catering managers and staff know what is expected of them and what standards are required.

Management should regularly monitor performance measurement to ensure that the control systems in place are adequate and effective. These control systems need to be contained in the policy documents relating to the catering department. The standards to be achieved may

originate from directives from the Department of Health and form part of the hospital's catering policy, or they may appear as part of the conditions of contract in a tender offer and to which a contract caterer would be legally bound. Figures 22.8(a) and (b) are from the Department of Health's Operational Policy Unit relating to management control systems and are examples of the type of stringent control systems relating to hygiene and food safety in NHS hospitals.

In hospitals good hygiene and food safety practices are of particular importance because of the potential vulnerability of the patients – the very young, the elderly and the infirm all have less resistance to infection than the general population. For this reason higher standards must be monitored and assessed and microbial testing performed at a very specific periods (see Figure 22.8 (c).

Accreditation within the hospital catering sector is now more common, where certain areas of the catering service are audited to examine the systems and controls being used and their efficiency. An example of a supplier accreditation can be seen in Figure 22.9, detailing such information as the supplier and the hospital's location and the grading system being used for evaluating various aspects of the catering department. This on-going form of control and raising of standards is already established in hospitals, and catering managers have study courses and meetings to exchange information; topics include devolving budgets, menus, service systems, quality assurance, etc. Catering departments also establish trading accounts and become responsible for their total costs. Where contract caterers are operating a hospital's catering service, the trading accounts would be produced by their own finance department (see Figure 22.10).

As changes are initiated within the NHS system and the individual hospitals, so will the areas of responsibility of hospital catering managers change. It is important to note that where hospital caterers are encompassing new fields of responsibility, sufficient training must also be given to enable the managers to integrate these new areas into their overall control systems and to learn to manage the large budgets that are being devolved to them.

Health Service
Guidelines

HSG(96)20
9 December 1996

Management of food hygiene and food services in the National Health Service
[Replacing HSG(92)34]

Action

All catering management, food handlers and NHS premises, in which food is stored, prepared or served must comply with the current food safety legislation. Due to the vulnerability of patients, good practice advice found in the approved Catering Industry Guides should be considered in appropriate circumstances.

• NHS management must ensure that food production and service complies with the requirements of current food safety legislation.

• Purchasing Authorities must ensure that contracts with provider units lay down the required standards of food provision including food hygiene.

• Providers must ensure they adopt standards of good hygiene practice to conform to current food safety legislation and that such standards are monitored.

Figure 22.8   *(a) and (b) Extracts from the Department of Health's Operational Policy Unit document, 'Hygiene Controls and Systems for Assuring Food Safety'; (c) An example of a microbial testing schedule as performed in a trust hospital*

3.1.2. The systems should be capable of identifying critical control points throughout food operations – receipt and storage of food, processing, preparation and distribution of food – including cleaning, pest control and waste disposal. Managers also need to develop programmes for the initial and refresher training and/or supervision and instruction of all food handlers (section 3.4.).

3.1.3. Where the food services are provided under contract, the contractor should be asked to demonstrate that they are able to provide and operate such systems (section 3.2).

3.1.4. Where foodstuffs are purchased from outside sources the purchasers should satisfy themselves that the foods meet and are maintained at the standards which conform to current food legislative requirements. The supplier should demonstrate that all reasonable precautions and due diligence have been taken to supply safe food.

3.2. Hygiene Controls

3.2.1. Managers need to ensure that there are written operational policies for safe food handling. The policies should cover all operational aspects, such as:

- the selection of raw ingredients;
- the selection of suppliers;
- the storage, preparation, cooking and cooling of food;
- procedures for washing up;
- procedures for the handling of food waste;
- systems which help identify potential food safety problems or substandard quality products (section 3.3.), which include procedures to ensure all internal users of the product can be notified if it is judged there are likely wider implications (paragraph 2.2.4);
- procedures for assessing the fitness to work of food handlers prior to appointment and during their employment (FOOD HANDLERS *Fitness to Work* – details in Bibliography);
- procedures for food handlers to report if they are suffering from certain infections and appropriate steps to be taken;
- procedures for instruction and/or training of supervisors and food handlers and annual refresher training;
- the carriage of food in delivery vehicles;
- the maintenance of building fabric and catering equipment;
- pest control procedures.

3.2.2. Managers will find it of value in drawing up or reviewing the procedures to refer to the Catering Industry Guide to Good Hygiene Practice, its supplement on temperature control of food and to seek expert advice from other sources where necessary.

Figure 22.8(b)

3.3. Systems for Assuring Food Safety

3.3.1. Although policies may be in place, a food business may still fail to produce safe food. To help ensure food safety and good hygiene practices a number of systems have been developed which can be adapted to meet the needs of the diverse food services. Two of these are outlined in the following paragraphs.

3.3.2. Hazard Analysis Critical Control Points (HACCP) is a technique which has been developed and is intended to help food providers to satisfy themselves that their products are safe. It is a structured approach to: analysing the potential hazards in an operation; identifying the points in the operation where the hazards may occur; deciding which are critical to consumer safety and implementing appropriate changes, and reviewing the system periodically. It is not only a written document, but a practical system which is kept up-to-date. Some of the principles of HACCP have been adapted for conventional catering operations. One system is called Assured Safe Catering. ("Assured Safe Catering – A Management System for Hazard Analysis" – details in Bibliography).

3.3.3. Where food production involves the use of cook-chill or cook-freeze catering systems the DH guidelines "CHILLED AND FROZEN: Guidelines on Cook-Chill and Cook-Freeze Catering Systems" should be followed in conjunction with the food hygiene regulations. (Details in Bibliography).

3.4. Staff Supervision, Instruction and/or Training

3.4.1. A management system can only meet its objectives or comply with relevant legal obligations if staff carry out procedures as laid down in the operational policy. It is therefore good practice to develop within operational policies appropriate programmes of supervision, instruction and/or training, including induction training for trainee or agency staff who have no previous training, and refresher courses, for all staff involved in food handling. Where agency staff are employed on a regular basis, discussions should be held with the agency to ensure that the staff are trained in the basic aspects of food hygiene.

3.4.2. Staff training should include instruction on hygiene practices. The knowledge base should match individual needs related to jobs and roles in the total operation. In formulating hygiene training, advice can be sought from appropriate training organisations. (Details of organisations offering training packages are given at the end of this Guidance).

3.4.3. All training – initial, refresher and updates – should be recorded. Detailed advice can be found in the Catering Industry Guide to Good Hygiene Practice.

Figure 22.8(b)

NAME OF BACTERIAL TEST	TYPE OF TEST	SIGNIFICANCE	APPROPRIATE TEST
TVC (total viable count)	Total bacterial estimation	Identifies a high total bacterial count	All food samples
Coliforms	Total Coliform species estimation	Identifies coliform contamination. Suggests poor standards of food handling or personal hygiene	
Escherichia Coli	Escherichia Coli estimation	Identifies contamination through poor personal hygiene	All food samples especially food requiring direct handling
Staphylococcus Aureus	Staphylococcus Aureus estimation	Identifies contamination through poor personal hygiene (especially nose and mouth)	All food samples especially food direct handling
Bacillus Cereus	Bacillus Cereus	Commonly associated with food poisoning boiled rice	Rice dishes only
Salmonella	Salmonella species estimation	Naturally presented in certain raw foods especially poultry and eggs	Poultry and egg dishes
Listeria	Listeria species estimation	Food poisoning risk especially in extended shelf life (cook chill) foods	Cheese sauce dishes

Notes
1. A minimum of three samples should be sent each week.
2. The production manager should designate and record the dishes to be sent and book up the transport arrangements.
3. The production manager should arrange that there is appropriate food produced to gain samples. Samples should be taken from a spare food tin (or dining room) so as to be representative of food to be consumed.
4. Each sample should weigh at least 100g.
5. Three microbial tests selected at random should be requested for sample.
6. The samples should be ready for dispatch for 2.00 pm on the day of production.
7. Each sample should be labelled with: name of product, production date, use by date, and the name of the three microbial tests to be carried out.

Figure 22.8(c)

SUPPLIER ACCREDITATION

The audit report is divided into two sections, firstly to examine the systems and controls established (reasonable precautions), and secondly, establishing that the system works properly (due diligence).

The marking for each item is divided into four standards as follows:

$$3 = \text{commendable}$$
$$2 = \text{acceptable}$$
$$1 = \text{undesirable but acceptable}$$
$$0 = \text{unacceptable}$$

The following guidelines will be followed as criteria for the particular mark awarded:

3   Commendable -   exemplary standard, work practices, procedures, equipment, etc cannot be faulted.

2   Acceptable -   good standard of hygiene, work practices and procedures, with modern equipment, etc.

1   Undesirable but -   standards, work practices and procedures, equipment, etc leave
     acceptable   something to be desired and could be improved upon, but they do not offer any threat to the safety of the product.

0   Unacceptable -   standards, work practices and procedures, equipment, etc with serious shortcomings where the safety of the product could be put at risk.

The award of a "0" mark would normally result in the supplier being graded "not approved" until such times that the matter is corrected.

Where an item is not applicable to the location being audited, a score of 2 will be entered and "N/A" entered in the Status column.

Figure 22.9(a)   *Extracts from a supplier accreditation audit*

SUPPLIER ACCREDITATION

SUPPLIER		DATE OF AUDIT	10 September 199

CONTACT		DATE OF LAST AUDIT	29 February 199
JOB TITLE	Catering Manager		

LOCATION		PRODUCTS	Cook-Chill

TEL NO.		PREVIOUS GRADE	N/A

PERCENTAGE	GRADE
91-100	A
81-90	B
71-80	C
61-70	D
51-60	E
50-below	F

STATUS AWARDED	Conditionally Approved	GRADE AWARDED	A	NEXT AUDIT	March 199

AUDITOR	

Figure 22.9(b) *Extracts from a supplier accreditation audit, in this example showing the grading system*

SUPPLIER ACCREDITATION

Page No		MAXIMUM ACHIEVABLE SCORE	SCORE ACHIEVED
REASONABLE PRECAUTIONS			
5	Documentation	30	22
6	Personnel	27	27
7	Raw Materials	18	18
8	Production	12	12
9	Finished Manufactured Products	30	30
10	Non-Conforming Product	42	42
11	Cleaning	12	12
12	Pest Control	18	18
13	Testing and Calibration	18	18
		207	199
DUE DILIGENCE			
14	Personnel	81	81
17	Raw Materials	36	34
18	Production	90	82
20	Finished Manufactured Products	24	24
21	Distribution	15	15
22	Cleaning	84	84
24	Pest Control	30	26
25	Structure/Equipment	147	143
	SUB TOTAL	507	489
	TOTAL	714	688
32	Closing Meeting		
33	Conclusions/Recommendations		
	Score achieved/Maximum achievable score x 100 =		96%

Figure 22.9(c)   *Extracts from a supplier accreditation audit, in this example showing the scores achieved compared against the maximum achievable score*

SUPPLIER ACCREDITATION

NO	STANDARD	STATUS	SCORE	FACTOR	TOTAL
	DOCUMENTATION				
1	A system of food safety and hygiene control covering all aspects of the food business.	Standard achieved. Operations Manual.	3	2	6
2	A system of hazard analysis (e.g. hazard analysis and critical control points [HACCP]). The system must identify the hazards, preventative measures, critical control points and deviation limits, the method of monitoring and action to be taken in the case of deviation.	Currently writing a simply safe system. To be completed and referenced against the Operations Manual and monitoring forms.	1	4	4
3	A clearly defined management structure should exist with responsibilities in respect of food safety and quality assurance clearly specified.	Standard achieved.	3	1	3
4	A system of internal hygiene audits of the food business by suitably qualified and experienced personnel.	Standard achieved. Daily cleaning checks and weekly hygiene audits - all documented.	3	2	6
5	An effective control system which ensures that all documents are kept up-to-date and all changes are controlled.	Standard achieved.	3	1	3
				TOTAL	22

Figure 22.9(d) *Extracts from a supplier accreditation audit, in this example for documentation*

SUPPLIER ACCREDITATION

NO	STANDARD	STATUS	SCORE	FACTOR	TOTAL
	PERSONNEL				
1	A system which ensures that a person who comes into contact with food, food equipment or enters a food room has, prior to employment, completed a comprehensive medical questionnaire which should be examined by a competent person to determine suitability for the food handling tasks. If appropriate, a medical examination should be undertaken.	Standard achieved. On-site Occupational Health Department carry out medical screening and reviews.	3	2	6
2	A system which ensures suitability of a person returning to work after sickness or returning from a trip abroad, for food handling tasks and that they have not had contact with persons suffering from food poisoning symptoms.	Standard achieved.	3	2	6
3	A system which ensures the suitability of visitors, maintenance personnel, etc, to enter food handling areas, including the provision of suitable protective clothing.	Standard achieved.	3	1	3
4	A standard of training for all persons who come into contact with food, food equipment or enter a food room, that is commensurate with their work activities. Records of the training received by each member of staff to be maintained.	Standard achieved. In-house training schedule for all staff.	3	4	12
				TOTAL	27

Figure 22.9(e)   *Extracts from a supplier accreditation audit, in this example for personnel*

MONTHLY ACTIVITY STATISTICS

| Month of December 199 | | | | 9 Months to 31st December 199 | | |

(YTD) LAST YEAR	ACTUAL	BUDGET	KEY ACTIVITY STATISTICS	ACTUAL	BUDGET	VARIANCE
				YEAR TO DATE		
			Estates			
			Help Desk Calls			
			Planned Preventative Maint. Events			
			Bournewood (£ 000's)			
			Other (£ 000's)			
			SDU			
			Packs processed (time weighted)			
			SPH (£ 000's) (pack cost)			
			Bournewood (£ 000's)			
			Other (£ 000's)			
			Telecomms.			
			Incoming Calls DDI			
			Incoming Calls Operator			
			of which :SPH			
			Bournewood			
			Domestics			
			Supplementary Activity (hours)			
			Catering			
			Patient Meals			
			Dining Room Meals			
			Bournewood (£ 000's)			
			Other (£ 000's)			
			Transport			
			Peterbus Passengers			
			2Serve Miles			
			Bournewood Miles			
			Other Miles (inc. Peterbus)			
			Portering			
			Requests			
£ K						
			FINANCIAL			
			INCOME			
			St. Peter's			
			Bournewood			
			Other			
			TOTAL INCOME			
			EXPENSES			
			PAY			
			Estates			
			SDU			
			Telecomms.			
			Domestic			
			Catering			
			Transport			
			Portering			
			Central Support			
			Security etc.			
			TOTAL PAY			
			NON - PAY			
			Estates			
			SDU			
			Telecomms.			
			Domestic			
			Catering			
			Transport			
			Portering			
			Central Support			
			Security etc.			
			TOTAL NON - PAY			
			TOTAL EXPENSES			
			PROFIT / (LOSS)			

Figure 22.10   *An example of a hospital trading account*

22.5   Contract catering in hospitals

With government policy actively encouraging competitive tendering within the welfare sector of the industry, more hospital and educational authorities are putting not only their catering needs out to tender but also their support services such as cleaning, laundering, portering, security, etc., so that contract caterers are now offering many hospitals complete facilities management (see Figure 22.11).

An invitation to tender to provide a catering service is usually advertised in the trade press, for example, *OJEC* the specification of the tender having been very carefully prepared in detail by the hospital. Both external contractors and in-house teams (DSOs) are eligible to apply.

An invitation to tender would begin with a general description of the hospital's size and the number of beds, followed by a very detailed description of the hospital's catering facilities and its requirements. It would cover such areas as the legal definitions of the contract, the contract period, the services needed, the quality of food and raw materials to be used, the menus for staff and patients, the ordering of meals, contract staff and their supervision, health and hygiene, food hygiene and inspections, equipment and materials, security and insurance, the contract price, monitoring and quality assurance, variations and terminations, arbitration and law.

There are various forms of contract used in the provision of catering services to health authorities which include:

1 *Unit price.* This is the most common form of contract used in the NHS. Essentially the cost of providing the service is fixed in advance, and the contract price consists of two cost elements. First, the base cost that does not vary with the number of meals provided; it represents labour, supervision and support costs of the contractor that are necessary regardless of the number of patients in the hospital. The second cost varies with output; it represents the provisions and ingredient costs that contribute to providing a meal. This cost is quoted and fixed per patient per meal, any surpluses or deficits go to the external contractors. For employee feeding the contractor is required to pay an agreed percentage to the health authority from its income from staff restaurants.

2 *Variable price.* This is similar to unit price contracts but involves regular adjustment according to price movements of the ingredients and provisions of the actual food used. This form of contract is not regularly used in the NHS.

3 *Management fee.* The health authority is charged for all costs incurred in providing the catering service including materials and labour. In addition to this, there is a management fee paid to the contractor representing the costs of administration, quality control, supervision, accounting, etc. Under this form of contract any loss arising from the inefficient use of labour or food wastage is borne by the health authority and monitoring is therefore important.

In order to ensure that the hospital is obtaining the best possible service in terms of quality and price, efficient monitoring procedures must be effected. The invitation to tender would also include the standards required of the catering service, the responsibilities of the catering and finance officers, and the control and performance evaluation procedures.

22.5.1   Compulsory competitive tendering

Compulsory competitive tendering (CCT) has contributed to a dramatic rise in the number of contract caterers managing hospital facilities. In 1991 eighty NHS and Trust hospitals were contracted out; in 1995 this figure rose from 131 to 142. Mintel estimates contractors now account for 20 per cent of all meals served in the NHS and this figure is increasing. This is due to a number of factors:

1 The introduction of CCT during the recession years prompted contract caterers to investigate the welfare sector more closely.
2 The experience gained by contract caterers as to hospitals' special demands and requirements has enabled them to offer a better and more competitive service and to build up credibility with the hospital service.
3 The complexity of the earlier documents and the uncertainty of hospitals' exact require-

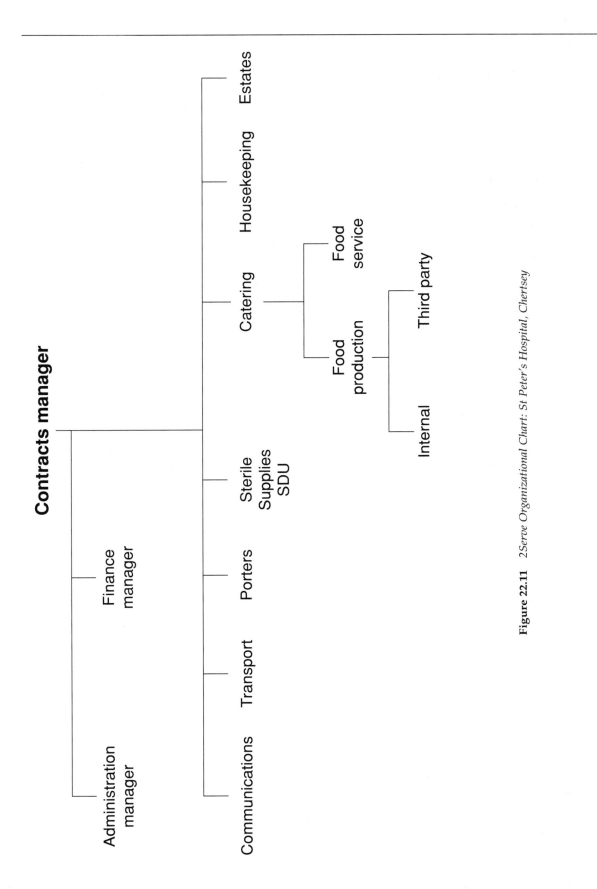

Figure 22.11 *2Serve Organizational Chart: St Peter's Hospital, Chertsey*

Contract Award Criteria

The contract will be awarded on the basis of the most economically advantageous offer judged on price, quality of product and service, delivery performance and overall cost effectiveness factors.

Unsuccessful Offerors will be given the opportunity to be debriefed on their submission.

INTERPRETATION

1.1   In these conditions:

1.1.1   "the Contract" means the agreement between the Authority and the Contractors, including all specifications, patterns, Contractor's samples, plans, drawings and other documents which are incorporated or referred to therein;

1.1.2   "the Contractor" means the person who by the Contract undertakes to supply the Goods to the Authority and/or Health Authority as is provided for in the Contract. Where the Contractor is an individual or partnership, the expression shall include the personal representatives of that individual or of the partners;

1.1.3   "the Authority" means the Health Authority placing the Contract.

1.1.4   "Health Authority" means a Regional Health Authority, District Health Authority, Family Health Services Authority, Special Health Authority (including the NHS Supplies Authority) or NHS trust as the case may be;

1.1.5   "the Goods" means all goods, materials or articles which the Contractor is required to supply under the Contract;

1.1.6   "the Contract Price" means the price exclusive of Value Added Tax payable to the Contractor by the Authority under the Contract for the full and proper performance by the Contractor of its part of the Contract.

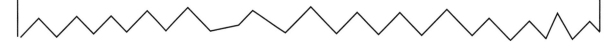

Figure 22.12   *Extracts from an invitation to tender: (a) contract award criteria and conditions*
Source: NHS Supplies

4. THE SERVICES

4.1 The Contractor shall during the Contract period provide, in accordance with the specification and the schedules, a range of pre-cooked chilled meals as detailed in the menu cycle.

4.2 The meals supplied shall be of good quality using quality ingredients and shall be provided at a cost effective price.

4.3 Offerers will need to demonstrate a thorough understanding of the Health Care Market. The Trust expects the Contractor to maintain stringent quality and hygiene controls throughout the production and delivery process. These aspects of the Contract will be rigorously monitored by the Trust or its agents throughout the Contract period.

4.4 Due to changes being introduced under the "Patient's Charter" and the sensitivity of the consumer, the Contract will be under constant review to ensure that the goods and services provided are meeting the needs of the Trust. The Contractor shall therefore advise the Trust, at the earliest opportunity of any changes in financial status or production methods or ingredients that may affect the quality or safety of the goods supplied.

5. MENUS

5.1 The Hospital is currently using a three week menu cycle.

5.2 The Contractor will be expected to provide specific Cook Chill products in accordance with their menu cycle. The range of products may be amended at any time during the Contract period due to changes at the earliest possible opportunity. The intention is that the hospital will amend the menus to take account of the Contractor's production cycle.

5.3 The number of meals required will vary in accordance with the number of patients being treated. Additionally the Patient's Charter will require the Trust to provide such meals as requested by the patients the day following the request. The Contractor shall be expected to provide a delivery service which will allow such flexibility.

5.4 The Trust has a reputation for providing a high quality Catering Service and the Contractor shall be required to maintain, and where possible, assist in the raising of the quality. The Trust will, providing the quality and service is not diminished, accept items from the standard range of meals produced by the Contractor. The menu cycle may be amended to suit the Contractor's production cycle.

5.5 The Contractor shall be expected to offer suitable seasonal variations to the menus for the Christmas period. Adjustments to the menus shall be made by the Trust in consultation with the Contractor.

5.6 A minimum number of six different main course dishes must be available each day so as to enable the compilation of menus which satisfy all of the Trust requirements.
Luncheon is to offer:

	Normal Textured Choice
	Hot Soft/Light Choice
	Hot Vegetarian Choice
	Salad Choice
	Main Vegetables
	Soft or Extended Vegetable
	Main Potato/Starch
	Soft Potato/Starch
	Dessert

Figure 22.12   *Extracts from an invitation to tender: (b) the services, menus, food quality and nutrition*
Source: NHS Supplies

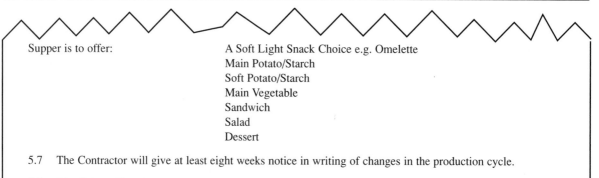

Supper is to offer: A Soft Light Snack Choice e.g. Omelette
Main Potato/Starch
Soft Potato/Starch
Main Vegetable
Sandwich
Salad
Dessert

5.7 The Contractor will give at least eight weeks notice in writing of changes in the production cycle.

5.8 The dishes offered will be from the standard range produced by the Contractor as detailed in their literature.

6. FOOD QUALITY

6.1 COOK CHILL

Cook Chill Foods shall mean prepared from raw ingredients and cooked/processed by the Contractor on the Contractor's premises. The products shall, after production, be chilled within 90 minutes and stored at a temperature of 0°C to 3°C with a life cycle of not more than 5 days including the day of preparation and the day of consumption.

6.2 Cook Chill Products supplied by a third party are not acceptable unless expressly agreed in writing by the Trust's Catering Services Manager.

6.3 All ingredients used in food provided under this agreement must meet in all respects the minimum standards specified in Schedule 1.

6.4 Irradiated foods may not be used without permission from the Trust's Catering Services Manager identifying the specific items. The Contractor shall be responsible for requesting such permission should the need arise.

7. NUTRITION

7.1 The Contractor shall be required to comply with the minimum portion sizes specified in Schedule 2 in accordance with DOH Dietary Reference Values (1991).

7.2 The choice of dishes should be suitable for the inclusion on menus similar to the choice of dishes shown included with this document and should state the following:-

Type of Choice	*Example*
Normal Textured Choice	Roast Chicken
Soft/Light Choice	Shepherd Pie
Vegetarian Choice	Vegetarian Hot Pie
Main Vegetable	Peas
Soft or Extended Cooked Vegetable	Carrots
Main Potato/Starch	Roast Potato
Soft Potato/Starch	Mashed Potato

7.3 Tenderers will be required to make recipes available for the Trust's Catering Services Manager to view and check in conjunction with the Trust's Dietitian.

Figure 22.12 *Extracts from an invitation to tender: (b) the services, menus, food quality and nutrition*
Source: NHS Supplies

ments initially led to high tendering costs for catering contractors; tendering documents have to a certain extent become more simplified.

4 The ability of contract caterers to raise and invest capital in a hospital's catering facilities can give them a competitive edge, for example, ISS Mediclean are investing £750,000 at Whipps Cross Hospital to upgrade the staff catering facilities.

5 The contract caterers' access to the latest information technology, computer-based systems and a company-wide information base on all tenders has enabled them to introduce those new ideas and systems to one trust which are working for another, to introduce in-house brands in different hospitals and to develop highly sophisticated costing systems to enable them to compete on cost which is still largely the key issue in the NHS.

Figure 22.12 shows examples of extracts from an invitation to tender detailing definitions of the conditions of the contract and the menu and food quality requirements, in this case of a cook-chill operation.

An alternative to a hospital's catering service being operated by either in-house catering or a contract caterer is for a partnership to be formed between the two. This innovative approach is being pioneered at St Peters Hospital, Chertsey, in collaboration with Serco Health Services and represents 'the first total facilities management contract covering both estates and hotel services awarded by an NHS Trust to a private sector company. The Trust identified the need for capital investment for the development of some support services, and following a series of budget cuts particularly in hotel service, it was realized that to make further improvements in quality and cost terms, skills from the private sector would be needed. The concept of a joint venture could, it was felt provide support services and be a vehicle to raise the necessary capital.'

St Peters Hospital is a District General Hospital of approximately 350 beds with 1400 staff and is situated on a 68-acre site with two other Trust hospitals. The £6-million contract began operating in April 1994 and has been awarded for five years with an option of a further two. 'The focus is on the identification of internal and external customer/supplier relationships, a process which has encouraged a greater awareness of customer needs.' The success of this joint venture has led to Serco discussing a similar arrangement with other Trusts and has proved to be a successful commercial alternative for both parties rather than an either/or choice between DSOs and contract caterers.

Hospital catering is a continually evolving service changing and adapting to new introductions and constraints, new markets, innovations and concepts, in particular that of total facilities management. The more traditionally organized hospital catering service is fast disappearing as more streamlined DSOs and contract caterers are competing against or working with each other to offer the customer a more efficient quality service.

22.6   References

British Hospitality Association (1996). *1996 Contract Catering Survey*.

NHS (1988). *Patients First*. London: HMSO.

Serco Health Services (1995). *Premises and Facilities Management*, Winning Team Serco.

The McCarthy Report. (1986) A *Review of Hospital Catering*. King Edward's Hospital Ward.

The Rayner Scrutiny Report. (1983) *The Cost of Catering Services in the National Health Service*.

Index